THE CANADIAN MOUNTAIN ASSESSMENT

The Canadian Mountain Assessment

WALKING TOGETHER TO ENHANCE UNDERSTANDING OF MOUNTAINS IN CANADA

Graham McDowell, Madison Stevens, Shawn Marshall, Eric Higgs, Aerin Jacob, Gùdia Mary Jane Johnson, Linda Johnson, Megan Dicker, Dani Inkpen, Michele Koppes, Keara Lightning, Brenda Parlee, Wanda Pascal, Joseph Shea, Daniel Sims, Niiyokamigaabaw Deondre Smiles, Leon Andrew, Caroline Aubry-Wake, David Borish, Ashley-Anne Churchill, Dawn Saunders Dahl, Goota Desmarais, Karine Gagné, Erika Gavenus, Stephan Gruber, Jiaao Guo, Katherine Hanly, Nina Hewitt, Murray Humphries, Rod Hunter, Lawrence Ignace, Pnnal Bernard Jerome, Patricia Joe, Stephen Johnston, Knut Kitching, Douglas Kootenay, Daniel Kraus, Sydney Lancaster, Rosemary Langford, Lachlan MacKinnon, Christopher Marsh, Brandy Mayes, Hayden Melting Tallow, Charlotte Mitchell, Tim Patterson, Sophie Pheasant, Karen Pheasant, Melissa Quesnelle, Rachel Reimer, Lauren Rethoret, Gabriella Richardson, Brooklyn Rushton, María Elisa Sánchez, Richard Schuster, Tonya Smith, Lauren Somers, Chris Springer, Kyra St. Pierre, Karson Sudlow, Yan Tapp, Julie M. Thériault, Andrew Trant, Vincent Vionnet, John Waldron, Gabrielle Weasel Head, Sonia Wesche, Nicole J. Wilson, Matthew Wiseman, Kristine Wray, Stephen Chignell, Thomas McIlwraith, PearlAnn Reichwein, Steven M. Vamosi

University of Calgary Press
2500 University Drive NW
Calgary, Alberta
Canada T2N 1N4
press.ucalgary.ca

Library and Archives Canada Cataloguing in Publication

Title: The Canadian Mountain Assessment : walking together to enhance understanding of mountains in Canada / Graham McDowell, Madison Stevens, Shawn Marshall, et al.
Names: McDowell, Graham, author. | Stevens, Madison, author. | Marshall, Shawn (Shawn J.), author.
Description: Statement of responsibility from cover. | Includes bibliographical references.
Identifiers: Canadiana (print) 20230542778 | Canadiana (ebook) 20230542883 | ISBN 9781773855080 (hardcover) | ISBN 9781773855097 (softcover) | ISBN 9781773855103 (Open Access PDF) | ISBN 9781773855110 (PDF) | ISBN 9781773855127 (EPUB)
Subjects: LCSH: Mountains—Canada. | LCSH: Mountain ecology—Canada. | LCSH: Traditional ecological knowledge—Canada.
Classification: LCC QH106 .M332 2023 | DDC 577.5/30971—dc23

The University of Calgary Press acknowledges the support of the Government of Alberta through the Alberta Media Fund for our publications. We acknowledge the financial support of the Government of Canada. We acknowledge the financial support of the Canada Council for the Arts for our publishing program.

The Canadian Mountain Assessment acknowledges support from the Canadian Mountain Network (CMN)—a member of the Networks of Centres of Excellence Canada program—and the Natural Sciences and Engineering Research Council of Canada (NSERC).

Copyediting by Brian Scrivener

Cover image: Storm Mountain and Arethusa Cirque in autumn, Canadian Rockies. Photo courtesy of Paul Zizka, 2020.

Cover design, page design, and typesetting by Garet Markvoort, zijn digital

We respectfully acknowledge that the mountains discussed herein, which inspire and sustain us, are the traditional and ancestral territories of First Nations, Métis, and Inuit Peoples who have cared for and known these homelands since time immemorial.

We recognize that present-day Canada was formed through colonial discrimination and dispossession of Indigenous Peoples, and that these legacies of colonial harm continue to perpetuate injustices against First Nations, Métis, and Inuit Peoples across Canada.

We affirm our individual and collective responsibilities to address these harms, work towards reconciliation and healing, and build relationships among Peoples and with the other-than-human world that are rooted in reciprocity, equity, and respect. This acknowledgement is only a first step in the journey.

We gratefully honour the ancestors who light our path ahead.

ACKNOWLEDGEMENTS

The Canadian Mountain Assessment (CMA) represents the first formal assessment of mountain systems in Canada, as well as an important effort to enhance understanding of mountains through the respectful inclusion of both Western academic and Indigenous ways of knowing. It is the outcome of over three years of work and was made possible by funding from the Canadian Mountain Network (CMN)—a member of the Networks of Centres of Excellence Canada program—and the Natural Sciences and Engineering Research Council of Canada (NSERC), institutional support from the University of Calgary, and the incredible commitment, effort, and care of an extensive and diverse group of individuals.

We acknowledge with deep gratitude those that have come together to prepare the CMA:

Project Leader: Graham McDowell
Project Assistant: Madison Stevens
Project Research Team: Jiaao Guo, Katherine Hanly, Graham McDowell
Canadian Advisors: Eric Higgs, Aerin Jacob, Gùdia Mary Jane Johnson, Linda Johnson, Shawn Marshall
International Advisors: Carolina Adler, Martin Price, Pasang Dolma Sherpa, Phillippus Wester
Chapter Co-Lead Authors: Megan Dicker, Eric Higgs, Dani Inkpen, Michele Koppes, Keara Lightning, Brenda Parlee, Wanda Pascal, Joseph Shea, Daniel Sims, Niiyokamigaabaw Deondre Smiles
Chapter Contributing Authors: Leon Andrew, Caroline Aubry-Wake, David Borish, Stephen Chignell, Ashley-Anne Churchill, Dawn Saunders Dahl, Goota Desmarais, Megan Dicker, Karine Gagné, Erika Gavenus, Stephan Gruber, Jiaao Guo, Katherine Hanly, Nina Hewitt, Eric Higgs, Murray Humphries, Rod Hunter, Lawrence Ignace, Aerin Jacob, Pnnal Bernard Jerome, Patricia Joe, Gùdia Mary Jane Johnson, Linda Johnson, Stephen Johnston, Knut Kitching, Douglas Kootenay, Michele Koppes, Daniel Kraus, Sydney Lancaster, Rosemary Langford, Keara Lightning, Lachlan MacKinnon, Christopher Marsh, Shawn Marshall, Brandy Mayes, Hayden Melting Tallow, Charlotte Mitchell, Wanda Pascal, Tim Patterson, Sophie Pheasant, Karen Pheasant, Melissa Quesnelle, PearlAnn Reichwein, Rachel Reimer, Lauren Rethoret, Gabriella Richardson, Brooklyn Rushton, María Elisa Sánchez, Richard Schuster, Joseph Shea, Daniel Sims, Niiyokamigaabaw Deondre Smiles, Tonya Smith, Lauren Somers, Chris Springer, Kyra St. Pierre, Madison Stevens, Karson Sudlow, Yan Tapp, Julie M. Thériault, Andrew Trant, Vincent Vionnet, John Waldron, Gabrielle Weasel Head, Sonia Wesche, Nicole J. Wilson, Matthew Wiseman, Kristine Wray
Chapter Review Editors: Stephen Chignell, Thomas McIlwraith, PearlAnn Reichwein, Steven M. Vamosi
Graphic Design: Annie Webb
Cartography: Chris Brackley and Angi Goodkey (As the Crow Flies cARTography), Jiaao Guo
Videography: David Borish

In addition to the core project team, we wish to acknowledge Robert Sandford and Kelly Bannister, who provided critical and constructive input, which played an important role in shaping our assessment process. We are also appreciative of 28 external reviewers, whose diverse perspectives and thoughtful suggestions improved the coherence and credibility of the CMA.

Matthew Berry and Stan Boutin—former CMN Interim Director and CMN Co-Research Director, respectively—were both champions of the CMA vision and were instrumental in securing financial and in-kind support from the CMN. We are also appreciative of helpful guidance received from Murray Humphries and Norma Kassi, current and former CMN Co-Research Directors, respectively.

Likewise, we thank Nicole Olivier, former CMN Programs Manager, for her encouragement and steadfast support with project operations and budgetary matters. Finally, Monique Dubé, Executive Director of the CMN, provided helpful assistance with project funding and supporting alignment with CMN priorities.

We are also thankful to those at the University of Calgary Press who have supported the publication process: Brian Scrivener, Alison Cobra, Helen Hajnoczky, Alan MacEachern, and Garet Markvoort. Their patience, attentiveness to the CMA's ethical and technical requirements, and skilful manuscript preparation efforts have led to a published work that is reflective of the spirit and intent of the CMA.

While the CMA is a national scale initiative, we note that many researchers; First Nations, Métis, and Inuit individuals; and mountain professionals with knowledge of mountains in Canada were not directly involved in the project. Nevertheless, our work was informed by the efforts of this broader community; we thank all of those that create, safeguard, and (where appropriate) share knowledge of mountains in Canada. Furthermore, while the CMA attempts to assess the state of mountain knowledge in Canada, we appreciate that knowledge of mountains is not only held by people. We recognize other-than-human Knowledge Holders in mountains and call attention to the importance and legitimacy of their knowledges, even if they are largely beyond the scope of the CMA and the realm of human experience more broadly.

Finally, we are grateful for the mountains themselves. Mountains are important to all of us involved in the CMA, in ways that are common, including as sources of freshwater, but also in ways that are distinctive and deeply personal. Regardless of our specific connections to mountains, they have inspired each of us to dedicate considerable time and effort to enhancing understanding of mountains in Canada. We benefit tremendously from mountains, and it has been an honour to work in the service of these special places.

FOREWORD

Jody Hilty, President and Chief Scientist, Yellowstone to Yukon Conservation Initiative

William (Bill) Snow, Acting Director of Consultation, Stoney Tribal Administration

Majestic and towering and yet uniquely fragile, mountains in Canada sit at the forefront of discussions about cultural regeneration, reversing biodiversity loss, and addressing climate change. Mountains are places of inspiration and rejuvenation for the mind, body, and the soul. For many Indigenous Peoples, they are also places of cultural sites and practices, and areas where cultures would meet and spend time together, to forge alliances and mark celebrations. Indigenous Peoples have long been stewards of mountain environments, and mountains have provided much in return. Today, questions about the guardianship of the mountain areas remains contentious as Indigenous Peoples assert their territories while the Government of Canada refers to much of these lands as "Crown Lands." In this context, Indigenous Peoples and the federal government are forging new ways forward that enable joint agreements on how lands should be cared for, consistent with the government's commitment to the United Nation's Declaration on the Rights of Indigenous Peoples and Canada's Truth and Reconciliation framework.

Mountains in Canada are also important centres of biodiversity; they are home to iconic species such as grizzly bears, wolverine, and mountain caribou, as well as less prominent but no less important flora and fauna. Historically, the general inaccessibility of mountains has meant that human development in the mountains—be it homes and towns, agriculture, or extractive activities—has been slower and less extensive than in more accessible valley bottoms and less topographically diverse regions. However, today mountains across Canada are seeing an increase of human activities and development, as population growth and new technologies result in development reaching ever further into the interior of mountains, up their slopes, and across their many folds. Given Indigenous Peoples' unique and significant knowledges of mountain ecosystems, it is promising that biodiversity conservation efforts are now advancing in more collaborative ways, leading to conservation efforts that are informed by both Western scientific and Indigenous knowledges of mountain environments, as well as the establishment of Indigenous-led protected areas in mountain regions.

Despite auspicious governance developments, climate change is rapidly transforming mountain areas in Canada, leading to growing concern about impacts on water resources, the structure and function of mountain ecosystems, and the safety and wellbeing of communities in and downstream of mountain areas. This, in turn, is raising awareness about the urgent need for both the mitigation of greenhouse gases as well as adaptation to emerging challenges and potential opportunities of climate change in mountain areas. However, changes are currently outpacing understanding of viable paths forward for mountain areas in Canada in a changing climate.

For these reasons and more, the timeliness of the Canadian Mountain Assessment (CMA) could not be better. It is more imperative than ever that we have clarity about what we know, do not know, and need to know about mountains areas across Canada. It is only with such knowledge that we can make prudent decisions about how we as a society—in all our diversity—can move forward to care for mountains into the future.

The CMA represents a tremendous effort to advance understanding of mountains in Canada, and assessment practices more broadly, through the respectful inclusion of multiple ways of knowing.

This involved developing new approaches to bring together Indigenous knowledges with insights from Western academics, including by organizing project governance through a 'Stewardship Circle'; convening a 'Learning Circle' with First Nations, Métis, and Inuit individuals from across mountain areas in Canada; ensuring that chapters were co-led by Indigenous and non-Indigenous authors to support equitable knowledge co-creation; and sharing oral knowledges through embedded videos to respect and support oral knowledge sharing traditions. It also involved significant attention to the protection of Indigenous knowledges, including by developing a publication model that allows for the removal of content into the future, if deemed necessary, consistent with the principle of ongoing consent. Another welcome aspect of the CMA is that those involved with the project explicitly recognize the limits of their individual and collective understanding across different mountain regions, Indigenous territories, and ways of knowing and connecting to mountains. This extends to the overall contribution of the CMA, which is framed as a beginning rather than the final word. Those involved with the CMA should be commended for their humility, and for leading the way in demonstrating how to engage respectfully with a diversity of knowledges in such a major assessment.

Given the many issues facing mountain areas in Canada, it is necessary to both broaden and deepen our understanding of mountains in the country. The CMA's thoughtful examination of diverse knowledges of mountains in Canada gives us an opportunity to do just this. It also gives us reasons to be hopeful about the future; it provides a very real example of how embracing multiple ways of knowing can enhance our collective understanding of mountains, while also leading to new insights about how we might move forward together in a good way. We are reminded of the words by the late ecologist E.O. Wilson who stated "We are drowning in information, while starving for wisdom." The Canadian Mountain Assessment provides ample food for thought.

EXECUTIVE SUMMARY

The Canadian Mountain Assessment (CMA) provides a first-of-its-kind look at what we know, do not know, and need to know about diverse and rapidly changing mountain systems in Canada. The assessment includes insights from both Indigenous and Western academic knowledge systems and represents a unique effort to enhance understanding of mountains through respectful inclusion of multiple bodies of knowledge. The CMA is a text-based document, but it also includes a variety of visual materials as well as access to video recordings of conversations with First Nations, Métis, and Inuit individuals from mountain areas in Canada. The CMA is the country's first formal assessment of mountain systems knowledge; it is guided by five overarching principles (Figure 0.1).

The CMA is composed of six chapters, summarised below.

Chapter 1. Introduction

This chapter provides the context and rationale for the assessment, as well as details about the CMA's governance, conceptual and ethical foundations, methodology, and structure. It also calls attention to important caveats and limitations as well as salient innovations and contributions of the CMA.

Chapter 2. Mountain Environments

The Mountain Environments chapter examines the biogeophysical characteristics of mountain regions in Canada. It assesses the state of knowledge for a wide range of environmental topics including geology; weather and climate; snow, ice, and permafrost; water; hazards; ecosystems and biodiversity; and connections between mountains and lowland/coastal environments. While demonstrating a significant amount of scientific work related to mountain environments in Canada, the chapter also illustrates the general lack of engagement with Indigenous knowledge systems in relation to mountain environments in existing Western academic research. Contributions from Indigenous Peoples are nevertheless included in the chapter by way of CMA authors

1 – Service

The CMA is guided by service to mountains and mountain-connected communities — Indigenous, non-Indigenous, and non-human — now and into the future.

2 – Inclusivity

The CMA celebrates the diversity, depth, and specificity of First Nations, Métis, Inuit, and Western academic knowledges related to mountains in Canada, and aspires to demonstrate the breadth of these knowledges, as well as points of tension, synergy, and emergence.

3 – Humility

The CMA aspires to collaboratively advance a good effort, acknowledging that our assessment of what we know, don't know, and need to know about mountains in Canada inherently reflects structural disparities, procedural limitations, and our own positionality.

4 – Responsibility

The CMA is committed to upholding the integrity of diverse knowledges shared into the assessment; respecting the privacy of culturally protected knowledges; enacting on-going consent; and ensuring open-access publication, traceability, and transparency.

5 – Action

The CMA aims to enhance understanding of the importance of mountains in Canada, and to stimulate relationships, research, and action that support the realization of desirable mountain futures.

Figure 0.1: CMA Guiding Principles

as well as knowledges shared during the CMA's Learning Circle. In its conclusion, the chapter identifies gaps in our current understanding of mountain environments and invites mountain researchers to engage with Indigenous communities to learn more about their unique perspectives and understandings of mountain environments in Canada.

Chapter 3. Mountains as Homelands

The Mountains as Homelands chapter considers how mountains in Canada are experienced and shaped as Homelands by Indigenous Peoples and homes by non-Indigenous people. The chapter approaches this broad topic by considering how mountainous environments are made into significant places through practice, representation, and relations among people. It weaves together knowledge from Indigenous Peoples and scholarly literature, and draws on conceptual approaches offered by relational thinking, multispecies scholarship, and ontologies studies. The chapter begins by examining storytelling as an important means of place-making in mountain Homelands. It then considers how an emerging field of mountain archaeology corroborates and supports Indigenous presence in mountain Homelands. Moving beyond strict divisions between nature and culture, a substantial portion of the chapter explores how multispecies relations underpin mountains as homes and Homelands. The chapter then examines the forms and ongoing impacts of colonialism and power in Canadian mountain places. This includes the role of parks and protected areas, and private land, in mountain regions, and how science, labour, recreation, and art have shaped perceptions and experiences of mountain places. It assesses how such practices can contribute to discrepancies in access to mountains as homes and Homelands. The chapter concludes with the topic of Indigenous governance in mountain places. Overall, the chapter finds that the literature on these topics is better represented in the western mountain regions, that the role of private land in constituting mountain places is generally under-examined, and that there are opportunities for scholarship that documents and explores Indigenous resistance to incursions on mountain Homelands and the reassertion of Indigenous governance in mountains.

Chapter 4. Gifts of the Mountains

The Gifts of the Mountains chapter explores the contributions of mountains to the wellbeing of human communities. It uses the framing of gifts as an alternative to the conventional descriptions of resources or ecosystem services, and reveals how, for many people in Canada, mountains provide material, artistic, pedagogical, emotional, and spiritual gifts. The chapter also discusses how particular users and communities receive benefits derived from energy, minerals, and forests found in mountains. Importantly, the chapter calls attention to the idea that many gifts from mountains are situated in reciprocal relationships where users receive foods, medicines, water, or recreational space, as personal gifts which, in turn, inspire wonder, awe, respect, and care. Such reciprocity is often, but not exclusively, associated with Indigenous worldviews. Ultimately, the chapter demonstrates that gifts from mountains are unevenly distributed and that some benefits derived from mountains may come at a cost to others seeking to enjoy the same mountain spaces. Furthermore, many gifts of the mountains are under increasing pressure from drivers of environmental and social change.

Chapter 5. Mountains Under Pressure

The Mountains Under Pressure chapter examines the drivers of recent and future change in mountain systems in Canada, as well as impacts to mountain ecosystems and communities, focusing on the period from the "great acceleration" of increasing human population and activity in 1950 out to 2100. Key issues assessed include climate change, land use development, resource extraction, pollution, tourism and recreation, population growth, invasive species, and governance practices, including associated threats to the sustainability of mountain environments, livelihoods, and gifts of the mountains. The chapter demonstrates that these pressures are often interconnected and compounding, and describes how each drives biophysical, political, socio-cultural, and ecological changes, with effects that vary from region to region. However, while changes have been acutely observed and felt by many Indigenous Peoples as well as non-Indigenous mountain communities, monitoring of both anthropogenic pressures and their implications is currently limited across mountain systems in Canada, making prediction of future threats difficult to assess, particularly in mountainous areas of northern Canada. The chapter concludes by calling attention to the need for enhanced research and monitoring efforts, as well as the importance of supporting adaptation to the challenges (and opportunities) posed by increasing rates of climate and anthropogenic change in mountain areas in Canada.

Chapter 6. Desirable Mountain Futures

The Desirable Mountain Futures chapter reflects on the CMA's knowledge co-creation process and the findings of its substantive chapters. It discusses how much was already known about mountains in Canada, but also how divides between Indigenous and Western knowledge systems have limited appreciation for the depth and diversity of existing mountain systems knowledge. It also describes how, in coming together across time, cultures, and landscapes, the CMA led to new insights about mountains in Canada. The chapter then discusses four cross-cutting themes that emerged from the CMA: Connectivity; elevating Indigenous knowledges; access and barriers to relationships with mountains; and humility. Ultimately, this chapter reveals how the CMA is only a beginning. It concludes by calling attention to opportunities for research, relationships, and actions that support ideals of the CMA.

By way of these chapters, the CMA aims to enhance appreciation for the diversity and significance of mountains in Canada; to clarify challenges and opportunities pertinent to mountain systems in the country; to motivate and inform mountain-focused research and policy; and, more broadly, to cultivate a community of practice related to mountains in Canada.

TABLE OF CONTENTS

River flowing into kokKuk (Southwest Arm), Saglek Fiord, Tongait KakKasuangita SilakKijapvinga (Torngat Mountains National Park). Photo courtesy of Darroch Whitaker (Parks Canada), 2013.

CHAPTER 1

Introduction

AUTHORS: Graham McDowell, Shawn Marshall, Madison Stevens, Eric Higgs, Aerin Jacob, Gùdia Mary Jane Johnson, Linda Johnson, David Borish, Jiaao Guo, Katherine Hanly, Daniel Sims, Murray Humphries, Lawrence Ignace

1.1 Mountains and Mountain Knowledge in Canada

Canada is a country of mountains. Around one-quarter (2.26 million km²) of the country is covered by mountainous terrain, an area large enough to encompass Switzerland 54 times and to position Canada as the fourth most mountainous country globally. Mountain areas in Canada—from high peaks of the St. Elias range in the northwest to the jagged Rocky Mountains of the western interior, and from Arctic ranges of Inuit Nunangat to the rolling hills of the Laurentian highlands—play an important role in shaping the biogeophysical and socio-cultural characteristics of the country (Fig. 1.1). Furthermore, the distribution of mountain areas across a wide range of latitudes, elevations, and climate zones in Canada produces a remarkable diversity of ecosystem types, sociocultural characteristics, and associated biocultural relationships and interdependencies. Since well before the country of Canada existed, these mountain places have sustained and been stewarded by Indigenous Peoples who continue to know and care for them. Mountain systems in Canada are therefore best understood as dynamic, living, and deeply relational spaces where physical, human, and other-than-human worlds are woven together across space and time.

Mountains in Canada contain unique geological features, play an important role in influencing regional weather and climate patterns, and are critical sources of freshwater for downstream ecosystems, communities, and economic activities. They also provide habitat, migration corridors, and refugia for plants and animals, including species that are endemic to mountain environments. Canada is also one of the most glacier-rich countries in the world, second only to Greenland, and the snow and ice adorning mountain tops in Canada from coast to coast to coast are defining features of these regions. For example, Canada hosts roughly 33,600 glaciers covering an area of 204,000 km² (Pfeffer et al., 2014).

Mountains have been homelands for Indigenous Peoples since time immemorial and, accordingly, many Indigenous territories and linguistic regions are associated with mountain areas in what is now referred to as Canada (Fig. 1.2 and 1.3). These connections highlight diverse, place-based, and long-standing relationships that Indigenous Peoples have with mountains in Canada. Today, around 1.3 million people live within the mountainous areas of the country (Fig. 1.4), a number equivalent to 3.5% of the total population of Canada but that is greater than the population of small countries such as Bhutan (McDowell & Guo 2021). A further 29 million people live within 100 km of mountains, indicating that 82% of the total population of the country lives within or adjacent to mountains. This value contains portions of populations in mountain-oriented cities in the west such as Vancouver and Calgary, as well as cities in the east such as Ottawa and Montreal

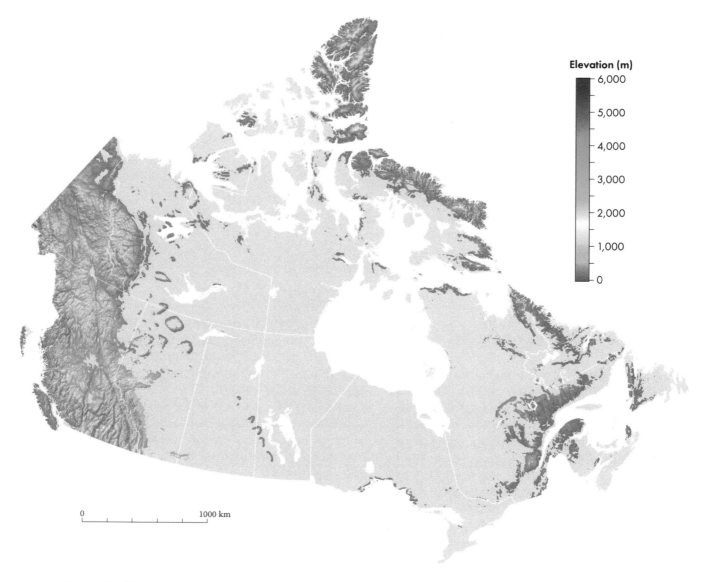

Figure 1.1: Mountainous areas in Canada based on McDowell & Guo (2021), following definition given by Kapos et al. (2000).

that are located within 100 km of minor mountainous features (note, this buffer distance has been used for population assessments in other contexts such as coasts, e.g., Millennium Ecosystem Assessment, 2005).

Mountains in Canada contribute to human well-being in myriad ways, including by providing freshwater, food, and medicine; sites of spiritual significance and places of solace and meaning; inspiration for art, literature, and storytelling; and destinations for recreation and mountain sports. These gifts from mountains play an important role in the culture, identity, and livelihoods of

people across Canada, even those who do not live in mountain areas. At the same time, mountains can be foreboding, with hostile winds, unpredictable weather, and dynamic landscapes and river courses that present challenges to safe passage. The rumbles of mountain hazards such as rockfall and avalanches freezes even seasoned alpine guides as they echo off mountain walls, a reminder of the volatility of these environments.

As in other mountain areas globally (see Adler et al., 2022; Hock et al., 2019), climate change is leading to transformative changes in mountain systems across Canada, with implications

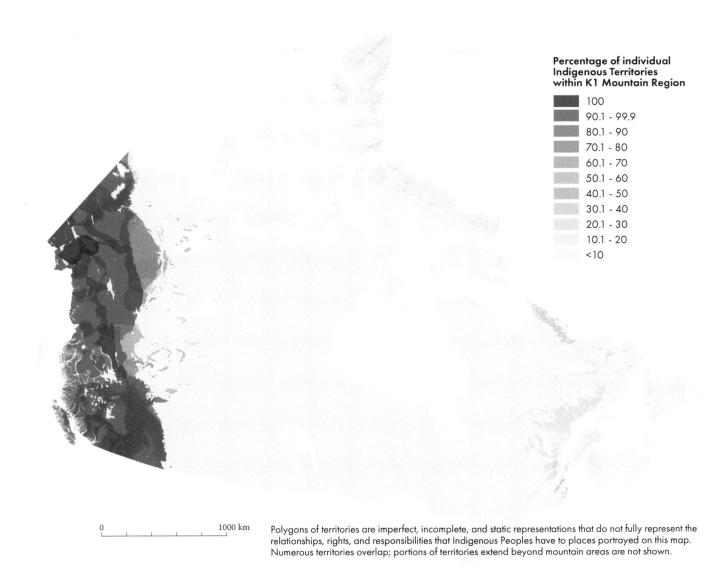

Percentage of individual Indigenous Territories within K1 Mountain Region

- 100
- 90.1 - 99.9
- 80.1 - 90
- 70.1 - 80
- 60.1 - 70
- 50.1 - 60
- 40.1 - 50
- 30.1 - 40
- 20.1 - 30
- 10.1 - 20
- <10

0   1000 km

Polygons of territories are imperfect, incomplete, and static representations that do not fully represent the relationships, rights, and responsibilities that Indigenous Peoples have to places portrayed on this map. Numerous territories overlap; portions of territories extend beyond mountain areas are not shown.

Figure 1.2: Indigenous territories associated with mountain areas in Canada. Based on McDowell & Guo (2021). Data from Native-Land.ca.

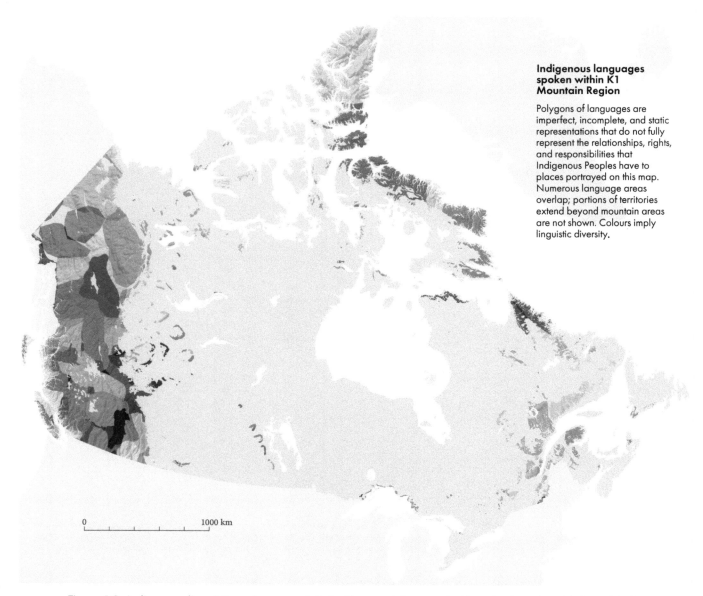

Indigenous languages spoken within K1 Mountain Region

Polygons of languages are imperfect, incomplete, and static representations that do not fully represent the relationships, rights, and responsibilities that Indigenous Peoples have to places portrayed on this map. Numerous language areas overlap; portions of territories extend beyond mountain areas are not shown. Colours imply linguistic diversity.

Figure 1.3: Indigenous linguistic regions associated with mountain areas in Canada. Based on McDowell & Guo (2021). Data from Native-Land.ca.

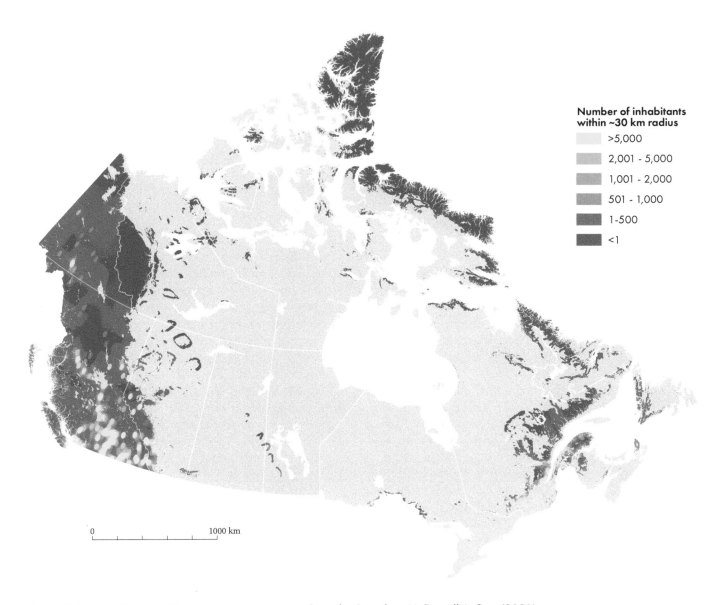

Figure 1.4: Population densities in mountain areas in Canada. Based on McDowell & Guo (2021).

for water resources, ecosystems, hazards, livelihoods, and the recreational, cultural, and spiritual values associated with these places. For example, what will the Icefields Parkway be named when the ice is gone, as expected by the end of this century (Clarke et al., 2015), and will this route through the Canadian Rockies evoke the same sense of wonder when the mountain peaks are bare? Climate change is also a threat to many alpine species that are adapted to the cooler temperatures or the snow regimes at high elevations. These species have nowhere higher to go in the face of increasing temperatures, and also face competitive pressures from lower-elevation species that are migrating upwards in search of respite from heat, wildfire, or population pressures. Similar to Arctic-adapted species, alpine flora and fauna might simply run out of habitat. This is also true in mountain streams and their downstream reaches, should water temperatures warm to conditions that support the upstream migration of lower-elevation aquatic ecosystems or invasive species.

The benefits mountains provide to people are increasingly threatened not only by climate change, but also other impacts related to human activities, such as land use development, resource extraction, and environmentally and socially damaging governance practices. The implications of these drivers of change are unevenly distributed within and across communities and ecosystems, but cumulatively are rapidly transforming mountain systems across Canada.

Despite the importance and sensitivity of mountain systems in Canada, there has never been a formal assessment of the state of mountain systems knowledge in the country. However, the lack of an existing assessment of mountain systems in Canada does not imply a paucity of knowledge about mountains. Indigenous Peoples have gathered profound bodies of knowledge through close connections to mountain places and by observing and experiencing the dynamics of weather and seasons, ecosystems and animal behaviour, water and rocks, and non-material features and presences in mountains. This has led to nuanced, holistic, and sophisticated knowledges of mountain systems across the continent, many of which focus on interconnectedness and purposefully include an ethic of care to honour past, current, and future generations of living and inanimate beings (Muller et al., 2019). These Indigenous knowledges, which in many traditions have been held by Elders and passed down intergenerationally following place-specific protocols for sharing stories and oral histories, often recognize the mountains and other-than-human beings as teachers and kin. Accordingly, environmental features in mountains (land, water, ice, biota) can be strongly connected to Indigenous identity (Berry, 1999; Downing & Cuerrier, 2011), or the knowledge and emotional significance of belonging to a group. Each Indigenous Nation or group has its own distinct knowledge system and Traditional Territory, including certain areas exclusive to them. Furthermore, based on their socio-cultural traditions, this territory is often subdivided, with certain areas associated with particular individuals and/or social groups like clans, moieties, or phratries. As such, First Nations, Métis, and Inuit knowledges of mountains are inextricably tied to relationships with their respective territories.

More recently, non-Indigenous settlers and migrants who have established communities in and adjacent to mountains in present-day Canada have come to know mountains through the lens of their own epistemologies. These individuals and their associated institutions typically applied the principles, techniques, and assumptions of Western sciences to measure and characterise mountain systems. Since the 1900s, this has led to an extensive and ever-growing body of research focused on mountains in Canada. Indeed, nearly 3000 peer-reviewed articles about mountain systems in Canada have been published to date (McDowell & Hanly, 2022). These publications are in addition to numerous scholarly books, literary texts, popular accounts, alpine journal reports, and artistic works that collectively contribute to a rich and diverse body of Western knowledge of mountain systems in Canada.

Much of the mountain research in Canada to date has been conducted in the mountain west and has focused on the physical environment and ecosystems that make these regions unique, including as homes to flora, fauna, landforms, glaciers, weather and climate regimes, and Earth system processes that can only be found in these environments. It has also shown that mountains in Canada serve as critical 'water towers'—locations that play an outsized role in providing freshwater for downstream populations and ecosystems (Vivrioli et al., 2007, Immerzeel et al., 2020)—for all of western Canada (e.g., Elmore et al., 2020), and much of the world's leading research into mountain snow, glaciers, and hydrological processes has been led out of long-term studies that trace to the 1960s in the St. Elias, Coast, and Rocky Mountains. Similar advances have been made through long-term study of alpine ecosystems (e.g., Krebs et al., 2014). Much of what we understand today about mountain ecological and landscape dynamics in Canada has its origins in this foundational research, including a legacy of student training and capacity building that has enabled ongoing advances in mountain research (Danby et al., 2014). While mountain research in Canada has been concentrated in the mountain west and has been focused primarily on the natural sciences to date, there is a strong foundation to build upon; there is also growing awareness of regional and topical gaps that warrant attention in the future (McDowell & Hanly, 2022).

Notwithstanding the contributions of Western academic mountain research activities, it is important to recognize that much of this work has tended to ignore or delegitimize other ways of knowing, and it has sometimes been explicitly linked to colonial ambitions of territorial control, including exploiting the resources of the Americas and subjugating and dispossessing Indigenous Peoples of their lands (Akena, 2012; Muller et al., 2019). Relevant examples of this colonial rationale can be found in information-gathering exercises such as surveying and characterising wildlife (Eichler & Baumeister, 2018; Hessami et al., 2021; Higgs et al., 2009).

In light of the fraught history of colonial settlement and its ongoing consequences, there are clear and repeated calls from Indigenous Peoples that Indigenous ways of knowing, doing, and being should be recognized as both equal to and distinct from Western academic knowledge. There is also widespread understanding that historical inequities, exclusions, and colonialism continue to create important obstacles to such inclusion and recognition (Fernández-Llamazares et al., 2021). Indigenous Peoples are seeking to level the playing field while overcoming colonial power asymmetries that have been reinforced by time, epistemic racism, and dominance (Battiste, 2002; Borrows, 2002; Kassi et al., 2022; McGregor, 2014; Reid et al., 2021; K. Whyte, 2017). There are likewise many vocal non-Indigenous advocates for more inclusive and just forms of engagement with Indigenous ways of knowing (Berkes et al., 2000; Cruickshank, 2005; Johnston & Mason, 2020; Lamb et al., 2022; Latulippe & Klenk, 2020; Nadasdy, 1999; Tengö et al., 2014). We recognize here that Indigenous and Western academic approaches to understanding mountain environments are both different and complementary. In this context, the Canadian Mountain Assessment was envisioned as an opportunity to work towards a more inclusive approach to characterising the state of mountain systems knowledge in Canada, while also acknowledging the impossibility of exhaustively assessing the state of Indigenous knowledges of mountains across Canada.

1.2 Introducing the Canadian Mountain Assessment

The Canadian Mountain Assessment (CMA) provides a first-of-its-kind look at what we know, do not know, and need to know about diverse and rapidly changing mountain systems in Canada. The assessment includes insights from both Indigenous and Western academic knowledge systems and represents a unique effort to enhance

understanding of mountains through the respectful inclusion of multiple bodies of knowledge. It is the country's first formal assessment of mountain systems knowledge. It was undertaken to:

- Provide a detailed account of the state of mountain systems knowledge in Canada
- Enhance appreciation of the diversity and significance of mountains in the country
- Deliver insights that are salient for a variety of end users (e.g., researchers, Indigenous communities, decision makers)
- Clarify challenges and opportunities pertinent to mountain systems in Canada
- Motivate and inform mountain-focused research and policy
- Cultivate a community of practice related to mountains in Canada
- Provide a tangible step towards reconciliation efforts in Canada

The CMA was inspired by the Hindu Kush Himalaya Assessment (Wester et al., 2019) and recent mountain-focused assessment activities by the Intergovernmental Panel on Climate Change (IPCC) (Adler et al., 2022; Hock et al., 2019), as well as prior efforts to elevate Indigenous knowledges in major assessment activities, such as the Arctic Climate Impact Assessment (ACIA), the Millennium Ecosystem Assessment (MEA), and work by the Intergovernmental Science-Policy Platform on Biodiversity and Ecosystem Services (IPBES) (ACIA, 2005; IPBES, 2019; Millennium Ecosystem Assessment, 2005). While the CMA was informed and motivated by these prior assessments, it was shaped by the specific priorities, challenges, and opportunities of the Canadian context.

The CMA was hosted at the University of Calgary, situated on the territories of the Peoples of Treaty 7, including the Blackfoot Confederacy (Siksika, Piikani, and Kainai First Nations), Îyârhe (Stoney) Nakoda (including the Chiniki, Bearspaw, and Goodstoney First Nations), and Tsuut'ina First Nation. The City of Calgary is also home to Métis Nation of Alberta, Region 3. The project was supported by funding from the Canadian Mountain Network (CMN) and the Natural Sciences and Engineering Research Council (NSERC). It was initiated in May 2020, and was prepared over the course of 3.5 years (Fig. 1.5). During this time, the CMA played an important role in catalysing

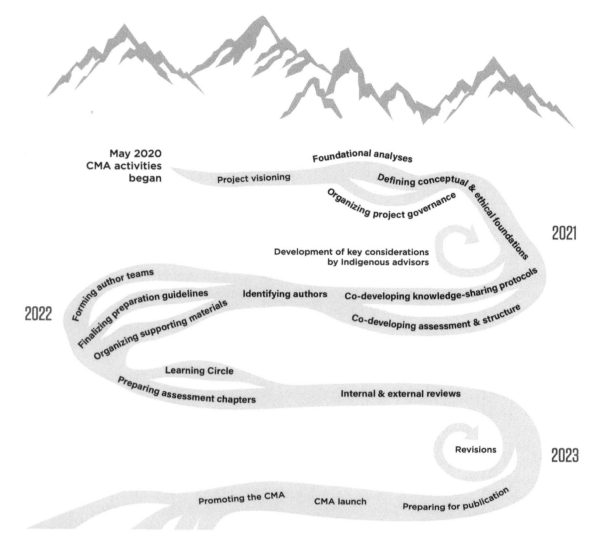

Figure 1.5: CMA timeline and key activities

Timeline labels:

May 2020 CMA activities began

Project visioning

Foundational analyses

Defining conceptual & ethical foundations

Organizing project governance

2021

Development of key considerations by Indigenous advisors

Forming author teams

Finalizing preparation guidelines

Identifying authors

Co-developing knowledge-sharing protocols

2022

Organizing supporting materials

Co-developing assessment & structure

Learning Circle

Preparing assessment chapters

Internal & external reviews

Revisions

2023

Promoting the CMA

CMA launch

Preparing for publication

a community of practice related to mountains by connecting and cultivating relationships between mountain knowledge holders from across Canada (Fig. 1.6).

The following sections detail the CMA's governance, visioning activities, and methodology, as well as key project innovations and limitations.

1.2.1 Project governance

The governance model for the CMA was conceptualised as a 'Stewardship Circle' (Fig. 1.7), a characterization that reflects the CMA's prioritisation of inclusivity, respectful dialogue, reciprocity, and shared responsibility. The Stewardship Circle—which included a Project Leader, Project Advisors, Assessment Authors, Project Assistants, and members of CMN leadership (Table 1.1)—was composed of a diverse group of Knowledge Holders and experts. Members worked collaboratively to enhance the integrity, relevance, and positive impact of the project and to work towards the inclusion of Indigenous Peoples' values and aspirations, which have historically been marginalised, misrepresented, or absent in knowledge assessment initiatives.

When inviting potential contributors to the assessment, efforts were made to balance representation according to First Nations, Métis, and Inuit/non-Indigenous identity; gender; career stage; and major mountain region of origin (Fig. 1.8). Despite some shortcomings, the overall composition of CMA's Stewardship Circle was relatively inclusive and diverse. For example, of the

Figure 1.6: CMA contributors coming together from across mountain geographies and knowledge systems (not all contributors pictured). Photos courtesy of David Borish and Graham McDowell, 2022.

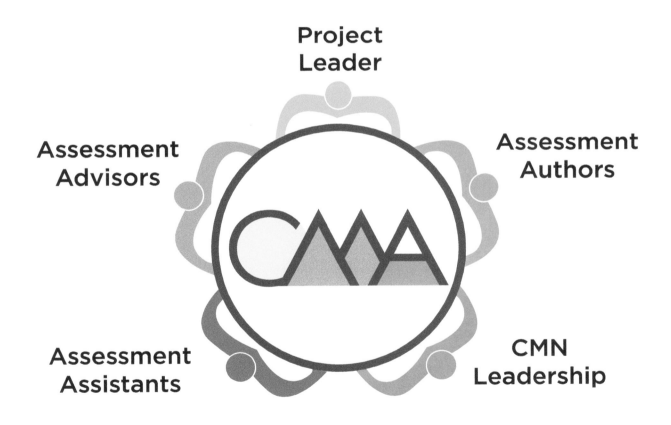

Figure 1.7: CMA Stewardship Circle

Table 1.1: Stewardship Circle: Roles and responsibilities.

PROJECT LEADER	The Project Leader conceptualised the project idea, secured project funding, and bore ultimate responsibility for defining, coordinating, and delivering the CMA. They worked closely with Project Advisors to co-develop key elements of the CMA, and with Authors and Project Assistants to operationalize the project vision and approach. The Project Leader also led foundational analyses/publications that underpin the CMA.
PROJECT ADVISORS	Project Advisors worked closely with the Project Leader to co-develop the vision and approach of the CMA, and to support the salience and impact of the project.
Canadian Advisors	Canadian Advisors were the primary individuals involved in providing guidance to the Project Leader. They played a key role in shaping the spirit, intent, and structure of the CMA, as well as providing guidance on practical, methodological, and strategic matters.
International Advisors	International Advisors supported the CMA by providing germane insights from prior mountain-focused assessments and other relevant international initiatives, as well as providing guidance on practical, methodological, and strategic matters.
ASSESSMENT AUTHORS	Assessment Authors worked to identify and engage with relevant information and knowledges, to prepare assessment chapters, and to adequately revise chapter content following external review.
Lead Authors	Lead Authors oversaw the coordination and preparation of specific chapters of the CMA.
Contributing Authors	Contributing Authors made specific contributions to one or more chapters of the CMA.
PROJECT ASSISTANTS	Project Assistants performed various essential tasks including conducting analyses, providing logistical support, and facilitating report preparation activities.
Project Assistant	The Project Assistant acted in a supportive capacity to implement the vision and approach of the CMA and was involved on a regular, ongoing basis in strategic planning and day-to-day activities. They worked closely with the Project Leader and communicated frequently with members of the Stewardship Circle.
Research Assistants	Research Assistants carried out specific research tasks to support the CMA.
CMN LEADERSHIP	CMN Leadership worked with the Project Leader to facilitate coherence between the CMA and the goals and priorities of the CMN.

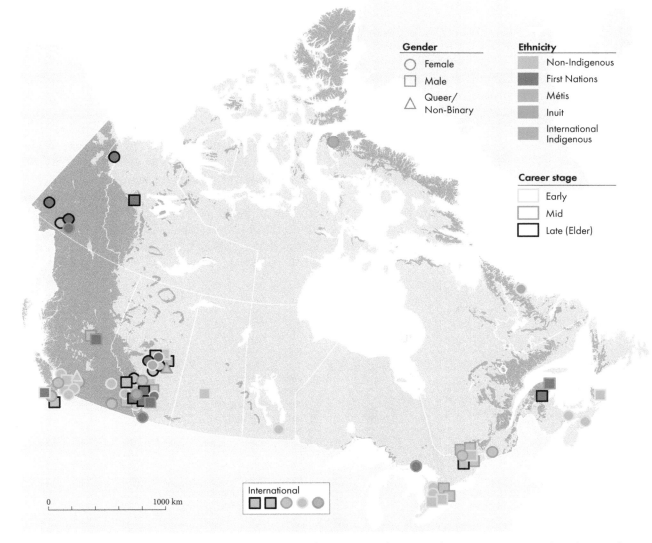

Figure 1.8: CMA contributors by First Nations, Métis, and Inuit/non-Indigenous identity; career stage; location; and gender (does not include external reviewers).

CMA's 80 core contributors, 30% of participants identified as First Nations, Métis, or Inuit, and 55% identified as female, queer, or non-binary. Furthermore, representation across career stages was nearly balanced and the overall geographical diversity of participants was fairly high. Contributor bios can be found in Appendix I.

1.2.2 Visioning

Visioning for the CMA involved members of the Stewardship Circle (primarily the Project Leader and Advisors) working collaboratively to define the spirit and intent of the project, the project's conceptual and ethical foundations, the kinds of

content that would be included in the CMA, and the structure of the Assessment. This period of the CMA process involved a diversity of perspectives from the outset. It was also informed by findings from a survey that was sent out to members of the CMN network, which asked for input on the assessment design and focal topics from potential end-users of the CMA (108 respondents), as well as guidance from an independent consultant on ethics and knowledge sharing.

During the visioning period of the CMA, formal Stewardship Circle meetings were convened regularly via Zoom (due to Covid restrictions). There were also numerous virtual meetings between individual project members, as well as members of a working group composed of Indigenous members of the Stewardship Circle. Meetings were conveyed with the intention of cultivating "ethical space" (Ermine, 2000, 2007; Ermine et al., 2004), which involved respecting individuals' diverse ways of knowing, being, and doing; making space for Indigenous protocols, including starting meetings with opening words or blessings (as appropriate) from Elders; providing reflexive land acknowledgments; and honouring the unique expertise and circumstances of individual participants. Through this highly intentional collaboration approach—which elicited moments of difficulty but also stimulated deep reflection, creativity thinking, and innovation—Stewardship Circle members successfully defined key elements of the project, as described below.

Conceptual foundations

The CMA's conceptual foundations were informed by a multiple evidence base (MEB) approach, which "emphasises the complementarity of knowledge systems and the values of letting each knowledge system speak for itself, within its own context, without assigning one dominant knowledge system with the role of external validator" (Tengö et al., 2014). This approach highlights the integrity of knowledge systems on their own terms, while also bringing attention to the possibility of respectfully braiding multiple sources of evidence together to enhance understanding of a particular issue (Fig. 1.9). This requires making space for diverse manifestations of knowledge (e.g., text, oral, visual), and ensuring

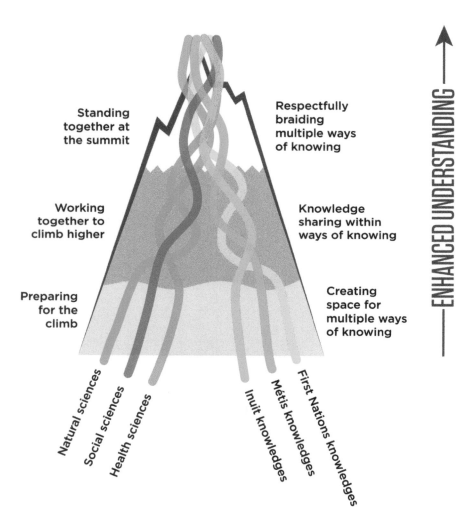

Figure 1.9: Simplified depiction of a multiple evidence base approach in the context of the CMA. Much like climbing to the summit of a mountain, respectfully braiding ways of knowing is an aspiration, but such an outcome is not guaranteed. The success of the effort can be determined not only by the point the climbers reach, but also by the learning along the way.

that determinations about which knowledge is appropriate, credible, and relevant occurs within knowledge systems (e.g., according to Indigenous protocols, according to scientific method). It also requires avoiding any attempt to integrate diverse knowledges into a unified truth (Kimmerer, 2020; Reid et al., 2021). The MEB therefore foregrounds issues of power involved in connecting different knowledge systems (and associated complexities, limitations, and opportunities), and emphasizes the need for deeply collaborative and reflexive co-creation processes from the outset. In these ways, an MEB approach aims to enhance the legitimacy and relevance of project outcomes for a broad range of groups, particularly those whose ways of knowing, being, and doing have tended to be marginalised.

Ethical foundations

The CMA's involvement with Indigenous Peoples and knowledges was guided by standards for ethical conduct described in the *Tri-Council Policy Statement: Ethical Conduct for Research Involving Humans TCPS 2* (2018) (Canadian Institutes of Health Research et al., 2018), particularly those elaborated in Chapter 9 'Research Involving the First Nations, Inuit and Métis Peoples of Canada'. However, members of the CMA aspired to exceed this guidance, and were particularly inspired and motivated by the transformative vision articulated in the United Nations Declaration on the Rights of Indigenous Peoples (UNDRIP, 2007), which was adopted by Canada in 2016. In particular, Article 31 states that "Indigenous peoples have the right to maintain, control, protect and develop their cultural heritage, traditional knowledge and traditional cultural expressions, as well as the manifestations of their sciences, technologies and cultures." We also drew guidance and motivation from the Truth and Reconciliation Commission of Canada's Calls to Action (Truth and Reconciliation Commission, 2015), which were endorsed by all levels of government in Canada, and OCAP® Principles (Ownership, Control, Access and Possession)[1] (First Nations Information

---

1 OCAP® is a registered trademark of the First Nations Information Governance Centre (FNIGC): https://fnigc.ca/ocap-training/

Governance Centre, n.d.), which are widely used and promoted by First Nations communities and organisations in Canada. The CMA's engagement with academic knowledge was guided by principles of scientific integrity—transparency, reproducibility, high quality, avoidance of conflict of interest, and adherence to research ethics—as elaborated in the Government of Canada's Policy on Scientific Integrity (Government of Canada, 2017).

Inclusion of diverse content

A cornerstone of the CMA is making space for diverse manifestations of knowledge about mountains. This approach is an outcome of the CMA's conceptual and ethical foundations and reflects recognition that knowledge about mountains is held in diverse forms and that text is not always a culturally appropriate way to convey such knowledges. Accordingly, while the CMA is a text-based document, it also includes a variety of visual materials (e.g., maps, paintings, photographs) as well as video recordings of knowledges and stories shared by First Nations, Métis, and Inuit individuals from across mountain areas in Canada. Video recordings of conversations—and the underpinning methodology (see 'First Nations, Métis, and Inuit knowledges' section below)—are specifically intended to respect and uplift oral knowledge transmission traditions, which are central for many Indigenous Peoples in Canada. We encourage the reader to engage with these videos, which can be found throughout the CMA, and which provide unique insights into the depth, specificity, and diversity of First Nations, Métis, and Inuit knowledges about mountains in Canada. The printed version of the CMA includes QR codes, which can be scanned to view videos on phones or tablets. The online version of the CMA has videos embedded in the text, which can be viewed within the document. Full URLs for videos are provided in Appendix II.

Guiding principles

Members of the Stewardship Circle elaborated five overarching principles that summarise the spirit and intent of the CMA, and that steered the efforts of those involved in preparing the assessment (Fig. 1.10).

1 – Service

The CMA is guided by service to mountains and mountain-connected communities — Indigenous, non-Indigenous, and non-human — now and into the future.

2 – Inclusivity

The CMA celebrates the diversity, depth, and specificity of First Nations, Métis, Inuit, and Western academic knowledges related to mountains in Canada, and aspires to demonstrate the breadth of these knowledges, as well as points of tension, synergy, and emergence.

3 – Humility

The CMA aspires to collaboratively advance a good effort, acknowledging that our assessment of what we know, don't know, and need to know about mountains in Canada inherently reflects structural disparities, procedural limitations, and our own positionality.

4 – Responsibility

The CMA is committed to upholding the integrity of diverse knowledges shared into the assessment; respecting the privacy of culturally protected knowledges; enacting on-going consent; and ensuring open-access publication, traceability, and transparency.

5 – Action

The CMA aims to enhance understanding of the importance of mountains in Canada, and to stimulate relationships, research, and action that support the realization of desirable mountain futures.

Figure 1.10: CMA Guiding Principles

1.2.3 *Methodology*

The CMA characterises the state of knowledge related to mountains in Canada based on the respectful consideration of multiple lines of evidence, including: peer-reviewed literature; First Nations, Métis, and Inuit knowledges; insights from select grey literature; and video recordings, artistic, and photographic content. Foundational analyses that underpin the CMA are described below, followed by information about the methodologies used to gather and consider distinct forms of evidence. The section concludes with information about the selection and roles of CMA authors.

Foundational analyses

At the outset of the CMA, numerous fundamental aspects of Canadian mountain systems had yet to be systematically characterised and quantified in a nationally coherent manner. In response, numerous geospatial analyses were conducted to advance understanding of the biogeography, people, and economic activities associated with mountains in Canada (see McDowell & Guo, 2021 for full details). The mountainous area of Canada was delineated according to the K1 definition provided by Kapos et al. (2000), which considers elevation, local elevation range, minimum elevation, and slope. This is the most commonly used set of criteria for defining mountain areas in the Western academic literature, and one that

provides a good approximation of regions generally considered mountainous in Canada. However, other valid approaches have been developed by Körner et al. (2011) and Karagulle et al. (2017), for example, which reflect differences in what is considered relevant in terms of attributes/criteria for delineation of mountainous terrain according to specific applications (see Sayer et al., 2018; Körner et al., 2021; Thornton et al., 2022). Results and maps based on the CMA's foundational analyses are found throughout this report. References for data used in these and other maps in the CMA are available in Appendix III.

To promote broad geographical consistency across CMA chapters, the CMA developed a classification scheme that divides the mountainous area of Canada into 10 major mountain regions (Fig. 1.11, interactive map here[2]). These regions are formed through an intersection of the K1 mountain area and the boundaries of existing 'terrestrial ecozones of Canada' (see Agriculture and Agri-Food Canada, 2016). Terrestrial ecozones represent areas with broadly consistent biophysical characteristics; they are not based on socio-economic or political criteria, which are inevitably contested. Authors were encouraged to use this framework as their primary geographical

2 https://www.arcgis.com/apps/webappviewer/ index.html?id=8b0239c85e62416b9f6ab11acfda5da8 &extent=-18755806.0455%2C4769580.2594%2C-3727 674.7884%2C11755313.1485%2C102100

Figure 1.11: Major mountain regions in Canada—The primary geographical framework used in the CMA. Based on McDowell & Guo, 2021.

framework when organising and assessing evidence. However, references to mountains in the west, north, and east (scaling up), or to specific mountain ranges or sub-ranges (scaling down), was also acceptable where relevant. Furthermore, First Nations, Métis, and Inuit authors were encouraged to reference mountain regions in other regionally/culturally appropriate ways, at their discretion (see 'Terminology' section below).

Peer-reviewed literature
The CMA aimed to provide a thorough assessment of peer-reviewed literature relevant to moun-

tains in Canada. Accordingly, the CMA conducted a national-scale systematic scoping review of peer-reviewed articles that are relevant to mountains in Canada. This effort yielded 2,888 articles, all of which were classified according to variables such as major mountain region, focal topics, and research approach (see McDowell & Hanly, 2022, for full details). Additionally, authors were asked to ensure that the 20 most influential publications in their respective area of expertise (that are relevant to mountains in Canada), as well as any relevant review articles were considered in their assessment activities. All publications relevant to the CMA were organised in a centralised and searchable cloud-based bibliography that was accessible to all authors.

Authors assessed the peer-reviewed academic literature with qualitative statements—supported by summary statistics as appropriate—about the state of knowledge/evidence in relation to key chapter themes and major mountain regions. Here, authors were asked to consider the amount of literature, the quality of literature, and the level of agreement in the literature within a particular domain of knowledge, as well as across mountain geographies. This approach was informed by the confidence language model of the IPCC (Mastrandrea et al., 2010). However, the CMA does not use formal confidence language, given concern that the lack of a comparable criteria for Indigenous knowledges would have the effect of undermining the perceived validity of insights from First Nations, Métis, and Inuit knowledges.

In addition to peer-reviewed articles, authors of some chapters also engaged with scholarly books as sources of information about mountains, especially for content from the humanities, arts, and literature. The identification and inclusion of scholarly books was based on the expertise of chapter authors.

When reviewing peer-reviewed literature, authors were asked to be cognizant of the processes originally used to gather and disseminate information, including the fact that some academic literature reporting insights from Indigenous Peoples in Canada has been produced without the free, prior, and informed consent of Knowledge Holders; has lacked due credit or attribution; and has misrepresented First Nations, Métis, and Inuit knowledges in ways that continue to be harmful to Indigenous communities. CMA authors were not in a position to comprehensively assess the extent of such issues, nor to make a determination that certain materials should be excluded on this basis. Instead, authors were asked to reflect critically and constructively on these issues when assessing the literature to enhance awareness about ethical concerns vis-à-vis the production of knowledge about mountains in Canada.

First Nations, Métis, and Inuit knowledges

A key aspiration of the CMA was to elevate Indigenous knowledges of mountains and to bring these knowledges into conversation with Western academic understandings of mountains. The co-creation of knowledge is fundamental to the Canadian response to the United Nations Declaration on the Rights of Indigenous Peoples and the Calls to Action of the Truth and Reconciliation Commission; it also reflects recent case law. Among other things, court cases such as Haida (2004), Taku (2004), and Blueberry (2021) have clearly established an obligation under Canada law for genuine consultation with Indigenous Peoples. This is true regardless of treaty and highlights that, while a treaty relationship can provide guidance in this situation, it is not mandatory for consultation to occur.

To provide a respectful and more culturally appropriate way of engaging with First Nations, Métis, and Inuit understandings of mountains, the CMA organised an in-person Learning Circle with Indigenous Knowledge Holders from across mountain areas in Canada. The gathering (the CMA's first in-person event) was held from from 23–26 May 2022 in Banff, Alberta—Traditional Territories of Treaty 7 Peoples, including Niitsitapi from the Blackfoot Confederacy (Siksika, Piikani, and Kainai First Nations), the Îyârhe (Stoney) Nakoda (including the Chiniki, Bearspaw, and Goodstoney First Nations), and the Tsuut'ina First Nation, as well as the Métis Nation of Alberta, Region 3. The gathering aimed to provide an ethical space where knowledges and stories that participants wished to contribute to the CMA could be shared and appropriately included under their guidance. The Learning Circle was informed by advice from members of the CMA's Stewardship Circle and an independent consultant on ethics and knowledge sharing, as well as wishes expressed during an online pre-meeting with participants; it was reviewed and approved by the University of Calgary's Research Ethics Review Board before being convened (REB22-0070).

The Learning Circle was attended by 20 First Nations, Métis, and Inuit individuals, including a Chief, numerous Elders, and several youths; some participants were also involved in the CMA as Authors and Advisors prior to the gathering. After offerings of tobacco, in adherence to Indigenous protocols of the Nations on whose territories we gathered, the Learning Circle was opened by Elders from the region (Blackfoot and Stoney Nakoda), followed by three days of conversations organised around the CMA's chapter themes. Following the guidance of Elders present, a chair at the circle was left open during the gathering as a sign of respect for the knowledge of, and responsibilities to, non-human kin that share mountain spaces. The Learning Circle conversations were facilitated by Indigenous CMA authors, the Project Leader, and the Project Assistant.

As Elder Pnnal Bernard Jerome, Micmacs of Gesgapegiag, shared during one of these conversations, the Learning Circle offered a space to reflect with humility on the mountains of his own home, to be reminded of his knowledge and identity as a Micmac person, and to learn from the stories and knowledges of diverse places shared during the gathering (LC 1.1). Offering closing words for the Learning Circle, Elder Hayden Melting Tallow of the Siksika Nation, Blackfoot Confederacy, affirmed the CMA efforts to follow protocol, honoured his ancestors, and reflected on the experience of visiting the mountains and Peoples of many Nations in Canada through the conversations held during the Learning Circle (LC 1.2). We closed the gathering with words of trust, coexistence, and shared aspiration to carry the sharing of knowledges forward with action.

With contributors' permission, conversations during the Learning Circle were video recorded by a videographer experienced in knowledge co-creation activities with Indigenous Peoples. After the event, these recordings were shared with participants, enabling them to request the removal of any culturally protected or otherwise sensitive content before it was shared more broadly. Shareable content was then uploaded to a video hosting and editing platform (frame.io), where video segments were time stamped by participants' name and Nation or community, as well as the themes and topics discussed during their remarks (Fig. 1.12). These searchable files were then shared with CMA authors, who were asked to weave videos into their respective chapters. With further guidance and review by Learning Circle participants, segments of these recordings have been included as videos in the CMA text (see videos in paragraph above, for example). Given their fundamental contributions to the CMA, Learning Circle participants are also recognized as CMA authors (all agreed to be recognized in this way).

Other manifestations of First Nations, Métis, and Inuit knowledges related to mountains in Canada were included in the CMA at the discretion of Indigenous chapter authors, including content reported in community reports and archival texts, as well as knowledge shared into the CMA by Indigenous chapter authors.

Unlike the CMA's engagement with academic literature, we did not aim to achieve a comprehensive understanding of First Nations, Métis, and Inuit knowledges of mountain systems across Canada. It would be impossible to include the diversity of First Nations, Métis, and Inuit knowledges of mountains in a single book. Moreover, as Learning Circle participant Gabrielle Weasel Head, Kainaiwa Nation, Blackfoot Confederacy, explains, learning from this knowledge requires heart-forward work to build meaningful relationships that advance specific Indigenous Nations' languages, protocols, and experiences (LC 1.3). In this spirit, the CMA approach reflects a commitment to confront colonial erasure of Indigenous lifeways and resist the imposition of *pan-Indigeneity* by

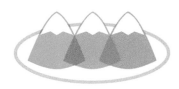

Pnnal Bernard Jerome, Micmacs of Gesgapegiag, 2022, LC 1.1

Hayden Melting Tallow, Siksika Nation, Blackfoot Confederacy, 2022, LC 1.2

Gabrielle Weasel Head, Kainaiwa Nation, Blackfoot Confederacy, 2022, LC 1.3

Figure 1.12: Learning Circle video with searchability according to participant name, community and/or Nation, themes, and topics

acknowledging and elevating the diversity of First Nations, Métis, and Inuit identities and ways of knowing mountains. In this context, the inclusion of certain First Nations, Métis, and Inuit knowledges should not be interpreted as endorsing those over others. Rather, the insights included in the CMA reflect the information that was available given the methodology described in this chapter, and decisions by authors about which knowledges were particularly effective in illustrating the depth, richness, and diversity of mountain-related experience and knowledges possessed by Indigenous Peoples in Canada.

Grey literature

Inclusion of credible information from grey literature—material not published in traditional academic outlets—is increasingly understood as a way to diversify and enhance assessment results (see Paez, 2017). While a comprehensive review of grey literature was beyond the scope of the CMA, authors were invited to engage with publicly available grey literature that was relevant to chapter themes. No formal inclusion/exclusion criteria were applied in relation to grey literature; instead, the selection of materials was based on the respective expertise of chapter authors. Authors were encouraged to comment briefly on the

nature and credibility of the grey literature referenced in the CMA.

Video, artistic, and photographic content

Video recordings and artistic and photographic content help to enrich and broaden understanding of mountains in Canada. The primary intention of video recordings was to present contributions from Indigenous Knowledge Holders in a more culturally appropriate way, as described above. In addition, the CMA recognizes that both Western academic and Indigenous knowledges of mountains are often presented in the form of art and photographs, and such content was therefore also included in the CMA. Authors used their own networks, knowledge, and expertise to identify relevant non-text content for inclusion in the CMA. There was no formal assessment process for such content.

Document management, bibliography, and citation formats

Documents related to the CMA were organised in a cloud-based 'Author Hub'. Notably, master copies of chapter drafts were hosted online and available to all authors. This facilitated real-time engagement with other chapter authors and the ability to check the content and status of other chapters on an ongoing basis, all of which supported collaborative writing and review activities and increased transparency.

The CMA also created a cloud-based project bibliography using Zotero, with searchability functions linked to codes from the systematic scoping review (e.g., major mountain regions, primary focal topic). This approach had important benefits for chapter preparation activities, including most literature being available to author teams from the outset of writing and assessment activities, real-time access to documents contributed by other authors, and the ability to have any changes to references updated simultaneously across chapter master documents.

The citation formats for different kinds of materials in the CMA vary according to content-appropriate protocols. Specifically, reference to Learning Circle content includes the contributor's name and community and/or Nation, as well as time brackets for the relevant segment of the video recording. (Note that recordings include full statements to ensure that comments are not taken out of context.) In addition, in-text contributions from Indigenous Knowledge Holders have been attributed to Knowledge Holders and their communities, as appropriate, using a citation format developed to acknowledge Indigenous oral teachings (MacLeod, 2021). Other text and non-text materials are cited using American Psychological Association (APA) output style.

Data management and copyright

The CMA Stewardship Circle devoted considerable attention to balancing a commitment to open-access publication with Indigenous data sovereignty considerations. The CMA has been published by the University of Calgary Press under a restricted Creative Commons licence (Attribution-NonCommercial-NoDerivatives) which allows for free, non-commercial distribution with proper attribution to contributors, but does not allow the material to be changed or distributed in derivative forms. Under this licence, authors and Learning Circle participants retain copyright to their contributions.

Recorded Learning Circle contributions are retained in perpetuity in a cloud-based repository accessible to all Learning Circle participants. Portions of the recordings included as embedded videos within this report were subject to a

rigorous review process to determine whether they were appropriate for inclusion and did not contain sensitive information which could pose risks to participants or their communities. Recognizing that such determinations can change over time, a data withdrawal process was developed with the University of Calgary Press, which allows for contributions to be removed beyond the publication date if they are deemed inappropriate to share. Such changes can be made quickly to content hosted on the University of Calgary Press web platform and will be reflected in future print runs of the CMA. The virtual component of this assessment is thus a living space, uniquely responsive to the principle of ongoing consent.

Author identification, roles, and activities

CMA authors were identified through a variety of strategies to support the establishment of an experienced, diverse, and capable author team. Members of the Stewardship Circle were asked to provide the names of potential authors, a review was conducted to identify Indigenous scholars with expertise relevant to mountains at Canadian universities, and an open call for authors was distributed through CMN social media and 64 departments/faculties within Canadian universities. These efforts yielded ~200 potential authors. The Project Leader and Project Assistant then extended invitations to a subset of potential authors, aiming to include individuals from diverse areas of expertise, geographies, career stages, and genders, and to balance participation by Indigenous and non-Indigenous individuals. This was a deeply intentional process that involved nearly a year of research and outreach. Nevertheless, some potentially appropriate authors were surely missed while others were not contacted given efforts to balance participation according to the criteria above. In other instances, potential authors were contacted but they did not have the capacity to join the project. Zoom meetings were held with most individuals to discuss the unique approach and aspirations of the CMA before confirming authorship roles. Learning Circle participants were also recognized as authors. In all, 75 individuals participated in the CMA as authors.

Individual CMA chapters were written by a group of chapter authors, with each chapter team being composed of both Indigenous and non-

Indigenous individuals. Each of the CMA's core chapters, chapters 2–6, had Co-Lead authors as well as contributing authors. Chapter co-leaders—one Indigenous and one non-Indigenous individual—oversaw the coordination and timely preparation of their respective chapters, while contributing authors contributed specific text and/or non-text content for key topics areas within each chapter. Several CMA authors contributed to multiple chapters where their expertise/knowledge pertained to topics that spanned multiple chapters. Note that Contributing Authors, which includes Learning Circle participants, are listed in alphabetical order in the author list for each chapter; thus, name order does not imply a hierarchy of contributions.

Initial chapter drafts were prepared between January–July 2022. Following the Learning Circle, a second in-person meeting was convened in Banff between 26–28 May 2022 with 20 of the CMA's authors. All other chapter preparation activities were coordinated through regular online meetings. Review and revision activities commenced in August 2022.

1.2.4 *Review and revision process*

The review process for the CMA focused on ensuring that the assessment of Western academic knowledge of mountains was consistent with scientific standards, and that culturally protected or otherwise sensitive Indigenous knowledges and stories were not shared publicly. It also sought to invite feedback about the appropriate representation and braiding of multiple forms of evidence. The review of the CMA involved three primary stages.

Internal review period
Following the completion of initial chapter drafts in July 2022, members of the Stewardship Circle undertook a month-long internal review of the CMA. This review stage focused on identifying and addressing remaining gaps in chapters, receiving further guidance from Learning Circle participants about the appropriate inclusion of their knowledges, increasing engagement with non-text materials, supporting discursive and structural continuity across chapters, and formatting.

External review period
Following internal review, the CMA underwent a six-week-long period of external review. Eligible reviewers included Indigenous Peoples in Canada and from other mountain regions globally, mountain researchers from Canada and abroad, and those with professional responsibilities pertinent to mountain areas in Canada. Potential reviewers were contacted through a variety of means, including outreach to the International Network of Mountain Indigenous Peoples (INMIP), notification through CMN and CMA social media, and announcements by the Mountain Research Initiative (MRI). To ensure potential reviewers had appropriate expertise, knowledge, and/or motivation, interested reviewers were asked to complete a form describing their relevant qualifications. In total, 28 individuals participated in the public review of the CMA, all of whom were either very familiar (79%) or somewhat familiar (21%) with mountains; 86% were mountain researchers, 11% were both mountain researchers and Indigenous Knowledge Holders, and 4% were involved with the NGO sector; 14% of reviewers self-identified as Indigenous individuals. 71% reviewers were based in Canada, 7% were living outside of Canada but had previously lived in Canada, and 21% were based outside of Canada and had never lived in Canada.

During the first week of external review, chapter drafts were available exclusively to Learning Circle participants and their communities, as an additional check to ensure that no sensitive content was shared with external reviewers. External reviewers were then sent the CMA manuscript and were given the opportunity to provide written or oral feedback, with the former being collated through Google Sheets (similar to the IPCC review model) and the latter being offered through Zoom meetings. In total, 773 comments and suggestions were received from external reviewers.

Revision and submission
Chapter revision and final report preparation activities took place between November 2022 and February 2023. Following external review, chapter teams were provided with comments and suggestions provided by reviewers. During revision activities, each chapter team was supported by a Chapter Review Editor (in addition to the

Project Leader and Project Assistant), who helped chapter authors engage appropriately and as thoroughly as possible with reviewer comments. Chapter Co-Lead authors, the Project Leader, Project Assistant, and select Chapter Review Editors then led the preparation of a penultimate CMA draft. This draft was shared with CMA Advisors for review prior to submission for publication. The final CMA manuscript was submitted for publication in July 2023.

Terminology

The CMA embraced a pluralistic approach to the use of terms and nomenclature, recognizing that diverse knowledge traditions have different conventions and approaches for using language. We did, however, aim for consistency in the use of certain key phrases and terms. For example, the term "mountain systems" is used throughout the CMA, and indicates that mountainous places are constituted through interconnected physical, social, and biological characteristics and processes. It is meant to broaden the view of mountains from immutable landscape features to dynamic, living, and deeply relational spaces. Furthermore, we followed the distinct major mountain regions in Canada defined by McDowell & Guo (2021) (see Figure 1.11).

Where First Nations, Métis, and Inuit place names were known to the author team, we strove to prioritise the use of these names, rather than defaulting to other colonial terms. Given the overlapping and often contested nature of Indigenous territories, we were not in a position to provide all applicable Indigenous toponyms for a given place or entity; in many cases, we referred to English and French names recognized by settler governments. Whether in Indigenous languages, English, or French, the names we chose were not intended to imply a hierarchy of one name above others, nor to align with one group's claim over others or replace other names and meanings. We used the name Canada, or terms such as "the place now known as Canada," to refer to the country established through colonisation of a continent which has held many different names through time. We avoided the use of the possessive "Canada's mountains" or "Canada's peoples" to eschew connotations of ownership.

Following from the work of scholars such as Max Liboiron (2021), we used capitalization intentionally to denote meaning in terms such as land/Land, where the use of "Land" refers to a context implying sacred meaning or identifying the Land as a living entity. For example, "I spend time on the land with my family," was written to be read as denoting a distinct meaning from "the Land has memory." Capitalization was also used to reflect respect, as in the case of capitalising the terms Elder, Nation, and Indigenous Peoples among others. Furthermore, to resist a default to assumptions of pan-Indigeneity, we aimed to prioritise use of the term First Nations, Métis, and Inuit to refer to the Peoples who have lived in the region now known as Canada since time immemorial. Likewise, we use the phrase Indigenous knowledges (plural) to denote an explicit recognition of the many distinct knowledges held by Indigenous Peoples in Canada. These choices reflect our best efforts to be consistent with emerging conventions within Indigenous Studies and the guidance of Indigenous authors and Advisors who contributed to this assessment.

1.2.5 *Innovations*

The CMA contributes numerous important innovations. For example, the CMA is the first formal assessment of the state of mountain systems knowledge in Canada; it also contributed several foundational analyses related to mountain systems in Canada (e.g. McDowell & Guo, 2021, McDowell & Hanly, 2022). Furthermore, CMA is the first 'national-scale' assessment of mountains in any country (importantly, the CMA can also be understood as an *inter*National assessment in that it brings together individuals from many Indigenous Nations across Canada). In addition, the CMA co-created and operationalized a pluralistic assessment approach that brings Indigenous and non-Indigenous individuals and knowledge systems into meaningful conversation to enhance understanding of a topic of shared interest. This is a first in the context of mountain-focused assessments and such approaches remain rare in large-scale assessment activities more broadly (see *Evaluación Nacional de Biodiversidad y Servicios Ecosistémicos de Colombia* (2021) for a notable recent example).

Specific elements of the CMA's pluralistic assessment approach warrant mention as important innovations. For example, the CMA's Stewardship Circle provides insights into how reimaging governance arrangements can increase the salience, credibility, and legitimacy of cross-cultural knowledge co-creation initiatives. Likewise, the CMA's implementation of a multiple evidence base approach and its foregrounding of ethics demonstrate pathways for enabling more respectful, inclusive, and generative assessment practices. The CMA's authorship model follows from these innovations and is significant in its inclusion of Indigenous and non-Indigenous chapter co-leaders, who are supported by authorship teams composed of both Indigenous and non-Indigenous individuals.

The CMA also makes several substantive methodological innovations. For example, while systematic reviews have been used for targeted purposes in prior assessments, the CMA appears to be the first major assessment to use a formal systematic scoping review a point of departure for identifying, collating, and characterising the relevant peer-review literature across all topics and geographies (i.e., the state of Western academic knowledge). This approach has considerable benefits for transparency, traceability, and reproducibility, as well as workflow (e.g., avoiding the need for authors to conduct their own time-consuming literature searches). The associated cloud-based bibliography and 'Author Hub' provided additional benefits for collaboration in the context of a large, distributed project team. The CMA's Learning Circle approach is also innovative in an assessment context, especially in its emphasis on cultivating a more culturally appropriate space for sharing First Nations, Métis, and Inuit knowledges of mountains. Relatedly, the CMA's inclusion of video recordings from conversations with Learning Circle participants is an important innovation that strives to honour and uplift oral knowledge sharing traditions.

A final set of innovations pertains to the publishing model of the CMA. For example, in recognition of the rightful ownership of Indigenous Peoples over their cultural knowledges, the CMA's copyright model places ownership solely with the knowledge contributor (not the publisher), and derivative works are not permissible without express consent of the contributor. Furthermore, contributors can withdraw material in the future if they deem that it is no longer appropriate to share, making the CMA uniquely responsive to the principle of ongoing consent.

1.2.6 *Caveats and limitations*

Notwithstanding its important innovations, enacting the CMA's commitment to the principle of humility (Guiding Principle 3, Figure 1.10) requires recognition of the project's limitations. CMA tried hard to be more inclusive of Indigenous knowledges and to generate a knowledge assessment that began to braid different ways of knowing within a space of equality and respect. That is a high mountain to climb. Beyond exchange and sharing of information, "knowledge braiding has to recognize and seek to redress historical and systemic injustices, and must be supported by a commitment to working together over the long term toward equity, self-determination, reconciliation, and transformation" (Kassi et al., 2022, p. 1). The chapters that follow show how far we have come up that mountain, as well as the fact that much of the mountain remains to be climbed.

The CMA encountered specific constraints in its efforts to advance a more inclusive mountain assessment. For example, the CMA was limited by its format as a text-based document written primarily in English. First Nations, Métis, and Inuit Peoples across Canada are the keepers of more than 60 Indigenous languages—many of which are found in mountain areas in Canada (Fig. 1.4)—each encoding specific knowledge of the landscape, including place-names and stories. Many are traditionally not written, and meanings may change when translated into English and transcribed into text. Moreover, using predominantly settler-colonial languages such as English reinforces structures of power and hierarchy among knowledge systems. Including video recordings of conversations from the Learning Circle throughout the assessment was a response to this issue, which endeavoured to provide a more culturally appropriate platform for sharing teachings and stories expressed orally and, in some instances, in Indigenous languages.

Despite efforts to advance the inclusion of Indigenous knowledges, academic literature and Western knowledge predominate across the CMA chapters. Furthermore, the CMA has only scratched the surface of First Nations, Métis, and Inuit knowledges of mountains, including the incredible diversity of traditions, laws, protocols, and ways of being encoded in these knowledge systems. This is related, importantly, to the fact that aspects of Indigenous knowledges are often kept private and therefore cannot and should not be included in publicly available materials like the CMA. It is also important to recognize that Indigenous Advisors, authors, and Learning Circle contributors do not represent all First Nations, Métis, and Inuit Peoples in mountain areas in Canada. In addition, the dichotomy between Indigenous and Western academic knowledge systems obscures the fact that many of those who contributed to this project hold multiple forms of knowledge, such as Indigenous individuals who have received Western academic training.

In addition, while the CMA aimed to comprehensively assess the peer-reviewed academic literature relevant to mountains in Canada, some pertinent peer-reviewed studies were undoubtedly missed by the systematic literature review (e.g., relevant studies that were missed due to their lack of terms used in the search protocol for the systematic review). Authors aimed to fill these gaps by adding additional relevant documents. Furthermore, other literature (e.g., grey literature, books) offers rich and meaningful insights about mountains in Canada, but a comprehensive review of such materials was beyond the scope of the project.

Notwithstanding the literature assessed and Indigenous knowledges included in the CMA, there are several content gaps in the chapters that follow. These gaps are largely related to difficulty in securing authors/subject experts for every topic the CMA intended to address. Each chapter contains a table that indicates a selection of topics that were not assessed. Finally, other sources of local and experiential knowledge of mountains including from mountain professionals and guides as well as non-Indigenous mountain community members largely fell outside the scope of the CMA due to time and resource constraints. We recognize and value these as important types of knowledge about mountains and encourage future assessment efforts to engage with these groups.

In view of these limitations, the CMA should be understood as an extensive but inevitably im-

perfect and incomplete assessment of the state of mountain systems knowledge in Canada.

1.3 Organisation of Assessment

The CMA includes six chapters that bring together Indigenous and Western academic knowledge of mountains in Canada. Each chapter provides a reflection of the unique approaches of diverse author teams, so chapters are distinctive in terms of content but also tone. This is a result of the CMA's support for experimentation and emergence within chapter teams and reflects the unique ways in which authors have brought together diverse knowledges of mountains within specific CMA chapters. Likewise, it is important to emphasise differences in the scope of engagement with First Nations, Métis, and Inuit knowledge in individual chapters, which is a reflection of the framing of specific chapters, the composition of author teams, and the availability of shareable Indigenous knowledges pertinent to the chapter theme (e.g., what was shared during the Learning Circle). An overview of content included in the CMA is provided below.

The Introduction to the CMA (Chapter 1) provides context and rationale for the assessment, as well as details about the CMA's governance, conceptual and ethical foundations, methodology, and innovations and limitations. Chapter 2, Mountain Environments, covers biogeophysical aspects of mountains in Canada, including origin stories; mountain geology; weather and climate; snow, ice, and permafrost; water; hazards; ecosystems and biodiversity; and connections between mountains and lowland/coastal environments. Chapter 3, Mountains as Homelands, examines the diverse connections that people have with mountain places, including as sites of homes and Homelands, spiritual importance, recreation, and parks and protected areas, as well as tensions and transformations associated with settler-colonialism. Chapter 4, Gifts of the Mountains, examines the benefits that people receive from mountains, including values, relationships, and uses associated with gifts provided by mountains. Chapter 5, Mountains Under Pressure, evaluates processes, drivers, and trajectories of environmental and social change in mountain systems. Chapter 6, Desirable Mountain Futures, reflects on the other chapters and on the CMA's knowledge co-creation process. It discusses cross-cutting themes that emerged from the project and concludes by calling attention to needs and opportunities for securing more desirable futures for mountain systems in Canada.

We hope that you enjoy, learn from, and are inspired by the Canadian Mountain Assessment.

Glossary

Canada: Canada is a country in North America composed of ten provinces and three territories. It is the world's second-largest country by total area globally. Confederated in 1867, Canada is a parliamentary democracy and a constitutional monarchy that is part of the British Commonwealth; it is premised on settler-colonial legal, economic, and political foundations. Now home to a highly diverse population of more than 40 million people, the state of Canada was imposed on the lands and territories of Indigenous Peoples, impacting but not erasing Indigenous governance systems and the stewardship, occupation, and use of lands under their care. Recognizing the complex meaning that the term "Canada" holds for different people, in the CMA we sometimes use phrases such as "the lands now referred to as Canada."

Canadian Mountain Network (CMN): The Canadian Mountain Network was established to support the resilience and health of mountain peoples and places in Canada through research partnerships based on Indigenous and Western ways of knowing that inform decision-making and action. It was funded by a five-year grant from the Government of Canada's Networks of Centres of Excellence (NCE) Program, and was operational between 2019-2024.

Elders: Elders are members of a community who hold important roles in sharing knowledge with future generations, gathered through their own experiences and knowledge often shared from their own Elders through ceremony, protocols, and land-based learning. In the context of the CMA, the term Elder is used as a respectful way to refer to Indigenous Knowledge Holders who play this role within their communities and who are acknowledged to be Elders in those contexts. The term Elder is capitalised to demonstrate respect and deference to the knowledge and authority held by these individuals.

Ethical space: Developed by Willie Ermine (2007), the term ethical space refers to a state of working across knowledge systems—in this case Western and Indigenous knowledges—that is characterised by "mutual respect, kindness, and generosity," and which involves ongoing conversation and active listening among actors with distinct worldviews and ethical norms. This process is rooted in relationship building and the development of trust, as well as a willingness to be adaptive and responsive to new information. Acknowledgement of each individual's positionality is a central step towards cultivating ethical space, because doing so requires recognizing power imbalances that shape access to and perceived legitimacy of knowledge. As Nikolakis and Hotte (2022) note, "ethical space has the potential to transform cross-cultural relations, from an asymmetrical social order to respectful partnerships between Indigenous and non-Indigenous peoples."

First Nations: First Nations is a collective term to refer to diverse Indigenous Peoples across what is now known as Canada who do not identify as Inuit or Métis. There are more than 630 federally recognized First Nations communities across Canada with distinct cultures and lifeways, who belong to more than 50 different Nations and speak more than 50 languages.

Grey literature: Information produced outside of traditional scholarly publishing and distribution channels, including policy literature, white papers, technical reports, government and community documents, newspaper, newsletters, and blogs, among other materials.

Indigenous Peoples: Indigenous Peoples are groups of culturally distinct people recognized as descendents of the earliest known human inhabitants of a particular region, who maintain enduring cultural and political connections to their ancestral lands and waters. There are thousands of distinct Indigenous Peoples worldwide who speak their own languages, have their own models of governance and law, and practise diverse ways of relating to and managing their surrounding environments. Note that the term "Indigenous Peoples" has no single agreed-upon definition and remains contested in many parts of the world. The United Nations Declaration on the Rights of Indigenous Peoples (UNDRIP, 2007) does not define indigeneity or which groups constitute Indigenous Peoples, leaving it to these groups and Nations to identify themselves as such. In the context of present-day Canada, and North America more broadly, the term Indigenous Peoples often refers to First Nations, Métis, and Inuit Peoples in juxtaposition to settlers (European and non-European) and their descendants.

Indigenous knowledges: Indigenous knowledges are understood in the CMA as the bodies of knowledge generated by and belonging to Indigenous Peoples, both collectively and individually. The plural form "knowledges" reflects the diversity of Indigenous ways of knowing, rather than implying that Indigenous

Peoples hold one collective form of knowledge. Indigenous knowledges often derive from longstanding relationships with the lands and water of Indigenous territories. While such knowledges are sometimes referred to as Traditional Knowledge or Traditional Ecological Knowledge, in the CMA we have generally moved away from this usage because Indigenous knowledges can also refer to knowledge gathered by Indigenous persons using diverse tools and approaches, including Western scientific approaches. Where the term "knowledge traditions" is applied, we use this to convey an "understanding of where we come from to move forward and share all we have to offer for our future generations" (Gùdia Mary Jane Johnson, personal communication, 26 April 2023), and to reference longstanding practices and protocols associated with knowledge gathering, safekeeping, and transmission.

Intergovernmental Panel on Climate Change (IPCC): The Intergovernmental Panel on Climate Change is the United Nations body for assessing the science related to climate change. The IPCC was established in 1988 by the World Meteorological Organization (WMO) and United Nations Environment Programme (UNEP) to provide policymakers with regular assessments of the scientific basis of climate change, its impacts and future risks, and options for adaptation and mitigation.

International Network of Mountain Indigenous Peoples (INMIP): The International Network of Mountain Indigenous Peoples brings together mountain communities from 11 countries as they seek to revitalise biocultural heritage for climate-resilient and sustainable food systems. It was established in Bhutan in May 2014 at the 14th Congress of the International Society for Ethnobiology.

Inuit: Inuit are a group of culturally related Indigenous Peoples whose territories across Inuit Nunangat (homeland) extend across Arctic and subarctic regions of present-day Canada, and who share the common language, Inuktitut. Inuit are among the three federally recognized groups of Indigenous Peoples in Canada (along with First Nations and Métis Peoples). Inuit territories include Nunavut, an independently governed territory since 1999, Nunavik in the northern third of what is now known as Quebec, Nunatsiavut and NunatuKavut in present-day Labrador, and portions of the Northwest Territories.

Knowledge braiding: A process of bringing together multiple ways of knowing, articulated by Robin Wall Kimmerer (2020) to think through a respectful process of sharing knowledge across Western academic and Indigenous knowledges. The metaphor of the sweetgrass braid suggests an approach in which each "strand" of knowledge remains distinct while contributing to the whole braid to strengthen and enrich understanding. The process of braiding knowledges is rooted in respect for the diverse strengths of many ways of knowing and sees these knowledge systems as complementary rather than incorporating or integrating one knowledge system within or beneath another.

Knowledge co-creation: Knowledge co-creation refers to a collaborative process among two or more communities (e.g., disciplines, ethnic or cultural groups) actively participating on equal footing in efforts to generate and share information that is coherent with each of their respective worldviews, disciplines, or perspectives. Effective knowledge co-creation requires trust among collaborators and respect for diverse ways of thinking and can also be understood as a process of mutual learning.

Knowledge Holders: Knowledge Holders, also referred to as Knowledge Keepers, are individuals within an Indigenous community who are responsible for learning, caring for, and transmitting knowledge. This may include information about cultural practices and lifeways, environmental conditions, governance and protocols, family traditions, and more. Knowledge Holders are entrusted to safeguard and responsibly carry knowledge important to their communities, and often hold formal responsibilities associated with its use and transmission.

Métis: Métis People are one of three federally recognized groups of Indigenous Peoples in Canada (in addition to First Nations and Inuit). The term Métis refers collectively to a group of Peoples who consider themselves culturally and ethnically distinct, with mixed European and Indigenous ancestry, who developed and maintained distinct cultures, languages, and communities in the post-contact era.

Mountain systems: The phrase mountain systems is used in the CMA to connote the intrinsic connectedness of the physical, social, and more-than-human dimensions of mountainous places, and to call attention to the dynamism of mountain areas across space and time. While the phrase mountain systems is preferred, terms such as mountains, mountain areas, mountain regions, mountainous are also used in the CMA; these should be understood as connoting similar ideas, unless stated otherwise.

Mountain Research Initiative (MRI): The Mountain Research Initiative serves as a coordination network for research collaboration, bringing the global mountain research community together. Since the establishment of the MRI Coordination Office in 2001, the MRI has striven to promote basic and applied research to understand how drivers and processes of global change present challenges and opportunities in mountain social-ecological systems. The MRI is hosted by the Centre for Development and Environment at the University of Bern.

Multiple Evidence Base (MEB) approach: A Multiple Evidence Base approach emphasises the complementarity of knowledge systems and the values of letting each knowledge system speak for itself, within its own context, without assigning one dominant knowledge system with the role of external validator. Complementary insights from different knowledge systems create an enriched picture of an issue of investigation. The approach acknowledges that there are power issues involved when connecting different knowledge systems, and that there are—despite similarities and overlaps—aspects of each knowledge system that cannot be fully translated into another. The MEB approach aims to promote and enable connections across knowledge systems in a respectful and equal manner. The approach stresses that the type of complementarity and co-production envisioned should be part of a collaborative process between those involved from the outset. The focus on the process may help to clarify the power dynamics, maintain integrity of knowledge systems, generate new questions, and thus enable assessments and knowledge generation activities that are salient, credible, and legitimate for a diversity of Knowledge Holders. Definition and text from Tengö et al. (2014).

Ongoing consent: In a research context, commitment to ongoing consent reflects an understanding that an initial process of obtaining informed consent (e.g., through an informed consent process guided by the Tri-Agency standards for ethical research conduct) is only the beginning of a continued consent process. Ongoing consent is an iterative process in which researchers maintain communication with research participants to provide updates and seek continued consent for participants' knowledge and data to be used and/or shared. The CMA enacts the principle of ongoing consent by maintaining dialogue throughout the CMA preparation process and ensuring through the publication contract that Learning Circle participants may—in perpetuity—withdraw knowledge shared into the assessment should they decide it is no longer appropriate to share.

Ownership, Access, Control, and Possession (OCAP®): OCAP® asserts that First Nations alone have control over data collection processes in their communities, and that they own and control how this information can be stored, interpreted, used, or shared. "Ownership" refers to the relationship of First Nations to their cultural knowledge, data, and information. This principle states that a community or group owns information collectively in the same way that an individual owns his or her personal information. "Control" affirms that First Nations, their communities, and representative bodies are within their rights to seek control over all aspects of research and information management processes that impact them. First Nations control of research can include all stages of a particular research project from start to finish. The principle extends to the control of resources and review processes, the planning process, management of the information and so on. "Access" refers to the fact that First Nations must have access to information and data about themselves and their communities regardless of where it is held. The principle of access also refers to

the right of First Nations' communities and organisations to manage and make decisions regarding access to their collective information. This may be achieved, in practice, through standardised, formal protocols. "Possession" While ownership identifies the relationship between a people and their information in principle, possession or stewardship is more concrete: it refers to the physical control of data. Possession is the mechanism by which ownership can be asserted and protected.

Peer-reviewed literature: Peer-reviewed literature has gone through an evaluation process in which expert scholars (peer reviewers) and journal editors critically assess the quality and scientific/academic merit of original research. Literature that passes this process is published in the academic journals (i.e., peer-reviewed articles) or scholarly presses (e.g. peer-reviewed books).

Systematic scoping review: Systematic scoping reviews use formal search procedures, inclusion/exclusion criteria, and classification protocols to provide an overview of the state of peer-review literature for a given topic. They prioritise transparency, traceability, and reproducibility, and aim to increase the credibility and thoroughness of literature-based assessment activities.

Traditional Territory: A legally defined term used in the modern-day treaties to refer to lands and waters historically used and occupied by First Nations, Métis, and Inuit Peoples.

Tri-Agency: Tri-Agency is the umbrella term used to describe the three Canadian Government research funding agencies: The Canadian Institutes of Health Research (CIHR), the Natural Sciences and Engineering Research Council (NSERC), and the Social Sciences and Humanities Research Council (SSHRC). The Tri-Agency is the primary mechanism through which the Government of Canada supports research and training at post-secondary institutions; it also provides guidance for the responsible and ethical conduct of research.

Truth and Reconciliation Commission of Canada (TRC): The Truth and Reconciliation Commission of Canada was created in 2008 as a result of the Indian Residential Schools Settlement Agreement. The purpose of the TRC was to document the history and lasting impacts of the Canadian Indian residential school system on Indigenous students and their families, including by providing residential school survivors opportunities to share their experiences during public and private meetings held across the country. The final report of the TRC, *Honouring the Truth, Reconciling for the Future* (2015), documents the tragic experiences of approximately 150,000 Canadian residential school students and outlines 94 "Calls to Action" regarding reconciliation between non-Indigenous Canadians and Indigenous Peoples.

United Nations Declaration on the Rights of Indigenous Peoples (UNDRIP): The United Nations Declaration on the Rights of Indigenous Peoples is the most comprehensive international instrument on the rights of Indigenous Peoples. It establishes a universal framework of minimum standards for the survival, dignity, and wellbeing of the Indigenous Peoples of the world and it elaborates on existing human rights standards and fundamental freedoms as they apply to the specific situation of Indigenous Peoples. It was adopted by the UN General Assembly on 13 September 2007 by a majority of member states. After initially opposing UNDRIP, the Government of Canada reversed its position and, as of 21 June 2021, now supports the implementation of the UNDRIP as a key step in renewing the Government's relationship with Indigenous Peoples.

Western academic knowledge: Western academic knowledge and ways of knowing have their intellectual roots in the Ancient Greek philosophers, including Socrates, Plato, and Aristotle, and extends through Roman philosophy, the European Renaissance, the Scientific Revolution, and the Age of Enlightenment. When we discuss Western academic knowledge or Western science, we do so to acknowledge the Western European knowledge traditions that underpin how universities understand, teach, and advance knowledge. Like Indigenous knowledges, Western academic knowledges are not monolithic and are informed by a wide range of assumptions, underpinning philosophies, approaches, methods, and contexts; often, though not always, Western academic practices aim to produce generalizable and reproducible insights based on analyses of observed phenomenon. These ways of producing knowledge are not static and reflect changing norms and principles for understanding what knowledge is legitimate.

References

ACIA. (2005). *Arctic Climate Impact Assessment: ACIA Overview Report* (pp. 1020). Cambridge University Press. https://www.amap.no/documents/doc/arctic-arctic-climate-impact-assessment/796

Adler, C., Wester, P., Bhatt, I., Huggel, C., Insarov, G., Morecroft, M., Muccione, V., Prakash, A., Alcántara-Ayala, I., Allen, S., Bader, M., Bigler, S., Camac, J., Chakraborty, R., Sanchez, A., Cuvi, N., Drenkhan, F., Hussain, A., Maharjan, A., & Werners, S. (2022). IPCC WGII Sixth Assessment Report Cross-Chapter Paper 5: Mountains. In H.-O. Pörtner, D. C. Roberts, M. Tignor, E. Poloczanska, K. Mintenbeck, A. Alegría, M. Craig, S. Langsdorf, V. Löschke, A. Möller, A. Okem, & B. Rama (Eds.), *Climate Change 2022: Impacts, Adaptation and Vulnerability. Contribution of Working Group II to the Sixth Assessment Report of the Intergovernmental Panel on Climate Change* (pp. 2273–2318). Cambridge University Press. doi:10.1017/9781009325844.022

Agriculture and Agri-Food Canada. (2016). *Terrestrial Ecozones of Canada.* https://open.canada.ca/data/en/dataset/7ad7ea01-eb23-4824-bccc-66adb7c5bdf8

Ahenakew, C. (2016). Grafting Indigenous Ways of Knowing onto Non-Indigenous Ways of Being: The (Underestimated) Challenges of a Decolonial Imagination. *International Review of Qualitative Research, 9*(3), 323–340. https://doi.org/10.1525/irqr.2016.9.3.323

Akena, F. A. (2012). Critical Analysis of the Production of Western Knowledge and Its Implications for Indigenous Knowledge and Decolonization. *Journal of Black Studies, 43*(6), 599–619. https://doi.org/10.1177/0021934712440448

Battiste, M. (2002). *Indigenous Knowledge and Pedagogy in First Nations Education: A Literature Review with Recommendations.* National Working Group on Education and the Minister of Indian Affairs, Indian and Northern Affairs Canada (INAC). http://www.afn.ca/uploads/files/education/24._2002_oct_marie_battiste_ indigenousknowledgeandpedagogy_lit_review_for_min_working_group.pdf

Berkes, F., Colding, J., & Folke, C. (2000). Rediscovery of Traditional Ecological Knowledge as Adaptive Management. *Ecological Applications, 10*(5), 1251–1262. https://doi.org/10.2307/2641280

Berry, J. (1999). Aboriginal cultural identity. *Canadian Journal of Native Studies, 19*(1), 1–36.

Borrows, J. (2002). *Recovering Canada: The Resurgence of Indigenous Law.* University of Toronto Press, Scholarly Publishing Division.

Canadian Institutes of Health Research, Natural Sciences and Engineering Research Council of Canada, & Social Sciences and Humanities Research Council. (2018). *Tri-Council Policy Statement on Ethical Conduct for Research Involving Humans (TCPS2)* (pp. 1–231). Secretariat on Responsible Conduct of Research. https://ethics.gc.ca/eng/documents/tcps2-2018-en-interactive-final.pdf

Clarke, G., Jarosch, A., Anslow, F., Radić, V., Menounos, B. (2015) Projected deglaciation of western Canada in the twenty-first century. *Nature Geoscience, 8*(5), 372–377. https://doi.org/10.1038/ngeo2407

Cravens, A. E., Jones, M. S., Ngai, C., Zarestky, J., & Love, H. B. (2022). Science facilitation: Navigating the intersection of intellectual and interpersonal expertise in scientific collaboration. *Humanities and Social Sciences Communications, 9*(1), Article 1. https://doi.org/10.1057/s41599-022-01217-1

Cruickshank, J. (2005). *Do Glaciers Listen?: Local Knowledge, Colonial Encounters, and Social Imagination.* UBC Press.

Danby, R.K., Williams, A., Hik, D.S. (2014). Fifty years of science at the Kluane Lake Research Station. *Arctic, 67*(1), iii–viii. http://dx.doi.org/10.14430/arctic4398

Dickson-Hoyle, S., Ignace, R. E., Ignace, M. B., Hagerman, S. M., Daniels, L. D., & Copes-Gerbitz, K. (2022). Walking on two legs: A pathway of Indigenous restoration and reconciliation in fire-adapted landscapes. *Restoration*

Ecology, 30(4), e13566. https://doi.org/10.1111/rec.13566

Downing, A., & Cuerrier, A. (2011). Synthesis of the impacts of climate change on the First Nations and Inuit of Canada. *Indian Journal of Traditional Knowledge, 10*(1), 57–70.

Eichler, L., & Baumeister, D. (2018). Hunting for Justice: An Indigenous Critique of the North American Model of Wildlife Conservation. *Environment and Society, 9*(1), 75–90. https://doi.org/10.3167/ares.2018.090106

Elmore, A.C., Alexiev, N., Craig, V. (2020). Understanding the World's Water Towers through High-Mountain Expeditions and Scientific Discovery. *One Earth, 3* (5), 561–563.

Ermine, W. (2000). *Ethical space: Transforming relations: A discussion paper.*

Ermine, W. (2007). The Ethical Space of Engagement. *Indigenous Law Journal, 6*(1), 193–204.

Ermine, W., Sinclair, R., & Jeffery, B. (2004). *The Ethics of Research Involving Indigenous Peoples.* Indigenous Peoples' Health Research Centre. https://doi.org/10.13140/RG.2.2.23069.31200

Fernández-Llamazares, Á., Lepofsky, D., Lertzman, K., Armstrong, C. G., Brondizio, E. S., Gavin, M. C., Lyver, P. O., Nicholas, G. P., Pascua, P., Reo, N. J., Reyes-García, V., Turner, N. J., Yletyinen, J., Anderson, E. N., Balée, W., Cariño, J., David-Chavez, D. M., Dunn, C. P., Garnett, S. C., … Vaughan, M. B. (2021). Scientists' Warning to Humanity on Threats to Indigenous and Local Knowledge Systems. *Journal of Ethnobiology, 41*(2), 144–169. https://doi.org/10.2993/0278-0771-41.2.144

Gómez, S. R., Chaves, M. E., Ramírez, W., Santamaría, M., Andrade, G., Solano, C., & Aranguren, S. (Eds.). (2021). *Evaluación Nacional de Biodiversidad y Servicios Ecosistémicos de Colombia* (pp. 1–1260). Instituto de Investigación de Recursos Biológicos Alexander von Humboldt, Programa de Naciones Unidas para el Desarrollo y el Centro Mundial de Monitoreo para la Conservación del Programa de las Naciones Unidas para el Medio Ambiente, Ministerio Federal de Medio Ambiente, Conservación de la Naturaleza y Seguridad Nuclear de la República Federal de Alemania. www.besnet.world_wp-content_uploads_2023_01_Colombia-NEA-Report.pdf

Government of Canada. (2017). *Model Policy on Scientific Integrity.* https://www.ic.gc.ca/eic/site/063.nsf/eng/h_97643.html

Hessami, M. A., Bowles, E., Popp, J. N., & Ford, A. T. (2021). Indigenizing the North American Model of Wildlife Conservation. *FACETS, 6*(1), 1285–1306. https://doi.org/10.1139/facets-2020-0088

Higgs, E., Bartley, G., & Fisher, A. C. (2009). *The Mountain Legacy Project.* (pp. 80) Blurb.ca. https://www.blurb.ca/b/586978-the-mountain-legacy-project

Hock, R., Rasul, G., Adler, C., Cáceres, B., Gruber, S., Hirabayashi, Y., Jackson, M., Kääb, A., Kang, S., Kutuzov, S., Milner, A., Molau, U., Morin, S., Orlove, B., & H. Steltzer. (2019). High Mountain Areas. In H.-O. Pörtner, D. C. Roberts, V. Masson-Delmotte, M. Zhai, M. Tignor, E.

Poloczanska, K. Mintenbeck, A. Alegría, M. Nicolai, A. Okem, J. Petzold, B. Rama, & N. M. Weyer (Eds.), *IPCC Special Report on the Ocean and Cryosphere in a Changing Climate* (pp. 131–202). Cambridge University Press. https://doi.org/10.1017/9781009157964.004

Immerzeel, W. W., Lutz, A. F., Andrade, M., Bahl, A., Biemans, H., Bolch, T., Hyde, S., Brumby, S., Davies, B. J., Elmore, A. C., Emmer, A., Feng, M., Fernández, A., Haritashya, U., Kargel, J. S., Koppes, M., Kraaijenbrink, P. D. A., Kulkarni, A. V., Mayewski, P. A., & Baillie, J. E. M. (2020). Importance and vulnerability of the world's water towers. *Nature, 577*(7790), 364–369. https://doi.org/10.1038/s41586-019-1822-y

IPBES. (2019). *Global assessment report on biodiversity and ecosystem services of the Intergovernmental Science-Policy Platform on Biodiversity and Ecosystem Services.* Zenodo. https://doi.org/10.5281/zenodo.641733

Johnston, J., & Mason, C. (2020). Eurocentric Lens to Indigenous Methods of Sharing Knowledge in Jasper National Park, Canada. *Journal of Park and Recreation Administration.* https://doi.org/10.18666/JPRA-2020-10251

Kapos, V., Rhind, J., Edwards, M., Price M.F., Ravilious, C. (2000) Developing a map of the world's mountain forests. In Price, M.F., Butt, N. (Eds.), *Forests in Sustainable Mountain Development* (pp. 4–9). (IUFRO research series 5). CABI Publishing.

Karagulle, D., Frye, C., Sayre, R., Breyer, S., Aniello, P., Vaughan, R., & Wright, D. (2017). Modeling global Hammond landform regions from 250-m elevation data. *Transactions in GIS, 21*(5), 1040–1060. https://doi.org/10.1111/tgis.12265

Kassi, N., Humphries, M. M., Dubé, M., Dragon, J., Olivier, N., Bowser, K., & Berry, M. (2022). Braiding Knowledges: The Canadian Mountain Network Experience. *Mountain Research and Development, 42*(4), P1–P6. https://doi.org/10.1659/mrd.2022.00026

Kimmerer, R. W. (2020). *Braiding sweetgrass: Indigenous wisdom, scientific knowledge, and the teachings of plants* (Second hardcover edition). Milkweed Editions.

Körner, C., Paulsen, J., & Spehn, E. M. (2011). A definition of mountains and their bioclimatic belts for global comparisons of biodiversity data. *Alpine Botany, 121*(2), 73. https://doi.org/10.1007/s00035-011-0094-4

Krebs, C. J., Boonstra, R., Boutin, S., Sinclair, A. R. E., Smith, J. N. M., Gilbert, B. S., Martin, K., O'Donoghue, M., Turkington, R. (2014). Trophic dynamics of the boreal forests of the Kluane Region. *Arctic, 67*(5), 71–81. doi:10.14430/arctic4350

Lamb, C., Willson, R., Richter, C., Owens-Beck, N., Napoleon, J., Muir, B., McNay, R. S., Lavis, E., Hebblewhite, M., Giguere, L., Dokkie, T., Boutin, S., & Ford, A. T. (2022). Indigenous-Led Conservation: Pathways to Recovery from the Nearly Extirpated Klinse-Za Mountain Caribou. *Ecological Applications, 32*(5), e2581-n/a. https://doi.org/10.1002/eap.2581

Latulippe, N., & Klenk, N. (2020). Making room and moving over: Knowledge co-production, Indigenous knowledge sovereignty and the politics of global environmental change decision-making. *Current Opinion in Environmental Sustainability*, *42*, 7–14. https://doi.org/10.1016/j.cosust.2019.10.010

Liboiron, M. (2021). *Pollution Is Colonialism*. Duke University Press.

MacLeod, L. (2021). More Than Personal Communication: Templates for Citing Indigenous Elders and Knowledge Keepers. *KULA: Knowledge Creation, Dissemination, and Preservation Studies*, *5*(1), Article 1. https://doi.org/10.18357/kula.135

Mastrandrea, M. D., Field, C. B., Stocker, T. F., Edenhofer, O., Ebi, K. L., Frame, D. J., Held, H., Kriegler, E., Mach, K. J., & Matschoss, P. R. (2010). *Guidance note for lead authors of the IPCC fifth assessment report on consistent treatment of uncertainties*.

McDowell, G., & Guo, J. (2021). A Nationally Coherent Characterization and Quantification of Mountain Systems in Canada. *Mountain Research and Development*, *41.0*(2), R21–R31. https://doi.org/10.1659/MRD-JOURNAL-D-20-00071.1

McDowell, G., & Hanly, K. (2022). The state of mountain research in Canada. *Journal of Mountain Science*, *19*(10), 3013–3025. https://doi.org/10.1007/s11629-022-7569-1

McGregor, D. (2014). Traditional Knowledge and Water Governance: The Ethic of Responsibility. *AlterNative: An International Journal of Indigenous Peoples*, *10*(5), 493–507. https://doi.org/10.1177/117718011401000505

Millennium Ecosystem Assessment (Ed.). (2005). *Ecosystems and human well-being: Synthesis*. Island Press.

Muller, S., Hemming, S., & Rigney, D. (2019). Indigenous sovereignties: Relational ontologies and environmental management. *Geographical Research*, *57*(4), 399–410. https://doi.org/10.1111/1745-5871.12362

Nadasdy, P. (1999). The Politics of Tek: Power and the "Integration" of Knowledge. *Arctic Anthropology*, *36*(1/2), 1–18.

Nikolakis, W., & Hotte, N. (2022). Implementing "ethical space": An exploratory study of Indigenous-conservation partnerships. *Conservation Science and Practice*, *4*(1), e580. https://doi.org/10.1111/csp2.580

Paez, A. (2017). Gray literature: An important resource in systematic reviews. *Journal of Evidence-Based Medicine*, *10*(3), 233–240. https://doi.org/10.1111/jebm.12266

Pfeffer, W., Arendt, A., Bliss, A., Bolch, T., Cogley, J., Gardner, A., . . . Sharp, M. (2014). The Randolph Glacier Inventory: A globally complete inventory of glaciers. *Journal of Glaciology*, *60*(221), 537-552. doi:10.3189/2014JoG13J176

Reid, A. J., Eckert, L. E., Lane, J.-F., Young, N., Hinch, S. G., Darimont, C. T., Cooke, S. J., Ban, N. C., & Marshall, A. (2021). "Two-Eyed Seeing": An Indigenous framework to transform fisheries research and management. *Fish and Fisheries*, *22*(2), 243–261. https://doi.org/10.1111/faf.12516

Tengö, M., Brondizio, E. S., Elmqvist, T., Malmer, P., & Spierenburg, M. (2014). Connecting Diverse Knowledge Systems for Enhanced Ecosystem Governance: The Multiple Evidence Base Approach. *Ambio*, *43*(5), 579–591.

The First Nations Principles of OCAP®. (n.d.). The First Nations Information Governance Centre. Retrieved 7 September 2022, from https://fnigc.ca/ocap-training/

Truth and Reconciliation Commission. (2015). Truth and Reconciliation Commission: Calls to action. Winnipeg: Truth and Reconciliation Commission.

United Nations Declaration on the Rights of Indigenous Peoples: Resolution/adopted by the General Assembly, A/RES/61/295 § General Assembly (2007). https://www.un.org/esa/socdev/unpfii/documents/DRIPS_en.pdf

Viviroli, D., Dürr, H. H., Messerli, B., Meybeck, M., & Weingartner, R. (2007). Mountains of the world, water towers for humanity: Typology, mapping, and global significance: *Water Resources Research*, *43*(7). https://doi.org/10.1029/2006WR005653

West, S., & Schill, C. (2022). Negotiating the ethical-political dimensions of research methods: A key competency in mixed methods, inter- and transdisciplinary, and co-production research. *Humanities and Social Sciences Communications*, *9*(1), Article 1. https://doi.org/10.1057/s41599-022-01297-z

Wester, P., Mishra, A., Mukherji, A., & Shrestha, A. B. (Eds.). (2019). *The Hindu Kush Himalaya Assessment: Mountains, Climate Change, Sustainability and People*. Springer Open.

Whyte, K. (2017). What do indigenous knowledges do for indigenous peoples? Forthcoming in *Keepers of the Green World: Traditional Ecological Knowledge and Sustainability*, Edited by Melissa K. Nelson and Dan Shilling.

Whyte, K. P. (2013). On the role of traditional ecological knowledge as a collaborative concept: A philosophical study. *Ecological Processes*, *2*(1), 7. https://doi.org/10.1186/2192-1709-2-7

A bull moose on the move in Kananaskis Country, Canadian Rockies, during the autumn rutting season.
Photo courtesy of Abdulla Moussa, 2021.

CHAPTER 2

Mountain Environments

CO-LEAD AUTHORS: Joseph Shea, Daniel Sims

CONTRIBUTING AUTHORS: Caroline Aubry-Wake, Megan Dicker, Stephan Gruber, Pnnal Bernard Jerome, Patricia Joe, Gùdia Mary Jane Johnson, Stephen Johnston, Michele Koppes, Daniel Kraus, Keara Lightning, Christopher Marsh, Shawn Marshall, Brandy Mayes, María Elisa Sánchez, Lauren Somers, Wanda Pascal, Kyra St. Pierre, Karson Sudlow, Hayden Melting Tallow, Julie M. Thériault, Andrew Trant, Vincent Vionnet, John Waldron

CHAPTER REVIEW EDITOR: Steven M. Vamosi

2.1 Introduction

Mountain environments are characterised by a wide range of geological features, climates, ecosystems, and landscapes. They can be viewed holistically, as regions that are greater than the sum of their individual parts, or they can be broken down into their constituents of rock, snow and ice, water, and plant and animal life. In this chapter, we take both viewpoints, and assess what is known—and not known—about mountain environments in Canada. We assess the state of scientific knowledge with respect to geology and mountain origins; mountain weather and climate; snow, ice, and permafrost; hydrology; ecosystems and biodiversity; hazards; and connections between mountain environments and the surrounding lowlands. Our assessment of the state of scientific understanding is complemented, where possible, with Indigenous knowledges of the same topics. The material in this chapter is foundational to subsequent chapters of the Canadian Mountain Assessment (CMA).

Mountain environments are defined partly by their elevation, which literally and figuratively

Due to the CMA's unique approach to engaging with multiple knowledge systems, we suggest that readers review the Introduction prior to reading subsequent chapters.

sets them apart from other landscapes. This elevation is a product of mountain-building processes that have occurred over hundreds of millions of years (Sec. 2.2). But mountains are also defined by their highly complex and heterogeneous nature. Large changes in elevation over relatively small horizontal distances lead to steep slopes and high relief that have cascading effects on weather (Sec. 2.3), water in both frozen (Sec. 2.4) and liquid (Sec. 2.5) forms, and plant and animal habitats and ecosystems (Sec. 2.7). The topographic and meteorological complexity of mountain environments also directly contributes to the hazards associated with these regions (Sec. 2.6). And while mountains may be set apart from their surrounding lowland regions, they are not isolated—viewed through a different lens, the two-way connections between upland and lowland regions can be brought into focus (Sec. 2.8).

Knowledge assessments impose divisions on the knowledge that is presented (Foucault, 1995), and each section of this chapter addresses a separate topic related to mountain environments. However, Indigenous Peoples' knowledges of mountain environments are typically holistic and not easily parsable along traditional scientific categories. Consider for example, connections to the diminutive Straw Mountain in Flagstaff County, Alberta, which are largely related to

Figure 2.1: Straw Mountain, Flagstaff County, Alberta. Photo courtesy of Daniel Sims, 2011.

Manitou Asinîy (the Manitou Stone) and the Viking Ribstones. Such importance or sacredness of mountain environments is, furthermore, often unique to particular Nations or communities. For example, while Siksika Elder Hayden Melting Tallow stated the mountains are sacred places he

Hayden Melting Tallow, Siksika Nation, Blackfoot Confederacy, 2022, LC 2.1

is quite clear that he is only speaking for himself and his Nation (LC 2.1).

Many Indigenous Peoples see a world full of animate entities. Beyond merely recognizing the personhood of other forms of life, many Indigenous Peoples see things that might not be viewed by Western science as animate as alive. This category can range from individual rocks— with perhaps the most famous example being the glacial erratic at Okotoks, Alberta (Fig. 2.2), that once chased Napi—to the planet itself, which Tsek'ehne Elders describe as a living entity. It has even been suggested that cryptids like sasquatch and the wendigo are personifications of the environment itself, although it could equally be said that this interpretation speaks more of settler

THE CANADIAN MOUNTAIN ASSESSMENT

perspectives than Indigenous worldviews (Blu Buhs, 2009). This perception of being in a very animate world informs Indigenous knowledges of mountains and makes it difficult to separate the "environment" from the other topics in this report. In this context, we have chosen to include some Indigenous knowledges of mountain environments that have been shared with the CMA in subsequent chapters, which are framed in more holistic ways (e.g., Gifts of the Mountains).

Ultimately, our assessment efforts are shaped by the availability of and access to knowledge, both of which impact our assessment of mountain environments in Canada. Indigenous knowledges of mountain environments are extensive, but when such knowledges have not been shared with CMA, have not been recorded in writing, or are expressly private, they cannot be incorporated into our assessment of mountain environments. Similarly, observational studies of mountains in Canada are limited given the expansiveness, remoteness, and challenges to access, which characterise many mountain regions across the country. Notwithstanding these caveats, this chapter provides the first formal assessment of what is known and not known about mountain environments in Canada.

2.2 Origins

"One of the things we all are raised up with, if we are First Nations, Inuit, or Métis people, is the creation of the World."—Gùdia Mary Jane Johnson, Lhu'àán Mân Ku Dań, LC 2.2

Gùdia Mary Jane Johnson, Lhu'àán Mân Ku Dań, 2022, LC 2.2

Figure 2.2: Big Rock (Okotoks Erratic) is a 16,500 tonne granite boulder found on the prairie south of Calgary, AB. It originated in the upper Athabasca valley, and was carried several hundred kilometres by an ice stream at the end of the Last Glacial Maximum. Photo by Coaxial, CC BY 3.0, 2007.

2.2.1 *Plate tectonics: The driving mechanism for mountain building*

Mountains are the products of a perpetual battle between the tectonic processes that uplift the Earth's surface and the processes of erosion that are constantly wearing it down. Most of these processes operate at rates that are too slow and on too large a scale for direct human observation. The result is that Earth's geography, its distribution of mountain belts and ocean basins, appears, from a human perspective, to be an almost permanent feature of our planet. But mountains and oceans are not permanent. Indigenous origin stories, which form the foundation of their culture and guide societal behaviours and decision making, also contain parallels to geological origin stories and the vastness of time.

The growth and demise of mountains involves tectonic processes that operate over many tens of millions of years (e.g., Müller et al., 2019). Many Indigenous creation stories talk about the creation of the world as well as certain natural features that were created or came into existence after the creation of the world (Snow, 2005). For example, the Fraser Valley contains hundreds of sites, known as transformer sites, where nations like the Stó:lō say their ancestors were turned

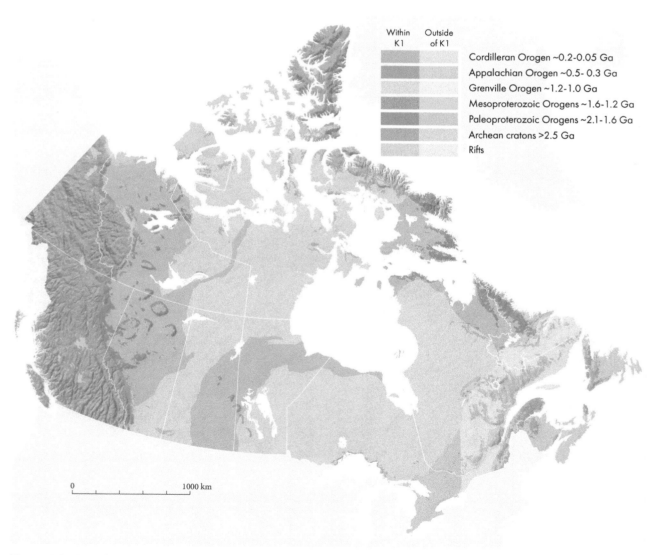

Figure 2.3: Canadian mountain regions (grey) based on McDowell & Guo (2021) superimposed on major crustal divisions and orogens Data from Hasterok et al., 2022.

THE CANADIAN MOUNTAIN ASSESSMENT

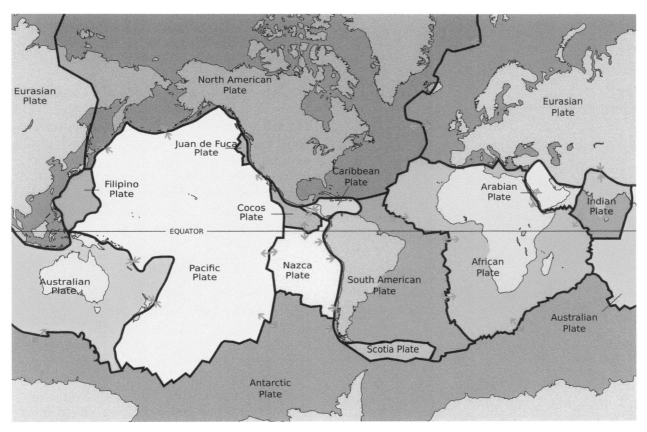

Figure 2.4: Principal plates of Earth's lithosphere at the present day. Image by Scott Nash.

to stone. James Hutton's demonstration, in 1788, of the extraordinarily slow rates of geological processes prompted the Scottish philosopher Playfair (Playfair, 1805) to write "The mind seemed to grow giddy by looking so far into the abyss of time." In our assessment of mountain regions within Canada, we need to be aware of the limits of our ability to understand such enormous spans of 'Deep Time' (McPhee, 1981).

Canada has a landscape defined by its geology. At its core is the Precambrian 'Canadian Shield'—a repository of ancient rocks formed between 4 and 1 billion years ago (e.g., Hoffman, 1988). The shield itself consists of cratons—blocks that have been stable for 2.5 billion years—stitched together and surrounded by mountain belts or orogens formed by the convergence of tectonic plates between 2.5 and 0.54 billion years ago. Time and erosion by water, wind, and ice have bevelled the Shield into a vast low-relief landscape of lakes, wandering rivers, and boreal forests. Surrounding the shield are much younger mountain regions: the Cordillera to the west, the Appalachians to the east and the Arctic Archipelago to the north (Fig. 2.3).

Plate-tectonic processes are responsible for mountain building. The Earth's rigid outer lithosphere is broken into a series of plates (Fig. 2.4) that move very slowly over the softer, more plastic asthenosphere below. Most of Canada lies in the North American Plate, which extends from the mid-Atlantic ridge to the edge of the Pacific Ocean. Tectonic plates are in motion as part of the 'supercontinent' cycle of continental growth, demise, and rebirth: a continual cycle of land and ocean evolution. Eastern Canada lies on a passive margin at the present day—it is in the middle of a plate and so experiences very limited seismic activity and has no volcanoes. In contrast the western margin of North America is an active margin; the continental margin is also a plate boundary. As a result, it has major earthquake-producing faults and numerous volcanoes that appear in the oral histories of First Nations groups in western Canada. The Nuu-chah-nulth peoples of the Pacific Maritime region, for example, speak of mountain dwarfs that not only cause earthquakes, but also warn people about them. In Heiltsuk (Bella Bella, Pacific Maritime region) traditions, earthquakes

Figure 2.5: View looking north over a slice of oceanic lithosphere preserved in the Tablelands, Gros Morne National Park, NL. Grey rocks on the left represent ancient oceanic crust. Orange-weathering rocks on the right are representative of the uppermost mantle. Photo courtesy of Phil McCausland, 2019.

occur when the being holding up the Earth with ropes periodically adjusts or loses their grip (McMillan & Hutchinson, 2002; Turkel, 2011).

2.2.2 Ancient orogens of eastern Canada

The precursor of the North American continent is known as Laurentia. Geological evidence from the eastern mountain regions of Canada indicate that Laurentia broke out of the supercontinent Rodinia between 800 and 550 million years ago (Ma) (Davidson, 2008). The ancient eastern margin of Laurentia is represented by thick limestone successions that record continental-shelf environments similar to the present-day Bahamas, showing that Atlantic Canada lay in the tropics at that time. As Laurentia split off and moved northward it was drawn into a plate collision and subduction zone that ultimately gave rise to the Appalachian mountains (Hibbard et al., 2007; van Staal et al., 1998; Waldron et al., 1998; Williams, 1979).

Maritime and Atlantic Canada, including much of the Atlantic Maritime and Boreal Shield mountain region, consists of the Appalachian orogen. Formed during the Paleozoic era (between 540 and 250 Ma), the Appalachians were once part of a single continuous mountain system extending from Texas to Svalbard. The opening of the Atlantic Ocean separated this orogen into the Appalachians in North America and the Caledonides of Greenland, Ireland, Britain, and Scandinavia. A continuation of the Caledonides into the Arctic basin is referred to as the Ellesmerian orogen and is at least in part responsible for the elevated topography of the northernmost portion of the Arctic Cordillera mountain region.

Evidence for the plate collision that formed the Appalachians and the volcanic arc that it produced occurs throughout the Atlantic Maritime and Boreal Shield region, particularly in the landscapes of the Bay of Islands and Gros Morne National Park. As the Laurentian margin was drawn into the subduction zone, the margin was pulled beneath a deformed mass of sedimentary, igneous, and metamorphic rock known as the 'Humber Arm allochthon'. Remnants of this geologic jumble form the famous Tablelands of Gros Morne National Park (Fig. 2.5). Mountain building continued for another 100 million years, incorporating multiple *terranes*—small crustal blocks with distinct geological histories—into the orogen (Cocks & Torsvik, 2011).

2.2.3 Younger orogens of western Canada

Together, the Montane Cordillera, Pacific Maritime, Boreal Cordillera, and Taiga Cordillera mountain regions (Fig. 2.6) form the Cordilleran orogen of western Canada. While Laurentia was being incorporated into eastern and northern North America, the future western Cordillera formed the western margin of the supercontinent Pangea, facing the vast expanse of the Panthalassic Ocean. As Pangea began to drift apart, a passive plate margin formed along North America's west coast. In the shallow sea waters within this passive margin the first complicated, multicellular life forms arose, and are preserved in the famous Burgess Shale fauna (Conway Morris, 1989). But it was not until the break-up of Pangea (at 200 Ma) that the Cordilleran ranges began to form. The rifting of North America away from Africa led to crustal thickening, metamorphism, and the formation of several ranges of mountains along the western margin. At ~75 Ma, the western Cordillera's most iconic ranges, the Rocky Mountains, were born.

Further north, strike-slip motion (where plates move horizontally past each other) pushed the 'Yakutat' continental block northward along the margin. This geologically recent continental collision (Mazzotti & Hyndman, 2002) formed the St. Elias Mountains, which include the highest peak in Canada, Mount Logan (5959 m). The Yakutat block collision was connected to the Cordilleran orogen but involved crustal shortening and uplift associated with continental plate convergence, in contrast to the subduction-zone convergence processes across much of the western cordillera.

The western mountains of Canada are all seismically active, with small- to moderate-sized earthquakes that occur infrequently from a human perspective, but on a regular basis geologically (Lamontagne et al., 2008). Subduction continues beneath Vancouver Island, periodically giving rise to great earthquakes and related tsunamis that have been recorded in First Nations oral histories (Ludwin et al., 2007; McMillan & Hutchinson, 2002). The most recent of these earthquakes occurred on 26 January 1700 (Clague et al., 2000) and was described by Chief Louis Clamhouse:

> This story is about the first !Anaqtl'a or "Pachena Bay" people. It is said that they were a big band at the time of him whose name was Hayoqwis7is, 'Ten-On-Head-On-Beach'. He was the Chief; he was of the Pachena Bay tribe; he owned the Pachena Bay country. Their village site was Loht'a; they of Loht'a live there. I think they numbered over a hundred persons ... there is no one left alive due to what this land does at times. They had practically no way or time to try to save themselves. I think it was at nighttime that the land shook ... They were at Loht 'a; and they simply had no time to get hold of canoes, no time to get awake. They sank at once, were all drowned; not one survived ... I think a big wave smashed into the beach. The Pachena Bay people were lost ... But they on their part who lived at Ma:lts'a:s, 'House-Up-Against-Hill', the wave did not reach because they were on high ground. Right against a cliff were the houses on high ground at M'a:l-sit, 'Coldwater Pool'. Because of that they came out alive. They did not drift out to sea along with the others ... (Arima et al., 1991, pp. 230–231).

Volcanoes are common in the western mountain regions, though less active and less well known. The Cascade volcanic province sits above the subduction zone in coastal British Columbia (Fig. 2.7) and includes the recently active Qw'elqw'elústen (Mount Meager) volcano (Hickson et al., 1999; Michol et al., 2008) and Nch'kaẏ (Mount Garibaldi), which last erupted when continental ice sheets covered the region (W. Mathews, 1952). The Anahim Volcanic Belt lies north of the Cascade volcanic province, and trends roughly east-west across the orogen. At the eastern edge of the belt sits the Nazko cone, which last erupted approximately 7200 years before present (Souther et al., 1987). This volcanic belt is thought to record the westward passage of the North American Plate above a mantle hotspot or plume (Kuehn et al., 2015). East of this lies the Wells Gray–Clearwater volcanic complex.

Figure 2.6: Map of the Canadian Cordillera showing terranes accreted to North America and features mentioned in the text. Modified from Colpron & Nelson, 2009.

Figure 2.7 (opposite): Map of volcanoes in western Canada, and volcanic belts and provinces. Volcano locations from the Geological Survey of Canada (http://gsc.nrcan.gc.ca/volcanoes/cat/volcano_e.php; last available June 2012) and the Smithsonian Global Volcanism Program (https://volcano.si.edu/ge/PlacemarkLinks.cfm; accessed April 2023). Locations of the volcanic provinces and belts modified from Edwards & Russell, 2000.

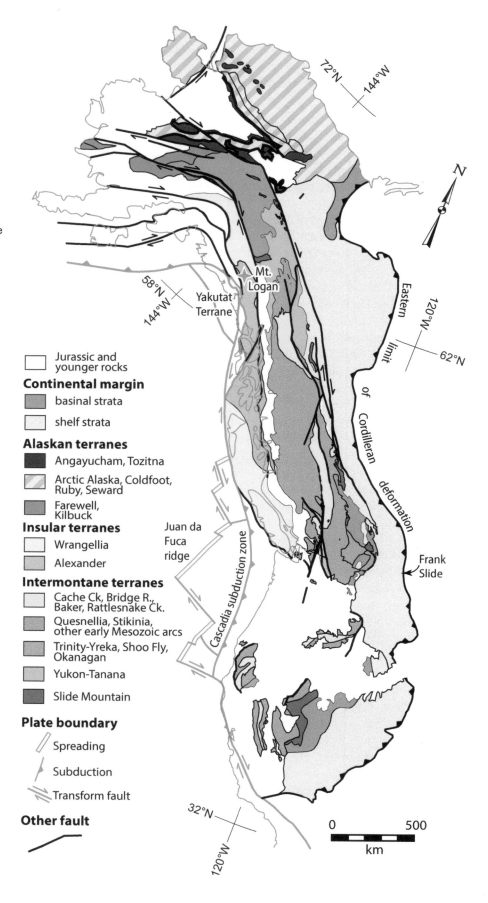

Jurassic and younger rocks

Continental margin
basinal strata
shelf strata

Alaskan terranes
Angayucham, Tozitna
Arctic Alaska, Coldfoot, Ruby, Seward
Farewell, Kilbuck

Insular terranes
Wrangellia
Alexander

Intermontane terranes
Cache Ck, Bridge R., Baker, Rattlesnake Ck.
Quesnellia, Stikinia, other early Mesozoic arcs
Trinity-Yreka, Shoo Fly, Okanagan
Yukon-Tanana
Slide Mountain

Plate boundary
Spreading
Subduction
Transform fault

Other fault

Mt. Logan

Yakutat Terrane

Juan da Fuca ridge

Cascadia subduction zone

Eastern limit of Cordilleran deformation

Frank Slide

72°N
144°W
58°N
144°W
120°W
62°N
32°N
120°W

N

0   500
km

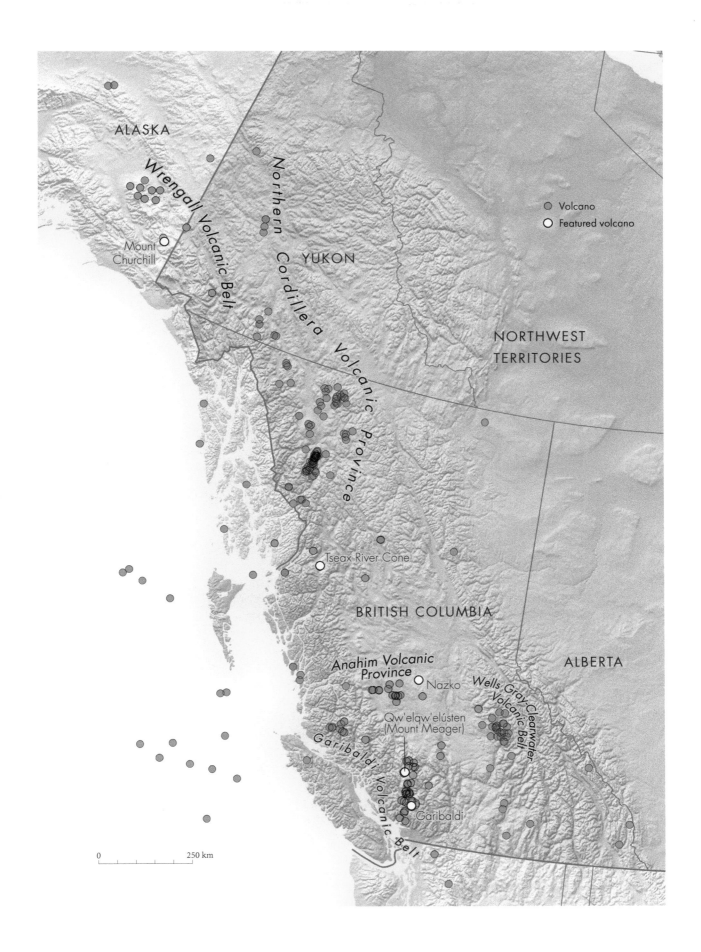

ALASKA

Wrengall Volcanic Belt

Northern Cordillera Volcanic Province

YUKON

Mount
Churchill

○ Volcano
◎ Featured volcano

NORTHWEST
TERRITORIES

Tseax River Cone

BRITISH COLUMBIA

ALBERTA

Anahim Volcanic
Province

Nazko

Wells Gray-Clearwater
Volcanic Belt

Qw'elqw'elústen
(Mount Meager)

Garibaldi Volcanic Belt

Garibaldi

0   250 km

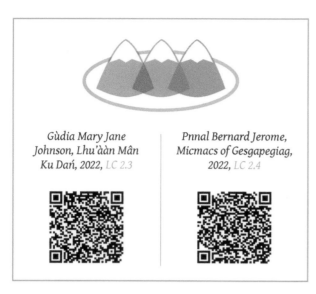

Gùdia Mary Jane Johnson, Lhu'ààn Mân Ku Dań, 2022, LC 2.3

Pnnal Bernard Jerome, Micmacs of Gesgapegiag, 2022, LC 2.4

Volcanic events in the Northern Cordilleran Volcanic Province (Stikine and Wrangell Volcanic Belts) have played an important part in the history of those who live in the mountains. Some Dene Nations, for example, speak of a volcanic eruption in the past that led to their ancestors leaving the Dene homeland, and which resulted in the subsequent emergence of the different Dene Nations (Moodie et al., 1992). As Lhu'ààn Mân Dań Elder Gùdia Mary Jane Johnson told the Learning Circle, her people speak of a year without summer (LC 2.3). While not definitively identified, it has been postulated that Elder Gùdia Mary Jane Johnson refers to the massive eruption of Mount Churchill around 720–850 CE (Mackay et al., 2022; Moodie et al., 1992), an event that may have driven southward migrations and declines in Indigenous groups in the region (Hare et al., 2004). The eruption of the Tseax cone around 1700 CE in the Nass River Valley (Fig. 2.8), is woven into Nisga'a oral histories, in part because it is the deadliest volcanic event in what became Canada (Corsiglia & Sniveky, 1997; Yannick, 2020). However, volcanic activity has also been thought to offer gifts to Indigenous Peoples. Elder Pnnal Bernard Jerome (Micmacs of Gesgapegiag) described the sacred stones, a form of perforated lava, offered up from the belly of Mother Earth to share her spirit with the people during ceremonies (LC 2.4).

Across all mountain regions, erosional processes continually sculpt the underlying geology of mountain landscapes. Erosion removes rock almost as fast as the mountains rise (Ford et al., 1981; Molnar & England, 1990). The interplay between relative sea level change and crustal rebound following the removal of continental scale ice sheets has led to dramatic changes in coastlines both in the Arctic (Müller & Barr, 1966) and along the Pacific coast (Shugar et al., 2014). The potential energy generated through the uplift and erosion of mountains can also lead to catastrophes for mountain inhabitants, where rockfall and landslides pose significant hazards (see Sec. 2.6).

2.2.4 *Ice sheet histories, landscape sculpting, and deglaciation*

Mountain ranges in the east, the north, and the west of Canada have served as centres of initiation for large ice sheets that repeatedly covered the northern half of North America over the past 2.6 million years (Batchelor et al., 2019; Clark et al., 1993). Flowing outwards from high-elevation regions lifted by tectonic forces, continental ice sheets and their associated erosional and depositional processes have repeatedly sculpted landscapes across Canada (Mathews, 1991), with comparable rates of erosion and sculpting from rivers during ice-free periods (CAINE, 1976; Koppes & Montgomery, 2009). The processes that shape mountain environments can be broadly summarised by elevation and slope angle (Slaymaker, 1990): at the highest elevations and on steeper mid-elevation slopes, glacial processes and mass wasting (i.e., rockfalls, landslides) dominate the landscape. At lower elevations and in valley bottoms, rivers control the sculpting process as they erode and rework the sediment deposited by glaciers and mass movements.

Glaciers and ice sheets are prolific landscape shapers: with each glaciation, the expansion of mountain glaciers and continental ice sheets widens and deepens existing river valleys, rounds lower elevation topography covered by ice sheets, and undercuts summits that remain above the ice (Mathews, 1991). These processes are reflected in the sharp peaks of the Pacific Maritime, Montane Cordillera, and Boreal Cordillera regions and the rounded hills of the interior and the Shield regions. Sediments eroded and carried by glaciers and ice sheets are deposited across the landscape as the ice sheets retreat, and water produced by the melting ice picks up, moves, and deposits these sediments in river valleys and lowland floodplains.

Figure 2.8: Lava beds in Nass Valley, Nisga'a territory, British Columbia. Photo by Darren Kirby, CC BY-SA 2.0, 2022.

Numerous inland lakes were formed during deglaciation in the Mountain, Pacific, and Boreal Cordillera. These lakes, created by temporary ice dams that blocked rivers draining the melting ice sheets, left thick deposits of sand and clay and scoured the landscape when the ice dams broke and the lakes drained catastrophically (Johnsen & Brennand, 2006; Ryder et al., 1991). In addition to shaping the landscape itself, repeated glaciations and deglaciations have impacted species distributions, biodiversity, and genetic diversity (Sec. 2.7) through habitat fragmentation, creation of glacial 'refuges', and exposure and subsequent flooding of continental shelves (Allen et al., 2012; Hewitt, 2000; Shafer et al., 2010).

The most recent period of glaciation peaked between 21,000 and 18,000 years ago, at what is known as the Last Glacial Maximum (LGM). At the LGM, two continental-scale ice sheets covered most of the Canadian landmass: the Cordilleran Ice Sheet, which was centred over the mountains of western Canada; and the Laurentide Ice Sheet, which originated from multiple ice domes centred east of Great Slave Lake, northern Ontario, and Quebec (Dyke & Prest, 1987; Gowan et al., 2016; Marshall et al., 2000). Thick ice sheets covered most of Canada at this time.

The timing of glacier and ice sheet retreat from their maximum LGM extents varies by mountain region. The earliest retreat of the Cordilleran Ice Sheet was likely initiated on the southern and western margins, with ice-free coastal sections possibly offering a viable corridor for human migration by approximately 18,000 years ago (Braje et al., 2020; Darvill et al., 2022; Dulfer et al., 2021; Dulfer et al., 2022; Wade, 2021). An ice-free corridor between the Cordilleran and the Laurentide Ice Sheets was likely not viable for human migration until somewhere between 13,800 and 12,600 years ago (Adler et al., 2022; Clark et al., 2022; Pedersen et al., 2016). There is some evidence to suggest a human presence on lands south of the continental ice sheets as long as 37,000 years ago (Rowe et al., 2022), although many Indigenous

Peoples understand their presence in these land-scapes as existing since time immemorial. The Laurentide Ice Sheet has a complex deglaciation history (Dyke & Prest, 1987), with ice domes persisting over northern Quebec and Labrador until approximately 7000 years ago (Ullman et al., 2016). Large icefields currently found on Baffin and Ellesmere Islands in the Arctic Cordillera are remnants of the last glaciation, as these contain residual Pleistocene-age ice (Koerner and Fisher, 2002; Zdanowicz et al., 2002).

While there may be a tension between scientific evidence for the first arrival of humans in North America, the chronology of continental ice sheets, and Indigenous concepts of being present on the land since time immemorial (Wynn, 2007), origin stories from the Blackfoot Nation of the Montane Cordillera clearly reflect the environmental processes related to deglaciation (Zedeno et al., 2021). These oral histories reference the great floods and lakes left behind by decaying ice sheets, the south to north re-vegetation of the deglaciated landscape, and the 'erratic train' of boulders (Fig. 2.2) that was left behind as the Cordilleran and Laurentide ice sheets retreated.

Following the retreat of the Cordilleran Ice Sheet in western Canada, global mean temperatures peaked approximately 8000 years before present. For a period of several thousand years, glaciers were absent over large areas that are now occupied by glacier ice in western Canada (Heusser, 1956; Menounos et al., 2009; Wood & Smith, 2004). In eastern and northern Canada, this thermal maximum was delayed by up to 4000 years due to the slower demise of the Laurentide Ice Sheet over eastern regions. This period of relative warmth prior to the re-establishment and expansion of mountain glaciers (Mood & Smith, 2015) and permafrost (Treat & Jones, 2018) has implications for the occupation of mountain regions by Indigenous Peoples and the establishment of mountain ecosystems over the past 10,000 years.

2.2.5 Gaps and challenges

Mountains exist because of a dynamic interplay between deep-time geological processes that lift land upwards, and the erosive effects of ice, water, and wind that grind them down under the force of gravity. They will continue to evolve both in ways that are beyond our ability to perceive, as well as those more rapid and visual processes involving snow, ice, hydrology, ecology, mountain hazards, and human interactions in these environments. A more holistic and integrated approach across these subject areas is needed to improve systems-based understanding of mountains and their future evolution.

In the younger mountain ranges of eastern and western Canada, mapping and biostratigraphy (correlation using fossils) has provided exceptional information on the ages of the rocks and the relationships between the main units. However, even in these relatively well understood orogens there are significant gaps and challenges. For example, controversy has surrounded the polarity of subduction—which slab of plate descended into the deeper mantle during convergence—in the evolution of both orogens (e.g., Johnston, 2008; McMechan et al., 2020; De Souza et al., 2014; van Staal et al., 2015), and more work is needed to resolve these questions. Also poorly understood is the relationship between the Appalachian Orogen and its continuation through the Caledonide Orogen of Europe, Svalbard, and Greenland into Arctic Canada as the Innuitian (or Ellesmerian) Orogen (Fig. 2.1) (e.g., Malone et al., 2019).

The older orogens in Canada pre-date most fossils, so unravelling their history is dependent on isotopic dating, and large areas have been mapped geologically only at reconnaissance scale. The tectonic history of the Canadian Shield records major episodes of mountain building for which the plate-tectonic processes are only beginning to be understood (e.g., Hoffman, 1988; Martins et al., 2022). Most of these former mountain belts have been worn down close to sea-level, but portions of the Grenville and Trans-Hudson orogens, formed during the amalgamation of earlier supercontinents, form the Laurentian and Torngat mountains in eastern Canada. Still more uncertainty surrounds the ancient Archean cratons (Fig. 2.1), which record a tectonic system prior to 2.5 billion years ago that may have been substantially different from modern plate tectonics (e.g., Hamilton, 1998).

2.3 Weather and Climate

Western science defines weather as the day-to-day changes in temperature, precipitation, wind, and clouds, and climate as the long-term average of weather. Or, as the Sami people of Finland have described it, "Climate is recorded. Weather is experienced" (Ingold & Kurtilla, 2000). Mountains are known for their unpredictable and extreme weather, and are on the front lines of climate change (Hock et al., 2019). While scientific research on mountain weather and climate focuses on quantifying and explaining spatial patterns in specific climate variables, this approach may be less relevant to Indigenous Peoples and others living in mountain areas than, for example, the lived experience of weather (Ingold & Kurtilla, 2000; Walsh et al., 2017), its predictability (Walsh et al., 2005; Wilson et al., 2015) or indicators of seasonal changes from animal behaviours (Turner & Clifton, 2009).

Millennia of accumulated experience on the land provide First Nations, Métis, and Inuit Peoples with intimate knowledge and understanding of "human-relevant environmental variables" (Fox et al., 2020; Simpson, 2002; Weatherhead et al., 2010). As Siksika (Blackfoot Confederacy) Elder Hayden Melting Tallow and Kwanlin Dün Elder Patricia Joe stated, the mountains themselves served as indicators of the weather and people learned to read them (LC 2.5, LC 2.6). In contrast, the observational networks used to measure, quantify, and model weather and climate were only established in the past century, and the climate reanalysis models used to describe broad spatial patterns have been developed and refined only in the past 20 years, although they have been applied retrospectively to past climate.

Hayden Melting Tallow, Siksika Nation, Blackfoot Confederacy, 2022, LC 2.5

Patricia Joe, Kwanlin Dün First Nation, 2022, LC 2.6

This section describes how air temperature, precipitation, and winds vary across mountain regions in Canada, and identifies the processes that make mountain weather both interesting and challenging. We use existing datasets to broadly characterise the climatology of mountain systems across Canada and assess the understanding of mountain-specific weather processes from both Indigenous and Western scientific perspectives. Few Indigenous perspectives on weather and climate in mountain regions across Canada were shared with us during the Assessment, so this section is limited in its representation of Indigenous understanding of mountain weather and climate processes. For the scientific perspective on mountain weather and climate, we refer throughout this section to the ERA5 global reanalysis dataset (Hersbach et al., 2020) which provides a more complete and consistent meteorological dataset than the sparse station networks often found in mountainous regions.

2.3.1 *Air temperature*

Mountain systems in Canada are characterised by large variations in near-surface air temperature in both space (Fig. 2.9) and time (Fig. 2.10). Mean seasonal and annual temperatures shown for the period 1991–2020 are based on the ERA5 reanalysis dataset (Hersbach et al., 2020) and are given in Table 2.1. From a climatological point of view, latitude and distance to the ocean control the spatial distribution of temperature across the different Canadian mountain regions (Fig. 2.9). The Pacific Maritime region stands out for being warm with mild winters (mean winter temperatures of -4.5°C) relative to the rest of Canada (mean winter temperatures of -20°C). The Arctic Cordillera region is on the other end of the spectrum, characterised by extremely cold conditions with mean annual temperatures of -16°C and mean winter temperatures of -30°C.

In mountain regions, the elevation of the 0°C temperature threshold is critically important for processes such as snow and ice melt, frozen ground, and precipitation phase (rain versus snow) at the surface (Mekis et al., 2020). Mountain regions in Canada that experience mean annual temperatures near 0°C are found in low-elevation and coastal regions of southern Canada (Pacific Cordillera and Atlantic Maritime).

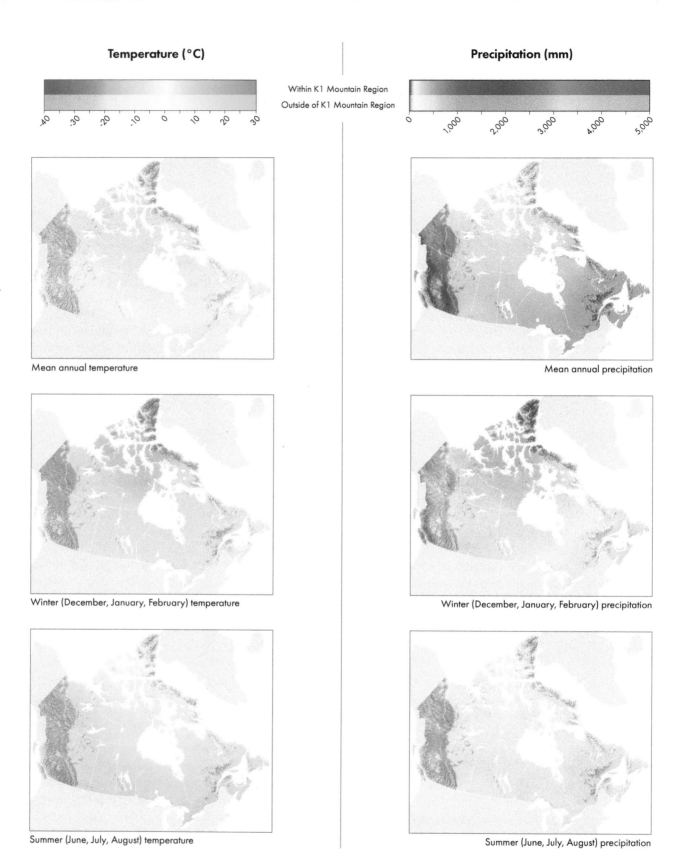

Temperature (°C)

-40 -30 -20 -10 0 10 20 30

Within K1 Mountain Region
Outside of K1 Mountain Region

Precipitation (mm)

0 1,000 2,000 3,000 4,000 5,000

Mean annual temperature

Mean annual precipitation

Winter (December, January, February) temperature

Winter (December, January, February) precipitation

Summer (June, July, August) temperature

Summer (June, July, August) precipitation

Figure 2.9: Maps showing the average annual, winter (December, January, and February), and summer (June, July, and August) air temperature (left) and precipitation (right) across Canada. This baseline climatology (1991–2020) is calculated from the ERA5 climate reanalysis. Data from Hersbach et al., 2020.

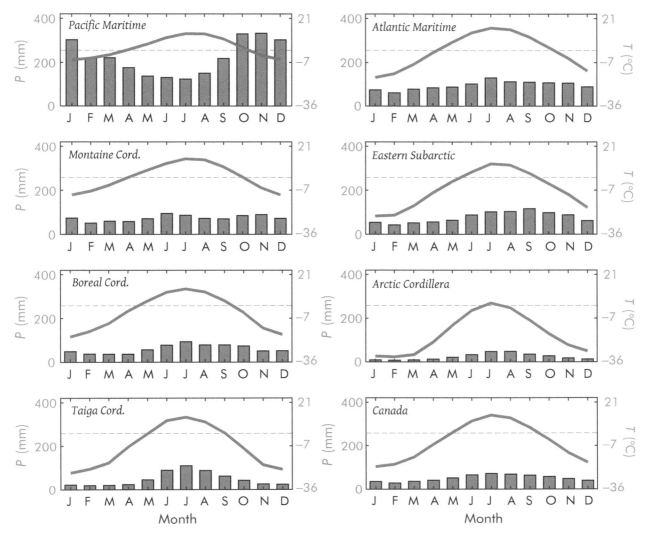

Figure 2.10: Baseline climatology (1991–2020) for monthly air temperature (red curve) and precipitation (blue bars) for the major mountain regions in Canada, calculated from the ERA5 climate reanalysis by averaging all ERA5 grid cells over each mountain region. Data from Hersbach et al., 2020.

Within a given mountain region, elevation strongly controls the spatial variability of temperature. On average, temperatures decrease with elevation at a rate known as a lapse rate or temperature gradient. In the Montane Cordillera, the mean annual lapse rate is -5.2°C km^{-1} (Shea et al., 2004), which means that on average the temperature decreases by 5.2°C for every 1000 m increase in elevation. A more negative lapse was found in springtime (-6.0°C km^{-1}) when strong temperature contrasts exist between snow-free valley bottoms and snow-covered peaks. In the eastern Montane Cordillera (Canadian Rockies) and the Pacific Cordillera, the lapse rate is generally larger for maximum temperatures than for minimum temperatures (Stahl & Moore, 2006; Wood et al., 2018). Lapse rates in the Arctic show similar ranges and are often weaker due to strong inversion structures, with links to atmospheric circulation patterns (Marshall et al., 2007).

Minimum temperatures in valley bottoms are particularly sensitive to the overnight accumulation of cold air in valley bottoms (Sakiyama, 1990), which reverses the lapse rate and leads to the formation of temperature *inversions* where colder air is found at lower elevation. Inversions are common in the eastern Canadian Rockies (Wood et al., 2018) and the Yukon (Burn, 1994), and are more frequent during winter when cold and continental polar air masses from northern Canada

Table 2.1: Average annual (ann), winter (DJF: December, January, and February), and summer (JJA: June, July, and August) temperature and precipitation in the main mountain regions of Canada and across all Canada (last row). The values were calculated from the ERA5 global climate reanalysis, with a resolution of 0.25 degrees and are based on all ERA5 grid cells covering Canada and each of the CMA mountain regions.

ERAS baseline climatology (1991–2020), Canadian Mountain Regions

Mountain Region	T (°C)			P (m)		
	DJF	JJA	ann	DJF	JJA	ann
Pacific Maritime	-4.5	11.2	2.9	0.84	0.38	2.60
Montane Cordillera	-9.1	12.4	1.5	0.21	0.25	0.92
Boreal Cordillera	-17.7	11.5	-3.1	0.13	0.27	0.73
Taiga Cordillera	-23.6	11.0	-7.1	0.07	0.31	0.62
Atlantic Maritime	-14.1	15.1	1.0	0.25	0.37	1.23
Eastern Subarctic	-19.3	9.5	-4.6	0.16	0.30	0.94
Arctic Cordillera	-30.0	1.4	-16.0	0.03	0.14	0.32
All of Canada	-20.0	12.3	-3.9	0.12	0.24	0.69

move southwards (Cullen & Marshall, 2011). The formation of valley cold pools represents a challenge for meteorological models, in particular in the Canadian Rockies (Vionnet et al., 2015). Temperature inversions are also very frequent in the Arctic, Taiga and Boreal Cordilleras (O'Neill et al., 2015; Smith & Bonnaventure, 2017) where they influence the spatial distribution of permafrost (Bonnaventure & Lewkowicz, 2013). Temperature inversions are not restricted to valley bottoms and can be observed at larger scales due to the continuous loss of heat from snow and ice-covered surfaces, particularly during dry and clear conditions. This is especially the case in the Arctic during the long and dark winter (Lesins et al., 2010).

Other weather phenomena, such as Chinook events in the eastern Canadian Rockies and the Foothills (Montane Cordillera), can also influence the lapse rate. During such events, air is warmed as it descends to the surface, and the lapse rate approaches -10°C km⁻¹ (Cullen & Marshall, 2011). Chinook events can bring rapid warming and snowmelt in the depths of winter in the Canadian Rockies (Nkemdirim, 1996, 1997; Mekis et al., 2020). More details about the Chinook, an iconic wind of the mountains in Canada, are given below in the section dedicated to mountain winds.

Mountain glaciers modify the distribution of air temperature in their vicinity. For example, during the melt season, the temperature of the snow and ice at the surface of glaciers cannot exceed 0°C. Observations from the Pacific Maritime region (Shea & Moore, 2010) and the Arctic Cordillera (Marshall et al., 2007) show that the air immediately above the glacier surface is cooled and, as it is denser, it flows downward in a thin layer above the glacier. Consequently, air temperatures above glaciers are typically lower than off-glacier temperatures at the same elevation during the summer months (i.e., when the surrounding terrain is snow-free).

Mountains in Canada are increasingly affected by extreme air temperatures in summertime. Recently, in June 2021, an unprecedented heat wave known in the media as the "heat dome" impacted the southern parts of the Pacific and Montane Cordilleras with local temperatures reaching values well above 40°C (Vasquez, 2022). During this heat wave, the all-time heat record in Canada was eclipsed three days in a row with air temperatures reaching 46.1°C, 47.9°C, and 49.6°C in the village of Lytton, located on the lee side of the Pacific Maritime ranges. This heat wave was associated with the presence of a large-scale and persistent high-pressure ridge centred over the region that prevented the transport of cooler, moist Pacific air into the region. Ridges are also associated with clear skies (i.e., sunny conditions) and sinking air that warms adiabatically, similar to Chinook winds, contributing to the hot, dry weather.

Similar circulation patterns are related to droughts in the Pacific and Montane Cordilleras and in the adjacent regions of interior British Columbia and of the Prairies (Bonsal et al., 2011;

Stewart et al., 2019). Droughts in mountains in Canada are a combination of anomalously low precipitation (Sec. 2.2.2) and high air temperatures (Bonsal et al., 2011). The occurrence of wildfires in the Montane Cordillera is also controlled by the same large-scale atmospheric circulation patterns that favour heat waves (Johnson & Wowchuk, 1993). Wildfires, in turn, can create their own thunderstorms—heat from intense wildfires causes humid air to rise rapidly into the atmosphere, producing pyrocumulus clouds (Stewart et al., 2019). In some conditions, lightning activity in pyrocumulus clouds can lead to new fire ignitions (Kochtubajda et al., 2017).

2.3.2 *Precipitation*

Precipitation can occur as liquid, ice, or a combination of the two when temperatures are near 0°C (Mekis et al., 2020; Stewart et al., 2015). We use total precipitation (the sum of all liquid and solid precipitation) extracted from ERA5 reanalysis data to compare precipitation across mountain regions in Canada. Average annual, summer, and winter precipitation data (Fig. 2.7, Fig. 2.8, and Table 2.1) for the period 1991–2020 highlight the importance of mountain regions as 'water towers' (Vivrioli et al., 2007).

The Pacific Maritime region stands out for being exceptionally wet, with annual precipitation four times greater than the rest of Canada (Table 2.1). The Pacific Maritime ranges are directly affected by moisture-laden westerly storms and atmospheric rivers coming off the Pacific Ocean. Atmospheric rivers, which transport warm and moist tropical air towards the West Coast in narrow bands, can contribute up to one-third of the total annual precipitation in coastal British Columbia (Sharma & Dery, 2020). The Arctic Cordillera is on the other end of the spectrum, characterised by dry conditions (0.32 m annual precipitation). The Taiga Cordillera region in northwestern Canada is also relatively dry, with a mean annual precipitation of 0.62 m. All other mountain regions in Canada receive precipitation totals that exceed the national average.

The ERA5 reanalysis data used to derive this precipitation climatology will underestimate precipitation in the high mountains (Mott et al., 2018). For instance, measurements from ice cores and glacier mass balance studies in the St. Elias

mountains, Yukon, indicate annual precipitation totals of ~2 m at elevations of 2500–3000 m in the St. Elias Icefields (Ochwat et al., 2021; Zdanowicz et al., 2014), which is an order of magnitude higher than the 0.28 m of precipitation received at Burwash Landing (806 m) in the adjacent valley bottom. Similar decreases in precipitation are observed going west to east across the continental divide of the Canadian Rockies (Adhikari & Marshall, 2013).

Mountain ranges are significant obstacles to atmospheric flow. When moist air encounters a mountain range it is forced to rise. This leads to cooling, condensation, and precipitation in a process known as orographic precipitation (Roe, 2005). Orographic precipitation is heaviest on windward sides of mountain ranges, with strong vertical gradients of precipitation given the right atmospheric conditions (Thériault et al., 2022). These gradients do not typically extend to the top of a mountain range, however, as the greatest rates of uplift, condensation, and precipitation tend to occur lower down the mountain. Orographic precipitation has been studied in the Arctic Cordillera (Fargey et al., 2014; Hanesiak et al., 2010), the Montane Cordillera (Liu et al., 2016; Milrad et al., 2015; Shea et al., 2004), and the Pacific Maritime (Jarosch et al., 2012; Mo et al., 2019; Sharma & Dery, 2020). In lower-elevation ranges, the mountains may not produce strong precipitation gradients, but they can affect the distribution and phase of precipitation, as shown in studies from the Atlantic Maritime and Boreal Shield region (Chartrand et al., 2022; Ressler et al., 2012).

While the windward sides of mountain ranges receive the highest precipitation totals, lee slopes can also experience heavy precipitation events associated with orographic forcing. The eastern side of the Montane Cordillera, for example, although associated with a drier climate, can experience frontal storm systems associated with easterly winds that lead to heavy precipitation and massive flooding (Liu et al., 2016). Convective precipitation, due to surface heating which lifts air parcels into the atmosphere, can also occur over complex terrain (Kirshbaum et al., 2018) and can weaken or reverse the standard precipitation gradient. For example, the highest amounts of precipitation observed in the 2013 Alberta floods were associated with convective precipitation at lower elevations (Kochtubajda et al., 2016). This convective activity was embedded in a three-day cyclonic storm (19–21 June 2013) during which more than 200 mm of rainfall was reported at locations on the eastern side of the Canadian Rockies (Pomeroy et al., 2016). Rainfall intensity plays a key role in the flooding risks associated with mountain precipitation (Weingartner et al., 2003), particularly in steep mountain creeks.

Atmospheric and meteorological factors that determine the *phase* of precipitation (rain, snow, or other) vary across mountain regions in Canada (Harder & Pomeroy, 2014; Poirier et al., 2019). The freezing level broadly describes the elevation where rain turns to snow. In atmospheric river events, shifts in the freezing level can determine whether flooding occurs or not (Newton et al., 2019). For example, in the atmospheric river event and flooding in southern British Columbia in November 2021, freezing levels were as high as 2000 m (Gillett et al., 2022). Anomalously warm conditions were also a factor during the June 2013 Alberta flooding, as precipitation fell as rain to elevations of up to 2500 m during the first two days of this storm event. Progressive cooling as the storm went on caused rain to change to snow at higher elevations, preventing an even more severe flooding event (Pomeroy et al., 2016). Rain-on-snow events can contribute to rapid snowmelt and downstream floods. Most of the melt during such events is due to the advection of warm and moist air over the snow surface, as opposed to melt energy in the rain itself (Sec. 2.4.1). Rain-on-snow events are common in the Pacific Maritime mountains, the Montane Cordillera, and eastern Canada (Cohen et al., 2015; Suriano, 2022), and are becoming more common in northern Canada. As described by Brandy Mayes of the Kwanlin Dün First Nation, precipitation regimes in mountain regions are being affected by climatic changes that include ocean warming (LC 2.7).

Brandy Mayes, Kwanlin Dün First Nation, 2022, LC 2.7

2.3.3 *Mountain wind systems*

Mountains modify large-scale atmospheric flows and create wind systems specific to mountain environments. For Indigenous people in the Arctic, winds affect all types of travel, and can be a significant safety consideration (Ford et al., 2019). Mountains of the Canadian Arctic Archipelago influence the wind patterns at some of the low-lying Arctic communities such as Iqaluit and Cape Dorset in Nunavut (Nawri & Stewart, 2008) and favour the occurrence of blizzards (Hanesiak et al., 2010). Cold air flows known as katabatic winds commonly descend off the large ice caps in the Arctic Cordillera due to high pressures created by cold, dense air that develops in the plateau regions of these ice caps (Gardner et al., 2009). This air flows downslope and can have a considerable fetch, building to strong and persistent off-glacier winds.

Similar winds are generated by the large ice-fields of western Canada (Stenntng et al., 1981; Shea & Moore, 2010; Ayala et al., 2015). The process is particularly strong in summer months, when the surrounding terrain and air heat up but the glacier surface does not warm beyond the melting point, 0°C. This creates a strong thermal and pressure gradient. The contrast of heating and cooling between the Rockies and the Prairies can also create atmospheric circulations between the mountain and the adjacent plains (Thyer, 1981). The interaction between large-scale, regional, and local wind systems can create complex atmospheric circulation patterns in the surroundings of large glaciers such as the Columbia Icefield in the Rockies (Conway et al., 2021). Katabatic winds also drive local cooling that suppresses the development of soil and vegetation in glacier forefields.

The complex topography of mountains presents many corridors that modify and channelize low-level winds. Strong winds due to wind channelling in mountain valleys can generate waves on valley lakes, affecting chemical and biological processes (e.g., Quesnel Lake in the Montane Cordillera; Thompson et al., 2020). Wind channelling also occurs in the St. Lawrence Valley, the Laurentian Mountains, and the Adirondack Mountains in the United States (Carrera et al., 2009). In winter, this channelling can produce a layer of cold air close to the surface, increasing the occurrence and intensity of freezing rain events such as the 1998 Ice Storm (Roebber & Gyakum, 2003) that occurred in and around the St. Lawrence Valley.

In the Coast Mountains of British Columbia (Pacific Maritime), winds are channelized in the deep valleys, fjords, and inlets that connect the interior of British Columbia to the coast (Bakri et al., 2017a; Jackson & Steyn, 1994). Depending on the gradient of pressure across the Coast Mountains, these winds can be inflows, with air moving from the coast to the interior, or outflows, with air moving from interior to the coast. Outflows are mainly observed during the winter when cold, high-pressure air masses sit over the interior east of the Coast Mountains. Combined with the warmer air at lower pressure found along the coast, it creates a pressure gradient that pushes the cold air through the valleys, fjords, and inlets. Large wind speeds (above 80 km h^{-1}) and associated extreme wind chill (below -30°C) can be observed during outflow events (Jackson, 1996).

The Squamish winds are common winter outflows in the Howe Sound region of British Columbia (Pacific Maritime), named after the Skwxwú7mesh (Squamish) First Nation of the region. Pressure gradients across the mountain passes of Vancouver Island create the Qualicum wind, an outflow that creates strong westerly winds and potentially dangerous sailing conditions in the Strait of Georgia on the eastern side of Vancouver Island (Bakri et al., 2017b).

CHINOOK WINDS

The most well-known mountain wind in Canada is the Chinook: a strong, warm, and dry westerly wind that descends the lee slopes of the Canadian Rocky Mountains in southern and central Alberta (Nkemdirim, 1996, 1997). Chinook winds on the eastern side of the Montane Cordillera are linked to orographic precipitation (Sec. 2.2.2) on the windward side. Warm and moist Pacific air that is forced to ascend the western side of the mountains cools, condenses, and loses moisture through precipitation. This adds latent heat to the air mass. As this drier air traverses the continental divide and descends on the eastern slopes, the descending air pressurises and warms faster than it cooled on the upslope side, which leads to warm winds at the surface. The phenomenon is associated with a wide band of clouds parallel to the mountains, known as the Chinook arch. The arch demarcates the precipitation bands over the mountains which help to fuel the Chinook. Many of the strongest Chinooks are associated with intense low pressure systems off the coast of British Columbia or the US Pacific Northwest, which can produce high winds and draw warm, moisture-laden air from the subtropical Pacific (also known as 'Pineapple Express' systems or atmospheric rivers).

Chinook winds occur all year around but are particularly noticeable in winter when they can lead to strong increases in near-surface air temperature (up to 25°C in less than a day) and high wind speeds in southern Alberta (Nkemdirim, 1991). In November 2011, successive Chinook wind-storms with gust wind speeds reaching more than 140 km h^{-1} led to massive damage in southern Alberta (Hugenholtz, 2013). On average, Chinooks occur about 50 days per winter (Nkemdirim, 1997) and the associated high temperatures and wind speeds can quickly remove large amounts of snow due to melt and sublimation (Sec. 2.3.1) (Golding, 1978; Macdonald et al., 2018). The term Chinook originates from the Lower Columbia River area, where the Chinookan nations experienced similar weather (Ballou, 1893; Costello, 1895). Commonly, Indigenous terminologies used in Western language are spatially disconnected from their origins. In the case of the Chinook, the local Indigenous term for this wind is *masta ganutha* in Nakoda[1] and *si'kssópoistsi* in Siksika (Frantz & Russell, 2017).

Daily (or diurnal) wind systems are also widely found in mountains in Canada at different scales. These wind systems are driven by heating and cooling cycles in the lower atmospheric layers. Slope wind systems can develop along the side walls of valleys, such as in the Kananaskis valley in Alberta (MacHattie, 1968). Slope winds are upslope in daytime when the sun warms the exposed slopes and the heated air rises above them. On the contrary, during nighttime, the cooled air near the surface flows downslope and collects in the valleys. Valley winds flowing along the valley axis are another manifestation of diurnal wind systems in mountains in Canada (Sakiyama, 1990).

1 https://dictionary.stoneynakoda.org/#/E/chinook

2.3.4 Gaps and challenges

Our understanding of mountain weather and climate is incomplete due to limited availability or inclusion of Indigenous knowledges within our assessment and a systematic lack of station observations. Ground-based observations of mountain weather are crucial for short-term weather forecasting, long-term climate assessment, and to improve our understanding of the complex interactions between mountains and the atmosphere. The density of active meteorological and hydrological stations varies across Canada (Fig. 2.11), with very few stations established at high elevations. The Montane Cordillera has more than 6 stations per 10,000 km² (Table 2.2), while high-latitude mountain regions show a very low density of stations (0.1 stations per 10 000 km² in the Eastern Subarctic).

Active stations used to forecast weather and streamflow belong to a range of federal, provincial, territorial, and municipal networks, and may have been deployed only recently. These active stations are not necessarily suitable for climate change assessments that require long-term and consistent meteorological data (Mekis & Vincent, 2011; Vincent et al., 2012). Consequently, the number of stations available for climate change assessments drops significantly across the country (Fig. 2.12) and for all mountain regions in Canada (Table 2.2). Only the Montane Cordillera has more than 1 station per 10,000 km² that can be used for climate assessment. The Pacific Maritime and Taiga Cordillera regions only have climate stations in nearby valleys and coastal areas. This lack of in-situ data makes climate change assessments a challenge for Canadian mountain regions.

Precipitation measurements, including amounts, intensity, and phase, are one of the greatest challenges in understanding and characterising the climate of mountainous regions (Lundquist et al., 2019). Most stations that measure precipitation are located in valleys, at lower elevations, where less precipitation generally occurs. At higher and colder elevations, precipitation measurements are challenged by winds (Kochendorfer et al., 2022) and snowfalls that cover gauges (Rasmussen et al., 2012). Local processes such as wind redistribution of snowfall (Mott et al., 2018) are not captured by typical measurement networks.

Low precipitation amounts also present a challenge to both measurement networks and models (Schirmer & Jamieson, 2015). This is the case in the Arctic, where light snow (known as diamond dust) can fall continuously but at a rate that is too low to be measured by standard all-weather gauges. A combination of ground instruments, new technologies such as hotplate precipitation gauges (Rasmussen et al., 2011; Thériault et al., 2021), and space-borne remote sensing is essential to map precipitation. However, satellite measurements of weather and climate conditions in mountainous terrain are limited by spatial resolution, repeat frequency, and the presence

Table 2.2: Number and density of stations measuring precipitation and/or temperature for the main CMA mountain regions. The information is provided for active stations that were used in the ECCC operational systems for weather and hydrological forecasting (Carrera et al., 2015; Fortin et al., 2018) between 1 January–31 May 2022 and for climatological stations from the Adjusted and Homogenized Canadian Climate Data (Mekis & Vincent, 2011; Vincent et al., 2012). The density represents the number of stations per 10,000 km².

Regions	Number (density) of active stations	Number (density) of climatological stations
Arctic Cordillera	_*	3 (0.1)
Atlantic Maritime and Boreal Shield	64 (3.3)	3 (0.2)
Boreal Cordillera	31 (0.6)	18 (0.4)
Interior Hills	17 (1.4)	3 (0.2)
Montane Cordillera	330 (6.4)	57 (1.1)
Pacific Maritime	37 (2.4)	0 (0.0)
Eastern Subarctic	1 (0.1)	1 (0.1)
Taiga Cordillera	6 (0.2)	0 (0.0)

* Not covered by the two ECCC operational forecast systems considered in this section.

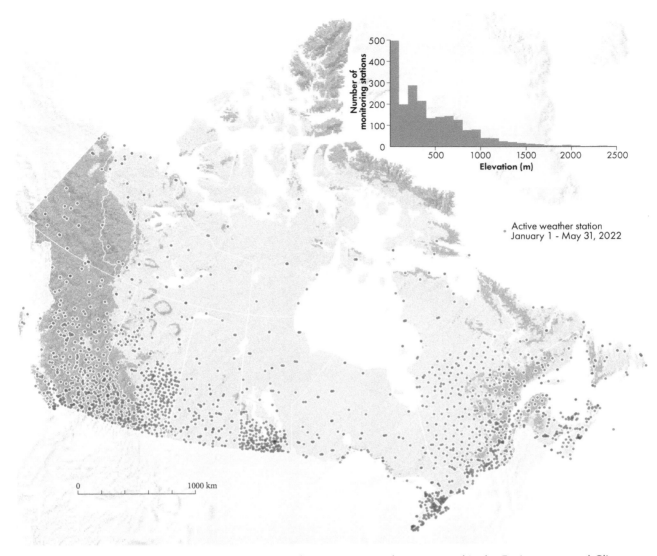

Figure 2.11: Active stations reporting precipitation and/or temperature that were used in the Environment and Climate Change Canada (ECCC) operational systems for weather and hydrological forecasting (Carrera et al., 2015; Fortin et al., 2018) between 1 January–31 May 2022. Inset histogram shows the elevation of these stations. Note that Nunavut, north of 70°N, is not covered by the two ECCC forecast systems considered in this section.

of clouds. New satellite missions aim to address the issue of low precipitation in the Arctic by deploying a far-infrared sensor sensitive enough to measure Arctic clouds and precipitation (Libois & Blanchet, 2017), and existing satellites are being used to map snow depths (Lievens et al., 2019).

As with precipitation and temperature, a full characterization of wind patterns across mountain regions in Canada remains a challenge due to a lack of observations. Atmospheric models have been used to simulate complex wind flows in the Bow River Valley (Vionnet et al., 2015) and snow

redistribution in the Montane Cordillera (Vionnet, Marsh et al., 2021). In both studies, the models were tested with observations from a dense network of meteorological stations deployed to cover a large range of elevation from valley bottom to alpine crests (Fang et al., 2019). The complexities of wind modelling make it difficult to provide accurate estimates of wind resources in the context of wind farm developments (Pinard et al., 2009) and accurate simulations of the mountain snow cover affected by wind-induced snow redistribution. These challenges are due to a still-limited

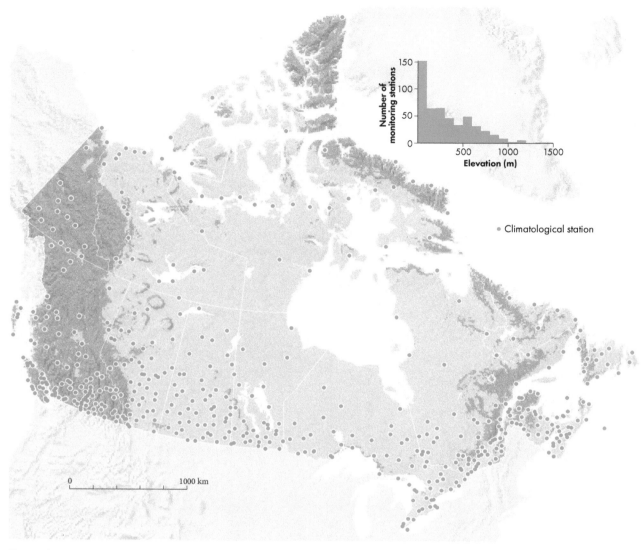

Figure 2.12: Long-term climatological stations reporting precipitation and/or temperature from the Adjusted and Homogenized Canadian Climate Data. Data from Mekis & Vincent, 2011; Vincent et al., 2012.

understanding of the complex multi-scale flows in mountainous terrain (Aksamit & Pomeroy, 2018a; Helgason & Pomeroy, 2012).

2.4 Snow, Ice, and Permafrost

Mountain regions in Canada are home to deep and prolonged winter snowpacks, glaciers, and permafrost (ground that remains below 0°C for at least two consecutive years). Elevation, proximity to oceans, and latitude determine winter snow accumulations and persistence: high-elevation snow that does not melt in the summer eventually becomes compressed into glacier ice and flows downhill. Mountain glaciers are both key

indicators of ongoing climate change and central figures in Indigenous oral knowledge systems (Cruikshank, 2001). The cryosphere figures prominently in the stories of the Tlingit and Champagne-Aishihik First Nations of the Boreal Cordillera (Cruikshank, 2007), and glacier-fed rivers in the Pacific Maritime region are home to the eulachon, a cultural keystone species for the Nuxalk Nation. While we have divided this section into snow, glaciers, and permafrost, this division may seem arbitrary to an Indigenous point of view. For example, given the life cycle of glaciers, where would we include the consciousness attributed to glaciers by Indigenous Peoples in Yukon (Cruikshank, 2005)?

Our assessment of mountain snow, ice, and permafrost (all part of the cryosphere) flows from the preceding assessment of mountain meteorology. However, we acknowledge that it is not possible to summarise all Indigenous knowledge of the cryosphere, given the way knowledge is transmitted and the broad diversity of Indigenous cultures and knowledge systems related to the mountain regions of Canada.

2.4.1 *Mountain snow*

Seasonal snow is a defining characteristic of our mountain regions and the rivers they feed (Immerzeel et al., 2020), and streamflows across much of Canada are dominated by seasonal snow melt. As a critical water resource (Dyer, 2008; Hamlet & Lettenmaier, 1999; Woo & Thorne, 2003, 2006), snow also has a wide range of ecosystem functions (Callaghan et al., 2011; Rand et al., 2006), regional climate impacts (Chapin et al., 2005; Pulliainen et al., 2020; Zhang, 2005), and socio-economic value (Sturm et al., 2017). For First Nations, Métis, and Inuit communities, snow can also be an essential material used to construct shelters (Furgal & Seguin, 2006), a predictor of animal behaviours (Turner & Clifton, 2009), a facilitator of winter transportation (Routledge, 2020), and an indicator of changing seasons (Turner et al., 2000).

While snow typically blankets Canadian mountain regions for much of the year (Mudryk et al., 2018), the actual amount of water stored in mountain snowpacks is a deceptively challenging question to answer. Snow can be measured directly at point locations through ground observations or through remote sensing observations from satellites or aircraft (both piloted and remotely piloted). Given the enormous spatial scales of mountain regions in Canada, snowpacks are also frequently modelled with inputs from regional climate networks or weather models (Largeron et al., 2020; Marsh et al., 2020; Wrzesien et al., 2018). Each approach—whether it is ground observations, remote sensing, or modelling—has its own unique challenges and limitations.

We focus here on snow accumulation and melt processes in mountain environments, discuss the ways that snow is measured or modelled, and examine what is known about the current distribution of snow, and how snowpacks are changing in Canadian mountain regions.

Snow accumulation

Snow can be measured in terms of its area, depth, density, and mass (also expressed as snow water equivalence, SWE). SWE is a function of snow depth and density, and it represents the amount of water stored in the snowpack, which is what matters for water managers, flood forecasters, and hydrologists (Sec. 2.5). Snow depths can be highly variable, and particularly so in mountain environments, due to complex terrain and weather patterns (Sec. 2.3). Snow density is generally less variable. Fresh snowfall has a lower density than a deep snowpack, and high- and low-elevation snowpacks in the same region can have very different densities depending on storm characteristics and the progression of the spring melt season.

Snowfall totals are governed by temperature and precipitation, which are ultimately a function of elevation, latitude, prevailing winds, and topography. In mountain environments snow can occur at temperatures well above 0°C (Kienzle, 2008), and orographic precipitation associated with mid-latitude or Arctic storm systems can bring solid precipitation to mountain systems in Canada year-round.

Snow accumulation on the ground varies with land cover and local wind patterns: forests can intercept up to 60% of the snow that falls, increase the spatial variability of snow on the ground, and decrease the amount of snow available for melt (Lv & Pomeroy, 2020; Pomeroy et al., 2007; Varhola et al., 2010). How much a forest affects snow accumulation depends largely on the forest type. In alpine environments, wind redistribution of snow is another critical process (Winstral et al., 2002) that produces complex snow distribution patterns that reflect the prevailing winds and the topography (Essery et al., 1999). Snow redistribution by wind enhances losses of snow directly back to the atmosphere through sublimation (see below), but also leads to the formation of perennial snow patches or aniuvat (Inuktitut) that persist through the summer months and are fundamental to the creation of alpine micro-habitats visited and used by a wide variety of mammals, birds, and insects (Rosvold, 2016). Archaeological evidence gathered from the margins of melting snow and ice patches in the southern Yukon, on or adjacent to the territories of Carcross-Tagish, Champagne and Aishihik, Kluane, and Kwanlin

Dun First Nations, indicate that snow patches were specialised hunting grounds for caribou, and feature prominently in the the traditions of all four First Nations (Farnell et al., 2004; Hare et al., 2004; Strand, 2003).

Avalanches also redistribute snow from high elevation (and low melt rate) regions to low elevation (and high melt rate) regions (Strasser et al., 2018), creating areas of extreme snow depth at the base of steep slopes (Bernhardt & Schulz, 2010). Avalanches occur in steep terrain where there is sufficient snow loading, and wind-transport of snow is often a key factor in avalanche formation (Bernhardt & Schulz, 2010). There can be tremendous human and economic costs of avalanches (Stethem et al., 2003) and they represent a significant hazard for winter recreation (e.g., ski touring, ice climbing) in mountain areas.

Ablation

The removal of snow from the landscape occurs through either melt (solid to liquid) or sublimation (solid to gas). Together, the processes of melt and sublimation are known as ablation. Our current scientific understanding of snow and ice ablation processes in Canadian mountain environments depends almost entirely on a handful of ground-based observations that are limited in both space and time (Table 2.3). Long-term and comprehensive observational networks in the mountains are exceedingly rare, with the Canadian Rockies Hydrological Observatory[1] a notable exception.

Ablation occurs when there is surplus energy at the snow or ice surface, and it is driven by the energy exchange between a snow/ice surface and its environment (Anderson, 1968). While sublimation can occur at any temperature, melt does not occur until the temperature of the snow/ice surface is raised to 0°C. Air temperatures can be used as a simple metric for snow and ice melt (Shea et al., 2009), but process-based studies use a surface energy balance approach which defines all the possible energy gains and losses from a volume of snow or ice.

Accounting for each energy component individually allows researchers to study what drives

melt in different environments, and to develop models that can be transferred to (and from) other regions. Shortwave radiation—the energy received from sun—has been identified as the main source of melt energy at Montane Cordillera sites in western Canada (Burles & Boon, 2011; Ebrahimi & Marshall, 2016; Marshall, 2014; Munro, 1991) and in the St. Elias Mountains (Wheeler & Flowers, 2011; Ochwat et al., 2021). Full energy balance studies in other Canadian mountain regions are largely absent. However, low-elevation Arctic and sub-Arctic studies (Ohmura, 1982) point to the balance between longwave (thermal) energy lost from the surface and gained from the atmosphere as a major component of the energy balance (Lackner et al., 2022). A warmer atmosphere increases the amount of longwave received at the surface.

Shortwave radiation changes with latitude, day of year, clouds, slope angle, and wildfire smoke (Aubry-Wake et al., 2022), but also with elevation: more energy reaches the surface at higher elevations due to the thinner atmosphere above (Saunders et al., 1997). And the net amount of shortwave energy at the surface is highly dependent on the reflectivity (or albedo) of the surface. Snowpacks with darker surfaces due to wildfires (Aubry-Wake et al., 2022), mineral dust, pollution, or snow algae (Engstrom et al., 2022) absorb more solar energy, and a reduced snow cover in Arctic and alpine regions due to ongoing climate warming may lead to an albedo feedback effect (Déry & Brown, 2007). Recent work has shown a strong connection between glacier albedo, snow-line elevation, and wildfire across western North America (Marshall & Miller, 2020; Williamson & Menounos, 2021). Significant advances in snow energy balance and hydrology have been made in the Prairie regions of Canada, with many of the principles directly transferable to mountain regions (Debeer & Pomeroy, 2017; Pomeroy & Essery, 1999; Pomeroy & Li, 2000).

Blowing snow entrains small snow particles into the atmosphere where they can quickly sublimate, so dry, windy environments that are typical of alpine or polar regions promote sublimation (Essery et al., 1999). Wintertime sublimation losses can range from 1% to 30–40% of total winter-time precipitation, but it is highly variable between studies (Mott et al., 2018a). In the

---

1 https://research-groups.usask.ca/hydrology/science/research-facilities/crho.php#Data

Table 2.3: Long-term snow and ice research sites within mountain regions of Canada.

Site	Region[1]	Latitude (°N)	Longitude (°W)	Elevation (m)	Notes / References
Wolf Creek, YT (1992–present)	BC/TC	61.52	135.52	660–2080	snow hydrology, energy balance, meteorology, permafrost (Janowicz et al., 2004; Rasouli et al., 2019)
Marmot Creek, AB (1962–1986; 2004–present)	MC	50.95	115.15	1600–2825	snow hydrology, snow energy balance, meteorology (Fang et al., 2019; Munn & Storr, 1967)
Conrad Glacier, BC (2015–present)	MC	50.81	116.92	1825–3235	glacier mass balance, energy balance, alpine permafrost, glacier dynamics (Pelto et al., 2019)
Fortress Mountain, AB (2013–present)	MC	50.83	115.21	2000–2300	snow accumulation and energy balance, hydrology, groundwater, RPAS (Schirmer & Pomeroy, 2020)
Place Glacier, BC (1965–present)	PM	50.43	122.60	1850–2550	glacier mass balance, meteorology, hydrology (Moore & Demuth, 2001)
Peyto Glacier, AB (1965–present)	MC	51.67	116.53	2150–3150	glacier mass balance, meteorology, hydrology (Demuth et al., 2006; Pradhananga et al., 2021)
Haig Glacier, AB (2000–present)	MC	50.72	115.30	2450–2800	glacier mass balance, meteorology, ice dynamics (Marshall & Miller, 2020)
Axel Heiberg Glacier, NU (1962–present)	AC	79.50	90.84	80–1782	glacier mass balance, meteorology (Thomson et al., 2017)
Foret Montmorency, QC	AMBS	47.32	71.15	600–1000	snow accumulation, snow melt, energy balance, snow chemistry (Plamondon et al., 1984)
Trapridge Glacier, YT (1969–2019)	TC	61.23	140.23	2250–2800	glacier dynamics, subglacial hydrology (Frappe & Clarke, 2007)
Rogers Pass, BC (1965–present)	MC	51.28	117.51	800–2800	meteorology, avalanche (Bellaire et al., 2016)

1 Regions: BC = Boreal Cordillera; TC = Taiga Cordillera; MC = Montane Cordillera; PM = Pacific Maritime; AMBS = Atlantic Maritime and Boreal Shield; AC = Arctic Cordillera

Boreal Cordillera in the Yukon, Marsh et al. (2019) found annual sublimation losses between 6 and 14%, while Pomeroy & Li (2000) reported losses of 22%, and Macdonald et al. (2009) reported losses between 19–81%. Snow losses due to sublimation in Arctic and sub-Arctic mountain environments (Arctic Cordillera, Taiga Cordillera, Interior Hills North) may be lower, as extreme cold temperatures limit sublimation (Ohmura, 1982).

Snowfall intercepted by forest canopies is susceptible to even greater rates of sublimation losses (Pomeroy et al., 2012). In the Okanagan basin, greater rates of sublimation were observed at higher elevations, where the winds are stronger, temperatures are colder, and there is less vapour pressure in the atmosphere (Jackson & Prowse, 2009). Forest composition, age, and disturbances such wildfire, logging, or pests alter the surface energy balance and affect both snow melt and snow accumulation patterns (Boon, 2012; Burles & Boon, 2011; Pomeroy et al., 2012; Winkler et al., 2014). Maximum SWE decreased up to 25% in pine-beetle defoliated stands in the Montane Cordillera (Winkler et al., 2015), and modelling experiments showed that snowpacks in the Montane Cordillera are highly sensitive to reductions in snow albedo following wildfires (Qian et al., 2009).

Rain-on-snow events can produce significant streamflow responses due to: warm rain advecting energy to the surface of the snowpack and infiltrating into the snowpack; the refreezing of this infiltrated water which releases latent heat; and large sensible and latent heat fluxes from the warm, humid air above the snow pack. Often the advected energy flux is small (Marks et al., 1998) and the turbulent heat fluxes to the snowcover are the dominant contributors to rain-on-snow melt events (Marks et al., 1998; Pomeroy et al., 2016). Pomeroy et al. (2016) identified that a late-spring and early-summer event in the Montane Cordillera had a greater ground heat-flux energy input than typical mid-winter events (e.g., Marks et al., 1998). In the Pacific Maritime and western Montane Cordillera, Trubilowicz and Moore (2017) found that large rain-on-snow events associated with atmospheric rivers can also include significant amounts of snow-melt runoff, contributing to flooding. A rain-on-snow event in the eastern Canadian Rockies contributed to one of the most expensive natural disasters in Canadian history at the time (June 2013 Bow River flood) (Pomeroy et al., 2016). This complex flooding event combined intense precipitation from active convective systems and enhanced runoff generation from snowmelt and rainfall runoff at higher elevations (Vionnet et al., 2020).

Continuous monitoring and detailed snow and ice energy balance studies across a range of elevations, land cover types, and mountain regions will improve our understanding of mountain snowpacks, and how they will respond in the future. Complex interactions between climate change, extreme heat events, and wildfire darkening of mountain snowpacks and glaciers also require further research.

Ground observations of snow

Direct observations of snow depth and snow mass are made by manual or automated methods (Kinar & Pomeroy, 2015). Snow depth is measured manually with simple snow rulers or automatically with acoustic or laser ranging sensors. Snow mass is measured automatically with snow pillows that record the weight of the overlying snowpack, or special sensors that measure the attenuation of cosmic (from the sky) or gamma (from the earth) radiation due to snow mass. Historically, snow mass has been measured manually and at regular intervals during accumulation and melt seasons with snow sampling tubes. Snow density is measured manually with calibrated snow sampling tubes or snow density pits, but it can also be calculated from automated measurements of snow depth and snow mass.

In mountain regions worldwide, direct observations of snow are sparse and biased towards lower elevation, lower latitude, and more accessible sites (Brown et al., 2021; DeBeer et al., 2021; Vionnet et al., 2021). Between 1 January and 31 May 2019, the total number of SWE observation sites in Canada was 1193. Of these 1193 sites, 1053 were manual snow course measurements, and 98 were automated snow pillows (Fig. 2.13). Snow measurement sites are concentrated in the southern populated regions of Canada with the majority located in Ontario and British Columbia. Manual and continuous snow monitoring sites in western Canada range in elevation between 500–2500 m, but manual observations in Ontario and Quebec are typically found below 750 m. There are no manual or automated snow measurements in the Torngats and no automated measurements in the Taiga Cordillera or Boreal Cordillera. Very few snow observations are made in the Arctic Cordillera. Citizen science efforts such as the Community Snow Observations project (Crumley et al., 2021) offer the potential for knowledge co-creation with recreational users and Indigenous communities in the mountain regions of Canada to help fill the gap in our measurement network.

Direct measurements of snowfall volumes can be made using weighing precipitation gauges, but these gauges typically undercatch snowfall amounts as wind blows snow across the top of the weighing gauge (Goodison, 1978; Rasmussen et al., 2012). Ground-penetrating radar (GPR) has been used to measure snow accumulation on Arctic glaciers (Sylvestre et al., 2013), but the technique has limited applicability for shallow snowpacks or forested areas.

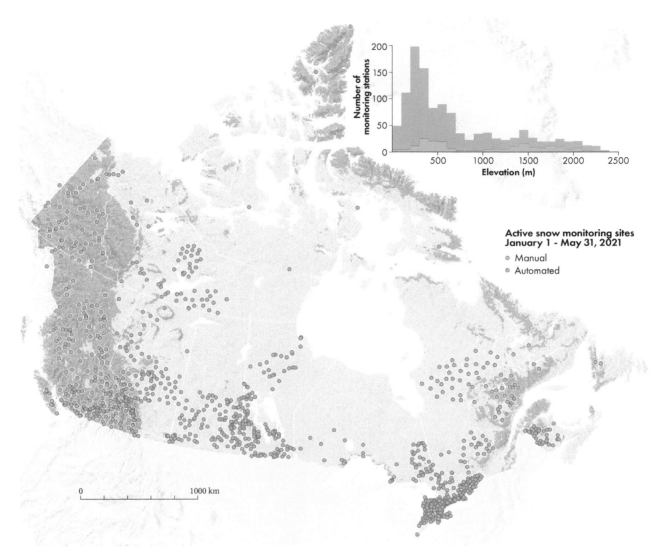

Figure 2.13: Manual (blue) and automated (orange) snow water equivalent measurement locations in Canada, that were active between 1 January–31 May 2021. Data from Vionnet et al., 2021.

Table 2.4: Number and density of snow monitoring sites in the main CMA mountain regions. The information is provided for stations that were active between 1 January–31 May 2021 and for climatological stations that have reported data for at least 30 years. The density represents the number of stations per 10,000 km².

Regions	Number (density) of active stations	Number (density) of climatological stations
Arctic Cordillera	0 (0.0)	0 (0.0)
Atlantic Maritime and Boreal Shield	23 (1.2)	8 (0.4)
Boreal Cordillera	57 (1.2)	50 (1.0)
Interior Hills	24 (1.9)	14 (1.1)
Montane Cordillera	245 (4.8)	231 (4.5)
Pacific Maritime	39 (2.5)	37 (2.4)
Eastern Subarctic	0 (0.0)	1 (0.1)
Taiga Cordillera	17 (0.5)	14 (0.4)

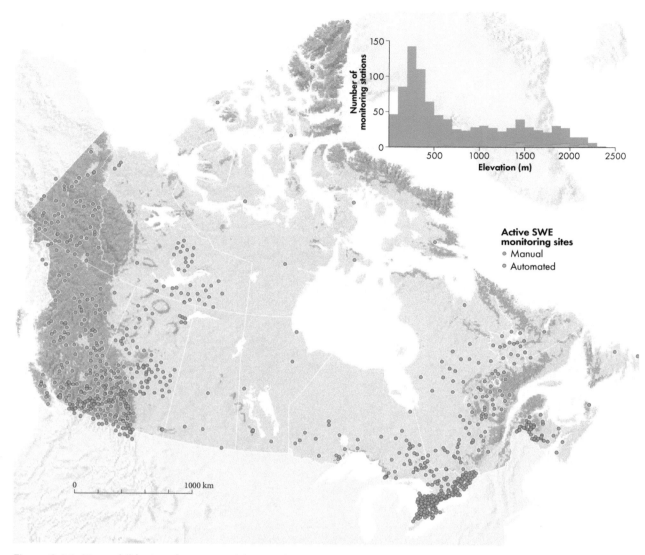

Figure 2.14: Manual (blue) and automated (orange) snow water equivalent (SWE) measurement locations that have reported data for at least 30 years. Data from Vionnet et al., 2021.

Remote sensing of snow

Snow is highly reflective (Warren, 1982), and this property allows snow-covered area to be reliably measured through satellite remote sensing (Rango, 1993; Rango, 1996). Persistent cloudiness in mountain environments (Sec. 2.3) and missing northern coverage through the polar winter present major obstacles to space-based observations of snow cover (Hall et al., 2002).

Until recently, there has been a tradeoff between satellite repeat intervals and spatial resolution: MODIS satellites have a spatial resolution of 250 m and acquire imagery daily over the entire planet, while higher spatial resolution satellites such as Landsat (30 m, Dozier, 1989) or Sentinel (20 m, Drusch et al., 2012) have repeat intervals on the order of 5–16 days. Snow monitoring from space is challenged by the substantial cloud cover in mountainous regions that often masks the snow surface (Gascoin et al., 2015). The high spatial variability of mountain snowpacks (Blöschl, 1999) also poses a challenge for coarse-resolution remote sensing platforms (Bormann et al., 2018), but recent increases in both spatial resolution and temporal frequency of lower-cost 'constellations' of satellites provides an avenue for detailed snow cover studies in mountain regions (Cannistra et al., 2021). However, there is currently no publicly available high-resolution snow cover product for mountain regions in Canada.

Remote sensing of snow depth with high precision and resolution is also possible through the use of (a) overlapping aerial photos and photogrammetry or (b) Light Detection and Ranging (LiDAR) laser scanners. Both technologies can be used from either piloted or remotely piloted aircraft, and snow depth studies from space are now feasible (Largeron et al., 2020). In these studies, a snow-free elevation map is first generated from a summer acquisition. By subtracting the snow-free elevation map from an elevation map created in winter, the snow depth can be mapped with high precision (Dozier et al., 2016). The snow density required to calculate SWE from remotely sensed snow depths can be obtained through coincident manual snow surveys (Brown et al., 2019), calculated from automated observations of snow depth and SWE, or modelled.

Snow depth surveys using LiDAR or photogrammetry have been conducted in the Montane Cordillera (Cartwright et al., 2021; Harder et al., 2020; Hopkinson et al., 2012; Mortezapour et al., 2020; Vionnet et al., 2021) and LiDAR is currently being used by water managers in some municipalities in the Pacific Maritime region (e.g., Floyd et al., 2020). Initial comparisons of LiDAR snow depths against ground observations in the Columbia Basin (Montane Cordillera) suggest that LiDAR may underestimate snow depths by 12% (Menounos et al., 2020). However, there are no published LiDAR snow depth surveys from other mountain regions, likely due to the cost of LiDAR scanners and aircraft time, and the challenges of conducting remotely piloted aircraft surveys in winter.

Satellite-based synthetic aperture radar (SAR) has been used to detect the presence of liquid water in snowpacks (Baghdadi et al., 1997), and recent improvements in spatial and temporal resolution have made it practical for mountain regions (Darychuk et al., 2022). There have been several attempts to use SAR to map SWE in mountain regions, with varying degrees of success (Bernier et al., 2002; Dozier et al., 2016). Reliable satellite-based observations of snow depth, SWE, and liquid water content across all of the mountain regions in Canada would be invaluable for a wide range of applications that include hydroelectric power generation, flood forecasting, and seasonal wildfire forecasting.

Modelling of snow

Models of snow accumulation and melt, combined with ground-based observations and remote sensing can be used to estimate snow pack development—and disappearance—across large, unmonitored regions (Mudryk et al., 2015; Vionnet et al., 2021; Wrzesien et al., 2018). These models are limited by the availability and quality of input data, and in many cases by their resolution: snow depths are incredibly varied across mountain landscapes, and high-resolution models that cover large areas can be computationally expensive. Coarse resolution models can underestimate SWE in alpine regions (Wrzesien et al., 2018).

A snowpack model that incorporates ground observations and remote sensing information to estimate peak SWE (Fig. 2.15) shows the greatest snowpack volumes in Pacific Maritime and Montane Cordillera regions, which corresponds with

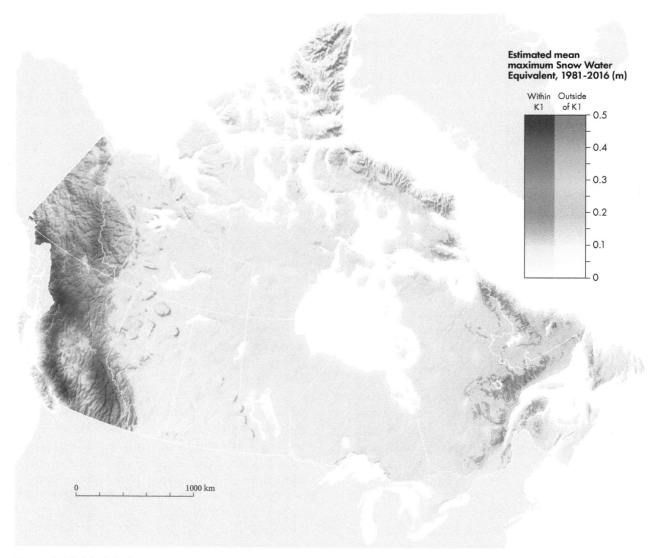

Figure 2.15: Modelled mean maximum snow water equivalent (SWE), 1981–2016. Data from Mudryk et al., 2015.

the high precipitation rates in these mountain regions (Sec. 2.3). However, this likely underestimates snow accumulation in the mountains as the ground resolution and model structure cannot capture mountain-specific processes of snow accumulation and redistribution (e.g., Sec. 2.3.6). Substantial progress in modelling snow in the complex terrain of western Canada (www.snowcast.ca) has been made with the next generation of hydrological models (Marsh et al., 2019, 2020). Combined with ground-based and satellite validation (Wayand et al., 2018), these models will advance our knowledge of current snow volumes and distribution, and how these might be expected to change in the future.

2.4.2 Mountain glaciers

In western and northern mountain regions, glaciers are a defining characteristic of mountain landscapes, and they have been meeting points for Indigenous and Western academic knowledge systems since the late 18th century (Cruikshank, 2005). For many Indigenous Peoples in these regions, glaciers figure prominently in oral traditions as sentient beings that "… listen, pay attention, and respond to human behaviour" (Cruikshank, 2001). In the case of the Champagne and Aishihik First Nations, the glaciers in Tatshenshini-Alsek Park provide a direct connection to the past when one of their ancestors,

Kwädāy Dän Ts'ìnchi, was found beside a glacier by hunters in 1999. Colloquially known as Canada's Iceman, Kwädāy Dän Ts'ìnchi succumbed to hypothermia while travelling from the coast into higher elevation regions inland (Beattie et al., 2000; Hebda et al., 2017; Holden, 1999). The location where Kwädāy Dän Ts'ìnchi was found, and the approximate time he lived (1450–1700 CE) provide important context for environmental and glacier change in the region (Cruikshank, 2005).

In the Montane Cordillera, the area covered by glaciers has reduced by over 25% from the maximum area that occurred in the Little Ice Age (LIA) in the 1850s (Luckman, 2000). There has been no systematic study of glacier area and volume declines since the LIA in any other mountain regions in Canada. The existence of glaciers, and their current distribution, depend on sufficiently cold temperatures, high quantities of snowfall, or some combination of the two (Shea et al., 2004). Wind redistribution and topographic shading can lead to the persistence of snow and ice year-round in regions that are otherwise unfavourable to the existence of glaciers (Debeer & Sharp, 2009). Glaciers across Canada come in a wide range of shapes and sizes: from endless Arctic icefields to long valley glaciers to small cirque glaciers that hide in the shadows of high mountain peaks. Decaying valley glaciers that are covered by debris, and rock glaciers related to slow downslope movements of buried frozen ground, are also characteristic in the mountain regions of Canada (Bevington & Menounos, 2022; Charbonneau & Smith, 2018; Evans, 1993; Luckman & Crockett, 1978).

Glaciers are typically measured by their area, their volume, and whether they are gaining or losing mass. Satellites offer relatively reliable methods for measuring glacier extents and areas (Bolch et al., 2009; Pfeffer et al., 2014; Sidjak, 1999) and how glacier areas have changed in the past (Chapter 5). According to the satellite-derived Randolph Glacier Inventory (RGI) there are over 33,600 glaciers in Canada, with a total area of approximately 204,000 km² (Table 2.5) (Pfeffer et al., 2014). For this assessment, we have grouped individual RGI glaciers into the CMA mountain regions and calculated their statistics. The largest concentrations of glacier ice are found in the Arctic Cordillera (11,740 glaciers with a total

area of 145,000 km²), the Pacific Maritime (10,129 glaciers with a total area of 34,559 km²) and the Boreal Cordillera (4150 glaciers with a total area of 18,385 km²). There are approximately 6244 glaciers with a total area of 5891 km² in the Montane Cordillera.

Glacier depth and volume can be measured directly with custom-designed ice radar systems or with low-frequency ground penetrating radar (Adhikari & Marshall, 2013; Pelto et al., 2020), though the logistics make it challenging to do so over large glaciers. Instead, glacier depth and volume are often modelled (Clarke et al., 2015) or approximated based on glacier area (Radić & Hock, 2010). Glacier mass and volume change can be measured on the ground (the glaciological approach) using a network of accumulation measurements at the end of winter and snow and ice ablation measurements at the end of summer (Beedle et al., 2014; Østrem & Brugman, 1993; Young & Ommanney, 1984). In recent years however, the geodetic approach, where changes in glacier surface elevations are calculated between two points in time, and then converted to a volume and mass change, have become prominent. Recent Canadian studies have derived surface elevations from topographic maps (Tennant & Menounos, 2013), air photo interpretation (Schiefer et al., 2007), LiDAR measurements (Pelto et al., 2019), and spaceborne radar and satellite imagery (Menounos et al., 2019). Most recently, elevation changes between 2000 and 2019 were calculated for all glaciers outside the Greenland and Antarctic ice sheets (Hugonnet et al., 2021), and this data has been used to compute average mass changes for glaciers in the CMA regions (Chapter 5).

Each year, a glacier will gain or lose mass (or remain the same) depending on the dominant weather conditions (Shea & Marshall, 2007). In years when glaciers lose mass, summers are typically warmer and drier, and winters have lower than average snow accumulation (or both). In years of mass gain, the opposite would be true. A wide range of glacier mass balance models have been applied in the Montane Cordillera and Pacific Maritime regions (Anslow et al., 2008; Clarke et al., 2015; Marshall et al., 2011; Munro, 1991; Shea et al., 2009), with relatively little work in the Boreal Cordillera (Wheler et al., 2014) and the Arctic Cordillera (Gardner et al., 2011; Sharp et al.,

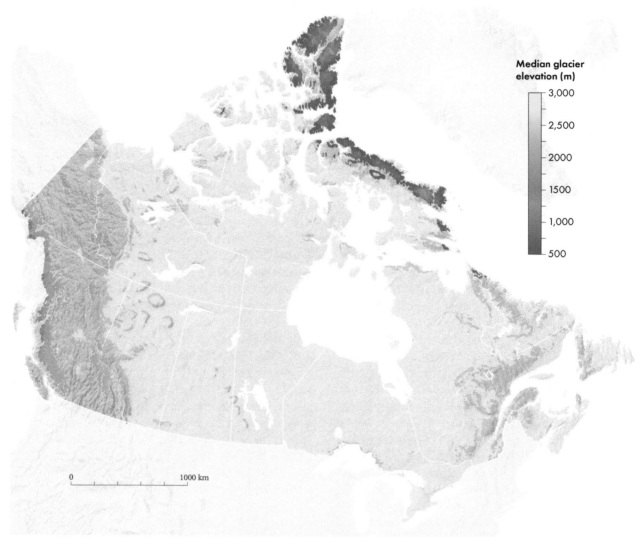

Median glacier elevation (m)

Figure 2.16: Median glacier elevations derived from the Randolph Glacier Inventory (Pfeffer et al., 2014). Each point represents an individual glacier.

Table 2.5: Glacier counts, total glacier area, and median glacier elevation for mountain regions in Canada, extracted from the Randolph Glacier inventory (Pfeffer et al., 2014) and the regional average surface elevation change rate from 2000–2019 (Hugonnet et al., 2021).

Region	Glacier count	Total glacier area (km²)	Median glacier elevation (m)	Average Rate of Glacier Mass Change (m w.e./yr)
Arctic Cordillera	11,740	145,617	908	-0.41 +/- 0.29
Atlantic Maritime	0	0	–	–
Boreal Cordillera	4150	18,385	1957	-0.45 +/- 0.37
Interior Hills Central	0	0	–	–
Interior Hills North	7	112	536	-0.48 +/- 0.36
Interior Hills West	0	0	–	–
Montane Cordillera	6244	5891	2314	-0.44 +/- 0.34
Pacific Maritime	10,129	34,559	1763	-0.38 +/- 0.34
Eastern Subarctic	103	20	813	-0.56 +/- 0.46
Taiga Cordillera	1234	656	1987	-0.36 +/- 0.38

2011). Recent modelling work is focused largely on projecting future glacier change and stream-flow response (Naz et al., 2014; .

The climatic setting of a glacier can be inferred from its median elevation (Fig. 2.16, Table 2.5). Glaciers in warmer and wetter climates, such as the Pacific Maritime, have lower median elevations than their continental counterparts in the Montane Cordillera. Glaciers at higher latitude settings (Arctic Cordillera, Boreal Cordillera, and Taiga Cordillera) exist at much lower elevations due to the colder climate, shorter melt season, and reduced shortwave radiation. The median glacier elevation is closely related to the long-term equilibrium line altitude (ELA), which varies between regions. The annual ELA shifts up and down each year in response to the glacier mass balance and is often approximated as the elevation of the transient snowline at the end of the summer melt season. Observational studies of glacier ELAs have been conducted in western Canada (Jiskoot et al., 2009; Schiefer & Menounos, 2010; Shea et al., 2013; Tennant et al., 2012), the Torngat Mountains of the Eastern Subarctic (Way et al., 2014), and the Arctic Cordillera (Miller et al., 1975, 2013).

2.4.3 *Mountain permafrost*

Nearly half of Canada is underlain by permafrost, and a significant proportion of this is in mountainous terrain (Gruber et al., 2015). Permafrost is hidden beneath a surface layer (the active layer) that undergoes seasonal freezing and thawing. As a subsurface phenomenon, permafrost cannot easily be observed remotely, and its distribution and change are less understood than for glaciers or snow. The presence and character of permafrost influence local hydrology (Sec. 2.4), ecosystems, infrastructure, as well as greenhouse gas emissions (Hock et al., 2019). Mountain permafrost thaw has been linked to large mass movement events (Deline et al., 2021; Gruber & Haeberli, 2007) in the mountains of western Canada (Chiarle et al., 2021; Cloutier et al., 2016; Friele et al., 2020; Geertsema et al., 2006) and nearby Alaska (Coe et al., 2018; Huggel et al., 2008).

The presence and character of permafrost is related to the interacting effects of climate, topography and ground conditions such as subsurface materials, vegetation, and snow depth (Davesne

et al., 2017; Gruber et al., 2015; Hasler et al., 2015; Péwé & Brown, 1973). Even though air temperature conventionally decreases with increasing elevation, wintertime inversions (Bonnaventure & Lewkowicz, 2013; O'Neill et al., 2015) and cold-air drainage and pooling can cause permafrost to exist in valley bottoms while adjacent slopes are warmer and permafrost free. These effects are especially strong in continental and polar environments and have been described in the Taiga Cordillera (Burn, 1994) and the Arctic Cordillera (Smith & Bonnaventure, 2017). In mountains, glaciers and alpine permafrost are often found in proximity. In wetter areas, glaciers would be expected to dominate the landscape, whereas in drier areas, permafrost will dominate (Haeberli & Burn, 2002). Rock glaciers are visible indicators of permafrost (Haeberli et al., 2006) and have been used to infer its presence in regions of Canada (Charbonneau & Smith, 2018), the United States (Janke, 2005), and other mountain ranges (Boeckli et al., 2012; Schmid et al., 2015).

Borehole temperature measurements are used to confirm the existence of permafrost. Only a few such studies from mountain regions in Canada exist: in the Boreal Cordillera (Bonnaventure & Lewkowicz, 2011; Lewkowicz & Ednie, 2004), the Montane Cordillera (Hall et al., 2001; Harris, 2001; Harris, 1997), and the Atlantic Maritime (Allard & Fortier, 1990; Davesne et al., 2017; Gray et al., 2017). The Global Terrestrial Network for Permafrost (GTN-P, as of 9 December 2022) identifies just over 50 borehole temperature measurement sites in these mountain regions, with most located in valleys and in Yukon (Taiga Cordillera). Only 10 of these are deeper than 10 m, and no data from these sites are available on GTN-P.

The simulation of permafrost in mountains is challenging because the steep topography causes micrometeorology, snow redistribution, ground materials, and temperatures to vary over short distances. Models have been used to estimate the distribution and likelihood of permafrost in mountains in Canada (Gruber, 2012b; Lewkowicz & Bonnaventure, 2008; Obu et al., 2019), but not to simulate permafrost depth, temperature, or future permafrost changes in detail. Climate re-analysis data (Sec. 2.2) has been used to drive global permafrost models with mountain components over multiple decades (Cao et al., 2019; Endrizzi et al., 2014; Fiddes & Gruber, 2014), and it

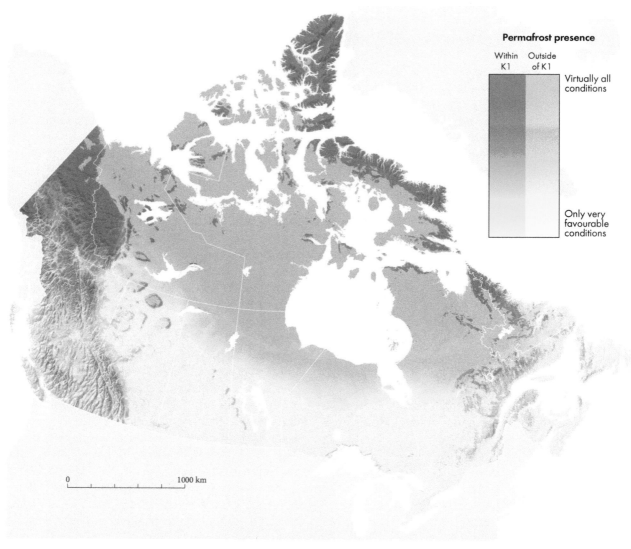

Permafrost presence

Within K1 | Outside of K1

Virtually all conditions

Only very favourable conditions

0   1000 km

Figure 2.17: Permafrost distribution in Canada. Data from Gruber, 2012.

is possible to simulate inversions/cold-air pooling (Cao et al., 2017) and to improve the computational efficiency in simulations with high spatial resolution (Fiddes et al., 2015; Fiddes & Gruber, 2012). However, soil temperatures produced directly in climate reanalyses are problematic due to the coarse spatial resolution and are subject to bias (Cao et al., 2020). Overall, even though suitable methods exist, permafrost in mountains in Canada is not yet represented well in simulation studies, and this is an active area of research.

2.4.4 Gaps and challenges

Inventories and monitoring of both snow and glaciers will provide downstream communities and water managers with critical information for understanding future changes in water supply. Improved observational networks for both snow accumulation and snow melt, combined with airborne and spaceborne observations, are needed in all mountain regions to develop and test models of wind redistribution of snow, surface energy exchange, and interactions between different mountain ecosystems and the cryosphere. High-resolution atmospheric and hydrological models of mountain snow accumulation, redistribution, and melt could be developed in conjunction with targeted field campaigns to provide the validation data that is needed to evaluate and calibrate models, towards operational forecast capabilities.

Ground-based monitoring of mountain snow-packs, glaciers, and permafrost conditions is logistically challenging, but critical. These observations should be supplemented with routine annual airborne or satellite-based observations with a systematic approach to monitoring surface changes as a function of altitude, and expanded to unmonitored regions. For glacier change, such studies should include a range of glacier sizes to evaluate the sensitivity of glaciers to future climate change. A detailed inventory of LIA glacier volumes and extents, as well as the timing of maximum extent could be used to test models of historical glacier mass balance and dynamics to improve future projections.

Five needs for permafrost research and development in mountain regions across Canada were identified in a 2014 workshop (Gruber et al., 2015). These needs include: (1) to understand processes and phenomena related to ground temperatures, ground ice, effects on water and rock-slope stability, and the interaction with vegetation in mountains; (2) to develop simulation capabilities that would support site assessment and hazard analysis; (3) long-term monitoring of permafrost and related phenomena to inform stakeholders, understand ongoing changes, and to develop and test models; (4) complementary baseline data to support permafrost research, such as high-elevation meteorological stations and snow observations; (5) communication and integration of research results in planning and decision-making. Though mountain permafrost can be highly variable, knowledge gained from polar permafrost studies can be applied as the governing physical principles are the same and many insights and tools may be transferred. Indigenous knowledges of mountain permafrost and permafrost thaw (e.g., CMA Learning Circle, Day 2) provides insights into the need for and benefits of more holistic knowledge co-creation approaches (Latulippe & Klenk, 2020; Wright et al., 2022).

2.5 Water

Mountains are the source of much of the world's freshwater resources (Viviroli et al., 2007), as they receive more precipitation than adjacent lowlands, experience less evapotranspiration, and can store water as snow and ice for short and long-term release. Mountain meltwater produces dry-season runoff and prolongs water availability downstream, which is why mountains are sometimes referred to as the world's water towers (Immerzeel et al., 2020). Many of the largest rivers in Canada have their headwaters in mountain regions and provide important water resources downstream. The South Saskatchewan River Basin exemplifies the role of mountains in water supply: 75% of the South Saskatchewan River flow as it crosses the Prairies is sourced from mountain sub-basins (Toth et al., 2009). CMA Learning Circle participant Hayden Melting Tallow of the Siksika Nation, Blackfoot Confederacy, identified the continuum between snow, ice, and streamflow on the eastern slopes of the Canadian Rockies: "And where does the water come from? It comes from the glaciers, melting it comes water. And what do the glaciers form from? It's the clouds, it rains and it comes down as rain or snow. And where do the clouds get the water from? It comes from the ocean. So there's a continuum there" (LC 2.8).

The vast majority of research on mountain water systems and generation has focused on the Montane Cordillera and Pacific Maritime Mountain regions (McDowell & Hanly, 2022). To understand how hydrological processes operate in the mountain regions of Canada, research has been centred on the measurement and simulation of processes like snowmelt, interflow, evapotranspiration, and groundwater flow in cold mountain regions with complex topography and steep slopes. Our understanding of how mountain groundwater and surface water systems are integrated remains somewhat limited and there are very few studies of mountain water systems in eastern Canada. As the climate changes, many studies are focused on measuring/simulating past and future changes to mountain hydrological systems in Canada given the potential impact on water resources.

Hayden Melting Tallow, Siksika Nation, Blackfoot Confederacy, 2022, LC 2.8

2.5.1 *Mountain flow regimes*

Seasonal changes in streamflow (the hydrological regime) are controlled by water inputs (e.g., rain and snowmelt), water losses (e.g., evaporation and plant transpiration), and storage changes in soils, lakes, wetlands, groundwater, or reservoirs (Woo & Thorne, 2003). Mountain hydrological regimes in Canada can be grouped according to the main driver of flow variation: snow-dominated (*nival*), rain-dominated (*pluvial*), glacier-dominated (*glacial*), and hybrid (Fig. 2.18).

Snow- and glacier-dominated systems have low flows during the winter when nearly all precipitation falls as snow, and experience peak flows in late spring and early summer when the snow melts, known as spring freshet (Pike, 2010; Woo & Thorne, 2003). Watersheds with significant glacier area (e.g., Pacific Maritime and Montane Cordillera) see high flows extended later into the summer (Déry et al., 2009). As glaciers store snow and ice during wet, cool years, and release more water in dry, warm years, they act as buffers against streamflow variability (Moore et al., 2020;

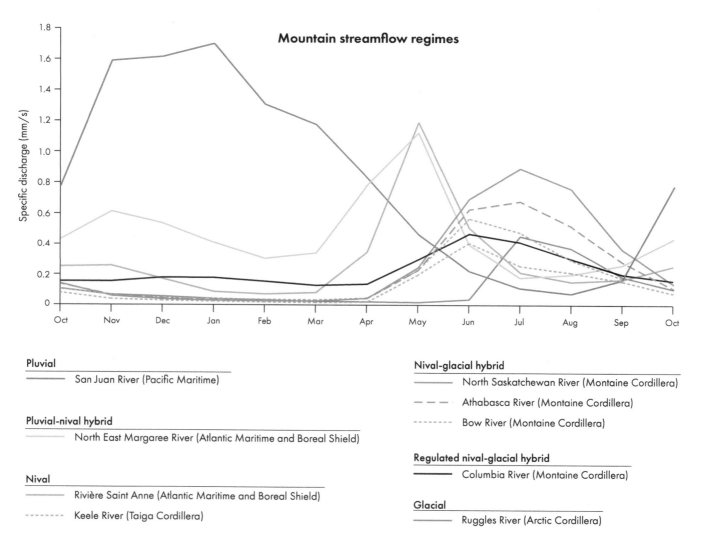

Figure 2.18: Annual hydrographs of specific monthly discharge for selected mountain rivers across Canada. Data from the Water Survey of Canada Historical Streamflow Data (https://wateroffice.ec.gc.ca/mainmenu/historical_data _index_e.html).

Van Tiel et al., 2021). River systems dominated by rain are found at lower elevations and near the coasts, including in the Pacific and Atlantic Maritime and Boreal Shield mountain regions. Here, streamflow patterns more closely follow precipitation patterns, and periodic high flows occur during the fall and winter (Déry et al., 2009; Pike, 2010). Many mountain watersheds, especially at larger scales, have hybrid hydrological regimes, and are influenced by some combination of rain, snow melt, and/or glacier melt.

Changes in watershed storage will affect the annual *hydrograph*, which illustrates seasonal changes in streamflow. The amount of water that is stored in a watershed depends on the physical characteristics of the catchment area including the thickness and texture of soils, geology, abundance, and volume of lakes (Woo & Thorne, 2003). River regulation in the form of dams and reservoirs—both human and natural—can reduce the peaks in an annual hydrograph and moderate both high and low flows on an annual basis

(Nazemi et al., 2017). Indigenous knowledge of the role of beavers in water storage and ecosystem management has led to their re-introduction to mountainous watersheds in Washington State (Jordan & Fairfax, 2022; Sherriff, 2021) for water regulation.

2.5.2 *Mountain surface hydrological processes*

The flow in mountain rivers is controlled by hydrological processes that occur throughout these complex watersheds. Our understanding of how these processes work has been developed through research in mountains and lowlands alike. However, mountains exhibit some unique hydrological behaviours owing to their cold temperatures, steep slopes, and soil and vegetation patterns. A wide range of studies in the mountain regions of Canada have sought to improve our understanding of key mountain hydrology processes (Fig. 2.19). These processes include:

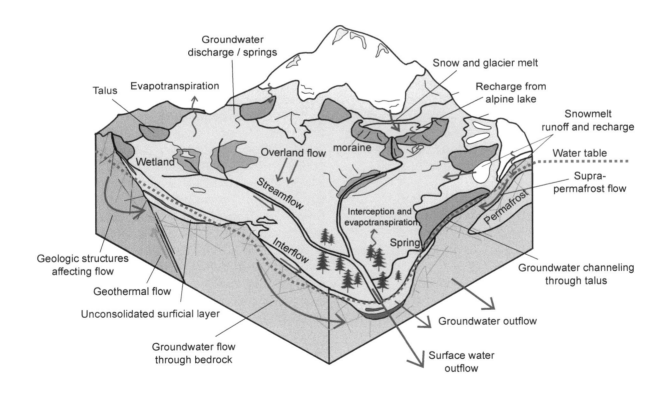

Figure 2.19: Schematic of hydrological processes with an emphasis on groundwater surface water interactions. Modified from Somers et al., 2019.

- Interception by vegetation, where precipitation does not reach the ground or is delayed (Lv & Pomeroy, 2019, 2020; Williams et al., 2019)
- Snow redistribution in the form of blowing snow and avalanches, which results in uneven snowpack and influences snowmelt timing (Aksamit & Pomeroy, 2018a, 2018b, 2020; Dery et al., 2010; Macdonald et al., 2009)
- Snowmelt, including the energy fluxes that control the rate and spatial variability of snowmelt and subsequent contribution to streamflow (Braun & Slaymaker, 1981; Debeer & Pomeroy, 2017; Dornes et al., 2008; Woo & Thorne, 2006)
- Glacier melt, including the energy fluxes that drive glacier melt, and the timing/pathways of streamflow contributions from glaciers (Henoch, 1971; Comeau et al., 2009; Jost et al., 2012; Hirose & Marshall, 2013; Bash & Marshall, 2014; Marshall, 2014; Brahney et al., 2017; Chernos et al., 2020)
- Infiltration of precipitation into the subsurface (Barrett & Slaymaker, 1989; Lilbaek & Pomeroy, 2007)
- Runoff/overland flow, where water travels along the ground surface during intense precipitation/rapid melt or over impermeable surfaces (Carey & Quinton, 2005; De Vries & Chow, 1978)
- *Interflow*, the lateral flow of water through the shallow subsurface, facilitated by larger pores in soil (Chanasyk & Verschuren, 1983; Kim et al., 2004)
- *Evapotranspiration*, the combined evaporation of water from the ground and water transpired through vegetation (Brown et al., 2014; Langs et al., 2021; Matheussen et al., 2000; Wang et al., 2015)
- Groundwater flow through the saturated zone of the subsurface (Campbell et al., 2021; Foster & Allen, 2015; Hood & Hayashi, 2015) and the hydrogeology of different mountain regions

Below we describe three research themes that have advanced our understanding of hydrological processes in the mountain watersheds in Canada: (1) the role of cold temperatures, (2) the importance of complex mountain topography,

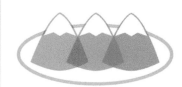

Patricia Joe, Kwanlin Dün First Nation, 2022, LC 2.9

and (3) peak flow regimes. While these themes speak to specific processes related to water in the mountains, the overall importance of mountains for downstream ecosystems and communities was described by Patricia Joe of the Kwanlin Dün First Nation, a river People whose wellbeing depends on the mountains upstream (LC 2.9).

The relatively cold temperatures experienced in many of the mountain ranges in Canada mean that cryosphere phenomena, like snowmelt, glacier melt, frozen soil, and permafrost are important controls on streamflow generation. Snowmelt makes a large, often dominant, contribution to mountain streamflow and groundwater recharge in nearly all mountain regions in Canada (Campbell & Ryan, 2021; Pomeroy et al., 2012; Woo & Thorne, 2006). In glacierized watersheds, glacier meltwater helps to sustain late summer streamflow after the snowpack has been depleted (Déry et al., 2009; Stahl & Moore, 2006). A variety of studies have quantified the contribution of glacier melt to streamflow in Alberta and British Columbia (Marshall et al., 2011; Bash & Marshall, 2014; Brahney et al., 2017; Chernos et al., 2020; Comeau et al., 2009; Henoch, 1971; Jost et al., 2012) most frequently using hydrological models. For example, approximately 10% of annual river flow comes from glacier ice and snow melt in the Illecillewaet River, in the unregulated headwaters of the Columbia River Basin, BC. In August, when snow has been depleted, glacier inputs account for 25% of streamflow despite glaciers only covering 4.9% of the watershed area (Hirose & Marshall, 2013). Permafrost and frozen soils in colder catchments act as low-permeability layers which limit the infiltration of rain or snowmelt into the soil and cause enhanced surface runoff compared to warmer catchments (Carey & Quinton, 2005; Woo et al., 2008).

Complex mountain topography causes slope, aspect, and shading to exert important controls on any hydrological process that is influenced directly or indirectly by solar radiation (Marsh et al., 2012). In the Northern Hemisphere, north-facing slopes receive less solar radiation than south-facing slopes, which allows snow and frozen soil to persist later into the spring, influences the types of vegetation, and increases the likelihood of permafrost occurrence (Woo et al., 2008). This effect is more pronounced at higher latitudes. Carey and Woo (2001) found that snow disappeared up to two months earlier on south-facing slopes in Wolf Creek, Yukon. The type and abundance of vegetation was found to differ according to slope and aspect—even more than elevation—in the Kluane Region of southwest Yukon (Dearborn & Danby, 2017). Differing vegetation on north- and south-facing slopes in turn affects evapotranspiration rates, soil moisture and interception patterns (Carey & Woo, 2001) with cascading influence on streamflow. Furthermore, aspect can be an important consideration in how mountain hydrological systems respond to perturbation like changes in forest cover (Ellis et al., 2011; Pomeroy et al., 2012).

Mountain basins in Canada present unique characteristics and risks related to floods. Several recent severe flooding events in Canada have centred on mountains, including the June 2013 Alberta and November 2021 southwestern British Columbia events that led to widespread flooding in both steep mountain creeks and large river floodplains. The 2021 heat dome event also led to extremely high flows in many mountain river systems in western Canada due to rapid snow and ice melt (White et al., 2022). *Debris flows* triggered by intense precipitation have been identified throughout the Boreal Cordillera, Pacific Maritime, and Montane Cordillera (VanDine, 1985).

While flooding is not unique to mountain regions, mountains receive more precipitation than lowlands (Sec. 2.3.2), are subject to atmospheric rivers that can drive high flows, particularly in the Pacific Maritime mountain region (Sharma & Dery, 2020), and have higher slope angles that move water rapidly into steep mountain creeks (Wohl, 2013). Rain-on-snow events can drive high river flows in mountain watersheds where rainfall partially melts the snowpack (Loukas et al., 2000; Musselman et al., 2018). In southwestern British Columbia, rain-on-snow events were found to enhance the total runoff of heavy rainfall events (> 40 mm) by 25% on average over rainfall alone

(Trubilowicz & Moore, 2017). Since snowpack and air temperatures vary widely with elevation (Sec. 2.2), the altitude-area distribution of a watershed (hypsometry) influences how quickly snowmelt happens and therefore the magnitude and timing of peak streamflow (Pomeroy et al., 2016; Shea et al., 2021). Saturated and frozen soils during snowmelt or intense rain limit infiltration into the subsurface and further enhance runoff and streamflow (Fang & Pomeroy, 2016; Mccartney et al., 2006; Pomeroy et al., 2016). Forest disturbances such as logging and wildfire affect the magnitude of peak flows in mountain river systems by reducing snowfall interception, allowing more snow accumulation, and altering the rate of snowmelt runoff (Ellis et al., 2013; Pomeroy et al., 2012; Schnorbus & Alila, 2004; Whitaker et al., 2002; Winkler et al., 2015; Zhang & Wei, 2014).

2.5.3 *Mountain lakes and reservoirs*

Several thousand alpine and subalpine lakes dot mountains across Canada. High-elevation alpine lakes of the Montane Cordillera tend to be small and nutrient-poor, with low dissolved carbon and species diversity (Hauer et al., 1997; Murphy et al., 2010). Proglacial lakes and glacier-fed lakes are often high in suspended sediment (Leonard, 1986), which gives these lakes their famous bright blue or green appearance. Snowmelt is the main water input to small high-elevation lakes which can be fully flushed in a matter of days during the snowmelt period (Hauer et al., 1997). Later in the year, groundwater can play an important role in the water balance of alpine lakes (Hood et al., 2006; Roy & Hayashi, 2008). Fish stocking in some high-elevation lakes previously barren of fish has caused nutrient levels to increase (Schindler, 2000). Larger valley bottom lakes of the Montane Cordillera are often deep (> 100 m), with retention times of 3–5 years (Hauer et al., 1997). A large survey of 560 lakes in coastal British Columbia (Pacific Maritime Mountain region) showed that evaporation accounts for a median of 9.6% of lake losses and that lake geochemistry was partly controlled by geology (Gibson et al., 2018). Bottom sediments from both small and large mountain lakes serve as indicators of past climatic and ecological variations (see Chapter 5).

Dams and reservoirs are constructed and operated in many mountain regions for hydroelectric generation, water supply and/or flood control. Both natural lakes and reservoirs can have a dampening effect on peak flows as they provide storage capacity to the watershed (Woo & Thorne, 2003). The Columbia River basin in Canada and the United States has the highest number of dams in the world, and those on the Canadian part of the river generate about half of British Columbia's hydroelectricity. Viewed through a historical lens, the construction of dams and flooding of traditional Indigenous territories without proper consultation or compensation, as in the case of the Williston Reservoir (Fig. 2.20) and Tsek'ehne lands and settlements in the Montane Cordillera, is highly problematic (Sims, 2010).

Dams alter the hydrological regime by storing water during times of high flow and releasing it during times of low flow, which results in a less variable annual hydrograph (Nazemi et al., 2017). On a daily basis, flows downstream of hydroelectric dams are affected by electricity demand (Rood et al., 1999). For example, the snow-dominated mountain headwaters of the Peace River saw lower peak flows and higher winter discharge after the construction of a major hydroelectric facility in 1968 (Peters & Prowse, 2001). Mountains in the Atlantic Maritime and Boreal Shield regions also host many hydroelectric dams, and studies here have shown that dam operation style also determines the impact on flows (Delisle, 2021; Landry et al., 2014). Dams that are operated as "run-of-the-river" dams aim to limit large changes in storage and therefore upstream and downstream flow patterns remain similar. Run-of-the-river dams also do not require large reservoirs and are now common throughout Canada (Olofsson et

Figure 2.20: The "Plug" at the north end of the Finlay Reach of the Williston Lake Reservoir where the Finlay River enters. Caused by strong south winds, the "Plug" completely blocks the river with logs created by the formation of the reservoir in 1968 (Yunker, 2022), until north winds unpack it. Photo courtesy of Daniel Sims, 2012.

THE CANADIAN MOUNTAIN ASSESSMENT

al., 2022). Dams have environmental, economic, and social impacts beyond hydrological changes of mountain rivers. This includes trapping sediment, impeding fish passage, and risks to water quality which are further discussed in Sec. 4.6 and Sec. 5.8.

2.5.4 *Mountain groundwater*

Groundwater (water stored underground in the saturated pore spaces of soil and rock) is an important source of streamflow in mountain systems, particularly during low flow conditions, making it an important resource in times of water stress (Hayashi, 2020). Furthermore, many mountain communities across Canada, like Banff and Jasper, Alberta, extract groundwater for municipal water supply (Anderson & Radic, 2020). Groundwater can be recharged by rain (pluvial), snowmelt (nival), both (hybrid) and/or from rivers, lakes, and wetlands (Allen et al., 2010). Groundwater moves slowly compared to surface water, so it continues to discharge to mountain streams and rivers when no precipitation is falling, and is known as *baseflow*. Groundwater increases the hydrological buffering capacity of mountains in a similar way to snow and ice storage, except that groundwater flows year-round (Somers & McKenzie, 2020). A baseflow index, which can be calculated as the ratio of long-term baseflow to total discharge (Beck et al., 2013, 2015; Smakhtin, 2001), gives an overview of the hydrogeologic regions in Canada and groundwater contributions to streamflow (Fig. 2.21). The baseflow index is an approximate measure of the amount of groundwater contributed to a stream or river over the long term. Western mountain regions shown in Fig. 2.21 tend to have a higher baseflow index than the adjacent prairies, but lower than the Canadian Shield.

Hydrogeologic studies in the mountain regions of Canada highlight the movement of groundwater through both shallower coarse deposits and underlying bedrock aquifers. Talus slopes, moraines, and alluvial deposits have been identified as zones of substantial groundwater storage in headwater catchments of the Montane Cordillera (Christensen et al., 2020; Hood & Hayashi, 2015; Kurylyk & Hayashi, 2017; Mcclymont et al., 2010; Roy & Hayashi, 2009; Szmigielski et al., 2018).

The coarse sediments of proglacial moraines, for example, were found to be a key store of groundwater in a small alpine headwater catchment in Yoho National Park, BC. Annual fluctuations in groundwater storage are much smaller than annual snowpack storage but are an important source of discharge during low flow periods in autumn and winter (Hood & Hayashi, 2015).

Groundwater also flows through bedrock aquifers, and geology is an important control on bedrock groundwater flow (Campbell et al., 2021; Campbell & Ryan, 2021; Smerdon et al., 2009; Spencer et al., 2021; Welch et al., 2012). Watersheds with more permeable/fractured bedrock in the Rocky and Columbia Mountains (Montane Cordillera) were found to have higher winter base flows than those with low-permeability bedrock (Paznekas & Hayashi, 2016). In the Okanagan region of British Columbia, groundwater recharge to bedrock was estimated at 27% of annual precipitation and approximately 2% of annual precipitation flowed out of the catchment through bedrock (Voeckler et al., 2014). A recent study of the Elbow River, AB, indicated that water residence time ranged from <5–10 years and that bedrock groundwater aquifers with high storage capacity and transmission rates may contribute 60% of annual streamflow (Campbell et al., 2021).

Groundwater outflow from mountain watersheds can contribute to groundwater resources downstream from the mountains themselves, in what is known as mountain block recharge. One study in the Pacific Maritime region estimated that 45% of a coastal aquifer recharge (used for municipal water supply) came from mountain block recharge (Doyle et al., 2015). Deep groundwater circulation does occur in the mountain regions of Canada, often associated with hot springs and highly deformed rock (Grasby & Lepitzki, 2002; Van Everdingen, 1991). Circulation depths of up to 3.8 km below ground surface have been estimated based on water chemistry, but deep circulation is rare relative to flow through shallow fractured bedrock (Grasby et al., 2016; Grasby & Lepitzki, 2002; Yonge & Lowe, 2017). Groundwater pollution in mountain environments (Chapter 5) can be an incredibly difficult problem to solve, given the relatively slow rates of groundwater transmission and connectivity of groundwater and surface water systems (Winter, 1995).

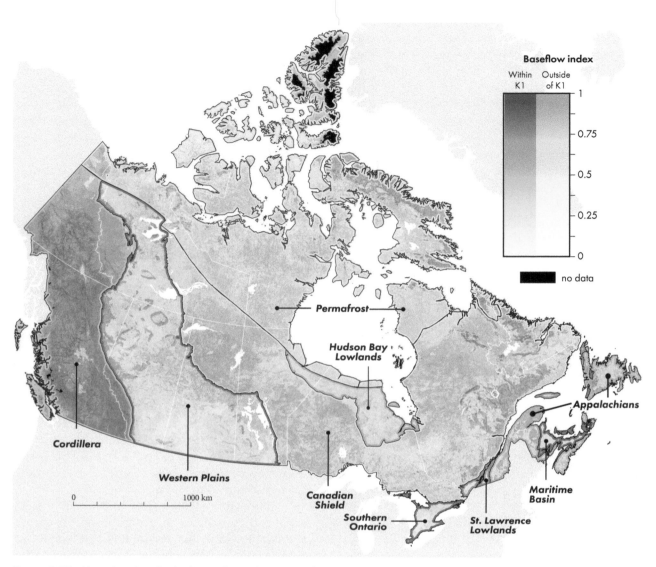

Figure 2.21: Map showing the hydrogeological regions of Canada (modified from (Sharpe et al., 2008) and a base-flow index (BI) that indicates areas of high (BI = 1) and low (BI = 0) groundwater contributions. Baseflow index (Beck et al., 2015) from the Global Streamflow Characteristics Dataset (https://www.gloh2o.org/gscd/).

While understanding of mountain groundwater in Canada has grown considerably in recent decades, observation wells are still lacking in mountains, particularly below 1–2 m depth, due to the difficulty in access and expense of drilling. The vast majority of mountain groundwater research in Canada is focused on the Montane Cordillera, and hydrogeological conditions in other Canadian mountain regions may be much different. Studies also tend to be local, with limited research on mountain block or mountain front recharge from the Montane Cordillera to the Prairies, or in any mountain regions in Canada.

2.5.5 *Mountain wetlands*

Wetlands occur in most ecoregions of the world and are characterised by a water table that is consistently near the ground surface. The connection between mountains and wetlands was noted by Pnnal Bernard Jerome of the Micmacs of Gesgapegiag on Day 2 of the CMA Learning Circle: "We gather medicines in the marshes...the marshes depend on the water that's coming from the mountains" (LC 2.10). Wetlands provide a wide variety of ecosystem services: water quality improvement, flood risk mitigation, water retention, support for biodiversity, and carbon management (Zedler & Kercher, 2005). While the cool temperatures and generally higher annual precipitation of high elevation regions favours the formation of wetlands and peatlands (Cooper et al., 2012), mountain wetlands are usually smaller in area than lower elevation wetlands and are confined by topography (Chimner et al., 2010).

Peatlands are a specific type of wetland that contribute significantly to the global carbon cycle. These ecosystems have effectively accumulated carbon through millennia and have had an overall cooling effect on the climate since the late Holocene (Frolking & Roulet, 2007; Yu et al., 2010). Peatlands cover only 3% of land on Earth (Gorham, 1991; Yu et al., 2010), and yet they accumulate more carbon than all other vegetation types in the world combined (IUCN, 2021). Small changes in the delicate balance between long-term climatic conditions, short-term weather events, ecology, hydrology, and geomorphology can cause shifts in the carbon dynamics of these ecosystems (Page & Baird, 2016) and can even reverse the sign (source or sink) of net carbon fluxes.

Despite their importance, wetlands and peatlands in the mountain regions of Canada have been largely overlooked in regional studies and inventories, possibly due to accessibility for data collection, and very little Indigenous knowledge of mountain wetlands has been reported. In the United States, the Rocky Mountains are home to several thousand square kilometres of peatland, most of which occur at elevations below 1500 m above sea level (Cooper et al., 2012; Morrison et al., 2014; Warner & Asada, 2006). Mountain regions in Canada contain an estimated 13,000 km² of peatlands, but this estimate, together with the Canadian Wetland Inventory, ignores a large portion of the Montane Cordillera, as well as the Boreal

Pnnal Bernard Jerome, Micmacs of Gesgapegiag, 2022, LC 2.10

and Taiga Cordilleras (Ducks Unlimited Canada, 2022; Tarnocai et al., 2011). A recent remote sensing approach to map wetlands performed poorly in the Boreal and Taiga Cordilleras due to a lack of training data for the model (Mahdianpari et al., 2020). Ground truthing in these areas, in direct partnership with local Indigenous communities, would help confirm the presence and characteristics of mountain wetlands. Without proper mapping and functional understanding, wetlands will be poorly represented in regional and global studies. The ecosystem services of mountain wetlands and projected changes are further discussed in Chapters 4 and 5, respectively.

2.5.6 *Mountain water quality*

Water quality can be considered from several perspectives that include temperature, sediment, and chemistry. Water pollution from human activities is addressed separately in Chapter 5. Water temperature dynamics have been studied in the Montane Cordillera and Pacific Maritime Mountain regions where cold-water fish and amphibians rely on cooler stream temperatures for survival (Friele et al., 2016; Mee et al., 2018). Solar radiation dominates the thermal regime of mountain streams and lakes (Harrington et al., 2017; Leach & Moore, 2011; Richards et al., 2012). Consequently, reduced shading from forest harvesting or wildfires can increase mountain stream temperatures (Moore et al., 2005; Wagner et al., 2014). The albedo of mountain streams is another important factor in heat absorption of mountain streams, which is influenced by turbidity and aeration (Mcmahon & Moore, 2017). Hydrological setting also controls mountain stream temperatures, as groundwater inputs cool streams during the summer (Macdonald et al., 2014). For example, springs emerging from an inactive *rock glacier* (small lenses of ice covered by seasonally frozen rock debris) in a headwater stream in Banff National Park were found to cool the peak summer stream temperature by 5°C, creating a thermal refuge for fish (Harrington et al., 2017). Evaporation from mountain streams also acts to limit daily maximum stream temperature in summer (Szeitz & Moore, 2020).

Sediment transport is a natural process in mountain streams and lakes. Landscape changes such as wildfire, forestry, hydropower development and river engineering can impact sediment loads, and increased sedimentation affects mountain stream ecosystems (Hedrick et al., 2013). Broadly speaking, the per area sediment yields of mountain regions in Canada are lower than the Prairies, given less erodible materials (Church et al., 1999). Periodic events such as flood flows, landslides and glacier changes account for large amounts of sediment transport in mountain systems (Heideman et al., 2018). For example, a study of suspended sediment concentrations and lake sediment cores in the Green Lake Basin, BC (Montane Cordillera) revealed that a summer rainstorm in 1991 transported more sediment than any other event in the previous 3000 years (Menounos et al., 2006). Wildfires in the Montane Cordillera region have been observed to increase total and peak streamflows (Mahat et al., 2016) and increased suspended sediment concentrations (Martens et al., 2019; Silins et al., 2009) and nutrient loads (Silins et al., 2014). Although hundreds of stream-gauging stations in Canada have some archival sediment data, continuous sediment data from the Water Survey of Canada is not available after the year 2000 (https://wateroffice.ec.gc.ca/search/sediment_e.html).

Turbidity refers to the clarity of a body of water and the amount of suspended sediment. Turbidity is an important water quality variable that relates to a suite of physical, chemical and biological processes. Mountain headwaters—with the exception of glacially fed streams (H. Slemmons et al., 2013)—tend to be relatively clear and turbidity increases downstream with erosion and the amalgamation of multiple tributaries (Whitfield, 1983). Light penetration into stream, river or lake waters is limited in high turbidity systems, which affects photosynthesis, primary production, and the ability of visual predators like fish to find their prey. Suspended sediment particles are active participants in chemical weathering reactions that may, in especially turbid waterways, overwhelm biological processes. Depending on which minerals are present, turbid systems can be sources (Interior Hills North; Zolkos et al., 2018) or sinks (St. Pierre et al., 2019) of greenhouse gases like carbon dioxide.

Water source and streamflow regime are key controls on the water quality in mountain rivers. A regional watershed classification across the Pacific Maritime region linked topography, streamflow regime, and water quality (quantified using dissolved organic carbon concentrations, (DOC)) to identify 12 major watershed types (Giesbrecht et al., 2022). Glacierized mountain watersheds were associated with the lowest DOC concentrations, while the small, lower elevation rain-dominated watersheds were recognized as DOC hotspots with snow-dominated and more continental (e.g., Fraser and Skeena Rivers) watersheds exhibiting intermediate DOC concentrations. Such differences in water quality likely extend to other organic matter-associated nutrients, like nitrogen and iron, and largely result from differences in climate that control soil accumulation and decomposition rates and the timing and intensity of peak flows that control contact times between waters and the surrounding soils and sediments (Bhatia et al., 2021). A glacial stream in the Montane Cordillera also had lower concentrations of other solutes, such as calcium, sodium, sulphate and chloride than a non-glacial stream due to higher specific discharge that limited water-rock contact times and solute supply from the surrounding soils (Lafreniere & Sharp, 2005). In contrast, a study of the Canadian Arctic Archipelago found that runoff from glacierized basins was an important source of iron and manganese to the ocean (Bhatia et al., 2021). Regional-level analyses of water quality and water quality characterizations similar to Giesbrecht et al. (2022) are lacking for other mountain regions in Canada.

2.5.7 *Hydrological modelling*

In tandem with advances in physical understanding of hydrological processes in mountains, a large body of research has worked to improve how these processes are modelled in mountain environments. Hydrological models can cover a wide range of complexities, from simple empirical models, to fully distributed physically based models. Hydrological models have been applied across different mountain regions in Canada to better understand streamflow dynamics (Fang et al., 2013; Pomeroy et al., 2016; Voeckler et al., 2014), forecast flood events (Quick & Pipes, 1977), and to simulate streamflow changes related to climate change (Kite, 1993; Shrestha et al., 2012; Islam et al., 2019; Whitfield et al., 2002) and/or land cover change (Ellis et al., 2013; Mahat et al., 2015; Pomeroy et al., 2012; Springer et al., 2015).

Past modelling efforts have established the value of breaking mountain basins into smaller areas (hydrological units) based on characteristics such as slope, aspect, elevation, soils, vegetation (Kite & Kouwen, 1992). For example, in a snow-dominated catchment in Wolf Creek, Yukon (Taiga Cordillera), snowmelt and streamflow simulations were improved by dividing the model domain into smaller units based on slope and aspect (Dornes et al., 2008). The incorporation of physically based energy balance equations also gives more accurate simulation of cold regions processes (Debeer & Pomeroy, 2017) and allows for stream temperature modelling which is of importance for ecosystems (Macdonald et al., 2014). The cold regions hydrological model (Pomeroy et al., 2007) has been applied to several study sites in the Montane Cordillera (Debeer & Pomeroy, 2017; Ellis et al., 2013; Fang & Pomeroy, 2020; Rasouli et al., 2019) and presents a method to use physically based hydrological formulations to improve process representation in cold regions.

Several challenges remain in simulating mountain hydrological systems in Canada. Despite the demonstrated importance of groundwater in feeding low flows, relatively few studies have coupled groundwater flow models to surface water models (Cochand et al., 2018; Foster & Allen, 2015; Voeckler et al., 2014), instead relying on a simple "bucket" parameterization for groundwater processes. We therefore do not have a clear understanding of how groundwater and surface water systems interact at different scales or the necessity of including distributed groundwater flow in mountain hydrological models. Additionally, uncertainty in meteorological model forcing leads to uncertainty in hydrological simulations (Thorne & Woo, 2006; Islam & Dery, 2017).

2.5.8 *Gaps and challenges*

While great progress has been made in characterising mountain water systems in Canada, several knowledge gaps remain. First, the vast majority of the literature reviewed in this section is focused on the Montane Cordillera and Pacific Maritime regions. A smaller but substantial body of research has focused on watersheds of the Boreal Cordillera in the Yukon. Very little research has been done on mountain hydrological systems in the Atlantic Maritime and Boreal Shield, Taiga Cordillera, and Interior Hills mountain regions. The focus on western Canada is not surprising given the size and abundance of mountainous terrain and the proximity to large population centres and downstream agricultural regions. However, this leaves a clear geographic knowledge gap where the mountain regions of eastern, central, and (to some extent) northern Canada have seen little hydrological research. Furthermore, mountains play a role in municipal water supplies, tourism, and conservation. The main water source for Quebec City (population of 300,000), for example, is a small mountain lake in the Atlantic Maritime and Boreal Shield region (Cochand et al., 2018; Ville de Québec, 2022)

Second, our understanding of mountain surface water and groundwater systems have advanced largely in parallel, and there remains a need to integrate groundwater and surface water studies. One challenge is that many mountain groundwater studies focus on small headwater catchments and are not easily scaled up to watershed or basin scales. We also lack observation wells in mountains, especially those deeper than a few metres, providing limited calibration targets for hydrological models. Hydrogeological models are also generally more computationally expensive than surface water models, and more research is needed to determine the adequacy of simplified groundwater flow modules in simulating low-flows. This may be particularly important when projecting future low-flow conditions under climate change, given the importance of groundwater in feeding rivers during dry periods.

Third, while a substantial body of work has focused on how mountain water systems are changing, there remain several knowledge gaps. Again, there is little analysis of how/if mountain streamflow is changing outside of the Montane and Boreal Cordilleras. There is very little research into how mountain groundwater systems are changing anywhere in Canada. In both surface and groundwater studies, trend analysis is limited in some cases by short observational records, which can sometimes be augmented with long-term proxy data. Expected future changes in mountain water systems and the consequences for downstream users and communities are explored in Chapter 5.

While we acknowledge the wide diversity of Indigenous viewpoints and cannot speak to all of them, water frequently emerges as a central theme in culture, health, spirituality, and sustainability of Indigenous communities within and downstream of mountain regions (Blackstock, 2001; Sanderson, 2008; Simms et al., 2016). Our assessment lacks direct examples of Indigenous knowledge with respect to mountain water systems, and it is clear that greater efforts must be made to co-generate knowledge with Indigenous and Western scientific viewpoints, with the goal of building more holistic approaches to understanding mountain water systems (Wilson et al., 2019).

2.6 Mountain Hazards

The mountain regions of Canada are subject to a host of natural hazards, including earthquakes and volcanoes, mass movements (landslides, rockfalls, debris flows, debris floods, and avalanches), floods and extreme precipitation events, wildfires and heatwaves, and extreme cold temperatures. The types and magnitude of risk from specific hazards vary significantly between mountain regions. Three components are important to understanding the regional diversity of mountain hazards and their impacts. First, mountain regions are tectonically, geomorphically, and hydrologically active due to elevation- and aspect-driven variability in relief, energy, and moisture, creating the conditions for active landscape change. Second, mountain regions are socio-culturally diverse, with settlements ranging from small, isolated communities to large population centres having distinctive social, cultural, economic, and political features that lead to differentiated experiences of mountain hazards (Chapters 3, 4, and 5). Third, mountains and adjacent lowlands are linked by flows of air, water, materials, wildlife, people, goods, and services (Sec. 2.8), and these highland-lowland linkages have increased in magnitude and importance in the past few decades.

2.6.1 *Indigenous perspectives on mountain hazards*

Recounting her experiences in the Richardson Mountains, Wanda Pascal of the Teetl'it Gwich'in Nation (a CMA Learning Circle participant) told a story of encountering a landslide path to illustrate the ways in which natural hazards affect the ways people move through the mountains, reshaping ancestral trails and the landscape of the mountains themselves (LC 2.11).

The "Frank Slide" of 29 April 1903 (Cruden & Martin, 2007) was another such event, in which ~80 Mt of rock fell from Turtle Mountain (Fig. 2.22) on the settler community of Frank, despite warnings from the Piikani Nation (Blackfoot Confederacy). Hayden Melting Tallow of the Siksika Nation (Blackfoot Confederacy) described the event at the CMA Learning Circle:

> Piikani people...have been in that area for thousands of years, and the Europeans came and found some coal in that area.... The Piikani people were warning the people there: 'Don't live (there), don't build your house (there). Build it farther, because that mountain is shaking' because they knew that. They didn't listen to them (saying): 'Oh they're just savages...' and stuff like that. They didn't believe in their way of thinking and their knowledge and their knowing. Then they all settled in that area, and one night, the whole thing came down. The mountain came down and it buried a whole town......Underneath, the town is still there, and there are some bodies down there too.....So our elders and our stories and our tales, they should be an addition to predicting what's going to happen. Those Blackfoots knew what was going to happen. That's why it's really important for us as

Wanda Pascal, Teetl'it Gwich'in, 2022, LC 2.11

Hayden Melting Tallow, Siksika Nation, Blackfoot Confederacy, 2022, LC 2.12

Figure 2.22: Turtle Mountain, showing the debris field of the 1903 Frank Slide. The debris from the Frank Slide is the white material spread over the valley floor. A new highway and railway have been built across the debris field since 1903. Photo courtesy of David J.F. Thomas and AlbertaSouthWest.com.

knowledge keepers to pass on that information and the technology that they were brought up with for thousands of years—how to use your sixth sense like the animals. They live with the animals and it's all in balance. That type of knowledge can be used today to predict a lot of things. (LC 2.12)

2.6.2 *Hazard types and frequency*

Scientific research on the risks and spatial and temporal dimensions of natural hazards in mountains in Canada is largely focused on the Montane Cordillera and Pacific Maritime Cordillera (Blown & Church, 1985; Church & Miles, 1987; Jakob et al., 2017; VanDine, 1985), and in particular on quantifying and mitigating hazards where they have disrupted or otherwise affected railway and pipeline corridors, roads, and mining activities (e.g., Gartner & Jakob, 2021; Kromer et al., 2015; Macciotta et al., 2015). There is also evidence to suggest that catastrophic landslides approximately 1000

years before present disrupted salmon runs on the Fraser River, which led to the abandonment of Tsilhqot'in settlements in the region (Hayden & Ryder, 1991).

Several high magnitude and damaging events have been studied extensively, such as the Mount Cayley volcanic eruptions (Evans & Brooks, 1991; Stasiuk et al., 2003), the Mount Meager and Mount Joffre landslides (Bovis & Jakob, 2000; Friele et al., 2020; Guthrie et al., 2012) on Lil'wat territory in southwestern British Columbia, the Frank Slide in 1903 on Nakoda/Blackfoot territory, and the Bow River watershed floods in 2013 (Whitfield & Pomeroy, 2016), which affected a number of territories in south-central Alberta. Chronic hazards along major infrastructure routes or in populated areas have also been studied. These include snow avalanches in the Rogers Pass area of Glacier National Park, BC (Bellaire et al., 2016), debris flows along the Sea to Sky Highway 99 north of Vancouver (Church & Miles, 1987; Clague et al., 2003; Hungr et al., 1999), and repeated high magnitude

Gùdia Mary Jane Johnson, Lhu'àán Mân Dań, 2022, LC 2.13

Keara Long Lightning, Nehiyaw, Samson Cree First Nation, 2022, LC 2.14

Daniel Sims, Tsay Keh Dene First Nation, 2022, LC 2.15

and damaging floods in the lower Fraser River Valley in 1898, 1948, and 2021.

Intense precipitation (Sec. 2.3.2) combined with steep mountain streams and creeks can produce rapid and damaging flood events (Jakob et al., 2016), such as the 2021 atmospheric river in southern British Columbia and the 2013 Bow River floods. Post-colonial development can also impact the severity of an event: Semá:th X̱ó:tsa (Sumas Lake), in the Fraser Valley, was both a form of natural flood protection and an incredibly valuable natural resource for the local Stó:lo people until it was drained in the 1920s for agriculture (Dick et al., 2022). In the 2021 floods, the lake was reconstituted with floodwaters that brought evacuations and large economic losses to farmers and communities that occupied the former lake bed (Olsen, 2021), but the event was also viewed by some members of the Semá:th First Nation as a sign that "the spirit of X̱ó:tsa was alive and well" (Ross et al., 2022).

Permafrost thaw poses a hazard for infrastructure and remote communities in the Taiga Cordillera and Arctic Cordillera (Arenson & Jakob, 2015; Ford et al., 2010), and has been linked to slope failures in the Boreal Cordillera (Huscroft et al., 2004). Alpine permafrost thaw specifically contributes to increased rockslides and slope failures (Clague, 2009) as the frozen water found in weathered rock and soils can act as a glue that holds unstable slopes together. In the CMA Learning Circle, Gùdia Mary Jane Johnson, a Lhu'àán Mân Dań Elder, spoke of creeks being blocked by 'big hills' and noted that "you could see where the mountainside had come down, and that's happened in all kinds of areas where I live because of the melting permafrost" (LC 2.13).

2.6.3 *Gaps and challenges*

Mountain hazards have not been systematically studied in most mountain regions of Canada, particularly through an interdisciplinary lens or through frameworks of vulnerability, adaptation, or loss and damages. There is emerging global attention to early warning systems around natural hazards and risks to vulnerable communities, and much of this is relevant to natural hazards in the populated mountain regions of Canada. Hazard assessment and warning systems require both increased surveillance capacity, near real-time monitoring systems, improved process-based models of mountain systems, and social science research to identify concerns and inform adaptation and mitigation activities that minimise vulnerability and risk. In particular, changes in hazard frequency and magnitude due to ongoing and future climate change (Beniston, 2003) need to be considered with respect to vulnerability assessments and emergency planning at community levels (Pearce, 2003).

2.7 Ecosystems and Biodiversity

This section assesses the state of knowledge with regards to the ecosystems and biodiversity of mountain environments and includes forests, alpine tundra, and alpine streams. According to Keara Lightning of the Samson Cree First Nation, the natural world is central to Indigenous societies (LC 2.14). It also offers many important gifts to people living in and beyond mountain areas, as described in Chapter 4. Across latitudinal and elevation gradients, abiotic (non-living) and biotic (living) factors that drive patterns of flora and faunal diversity are explored. Ongoing changes in mountain ecosystems—particularly, those driven by humans—were also recurring themes in the CMA Learning Circle. Daniel Sims, Tsay Keh Dene First Nation, shared that "[If] we don't share the proper respect to the animals, the animals will get their revenge...It could be them disappearing, it could also be them just getting their revenge in that sense" (LC 2.15). Changes in mountain ecosystems and biodiversity, and the drivers of change, are discussed in Chapter 5.

2.7.1 *Terrestrial mountain ecosystems*

Mountains are home to a wide range of ecosystems (Fig. 2.23). This includes snow and ice, lakes and rivers, wetlands, forests, and alpine-tundra with transition 'ecotones' between them. These ecosystems, depending on their latitude, elevation, and proximity to the ocean or large lakes, vary significantly in their structure and function. For example, the above-ground biomass and carbon storage is highest in low-elevation productive forested ecosystems (Hagedorn et al., 2019). Conversely, for below-ground carbon storage, the highest values are found in montane wetland ecosystems where nutrient poor conditions and cold temperatures result in low rates of organic matter decomposition (Xiao et al., 2019). Functional attributes also vary by ecosystem type, including differences in habitat and resource availability. Species composition, one important metric of biodiversity, is strongly associated with ecosystem type, and thus the distribution of these ecosystems informs biodiversity across mountain landscapes. Other ways

Figure 2.23: The Blakiston Valley in Waterton Lakes (Paahtómahksikimi) National Park and the Traditional Territory of Niitsitapii (Blackfoot) and K'tunaxa is home to a diverse range of ecosystems and land cover types. Scars from the Kenow wildfire can be seen at the end of the valley. Photo courtesy of Charles Hayes, Mountain Legacy Project.

of understanding biodiversity, including cultural values, species distributions, and abundance are expanded upon in Sec. 2.6.3.

Land cover

Broadly classified land cover types can be mapped over large regions from satellite data. A recently published dataset (Hermosilla et al., 2022) that builds on a decade of land cover classification work (Coops et al., 2020; Gómez et al., 2016; White et al., 2014; Wulder et al., 2018) provides annual (1985–2019) land cover classifications for regions south of the treeline, yielding the ability to track land cover changes through time (Chapter 5).

While mountains are often imagined as rocky, snow-covered peaks, the mountain regions of Canada included in this satellite-based classification are predominantly forested (Fig. 2.24). These include coniferous, broadleaf, and mixed wood forests. Other land cover classes include herbs, shrubs, and bryoids; wetland and wetland-treed; and barren, rock, snow/ice, and water. The Boreal Cordillera region (Fig. 2.25), for example, contains

snow, rock, and barren ground at its highest elevations, but is defined by extensive coniferous forests, shrubs, and wetlands. Broadleaf and mixed-wood forests dominate the Interior Hills Central region, while coniferous forests are the largest component of the Atlantic Maritime and Boreal Shield, the Interior Hills West, Montane Cordillera, and Pacific Maritime regions.

Compared to terrestrial land cover types, ice, snow, and water cover a small portion of Canadian mountain environments. However, these cryo- and hydrological features are crucial for the supply of freshwater and support diverse aquatic ecosystems. Here, we briefly outline snow and ice, and water contributions to the land cover composition of mountain landscapes in Canada. Changes in land cover types are examined in Chapter 5.

Glaciers are an important feature in most of the mountain regions in Canada. In the Arctic and high elevation regions, such as the Arctic Cordillera, Boreal Cordillera, and Pacific Maritime, glaciers cover more than 10,000 km² , respectively (Table 2.5) but make up a very small proportion of

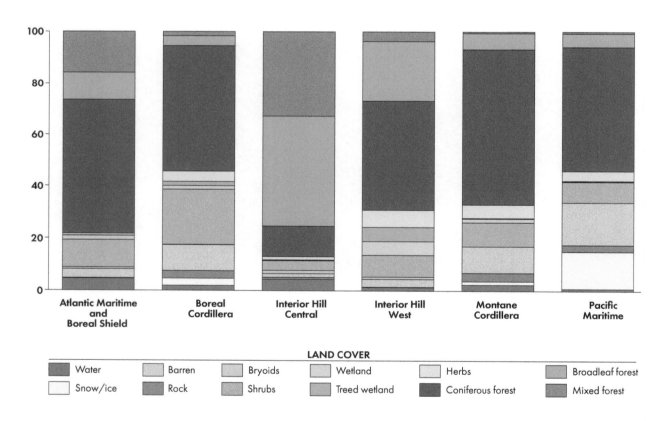

Figure 2.24: Percent total land cover for six CMA major mountain regions in 2019, following the classification of Hermosilla et al., 2022. Data from https://opendata.nfis.org/mapserver/nfis-change_eng.html.

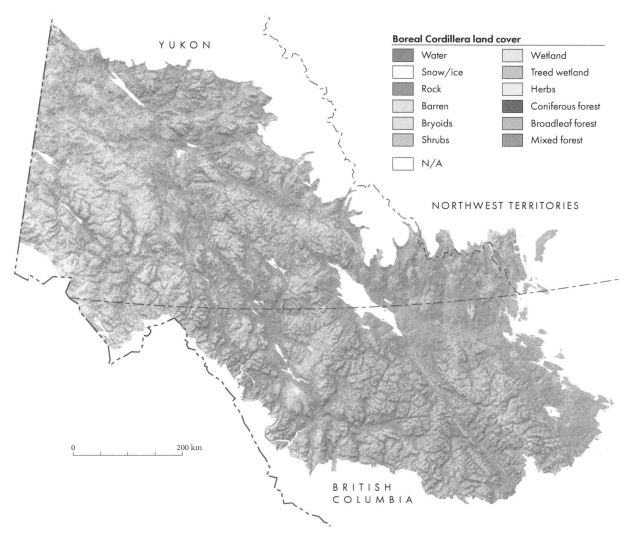

Boreal Cordillera land cover

■	Water	□	Wetland
□	Snow/ice	▦	Treed wetland
■	Rock	□	Herbs
▨	Barren	■	Coniferous forest
▨	Bryoids	▨	Broadleaf forest
▨	Shrubs	▨	Mixed forest
□	N/A		

YUKON

NORTHWEST TERRITORIES

0   200 km

BRITISH COLUMBIA

Figure 2.25: Classified land cover for the Boreal Cordillera mountain region in 2019, following the classification of Hermosilla et al., 2022.

the total land cover. Seasonal snow, on the other hand, covers a substantial portion of all mountain regions in Canada in winter, and transitions to barren and vegetated landscapes in summer. However, Arctic and alpine landscapes support many perennial or semi-permanent snowpacks that persist into summer, and adjacent ecosystems are adapted to snow cover and colder conditions.

Glaciers and snowfields supply networks of lakes, streams, and rivers which transport water, nutrients, sediment, and organisms from alpine regions to landscapes below (Sec. 2.4). Freshwater features are found in all mountain systems in Canada, though again cover a small fraction of mountain landscapes compared to terrestrial cover types. Mountain lakes and rivers are fed by a mix of glacier and snow melt, groundwater,

and precipitation, and the relative proportions of these differing inputs can alter the biodiversity and services supplied by water bodies (Milner et al., 2017) .

Ecological gradients

The most pronounced ecological gradient across mountain regions occurs with changes in elevation. The structure and function of ecosystems across elevation gradients depends on several factors, including aspect, latitude and proximity to coastal environments. For mountains in southern Canada, the low elevation ecosystems are predominantly covered by coniferous closed-canopy forests, with some exceptions in the Atlantic Maritime and Boreal Shield region, where deciduous species can comprise the majority of the forests (Fig. 2.24). For mountains that extend above the elevational limit of trees, tree density decreases with elevation, resulting in a more open canopy forest as you move up the mountain. The 'treeline' is referred to as the upper elevation limit of trees growing over 3 m in height (Körner, 2012). The upper elevational limit of trees is thought to be controlled by climate factors, whereas lower in elevation, non-climate (likely biotic factors) may be more important (Ettinger et al., 2011). Species that grow as trees at lower elevations often have stunted growth forms above the treeline, such as krummholz, which will be discussed below. The combined high-elevation open canopy forest, treeline, and trees with a growth form less than 3 m in height, are referred to as the forest-alpine-tundra ecotone. Above the forest-alpine-tundra ecotone, the alpine-tundra extends towards the mountain top, though the distribution of vegetation is often quite variable, driven by soil availability and other site characteristics. Northern mountains, such as those in the Arctic Cordillera, and parts of the Eastern Subarctic and Taiga Cordillera mountain regions, are either north of the latitudinal limit of trees or north of where closed-canopy forests occur. In these northern regions, the dominant woody vegetation is deciduous shrub species, including dwarf birch, willows, and alders.

In addition to latitudinal and elevational gradients, aspect can also play an important role in mountain ecosystems. North-facing slopes, particularly in more northern mountain regions (Arctic Cordillera, Taiga Cordillera, Boreal Cordillera) generally have more persistent late-lying snow patches which results in a shorter growing season but potentially more protection for low-lying vegetation from spring frost events. Conversely, south-facing slopes have higher levels of solar radiation, which, in addition to a longer growing season, can increase soil temperature and have a deeper active layer (Dearborn & Danby, 2017). Aspect influences the position of the treeline with, generally, south-facing slopes having higher treelines than north-facing slopes, and also strongly influences the composition of plant communities (Dearborn & Danby, 2017).

Another important factor that shapes mountain ecosystems lies below the ground. For trees, there is a significant body of scholarship that demonstrates a hidden mycorrhizal fungal network that allows different tree species (*Betula papyrifera* and *Pseudotsuga menziesii*) to communicate and share nutrients (Simard, 2021; Simard et al., 1997). This recent holistic approach has important implications for understanding how mountain ecosystems function and respond to disturbance and climate change (Reithmeier & Kernaghan, 2013), and it mirrors long-standing Indigenous perspectives on the importance of holistic monitoring and knowing of associations among ecosystem components (Jessen et al., 2022).

Mountain corridors

Whether it is in the higher elevation alpine-tundra or in the lower elevation forest ecosystems, mountains provide important corridors for people and wildlife. Indigenous Peoples, for millennia, have moved through mountain landscapes for a variety of purposes including for trading and hunting. In Nunatsiavut and Nunavik (Eastern Subarctic mountain region), Inuit travelled between communities in northern Labrador and Kangiqsualujjuaq along the Koroc River, through the Torngat Mountains for trade, social, and other cultural reasons (Cuerrier et al., 2019). Megan Dicker, Inuit, Nunatsiavut, described the ongoing importance of mountain paths in northern Labrador for helping people to travel safely and reach their homes (LC 2.16). Glaciers in the St. Elias range were described as travel corridors by Eyak, Athapaskan, and Tlingit groups in the region (Cruikshank, 2001). For many wildlife species, high- and low-elevation mountain corridors in Canada are important for habitat connectivity that is needed to satisfy a variety of requirements. These corridors can provide seasonal or daily access to climates and habitats that offer adaptive benefits for thermoregulation and increased access and variation of food. Mountain corridors are critically important large-scale landscape

Megan Dicker, Inuit, Nunatsiavut, 2022, LC 2.16

connectivity features and are the focus of ongoing conservation efforts (Hilty & Jacob, 2021).

2.7.2 Landscape management and disturbances

Mountain landscapes have been managed and stewarded by Indigenous Peoples for millennia in a diversity of ways that cannot be fully represented here. In this section we provide examples of landscape management from different mountain regions of Canada. Indigenous fire stewardship—also referred to as 'cultural' or 'good' fire—has been practised by most Indigenous Peoples in the mountains of what is now called Canada. The reasons for using fire vary tremendously but include clearing of land and enhanced food production with the added benefit of limiting catastrophic wildfires (Brookes et al., 2021) and enhancing overall biodiversity (Hoffman et al., 2021). In the Pacific Maritime mountain region, Indigenous Peoples used fire to increase resource productivity and predictability (Turner et al., 2011). In the Eastern Subarctic mountain region, fire was also used by Inuit in Labrador to manage plant communities and improve soil fertility (Oberndorfer, 2020). Across Canada, including the mountain regions, the use of fire by Indigenous Peoples was actively suppressed by colonial policies and practices, which can affect the harvest of berries, for example (Gottesfeld, 1994). While Indigenous fire stewardship continued in some regions, despite colonialism, there has been a resurgence of Indigenous communities using fire to manage landscapes (Hoffman et al., 2022).

Historically, natural wildfires have played an important role in many Canadian mountain regions, especially in the Montane Cordillera and the Boreal Cordillera (Amoroso et al., 2011; Chavardes et al., 2018; Van Wagner et al., 2006). In some of the mountain regions across Canada, there are detailed fire histories, though the majority are concentrated in the western areas of mountains in Canada (Hallett et al., 2003; Harvey et al., 2017; Power et al., 2011), with some from eastern Canada (Lauzon et al., 2007). A century of forest fire suppression policies at provincial and federal levels has transformed the overall forest structure. A high frequency of fires cleared the understory of young trees, resulting in an open forest dominated by older, larger trees with thick,

fire-retardant bark (Naficy et al., 2010). With the suppression of fire, forests became denser with greatly reduced understory vegetation as little light reaches the forest floor (Van Couwenberghe et al., 2011). For higher elevation subalpine ecosystems, fire drives increases in plant diversity, though this pattern decreases with elevation (Coop et al., 2010). Another important factor influencing fire in mountain ecosystems is that over a century of livestock grazing reduced fine fuels, such as grasses and forbs (Keane et al., 2002), and allowed the establishment of more flammable species such as cheatgrass (*Bromus tectorum*; Diamond et al., 2009). From a management perspective, the accumulation of wood fuel and more flammable species in the understory of most forests, combined with warmer, drier summers related to climate change, has resulted in an increased frequency, severity and extent of wildfires. The frequency of catastrophic fires is a significant concern for many mountain communities (Hoffman et al., 2022).

Insect herbivory is also a significant disturbance factor in mountain ecosystems across Canada. For example, periodic outbreaks of mountain pine beetle in the Montane Cordillera region have been documented over the past century (Axelson et al., 2018; Taylor & Carroll, 2003) with a large-scale outbreak, beginning in the late 1990s to 2015, killed more than half of British Columbia's merchantable pine (Dhar et al., 2016). While carbon storage in pine beetle-affected areas is recovering (Mcewen et al., 2020), the interaction between fire severity and outbreak severity influences, and complicates, the recovery trajectories (Talucci and Krawchuk 2019). In mountain regions of eastern Canada, some insect species have outbreaks in higher elevation open-canopy forests. For example, at Mont Mégantic, QC, in the Atlantic Maritime and Boreal Shield mountain region, reconstructed insect outbreaks of spruce budworm have been observed every 20–40 years over the past century (Filion et al., 1998). In the northern mountain regions, insect herbivory occurs more often at non-outbreak levels but is still an important factor for understanding ecosystem dynamics and the consequences for carbon storage (Silfver et al., 2020). In addition to fire and the insect species discussed above, mountain regions are affected by a range of other natural and human disturbance factors.

2.7.3 *Mountain biodiversity*

Many wild species make the mountains their home, either exclusively or seasonally, each with varying but important levels of ecological and cultural significance. Mountains not only support a richness of wildlife and ecosystems, but many of these are rare, rapidly declining, or at risk of disappearing in a rapidly changing world. Despite the iconic status of many mountain ecosystems and species, much of the mountain biodiversity in Canada is poorly documented and remains to be described. At times public perception is shaped more by romanticism and/or myth than reality.

While we are unable to provide an exhaustive list of the biodiversity in each mountain region, we explore terrestrial and aquatic mountain ecosystems, some of the iconic mountain species, threatened ecosystems and species, and the need to conserve mountain biodiversity.

Mountain ecosystems

Mountain ecosystems are diverse, and this diversity is often compressed into relatively small areas as ecosystems rapidly transition in response to changes in altitude. From floodplain forests and wetlands along river valleys to high alpine meadows and snow-covered peaks, the high diversity of mountain ecosystems can often be witnessed by simply looking at the mountain. While the classification and description of mountain ecosystems is incomplete in Canada, each mountain region often has distinct altitudinal zones that drive the types of the ecosystems that occur:

Valleylands in mountains often include lakes, rivers, streams, and wetlands. These range from the rocky and barren river valley of the Akshayuk Pass in Auyuittuq National Park in the Arctic to the rich bottomlands of the Creston Valley, BC. Valleylands often have lowland ecosystems not found at higher elevations such as Black Cottonwood (*Populus balsamifera ssp. trichocarpa*) riparian forests in the Rocky Mountains, and seasonal flooding can be an important natural process.

Foothills occur along the base of mountains. In the southern mountain regions of Canada, the foothills can be a wide forested transition zone between valleylands and montane zones. Foothills in the rain shadow of the mountain are often grassland or shrubland. In the Rocky Mountains, the foothill zone extends along the eastern flank of the mountains and is dominated by rolling Rough Fescue (*Festuca hallii*) grasslands.

Montane ecosystems occur on the slope of the mountain. There can be high diversity of ecosystems within this zone with warmer temperatures, more moisture, and less snow in the lower regions. Aspect and wildfire can also play an important role in shaping ecosystems in the montane zone. Montane ecosystems range from British Columbia's inland temperate rainforests dominated by Western Cedar (*Thuja plicata*) and Western Hemlock (*Tsuga heterophylla*) to the Trembling Aspen (*Populus tremuloides*) and Balsam Poplar (*Populus balsamifera*) forests of the Boreal Cordillera. In treeless mountain regions such as the Torngat Mountains in Labrador, the montane zone is dominated by alpine heath of Dwarf Huckleberry (*Vaccinium caespitosum*), Mountain Cranberry (*Vaccinium vitis-idaea*), bearberry (*Arctostaphylos uva-ursi*), and Black Crowberry (*Empetrum nigrum*).

Subalpine ecosystems mark a transition between the alpine and montane zones. In treed environments there is typically a marked difference in the character and composition of forest ecosystems. Wind, cloud and fog cover, and avalanches play an increasingly important role in ecosystem dynamics in the subalpine zone. In the Atlantic Maritimes and Boreal Shield region, subalpine communities can include stunted Black Spruce (*Picea mariana*) mixed with heath shrubs including Sheep Laurel (*Kalmia angustifolia*), Labrador Tea (*Ledum groenlandicum*), and Alpine Blueberry (*Vaccinium uliginosum*). In the Montane Cordillera, the subalpine zone is often characterized by Lodgepole Pine (*Pinus contorta*), Engelmann Spruce (*Picea engelmannii*), and Subalpine Fir (*Abies lasiocarpa*).

Alpine ecosystems occur at the top of the mountain above the treeline (in forested regions). In the Northern Appalachians, such as the Chic-Choc Mountains on the Gaspé Peninsula in eastern Québec, dominant vegetation includes low heath shrubs such as Alpine Blueberry and arctic-alpine wildflowers including Lapland Diapensia (*Diapensia lapponica*). In the Boreal and Taiga Cordillera, such as the Selwyn Mountains along the Yukon-Northwest Territories border, alpine vegetation is characterised by of crustose lichens, mountain avens (*Dryas* spp.), and heath shrubs with sedges (*Carex* spp.) and cottongrasses (*Eriophorum* spp.) associated with wetter sites.

Mountain systems in Canada contain a high diversity of other ecosystems. For example, in the northernmost mountain ranges in Canada, the Arctic Cordillera on Ellesmere and Devon Islands, the mountains are largely ice covered, with arctic-alpine plants, mosses, and lichens in the lowlands. Many mountains such as the Richardson and Ogilvie Mountains in the Yukon have large areas characterised by barren talus slopes and steep cliffs.

Threatened mountain ecosystems

Mountain ecosystems across Canada are at risk because of industrial forestry, mining, energy development, expanding urban and second home areas, and recreation. Climate change is also resulting in increased temperatures, extreme heat, drought, and extreme winds (Pörtner et al. 2022).

There are more than 120 mountain ecosystems documented from Canada that are ranked as globally imperilled or vulnerable (Table 2.6 (*NatureServe Explorer*, 2023)). This represents almost 40% of all the threatened ecosystems that are currently documented in Canada. The International Union for the Conservation of Nature (IUCN) lists an additional seven mountain ecosystems from Canada that are now on the *IUCN Red List of Ecosystems*, including Rocky Mountain Dry Lower Montane and Foothill Forest and Rocky Mountain Subalpine and High Montane Conifer Forest (Ferrer-Paris et al., 2019). Several other ecosystems including Northern Rocky Mountain Subalpine Woodland and Parkland and Rocky Mountain Aspen Forest and Woodland are assessed as Near Threatened (Comer et al., 2022).

The number of threatened mountain ecosystems is likely higher. Many ecosystems, particularly in the north of Canada, have not been described and assigned status ranks. Threatened

Table 2.6: Examples of threatened mountain ecosystems from Canada.

Common Name	Mountain Zone	NatureServe Rounded Global Rank*	Distribution in Canada
Sitka Spruce—Bigleaf Maple / Devil's-club—Salmonberry / False Lily-of-the-Valley Forest	Forest and Woodland	G1	BC
Limber Pine / Rough Fescue Woodland	Foothills	G3	AB
Black Cottonwood / Bluejoint Riparian Forest	Valleyland	G2	AB
Subalpine Fir—White Spruce—(Lodgepole Pine) / Splendid Feathermoss Forest	Montane	G3	AB, BC, YT
Subalpine Fir—Engelmann Spruce / Rusty Menziesia—Grouse Whortleberry Forest	Subalpine	G3	AB, BC
Limber Pine Scree Slope	Subalpine	G3	AB
Eastern Lichen Fell-field	Alpine	G3	QC
Eight-petal Mountain-avens—Alpine Bistort Alpine Dwarf-shrub Meadow	Alpine	G3	AB
Parry's Rush / Creeping Sibbaldia Alpine Snowbed	Alpine	G3	AB
Northern Appalachian Alpine Tundra	Alpine	G3	NB, QC

*NatureServe Ranks

Rank	Definition
G1	Critically Imperilled—At very high risk of extinction or elimination due to very restricted range, very few populations or occurrences, very steep declines, very severe threats, or other factors.
G2	Imperilled—At high risk of extinction or elimination due to restricted range, few populations or occurrences, steep declines, severe threats, or other factors.
G3	Vulnerable—At moderate risk of extinction or elimination due to a fairly restricted range, relatively few populations or occurrences, recent and widespread declines, threats, or other factors.

mountain ecosystems range from ecosystems that are restricted to small areas of Canada to ecosystems that once occurred over large areas but are threatened because of historical and continuing habitat degradation and loss.

Mountain wildlife

There are thousands of species in Canada that inhabit mountain ecosystems ranging from alpine plants such Pink Mountain-heather (*Phyllodoce empetriformis*) to iconic mammals including Mountain Caribou (*Rangifer tarandus caribou*). Some species are restricted to mountain habitats, while other species inhabit mountains seasonally or during migration. Biodiversity, in terms of the number of unique species, generally decreases with elevation and latitude. However, if land area is taken into account (i.e., there is significantly less alpine-tundra habitat compared to forest habitat, given the conical shape of mountains), then mountain biodiversity actually increases with elevation (Körner & Spehn, 2019).

Many species of mountain wildlife are restricted to specific mountain zones and ecosystems. For example, Collared Pika (*Ochotona collaris*) are only found in alpine talus slopes interspersed with small meadows in Yukon and neighbouring Alaska. However, many mammals and birds have seasonal mountain migrations or move between altitudinal zones. Dall Sheep (*Ovis dalli*) spend summers grazing in alpine meadows, move to steep cliffs to give birth, and spend winters at lower, south-facing elevations that have less snow depth. A review of mountain habitat in British Columbia found that 95 species of migratory birds used alpine, subalpine, and montane forests, 25% of which have conservation status (Boyle & Martin, 2015).

Bears are one of the most iconic mountain species, and three species of bear are found in the mountain regions of Canada. Black Bear (*Ursus americanus*) are the most common and widespread, while Polar Bear (*Ursus maritimus*) are restricted to the mountain habitats of the Arctic Cordillera and the Eastern Subarctic. Grizzly Bear (*Ursus arctos horribilis*) are perhaps the most iconic of mountain bears and have seasonal migration patterns based on food availability. Most Grizzly Bears found in southern Canada are now restricted to mountain regions that include the

Pacific Maritime, Montane Cordillera, Boreal Cordillera, and Taiga Cordillera (COSEWIC, 2012).

Both grizzly bears and caribou showcase the important role of mountains as a refuge for wildlife, as their formerly large ranges have been dramatically reduced to isolated mountain regions. Other mammals that require large home ranges and have been pushed into the refugia mountain environments include Grey Wolf (*Canis lupus*), Wolverine (*Gulo gulo*), and Cougar (*Puma concolor*). As a result, the Rocky Mountains are one of the last regions in North America to have maintained intact assemblages of large mammals (Sanjayan et al., 2012).

The refugia of intact habitats that have been retained in mountain ecosystems are also important ecological corridors. The Yellowstone to Yukon corridor that winds through the Montane and Boreal Cordillera (Chester, 2015) and the Two Countries One Forest corridor that connect the Appalachians with the Atlantic Maritime and Boreal Shield mountain region (Bateson, 2005) provide important north-south corridors for wildlife. In addition to animal movements, these mountain corridors are important to help plants and ecosystems shift to changing climate (Chester & Hilty, 2019).

Threatened mountain species

Mountain regions comprise 24% of the land area of Canada (McDowell & Guo, 2021) but support approximately one-third of species assessed as at risk[2] by the Committee on the Status of Endangered Wildlife in Canada (Canada, 2018). Many of these threatened species are primarily restricted to mountain ecosystems.

Porsild's Bryum (*Haplodontium macrocarpum*) (Threatened) is a moss that is most common in western mountain ranges, preferring sites that are constantly moist during the growing season. Mountain Holly Fern (*Polystichum scopulinum*) (Threatened) grows on rock outcrops in the mountains of the Tulameen River area in southwestern

---

2 233/705. Species at Risk Registry database. Species assessed as Extirpated, Endangered, Threatened, or Special Concern. Excluding marine mammals and marine fishes from total number. Query completed in January 2023.

CONSERVING THE ICONIC MOUNTAIN CARIBOU

While widespread, caribou are often associated with mountains (Fig. 2.26). Mountain caribou is an important subsistence and cultural species for Indigenous Peoples of the Montane Cordillera region and Indigenous-led conservation efforts are supporting recovery efforts of this iconic species (Lamb et al., 2022). In eastern Canada, the last herd of the Caribou-Atlantic-Gaspésie population can be found in the mountains of Gaspe. In the 19th century, this eastern population of caribou was distributed throughout New England and the Canadian Maritimes but is now restricted to fewer than 120 adults that inhabit mountain plateaus in the Atlantic Maritime and Boreal Shield region (COSEWIC, 2014b), and its numbers continue to decline (Webb, 2021). As Elder Pnnal Bernard Jerome, of the Micmacs of Gesgapegiag, explained: "We used to have caribou, like everybody else. But back in 1935 they started to dwindle. It's even worse now...the environment that the caribou lives on is being depleted" (LC 2.17).

Mountain caribou have adapted to the deep snow of mountains. Historically, Mountain caribou spend the winter foraging at lower elevations and move to higher elevation in the spring and summer to feed and have their calves. Recently, these migrations have been disrupted, or even abandoned, by some herds (COSEWIC, 2014a) (COSEWIC 2014b). Despite being listed under Canada's *Species at Risk Act*, Mountain caribou have continued to decline rapidly as a result of industrial forestry and energy development that has greatly reduced the amount and quality of habitat (Nagy-Reis et al., 2021; Palm et al., 2020).

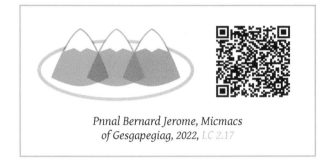

Pnnal Bernard Jerome, Micmacs of Gesgapegiag, 2022, LC 2.17

Figure 2.26: Mountain caribou (*Rangifer tarandus caribou*) in the interior temperate rainforest of central British Columbia. Photo courtesy of David Moskowitz, www.davidmoskowitz.net.

British Columbia and on Mont Albert in the Gaspé Peninsula, Quebec.

Many species use mountain regions for breeding, including several populations of Sockeye Salmon (*Oncorhynchus nerka*) in British Columbia and at-risk species such as Bicknell's Thrush (*Catharus bicknelli*) (Threatened) in Quebec, Black Swift (*Cypseloides niger*) (Endangered) in Alberta, and Westslope Cutthroat Trout (*Oncorhynchus clarkii lewisi*), Threatened in Alberta and of Special Concern in British Columbia. Many threatened birds and insects are found in mountain regions as part of a broader range such as Bank Swallow (*Riparia riparia*) (Threatened) and Wood Thrush (*Hylocichla mustelina*) (Threatened).

More than 100 species are restricted (endemic) to mountain regions in Canada. These comprise approximately 40% of all of the nationally endemic species that have been documented to date (Kraus et al., 2023). These include the Vancouver Island Marmot (*Marmota vancouverensis*) of the Pacific Maritime mountain region, Lake Louise Arnica (*Arnica louiseana*) in the Montane Cordillera, Mont Albert Goldenrod in the Atlantic Maritime region in Quebec, and the Ogilvie Mountains Collared Lemming (*Dicrostonyx nunatakensis*) that is restricted to the Ogilvie Mountains in north-central Yukon. Less than 10% of mountain endemic species in Canada have been assessed as secure in terms of their conservation status, and an unknown number are vital to Indigenous lifeways. For example, Elder Gùdia Mary Jane Johnson, Lhu'ààn Mân Ku Dań Nation, described the importance of caribou leaves, a species of sage (*Artemisia spp.*) used as medicine and traded across many Nations in the Pacific Maritime region, which is threatened by development of mining access infrastructure in her Traditional Territory (LC 2.18).

Gùdia Mary Jane Johnson, Lhu'ààn Mân Dań, 2022, LC 2.18

Mountain regions in Canada are hotspots of nationally endemic species as well. These include Haida Gwaii, Ogilvie Mountains, Kluane, Gaspésie, Vancouver Island, Okanagan Similkameen, Central Yukon Plateau, and sites in western mountain parks in Canada (Banff, Jasper, Waterton) (Kraus et al., 2023). Several of the hotspots coincide with glacial refugia that were likely ice-free during the Last Glacial Maximum (Fernald, 1925). The best known of these is the unglaciated region called Beringia, which extends from the Lena River in Russia east to the Mackenzie River in the Northwest Territories (Hultén, 1937) and is part of the Taiga Cordillera. This region formed a broad connection between Asia and North America during the last glaciation. Refugia have also been described from multiple sites in the northwestern Canadian Arctic Archipelago (Dyke, 2004), the west coast and islands of the Pacific Maritime region, and possibly in the Montane Cordillera (Clark et al., 1993; Marr et al., 2008).

2.7.4 *Aquatic ecosystems and biodiversity*

As with terrestrial ecosystems, diverse aquatic ecosystems are also found throughout mountain regions in Canada, and many aquatic ecosystems include species endemic to mountain environments. Mountain stream ecosystems are typically composed of fish and communities of bacteria, algae, and aquatic macroinvertebrates that grow attached to the rocks of streambeds. Water source (Sec. 2.4) is a critical determinant of aquatic biodiversity: glacier melt, snow melt, and groundwater sources form distinct environments with varying temperature, discharge, turbidity, and nutrient availability, all of which affect ecosystem complexity (Milner et al., 2017).

Rivers

Algae, along with bacteria, serve as the dominant primary producer in many mountain streams. These photosynthetic organisms form the base of mountain stream food webs and are critical to the success of higher trophic levels in environments with little other productivity. Glacial meltwater (Fig. 2.27) has a strong effect on the composition of algal communities, as few species tolerate frigid, rapid, and turbid glacial flows. These harsh conditions shape distinct communities compared to streams fed by more benign sources, like groundwater (Brahney et al., 2021; Roy et al., 2010). Low algal diversity is common in glacial streams as only few diatom specialists can tolerate the frequent stream disturbances (Gesierich & Rott, 2012). As the influence of glacial meltwater wanes and snowmelt and groundwater increasingly contribute to stream flow, chlorophytes (i.e., green algae), chrysophytes, and cyanobacteria colonise mountain streams, contributing to diverse and productive algal communities (Roy et al., 2010).

Evidence from alpine streams globally indicates that water source is also an important determinant of benthic macroinvertebrate community structure (Milner et al., 2017). Temperature is a particularly strong filter of macroinvertebrate communities in mountain streams. Only cold-water specialists, such as *Diamesa*, are typically found in frigid glacial meltwaters (Milner et al., 2001). In snow and groundwater fed streams, warmer temperatures support the colonisation of temperature sensitive stoneflies, mayflies, and caddisflies (Milner et al., 2001). Although these patterns are well documented in mountain regions around the world, studies focused on benthic macroinvertebrate communities in Canadian mountain streams are lacking, and a key knowledge gap persists as to the extent of macroinvertebrate diversity endemic to Canadian mountain streams. Two stonefly species endemic to alpine streams in Northern Montana and Wyoming, just south of the Montane Cordillera region in Canada, have recently been listed under the U.S. Endangered Species Act (Giersch et al., 2017; Muhlfeld et al., 2020). However, it is unknown whether the range of these endangered species extends into Canada.

Mountain streams provide habitat to diverse fishes across Canada. Although the steep, turbulent flows inherent to high-alpine streams impede fish colonisation, many species are found in lower elevation montane streams with gentle gradients and stable streambeds (Pitman et al., 2020). Again, cold temperatures are a key feature that enable healthy fish populations, particularly for species endemic to mountain waters. For example, the endangered Westslope Cutthroat trout (*Oncorhynchus clarkii lewisi*) of the Montane Cordillera

Figure 2.27: Glacier meltwater from the Saskatchewan Glacier in Banff National Park. Photo courtesy of Joseph Shea, 2021.

thrive in mountain streams with specific thermal zones bookended by frigid glacial waters and mild low-elevation waters (Heinle et al., 2021). Bull trout (*Salvelinus confluentus*), whose range extends northwards from the Montane Cordillera into the Taiga Cordillera, are similarly constrained to cold-water streams (Heinle et al., 2021; Mochnacz et al., 2021). In the Atlantic Maritime region, mountain streams provide critical spawning habitat for Atlantic salmon, as Elder Pnnal Bernard Jerome, Micmacs of Gesgapegiag, shared during the Learning Circle (LC 2.19). To the west, Pacific salmon migrate up mountain streams to reproduce each fall in the Pacific Maritime (Pitman et

Pnnal Bernard Jerome, Micmacs of Gesgapegiag, 2022, LC 2.19

al., 2020). Pacific salmon rely on mountain glaciers to provide and maintain critical spawning habitat. Streams within previously glaciated valleys also provide salmon low-gradient streams with stable streambeds necessary for reproduction (Pitman et al., 2021). Glacial meltwater inputs also cool important salmon migratory paths, keeping stream temperatures within the thermal tolerance range of salmon (Pitman & Moore, 2021).

Lakes

Mountain lakes are diverse aquatic ecosystems with distinct benthic (bottom) and pelagic (water column) communities. In addition to algal and macroinvertebrate communities living along lake bottoms, fish, phyto- and zooplankton communities are all commonly found in mountain lakes.

Phytoplankton are primary producers that live in the water columns of mountain lakes and ponds. Like algae in mountain streams, phytoplankton form the base of mountain lake food webs and are an important source of energy for grazing macroinvertebrates and zooplankton (Mcnaught et al., 1999). Planktonic algae additionally serve as crucial sentinels of climate change in mountain lakes (Moser et al., 2019; Parker et al., 2008). Phytoplankton produce photosynthetic pigments that are readily preserved in the sediment of lake bottoms (Vinebrooke & Leavitt, 1999). As lake environments change over time, fossilised pigments record phytoplankton responses, providing a proxy for how changing climates impact mountain lake ecosystems across millennia (Karst-Riddoch et al., 2005; Vinebrooke et al., 2010). For example, novel sediment core research on alpine lakes in the Montane Cordillera identified that phytoplankton community structure rapidly shifted following the last glacial maxima (Vinebrooke et al., 2010). This sensitivity to climate change makes phytoplankton a useful tool for further studying climate change in

mountain environments. Similarly, phytoplankton are useful bioindicators of more local lake processes, like fish stocking, catchment glacier loss, and nutrient deposition (Moser et al., 2019; Parker et al., 2008).

Zooplankton, a group of animal plankton, also contribute to the biodiversity of mountain lakes. These plankton feed on phytoplankton and serve as important food sources themselves for alpine fishes. This integration of top-down and bottom-up food web dynamics make zooplankton a strong target against which to measure environmental change. Many studies use zooplankton as biomonitors to measure the ecological effects of historic non-native fish stocking (Donald et al., 2001; Redmond et al., 2018) and eradication (Beaulieu et al., 2021; Parker et al., 2001; Parker & Schindler, 2006) in alpine lakes in the Montane Cordillera. Zooplankton are also used as a model group to study how climate (Loewen et al., 2019; Strecker et al., 2004), geography (Loewen et al., 2019; Strecker et al., 2004) and water quality (Swadling et al., 2000) impact mountain lake ecosystems.

Little is known about the extent of phyto- and zooplankton diversity across mountain regions in Canada. Although regional surveys in western Canada have contributed knowledge to zooplankton diversity in the Pacific Maritime (Loewen et al., 2019; Strecker et al., 2004) and Montane Cordillera regions (Anderson, 1974; Loewen et al., 2019), this group remains understudied in most other mountain regions in Canada. Phytoplankton diversity is similarly poorly studied. Given the importance of these planktonic groups in alpine lake food webs and their sensitivity to environmental change, there is an urgent need to further monitor phyto- and zooplankton throughout Canada as mountain ecosystems continue to change.

2.7.5 *Gaps and challenges*

Regarding mountain environments, knowledge co-creation has been best developed with respect to mountain biodiversity and conservation. Recent examples include grizzly bear monitoring and conservation by the Heiltsuk First Nation, mountain goat monitoring by the Kitasoo Xai'xais First Nation in the Pacific Maritime (Housty et al., 2014; Jessen et al., 2022), and mountain caribou conservation by the West Moberly First Nations and Saulteau First Nations in the Montane Cordillera (Lamb et al., 2022). Paleoecological studies are largely absent from our assessment and represent a significant gap in our understanding of mountain ecosystems. Another significant exclusion were the detailed fire histories that exist for some sites in some mountain regions, though a compilation of paleoecological and fire history data as a knowledge co-generation project would be an invaluable contribution. One of the most significant gaps when preparing this section was the lack of species-specific and mountain species data, especially in the biodiversity section. Many biodiversity studies are limited spatially and thus hard to extrapolate across entire mountain regions. These same studies are also often taxa specific. Another interesting area of inquiry that is not presented in this section is the 'sky island' hypothesis (McCormack et al., 2009) that considers high elevation areas in terms of their relative isolation to other sky islands and could be explored to answer questions around endemic species and speciation more broadly. There was little information found on sky islands in the Canadian context.

2.8 Connections between Mountains and Lowland/Coastal Environments

Mountains shape the way that air moves and water flows, and in turn, how and whether animals (including humans) and plants disperse across their slopes. Connections between mountains and lowland/coastal environments are therefore omnipresent and fundamental to the health and wellbeing of people and ecosystems across Canada. Elder Patricia Joe, Kwanlin Dün First Nation, spoke to this connection during the CMA Learning Circle gathering: "We would not be river people if it wasn't for the mountain people. It's the mountains that make the river" (LC 2.20).

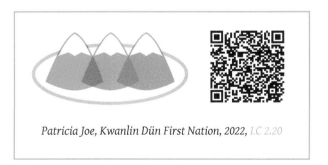

Patricia Joe, Kwanlin Dün First Nation, 2022, LC 2.20

While alpine valley communities immediately recognize the role that mountains play in their day-to-day life, the role of mountains in affecting people and places can extend hundreds to thousands of kilometres downstream, where their importance may be more often overlooked (see Chapter 4).

At a basic level, highland-lowland connections occur in two directions: 1) air masses that originate and organisms that move from marine and other lowland areas, transporting water, nutrients and contaminants to the mountains; and 2) fluxes of air, water and materials from the mountains to lakes, rivers, and coastal waters downstream. Upstream movements and fluxes are closely coupled with those downstream and in many cases operate as a cycle, such that changes in the larger earth system (e.g., oceanic changes) have implications for the mountains and the ecosystems that depend on them.

The nature and strength of the connections between mountain and lowland environments may differ substantially over time and space, driven by local combinations of weather, climate, hydrology, and biology. For example, along the Pacific coast, connectivity is simultaneously defined by annual cycles in rainfall, snow, and/or glacial melt that determine river hydrology (Moore, 1992), the atmospheric transport of pollutants to high mountain regions (Blais et al., 1998), and subsequent chemical export downstream to networks of lakes and rivers (Milner et al., 2017), as well as the migration of anadromous fish species out to their oceanic feeding grounds and their ultimate return to freshwaters to spawn. In inland mountain regions, connections are largely defined by annual cycles of snow and ice melt that control river/lake hydrology. This is also true in the Arctic, but with the additional influence of the transition between polar day and night that affects biological production and atmospheric deposition of compounds from distant locales (Law & Stohl, 2007). Along the Atlantic coast, the snowmelt season is a primary driver of river hydrology (Sec. 2.5), whereas local weather, sea ice formation, and oceanography impact fog formation and atmospheric deposition at higher elevations. In coastal mountain regions, one additional factor to consider is that the impact of alpine exports on receiving marine environments also depends on largely seasonal oceanographic processes like upwelling/downwelling and sea ice formation/melt.

Connections between mountain and lowland environments are implicit throughout this chapter (e.g., Chinook and gap/outflow winds in Sec. 2.3; river and stream flow in Sec. 2.5) and elsewhere in the assessment. The idea of connection between mountain and lowland environments is, however, rarely considered explicitly in the peer-reviewed literature. In this section, we therefore highlight major themes that allude to the impact that broader earth system processes have on mountain environments and the role of mountains in structuring downstream ecosystems. Oftentimes, these themes reflect regional interests and concerns, rather than processes common to all—or even multiple—mountain regions in Canada.

2.8.1 *Upstream movements of air, water, materials, and organisms*

Long range transport and atmospheric deposition

Orographic processes are crucial in both generating and intercepting air masses. Along with water, these air masses are also responsible for the long-range transport and subsequent deposition of nutrients, metals and organic contaminants to alpine forests (Evans & Hutchinson, 1996; Lin et al., 1997), snow (Blais et al., 1998) and ice (Beal et al., 2015). Air masses transport metals and contaminants released by both natural and anthropogenic (industrial activities, metropolitan areas) processes over long distances before these compounds are deposited at high elevations, where cold temperatures and precipitation can favour deposition. For example, the deposition of persistent organochlorine compounds to western Canadian snowpacks increases 10- to 100-fold between 770 and 3100 metres above sea level (m.a.s.l.) due to colder temperatures that prevent re-volatilization (Blais et al., 1998). In the Arctic, the annual transition from 24-h daylight to 24-h darkness can also promote the deposition of light sensitive compounds, like mercury, to snow and ice in alpine environments (Environment and Climate Change Canada, 2016). In the Atlantic Maritime and Boreal Shield regions, particular attention has been paid to the role of fog in transporting metals and hydrogen ions (responsible for acidification) to the mountains (Schemenauer, 1986; Schemenauer et al., 1995).

Anadromous fish migration

The annual migration of anadromous fish species from the ocean to upland environments to spawn represent crucial events for mountain ecosystems. This is especially true in the Pacific Maritime and Boreal Cordillera regions, where the annual return of Pacific salmon species (*Oncorhynchus* sp.) from oceanic feeding areas to their natal streams is of immense cultural and ecological significance (Chapter 4). As spawning fish die, their remains decompose, acting as an important source of marine-derived nutrients to both freshwater and terrestrial mountain headwater ecosystems (Gende et al., 2002). Salmon-derived nutrients permeate the soils, insects, trees, influencing terrestrial and freshwater food webs of the coastal temperate rainforest (Gende et al., 2002; Reimchen et al., 2003). Bears, in particular, play a critical role in facilitating the "salmon resource wave," transferring 50% or more of spawning salmon to streamside areas (Levi et al., 2020). The resource wave is associated with changes in riparian plant community composition and diversity (Hocking & Reynolds, 2011), increases in bird abundance and diversity near salmon-bearing streams (Wagner & Reynolds, 2019) and strongly influences bears' abilities to build fat stores for the winter months (Levi et al., 2020). Changing water temperatures and levels, combined with dam construction and other forms of intensive human activities (e.g., commercial fishing), are devastating Pacific salmon populations along the Pacific coastline with biological, social and cultural ramifications for the communities (human, trees, bears) that depend on them, as Brandy Mayes, Kwanlin Dün First Nation, described during the CMA Learning Circle gathering (LC 2.21).

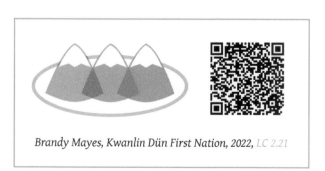

Brandy Mayes, Kwanlin Dün First Nation, 2022, LC 2.21

Figure 2.28: Sun-dried eulachon, Fishery Bay, Nisga'a Nation. Photo courtesy of Brodie Guy, www.brodieguy.com, 2018.

While the resource wave associated with Pacific salmon species is well understood, Western academic literature lacks knowledge in the role that other anadromous fish species play in the coastal mountain regions of Canada. The annual migration of eulachon (*Thaleichthys pacificus*, Fig. 2.28) to the lower reaches of mountain rivers and streams along the Pacific coast is of huge cultural significance (Moody, 2008). Early spring eulachon runs historically provided humans and other animals with a high fat food source when food was otherwise scarce (Moody, 2008). In recent decades, eulachon populations have declined significantly and become extirpated in some streams and rivers. Although the exact reasons for these declines are unknown, climate change, fisheries practices and bycatch, forestry, and pollution may all have played a role (COSEWIC, 2013; Moody, 2008).

In parts of the Columbia River basin, the migration of American shad (*Alosa sapidissima*) may also represent an increasingly important source of marine-derived nutrients as salmon populations decline (Haskell, 2018). In the Atlantic Maritime and Boreal Shield region, the role of marine-derived nutrients and contaminants in mountain systems is less well known, though recent studies from non-mountainous areas of New Brunswick and Prince Edward Island have demonstrated food web incorporation of marine-derived nutrients from both rainbow smelt (*Osmerus mordax*; Landsman et al., 2018) and Atlantic salmon (*Salmo salar*; Bryson et al., 2022). In the Arctic, the migration of arctic char (*Salvelinus alpinus*) may have a more subtle effect on freshwater food webs, and specific nutrient subsidies were undetectable in the study lakes (Swanson et al., 2010). Additional work is needed to fully resolve the complexity of these subsidies for mountain ecosystems, especially for non-Pacific salmon species and areas outside of the Pacific Maritime and Boreal Cordillera regions.

2.8.2 *Downstream movements of air, water, materials, and organisms*

Downstream impacts of glacial meltwaters
The impacts of glacial meltwaters on downstream ecosystems and communities are growing areas of study in Canadian mountain systems, given the changes that have already occurred and are predicted to occur in glacierized systems. Many western Canadian communities rely on glacier-fed systems as drinking water and irrigation sources and are highly vulnerable to the impacts of glacial retreat on water supply (Anderson & Radić, 2020; Schindler & Donahue, 2006). In some cases, glacial retreat is associated with the complete hydrological reorganisation of mountain watersheds with important implications for downstream ecosystems. The 2016 redirection of 'A'ąy Chù' (Slims River) away from Lhù'ààn Mân' (Kluane Lake) following the retreat of the Kaskawulsh Glacier is one such example. As the primary inflow to the lake, the redirection of 'A'ąy Chù' towards the Alsek River significantly lowered lake water levels (Shugar et al., 2017) with potential implications for temperature and productivity in the southern basin of the lake (McKnight et al., 2021).

As repositories for atmospherically deposited nutrients and contaminants, glacial meltwater fluxes also have potentially important implications for the health and function of downstream aquatic ecosystems. Between 2007 and 2012, a 1°C increase in temperature resulted in a ~10-fold increase in the delivery of glacial meltwater from the Northern Ellesmere Icefield (Grant Land Mountains) to Lake Hazen in the Arctic Cordillera (Lehnherr et al., 2018). Changes in the glacial headwaters were associated with changes in lake turnover, increasing fluxes of mercury (St. Pierre et al., 2019), organic contaminants to the lake (MacInnis et al., 2022; Sun et al., 2020), and enhanced carbon dioxide consumption by chemical weathering in the turbid meltwater-fed rivers (St. Pierre et al., 2019).

In the Montane Cordillera, glacial meltwaters have also been found to be important sources of persistent organic pollutants to alpine lakes (Blais et al., 2001; Lafreniere et al., 2006), impacting bio-accumulation in resident aquatic invertebrates (Blais et al., 2003). Differences in water quality between glacial and non-glacial streams represent important functional differences for downstream ecosystems, affecting whether freshwater ecosystems are sinks or sources of carbon dioxide from the atmosphere and the bacteria, phytoplankton, zooplankton, invertebrates, and fish that call these systems home. In more temperate mountain ranges, the complete loss of glaciers has the potential to alter water quality in downstream ecosystems, as well as impact the habitat suitability for key fish species (e.g., thermal refugia important for such cold-water species as Pacific salmon (Pitman et al., 2020).

Downstream impacts of permafrost thaw
Northern mountain regions like the Taiga Cordillera, and Interior Hills North and West, are increasingly being impacted by permafrost thaw. Hillslope thermokarst processes like retrogressive thaw slumps have the ability to rapidly move large amounts of materials previously immobilised in frozen soils to downstream ecosystems. For example, over 100 million tons of sediment is deposited in the Mackenzie Delta, NWT, yearly (Carson et al., 1998). These materials make their way into waterways across the region (Keskitalo et al., 2021; Kokelj et al., 2021; Zolkos & Tank, 2020) and act as significant barriers and hazards to human and animal travel across these mountain landscapes. According to Wanda Pascal of the Teetl'it Gwich'in Nation (a CMA Learning Circle participant), "[Everything is] going to be affected one way or another because we're downstream" (LC 2.22).

At least initially, thaw slumps tend to increase the concentrations of particle-bound organic

Wanda Pascal, Teetl'it Gwich'in, 2022, LC 2.22

carbon (Keskitalo et al., 2021; Shakil et al., 2020) and mercury (St. Pierre et al., 2018), which can persist through stream and river networks over tens of kilometres. The cumulative impacts of these headwater dynamics have important consequences for large river systems like the Mackenzie River, where increases in the flux of both dissolved inorganic and organic carbon since the 1970s are consistent with permafrost thaw dynamics across its watershed (Tank et al., 2016). The effects of these mountain/hillslope processes are then exported to nearshore environments in the Beaufort Sea (Kokelj et al., 2021).

Landslide effects on freshwater and coastal environments

Extreme events, like landslides, can completely alter the connections between the mountains and downstream ecosystems. In some cases, the impacts of these events may be short-lived (weeks to months), whereas other impacts may last much longer (years to decades or longer). In November 2020, ~13.3 million m³ of rock fell into proglacial Elliot Lake in the Cascade Mountains of the British Columbia coast (Geertsema et al., 2022). The resultant outburst flood and tsunami cascaded through Elliot Creek and the Southgate River, destroying key salmon spawning habitats and generating a turbidity current more than 60 km downstream in Bute Inlet. The turbidity current increased deep-water turbidity in the fjord by 200%, reduced salinity and reversed 70-year trends of warming waters and oxygen loss at depth (Geertsema et al., 2022). Although climate change may have contributed to the Elliot Creek event, landslides have been a feature of coastal mountain environments on both the Pacific and Atlantic coasts of Canada since time immemorial. In 1663, a large earthquake triggered the collapse of the Saguenay Fjord basin, widespread landslides, the damming of the Saguenay River, and a turbidity current in the fjord that lasted 28 days as the river eroded landslide debris (Syvitski & Schafer, 1996). While turbidity currents may be relatively short-lived effects of these events, they can efficiently transport and bury large quantities of organic matter from mountain landscapes, effectively augmenting the role of fjords as global carbon sinks over long periods of time (Hage et al., 2020, 2022).

Biological communities impacted by these events can take much longer to recover. Such events can destroy fish spawning and rearing habitat and act as a barrier to fish reaching their spawning grounds. In 2018, the Big Bar Landslide along the Fraser River in the British Columbia Interior effectively prevented the passage of threatened Pacific salmon stocks to their spawning grounds. Extensive interventions, in close collaboration between local First Nations and the federal and provincial governments, including transport of salmon past the slide site, have been undertaken to secure salmon recovery to the upper reaches of the Fraser River.

Impacts of mountains on oceanic circulation

The impacts of mountain systems on ocean environments, though, are much broader than turbidity currents in fjords. Along the Pacific coast, high rainfall, deep snowpacks, and glacial meltwaters from the region's mountains result in consistently large, but seasonally variable freshwater fluxes to the northeast Pacific Ocean. Large freshwater fluxes to the coastal Pacific Ocean are also responsible for the formation of eddies that transport land-derived nutrients and iron to the ocean interior (Cullen et al., 2009; Ladd et al., 2009). The cumulative impact of these freshwater fluxes is sufficient to generate a contiguous boundary current that moves clockwise around northern North America (Carmack et al., 2015). The boundary current, coined the "riverine coastal domain," is perpetuated through the Arctic by freshwater inflows like the Mackenzie River and the annual sea ice cycle (Carmack et al., 2016). Freshwater sources in the Arctic, some of which originate in the Taiga Cordillera, Interior Hills North, Arctic Cordillera, and neighbouring Greenlandic mountain regions, are detectable within the Labrador Current, which is a major driver of oceanic circulation and climate across the Atlantic (Khatiwala et al., 1999). Exports from the Atlantic Maritime and Boreal Shield regions contribute water and materials to the St. Lawrence River and some smaller rivers that discharge to the St. Lawrence Estuary. These riverine inputs affect stratification and circulation in the estuary, ultimately influencing the estuary's connections to the Gulf of St. Lawrence and the Atlantic Ocean (Khatiwala et al., 1999).

2.8.3 *Gaps and challenges*

Geographic coverage and regional interests

Mountain systems in Canada and the environments to which they are connected inevitably are incredibly diverse. The available scientific literature therefore often reflects specific regional interests, like the role of fog in the Atlantic Maritime region or the role of permafrost thaw in the mobilisation of carbon in the Interior Hills North and West regions. Arguably, the most well understood of the regions with regard to connections is the Pacific Maritime, where the cultural, ecological and economic importance of anadromous fish species has expedited our still evolving understanding of highland/lowland connections. While highland/lowland connections in most other regions (e.g., Arctic Cordillera, Taiga Cordillera, Boreal Cordillera) are less well understood—or described scientifically—than the Pacific Maritime, there was a near complete paucity of peer-reviewed literature on connectivity from the Interior Hills Central and Eastern Subarctic regions, which warrants immediate attention.

A prime opportunity for transdisciplinarity

In all respects, Western science lags behind Indigenous knowledge systems when it comes to recognizing and understanding the importance of the connections between highland and lowland areas. Elder Gùdia Mary Jane Johnson, Lhu'ààn Mân Ku Dán, describes the importance of viewing these systems as interconnected: "We can't just think of mountain environments as being singular. We need to think of it as a whole. When we're thinking of one mountain, it doesn't mean that we isolate that one mountain, we're thinking of what is happening on that whole mountain area" (LC 2.23).

Gùdia Mary Jane Johnson, Lhu'ààn Mân Ku Dán, 2022, LC 2.23

Table 2.7: Examples of topics not comprehensively assessed in this chapter

Findings from other biodiversity assessments
Indigenous knowledges of mountain geology, meteorology, hydrology, and ecology
Snow avalanches
Alpine lake and river ice
Spatial variability of mountain snowpacks
Mountain paleoenvironments
Hydrogeology of mountain regions
Advances in high-resolution modelling of mountain weather and hydrology
Mountain wildfire causes and impacts

To better understand and appreciate the reciprocal connections between mountain and low-lying and coastal environments requires holistic thinking and transdisciplinary approaches—the meaningful engagement with different scientific disciplines and ways of knowing, bridging atmospheric sciences, geomorphology, freshwater and marine sciences, and ecology with Indigenous knowledge systems.

2.9 Conclusions

Mountain regions in Canada may occupy a small area, but they fill many critical roles: as archives of the geological history that has shaped the landscape (Sec. 2.2); as weather generators and influencers (Sec. 2.3); as hosts for glaciers and snowpacks (Sec. 2.4); as sources of streamflow (Sec. 2.5); as dynamic terrain that presents numerous hazards (Sec. 2.6); as homes for complex ecosystems and endangered species (Sec. 2.7), and as corridors for migration and travel, both upstream and downstream (Sec. 2.8). Our assessment is not exhaustive (Table 2.7). Rather, it attempts to cover a broad range of subjects related to Mountain Environments, to provide examples from both Indigenous knowledges and scientific expertise, and to identify where gaps in knowledge and challenges in understanding mountain environments exist. The gaps and challenges are many.

First and foremost, we cannot speak for the Indigenous groups that have not shared or cannot share their knowledge of mountain environments. This is apparent in the imbalance between scientific literature and Indigenous viewpoints throughout the chapter. Western science has, for many years, worked to understand different aspects of mountain environments in isolation, without consideration of more holistic approaches. Co-generation of knowledge, let alone proper consultation with local Indigenous leaders and communities, is absent from most mountain research projects (Wong et al., 2020).

It is easy to say that "more research is needed," but it might be more useful to say that "better research is needed." Future research should aim to address issues and subjects that are of direct relevance to communities within and downstream of the mountains, and should work across disciplines, rather than within. For example, the impacts of climate change on glaciers and snowpacks, combined with models of hydrology and streamflow chemistry, could be used to bracket future changes in stream properties (e.g., flow, temperature, chemistry) with direct linkages to ecosystem function. Improved observational networks—for weather, streamflow, water quality, ecosystem health—are a common thread. Remote sensing, modelling, and machine-learning methods offer the possibility to fill knowledge gaps within remote mountain regions, but these rarely capture the true complexity of physical and biological systems in the mountains, and data are essential to train and test these methods. Current scientific methods also fail to capture holistic viewpoints and the animate characteristics of mountain environments, which is why co-generation of knowledge will be critical for future research examining mountain environments in Canada.

Glossary

Ablation: Processes that remove mass from a glacier, such as melt, sublimation, and calving.

Active margin: Active transition zone between continental and oceanic tectonic plates.

Albedo: The amount of light reflected by a surface; affects the amount of solar energy absorbed by the surface.

Asthenosphere: A high pressure and high temperature layer of the mantle that lies directly below the lithosphere.

Atmospheric deposition: Process whereby precipitation, aerosols, and pollutants are moved from the atmosphere to the surface.

Atmospheric river: A narrow band of warm and moist air that can extend from the tropics to sub-polar regions.

Baseflow: Portion of streamflow that is sustained between precipitation or snow/ice melt inputs to a river system.

Benthic: Ecological region associated with the bottom of a water body.

Chinook: A term commonly referring to warm dry winds blowing east out of the Rockies in southern Alberta during the winter months; they exist due to the physical environment of the area and as such are not limited to a particular time of year, although their impact is most pronounced when it is cold. Similar winds exist in other parts of the world, including the Puget Sound area of Washington State, which is the Traditional Territory of the Chinook Nation.

Craton: A stable and relatively unchanging portion the Earth's crust that forms the core of continents.

Cryosphere: Components of the Earth's climate system that are frozen: snow, glaciers, ice sheets, permafrost, sea ice.

Debris flows: Masses of water, soil, and fragmented rock that move rapidly down hillslopes and channels.

Endemic: A plant or animal species that is restricted to a certain area.

Evapotranspiration: Loss of water from a surface through evaporation and plant transpiration.

Glacial refugia: Areas that remained ice-free during the Last Glacial Maximum, and permitted the survival of flora and fauna for post-glacial succession.

Glacier mass balance: The change in mass of a glacier over a given time period; a positive balance means the glacier is gaining mass, while a negative balance means the glacier is losing mass. Often used to discuss glacier health.

Hydrograph: A graph of water flow (e.g., cubic metres per second) past a specific point over time.

Hydrological regimes: Seasonal distribution of flow over time in a river system. The main flow regimes in mountain environments include snow-dominated (*nival*), rain dominated (*pluvial*), glacier-dominated (*glacial*), and hybrid systems.

Inversion: An atmospheric condition in which temperatures increase with altitude above the surface; common in winter and in mountain valleys.

Last Glacial Maximum (LGM): Most recent period of continental scale glaciation, which peaked approximately 24,000 years before present.

Lapse rate: The rate of temperature change with increasing altitude (often expressed as a positive, though temperatures generally decrease with increasing altitude). Lapse rates are sometimes applied to other meteorological variables as well, e.g., changes in precipitation with altitude.

Lithosphere: The solid outer part of the Earth, composed of brittle continental and oceanic crust and the upper part of the mantle.

Manitou Asinîy: Also known as the Manitou Stone or Iron Creek Meteorite. This 145 kg iron meteorite was originally located near Straw Mountain, AB, and was part of a religious complex including the Viking Ribstones. It was stolen by Methodist missionary George McDougall in 1866 in an attempt to attract people to his mission at Pakan and is currently at the Royal Alberta Museum.

Orographic precipitation: Precipitation that occurs when moist air masses encounter hills and mountains and are forced to rise, causing cooling, condensation, and precipitation.

Orogen: Elongated regions of deformation that border *cratons*; product of mountain building (*orogeny*) that occurs in convergence zones along continental margins.

Passive margin: Inactive transition between continental and oceanic tectonic plates.

Pelagic: Ecological region associated with the water column.

Permafrost: Ground that is permanently frozen (less than 0°C).

Sublimation: Phase change of water from solid to gas, or gas to solid.

Turbidity: A measure of the clarity of a waterbody. High turbidity streams carry higher concentrations of suspended sediment.

Viking Ribstones: Located south of Philips, AB, in Beaver County, the "ribstones" are three quartzite bounders carved to look like stylized bison. Part of the same religious complex as Manitou Asinîy, the two largest stones remain in place and now form the centre of an Alberta Historic Place.

Wetlands: A distinct ecosystem characterised by a water table that is at or near the surface.

References

Adhikari, S., & Marshall, S. J. (2013). Influence of High-Order Mechanics on Simulation of Glacier Response to Climate Change: Insights from Haig Glacier, Canadian Rocky Mountains. *Cryosphere*, 7(5), 1527–1541. https://doi.org/10.5194/tc-7-1527-2013

Adler, C., Wester, P., Bhatt, I., Huggel, C., Insarov, G., Morecroft, M., Muccione, V., Prakash, A., Alcántara-Ayala, I., Allen, S., Bader, M., Bigler, S., Camac, J., Chakraborty, R., Sanchez, A., Cuvi, N., Drenkhan, F., Hussain, A., Maharjan, A., & Werners, S. (2022). IPCC WGII Sixth Assessment Report Cross-Chapter Paper 5: Mountains. In H.-O. Pörtner, D. C. Roberts, M. Tignor, E. Poloczanska, K. Mintenbeck, A. Alegría, M. Craig, S. Langsdorf, V. Löschke, A. Möller, A. Okem, & B. Rama (Eds.), *Climate Change 2022: Impacts, Adaptation and Vulnerability. Contribution of Working Group II to the Sixth Assessment Report of the Intergovernmental Panel on Climate Change* (pp. 2273–2318). Cambridge University Press. doi:10.1017/9781009325844.022

Aksamit, N. O., & Pomeroy, J. W. (2018a). Scale Interactions in Turbulence for Mountain Blowing Snow. *Journal of Hydrometeorology*, 19(2), 305–320. https://doi.org/10.1175/JHM-D-17-0179.1

Aksamit, N. O., & Pomeroy, J. W. (2018b). The Effect of Coherent Structures in the Atmospheric Surface Layer on Blowing-Snow Transport. *Boundary-Layer Meteorology*, 167(2), 211–233. https://doi.org/10.1007/s10546-017-0318-2

Aksamit, N. O., & Pomeroy, J. W. (2020). Warm-Air Entrainment and Advection during Alpine Blowing Snow Events. *Cryosphere*, 14(9), 2795–2807. https://doi.org/10.5194/tc-14-2795-2020

Allard, M., & Fortier, R. (1990). The Thermal Regime of a Permafrost Body at Mont du Lac des Cygnes, Quebec. *Canadian Journal of Earth Sciences*, 27(5), 694–697. https://doi.org/10.1139/e90-067

Allen, D. M., Whitfield, P. H., & Werner, A. (2010). Groundwater Level Responses in Temperate Mountainous Terrain: Regime Classification, and Linkages to Climate and Streamflow. *Hydrological Processes*, 24(23), 3392–3412. https://doi.org/10.1002/hyp.7757

Allen, G. A., Marr, K. L., McCormick, L. J., & Hebda, R. J. (2012). The impact of Pleistocene climate change on an ancient arctic–alpine plant: Multiple lineages of disparate history in Oxyria digyna. *Ecology and Evolution*, 2(3), 649–665. https://doi.org/10.1002/ece3.213

Amoroso, M. M., Daniels, L. D., Bataineh, M., & Andison, D. W. (2011). Evidence of Mixed-Severity Fires in the Foothills of the Rocky Mountains of West-Central Alberta, Canada. *Forest Ecology and Management*, 262(12), 2240–2249. https://doi.org/10.1016/j.foreco.2011.08.016

Anderson, E. A. (1968). Development and testing of snow pack energy balance equations. *Water Resources Research*, 4(1), 19–37. https://doi.org/10.1029/WR004i001p00019

Anderson, R. (1974). Crustacean Plankton Communities of 340 Lakes and Ponds in and near National Parks of Canadian Rocky Mountains. *Journal of the Fisheries Research Board of Canada*, *31*(5), 855–869. https://doi.org/10.1139/f74-105

Anderson, S., & Radić, V. (2020). Identification of local water resource vulnerability to rapid deglaciation in Alberta. *Nature Climate Change*, *10*(10), 933–938. https://doi.org/10.1038/s41558-020-0863-4

Anslow, F. S., Hostetler, S., Bidlake, W. R., & Clark, P. U. (2008). Distributed energy balance modeling of South Cascade Glacier, Washington and assessment of model uncertainty. *Journal of Geophysical Research: Earth Surface*, *113*(2). https://doi.org/10.1029/2007JF000850

Arenson, L. U., & Jakob, M. (2015). Periglacial Geohazard Risks and Ground Temperature Increases. In G. Lollino, A. Manconi, J. Clague, W. Shan, & M. Chiarle (Eds.), *Engineering Geology for Society and Territory—Volume 1* (pp. 233–237). Springer International Publishing. https://doi.org/10.1007/978-3-319-09300-0_44

Arima, E. Y., St. Claire, D., Clamhouse, L., & Edgar, J. (1991). *Between Ports Alberni and Renfrew: Notes on West Coast peoples*. University of Ottawa Press.

Aubry-Wake, C., Bertoncini, A., & Pomeroy, J. W. (2022). Fire and Ice: The Impact of Wildfire-Affected Albedo and Irradiance on Glacier Melt. *Earth's Future*, *10*(4), e2022EF002685. https://doi.org/10.1029/2022EF002685

Axelson, J. N., Hawkes, B. C., van Akker, L., & Alfaro, R. I. (2018). Stand dynamics and the mountain pine beetle—30 years of forest change in Waterton Lakes National Park, Alberta, Canada. *Canadian Journal of Forest Research*, *48*(10), 1159–1170. https://doi.org/10.1139/cjfr-2018-0161

Ayala, A., Pellicciotti, F., & Shea, J. M. (2015). Modeling 2M Air Temperatures Over Mountain Glaciers: Exploring the Influence of Katabatic Cooling and External Warming. *Journal of Geophysical Research-Atmospheres*, *120*(8), 3139–3157. https://doi.org/10.1002/2015JD023137

Baghdadi, N., Gauthier, Y., & Bernier, M. (1997). Capability of multitemporal ERS-1 SAR data for wet-snow mapping. *Remote Sensing of Environment*, *60*(2), 174–186. https://doi.org/10.1016/S0034-4257(96)00180-0

Bakri, T., Jackson, P., & Doherty, F. (2017a). Along-Channel Winds in Howe Sound: Climatological Analysis and Case Studies. *Atmosphere-Ocean*, *55*(1), 12–30. https://doi.org/10.1080/07055900.2016.1233094

Bakri, T., Jackson, P., & Doherty, F. (2017b). A synoptic climatology of strong along-channel winds on the Coast of British Columbia, Canada: A climatology of strong along-channel winds. *International Journal of Climatology*, *37*(5), 2398–2412. https://doi.org/10.1002/joc.4853

Ballou, H. (1893). The Chinook Wind. *American Meteorological Journal*, *9*(12), 541.

Barrett, G., & Slaymaker, O. (1989). Identification, Characterization, and Hydrological Implications of Water Repellency in Mountain Soils, Southern British Columbia. *Catena*, *16*(4), 477–489. https://doi.org/10.1016/0341-8162(89)90029-5

Bash, E. A., & Marshall, S. J. (2014). Estimation of Glacial Melt Contributions to the Bow River, Alberta, Canada, Using a Radiation-Temperature Melt Model. *Annals of Glaciology*, *55*(66), 138–152. https://doi.org/10.3189/2014AoG66A226

Batchelor, C. L., Margold, M., Krapp, M., Murton, D. K., Dalton, A. S., Gibbard, P. L., Stokes, C. R., Murton, J. B., & Manica, A. (2019). The configuration of Northern Hemisphere ice sheets through the Quaternary. *Nature Communications*, *10*(1), Article 1. https://doi.org/10.1038/s41467-019-11601-2

Bateson, E. M. (2005). Two Countries, One Forest—Deux Pays, Une Forêt: Launching a Landscape-Scale Conservation Collaborative in the Northern Appalachian Region of the United States and Canada. *The George Wright Forum*, *22*(1), 35–45.

Beal, S. A., Osterberg, E. C., Zdanowicz, C. M., & Fisher, D. A. (2015). Ice Core Perspective on Mercury Pollution during the Past 600 Years. *Environmental Science & Technology*, *49*(13), 7641–7647. https://doi.org/10.1021/acs.est.5b01033

Beattie, O., Apland, B., Blake, E., Cosgrove, J., Gaunt, S., Greer, S., Mackie, A., Mackie, K., Straathof, D., Thorp, V., & Troffe, P. (2000). The Kwaday Dan Ts'inchi Discovery from a Glacier in British Columbia. *Canadian Journal of Archaeology*, *24*(1–2), 129–147.

Beaulieu, J., Trépanier-Leroux, D., Fischer, J. M., Olson, M. H., Thibodeau, S., Humphries, S., Fraser, D. J., & Derry, A. M. (2021). Rotenone for exotic trout eradication: Nontarget impacts on aquatic communities in a mountain lake. *Lake and Reservoir Management*, *37*(3), 323–338. https://doi.org/10.1080/10402381.2021.1912864

Beck, H. E., Roo, A. de, & Dijk, A. I. J. M. van. (2015). Global Maps of Streamflow Characteristics Based on Observations from Several Thousand Catchments. *Journal of Hydrometeorology*, *16*(4), 1478–1501. https://doi.org/10.1175/JHM-D-14-0155.1

Beck, H. E., van Dijk, A. I. J. M., Miralles, D. G., de Jeu, R. A. M., (Sampurno) Bruijnzeel, L. A., McVicar, T. R., & Schellekens, J. (2013). Global patterns in base flow index and recession based on streamflow observations from 3394 catchments. *Water Resources Research*, *49*(12), 7843–7863. https://doi.org/10.1002/2013WR013918

Beedle, M. J., Menounos, B., & Wheate, R. (2014). An Evaluation of Mass-Balance Methods Applied to Castle Creek Glacier, British Columbia, Canada. *Journal of Glaciology*, *60*(220), 262–276. https://doi.org/10.3189/2014JoG13J091

Bellaire, S., Jamieson, B., Thumlert, S., Goodrich, J., & Statham, G. (2016). Analysis of Long-Term Weather, Snow and Avalanche Data at Glacier National Park, B.C., Canada. *Cold Regions Science and Technology*, *121*, 118–125. https://doi.org/10.1016/j.coldregions.2015.10.010

Beniston, M. (2003). Climatic change in mountain regions: A review of possible impacts. *Climatic Change, 59*(1–2), 5–31. https://doi.org/10.1023/A:1024458411589

Bernhardt, M., & Schulz, K. (2010). SnowSlide: A simple routine for calculating gravitational snow transport. *Geophysical Research Letters, 37*(11). https://doi.org/10.1029/2010GL043086

Bernier, M., Gauthier, Y., Briand, P., Coulombe-Simoneau, J., Hurley, J., & Weber, F. (2002). Radiometric correction of RADARSAT-1 images for mapping the snow water equivalent (SWE) in a mountainous environment. *IEEE International Geoscience and Remote Sensing Symposium, 1*(1), 227–230. https://doi.org/10.1109/IGARSS.2002.1024995

Bevington, A. R., & Menounos, B. (2022). Accelerated change in the glaciated environments of western Canada revealed through trend analysis of optical satellite imagery. *Remote Sensing of Environment, 270*, 112862. https://doi.org/10.1016/J.RSE.2021.112862

Bhatia, M. P., Waterman, S., Burgess, D. O., Williams, P. L., Bundy, R. M., Mellett, T., Roberts, M., & Bertrand, E. M. (2021). Glaciers and Nutrients in the Canadian Arctic Archipelago Marine System. *Global Biogeochemical Cycles, 35*(8). https://doi.org/10.1029/2021GB006976

Blackstock, M. (2001). Water: A First Nations' Spiritual and Ecological Perspective. *Journal of Ecosystems and Management, 1*(1). https://doi.org/10.22230/jem.2001v1n1a216

Blais, J. M., Schindler, D. W., Muir, D. C. G., Kimpe, L. E., Donald, D. B., & Rosenberg, B. (1998). Accumulation of Persistent Organochlorine Compounds in Mountains of Western Canada. *Nature, 395*(6702), 585–588. https://doi.org/10.1038/26944

Blais, J. M., Schindler, D. W., Muir, D. C., Sharp, M., Donald, D., Lafreniere, M., Braekevelt, E., & Strachan, W. M. (2001). Melting Glaciers: A Major Source of Persistent Organochlorines to Subalpine Bow Lake in Banff National Park, Canada. *Ambio, 30*(7), 410–415.

Blais, J., Schindler, D., Sharp, M., Braekevelt, E., Lafreniere, M., Mcdonald, K., Muir, D., & Strachan, W. (2001). Fluxes of Semivolatile Organochlorine Compounds in Bow Lake, a High-Altitude, Glacier-Fed, Subalpine Lake in the Canadian Rocky Mountains. *Limnology and Oceanography, 46*(8), 2019–2031. https://doi.org/10.4319/lo.2001.46.8.2019

Blais, J. M., Wilhelm, F., Kidd, K. A., Muir, D. C., Donald, D. B., & Schindler, D. W. (2003). Concentrations of organochlorine pesticides and polychlorinated biphenyls in amphipods (Gammarus lacustris) along an elevation gradient in mountain lakes of western Canada. *Environmental Toxicology and Chemistry: An International Journal, 22*(11), 2605–2613.

Blöschl, G. (1999). Scaling issues in snow hydrology. *Hydrological Processes, 13*(14–15), 2149–2175. https://doi.org/10.1002/(SICI)10991085(199910)13:14/15<2149::AID-HYP847>3.0.CO;2-8

Blown, I., & Church, M. (1985). Catastrophic Lake Drainage within the Homathko River Basin, British Columbia. *Canadian Geotechnical Journal, 22*(4), 551–563. https://doi.org/10.1139/t85-075

Blu Buhs, J. (2009). *Bigfoot: The Life and Times of a Legend.* University of Chicago Press.

Boeckli, L., Brenning, A., Gruber, S., & Noetzli, J. (2012). A statistical approach to modelling permafrost distribution in the European Alps or similar mountain ranges. *The Cryosphere, 6*(1), 125–140. https://doi.org/10.5194/tc-6-125-2012

Bolch, T., Menounos, B., & Wheate, R. (2009). Landsat-Based Inventory of Glaciers in Western Canada, 1985–2005. *Remote Sensing of Environment, 114*(1), 127–137. https://doi.org/10.1016/j.rse.2009.08.015

Bonnaventure, P. P., & Lewkowicz, A. G. (2011). Modelling Climate Change Effects on the Spatial Distribution of Mountain Permafrost at Three Sites in Northwest Canada. *Climatic Change, 105*(1–2), 293–312. https://doi.org/10.1007/s10584-010-9818-5

Bonnaventure, P. P., & Lewkowicz, A. G. (2013). Impacts of Mean Annual Air Temperature Change on a Regional Permafrost Probability Model for the Southern Yukon and Northern British Columbia, Canada. *Cryosphere, 7*(3), 935–946. https://doi.org/10.5194/tc-7-935-2013

Bonsal, B. R., Wheaton, E. E., Chipanshi, A. C., Lin, C., Sauchyn, D. J., & Wen, L. (2011). Drought Research in Canada: A Review. *Atmosphere-Ocean, 49*(4), 303–319. https://doi.org/10.1080/07055900.2011.555103

Boon, S. (2012). Snow Accumulation Following Forest Disturbance. *Ecohydrology, 5*(3), 279–285. https://doi.org/10.1002/eco.212

Bormann, K. J., Brown, R. D., Derksen, C., & Painter, T. H. (2018). Estimating snow-cover trends from space. *Nature Climate Change, 8*(11), Article 11. https://doi.org/10.1038/s41558-018-0318-3

Bovis, M., & Jakob, M. (2000). The July 29, 1998, Debris Flow and Landslide Dam at Capricorn Creek, Mount Meager Volcanic Complex, Southern Coast Mountains, British Columbia. *Canadian Journal of Earth Sciences, 37*(10), 1321–1334. https://doi.org/10.1139/e00-042

Boyle, W. A., & Martin, K. (2015). The Conservation Value of High Elevation Habitats to North American Migrant Birds. *Biological Conservation, 192*, 461–476. https://doi.org/10.1016/j.biocon.2015.10.008

Brahney, J., Bothwell, M. L., Capito, L., Gray, C. A., Null, S. E., Menounos, B., & Curtis, P. J. (2021). Glacier recession alters stream water quality characteristics facilitating bloom formation in the benthic diatom Didymosphenia geminata. *Science of the Total Environment, 764.* https://doi.org/10.1016/j.scitotenv.2020.142856

Brahney, J., Menounos, B., Wei, X., & Curtis, P. J. (2017). Determining Annual Cryosphere Storage Contributions to Streamflow Using Historical Hydrometric Records. *Hydrological Processes, 31*(8), 1590–1601. https://doi.org/10.1002/hyp.11128

Braje, T. J., Erlandson, J. M., Rick, T. C., Davis, L., Dillehay, T., Fedje, D. W., Froese, D., Gusick, A., Mackie, Q., McLaren, D., Pitblado, B., Raff, J., Reeder-Myers, L., & Waters, M. R. (2020). Fladmark + 40: What Have We

Learned about a Potential Pacific Coast Peopling of the Americas? *American Antiquity*, *85*(1), 1–21. https://doi.org/10.1017/aaq.2019.80

Braun, L. N., & Slaymaker, H. O. (1981). Effect of Scale on the Complexity of Snowmelt Systems (Coast Mountains British Columbia). *Nordic Hydrology*, *12*(44291), 225–234. https://doi.org/10.2166/nh.1981.0018

Brookes, W., Daniels, L. D., Copes-Gerbitz, K., Baron, J. N., & Carroll, A. L. (2021). A Disrupted Historical Fire Regime in Central British Columbia. *Frontiers in Ecology and Evolution*, *9*. https://doi.org/10.3389/fevo.2021.676961

Brown, M. G., Black, T. A., Nesic, Z., Foord, V. N., Spittlehouse, D. L., Fredeen, A. L., Bowler, R., Grant, N. J., Burton, P. J., Trofymow, J. A., Lessard, D., & Meyer, G. (2014). Evapotranspiration and Canopy Characteristics of Two Lodgepole Pine Stands Following Mountain Pine Beetle Attack. *Hydrological Processes*, *28*(8), 3326–3340. https://doi.org/10.1002/hyp.9870

Brown, R. D., Fang, B., & Mudryk, L. (2019). Update of Canadian Historical Snow Survey Data and Analysis of Snow Water Equivalent Trends, 1967–2016. *Atmosphere-Ocean*, *57*(2), 149–156. https://doi.org/10.1080/07055900.2019.1598843

Brown, R. D., Smith, C., Derksen, C., & Mudryk, L. (2021). Canadian In Situ Snow Cover Trends for 1955–2017 Including an Assessment of the Impact of Automation. *Atmosphere-Ocean*, *59*(2), 77–92. https://doi.org/10.1080/07055900.2021.1911781

Bryson, G. E., Kidd, K. A., & Samways, K. M. (2022). Food web incorporation of marine-derived nutrients after the reintroduction of endangered inner Bay of Fundy Atlantic salmon (Salmo salar). *Canadian Journal of Fisheries and Aquatic Sciences*, *79*(6), 875–882. https://doi.org/10.1139/cjfas-2020-0326

Burles, K., & Boon, S. (2011). Snowmelt energy balance in a burned forest plot, Crowsnest Pass, Alberta, Canada. *Hydrological Processes*, *25*(19), 3012–3029. https://doi.org/10.1002/hyp.8067

Burn, C. R. (1994). Permafrost, Tectonics, and Past and Future Regional Climate Change, Yukon and Adjacent Northwest Territories. *Canadian Journal of Earth Sciences*, *31*(1), 182–191. https://doi.org/10.1139/e94-015

CAINE, N. (1976). A uniform measure of subaerial erosion. *GSA Bulletin*, *87*(1), 137–140. https://doi.org/10.1130/0016-7606(1976)87<137:AUMOSE>2.0.CO;2

Callaghan, T. V., Johansson, M., Brown, R. D., Groisman, P. Ya., Labba, N., Radionov, V., Bradley, R. S., Blangy, S., Bulygina, O. N., Christensen, T. R., Colman, J. E., Essery, R. L. H., Forbes, B. C., Forchhammer, M. C., Golubev, V. N., Honrath, R. E., Juday, G. P., Meshcherskaya, A. V., Phoenix, G. K., … Wood, E. F. (2011). Multiple Effects of Changes in Arctic Snow Cover. *AMBIO*, *40*(1), 32–45. https://doi.org/10.1007/s13280-011-0213-x

Campbell, É.M.S., Lagasca, P. A., Stanic, S., Zhang, Y., & Ryan, M. C. (2021). Insight into watershed hydrodynamics using silica, sulfate, and tritium: Source aquifers and water age in a mountain river. *Applied Geochemistry*, *132*(105070) https://doi.org/10.1016/j.apgeochem.2021.105070

Campbell, É.M.S., & Ryan, M. C. (2021). Nested recharge systems in mountain block hydrology: High-elevation snowpack generates low-elevation overwinter baseflow in a rocky mountain river. *Water (Switzerland)*, *13*(16), 2249. https://doi.org/10.3390/w13162249

Canada, E. and C. C. (2018, January 8). *Species at risk public registry* [Navigation page]. https://www.canada.ca/en/environment-climate-change/services/species-risk-public-registry.html

Cannistra, A. F., Shean, D. E., & Cristea, N. C. (2021). High-resolution CubeSat imagery and machine learning for detailed snow-covered area. *Remote Sensing of Environment*, *258*, 112399. https://doi.org/10.1016/j.rse.2021.112399

Cao, B., Gruber, S., & Zhang, T. (2017). REDCAPP (v1.0): Parameterizing valley inversions in air temperature data downscaled from reanalyses. *Geoscientific Model Development*, *10*(8), 2905–2923. https://doi.org/10.5194/gmd-10-2905-2017

Cao, B., Gruber, S., Zheng, D., & Li, X. (2020). The ERA5-Land soil temperature bias in permafrost regions. *The Cryosphere*, *14*(8), 2581–2595. https://doi.org/10.5194/tc-14-2581-2020

Cao, B., Quan, X., Brown, N., Stewart-Jones, E., & Gruber, S. (2019). GlobSim (v1.0): Deriving meteorological time series for point locations from multiple global reanalyses. *Geoscientific Model Development* *12*(11). 4661–4679. https://doi.org/10.5194/gmd-12-4661-2019

Carey, S. K., & Quinton, W. (2005). Evaluating Runoff Generation during Summer Using Hydrometric, Stable Isotope and Hydrochemical Methods in a Discontinuous Permafrost Alpine Catchment. *Hydrological Processes*, *19*(1), 95–114. https://doi.org/10.1002/hyp.5764

Carey, S. K., & Woo, M. (2001). Spatial variability of hillslope water balance, wolf creek basin, subarctic yukon. *Hydrological Processes*, *15*(16), 3113–3132. https://doi.org/10.1002/hyp.319

Carmack, E. C., Yamamoto-Kawai, M., Haine, T. W. N., Bacon, S., Bluhm, B. A., Lique, C., Melling, H., Polyakov, I. V., Straneo, F., Timmermans, M.-L., & Williams, W. J. (2016). Freshwater and its role in the Arctic Marine System: Sources, disposition, storage, export, and physical and biogeochemical consequences in the Arctic and global oceans. *Journal of Geophysical Research: Biogeosciences*, *121*(3), 675–717. https://doi.org/10.1002/2015JG003140

Carmack, E., Winsor, P., & Williams, W. (2015). The contiguous panarctic Riverine Coastal Domain: A unifying concept. *Overarching Perspectives of Contemporary and Future Ecosystems in the Arctic Ocean*, *139*, 13–23. https://doi.org/10.1016/j.pocean.2015.07.014

Carrera, M. L., Bélair, S., & Bilodeau, B. (2015). The Canadian Land Data Assimilation System (CaLDAS): Description and Synthetic Evaluation Study. *Journal of Hydrometeorology*, *16*(3), 1293–1314. https://doi.org/10.1175/JHM-D-14-0089.1

Carrera, M. L., Gyakum, J. R., & Lin, C. A. (2009). Observational Study of Wind Channeling within the St. Lawrence River Valley. *Journal of Applied Meteorology and Climatology, 48*(11), 2341–2361. https://doi.org/10.1175/2009JAMC2061.1

Carson, M. A., Jasper, J. N., & Conly, F. M. (1998). Magnitude and Sources of Sediment Input to the Mackenzie Delta, Northwest Territories, 1974–94. *ARCTIC, 51*(2), 116–124. https://doi.org/10.14430/arctic1053

Cartwright, K., Mahoney, C., & Hopkinson, C. (2022). Machine Learning Based Imputation of Mountain Snowpack Depth within an Operational LiDAR Sampling Framework in Southwest Alberta. *Canadian Journal of Remote Sensing, 48*(1), 107–125. https://doi.org/10.1080/07038992.2021.1988540

Chanasyk, D. S., & Verschuren, J. P. (1983). An Interflow Model: Ii. Model Validation. *Canadian Water Resources Journal, 8*(2), 44214. https://doi.org/10.4296/cwrj0802001

Chapin, F. S., Sturm, M., Serreze, M. C., McFadden, J. P., Key, J. R., Lloyd, A. H., McGuire, A. D., Rupp, T. S., Lynch, A. H., Schimel, J. P., Beringer, J., Chapman, W. L., Epstein, H. E., Euskirchen, E. S., Hinzman, L. D., Jia, G., Ping, C.-L., Tape, K. D., Thompson, C. D. C., ... Welker, J. M. (2005). Role of Land-Surface Changes in Arctic Summer Warming. *Science, 310*(5748), 657–660. https://doi.org/10.1126/science.1117368

Charbonneau, A. A., & Smith, D. J. (2018). An inventory of rock glaciers in the central British Columbia Coast Mountains, Canada, from high resolution Google Earth imagery. *Arctic, Antarctic, and Alpine Research, 50*(1), 1489026. https://doi.org/10.1080/15230430.2018.1489026

Charbonneau, R., & David, P. P. (1993). Glacial Dispersal of Rock Debris in Central Gaspesie, Quebec, Canada. *Canadian Journal of Earth Sciences, 30*(8), 1697–1707. https://doi.org/10.1139/e93-148

Chartrand, J., Thériault, J. M., & Marinier, S. (2023). Freezing Rain Events that Impacted the Province of New Brunswick, Canada, and Their Evolution in a Warmer Climate. *Atmosphere-Ocean, 61*(1), 40–56. https://doi.org/10.1080/07055900.2022.2092444

Chavardes, R. D., Daniels, L. D., Gedalof, Z., & Andison, D. W. (2018). Human Influences Superseded Climate to Disrupt the 20th Century Fire Regime in Jasper National Park, Canada. *Dendrochronologia, 48*, 10–19. https://doi.org/10.1016/j.dendro.2018.01.002

Chernos, M., Macdonald, R. J., Nemeth, M. W., & Craig, J. R. (2020). Current and Future Projections of Glacier Contribution to Streamflow in the Upper Athabasca River Basin. *Canadian Water Resources Journal, 45*(4), 324–344. https://doi.org/10.1080/07011784.2020.1815587

Chester, C. C. (2015). Yellowstone to Yukon: Transborder conservation across a vast international landscape. *Environmental Science & Policy, 49*, 75–84. https://doi.org/10.1016/j.envsci.2014.08.009

Chester, C. C., & Hilty, J. A. (2019). The Yellowstone to Yukon Conservation Initiative as an Adaptive Response to Climate Change. In W. Leal Filho, J. Barbir, & R. Preziosi (Eds.), *Handbook of Climate Change and Biodiversity* (pp. 179–193). Springer International Publishing. https://doi.org/10.1007/978-3-319-98681-4_11

Chiarle, M., Geertsema, M., Mortara, G., & Clague, J. J. (2021). Relations between climate change and mass movement: Perspectives from the Canadian Cordillera and the European Alps. *Global and Planetary Change, 202*, 103499. https://doi.org/10.1016/j.gloplacha.2021.103499

Chimner, R. A., Lemly, J. M., & Cooper, D. J. (2010). Mountain Fen Distribution, Types and Restoration Priorities, San Juan Mountains, Colorado, USA. *Wetlands, 30*(4), 763–771. https://doi.org/10.1007/s13157-010-0039-5

Christensen, C. W., Hayashi, M., & Bentley, L. R. (2020). Hydrogeological Characterization of an Alpine Aquifer System in the Canadian Rocky Mountains. *Hydrogeology Journal, 28*(5), 1871–1890. https://doi.org/10.1007/s10040-020-02153-7

Church, M., Ham, D., Hassan, M., & Slaymaker, O. (1999). Fluvial clastic sediment yield in Canada: Scaled analysis. *Canadian Journal of Earth Sciences, 36*(8), 1267–1280. https://doi.org/10.1139/e99-034

Church, M., & Miles, M. J. (1987). Meteorological Antecedents to Debris Flow in Southwestern British Columbia; Some Case Studies. *Gsa Reviews in Engineering Geology, 7*, 63.

Clague, J., Friele, P., & Hutchinson, I. (2003). Chronology and Hazards of Large Debris Flows in the Cheekye River Basin, British Columbia, Canada. *Environmental & Engineering Geoscience, 9*(2), 99–115. https://doi.org/10.2113/9.2.99

Clague, J. J. (2009). Climate Change and Slope Instability. In K. Sassa & P. Canuti (Eds.), *Landslides—Disaster Risk Reduction* (pp. 557–572). Springer. https://doi.org/10.1007/978-3-540-69970-5_29

Clague, J. J., Bobrowsky, P. T., & Hutchinson, I. (2000). A review of geological records of large tsunamis at Vancouver Island, British Columbia, and implications for hazard. *Quaternary Science Reviews, 19*(9), 849–863. https://doi.org/10.1016/S0277-3791(99)00101-8

Clark, J., Carlson, A. E., Reyes, A. V., Carlson, E. C. B., Guillaume, L., Milne, G. A., Tarasov, L., Caffee, M., Wilcken, K., & Rood, D. H. (2022). The age of the opening of the Ice-Free Corridor and implications for the peopling of the Americas. *Proceedings of the National Academy of Sciences, 119*(14), e2118558119. https://doi.org/10.1073/pnas.2118558119

Clark, P. U., Clague, J. J., Curry, B. B., Dreimanis, A., Hicock, S. R., Miller, G. H., Berger, G. W., Eyles, N., Lamothe, M., Miller, B. B., Mott, R. J., Oldale, R. N., Stea, R. R., Szabo, J. P., Thorleifson, L. H., & Vincent, J.-S. (1993). Initiation and development of the Laurentide and Cordilleran Ice Sheets following the last interglaciation. *Quaternary Science Reviews, 12*(2), 79–114. https://doi.org/10.1016/0277-3791(93)90011-A

Clarke, G. K. C., Jarosch, A. H., Anslow, F. S., Radic, V., & Menounos, B. (2015). Projected Deglaciation of Western

Canada in the Twenty-First Century. *Nature Geoscience*, *8*(5), 372–377. https://doi.org/10.1038/NGEO2407

Cloutier, C., Locat, J., Geertsema, M., Jakob, M., & Schnorbus, M. (2016). Potential impacts of climate change on landslides occurrence in Canada. In *Slope Safety Preparedness for Impact of Climate Change* (pp. 71–104). CRC Press. https://doi.org/10.1201/9781315387789-3

Cochand, F., Therrien, R., & Lemieux, J.-M. (2018). Integrated Hydrological Modeling of Climate Change Impacts in a Snow-Influenced Catchment. *Ground Water*, *57*(1), 44275. https://doi.org/10.1111/gwat.12848

Cocks, L. R. M., & Torsvik, T. H. (2011). The Palaeozoic geography of Laurentia and western Laurussia: A stable craton with mobile margins. *Earth-Science Reviews*, *106*(1), 1–51. https://doi.org/10.1016/j.earscirev.2011.01.007

Coe, J. A., Bessette-Kirton, E. K., & Geertsema, M. (2018). Increasing rock-avalanche size and mobility in Glacier Bay National Park and Preserve, Alaska detected from 1984 to 2016 Landsat imagery. *Landslides*, *15*(3), 393–407. https://doi.org/10.1007/s10346-017-0879-7

Cohen, J., Ye, H., & Jones, J. (2015). Trends and variability in rain-on-snow events. *Geophysical Research Letters*, *42*(17), 7115–7122. https://doi.org/10.1002/2015GL065320

Colpron, M., & Nelson, J. L. (2009). A Palaeozoic Northwest Passage: Incursion of Caledonian, Baltican and Siberian terranes into eastern Panthalassa, and the early evolution of the North American Cordillera. *Geological Society, London, Special Publications*, *318*(1), 273–307. https://doi.org/10.1144/sp318.10

Comeau, L. E. L., Pietroniro, A., & Demuth, M. N. (2009). Glacier Contribution to the North and South Saskatchewan Rivers. *Hydrological Processes*, *23*(18, SI), 2640–2653. https://doi.org/10.1002/hyp.7409

Comer, P. J., Hak, J. C., & Seddon, E. (2022). Documenting at-risk status of terrestrial ecosystems in temperate and tropical North America. *Conservation Science and Practice*, *4*(2), e603. https://doi.org/10.1111/csp2.603

Conway, J. P., Helgason, W. D., Pomeroy, J. W., & Sicart, J. E. (2021). Icefield Breezes: Mesoscale Diurnal Circulation in the Atmospheric Boundary Layer Over an Outlet of the Columbia Icefield, Canadian Rockies. *Journal of Geophysical Research: Atmospheres*, *126*(6), 1–17. https://doi.org/10.1029/2020JD034225

Conway Morris, S. (1989). Burgess Shale Faunas and the Cambrian Explosion. *Science*, *246*(4928), 339–346. https://doi.org/10.1126/science.246.4928.339

Coop, J. D., Massatti, R. T., & Schoettle, A. W. (2010). Subalpine vegetation pattern three decades after stand-replacing fire: Effects of landscape context and topography on plant community composition, tree regeneration, and diversity. *Journal of Vegetation Science*, *21*(3), 472–487. https://doi.org/10.1111/j.1654-1103.2009.01154.x

Cooper, D. J., Chimner, R. A., & Merritt, D. M. (2012). Western Mountain Wetlands. In *Wetland Habitats of North America* (pp. 313–328). University of California Press. https://doi.org/10.1525/9780520951419-024

Coops, N. C., Shang, C., Wulder, M. A., White, J. C., & Hermosilla, T. (2020). Change in Forest Condition: Characterizing Non-Stand Replacing Disturbances Using Time Series Satellite Imagery. *Forest Ecology and Management*, *474*, 1–13. https://doi.org/10.1016/j.foreco.2020.118370

Corsiglia, J., & Sniveky, G. (1997). Knowing Home: NisGa'a traditional knowledge and wisdom improve environmental decision making. *Alternatives Journal*, *23*(3), 22.

COSEWIC. (2012). *COSEWIC assessment and status report on the Grizzly Bear Ursus arctos in Canada* (p. 84). Committee on the Status of Endangered Wildlife. https://www.sararegistry.gc.ca/virtual_sara/files/cosewic/sr_ours_grizz_bear_1012_e.pdf

COSEWIC. (2013). *COSEWIC Assessment and Status Report on the Eulachon, Nass/Skeena population, Thaleichthys pacificus in Canada* (p. xi + 18 pp.). https://wildlife-species.canada.ca/species-risk-registry/virtual_sara/files/cosewic/sr_eulakane_eulachon_nass-skeena_1213_e.pdf

COSEWIC. (2014a). *COSEWIC assessment and status report on the Caribou Rangifer tarandus, Newfoundland population, Atlantic-Gaspésie population and Boreal population, in Canada* (p. 128). Committee on the Status of Endangered Wildlife. https://wildlife-species.canada.ca/species-risk-registry/virtual_sara/files/cosewic/sr_Caribou_NF_Boreal_Atlantic_2014_e.pdf

COSEWIC. (2014b). *COSEWIC assessment and status report on the Caribou Rangifer tarandus, Northern Mountain population, Central Mountain population and Southern Mountain population in Canada.* (p. 113). Committee on the Status of Endangered Wildlife. https://wildlife-species.canada.ca/species-risk-registry/virtual_sara/files/cosewic/sr_Caribou_Northern_Central_Southern_2014_e.pdf

Costello, J. A. (1895). *The Siwash: Their Life Legends and Tales.* The Calvert Company.

Cruden, D. M., & Martin, C. D. (2007). Before the Frank Slide. *Canadian Geotechnical Journal*, *44*(7), 765–780. https://doi.org/10.1139/t07-030

Cruikshank, J. (2001). Glaciers and Climate Change: Perspectives from Oral Tradition. *Arctic*, *54*(4), 377–393.

Cruikshank, J. (2005). *Do Glaciers Listen?: Local Knowledge, Colonial Encounters, and Social Imagination.* UBC Press.

Cruikshank, J. (2007). Melting Glaciers and Emerging Histories in the Saint Elias Mountains. In *Indigenous Experience Today* (pp. 355–378). Taylor & Francis.

Crumley, R. L., Hill, D. F., Wikstrom Jones, K., Wolken, G. J., Arendt, A. A., Aragon, C. M., Cosgrove, C., & Community Snow Observations Participants. (2021). Assimilation of citizen science data in snowpack modeling using a new snow data set: Community Snow Observations. *Hydrology and Earth System Sciences*, *25*(9), 4651–4680. https://doi.org/10.5194/hess-25-4651-2021

Cuerrier, A., Clark, C., & Norton, C. H. (2019). Inuit plant use in the eastern Subarctic: Comparative ethnobotany in Kangiqsualujjuaq, Nunavik, and in Nain, Nunatsiavut.

Botany, *97*(5), 272–282. https://doi.org/dx.doi.org/10.1139/cjb-2018-0195

Cullen, J. T., Chong, M., & Ianson, D. (2009). British Columbian continental shelf as a source of dissolved iron to the subarctic northeast Pacific Ocean. *Global Biogeochemical Cycles*, *23*(4). https://doi.org/10.1029/2008GB003326

Cullen, R. M., & Marshall, S. J. (2011). Mesoscale Temperature Patterns in the Rocky Mountains and Foothills Region of Southern Alberta. *Atmosphere-Ocean*, *49*(3), 189–205. https://doi.org/10.1080/07055900.2011.592130

Darvill, C. M., Menounos, B., Goehring, B. M., & Lesnek, A. J. (2022). Cordilleran Ice Sheet Stability During the Last Deglaciation. *Geophysical Research Letters*, *49*(10), e2021GL097191. https://doi.org/10.1029/2021GL097191

Darychuk, S. E., Shea, J. M., Menounos, B., Chesnokova, A., Jost, G., & Weber, F. (2022). Snowmelt Characterization from Optical and Synthetic Aperture Radar Observations in the Lajoie Basin, British Columbia. *The Cryosphere Discussions*, 1–27. https://doi.org/10.5194/tc-2022-89

Davesne, G., Fortier, D., Domine, F., & Gray, J. T. (2017). Wind-Driven Snow Conditions Control the Occurrence of Contemporary Marginal Mountain Permafrost in the Chic-Choc Mountains, South-Eastern Canada: A Case Study from Mont Jacques-Cartier. *Cryosphere*, *11*(3), 1351–1370. https://doi.org/10.5194/tc-11-1351-2017

Davidson, A. (2008). Late Paleoproterozoic to mid-Neoproterozoic history of northern Laurentia: An overview of central Rodinia. *Precambrian Research*, *160*(1), 5–22. https://doi.org/10.1016/j.precamres.2007.04.023

De Souza, S., Tremblay, A., & Ruffet, G. (2014). Taconian orogenesis, sedimentation and magmatism in the southern Quebec–northern Vermont Appalachians: Stratigraphic and detrital mineral record of Iapetan suturing. *American Journal of Science*, *314*(7), 1065–1103.

De Vries, J., & Chow, T. L. (1978). Hydrologic Behavior of a Forested Mountain Soil in Coastal British Columbia. *Water Resources Research*, *14*(5), 935–942. https://doi.org/10.1029/WR014i005p00935

Dearborn, K. D., & Danby, R. K. (2017). Aspect and Slope Influence Plant Community Composition More Than Elevation Across Forest-Tundra Ecotones in Subarctic Canada. *Journal of Vegetation Science*, *28*(3), 595–604. https://doi.org/10.1111/jvs.12521

Debeer, C. M., & Pomeroy, J. W. (2017). Influence of Snowpack and Melt Energy Heterogeneity on Snow Cover Depletion and Snowmelt Runoff Simulation in a Cold Mountain Environment. *Journal of Hydrology*, *553*, 199–213. https://doi.org/10.1016/j.jhydrol.2017.07.051

Debeer, C. M., & Sharp, M. J. (2009). Topographic Influences on Recent Changes of Very Small Glaciers in the Monashee Mountains, British Columbia, Canada. *Journal of Glaciology*, *55*(192), 691–700. https://doi.org/10.3189/002214309789470851

DeBeer, C. M., Wheater, H. S., Pomeroy, J. W., Barr, A. G., Baltzer, J. L., Johnstone, J. F., Turetsky, M. R., Stewart, R.

E., Hayashi, M., van der Kamp, G., Marshall, S., Campbell, E., Marsh, P., Carey, S. K., Quinton, W. L., Li, Y., Razavi, S., Berg, A., McDonnell, J. J., … Pietroniro, A. (2021). Summary and synthesis of Changing Cold Regions Network (CCRN) research in the interior of western Canada—Part 2: Future change in cryosphere, vegetation, and hydrology. *Hydrology and Earth System Sciences*, *25*(4), 1849–1882. https://doi.org/10.5194/hess-25-1849-2021

Deline, P., Gruber, S., Amann, F., Bodin, X., Delaloye, R., Failletaz, J., Fischer, L., Geertsema, M., Giardino, M., Hasler, A., Kirkbride, M., Krautblatter, M., Magnin, F., McColl, S., Ravanel, L., Schoeneich, P., & Weber, S. (2021). Chapter 15—Ice loss from glaciers and permafrost and related slope instability in high-mountain regions. In W. Haeberli & C. Whiteman (Eds.), *Snow and Ice-Related Hazards, Risks, and Disasters (Second Edition)* (pp. 501–540). Elsevier. https://doi.org/10.1016/B978-0-12-817129-5.00015-9

Delisle, F. (2021). Comparison of Seasonal Flow Rate Change Indices Downstream of Three Types of Dams in Southern Quebec (Canada). *Water*, *13*(18), 2555. https://doi-org.ezproxy.library.dal.ca/10.3390/w13182555

Demuth, M. N., Munro, D. S., & Young, G. J. (2006). *Peyto Glacier: One century of science*. Environment Canada.

Déry, S. J., & Brown, R. D. (2007). Recent Northern Hemisphere snow cover extent trends and implications for the snow-albedo feedback. *Geophysical Research Letters*, *34*(22). https://doi.org/10.1029/2007GL031474

Dery, S. J., Clifton, A., Macleod, S., & Beedle, M. J. (2010). Blowing Snow Fluxes in the Cariboo Mountains of British Columbia, Canada. *Arctic Antarctic and Alpine Research*, *42*(2), 188–197. https://doi.org/10.1657/1938-4246-42.2.188

Déry, S. J., Stahl, K., Moore, R. D., Whitfield, P. H., Menounos, B., & Burford, J. E. (2009). Detection of runoff timing changes in pluvial, nival, and glacial rivers of western Canada. *Water Resources Research*, *45*(4). https://doi.org/10.1029/2008WR006975

Dhar, A., Parrott, L., & Heckbert, S. (2016). Consequences of Mountain Pine Beetle Outbreak on Forest Ecosystem Services in Western Canada. *Canadian Journal of Forest Research*, *46*(8), 987–999. https://doi.org/10.1139/cjfr-2016-0137

Diamond, J. M., Call, C. A., Devoe, N., Diamond, J. M., Call, C. A., & Devoe, N. (2009). Effects of targeted cattle grazing on fire behavior of cheatgrass-dominated rangeland in the northern Great Basin, USA. *International Journal of Wildland Fire*, *18*(8), 944–950. https://doi.org/10.1071/WF08075

Dick, C. A., Sewid-Smith, D., Recalma-Clutesi, K., Deur, D., & Turner, N. J. (2022). "From the beginning of time": The colonial reconfiguration of native habitats and Indigenous resource practices on the British Columbia Coast. *FACETS*, *7*, 543–570. https://doi.org/10.1139/facets-2021-0092

Donald, D., Vinebrooke, R., Anderson, R., Syrgiannis, J., & Graham, M. (2001). Recovery of Zooplankton Assemblages in Mountain Lakes from the Effects of Introduced Sport Fish. *Canadian Journal of Fisheries and Aquatic Sciences, 58*(9), 1822–1830. https://doi.org/10.1139/f01-121

Dornes, P. F., Pomeroy, J. W., Pietroniro, A., Carey, S. K., & Quinton, W. L. (2008). Influence of Landscape Aggregation in Modelling Snow-Cover Ablation and Snowmelt Runoff in a Sub-Arctic Mountainous Environment. *Hydrological Sciences Journal/Journal des sciences hydrologiques, 53*(4), 725–740. https://doi.org/10.1623/hysj.53.4.725

Dornes, P. F., Pomeroy, J. W., Pietroniro, A., & Verseghy, D. L. (2008). Effects of Spatial Aggregation of Initial Conditions and Forcing Data on Modeling Snowmelt Using a Land Surface Scheme. *Journal of Hydrometeorology, 9*(4), 789–803. https://doi.org/10.1175/2007JHM958.1

Doyle, J. M., Gleeson, T., Manning, A. H., & Mayer, K. U. (2015). Using Noble Gas Tracers to Constrain a Groundwater Flow Model with Recharge Elevations: A Novel Approach for Mountainous Terrain. *Water Resources Research, 51*(10), 8094–8113. https://doi.org/10.1002/2015WR017274

Dozier, J. (1989). Spectral signature of alpine snow cover from the landsat thematic mapper. *Remote Sensing of Environment, 28*, 9–22. https://doi.org/10.1016/0034-4257(89)90101-6

Dozier, J., Bair, E. H., & Davis, R. E. (2016). Estimating the spatial distribution of snow water equivalent in the world's mountains. *WIREs Water, 3*(3), 461–474. https://doi.org/10.1002/wat2.1140

Drusch, M., Del Bello, U., Carlier, S., Colin, O., Fernandez, V., Gascon, F., Hoersch, B., Isola, C., Laberinti, P., Martimort, P., Meygret, A., Spoto, F., Sy, O., Marchese, F., & Bargellini, P. (2012). Sentinel-2: ESA's Optical High-Resolution Mission for GMES Operational Services. *Remote Sensing of Environment, 120*, 25–36. https://doi.org/10.1016/j.rse.2011.11.026

Ducks Unlimited Canada. (2022). *Canadian Wetlands Inventory*. Canadian Wetland Inventory – Ducks Unlimited. https://www.ducks.ca/initiatives/canadian-wetland-inventory/#cwi-progress-map

Dulfer, H. E., Margold, M., Darvill, C. M., & Stroeven, A. P. (2022). Reconstructing the advance and retreat dynamics of the central sector of the last Cordilleran Ice Sheet. *Quaternary Science Reviews, 284*, 107465. https://doi.org/10.1016/j.quascirev.2022.107465

Dulfer, H., Margold, M., Engel, Z., Braucher, R., Aumaitre, G., Bouries, D., & Keddadouche, K. (2021). Using Be-10 dating to determine when the Cordilleran Ice Sheet stopped flowing over the Canadian Rocky Mountains. *Quaternary Research, 102*, 222–233. https://doi.org/10.1017/qua.2020.122

Dyer, J. (2008). Snow depth and streamflow relationships in large North American watersheds. *Journal of Geophysical Research: Atmospheres, 113*(D18). https://doi.org/10.1029/2008JD010031

Dyke, A., & Prest, V. (1987). Late Wisconsinan and Holocene History of the Laurentide Ice Sheet. *Géographie Physique et Quaternaire, 41*(2), 237–263. https://doi.org/10.7202/032681ar

Dyke, A. S. (2004). An outline of North American deglaciation with emphasis on central and northern Canada. In J. Ehlers & P. L. Gibbard (Eds.), *Developments in Quaternary Sciences* (Vol. 2, pp. 373–424). Elsevier. https://doi.org/10.1016/S1571-0866(04)80209-4

Ebrahimi, S., & Marshall, S. J. (2016). Surface Energy Balance Sensitivity to Meteorological Variability on Haig Glacier, Canadian Rocky Mountains. *Cryosphere, 10*(6), 2799–2819. https://doi.org/10.5194/tc-10-2799-2016

Edwards, B. R., & Russell, J. K. (2000). Distribution, nature, and origin of Neogene–Quaternary magmatism in the northern Cordilleran volcanic province, Canada. *GSA Bulletin, 112*(8), 1280–1295. https://doi.org/10.1130/0016-7606(2000)112<1280:DNAOON>2.0.CO;2

Ellis, C. R., Pomeroy, J. W., Essery, R. L. H., & Link, T. E. (2011). Effects of Needleleaf Forest Cover on Radiation and Snowmelt Dynamics in the Canadian Rocky Mountains. *Canadian Journal of Forest Research, 41*(3), 608–620. https://doi.org/10.1139/X10-227

Ellis, C. R., Pomeroy, J. W., & Link, T. E. (2013). Modeling Increases in Snowmelt Yield and Desynchronization Resulting from Forest Gap-Thinning Treatments in a Northern Mountain Headwater Basin. *Water Resources Research, 49*(2), 936–949. https://doi.org/10.1002/wrcr.20089

Endrizzi, S., Gruber, S., Dall'Amico, M., & Rigon, R. (2014). GEOtop 2.0: Simulating the combined energy and water balance at and below the land surface accounting for soil freezing, snow cover and terrain effects. *Geoscientific Model Development, 7*(6), 2831–2857. https://doi.org/10.5194/gmd-7-2831-2014

Engstrom, C. B., Williamson, S. N., Gamon, J. A., & Quarmby, L. M. (2022). Seasonal development and radiative forcing of red snow algal blooms on two glaciers in British Columbia, Canada, summer 2020. *Remote Sensing of Environment, 280*, 113164. https://doi.org/10.1016/j.rse.2022.113164

Environment and Climate Change Canada. (2016). *Canadian Mercury Science Assessment Report* (pp. 795). https://publications.gc.ca/collections/collection_2017/eccc/En84-130-3-2016-eng.pdf

Essery, R., Li, L., & Pomeroy, J. (1999). A distributed model of blowing snow over complex terrain. *Hydrological Processes, 13*(14–15), 2423–2438. https://doi.org/10.1002/(SICI)1099-1085(199910)13:14/15<2423::AID-HYP853>3.0.CO;2-U

Ettinger, A. K., Ford, K. R., & HilleRisLambers, J. (2011). Climate determines upper, but not lower, altitudinal range limits of Pacific Northwest conifers. *Ecology, 92*(6), 1323–1331. https://doi.org/10.1890/10-1639.1

Evans, C., & Hutchinson, T. (1996). Mercury Accumulation in Transplanted Moss and Lichens at High Elevation Sites in Quebec. *Water Air and Soil Pollution, 90*(44259), 475–488. https://doi.org/10.1007/BF00282663

Evans, D. J. A. (1993). High-latitude rock glaciers: A case study of forms and processes in the Canadian arctic. *Permafrost and Periglacial Processes, 4*(1), 17–35. https://doi.org/10.1002/ppp.3430040103

Evans, S., & Brooks, G. (1991). Prehistoric Debris Avalanches from Mount Cayley Volcano, British-Columbia. *Canadian Journal of Earth Sciences, 28*(9), 1365–1374. https://doi.org/10.1139/e91-120

Fang, X., & Pomeroy, J. W. (2016). Impact of Antecedent Conditions on Simulations of a Flood in a Mountain Headwater Basin. *Hydrological Processes, 30*(16), 2754–2772. https://doi.org/10.1002/hyp.10910

Fang, X., & Pomeroy, J. W. (2020). Diagnosis of Future Changes in Hydrology for a Canadian Rockies Headwater Basin. *Hydrology and Earth System Sciences, 24*(5), 2731–2754. https://doi.org/10.5194/hess-24-2731-2020

Fang, X., Pomeroy, J. W., DeBeer, C. M., Harder, P., & Siemens, E. (2019). Hydrometeorological data from Marmot Creek Research Basin, Canadian Rockies. *Earth System Science Data, 11*(2), 455–471. https://doi.org/10.5194/essd-11-455-2019

Fang, X., Pomeroy, J. W., Ellis, C. R., Macdonald, M. K., Debeer, C. M., & Brown, T. (2013). Multi-Variable Evaluation of Hydrological Model Predictions for a Headwater Basin in the Canadian Rocky Mountains. *Hydrology and Earth System Sciences, 17*(4), 1635–1659. https://doi.org/10.5194/hess-17-1635-2013

Fargey, S., Hanesiak, J., Stewart, R., & Wolde, M. (2014). Aircraft Observations of Orographic Cloud and Precipitation Features over Southern Baffin Island, Nunavut, Canada. *Atmosphere-Ocean, 52*(1), 54–76. https://doi.org/10.1080/07055900.2013.855624

Farnell, R., Hare, P. G., Blake, E., Bowyer, V., Schweger, C., Greer, S., & Gotthardt, R. (2004). Multidisciplinary Investigations of Alpine Ice Patches in Southwest Yukon, Canada: Paleoenvironmental and Paleobiological Investigations. *Arctic, 57*(3), 247–259.

Fernald, M. L. (1925). Persistence of Plants in Unglaciated Areas of Boreal America. *Memoirs of the American Academy of Arts and Sciences, 15*(3), 239–342. https://doi.org/10.2307/25058128

Ferrer-Paris, J. R., Zager, I., Keith, D. A., Oliveira-Miranda, M. A., Rodríguez, J. P., Josse, C., González-Gil, M., Miller, R. M., Zambrana-Torrelio, C., & Barrow, E. (2019). An ecosystem risk assessment of temperate and tropical forests of the Americas with an outlook on future conservation strategies. *Conservation Letters, 12*(2), e12623. https://doi.org/10.1111/conl.12623

Fiddes, J., Endrizzi, S., & Gruber, S. (2015). Large-area land surface simulations in heterogeneous terrain driven by global data sets: Application to mountain permafrost. *The Cryosphere, 9*(1), 411–426. https://doi.org/10.5194/tc-9-411-2015

Fiddes, J., & Gruber, S. (2012). TopoSUB: a tool for efficient large area numerical modelling in complex topography at sub-grid scales. *Geoscientific Model Development, 5*(5), 1245–1257. https://doi.org/10.5194/gmd-5-1245-2012

Fiddes, J., & Gruber, S. (2014). TopoSCALE v.1.0: Downscaling gridded climate data in complex terrain. *Geoscientific Model Development, 7*(1), 387–405. https://doi.org/10.5194/gmd-7-387-2014

Filion, L., Payette, S., Delwaide, A., & Bhiry, N. (1998). Insect Defoliators as Major Disturbance Factors in the High-Altitude Balsam Fir Forest of Mount Megantic, Southern Quebec. *Canadian Journal of Forest Research-Revue canadienne de recherche forestiere, 28*(12), 1832–1842. https://doi.org/10.1139/cjfr-28-12-1832

Floyd, W., Bishop, A., Menounos, B., Heathfield, D., Beffort, S., & Arriola, S. (2020). *Fixed Wing LiDAR Snow Mapping in the Upper Englishman and Little Qualicum River Watershed: 2020 Progress Report* (pp. 25). Vancouver Island University. https://www.rdn.bc.ca/sites/default/files/inline-files/RDN%20Snow%20Mapping%20Progress%20Report%202020.pdf

Ford, D. C., Schwarcz, H. P., Drake, J. J., Gascoyne, M., Harmon, R. S., & Latham, A. G. (1981). Estimates of the Age of the Existing Relief within the Southern Rocky Mountains of Canada. *Arctic & Alpine Research, 13*(1), 44206. https://doi.org/10.2307/1550621

Ford, J. D., Bell, T., & St-Hilaire-Gravel, D. (2010). Vulnerability of Community Infrastructure to Climate Change in Nunavut: A Case Study from Arctic Bay. In G. K. Hovelsrud & B. Smit (Eds.), *Community Adaptation and Vulnerability in Arctic Regions* (pp. 107–130). Springer Netherlands. https://doi.org/10.1007/978-90-481-9174-1_5

Ford, J. D., Clark, D., Pearce, T., Berrang-Ford, L., Copland, L., Dawson, J., New, M., & Harper, S. L. (2019). Changing access to ice, land and water in Arctic communities. *Nature Climate Change, 9*(4), Article 4. https://doi.org/10.1038/s41558-019-0435-7

Fortin, V., Roy, G., Stadnyk, T., Koenig, K., Gasset, N., & Mahidjiba, A. (2018). Ten Years of Science Based on the Canadian Precipitation Analysis: A CaPA System Overview and Literature Review. *Atmosphere-Ocean, 56*(3), 178–196. https://doi.org/10.1080/07055900.2018.1474728

Foster, S. B., & Allen, D. M. (2015). Groundwater-Surface Water Interactions in a Mountain-to-Coast Watershed: Effects of Climate Change and Human Stressors. *Advances in Meteorology, 2015*, 1–22. https://doi.org/10.1155/2015/861805

Foucault, M. (1995). *Discipline and Power: The Birth of the Prison*. Vintage Books.

Fox, S., Qillaq, E., Angutikjuak, I., Tigullaraq, D. J., Kautuk, R., Huntington, H., Liston, G. E., & Elder, K. (2020). Connecting understandings of weather and climate: Steps towards co-production of knowledge and collaborative environmental management in Inuit Nunangat. *Arctic Science, 6*(3), 267–278. https://doi.org/10.1139/as-2019-0010

Frantz, D. G., & Russell, N. J. (2017). *Blackfoot Dictionary of Stems, Roots, and Affixes: Third Edition*. University of Toronto Press.

Frappe, T.-P., & Clarke, G. K. C. (2007). Slow Surge of Trapridge Glacier, Yukon Territory, Canada. *Journal of Geophysical Research-Earth Surface*, 112(F3). https://doi.org/10.1029/2006JF000607

Friele, P. A., Paige, K., & Moore, R. D. (2016). Stream Temperature Regimes and the Distribution of the Rocky Mountain Tailed Frog at Its Northern Range Limit, Southeastern British Columbia. *Northwest Science*, 90(2), 159–175. https://doi.org/10.3955/046.090.0208

Friele, P., Millard, T. H., Mitchell, A., Allstadt, K. E., Menounos, B., Geertsema, M., & Clague, J. J. (2020). Observations on the May 2019 Joffre Peak Landslides, British Columbia. *Landslides*, 17(4), 913–930. https://doi.org/10.1007/s10346-019-01332-2

Frolking, S., & Roulet, N. T. (2007). Holocene radiative forcing impact of northern peatland carbon accumulation and methane emissions. *Global Change Biology*, 13(5), 1079–1088. https://doi.org/10.1111/j.1365-2486.2007.01339.x

Furgal, C., & Seguin, J. (2006). Climate Change, Health, and Vulnerability in Canadian Northern Aboriginal Communities. *Environmental Health Perspectives*, 114(12), 1964–1970. https://doi.org/10.1289/ehp.8433

Gardner, A. S., Sharp, M. J., Koerner, R. M., Labine, C., Boon, S., Marshall, S. J., Burgess, D. O., & Lewis, D. (2009). Near-Surface Temperature Lapse Rates over Arctic Glaciers and Their Implications for Temperature Downscaling. *Journal of Climate*, 22(16), 4281–4298. https://doi.org/10.1175/2009JCLI2845.1

Gardner, A. S., Moholdt, G., Wouters, B., Wolken, G. J., Burgess, D. O., Sharp, M. J. & Labine, C. (2011). Sharply increased mass loss from glaciers and ice caps in the Canadian Arctic Archipelago. *Nature*, 473(7347), 357–360.

Gartner, J. E., & Jakob, M. (2021). Steep Creek risk assessment for pipeline design: A case study from British Columbia, Canada. *Environmental and Engineering Geoscience*, 27(2), 167–178. https://doi.org/10.2113/EEG-D-20-00016

Gascoin, S., Hagolle, O., Huc, M., Jarlan, L., Dejoux, J.-F., Szczypta, C., Marti, R., & Sánchez, R. (2015). A snow cover climatology for the Pyrenees from MODIS snow products. *Hydrology and Earth System Sciences*, 19(5), 2337–2351. https://doi.org/10.5194/hess-19-2337-2015

Geertsema, M., Clague, J., Schwab, J., & Evans, S. (2006). An Overview of Recent Large Catastrophic Landslides in Northern British Columbia, Canada. *Engineering Geology*, 83(44199), 120–143. https://doi.org/10.1016/j.enggeo.2005.06.028

Geertsema, M., Menounos, B., Bullard, G., Carrivick, J. L., Clague, J. J., Dai, C., Donati, D., Ekstrom, G., Jackson, J. M., Lynett, P., Pichierri, M., Pon, A., Shugar, D. H., Stead, D., Del Bel Belluz, J., Friele, P., Giesbrecht, I., Heathfield, D., Millard, T., ... Sharp, M. A. (2022). The 28 November 2020 Landslide, Tsunami, and Outburst Flood—A Hazard Cascade Associated With Rapid Deglaciation at Elliot Creek, British Columbia, Canada. *Geophysical Research Letters*, 49(6), e2021GL096716. https://doi.org/10.1029/2021GL096716

Gende, S. M., Edwards, R. T., Willson, M. F., & Wipfli, M. S. (2002). Pacific Salmon in Aquatic and Terrestrial Ecosystems: Pacific salmon subsidize freshwater and terrestrial ecosystems through several pathways, which generates unique management and conservation issues but also provides valuable research opportunities. *BioScience*, 52(10), 917–928. https://doi.org/10.1641/0006-3568(2002)052[0917:PSIAAT]2.0.CO;2

Gesierich, D., & Rott, E. (2012). Is Diatom Richness Responding to Catchment Glaciation? A Case Study from Canadian Headwater Streams. *Journal of Limnology*, 71(1), 72–83. https://doi.org/10.4081/jlimnol.2012.e7

Gibson, J. J., Birks, S. J., Yi, Y., Shaw, P., & Moncur, M. C. (2018). Isotopic and Geochemical Surveys of Lakes in Coastal B.C.: Insights into Regional Water Balance and Water Quality Controls. *Journal of Hydrology-Regional Studies*, 17, 47–63. https://doi.org/10.1016/j.ejrh.2018.04.006

Giersch, J. J., Hotaling, S., Kovach, R. P., Jones, L. A., & Muhlfeld, C. C. (2017). Climate-induced glacier and snow loss imperils alpine stream insects. *Global Change Biology*, 23(7), 2577–2589. https://doi.org/10.1111/gcb.13565

Giesbrecht, I. J. W., Tank, S. E., Frazer, G. W., Hood, E., Gonzalez Arriola, S. G., Butman, D. E., D'Amore, D. V., Hutchinson, D., Bidlack, A., & Lertzman, K. P. (2022). Watershed Classification Predicts Streamflow Regime and Organic Carbon Dynamics in the Northeast Pacific Coastal Temperate Rainforest. *Global Biogeochemical Cycles*, 36(2), e2021GB007047. https://doi.org/10.1029/2021GB007047

Gillett, N. P., Cannon, A. J., Malinina, E., Schnorbus, M., Anslow, F., Sun, Q., Kirchmeier-Young, M., Zwiers, F., Seiler, C., Zhang, X., Flato, G., Wan, H., Li, G., & Castellan, A. (2022). Human influence on the 2021 British Columbia floods. *Weather and Climate Extremes*, 36, 100441. https://doi.org/10.1016/j.wace.2022.100441

Golding, D. (1978). Calculated Snowpack Evaporation during Chinooks along Eastern Slopes of Rocky Mountains in Alberta. *Journal of Applied Meteorology*, 17(11), 1647–1651. https://doi.org/10.1175/1520-0450(1978)017<1647:CSEDCA>2.0.CO;2

Gómez, C., White, J. C., & Wulder, M. A. (2016). Optical remotely sensed time series data for land cover classification: A review. *ISPRS Journal of Photogrammetry and Remote Sensing*, 116, 55–72. https://doi.org/10.1016/j.isprsjprs.2016.03.008

Goodison, B. E. (1978). Accuracy of Canadian Snow Gage Measurements. *Journal of Applied Meteorology and Climatology*, 17(10), 1542–1548. https://doi.org/10.1175/1520-0450(1978)017<1542:AOCSGM>2.0.CO;2

Gorham, E. (1991). Northern Peatlands: Role in the Carbon Cycle and Probable Responses to Climatic Warming. *Ecological Applications*, 1(2), 182–195. https://doi.org/10.2307/1941811

Gottesfeld, L. M. J. (1994). Aboriginal burning for vegetation management in northwest British Columbia.

Human Ecology, 22(2), 171–188. https://doi.org/10.1007/BF02169038

Gowan, E. J., Tregoning, P., Purcell, A., Montillet, J.-P., & McClusky, S. (2016). A model of the western Laurentide Ice Sheet, using observations of glacial isostatic adjustment. *Quaternary Science Reviews, 139*, 1–16. https://doi.org/10.1016/j.quascirev.2016.03.003

Grasby, S. E., Ferguson, G., Brady, A., Sharp, C., Dunfield, P., & Mcmechan, M. (2016). Deep Groundwater Circulation and Associated Methane Leakage in the Northern Canadian Rocky Mountains. *Applied Geochemistry, 68*, 44487. https://doi.org/10.1016/j.apgeochem.2016.03.004

Grasby, S., & Lepitzki, D. (2002). Physical and Chemical Properties of the Sulphur Mountain Thermal Springs, Banff National Park, and Implications for Endangered Snails. *Canadian Journal of Earth Sciences, 39*(9), 1349–1361. https://doi.org/10.1139/E02-056

Gray, J., Davesne, G., Fortier, D., & Godin, E. (2017). The Thermal Regime of Mountain Permafrost at the Summit of Mont Jacques-Cartier in the Gaspe Peninsula, Quebec, Canada: A 37 Year Record of Fluctuations Showing an Overall Warming Trend. *Permafrost and Periglacial Processes, 28*(1), 266–274. https://doi.org/10.1002/ppp.1903

Gruber, S. (2012). Derivation and analysis of a high-resolution estimate of global permafrost zonation. *The Cryosphere, 6*(1), 221–233. https://doi.org/10.5194/tc-6-221-2012

Gruber, S., Burn, C. R., Arenson, L., Geertsema, M., Harris, S., Smith, S. L., Bonnaventure, P., & Benkert, B. (2015). Permafrost in mountainous regions of Canada. *Proceedings of GeoQuebec 2015*. GeoQuebec, 20–23 September 2015, Quebec, Canada.

Gruber, S., & Haeberli, W. (2007). Permafrost in steep bedrock slopes and its temperature-related destabilization following climate change. *Journal of Geophysical Research, 112*(F2), F02S18. https://doi.org/10.1029/2006JF000547

Guthrie, R. H., Friele, P., Allstadt, K., Roberts, N., Evans, S. G., Delaney, K. B., Roche, D., Clague, J. J., & Jakob, M. (2012). The 6 August 2010 Mount Meager Rock Slide-Debris Flow, Coast Mountains, British Columbia: Characteristics, Dynamics, and Implications for Hazard and Risk Assessment. *Natural Hazards and Earth System Sciences, 12*(5), 1277–1294. https://doi.org/10.5194/nhess-12-1277-2012

Haeberli, W., & Burn, C. R. (2002). Natural hazards in forests: Glacier and permafrost effects as related to climate change. In *Environmental change and geomorphic hazards in forests* (pp. 241). CABI.

Haeberli, W., Hallet, B., Arenson, L., Elconin, R., Humlum, O., & Ka, A. (2006). Permafrost creep and rock glacier dynamics. *Permafrost and Periglacial Processes, 17*(3), 189–214. https://doi.org/10.1002/ppp

Hage, S., Galy, V. V., Cartigny, M. J. B., Acikalin, S., Clare, M. A., Gröcke, D. R., Hilton, R. G., Hunt, J. E., Lintern, D. G., McGhee, C. A., Parsons, D. R., Stacey, C. D., Sumner, E. J.,

& Talling, P. J. (2020). Efficient preservation of young terrestrial organic carbon in sandy turbidity-current deposits. *Geology, 48*(9), 882–887. https://doi.org/10.1130/G47320.1

Hage, S., Galy, V. V., Cartigny, M. J. B., Heerema, C., Heijnen, M. S., Acikalin, S., Clare, M. A., Giesbrecht, I., Gröcke, D. R., Hendry, A., Hilton, R. G., Hubbard, S. M., Hunt, J. E., Lintern, D. G., McGhee, C., Parsons, D. R., Pope, E. L., Stacey, C. D., Sumner, E. J., ... Talling, P. J. (2022). Turbidity Currents Can Dictate Organic Carbon Fluxes Across River-Fed Fjords: An Example from Bute Inlet (BC, Canada). *Journal of Geophysical Research: Biogeosciences, 127*(6), e2022JG006824. https://doi.org/10.1029/2022JG006824

Hagedorn, F., Gavazov, K., & Alexander, J. M. (2019). Above- and belowground linkages shape responses of mountain vegetation to climate change. *Science, 365*(6458), 1119–1123. https://doi.org/10.1126/science.aax4737

Hall, D. K., Riggs, G. A., Salomonson, V. V., DiGirolamo, N. E., & Bayr, K. J. (2002). MODIS snow-cover products. *Remote Sensing of Environment, 83*(1), 181–194. https://doi.org/10.1016/S0034-4257(02)00095-0

Hall, K., Boelhouwers, J., & Driscoll, K. (2001). Some Morphometric Measurements on Ploughing Blocks in the Mcgregor Mountains, Canadian Rockies. *Permafrost and Periglacial Processes, 12*(2), 219–225. https://doi.org/10.1002/ppp.368

Hallett, D. J., Mathewes, R. W., & Walker, R. C. (2003). A 1000-year record of forest fire, drought and lake-level change in southeastern British Columbia, Canada. *The Holocene, 13*(5), 751–761. https://doi.org/10.1191/0959683603hl660rp

Hamilton, W. B. (1998). Archean magmatism and deformation were not products of plate tectonics. *Precambrian Research, 91*(1–2), 143–179. https://doi.org/10.1016/S0301-9268(98)00042-4

Hamlet, A. F., & Lettenmaier, D. P. (1999). Effects of Climate Change on Hydrology and Water Resources in the Columbia River Basin. *JAWRA Journal of the American Water Resources Association, 35*(6), 1597–1623. https://doi.org/10.1111/j.1752-1688.1999.tb04240.x

Hanesiak, J., Stewart, R., Taylor, P., Moore, K., Barber, D., McBean, G., Strapp, W., Wolde, M., Goodson, R., Hudson, E., Hudak, D., Scott, J., Liu, G., Gilligan, J., Biswas, S., Desjardins, D., Dyck, R., Fargey, S., Field, R., ... Zhang, S. (2010). Storm Studies in the Arctic (STAR). *Bulletin of the American Meteorological Society, 91*(1), 47–68. https://doi.org/10.1175/2009BAMS2693.1

Harder, P., & Pomeroy, J. W. (2014). Hydrological Model Uncertainty Due to Precipitation-Phase Partitioning Methods. *Hydrological Processes, 28*(14, SI), 4311–4327. https://doi.org/10.1002/hyp.10214

Harder, P., Pomeroy, J. W., & Helgason, W. D. (2020). Improving Sub-Canopy Snow Depth Mapping with Unmanned Aerial Vehicles: Lidar Versus Structure-from-Motion Techniques. *Cryosphere, 14*(6), 1919–1935. https://doi.org/10.5194/tc-14-1919-2020

Hare, P. G., Greer, S., Gotthardt, R., Farnell, R., Bowyer, V., Schweger, C., & Strand, D. (2004). Ethnographic and Archaeological Investigations of Alpine Ice Patches in Southwest Yukon, Canada. *Arctic*, 57(3), 260–272.

Harrington, J. S., Hayashi, M., & Kurylyk, B. L. (2017). Influence of a rock glacier spring on the stream energy budget and cold-water refuge in an alpine stream. *Hydrological Processes*, 31(26), 4719–4733. https://doi.org/10.1002/hyp.11391

Harris, S. (2001). Twenty Years of Data on Climate-Permafrost-Active Layer Variations at the Lower Limit of Alpine Permafrost, Marmot Basin, Jasper National Park, Canada. *Geografiska Annaler Series A-Physical Geography*, 83A(44198), 44209.

Harris, S. A. (1997). Relict Late Quaternary Permafrost on a Former Nunatak at Plateau Mountain, S. W. Alberta, Canada. *Biuletyn Peryglacjalny*, 36, 47–72.

Harvey, J. E., Smith, Dan. J., & Veblen, T. T. (2017). Mixed-severity fire history at a forest—Grassland ecotone in west central British Columbia, Canada. *Ecological Applications*, 27(6), 1746–1760.

Haskell, C. A. (2018). From salmon to shad: Shifting sources of marine-derived nutrients in the Columbia River Basin. *Ecology of Freshwater Fish*, 27(1), 310–322. https://doi.org/10.1111/eff.12348

Hasler, A., Geertsema, M., Foord, V., Gruber, S., & Noetzli, J. (2015). The Influence of Surface Characteristics, Topography and Continentality on Mountain Permafrost in British Columbia. *Cryosphere*, 9(3), 1025–1038. https://doi.org/10.5194/tc-9-1025-2015

Hasterok, D., Halpin, J. A., Collins, A. S., Hand, M., Kreemer, C., Gard, M. G., & Glorie, S. (2022). New Maps of Global Geological Provinces and Tectonic Plates. *Earth-Science Reviews*, 231, 104069. https://doi.org/10.1016/j.earscirev.2022.104069

Hauer, F., Baron, J., Campbell, D., Fausch, K., Hostetler, S., Leavesley, G., Leavitt, P., Mcknight, D., & Stanford, J. (1997). Assessment of Climate Change and Freshwater Ecosystems of the Rocky Mountains, USA and Canada. *Hydrological Processes*, 11(8), 903–924.

Hayashi, M. (2020). Alpine Hydrogeology: The Critical Role of Groundwater in Sourcing the Headwaters of the World. *Groundwater*, 58(4), 498–510. https://doi.org/10.1111/gwat.12965

Hayden, B., & Ryder, J. M. (1991). Prehistoric Cultural Collapse in the Lillooet Area. *American Antiquity*, 56(1), 50–65. https://doi.org/10.2307/280972

Hebda, R., Greer, S., & Mackie, A. (Eds.). (2017). *Kwäday Dän Ts'ìnchį: Teachings from Long Ago Person Found*. Royal BC Museum.

Hedrick, L. B., Anderson, J. T., Welsh, S. A., & Lin, L.-S. (2013). *Sedimentation in Mountain Streams: A Review of Methods of Measurement. 2013*. https://doi.org/10.4236/nr.2013.41011

Heideman, M., Menounos, B., & Clague, J. J. (2018). A Multi-Century Estimate of Suspended Sediment Yield from Lillooet Lake, Southern Coast Mountains, Canada. *Canadian Journal of Earth Sciences*, 55(1), 18–32. https://doi.org/10.1139/cjes-2017-0025

Heinle, K. B., Eby, L. A., Muhlfeld, C. C., Steed, A., Jones, L., D'Angelo, V., Whiteley, A. R., & Hebblewhite, M. (2021). Influence of water temperature and biotic interactions on the distribution of westslope cutthroat trout (Oncorhynchus clarkia lewisi) in a population stronghold under climate change. *Canadian Journal of Fisheries and Aquatic Sciences*, 78(4), 444–456. https://doi.org/10.1139/cjfas-2020-0099

Helgason, W., & Pomeroy, J. W. (2012). Characteristics of the Near-Surface Boundary Layer within a Mountain Valley during Winter. *Journal of Applied Meteorology and Climatology*, 51(3), 583–597. https://doi.org/10.1175/JAMC-D-11-058.1

Henoch, W. E. S. (1971). Estimate of Glaciers Secular (1948-1966) Volumetric Change and Its Contribution to the Discharge in the Upper North Saskatchewan River Basin. *Journal of Hydrology*, 12(2), 145–160. https://doi.org/10.1016/0022-1694(71)90106-5

Hermosilla, T., Wulder, M. A., White, J. C., & Coops, N. C. (2022). Land cover classification in an era of big and open data: Optimizing localized implementation and training data selection to improve mapping outcomes. *Remote Sensing of Environment*, 268, 112780. https://doi.org/10.1016/j.rse.2021.112780

Hersbach, H., Bell, B., Berrisford, P., Hirahara, S., Horányi, A., Muñoz-Sabater, J., Nicolas, J., Peubey, C., Radu, R., Schepers, D., Simmons, A., Soci, C., Abdalla, S., Abellan, X., Balsamo, G., Bechtold, P., Biavati, G., Bidlot, J., Bonavita, M., … Thépaut, J.-N. (2020). The ERA5 global reanalysis. *Quarterly Journal of the Royal Meteorological Society*, 146(730), 1999–2049. https://doi.org/10.1002/qj.3803

Heusser, C. J. (1956). Postglacial Environments in the Canadian Rocky Mountains. *Ecological Monographs*, 26(4), 263–302. https://doi.org/10.2307/1948543

Hewitt, G. (2000). The genetic legacy of the Quaternary ice ages. *Nature*, 405(6789), Article 6789. https://doi.org/10.1038/35016000

Hibbard, J. P., Van Staal, C. R., & Rankin, D. W. (2007). A comparative analysis of pre-Silurian crustal building blocks of the northern and the southern Appalachian orogen. *American Journal of Science*, 307(1), 23–45. https://doi.org/10.2475/01.2007.02

Hickson, C., Russell, J., & Stasiuk, M. (1999). Volcanology of the 2350 Bp Eruption of Mount Meager Volcanic Complex, British Columbia, Canada: Implications for Hazards from Eruptions in Topographically Complex Terrain. *Bulletin of Volcanology*, 60(7), 489–507. https://doi.org/10.1007/s004450050247

Hilty, J., & Jacob, A. (2021). Connectivity Conservation. *The Yellowstone to Yukon (Y2Y) Conservation Initiative*, 83.

Hirose, J. M. R., & Marshall, S. J. (2013). Glacier Meltwater Contributions and Glaciometeorological Regime of the Illecillewaet River Basin, British Columbia, Canada. *Atmosphere-Ocean*, 51(4), 416–435. https://doi.org/10.1080/07055900.2013.791614

Hock, R., Rasul, G., Adler, C., Cáceres, B., Gruber, S., Hirabayashi, Y., Jackson, M., Kääb, A., Kang, S., Kutuzov, S., Milner, A., Molau, U., Morin, S., Orlove, B., & H. Steltzer. (2019). High Mountain Areas. In N. M. W. H.-O. Pörtner, D.C. Roberts, V. Masson-Delmotte, P. Zhai, M. Tignor, E. Poloczanska, K. Mintenbeck, A. Alegría, M. Nicolai, A. Okem, J. Petzold, B. Rama (Ed.), *IPCC Special Report on the Ocean and Cryosphere in a Changing Climate [H.-O.]* (pp. 131–202). Cambridge University Press. https://doi.org/10.1017/9781009157964.004

Hocking, M. D., & Reynolds, J. D. (2011). Impacts of Salmon on Riparian Plant Diversity. *Science, 331*(6024), 1609–1612. https://doi.org/10.1126/science.1201079

Hoffman, K. M., Christianson, A. C., Dickson-Hoyle, S., Copes-Gerbitz, K., Nikolakis, W., Diabo, D. A., McLeod, R., Michell, H. J., Mamun, A. A., & Zahara, A. (2022). The right to burn: Barriers and opportunities for Indigenous-led fire stewardship in Canada. *FACETS, 7*(1), 464–481.

Hoffman, K. M., Christianson, A. C., Gray, R. W., & Daniels, L. (2022). Western Canada's new wildfire reality needs a new approach to fire management. *Environmental Research Letters, 17*(6), 061001. https://doi.org/10.1088/1748-9326/ac7345

Hoffman, K. M., Davis, E. L., Wickham, S. B., Schang, K., Johnson, A., Larking, T., Lauriault, P. N., Quynh Le, N., Swerdfager, E., & Trant, A. J. (2021). Conservation of Earth's biodiversity is embedded in Indigenous fire stewardship. *Proceedings of the National Academy of Sciences, 118*(32), e2105073118. https://doi.org/10.1073/pnas.2105073118

Hoffman, P. F. (1988). United plates of America, The birth of a craton: Early Proterozoic assembly and growth of Laurentia. *Annual Review of Earth and Planetary Sciences, 16*(1), 543–603.

Holden, C. (1999). Canadians Find "Ice Man" in Glacier. *Science, 285*(5433), 1485.

Hood, J. L., & Hayashi, M. (2015). Characterization of Snowmelt Flux and Groundwater Storage in an Alpine Headwater Basin. *Journal of Hydrology, 521*, 482–497. https://doi.org/10.1016/j.jhydrol.2014.12.041

Hood, J. L., Roy, J. W., & Hayashi, M. (2006). Importance of Groundwater in the Water Balance of an Alpine Headwater Lake. *Geophysical Research Letters, 33*(L13405,). https://doi.org/10.1029/2006GL026611

Hopkinson, C., Collins, T., Anderson, A., Pomeroy, J., & Spooner, I. (2012). Spatial Snow Depth Assessment Using LiDAR Transect Samples and Public GIS Data Layers in the Elbow River Watershed, Alberta. *Canadian Water Resources Journal / Revue Canadienne Des Ressources Hydriques, 37*(2), 69–87. https://doi.org/10.4296/cwrj3702893

Housty, W. G., Noson, A., Scoville, G. W., Boulanger, J., Jeo, R. M., Darimont, C. T., & Filardi, C. E. (2014). Grizzly bear monitoring by the Heiltsuk people as a crucible for First Nation conservation practice. *Ecology and Society, 19*(2), 1–16. https://www.jstor.org/stable/26269572

Hugenholtz, C. H. (2013). Anatomy of the November 2011 windstorms in southern Alberta, Canada. *Weather, 68*(11), 295–299. https://doi.org/10.1002/wea.2171

Huggel, C., Gruber, S., & Wessels, R. L. (2008). The 2005 Mt. Steller, Alaska, rock-ice avalanche: A large slope failure in cold permafrost. *Proceedings of the 9th International Conference on Permafrost 2008*, 747–752.

Hugonnet, R., McNabb, R., Berthier, E., Menounos, B., Nuth, C., Girod, L., Farinotti, D., Huss, M., Dussaillant, I., Brun, F., & Kääb, A. (2021). Accelerated global glacier mass loss in the early twenty-first century. *Nature, 592*(7856), 726–731. https://doi.org/10.1038/s41586-021-03436-z

Hultén, E. (1937). *Outline of the history of Arctic and boreal biota during the Quaternary Period: Their evolution during and after the glacial period as indicated by the equiformal progressive areas of present plant species.* Bokförlags aktiebolaget Thule.

Hungr, O., Evans, S. G., & Hazzard, J. (1999). Magnitude and frequency of rock falls and rock slides along the main transportation corridors of southwestern British Columbia. *Canadian Geotechnical Journal, 36*(2), 224–238. https://doi.org/10.1139/t98-106

Huscroft, C., Lipovsky, P. S., & Bond, J. D. (2004). *Permafrost and landslide activity: Case studies from southwestern Yukon Territory* (Yukon Exploration and Geology 2003, pp. 107–119). Yukon Geological Survey.

Immerzeel, W. W., Lutz, A. F., Andrade, M., Bahl, A., Biemans, H., Bolch, T., Hyde, S., Brumby, S., Davies, B. J., Elmore, A. C., Emmer, A., Feng, M., Fernández, A., Haritashya, U., Kargel, J. S., Koppes, M., Kraaijenbrink, P. D. A., Kulkarni, A. V., Mayewski, P. A., & Baillie, J. E. M. (2020). Importance and vulnerability of the world's water towers. *Nature, 577*(7790), 364–369. https://doi.org/10.1038/s41586-019-1822-y

Ingold, T., & Kurtilla, T. (2000). Perceiving the Environment in Finnish Lapland. *Body & Society, 6*(3–4), 183–196. https://doi.org/10.1177/1357034X00006003010

Islam, S.U., Curry, C. L., Dery, S. J., & Zwiers, F. W. (2019). Quantifying Projected Changes in Runoff Variability and Flow Regimes of the Fraser River Basin, British Columbia. *Hydrology and Earth System Sciences, 23*(2), 811–828. https://doi.org/10.5194/hess-23-811-2019

Islam, S.U., & Dery, S. J. (2017). Evaluating Uncertainties in Modelling the Snow Hydrology of the Fraser River Basin, British Columbia, Canada. *Hydrology and Earth System Sciences, 21*(3), 1827–1847. https://doi.org/10.5194/hess-21-1827-2017

IUCN. (2021). *Peatlands and Climate Change.* IUCN. https://www.iucn.org/sites/default/files/2022-04/iucn_issues_brief_peatlands_and_climate_change_final_nov21.pdf

Jackson, P. L. (1996). Surface winds during an intense outbreak of arctic air in Southwestern British Columbia. *Atmosphere-Ocean, 34*(2), 285–311. https://doi.org/10.1080/07055900.1996.9649566

Jackson, P. L., & Steyn, D. G. (1994). Gap Winds in a Fjord. Part I: Observations and Numerical Simulation. *Monthly*

Weather Review, 122(12), 2645–2665. https://doi.org/10.1175/1520-0493(1994)122<2645:GWIAFP>2.0.CO;2

Jackson, S. I., & Prowse, T. D. (2009). Spatial Variation of Snowmelt and Sublimation in a High-Elevation Semi-Desert Basin of Western Canada. *Hydrological Processes, 23*(18), 2611–2627. https://doi.org/10.1002/hyp.7320

Jakob, M., Clague, J. J., & Church, M. (2016). Rare and Dangerous: Recognizing Extra-Ordinary Events in Stream Channels. *Canadian Water Resources Journal, 41*(44198), 161–173. https://doi.org/10.1080/07011784.2015.1028451

Jakob, M., Weatherly, H., Bale, S., Perkins, A., & MacDonald, B. (2017). A Multi-Faceted Debris-Flood Hazard Assessment for Cougar Creek, Alberta, Canada. *Hydrology, 4*(1), Article 1. https://doi.org/10.3390/hydrology4010007

Janke, J. R. (2005). Modeling past and future alpine permafrost distribution in the Colorado Front Range. *Earth Surface Processes and Landforms, 30*(12), 1495–1508. https://doi.org/10.1002/esp.1205

Janowicz, J. R., Hedstrom, N., Pomeroy, J., Granger, R., & Carey, S. (2004). Wolf Creek Research basin water balance studies. *Northern Research Basins Water Balance, 290*, 195–204.

Jarosch, A. H., Anslow, F. S., & Clarke, G. K. C. (2012). High-resolution precipitation and temperature downscaling for glacier models. *Climate Dynamics, 38*(1), 391–409. https://doi.org/10.1007/s00382-010-0949-1

Jessen, T. D., Ban, N. C., Claxton, N. X., & Darimont, C. T. (2022). Contributions of Indigenous Knowledge to ecological and evolutionary understanding. *Frontiers in Ecology and the Environment, 20*(2), 93–101. https://doi.org/10.1002/fee.2435

Jessen, T. D., Service, C. N., Poole, K. G., Burton, A. C., Bateman, A. W., Paquet, P. C., & Darimont, C. T. (2022). Indigenous peoples as sentinels of change in human-wildlife relationships: Conservation status of mountain goats in Kitasoo Xai'xais territory and beyond. *Conservation Science and Practice, 4*(4), e12662. https://doi.org/10.1111/csp2.12662

Jiskoot, H., Curran, C. J., Tessler, D. L., & Shenton, L. R. (2009). Changes in Clemenceau Icefield and Chaba Group glaciers, Canada, related to hypsometry, tributary detachment, length–slope and area–aspect relations. *Annals of Glaciology, 50*(53), 133–143. https://doi.org/10.3189/172756410790595796

Johnsen, T. F., & Brennand, T. A. (2006). The environment in and around ice-dammed lakes in the moderately high relief setting of the southern Canadian Cordillera. *Boreas, 35*(1), 106–125. https://doi.org/10.1111/j.1502-3885.2006.tb01116.x

Johnson, E., & Wowchuk, D. (1993). Wildfires in the Southern Canadian Rocky-Mountains and their Relationship to Midtropospheric Anomalies. *Canadian Journal of Forest Research, 23*(6), 1213–1222. https://doi.org/10.1139/x93-153

Johnston, S. T. (2008). The Cordilleran ribbon continent of North America. *Annual Review of Earth and Planetary Sciences, 36*(1), 495–530. GeoRef. https://doi.org/10.1146/annurev.earth.36.031207.124331

Jordan, C. E., & Fairfax, E. (2022). Beaver: The North American freshwater climate action plan. *WIREs Water, 9*(4), e1592. https://doi.org/10.1002/wat2.1592

Jost, G., Moore, R. D., Menounos, B., & Wheate, R. (2012). Quantifying the Contribution of Glacier Runoff to Streamflow in the Upper Columbia River Basin, Canada. *Hydrology and Earth System Sciences, 16*(3), 849–860. https://doi.org/10.5194/hess-16-849-2012

Karst-Riddoch, T., Pisaric, M., & Smol, J. (2005). Diatom Responses to 20th Century Climate-Related Environmental Changes in High-Elevation Mountain Lakes of the Northern Canadian Cordillera. *Journal of Paleolimnology, 33*(3), 265–282. https://doi.org/10.1007/s10933-004-5334-9

Keane, R., Veblen, T., Ryan, K., Logan, J., Allen, C., & Hawkes, B. (2002). *The cascading effects of fire exclusion in the Rocky Mountains.* 133–152.

Keskitalo, K. H., Bröder, L., Shakil, S., Zolkos, S., Tank, S. E., van Dongen, B. E., Tesi, T., Haghipour, N., Eglinton, T. I., Kokelj, S. V., & Vonk, J. E. (2021). Downstream Evolution of Particulate Organic Matter Composition from Permafrost Thaw Slumps. *Frontiers in Earth Science, 9.* https://www.frontiersin.org/articles/10.3389/feart.2021.642675

Khatiwala, S. P., Fairbanks, R. G., & Houghton, R. W. (1999). Freshwater sources to the coastal ocean off northeastern North America: Evidence from H2 18O/H2 16O. *Journal of Geophysical Research: Oceans, 104*(C8), 18241–18255. https://doi.org/10.1029/1999JC900155

Kienzle, S. W. (2008). A new temperature based method to separate rain and snow. *Hydrological Processes, 22*(26), 5067–5085. https://doi.org/10.1002/hyp.7131

Kim, H., Sidle, R., Moore, R., & Hudson, R. (2004). Throughflow Variability during Snowmelt in a Forested Mountain Catchment, Coastal British Columbia, Canada. *Hydrological Processes, 18*(7), 1219–1236. https://doi.org/10.1002/hyp.1396

Kinar, N. J., & Pomeroy, J. W. (2015). Measurement of the physical properties of the snowpack. *Reviews of Geophysics, 53*(2), 481–544. https://doi.org/10.1002/2015RG000481

Kirshbaum, D. J., Adler, B., Kalthoff, N., Barthlott, C., & Serafin, S. (2018). Moist Orographic Convection: Physical Mechanisms and Links to Surface-Exchange Processes. *Atmosphere, 9*(3), Article 3. https://doi.org/10.3390/atmos9030080

Kite, G., & Kouwen, N. (1992). Watershed Modeling Using Land Classifications. *Water Resources Research, 28*(12), 3193–3200. https://doi.org/10.1029/92WR01819

Kite, G. W. (1993). Application of a Land Class Hydrological Model to Climatic Change. *Water Resources Research, 29*(7), 2377–2384. https://doi.org/10.1029/93WR00582

Kochendorfer, J., Earle, M., Rasmussen, R., Smith, C., Yang, D., Morin, S., Mekis, E., Buisan, S., Roulet, Y.-A., Landolt,

S., Wolff, M., Hoover, J., Thériault, J. M., Lee, G., Baker, B., Nitu, R., Lanza, L., Colli, M., & Meyers, T. (2022). How Well Are We Measuring Snow Post-SPICE? *Bulletin of the American Meteorological Society*, 103(2), E370–E388. https://doi.org/10.1175/BAMS-D-20-0228.1

Kochtubajda, B., Brimelow, J., Flannigan, B., Morrow, M., & Greenhough, M. D. (2017). The extreme 2016 wildfire in Fort McMurray, Alberta, Canada. In *State of the Climate in 2016, Bulletin of the American Meteorological Society* Vol. 98, pp. 176–177.

Kochtubajda, B., Stewart, R. E., Boodoo, S., Thériault, J. M., Li, Y., Liu, A., Mooney, C., Goodson, R., & Szeto, K. (2016). The June 2013 Alberta catastrophic flooding event—part 2: Fine-scale precipitation and associated features. *Hydrological Processes*, 30(26), 4917–4933. https://doi.org/10.1002/hyp.10855

Koerner, R. M., & Fisher, D. A. (2002). Ice-core evidence for widespread Arctic glacier retreat in the Last Interglacial and the early Holocene. Annals of Glaciology, 35, 19–24.

Kokelj, S., Kokoszka, J., Van der Sluijs, J., Rudy, A., Tunnicliffe, J., Shakil, S., Tank, S., & Zolkos, S. (2021). Thaw-driven mass wasting couples slopes with downstream systems, and effects propagate through Arctic drainage networks. *Cryosphere*, 15(7), 3059–3081. https://doi.org/10.5194/tc-15-3059-2021

Koppes, M. N., & Montgomery, D. R. (2009). The relative efficacy of fluvial and glacial erosion over modern to orogenic timescales. *Nature Geoscience*, 2(9), Article 9. https://doi.org/10.1038/ngeo616

Körner, C. (2012). *Alpine treelines*. Springer.

Körner, C., & Spehn, E. M. (2019). *Mountain Biodiversity: A Global Assessment*. Routledge.

Kraus, D., Enns, A., Hebb, A., Murphy, S., Drake, D. A. R., & Bennett, B. (2023). Prioritizing nationally endemic species for conservation. *Conservation Science and Practice*, 5(1), e12845. https://doi.org/10.1111/csp2.12845

Kromer, R., Hutchinson, J., Lato, M., & Edwards, T. (2015). Geohazard Management: on the Canadian National Railway Corridor. *Gim International*, 29(12), 17–19.

Kuehn, C., Guest, B., Russell, J. K., & Benowitz, J. A. (2015). The Satah Mountain and Baldface Mountain volcanic fields: Pleistocene hot spot volcanism in the Anahim Volcanic Belt, west-central British Columbia, Canada. *Bulletin of Volcanology*, 77(3), 19. https://doi.org/10.1007/s00445-015-0907-1

Kurylyk, B. L., & Hayashi, M. (2017). Inferring hydraulic properties of alpine aquifers from the propagation of diurnal snowmelt signals. *Water Resources Research*, 53(5), 4271–4285. https://doi.org/10.1002/2016WR019651

Lackner, G., Domine, F., Nadeau, D. F., Parent, A.-C., Anctil, F., Lafaysse, M., & Dumont, M. (2022). On the energy budget of a low-Arctic snowpack. *The Cryosphere*, 16(1), 127–142. https://doi.org/10.5194/tc-16-127-2022

Ladd, C., Crawford, W. R., Harpold, C. E., Johnson, W. K., Kachel, N. B., Stabeno, P. J., & Whitney, F. (2009). A synoptic survey of young mesoscale eddies in the Eastern Gulf of Alaska. *Physical and Biological Patterns, Processes, and Variability in the Northeast Pacific.*, 56(24), 2460–2473. https://doi.org/10.1016/j.dsr2.2009.02.007

Lafreniere, M. J., Blais, J. M., Sharp, M. J., & Schindler, D. W. (2006). Organochlorine Pesticide and Polychlorinated Biphenyl Concentrations in Snow, Snowmelt, and Runoff at Bow Lake, Alberta. *Environmental Science & Technology*, 40(16), 4909–4915. https://doi.org/10.1021/es060237g

Lafreniere, M., & Sharp, M. (2005). A Comparison of Solute Fluxes and Sources from Glacial and Non-Glacial Catchments over Contrasting Melt Seasons. *Hydrological Processes*, 19(15), 2991–3012. https://doi.org/10.1002/hyp.5812

Lamb, C., Willson, R., Richter, C., Owens-Beck, N., Napoleon, J., Muir, B., McNay, R. S., Lavis, E., Hebblewhite, M., Giguere, L., Dokkie, T., Boutin, S., & Ford, A. T. (2022). Indigenous-Led Conservation: Pathways to Recovery for the Nearly Extirpated Klinse-Za Mountain Caribou. *Ecological Applications* 32(5). https://doi.org/10.1002/eap.2581

Lamontagne, M., Halchuk, S., Cassidy, J. F., & Rogers, G. C. (2008). Significant Canadian Earthquakes of the Period 1600–2006. *Seismological Research Letters*, 79(2), 211–223. https://doi.org/10.1785/gssrl.79.2.211

Landry, R., Assani, A. A., Biron, S., & Quessy, J.-F. (2014). The Management Modes of Seasonal Floods and Their Impact on the Relationship Between Climate and Streamflow Downstream from Dams in Quebec (Canada). *River Research and Applications*, 30(3), 287–298. https://doi.org/10.1002/rra.2644

Landsman, S. J., Samways, K. M., Hayden, B., Knysh, K. M., & Heuvel, M. R. van den. (2018). Assimilation of marine-derived nutrients from anadromous Rainbow Smelt in an eastern North American riverine food web: Evidence from stable-isotope and fatty acid analysis. *Freshwater Science*, 37(4), 747–759. https://doi.org/10.1086/700598

Langs, L. E., Petrone, R. M., & Pomeroy, J. W. (2021). Sub-alpine forest water use behaviour and evapotranspiration during two hydrologically contrasting growing seasons in the Canadian Rockies. *Hydrological Processes*, 35(5). https://doi.org/10.1002/hyp.14158

Largeron, C., Dumont, M., Morin, S., Boone, A., Lafaysse, M., Metref, S., Cosme, E., Jonas, T., Winstral, A., & Margulis, S. A. (2020). Toward Snow Cover Estimation in Mountainous Areas Using Modern Data Assimilation Methods: A Review. *Frontiers in Earth Science*, 8, 325. https://www.frontiersin.org/article/10.3389/feart.2020.00325

Latulippe, N., & Klenk, N. (2020). Making room and moving over: Knowledge co-production, Indigenous knowledge sovereignty and the politics of global environmental change decision-making. *Current Opinion in Environmental Sustainability*, 42, 7–14. https://doi.org/10.1016/j.cosust.2019.10.010

Lauzon, È., Kneeshaw, D., & Bergeron, Y. (2007). Reconstruction of fire history (1680–2003) in Gaspesian mixedwood boreal forests of eastern Canada. *Forest Ecology and Management*, 244(1–3), 41–49. https://doi.org/10.1016/j.foreco.2007.03.064

Law, K. S., & Stohl, A. (2007). Arctic Air Pollution: Origins and Impacts. *Science*, 315(5818), 1537–1540. https://doi.org/10.1126/science.1137695

Leach, J. A., & Moore, R. D. (2011). Stream temperature dynamics in two hydrogeomorphically distinct reaches. *Hydrological Processes*, 25(5), 679–690. https://doi.org/10.1002/hyp.7854

Lehnherr, I., St. Louis, V. L., Sharp, M., Gardner, A. S., Smol, J. P., Schiff, S. L., Muir, D. C. G., Mortimer, C. A., Michelutti, N., Tarnocai, C., St. Pierre, K. A., Emmerton, C. A., Wiklund, J. A., Köck, G., Lamoureux, S. F., & Talbot, C. H. (2018). The world's largest High Arctic lake responds rapidly to climate warming. *Nature Communications*, 9(1), 1290. https://doi.org/10.1038/s41467-018-03685-z

Leonard, E. M. (1986). Use of lacustrine sedimentary sequences as indicators of Holocene glacial history, Banff National Park, Alberta, Canada. *Quaternary Research*, 26(2), 218–231. https://doi.org/10.1016/0033-5894(86)90106-7

Lesins, G., Duck, T. J., & Drummond, J. R. (2010). Climate trends at Eureka in the Canadian high arctic. *Atmosphere-Ocean*, 48(2), 59–80. https://doi.org/10.3137/AO1103.2010

Levi, T., Hilderbrand, G. V., Hocking, M. D., Quinn, T. P., White, K. S., Adams, M. S., Armstrong, J. B., Crupi, A. P., Darimont, C. T., Deacy, W., Gilbert, S. L., Ripple, W. J., Shakeri, Y. N., Wheat, R. E., & Wilmers, C. C. (2020). Community Ecology and Conservation of Bear-Salmon Ecosystems. *Frontiers in Ecology and Evolution*, 8. https://www.frontiersin.org/article/10.3389/fevo.2020.513304

Lewkowicz, A., & Ednie, M. (2004). Probability Mapping of Mountain Permafrost Using the Bts Method, Wolf Creek, Yukon Territory, Canada. *Permafrost and Periglacial Processes*, 15(1), 67–80. https://doi.org/10.1002/ppp.480

Lewkowicz, A. G., & Bonnaventure, P. R. (2008). Interchangeability of Mountain Permafrost Probability Models, Northwest Canada. *Permafrost and Periglacial Processes*, 19(1), 49–62. https://doi.org/10.1002/ppp.612

Libois, Q., & Blanchet, J.-P. (2017). Added value of farinfrared radiometry for remote sensing of ice clouds. *Journal of Geophysical Research: Atmospheres*, 122(12), 6541–6564. https://doi.org/10.1002/2016JD026423

Lievens, H., Demuzere, M., Marshall, H.-P., Reichle, R. H., Brucker, L., Brangers, I., de Rosnay, P., Dumont, M., Girotto, M., Immerzeel, W. W., Jonas, T., Kim, E. J., Koch, I., Marty, C., Saloranta, T., Schöber, J., & De Lannoy, G. J. M. (2019). Snow depth variability in the Northern Hemisphere mountains observed from space. *Nature Communications*, 10(1), 4629. https://doi.org/10.1038/s41467-019-12566-y

Lilbaek, G., & Pomeroy, J. W. (2007). Modelling Enhanced Infiltration of Snowmelt Ions into Frozen Soil. *Hydrological Processes*, 21(19), 2641–2649. https://doi.org/10.1002/hyp.6788

Lin, Z., Schemenauer, R., Schuepp, P., Barthakur, N., & Kennedy, G. (1997). Airborne Metal Pollutants in High Elevation Forests of Southern Quebec, Canada, and Their Likely Source Regions. *Agricultural and Forest Meteorology*, 87(1), 41–54. https://doi.org/10.1016/S0168-1923(97)00005-1

Liu, A. Q., Mooney, C., Szeto, K., Theriault, J. M., Kochtubajda, B., Stewart, R. E., Boodoo, S., Goodson, R., Li, Y., & Pomeroy, J. (2016). The June 2013 Alberta Catastrophic Flooding Event: Part 1 Climatological Aspects and Hydrometeorological Features. *Hydrological Processes*, 30(26), 4899–4916. https://doi.org/10.1002/hyp.10906

Loewen, C. J. G., Strecker, A. L., Larson, G. L., Vogel, A., Fischer, J. M., & Vinebrooke, R. D. (2019). Macroecological Drivers of Zooplankton Communities across the Mountains of Western North America. *Ecography*, 42(4), 791–803. https://doi.org/10.1111/ecog.03817

Loukas, A., Vasiliades, L., & Dalezios, N. (2000). Flood Producing Mechanisms Identification in Southern British Columbia, Canada. *Journal of Hydrology*, 227(44200), 218–235. https://doi.org/10.1016/S0022-1694(99)00182-1

Luckman, B. H. (2000). The Little Ice Age in the Canadian Rockies. *Geomorphology*, 32(44259), 357–384. https://doi.org/10.1016/S0169-555X(99)00104-X

Luckman, B. H., & Crockett, K. J. (1978). Distribution and characteristics of rock glaciers in the southern part of Jasper National Park, Alberta. *Canadian Journal of Earth Sciences*, 15(4), 540–550. https://doi.org/10.1139/e78-060

Ludwin, R. S., Smits, G. J., & et al. (2007). Folklore and earthquakes: Native American oral traditions from Cascadia compared with written traditions from Japan. *Myths and Geology*, 273(1), 67–94.

Lundquist, J., Hughes, M., Gutmann, E., & Kapnick, S. (2019). Our Skill in Modeling Mountain Rain and Snow is Bypassing the Skill of Our Observational Networks. *Bulletin of the American Meteorological Society*, 100(12), 2473–2490. https://doi.org/10.1175/BAMS-D-19-0001.1

Lv, Z., & Pomeroy, J. W. (2019). Detecting Intercepted Snow on Mountain Needleleaf Forest Canopies Using Satellite Remote Sensing. *Remote Sensing of Environment*, 231(111222). https://doi.org/10.1016/j.rse.2019.111222

Lv, Z., & Pomeroy, J. W. (2020). Assimilating Snow Observations to Snow Interception Process Simulations. *Hydrological Processes*, 34(10), 2229–2246. https://doi.org/10.1002/hyp.13720

Macciotta, R., Martin, C. D., Edwards, T., Cruden, D. M., & Keegan, T. (2015). Quantifying Weather Conditions for Rock Fall Hazard Management. *Georisk*, 9(3), 171–186. https://doi.org/10.1080/17499518.2015.1061673

Macdonald, M. K., Pomeroy, J. W., & Essery, R. L. H. (2018). Water and Energy Fluxes over Northern Prairies as Affected by Chinook Winds and Winter Precipitation.

Agricultural and Forest Meteorology, 248, 372–385. https://doi.org/10.1016/j.agrformet.2017.10.025

Macdonald, M. K., Pomeroy, J. W., & Pietroniro, A. (2009). Parameterizing Redistribution and Sublimation of Blowing Snow for Hydrological Models: Tests in a Mountainous Subarctic Catchment. *Hydrological Processes, 23*(18), 2570–2583. https://doi.org/10.1002/hyp.7356

Macdonald, R. J., Boon, S., & Byrne, J. M. (2014). A Process-Based Stream Temperature Modelling Approach for Mountain Regions. *Journal of Hydrology, 511*, 920–931. https://doi.org/10.1016/j.jhydrol.2014.02.009

Macdonald, R. J., Boon, S., Byrne, J. M., & Silins, U. (2014). A Comparison of Surface and Subsurface Controls on Summer Temperature in a Headwater Stream. *Hydrological Processes, 28*(4), 2338–2347. https://doi.org/10.1002/hyp.9756

MacHattie, L. B. (1968). Kananaskis Valley Winds in Summer. *Journal of Applied Meteorology, 7*(3), 348–352. https://doi.org/10.1175/1520-0450(1968)007<0348:KVWIS>2.0.CO;2

MacInnis, J., De Silva, A. O., Lehnherr, I., Muir, D. C. G., St. Pierre, K. A., St. Louis, V. L., & Spencer, C. (2022). Investigation of perfluoroalkyl substances in proglacial rivers and permafrost seep in a high Arctic watershed. *Environmental Science: Processes & Impacts 24*(1), 42–51. https://doi.org/10.1039/D1EM00349F

Mackay, H., Plunkett, G., Jensen, B. J. L., Aubry, T. J., Corona, C., Kim, W. M., Toohey, M., Sigl, M., Stoffel, M., Anchukaitis, K. J., Raible, C., Bolton, M. S. M., Manning, J. G., Newfield, T. P., Di Cosmo, N., Ludlow, F., Kostick, C., Yang, Z., Coyle McClung, L., … Swindles, G. T. (2022). The 852/3 CE Mount Churchill eruption: Examining the potential climatic and societal impacts and the timing of the Medieval Climate Anomaly in the North Atlantic region. *Climate of the Past, 18*(6), 1475–1508. https://doi.org/10.5194/cp-18-1475-2022

Mahat, V., Anderson, A., & Silins, U. (2015). Modelling of Wildfire Impacts on Catchment Hydrology Applied to Two Case Studies. *Hydrological Processes, 29*(17), 3687–3698. https://doi.org/10.1002/hyp.10462

Mahat, V., Silins, U., & Anderson, A. (2016). Effects of Wildfire on the Catchment Hydrology in Southwest Alberta. *Catena, 147*, 51–60. https://doi.org/10.1016/j.catena.2016.06.040

Mahdianpari, M., Brisco, B., Granger, J. E., Mohammadimanesh, F., Salehi, B., Banks, S., Homayouni, S., Bourgeau-Chavez, L., & Weng, Q. (2020). The Second Generation Canadian Wetland Inventory Map at 10 Meters Resolution Using Google Earth Engine. *Canadian Journal of Remote Sensing, 46*(3), 360–375. https://doi.org/10.1080/07038992.2020.1802584

Malone, S. J., McClelland, W. C., Gosen, W. von, & Piepjohn, K. (2019). Detrital zircon U-Pb and Lu-Hf analysis of Paleozoic sedimentary rocks from the Pearya terrane and Ellesmerian Fold Belt (northern Ellesmere Island):

A comparison with Circum-Arctic datasets and their implications on terrane tectonics. In K. Piepjohn, J. V. Strauss, L. Reinhardt, & W. C. McClelland, *Circum-Arctic Structural Events: Tectonic Evolution of the Arctic Margins and Trans-Arctic Links with Adjacent Orogens* (pp. 231–254). Geological Society of America. https://doi.org/10.1130/2018.2541(12)

Marks, D., Kimball, J., Tingey, D., & Link, T. (1998). The sensitivity of snowmelt processes to climate conditions and forest cover during rain-on-snow: A case study of the 1996 Pacific Northwest flood. *Hydrological Processes, 12*(10–11), 1569–1587. https://doi.org/10.1002/(sici)1099-1085(199808/09)12:10/11<1569::aid-hyp682>3.0.co;2-l

Marr, K. L., Allen, G. A., & Hebda, R. J. (2008). Refugia in the Cordilleran ice sheet of western North America: Chloroplast DNA diversity in the Arctic–alpine plant Oxyria digyna. *Journal of Biogeography, 35*(7), 1323–1334. https://doi.org/10.1111/j.1365-2699.2007.01879.x

Marsh, C. B., Pomeroy, J. W., & Spiteri, R. J. (2012). Implications of Mountain Shading on Calculating Energy for Snowmelt Using Unstructured Triangular Meshes. *Hydrological Processes, 26*(12), 1767–1778. https://doi.org/10.1002/hyp.9329

Marsh, C. B., Pomeroy, J. W., Spiteri, R. J., & Wheater, H. S. (2019). A Finite Volume Blowing Snow Model for Use with Variable Resolution Meshes. *Water Resources Research, 56*(2). https://doi.org/10.1029/2019wr025307

Marsh, C. B., Pomeroy, J. W., & Wheater, H. S. (2020). The Canadian Hydrological Model (CHM) v1.0: A multi-scale, multi-extent, variable-complexity hydrological model—design and overview. *Geoscientific Model Development, 13*(1), 225–247. https://doi.org/10.5194/gmd-13-225-2020

Marshall, S. J. (2014). Meltwater Run-Off from Haig Glacier, Canadian Rocky Mountains, 2002–2013. *Hydrology and Earth System Sciences, 18*(12), 5181–5200. https://doi.org/10.5194/hess-18-5181-2014

Marshall, S. J., & Miller, K. (2020). Seasonal and Interannual Variability of Melt-Season Albedo at Haig Glacier, Canadian Rocky Mountains. *The Cryosphere, 14*(10), 3249–3267. https://doi.org/10.5194/tc-14-3249-2020

Marshall, S. J., Sharp, M. J., Burgess, D. O., & Anslow, F. S. (2007). Near-surface-temperature lapse rates on the Prince of Wales Icefield, Ellesmere Island, Canada: Implications for regional downscaling of temperature. *International Journal of Climatology, 27*(3), 385–398. https://doi.org/10.1002/joc.1396

Marshall, S. J., Tarasov, L., Clarke, G. K. C., & Peltier, W. R. (2000). Glaciological reconstruction of the Laurentide Ice Sheet: Physical processes and modelling challenges. *Canadian Journal of Earth Sciences, 37*(5), 769–793. https://doi.org/10.1139/e99-113

Marshall, S. J., White, E. C., Demuth, M. N., Bolch, T., Wheate, R., Menounos, B., Beedle, M. J., & Shea, J. M. (2011). Glacier Water Resources on the Eastern Slopes of the Canadian Rocky Mountains. *Canadian Water Resources Journal*, 36(2), 109–133. https://doi.org/10.4296/cwrj3602823

Martens, A. M., Silins, U., Proctor, H. C., Williams, C. H. S., Wagner, M. J., Emelko, M. B., & Stone, M. (2019). Long-Term Impact of Severe Wildfire and Post-Wildfire Salvage Logging on Macroinvertebrate Assemblage Structure in Alberta's Rocky Mountains. *International Journal of Wildland Fire*, 28(10), 738–749. https://doi.org/10.1071/WF18177

Martins, T., Rayner, N., Corrigan, D., & Kremer, P. (2022). Regional geology and tectonic framework of the Southern Indian domain, Trans-Hudson orogen, Manitoba. *Canadian Journal of Earth Sciences*, 59(6), 371–388. https://doi.org/10.1139/cjes-2020-0142

Matheussen, B., Kirschbaum, R. L., Goodman, I. A., O'Donnell, G. M., & Lettenmaier, D. P. (2000). Effects of land cover change on streamflow in the interior Columbia River Basin (USA and Canada). *Hydrological Processes*, 14(5), 867–885. https://doi.org/10.1002/(SICI)1099-1085(20000415)14:5<867::AID-HYP975>3.0.CO;2-5

Mathews, W. (1952). Mount Garibaldi, a Supraglacial Pleistocene Volcano in South-Western British-Columbia. *American Journal of Science*, 250(2), 81–103. https://doi.org/10.2475/ajs.250.2.81

Mathews, W. H. (1991). *Physiographic Evolution of the Canadian Cordillera*. https://doi.org/10.1130/DNAG-GNA-G2.403

Mazzotti, S., & Hyndman, R. D. (2002). Yakutat collision and strain transfer across the northern Canadian Cordillera. *Geology (Boulder)*, 30(6), 495–498. GeoRef. https://doi.org/10.1130/0091-7613(2002)030<0495:YCASTA>2.0.CO;2

Mccartney, S., Carey, S., & Pomeroy, J. (2006). Intra-Basin Variability of Snowmelt Water Balance Calculations in a Subarctic Catchment. *Hydrological Processes*, 20(4), 1001–1016. https://doi.org/10.1002/hyp.6125

Mcclymont, A. F., Hayashi, M., Bentley, L. R., Muir, D., & Ernst, E. (2010). Groundwater Flow and Storage within an Alpine Meadow-Talus Complex. *Hydrology and Earth System Sciences*, 14(6), 859–872. https://doi.org/10.5194/hess-14-859-2010

McCormack, J. E., Huang, H., Knowles, L. L., Gillespie, R., & Clague, D. (2009). Sky Islands. *Encyclopedia of Islands*, University of California Press, 841–843.

McDowell, G., & Guo, J. (2021). A Nationally Coherent Characterization and Quantification of Mountain Systems in Canada. *Mountain Research and Development*, 41(2), R21–R31. https://doi.org/10.1659/MRD-JOURNAL-D-20-00071.1

McDowell, G., & Hanly, K. (2022). The state of mountain research in Canada. *Journal of Mountain Science*, 19(10), 3013–3025. https://doi.org/10.1007/s11629-022-7569-1

Mcewen, J., Fredeen, A. L., Pypker, T. G., Foord, V. N., Black, T. A., Jassal, R. S., & Nesic, Z. (2020). Carbon Storage Recovery in Surviving Lodgepole Pine (Pinus Contorta Var. Latifolia) 11 Years after Mountain Pine Beetle Attack in Northern British Columbia, Canada. *Canadian Journal of Forest Research*, 50(12), 1383–1390. https://doi.org/10.1139/cjfr-2019-0394

McKnight, E. A., Swanson, H., Brahney, J., & Hik, D. S. (2021). The physical and chemical limnology of Yukon's largest lake, Lhù'ààn Mân' (Kluane Lake), prior to the 2016 'A'äy Chù' diversion. *Arctic Science*, 7(3), 655–678. https://doi.org/10.1139/as-2020-0012

Mcmahon, A., & Moore, R. D. (2017). Influence of Turbidity and Aeration on the Albedo of Mountain Streams. *Hydrological Processes*, 31(25), 4477–4491. https://doi.org/10.1002/hyp.11370

McMechan, M. E., Root, K. G., Simony, P. S., & Pattison, D. R. M. (2020). Nailed to the craton: Stratigraphic continuity across the southeastern Canadian Cordillera with tectonic implications for ribbon continent models. *Geology*, 49(1), 101–105. https://doi.org/10.1130/G48060.1

McMillan, A. D., & Hutchinson, I. (2002). When the Mountain Dwarfs Danced: Aboriginal Traditions of Paleoseismic Events along the Cascadia Subduction Zone of Western North America. *Ethnohistory*, 49(1), 41–68.

Mcnaught, A., Schindler, D., Parker, B., Paul, A., Anderson, R., Donald, D., & Agbeti, M. (1999). Restoration of the Food Web of an Alpine Lake Following Fish Stocking. *Limnology and Oceanography*, 44(1), 127–136. https://doi.org/10.4319/lo.1999.44.1.0127

McPhee, J. (1981). *Basin and Range*. Farrar, Straus & Giroux.

Mee, J. A., Robins, G. L., & Post, J. R. (2018). Patterns of Fish Species Distributions Replicated across Three Parallel Rivers Suggest Biotic Zonation in Response to a Longitudinal Temperature Gradient. *Ecology of Freshwater Fish*, 27(1), 44–61. https://doi.org/10.1111/eff.12322

Mekis, E., Stewart, R. E., Theriault, J. M., Kochtubajda, B., Bonsal, B. R., & Liu, Z. (2020). Near-0°C surface temperature and precipitation type patterns across Canada. *Hydrology and Earth System Sciences*, 24(4), 1741–1761. https://doi.org/10.5194/hess-24-1741-2020

Mekis, É., & Vincent, L. A. (2011). An Overview of the Second Generation Adjusted Daily Precipitation Dataset for Trend Analysis in Canada. *Atmosphere-Ocean*, 49(2), 163–177. https://doi.org/10.1080/07055900.2011.583910

Menounos, B., Hugonnet, R., Shean, D., Gardner, A., Howat, I., Berthier, E., Pelto, B., Tennant, C., Shea, J., Noh, M.-J., Brun, F., & Dehecq, A. (2019). Heterogeneous Changes in Western North American Glaciers Linked to Decadal Variability in Zonal Wind Strength. *Geophysical Research Letters*, 46(1), 200–209. https://doi.org/10.1029/2018GL080942

Menounos, B., Osborn, G., Clague, J. J., & Luckman, B. H. (2009). Latest Pleistocene and Holocene Glacier Fluctuations in Western Canada. *Quaternary Science Reviews*, 28(21–22), 2049–2074. https://doi.org/10.1016/j.quascirev.2008.10.018

Menounos, B., Pelto, B., Fleming, S., Moore, R. D., Weber, F., & Hutchinson, D. (2020). *Glaciers in the Canadian Columbia Basin* [Technical Report]. Canadian Columbia Basin Glacier and Snow Research Network. https://ourtrust.org/wp-content/uploads/downloads/2020-03_Glaciers-Canadian-ColumbiaBasin-Technical-Full-Report_FINAL.pdf

Menounos, B., Schiefer, E., & Slaymaker, O. (2006). Nested Temporal Suspended Sediment Yields, Green Lake Basin, British Columbia, Canada. *Geomorphology*, *79*(44198), 114–129. https://doi.org/10.1016/j.geomorph.2005.09.020

Michol, K. A., Russell, J. K., & Andrews, G. D. M. (2008). Welded Block and Ash Flow Deposits from Mount Meager, British Columbia, Canada. *Journal of Volcanology and Gemal Research*, *169*(44259), 121–144. https://doi.org/10.1016/j.jvolgeores.2007.08.010

Miller, G. H., Bradley, R. S., & Andrews, J. T. (1975). The Glaciation Level and Lowest Equilibrium Line Altitude in the High Canadian Arctic: Maps and Climatic Interpretation. *Arctic and Alpine Research*, *7*(2), 155–168. https://doi.org/10.1080/00040851.1975.12003819

Miller, G. H., Lehman, S. J., Refsnider, K. A., Southon, J. R., & Zhong, Y. (2013). Unprecedented recent summer warmth in Arctic Canada. *Geophysical Research Letters*, *40*(21), 5745–5751. https://doi.org/10.1002/2013GL057188

Milner, A. M., Brittain, J. E., Castella, E., & Petts, G. E. (2001). Trends of macroinvertebrate community structure in glacier-fed rivers in relation to environmental conditions: A synthesis. *Freshwater Biology*, *46*(12), 1833–1847. https://doi.org/10.1046/j.1365-2427.2001.00861.x

Milner, A. M., Khamis, K., Battin, T. J., Brittain, J. E., Barrand, N. E., Füreder, L., Cauvy-Fraunié, S., Gíslason, G. M., Jacobsen, D., Hannah, D. M., Hodson, A. J., Hood, E., Lencioni, V., Ólafsson, J. S., Robinson, C. T., Tranter, M., & Brown, L. E. (2017). Glacier shrinkage driving global changes in downstream systems. *Proceedings of the National Academy of Sciences of the United States of America*, *114*(37), 9770–9778. https://doi.org/10.1073/pnas.1619807114

Milrad, S. M., Gyakum, J. R., & Atallah, E. H. (2015). A Meteorological Analysis of the 2013 Alberta Flood: Antecedent Large-Scale Flow Pattern and Synoptic-Dynamic Characteristics. *Monthly Weather Review*, *143*(7), 2817–2841. https://doi.org/10.1175/MWR-D-14-00236.1

Mo, R., Brugman, M. M., Milbrandt, J. A., Goosen, J., Geng, Q., Emond, C., Bau, J., & Erfani, A. (2019). Impacts of Hydrometeor Drift on Orographic Precipitation: Two Case Studies of Landfalling Atmospheric Rivers in British Columbia, Canada. *Weather and Forecasting*, *34*(5), 1211–1237. https://doi.org/10.1175/WAF-D-18-0176.1

Mochnacz, N. J., Mackenzie, D. I., Koper, N., Docker, M. F., & Isaak, D. J. (2021). Fringe effects: Detecting bull trout (salvelinus confluentus) at distributional boundaries in a montane watershed. *Canadian Journal of Fisheries and Aquatic Sciences*, *78*(8), 1030–1044. https://doi.org/10.1139/cjfas-2020-0219

Molnar, P., & England, P. (1990). Late Cenozoic uplift of mountain ranges and global climate change: Chicken or egg? *Nature*, *346*(6279), Article 6279. https://doi.org/10.1038/346029a0

Mood, B. J., & Smith, D. J. (2015). Holocene Glacier Activity in the British Columbia Coast Mountains, Canada. *Quaternary Science Reviews*, *128*, 14–36. https://doi.org/10.1016/j.quascirev.2015.09.002

Moodie, D. W., Catchpole, A. J. W., & Abel, K. (1992). Northern Athapaskan Oral Traditions and the White River Volcano. *Ethnohistory*, *39*(2), 148–171.

Moody, Megan. (2008). *Eulachon past and present* [University of Victoria]. http://nuxalk.net/media/eulachon_moody.pdf

Moore, R. D. (1992). The Influence of Glacial Cover on the Variability of Annual Runoff, Coast Mountains, British Columbia, Canada. *Canadian Water Resources Journal*, *17*(2), 101–109. https://doi.org/10.4296/cwrj1702101

Moore, R. D., Pelto, B., Menounos, B., & Hutchinson, D. (2020). Detecting the Effects of Sustained Glacier Wastage on Streamflow in Variably Glacierized Catchments. *Frontiers in Earth Science*, *8*(May), 136. https://doi.org/10.3389/feart.2020.00136

Moore, R. D., Spittlehouse, D. L., & Story, A. (2005). Riparian Microclimate and Stream Temperature Response to Forest Harvesting: A Review. *Journal of the American Water Resources Association*, *41*(4), 813–834.

Moore, R., & Demuth, M. (2001). Mass Balance and Streamflow Variability at Place Glacier, Canada, in Relation to Recent Climate Fluctuations. *Hydrological Processes*, *15*(18), 3473–3486. https://doi.org/10.1002/hyp.1030

Morrison, A., Westbrook, C. J., & Bedard-Haughn, A. (2014). Distribution of Canadian Rocky Mountain Wetlands Impacted by Beaver. *Wetlands*, *35*(1), 95–104. https://doi.org/10.1007/s13157-014-0595-1

Mortezapour, M., Menounos, B., Jackson, P. L., Erler, A. R., & Pelto, B. M. (2020). The Role of Meteorological Forcing and Snow Model Complexity in Winter Glacier Mass Balance Estimation, Columbia River Basin, Canada. *Hydrological Processes*, *34*(25), 5085–5103. https://doi.org/10.1002/hyp.13929

Moser, K. A., Baron, J. S., Brahney, J., Oleksy, I. A., Saros, J. E., Hundey, E. J., Sadro, S., Kopáček, J., Sommaruga, R., Kainz, M. J., Strecker, A. L., Chandra, S., Walters, D. M., Preston, D. L., Michelutti, N., Lepori, F., Spaulding, S. A., Christianson, K. R., Melack, J. M., & Smol, J. P. (2019). Mountain lakes: Eyes on global environmental change. *Global and Planetary Change*, *178*, 77–95. https://doi.org/10.1016/j.gloplacha.2019.04.001

Mott, R., Vionnet, V., & Grünewald, T. (2018). The Seasonal Snow Cover Dynamics: Review on Wind-Driven Coupling Processes. *Frontiers in Earth Science*, *6*, 197. https://doi.org/10.3389/feart.2018.00197

Mudryk, L. R., Derksen, C., Howell, S., Laliberté, F., Thackeray, C., Sospedra-Alfonso, R., Vionnet, V., Kushner, P. J., & Brown, R. (2018). Canadian snow and sea ice: Historical trends and projections. *The Cryosphere*, *12*(4), 1157–1176. https://doi.org/10.5194/tc-12-1157-2018

Mudryk, L. R., Derksen, C., Kushner, P. J., & Brown, R. (2015). Characterization of Northern Hemisphere Snow Water Equivalent Datasets, 1981–2010. *Journal of Climate*, *28*(20), 8037–8051. https://doi.org/10.1175/JCLI-D-15-0229.1

Muhlfeld, C. C., Cline, T. J., Giersch, J. J., Peitzsch, E., Florentine, C., Jacobsen, D., & Hotaling, S. (2020). Specialized meltwater biodiversity persists despite widespread deglaciation. *Proceedings of the National Academy of Sciences*, *117*(22), 12208–12214. https://doi.org/10.1073/pnas.2001697117

Müller, F., & Barr, W. (1966). Postglacial Isostatic Movement in Northeastern Devon Island, Canadian Arctic Archipelago. *Arctic*, *19*(3), 263–269.

Müller, R.D., Zahirovic, S., Williams, S.E., Cannon, J., Seton, M., Bower, D.J., Tetley, M.G., Heine, C., Le Breton, E., Liu, S. & Russell, S.H., 2019. A global plate model including lithospheric deformation along major rifts and orogens since the Triassic. *Tectonics*, 38(6), 1884-1907. https://doi.org/10.1029/2018TC005462

Munn, R. E., & Storr, D. (1967). Meteorological Studies in the Marmot Creek Watershed, Alberta, Canada, in August 1965. *Water Resources Research*, *3*(3), 713–722. https://doi.org/10.1029/WR003i003p00713

Munro, D. (1991). A Surface-Energy Exchange Model of Glacier Melt and Net Mass Balance. *International Journal of Climatology*, *11*(6), 689–700.

Murphy, C. A., Thompson, P. L., & Vinebrooke, R. D. (2010). Assessing the Sensitivity of Alpine Lakes and Ponds to Nitrogen Deposition in the Canadian Rocky Mountains. *Hydrobiologia*, *648*(1), 83–90. https://doi.org/10.1007/s10750-010-0146-6

Musselman, K. N., Lehner, F., Ikeda, K., Clark, M. P., Prein, A. F., Liu, C., Barlage, M., & Rasmussen, R. (2018). Projected Increases and Shifts in Rain-on-Snow Flood Risk over Western North America. *Nature Climate Change*, *8*(9), 808–812. https://doi.org/10.1038/s41558-018-0236-4

Naficy, C., Sala, A., Keeling, E. G., Graham, J., & DeLuca, T. H. (2010). Interactive effects of historical logging and fire exclusion on ponderosa pine forest structure in the northern Rockies. *Ecological Applications*, *20*(7), 1851–1864. https://doi.org/10.1890/09-0217.1

Nagy-Reis, M., Dickie, M., Calvert, A. M., Hebblewhite, M., Hervieux, D., Seip, D. R., Gilbert, S. L., Venter, O., DeMars, C., Boutin, S., & Serrouya, R. (2021). Habitat loss accelerates for the endangered woodland caribou in western Canada. *Conservation Science and Practice*, *3*(7), e437. https://doi.org/10.1111/csp2.437

NatureServe Explorer. (2023). https://explorer.natureserve.org/

Nawri, N., & Stewart, R. E. (2008). Channelling of high-latitude boundary-layer flow. *Nonlinear Processes in Geophysics*, *15*(1), 33–52. https://doi.org/10.5194/npg-15-33-2008

Naz, B. S., Frans, C. D., Clarke, G. K. C., Burns, P., & Lettenmaier, D. P. (2014). Modeling the effect of glacier recession on streamflow response using a coupled glacio-hydrological model. *Hydrology and Earth System Sciences*, 18(2), 787–802.

Nazemi, A., Wheater, H. S., Chun, K. P., Bonsal, B., & Mekonnen, M. (2017). Forms and Drivers of Annual Streamflow Variability in the Headwaters of Canadian Prairies during the 20th Century. *Hydrological Processes*, *31*(1), 221–239. https://doi.org/10.1002/hyp.11036

Newton, B. W., Bonsal, B. R., Edwards, T. W. D., Prowse, T. D., & Mcgregor, G. R. (2019). Atmospheric Drivers of Winter Above-Freezing Temperatures and Associated Rainfall in Western Canada. *International Journal of Climatology*, *39*(15), 5655–5671. https://doi.org/10.1002/joc.6178

Nkemdirim, L. (1991). Chinooks and Winter Evaporation. *Theoretical and Applied Climatology*, *43*(3), 129–136. https://doi.org/10.1007/BF00867470

Nkemdirim, L. (1996). Canada'S Chinook Belt. *International Journal of Climatology*, *16*(4), 441–462. https://doi.org/10.1002/(SICI)1097-0088(199604)16:4<441::AID-JOC21>3.0.CO;2-T

Nkemdirim, L. (1997). On the Frequency and Sequencing of Chinook Events. *Physical Geography*, *18*(2), 101–113. https://doi.org/10.1080/02723646.1997.10642610

Oberndorfer, E. (2020). What the Blazes!? A People's History of Fire in Labrador. *Journal of the North Atlantic*, *2020*(40), 1–16. https://doi.org/10.3721/037.006.4001

Obu, J., Westermann, S., Bartsch, A., Berdnikov, N., Christiansen, H. H., Dashtseren, A., Delaloye, R., Elberling, B., Etzelmüller, B., Kholodov, A., Khomutov, A., Kääb, A., Leibman, M. O., Lewkowicz, A. G., Panda, S. K., Romanovsky, V., Way, R. G., Westergaard-Nielsen, A., Wu, T., ... Zou, D. (2019). Northern Hemisphere permafrost map based on TTOP modelling for 2000–2016 at 1 km 2 scale. *Earth-Science Reviews*, 193, 299–316. https://doi.org/10.1016/j.earscirev.2019.04.023

Ochwat, N. E., Marshall, S. J., Moorman, B. J., Criscitiello, A. S., & Copland, L. (2021). Evolution of the firn pack of Kaskawulsh Glacier, Yukon: Meltwater effects, densification, and the development of a perennial firn aquifer. *Cryosphere*, 15(4), 2021–2040. https://doi.org/10.5194/tc-15-2021-2021

Ohmura, A. (1982). Climate and energy balance on the arctic tundra. *Journal of Climatology*, *2*(1), 65–84. https://doi.org/10.1002/joc.3370020106

Olofsson, M., Önskog, T., & Lundström, N. L. P. (2022). Management strategies for run-of-river hydropower plants: An optimal switching approach. *Optimization and Engineering*, 23(3), 1707–1731. https://doi.org/10.1007/s11081-021-09683-3

Olsen, T. (2021, November 17). Abbotsford's flood crisis could revive Sumas Lake. *Fraser Valley Current*. https://fvcurrent.com/article/sumas-lake-flooding-history/

O'Neill, H. B., Burn, C. R., Kokelj, S. V., & Lantz, T. C. (2015). 'Warm' Tundra: Atmospheric and Near-Surface Ground Temperature Inversions Across an Alpine Treeline in Continuous Permafrost, Western Arctic, Canada.

Permafrost and Periglacial Processes, 26(2), 103–118. https://doi.org/10.1002/ppp.1838

Østrem, G., & Brugman, M. (1993). *Glacier mass-balance measurements: A manual for field and office work*. National Hydrology Research Institute.

Palm, E. C., Fluker, S., Nesbitt, H. K., Jacob, A. L., & Hebblewhite, M. (2020). The long road to protecting critical habitat for species at risk: The case of southern mountain woodland caribou. *Conservation Science and Practice, 2*(7), e219. https://doi.org/10.1111/csp2.219

Parker, B. R., Vinebrooke, R. D., & Schindler, D. W. (2008). Recent Climate Extremes Alter Alpine Lake Ecosystems. *Proceedings of the National Academy of Sciences of the United States of America, 105*(35), 12927–12931. https://doi.org/10.1073/pnas.0806481105

Parker, B., & Schindler, D. (2006). Cascading Trophic Interactions in an Oligotrophic Species-Poor Alpine Lake. *Ecosystems, 9*(2), 157–166. https://doi.org/10.1007/s10021-004-0016-z

Parker, B., Schindler, D., Donald, D., & Anderson, R. (2001). The Effects of Stocking and Removal of a Nonnative Salmonid on the Plankton of an Alpine Lake. *Ecosystems, 4*(4), 334–345. https://doi.org/10.1007/s10021-001-0015-2

Paznekas, A., & Hayashi, M. (2016). Groundwater Contribution to Winter Streamflow in the Canadian Rockies. *Canadian Water Resources Journal, 41*(4), 484–499. https://doi.org/10.1080/07011784.2015.1060870

Pearce, L. (2003). Disaster Management and Community Planning, and Public Participation: How to Achieve Sustainable Hazard Mitigation. *Natural Hazards, 28*(2), 211–228. https://doi.org/10.1023/A:1022917721797

Pedersen, M. W., Ruter, A., Schweger, C., Friebe, H., Staff, R. A., Kjeldsen, K. K., Mendoza, M. L. Z., Beaudoin, A. B., Zutter, C., Larsen, N. K., Potter, B. A., Nielsen, R., Rainville, R. A., Orlando, L., Meltzer, D. J., Kjær, K. H., & Willerslev, E. (2016). Postglacial viability and colonization in North America's ice-free corridor. *Nature, 537*(7618), Article 7618. https://doi.org/10.1038/nature19085

Pelto, B. M., Maussion, F., Menounos, B., Radić, V., & Zeuner, M. (2020). Bias-Corrected Estimates of Glacier Thickness in the Columbia River Basin, Canada. *American Meteorological Society, 4*(5), 937–953. https://doi.org/10.1175/2010JAMC2315.1

Pelto, B. M., Menounos, B., & Marshall, S. J. (2019). Multi-Year Evaluation of Airborne Geodetic Surveys to Estimate Seasonal Mass Balance, Columbia and Rocky Mountains, Canada. *Cryosphere, 13*(6), 1709–1727. https://doi.org/10.5194/tc-13-1709-2019

Peters, D. L., & Prowse, T. D. (2001). Regulation effects on the lower Peace River, Canada. *Hydrological Processes, 15*(16), 3181–3194. Scopus. https://doi.org/10.1002/hyp.321

Péwé, R., & Brown, T. (1973). Distribution of permafrost in North America and its relationship to the environment: A review, 1963–1973. In *Permafrost: North American

Contribution to the Second International Conference* (Vol. 2, pp. 71–100). National Academies.

Pfeffer, W. T., Arendt, A. A., Bliss, A., Bolch, T., Cogley, J. G., Gardner, A. S., Hagen, J.-O., Hock, R., Kaser, G., Kienholz, C., Miles, E. S., Moholdt, G., Mölg, N., Paul, F., Radić, V., Rastner, P., Raup, B. H., Rich, J., Sharp, M. J., & Consortium, T. R. (2014). The Randolph Glacier Inventory: A globally complete inventory of glaciers. *Journal of Glaciology, 60*(221), 537–552. https://doi.org/10.3189/2014JoG13J176

Pike, R. G. (2010). *Compendium of forest hydrology and geomorphology in British Columbia*. Ministry of Forests and Range.

Pinard, J.-P., Benoit, R., & Wilson, J. D. (2009). Mesoscale Wind Climate Modelling in Steep Mountains. *Atmosphere-Ocean, 47*(1), 63–78. https://doi.org/10.3137/AO922.2009

Pitman, K. J., & Moore, J. W. (2021). The role of large, glaciated tributaries in cooling an important Pacific salmon migration corridor: A study of the Babine River. *Environmental Biology of Fishes, 104*(10), 1263–1277. https://doi.org/10.1007/s10641-021-01152-1

Pitman, K. J., Moore, J. W., Huss, M., Sloat, M. R., Whited, D. C., Beechie, T. J., Brenner, R., Hood, E. W., Milner, A. M., Pess, G. R., Reeves, G. H., & Schindler, D. E. (2021). Glacier retreat creating new Pacific salmon habitat in western North America. *Nature Communications, 12*(1), 6816. https://doi.org/10.1038/s41467-021-26897-2

Pitman, K. J., Moore, J. W., Sloat, M. R., Beaudreau, A. H., Bidlack, A. L., Brenner, R. E., Hood, E. W., Pess, G. R., Mantua, N. J., Milner, A. M., Radić, V., Reeves, G. H., Schindler, D. E., & Whited, D. C. (2020). Glacier Retreat and Pacific Salmon. *BioScience, 70*(3), 220–236. https://doi.org/10.1093/biosci/biaa015

Plamondon, A., Prévost, M., & C. Naud, R. (1984). Accumulation et fonte de la neige en milieux boisé et déboisé. *Géographie physique et Quaternaire, 38*(1), 27–35.

Playfair, J. (1805). Biographical Account of the Late Dr James Hutton, F.R.S. Edin. *Transactions of the Royal Society of Edinburgh, 5*, 71–73.

Poirier, É., Thériault, J. M., & Leriche, M. (2019). Role of Sublimation and Riming in the Precipitation Distribution in the Kananaskis Valley, Alberta, Canada. *Hydrology and Earth System Sciences, 23*(10), 4097–4111. https://doi.org/10.5194/hess-23-4097-2019

Pomeroy, J., Fang, X., & Ellis, C. (2012). Sensitivity of Snowmelt Hydrology in Marmot Creek, Alberta, to Forest Cover Disturbance. *Hydrological Processes, 26*(12), 1892–1905. https://doi.org/10.1002/hyp.9248

Pomeroy, J. W., & Essery, R. L. H. (1999). Turbulent fluxes during blowing snow: Field tests of model sublimation predictions. *Hydrological Processes, 13*(18), 2963–2975. https://doi.org/10.1002/(SICI)1099-1085(19991230)13:18<2963::AID-HYP11>3.0.CO;2-9

Pomeroy, J. W., Fang, X., & Marks, D. G. (2016). The Cold Rain-on-Snow Event of June 2013 in the Canadian Rockies Characteristics and Diagnosis. *Hydrological Processes, 30*(17), 2899–2914. https://doi.org/10.1002/hyp.10905

Pomeroy, J. W., Gray, D. M., Brown, T., Hedstrom, N. R., Quinton, W. L., Granger, R. J., & Carey, S. K. (2007). The Cold Regions Hydrological Process Representation and Model: A Platform for Basing Model Structure on Physical Evidence. *Hydrological Processes*, 21(19), 2650–2667. https://doi.org/10.1002/hyp.6787

Pomeroy, J. W., & Li, L. (2000). Prairie and arctic areal snow cover mass balance using a blowing snow model. *Journal of Geophysical Research: Atmospheres*, 105(D21), 26619–26634. https://doi.org/10.1029/2000JD900149

Pomeroy, J. W., Stewart, R. E., & Whitfield, P. H. (2016). The 2013 Flood Event in the South Saskatchewan and Elk River Basins: Causes, Assessment and Damages. *Canadian Water Resources Journal*, 41(44198), 105–117. https://doi.org/10.1080/07011784.2015.1089190

Power, M. J., Whitlock, C., & Bartlein, P. J. (2011). Postglacial fire, vegetation, and climate history across an elevational gradient in the Northern Rocky Mountains, USA and Canada. *Quaternary Science Reviews*, 30(19–20), 2520–2533. https://doi.org/10.1016/j.quascirev.2011.04.012

Pradhananga, D., Pomeroy, J., Aubry-Wake, C., Munro, D., Shea, J., Demuth, M., Kirat, N., Menounos, B., & Mukherjee, K. (2021). Hydrometeorological, glaciological and geospatial research data from the Peyto Glacier Research Basin in the Canadian Rockies. *Earth System Science Data*, 13(6), 2875–2894. https://doi.org/10.5194/essd-13-2875-2021

Pulliainen, J., Luojus, K., Derksen, C., Mudryk, L., Lemmetyinen, J., Salminen, M., Ikonen, J., Takala, M., Cohen, J., Smolander, T., & Norberg, J. (2020). Patterns and trends of Northern Hemisphere snow mass from 1980 to 2018. *Nature*, 581(7808), Article 7808. https://doi.org/10.1038/s41586-020-2258-0

Qian, Y., Gustafson Jr., W. I., Leung, L. R., & Ghan, S. J. (2009). Effects of soot-induced snow albedo change on snowpack and hydrological cycle in western United States based on Weather Research and Forecasting chemistry and regional climate simulations. *Journal of Geophysical Research: Atmospheres*, 114(D3). https://doi.org/10.1029/2008JD011039

Quick, M. C., & Pipes, A. (1977). U.B.C. Watershed Model. *Hydrological Sciences Bulletin*, 22(1), 153–161. https://doi.org/10.1080/02626667709491701

Radić, V., & Hock, R. (2010). Regional and global volumes of glaciers derived from statistical upscaling of glacier inventory data. *Journal of Geophysical Research: Earth Surface*, 115(F1). https://doi.org/10.1029/2009JF001373

Rand, P. S., Hinch, S. G., Morrison, J., Foreman, M. G. G., MacNutt, M. J., Macdonald, J. S., Healey, M. C., Farrell, A. P., & Higgs, D. A. (2006). Effects of River Discharge, Temperature, and Future Climates on Energetics and Mortality of Adult Migrating Fraser River Sockeye Salmon. *Transactions of the American Fisheries Society*, 135(3), 655–667. https://doi.org/10.1577/T05-023.1

Rango, A. (1993). II. Snow hydrology processes and remote sensing. *Hydrological Processes*, 7(2), 121–138. https://doi.org/10.1002/hyp.3360070204

Rango, A. (1996). Spaceborne remote sensing for snow hydrology applications. *Hydrological Sciences Journal*, 41(4), 477–494. https://doi.org/10.1080/02626669609491521

Rasmussen, J. B., Krimmer, A. N., Paul, A. J., & Hontela, A. (2012). Empirical Relationships between Body Tissue Composition and Bioelectrical Impedance of Brook Trout Salvelinus Fontinalis from a Rocky Mountain Stream. *Journal of Fish Biology*, 80(6), 2317–2327. https://doi.org/10.1111/j.1095-8649.2012.03295.x

Rasmussen, R., Baker, B., Kochendorfer, J., Meyers, T., Landolt, S., Fischer, A. P., Black, J., Thériault, J. M., Kucera, P., Gochis, D., Smith, C., Nitu, R., Hall, M., Ikeda, K., & Gutmann, E. (2012). How Well Are We Measuring Snow: The NOAA/FAA/NCAR Winter Precipitation Test Bed. *Bulletin of the American Meteorological Society*, 93(6), 811–829. https://doi.org/10.1175/bams-d-11-00052.1

Rasmussen, R. M., Hallett, J., Purcell, R., Landolt, S. D., & Cole, J. (2011). The Hotplate Precipitation Gauge. *Journal of Atmospheric and Oceanic Technology*, 28(2), 148–164. https://doi.org/10.1175/2010JTECHA1375.1

Rasouli, K., Pomeroy, J. W., Janowicz, J. R., Williams, T. J., & Carey, S. K. (2019). A Long-Term Hydrometeorological Dataset (1993–2014) of a Northern Mountain Basin: Wolf Creek Research Basin, Yukon Territory, Canada. *Earth System Science Data*, 11(1), 89–100. https://doi.org/10.5194/essd-11-89-2019

Rasouli, K., Pomeroy, J. W., & Whitfield, P. H. (2019). Hydrological Responses of Headwater Basins to Monthly Perturbed Climate in the North American Cordillera. *Journal of Hydrometeorology*, 20(5), 863–882. https://doi.org/10.1175/JHM-D-18-0166.1

Redmond, L. E., Loewen, C. J. G., & Vinebrooke, R. D. (2018). A Functional Approach to Zooplankton Communities in Mountain Lakes Stocked with Non-Native Sportfish under a Changing Climate. *Water Resources Research*, 54(3), 2362–2375. https://doi.org/10.1002/2017WR021956

Reimchen, T. E., Mathewson, D., Hocking, M. D., & Moran, J. (2003). Isotopic Evidence for Enrichment of Salmon-Derived Nutrients in Vegetation, Soil, and Insects in Riparian Zones in Coastal British Columbia. *American Fisheries Society Symposium*, 59–70.

Reithmeier, L., & Kernaghan, G. (2013). Availability of Ectomycorrhizal Fungi to Black Spruce above the Present Treeline in Eastern Labrador. *PLoS ONE*, 8(10), e77527. https://doi.org/10.1371/journal.pone.0077527

Ressler, G. M., Milrad, S. M., Atallah, E. H., & Gyakum, J. R. (2012). Synoptic-Scale Analysis of Freezing Rain Events in Montreal, Quebec, Canada. *Weather and Forecasting*, 27(2), 362–378. https://doi.org/10.1175/WAF-D-11-00071.1

Richards, J., Moore, R. D., & Forrest, A. L. (2012). Late-Summer Thermal Regime of a Small Proglacial Lake. *Hydrological Processes*, 26(18), 2687–2695. https://doi.org/10.1002/hyp.8360

Roe, G. H. (2005). Orographic Precipitation. *Annual Review of Earth and Planetary Sciences*, 33(1), 645–671. https://doi.org/10.1146/annurev.earth.33.092203.122541

Roebber, P. J., & Gyakum, J. R. (2003). Orographic Influences on the Mesoscale Structure of the 1998 Ice Storm. *Monthly Weather Review, 131*(1), 27–50. https://doi.org/10.1175/1520-0493(2003)131<0027:OIOTMS>2.0.CO;2

Rood, S., Taboulchanas, K., Bradley, C. E., & Kalischuk, A. (1999). Influence of flow regulation on channel dynamics and riparian cottonwoods along the Bow River, Alberta. *Rivers, 7*, 36–48.

Ross, P., Walters, K., Yunker, M., & Lo, B. (2022). *A lake re-emerges: Analysis of contaminants in the Semá: Th X̱ó: Tsa (Sumas Lake) region following the BC floods of 2021.* (pp. 84). Raincoast Conservation Foundation. https://www.raincoast.org/wp-content/uploads/2022/11/Contaminants-BC-Floods-Full-Report-Raincoast.pdf

Rosvold, J. (2016). Perennial ice and snow-covered land as important ecosystems for birds and mammals. *Journal of Biogeography, 43*(1), 3–12. https://doi.org/10.1111/jbi.12609

Routledge, K. (2020). *Do you see ice?: Inuit and Americans at home and away.* University of Chicago Press.

Rowe, T. B., Stafford, T. W., Fisher, D. C., Enghild, J. J., Quigg, J. M., Ketcham, R. A., Sagebiel, J. C., Hanna, R., & Colbert, M. W. (2022). Human Occupation of the North American Colorado Plateau ~37,000 Years Ago. *Frontiers in Ecology and Evolution, 10.* https://www.frontiersin.org/articles/10.3389/fevo.2022.903795

Roy, A. H., Paul, M. J., & Wenger, S. J. (2010). Urban Stream Ecology. In *Urban Ecosystem Ecology* (pp. 341–352). John Wiley & Sons, Ltd. https://doi.org/10.2134/agronmonogr55.c16

Roy, J. W., & Hayashi, M. (2008). Groundwater Exchange with Two Small Alpine Lakes in the Canadian Rockies. *Hydrological Processes, 22*(15), 2838–2846. https://doi.org/10.1002/hyp.6995

Roy, J. W., & Hayashi, M. (2009). Multiple, Distinct Groundwater Flow Systems of a Single Moraine-Talus Feature in an Alpine Watershed. *Journal of Hydrology, 373* (44198), 139–150. https://doi.org/10.1016/j.jhydrol.2009.04.018

Ryder, J., Fulton, R., & Clague, J. (1991). The Cordilleran Ice Sheet and the Glacial Geomorphology of Southern and Central British Columbia. *Géographie Physique et Quaternaire, 45*(3), 365–377. https://doi.org/10.7202/032882ar

Sakiyama, S. K. (1990). Drainage Flow Characteristics and Inversion Breakup in Two Alberta Mountain Valleys. *Journal of Applied Meteorology, 29*(10), 1015–1030. https://doi.org/10.1175/1520-0450(1990)029<1015:DFCAIB>2.0.CO;2

Sanderson, C. (2008). *Nipiy wasekimew/clear water: The Meaning of Water, from the Words of the Elders the Interconnections of Health, Education, Law, and the Environment* [PhD Thesis]. Simon Fraser University.

Sanjayan, M., Samberg, L. H., Boucher, T., & Newby, J. (2012). Intact Faunal Assemblages in the Modern Era. *Conservation Biology, 26*(4), 724–730. https://doi.org/10.1111/j.1523-1739.2012.01881.x

Saunders, I. R., Munro, D. S., & Bailey, W. G. (1997). Alpine Environments. In *The Surface Climates of Canada.* McGill-Queen's University Press.

Schemenauer, R. S. (1986). Acidic Deposition to Forests: The 1985 Chemistry of High Elevation Fog (Chef) Project. *Atmosphere-Ocean, 24*(4), 303–328. https://doi.org/10.1080/07055900.1986.9649254

Schemenauer, R. S., Banic, C. M., & Urquizo, N. (1995). High Elevation Fog and Precipitation Chemistry in Southern Quebec, Canada. *Atmospheric Environment, 29*(17), 2235–2252. https://doi.org/10.1016/1352-2310(95)00153-P

Schiefer, E., & Menounos, B. (2010). Climatic and Morphometric Controls on the Altitudinal Range of Glaciers, British Columbia, Canada. *Holocene, 20*(4), 517–523. https://doi.org/10.1177/0959683609356583

Schiefer, E., Menounos, B., & Wheate, R. (2007). Recent Volume Loss of British Columbian Glaciers, Canada. *Geophysical Research Letters, 34*(16). https://doi.org/10.1029/2007GL030780

Schindler, D. (2000). Aquatic Problems Caused by Human Activities in Banff National Park, Alberta, Canada. *Ambio, 29*(7), 401–407. https://doi.org/10.1639/0044-7447(2000)029[0401:APCBHA]2.0.CO;2

Schindler, D. W., & Donahue, W. F. (2006). An impending water crisis in Canada's western prairie provinces. *Proceedings of the National Academy of Sciences, 103*(19), 7210–7216. https://doi.org/10.1073/pnas.0601568103

Schirmer, M., & Jamieson, B. (2015). Verification of Analysed and Forecasted Winter Precipitation in Complex Terrain. *Cryosphere, 9*(2), 587–601. https://doi.org/10.5194/tc-9-587-2015

Schirmer, M., & Pomeroy, J. W. (2020). Processes Governing Snow Ablation in Alpine Terrain Detailed Measurements from the Canadian Rockies. *Hydrology and Earth System Sciences, 24*(1), 143–157. https://doi.org/10.5194/hess-24-143-2020

Schmid, M.-O., Baral, P., Gruber, S., Shahi, S., Shrestha, T., Stumm, D., & Wester, P. (2015). Assessment of permafrost distribution maps in the Hindu Kush Himalayan region using rock glaciers mapped in Google Earth. *The Cryosphere, 9*(6), 2089–2099. https://doi.org/10.5194/tc-9-2089-2015

Schnorbus, M., & Alila, Y. (2004). Generation of an Hourly Meteorological Time Series for an Alpine Basin in British Columbia for Use in Numerical Hydrologic Modeling. *Journal of Hydrometeorology, 5*(5), 862–882. https://doi.org/10.1175/1525-7541(2004)005<0862:GOAHMT>2.0.CO;2

Shafer, A. B. A., Cullingham, C. I., Cote, S. D., & Coltman, D. W. (2010). Of Glaciers and Refugia: A Decade of Study Sheds New Light on the Phylogeography of Northwestern North America. *Mol Ecol, 19*(21), 4589–4621. https://doi.org/10.1111/j.1365-294X.2010.04828.x

Shakil, S., Tank, S. E., Kokelj, S. V., Vonk, J. E., & Zolkos, S. (2020). Particulate dominance of organic carbon mobilization from thaw slumps on the Peel Plateau, NT: Quantification and implications for stream systems and permafrost carbon release. *Environmental Research Letters*, 15(11), 114019. https://doi.org/10.1088/1748-9326/abac36

Sharma, A. R., & Déry, S. J. (2020). Contribution of Atmospheric Rivers to Annual, Seasonal, and Extreme Precipitation across British Columbia and Southeastern Alaska. *Journal of Geophysical Research-Atmospheres*, 125(9). https://doi.org/10.1029/2019JD031823

Sharp, M., Burgess, D. O., Cogley, J. G., Ecclestone, M., Labine, C., & Wolken, G. J. (2011). Extreme melt on Canada's Arctic ice caps in the 21st century. *Geophysical Research Letters*, 38(11).

Sharpe, D., Russel, H., & Wozniak, P. (2008). *Hydrogeologial regions of Canada: Data release* (No. 5893; Open File, p. 20). Geological Survey of Canada. https://ftp.maps.canada.ca/pub/nrcan_rncan/publications/STPublications_PublicationsST/226/226194/of_5893.zip

Shea, J. M., & Marshall, S. J. (2007). Atmospheric Flow Indices, Regional Climate, and Glacier Mass Balance in the Canadian Rocky Mountains. *International Journal of Climatology*, 27(2), 233–247. https://doi.org/10.1002/joc.1398

Shea, J. M., Marshall, S. J., & Livingston, J. M. (2004). Glacier Distributions and Climate in the Canadian Rockies. *Arctic, Antarctic, and Alpine Research*, 36(2), 272–279. https://doi.org/10.1657/1523-0430(2004)036[0272:GDACIT]2.0.CO;2

Shea, J. M., Menounos, B., Moore, R. D., & Tennant, C. (2013). An Approach to Derive Regional Snow Lines and Glacier Mass Change from Modis Imagery, Western North America. *Cryosphere*, 7(2), 667–680. https://doi.org/10.5194/tc-7-667-2013

Shea, J. M., & Moore, R. D. (2010). Prediction of Spatially Distributed Regional-Scale Fields of Air Temperature and Vapor Pressure over Mountain Glaciers. *Journal of Geophysical Research-Atmospheres*, 115. https://doi.org/10.1029/2010JD014351

Shea, J. M., Moore, R. D., & Stahl, K. (2009). Derivation of Melt Factors from Glacier Mass-Balance Records in Western Canada. *Journal of Glaciology*, 55(189), 123–130. https://doi.org/10.3189/002214309788608886

Shea, J. M., Whitfield, P. H., Fang, X., & Pomeroy, J. W. (2021). The Role of Basin Geometry in Mountain Snowpack Responses to Climate Change. *Frontiers in Water*, 3. https://doi.org/10.3389/frwa.2021.604275

Sherriff, L. (2021, February 23). Beaver believers: Native Americans promote resurgence of "nature's engineers." *The Guardian*. https://www.theguardian.com/environment/2021/feb/23/beavers-native-american-tribes-washington-california

Shrestha, R. R., Schnorbus, M. A., Werner, A. T., & Berland, A. J. (2012). Modelling Spatial and Temporal Variability of Hydrologic Impacts of Climate Change in the Fraser River Basin, British Columbia, Canada. *Hydrological Processes*, 26(12), 1841–1861. https://doi.org/10.1002/hyp.9283

Shugar, D. H., Clague, J. J., Best, J. L., Schoof, C., Willis, M. J., Copland, L., & Roe, G. H. (2017). River Piracy and Drainage Basin Reorganization Led by Climate-Driven Glacier Retreat. *Nature Geoscience*, 10(5), 370–375. https://doi.org/10.1038/NGEO2932

Shugar, D. H., Walker, I. J., Lian, O. B., Eamer, J. B. R., Neudorf, C., McLaren, D., & Fedje, D. (2014). Post-glacial sea-level change along the Pacific coast of North America. *Quaternary Science Reviews*, 97, 170–192. https://doi.org/10.1016/j.quascirev.2014.05.022

Sidjak, R. W. (1999). Glacier mapping of the Illecillewaet icefield, British Columbia, Canada, using Landsat TM and digital elevation data. *International Journal of Remote Sensing*, 20(2), 273–284. https://doi.org/10.1080/014311699213442

Silfver, T., Heiskanen, L., Aurela, M., Myller, K., Karhu, K., Meyer, N., Tuovinen, J.-P., Oksanen, E., Rousi, M., & Mikola, J. (2020). Insect herbivory dampens Subarctic birch forest C sink response to warming. *Nature Communications*, 11(1), 2529. https://doi.org/10.1038/s41467-020-16404-4

Silins, U., Bladon, K. D., Kelly, E. N., Esch, E., Spence, J. R., Stone, M., Emelko, M. B., Boon, S., Wagner, M. J., Williams, C. H. S., & Tichkowsky, I. (2014). Five-Year Legacy of Wildfire and Salvage Logging Impacts on Nutrient Runoff and Aquatic Plant, Invertebrate, and Fish Productivity. *Ecohydrology*, 7(6), 1508–1523. https://doi.org/10.1002/eco.1474

Silins, U., Stone, M., Emelko, M. B., & Bladon, K. D. (2009). Sediment Production following Severe Wildfire and Post-Fire Salvage Logging in the Rocky Mountain Headwaters of the Oldman River Basin, Alberta. *Catena*, 79(3), 189–197. https://doi.org/10.1016/j.catena.2009.04.001

Simard, S. (2021). *Finding the mother tree: Discovering the wisdom of the forest* (First edition). Alfred A. Knopf.

Simard, S. W., Perry, D. A., Jones, M. D., Myrold, D. D., Durall, D. M., & Molina, R. (1997). Net transfer of carbon between ectomycorrhizal tree species in the field. *Nature*, 388(6642), Article 6642. https://doi.org/10.1038/41557

Simms, R., Harris, L., Joe, N., & Bakker, K. (2016). Navigating the tensions in collaborative watershed governance: Water governance and Indigenous communities in British Columbia, Canada. *Geoforum*, 73, 6–16. https://doi.org/10.1016/j.geoforum.2016.04.005

Simpson, Kirstie E.M. (2002). The use of Traditional Aboriginal Knowledge in avalanche forecasting (Canada and Alaska). *International Snow Science Workshop Proceedings*. International Snow Science Workshop, Penticton, B.C. https://arc.lib.montana.edu/snow-science/objects/issw-2002-228-236.pdf

Sims, D. (2010). *Tse Keh Nay-European Relations and Ethnicity: 1790s–2009* [University of Alberta]. https://doi.org/10.7939/R3533K

Slaymaker, O. (1990). Climate Change and Erosion Processes in Mountain Regions of Western Canada. *Mountain Research and Development*, 10(2), 171–182. https://doi.org/10.2307/3673427

Slemmons, K. E., Saros, J., & Simon, K. (2013). The influence of glacial meltwater on alpine aquatic ecosystems: A review. *Environmental Science: Processes & Impacts*, *15*(10), 1794–1806. https://doi.org/10.1039/C3EM00243H

Smakhtin, V. U. (2001). Low flow hydrology: A review. *Journal of Hydrology*, *240*(3), 147–186. https://doi.org/10.1016/S0022-1694(00)00340-1

Smerdon, B. D., Allen, D. M., Grasby, S. E., & Berg, M. A. (2009). An Approach for Predicting Groundwater Recharge in Mountainous Watersheds. *Journal of Hydrology*, *365*(44259), 156–172. https://doi.org/10.1016/j.jhydrol.2008.11.023

Smith, S. L., & Bonnaventure, P. P. (2017). Quantifying Surface Temperature Inversions and Their Impact on the Ground Thermal Regime at a High Arctic Site. *Arctic, Antarctic, and Alpine Research*, *49*(1), 173–185. https://doi.org/10.1657/AAAR0016-039

Snow, J. (2005). *These Mountains are Our Sacred Places: The Story of the Stoney People*. Fifth House.

Somers, L. D., & McKenzie, J. M. (2020). A review of groundwater in high mountain environments. *WIREs Water*, *7*(6), e1475. https://doi.org/10.1002/wat2.1475

Somers, L. D., McKenzie, J. M., Mark, B. G., Lagos, P., Ng, G. H. C., Wickert, A. D., Yarleque, C., Baraer, M., & Silva, Y. (2019). Groundwater Buffers Decreasing Glacier Melt in an Andean Watershed—But Not Forever. *Geophysical Research Letters*, *46*(22), 13016–13026. https://doi.org/10.1029/2019GL084730

Souther, J. G., Clague, J. J., & Mathewes, R. W. (1987). Nazko cone: A Quaternary volcano in the eastern Anahim Belt. *Canadian Journal of Earth Sciences*, *24*(12), 2477–2485. https://doi.org/10.1139/e87-232

Spencer, S. A., Anderson, A. E., Silins, U., & Collins, A. L. (2021). Hillslope and groundwater contributions to streamflow in a Rocky Mountain watershed underlain by glacial till and fractured sedimentary bedrock. *Hydrology and Earth System Sciences*, *25*(1), 237–255. https://doi.org/10.5194/hess-25-237-2021

Springer, J., Ludwig, R., & Kienzle, S. W. (2015). Impacts of Forest Fires and Climate Variability on the Hydrology of an Alpine Medium Sized Catchment in the Canadian Rocky Mountains. *Hydrology*, *2*(1), 23–47. https://doi.org/10.3390/hydrology2010023

St. Pierre, K. A., St. Louis, V. L., Lehnherr, I., Gardner, A. S., Serbu, J. A., Mortimer, C. A., Muir, D. C. G., Wiklund, J. A., Lemire, D., Szostek, L., & Talbot, C. (2019). Drivers of Mercury Cycling in the Rapidly Changing Glacierized Watershed of the High Arctic's Largest Lake by Volume (Lake Hazen, Nunavut, Canada). *Environmental Science & Technology*, *53*(3), 1175–1185. https://doi.org/10.1021/acs.est.8b05926

St. Pierre, K. A., St. Louis, V. L., Schiff, S. L., Lehnherr, I., Dainard, P. G., Gardner, A. S., Aukes, P. J. K., & Sharp, M. J. (2019). Proglacial freshwaters are significant and previously unrecognized sinks of atmospheric CO_2. *Proceedings of the National Academy of Sciences*, *116*(36), 17690. https://doi.org/10.1073/pnas.1904241116

St. Pierre, K. A., Zolkos, S., Shakil, S., Tank, S. E., St. Louis, V. L., & Kokelj, S. V. (2018). Unprecedented Increases in Total and Methyl Mercury Concentrations Downstream of Retrogressive Thaw Slumps in the Western Canadian Arctic. *Environmental Science & Technology*, *52*(24), 14099–14109. https://doi.org/10.1021/acs.est.8b05348

Stahl, K., & Moore, R. D. (2006). Influence of watershed glacier coverage on summer streamflow in British Columbia, Canada. *Water Resources Research*, *42*(6). https://doi.org/10.1029/2006WR005022

Stasiuk, M., Hickson, C., & Mulder, T. (2003). The Vulnerability of Canada to Volcanic Hazards. *Natural Hazards*, *28*(44230), 563–589. https://doi.org/10.1023/A:1022954829974

Stenntng, A. J., Banfield, C. E., & Young, G. J. (1981). Synoptic controls over katabatic layer characteristics above a melting glacier. *Journal of Climatology*, *1*(4), 309–324. https://doi.org/10.1002/joc.3370010404

Stethem, C., Jamieson, B., Schaerer, P. a., Liverman, D., Germain, D., & Walker, S. (2003). Snow avalanche hazard in Canada—A review. *Natural Hazards*, *28*(2–3), 487–515. https://doi.org/10.1023/A:1022998512227

Stewart, R. E., Szeto, K. K., Bonsal, B. R., Hanesiak, J. M., Kochtubajda, B., Li, Y., Thériault, J. M., DeBeer, C. M., Tam, B. Y., Li, Z., Liu, Z., Bruneau, J. A., Duplessis, P., Marinier, S., & Matte, D. (2019). Summary and synthesis of Changing Cold Regions Network (CCRN) research in the interior of western Canada—Part 1: Projected climate and meteorology. *Hydrology and Earth System Sciences*, *23*(8), 3437–3455. https://doi.org/10.5194/hess-23-3437-2019

Stewart, R. E., Thériault, J. M., & Henson, W. (2015). On the Characteristics of and Processes Producing Winter Precipitation Types near 0°C. *Bulletin of the American Meteorological Society*, *96*(4), 623–639. https://doi.org/10.1175/BAMS-D-14-00032.1

Strand, D. (2003). Southern Yukon alpine ice patches: Climate change records, caribou history, ancient hunters and much more. *Historic Environment*. https://search.informit.org/doi/abs/10.3316/ielapa.876318454413350

Strasser, U., Marke, T., Braun, L., Escher-Vetter, H., Juen, I., Kuhn, M., Maussion, F., Mayer, C., Nicholson, L., Niedertscheider, K., Sailer, R., Stötter, J., Weber, M., & Kaser, G. (2018). The Rofental: A high Alpine research basin (1890–3770 m a.s.l.) in the Ötztal Alps (Austria) with over 150 years of hydrometeorological and glaciological observations. *Earth System Science Data*, *10*(1), 151–171. https://doi.org/10.5194/essd-10-151-2018

Strecker, A., Cobb, T., & Vinebrooke, R. (2004). Effects of Experimental Greenhouse Warming on Phytoplankton and Zooplankton Communities in Fishless Alpine Ponds. *Limnology and Oceanography*, *49*(4), 1182–1190. https://doi.org/10.4319/lo.2004.49.4.1182

Sturm, M., Goldstein, M. A., & Parr, C. (2017). Water and life from snow: A trillion dollar science question. *Water Resources Research*, *53*(5), 3534–3544. https://doi.org/10.1002/2017WR020840

Sun, Y., De Silva, A. O., St Pierre, K. A., Muir, D. C. G., Spencer, C., Lehnherr, I., & MacInnis, J. J. (2020). Glacial Melt Inputs of Organophosphate Ester Flame Retardants to the Largest High Arctic Lake. *Environmental Science &*

Technology, 54(5), 2734–2743. https://doi.org/10.1021/acs.est.9b06333

Suriano, Z. J. (2022). North American rain-on-snow ablation climatology. Climate Research, 87, 133–145. https://doi.org/10.3354/cr01687

Swadling, K., Pienitz, R., & Nogrady, T. (2000). Zooplankton Community Composition of Lakes in the Yukon and Northwest Territories (Canada): Relationship to Physical and Chemical Limnology. Hydrobiologia, 431(44230), 211–224. https://doi.org/10.1023/A:1004056715976

Swanson, H. K., Kidd, K. A., & Reist, J. D. (2010). Effects of Partially Anadromous Arctic Charr (Salvelinus alpinus) Populations on Ecology of Coastal Arctic Lakes. Ecosystems, 13(2), 261–274. https://doi.org/10.1007/s10021-010-9316-7

Sylvestre, T., Copland, L., Demuth, M. N., & Sharp, M. (2013). Spatial patterns of snow accumulation across Belcher Glacier, Devon Ice Cap, Nunavut, Canada. Journal of Glaciology, 59(217), 874–882. https://doi.org/10.3189/2013JoG12J227

Syvitski, J. P. M., & Schafer, C. T. (1996). Evidence for an earthquake-triggered basin collapse in Saguenay Fjord, Canada. Marine Sedimentary Events and Their Records, 104(1), 127–153. https://doi.org/10.1016/0037-0738(95)00125-5

Szeitz, A. J., & Moore, R. D. (2020). Predicting Evaporation from Mountain Streams. Hydrological Processes, 34(22), 4262–4279. https://doi.org/10.1002/hyp.13875

Szmigielski, J. T., Barbour, S. L., Carey, S. K., Kurylo, J., Mcclymont, A. F., & Hendry, M. J. (2018). Hydrogeology of a Montane Headwater Groundwater System Downgradient of a Coal-Mine Waste Rock Dump: Elk Valley, British Columbia, Canada. Hydrogeology Journal, 26(7), 2341–2356. https://doi.org/10.1007/s10040-018-1809-z

Talucci, A. C., & Krawchuk, M. A. (2019). Dead Forests Burning: The Influence of Beetle Outbreaks on Fire Severity and Legacy Structure in Sub-Boreal Forests. Ecosphere, 10(5). https://doi.org/10.1002/ecs2.2744

Tank, S. E., Striegl, R. G., McClelland, J. W., & Kokelj, S. V. (2016). Multi-decadal increases in dissolved organic carbon and alkalinity flux from the Mackenzie drainage basin to the Arctic Ocean. Environmental Research Letters, 11(5), 054015. https://doi.org/10.1088/1748-9326/11/5/054015

Tarnocai, C., Kettles, I. M., & Lacelle, B. (2011). Peatlands of Canada (No. 6561). https://doi.org/10.4095/288786

Taylor, S. W., & Carroll, A. (2003). Disturbance, Forest Age, and Mountain Pine Beetle Outbreak Dynamics in BC: A Historical Perspective. In Mountain Pine Beetle Symposium: Challenges and Solutions.

Tennant, C., & Menounos, B. (2013). Glacier Change of the Columbia Icefield, Canadian Rocky Mountains, 1919–2009. Journal of Glaciology, 59(216), 671–686. https://doi.org/10.3189/2013JoG12J135

Tennant, C., Menounos, B., Wheate, R., & Clague, J. J. (2012). Area Change of Glaciers in the Canadian Rocky Mountains, 1919 to 2006. Cryosphere, 6(6), 1541–1552. https://doi.org/10.5194/tc-6-1541-2012

Thériault, J. M., Leroux, N. R., & Rasmussen, R. M. (2021). Improvement of Solid Precipitation Measurements Using a Hotplate Precipitation Gauge. Journal of Hydrometeorology, 22(4), 877–885. https://doi.org/10.1175/JHM-D-20-0168.1

Thériault, J. M., Leroux, N. R., Stewart, R. E., Bertoncini, A., Déry, S. J., Pomeroy, J. W., Thompson, H. D., Smith, H., Mariani, Z., Desroches-Lapointe, A., Mitchell, S., & Almonte, J. (2022). Storms and Precipitation Across the continental Divide Experiment (SPADE). Bulletin of the American Meteorological Society, 103(11), E2628–E2649. https://doi.org/10.1175/BAMS-D-21-0146.1

Thompson, H. D., Dery, S. J., Jackson, P. L., & Laval, B. E. (2020). A Synoptic Climatology of Potential Seiche-Inducing Winds in a Large Intermontane Lake: Quesnel Lake, British Columbia, Canada. International Journal of Climatology, 40(14), 5973–5986. https://doi.org/10.1002/joc.6560

Thomson, L. I., Zemp, M., Copland, L., Cogley, J. G., & Ecclestone, M. A. (2017). Comparison of geodetic and glaciological mass budgets for White Glacier, Axel Heiberg Island, Canada. Journal of Glaciology, 63(237), 55–66. https://doi.org/10.1017/jog.2016.112

Thorne, R., & Woo, M.-K. (2006). Efficacy of a Hydrologic Model in Simulating Discharge from a Large Mountainous Catchment. Journal of Hydrology, 330(44198), 301–312. https://doi.org/10.1016/j.jhydrol.2006.03.031

Thyer, N. (1981). Diurnal Variations of Upper Winds in Summer in Alberta. Atmosphere-Ocean, 19(4), 337–344. https://doi.org/10.1080/07055900.1981.9649119

Toth, B., Corkal, D. R., Sauchyn, D., Van Der Kamr, G., & Pietroniro, E. (2009). The Natural Characteristics of the South Saskatchewan, River Basin: Climate, Geography and Hydrology. Prairie Forum, 34(1), 95–127.

Treat, C. C., & Jones, M. C. (2018). Near-surface permafrost aggradation in Northern Hemisphere peatlands shows regional and global trends during the past 6000 years. The Holocene, 28(6), 998–1010. https://doi.org/10.1177/0959683617752858

Trubilowicz, J. W., & Moore, R. D. (2017). Quantifying the Role of the Snowpack in Generating Water Available for Run-Off during Rain-on-Snow Events from Snow Pillow Records. Hydrological Processes, 31(23), 4136–4150. https://doi.org/10.1002/hyp.11310

Turkel, W. (2011). The Archive of Place: Unearthing the Pasts of the Chilcotin Plateau. UBC Press.

Turner, N. J., & Clifton, H. (2009). "It's so different today": Climate change and indigenous lifeways in British Columbia, Canada. Global Environmental Change, 19(2), 180–190. https://doi.org/10.1016/j.gloenvcha.2009.01.005

Turner, N. J., Deur, D., & Mellott, C. R. (2011). "Up on the Mountain": Ethnobotanical Importance of Montane Sites in Pacific Coastal North America. Journal of Ethnobiology, 31(1), 4–43. https://doi.org/10.2993/0278-0771-31.1.4

Turner, N. J., Ignace, M. B., & Ignace, R. (2000). Traditional Ecological Knowledge and Wisdom of Aboriginal

Peoples in British Columbia. *Ecological Applications*, *10*(5), 1275–1287. https://doi.org/10.1890/1051-0761 (2000)010[1275:TEKAWO]2.0.CO;2

Ullman, D. J., Carlson, A. E., Hostetler, S. W., Clark, P. U., Cuzzone, J., Milne, G. A., Winsor, K., & Caffee, M. (2016). Final Laurentide ice-sheet deglaciation and Holocene climate-sea level change. *Quaternary Science Reviews*, *152*, 49–59. https://doi.org/10.1016/j.quascirev.2016.09.014

Van Couwenberghe, R., Collet, C., Lacombe, E., & Gégout, J.-C. (2011). Abundance response of western European forest species along canopy openness and soil pH gradients. *Forest Ecology and Management*, *262*(8), 1483–1490. https://doi.org/10.1016/j.foreco.2011.06.049

Van Everdingen, R. (1991). Physical, Chemical, and Distributional Aspects of Canadian Springs. *Memoirs of the Entomological Society of Canada*, *123*(155), 7–28. https://doi.org/10.4039/entm123155007-1

van Staal, C. R., Dewey, J. F., MacNiocaill, C., & McKerrow, W. S. (1998). The Cambrian-Silurian tectonic evolution of the northern Appalachians and British Caledonides: History of a complex, west and southwest Pacific-type segment of Iapetus. In D. J. Blundell & A. C. Scott (Eds.), *Lyell: The Past is the Key to the Present* (Vol. 143, pp. 199–242). Geological Society.

van Staal, C. R., Wilson, R. A., & McClelland, W. (2015). Discussion: Taconian orogenesis, sedimentation and magmatism in the southern Quebec-northern Vermont Appalachians: Stratigraphic and detrital mineral record of Iapetan suturing. *American Journal of Science*, *315*(5), 486–500. https://doi.org/10.2475/05.2015.04

Van Tiel, M., Van Loon, A. F., Seibert, J., & Stahl, K. (2021). Hydrological response to warm and dry weather: Do glaciers compensate? *Hydrology and Earth System Sciences*, *25*(6), 3245–3265. https://doi.org/10.5194/hess-25-3245-2021

Van Wagner, C. E., Finney, M. A., & Heathcott, M. (2006). Historical Fire Cycles in the Canadian Rocky Mountain Parks. *Forest Science*, *52*(6), 704–717.

VanDine, D. F. (1985). Debris flows and debris torrents in the Southern Canadian Cordillera. *Canadian Geotechnical Journal*, *22*(1), 44–68. https://doi.org/10.1139/t85-006

Varhola, A., Coops, N. C., Weiler, M., & Moore, R. D. (2010). Forest canopy effects on snow accumulation and ablation: An integrative review of empirical results. *Journal of Hydrology*, *392*(3), 219–233. https://doi.org/10.1016/j.jhydrol.2010.08.009

Vasquez, T. (2022). An Unprecedented Pacific Northwest Heat Wave Rings Alarm Bells. *Weatherwise*, *75*(1), 22–27. https://doi.org/10.1080/00431672.2022.1996146

Ville de Québec. (2022). *Bassins Versants et Sources d'eau Potable*. https://www.ville.quebec.qc.ca/citoyens/environnement/eau/protection-cours-deau/bassins-versants-et-sources-deau-potable/

Vincent, L. A., Wang, X. L., Milewska, E. J., Wan, H., Yang, F., & Swail, V. (2012). A second generation of homogenized Canadian monthly surface air temperature for

climate trend analysis: Homogenized Canadian temperature. *Journal of Geophysical Research: Atmospheres*, *117*(D18), n/a-n/a. https://doi.org/10.1029/2012JD017859

Vinebrooke, R. D., Thompson, P. L., Hobbs, W., Luckman, B. H., Graham, M. D., & Wolfe, A. P. (2010). Glacially mediated impacts of climate warming on alpine lakes of the Canadian Rocky Mountains. *SIL Proceedings, 1922-2010*, *30*(9), 1449–1452. https://doi.org/10.1080/03680770.2009.11902351

Vinebrooke, R., & Leavitt, P. (1999). Phytobenthos and Phytoplankton as Potential Indicators of Climate Change in Mountain Lakes and Ponds: A Hplc-Based Pigment Approach. *Journal of the North American Benthological Society*, *18*(1), 15–33. https://doi.org/10.2307/1468006

Vionnet, V., Belair, S., Girard, C., & Plante, A. (2015). Wintertime Subkilometer Numerical Forecasts of Near-Surface Variables in the Canadian Rocky Mountains. *Monthly Weather Review*, *143*(2), 666–686. https://doi.org/10.1175/MWR-D-14-00128.1

Vionnet, V., Fortin, V., Gaborit, E., Roy, G., Abrahamowicz, M., Gasset, N., & Pomeroy, J. W. (2020). Assessing the Factors Governing the Ability to Predict Late-Spring Flooding in Cold-Region Mountain Basins. *Hydrology and Earth System Sciences*, *24*(4), 2141–2165. https://doi.org/10.5194/hess-24-2141-2020

Vionnet, V., Marsh, C. B., Menounos, B., Gascoin, S., Wayand, N. E., Shea, J., Mukherjee, K., & Pomeroy, J. W. (2021). Multi-scale snowdrift-permitting modelling of mountain snowpack. *Cryosphere*, *15.0*(2), 743–769. https://doi.org/10.5194/tc-15-743-2021

Vionnet, V., Mortimer, C., Brady, M., Arnal, L., & Brown, R. (2021). Canadian historical Snow Water Equivalent dataset (CanSWE, 1928–2020). *Earth System Science Data*, *13*(9), 4603–4619. https://doi.org/10.5194/essd-13-4603-2021

Viviroli, D., Dürr, H. H., Messerli, B., Meybeck, M., & Weingartner, R. (2007). Mountains of the world, water towers for humanity: Typology, mapping, and global significance: *Water Resources Research*, *43*(7). https://doi.org/10.1029/2006WR005653

Voeckler, H. M., Allen, D. M., & Alila, Y. (2014). Modeling Coupled Surface Water—Groundwater Processes in a Small Mountainous Headwater Catchment. *Journal of Hydrology*, *517*, 1089–1106. https://doi.org/10.1016/j.jhydrol.2014.06.015

Wade, L. (2021). Human footprints near ice age lake suggest surprisingly early arrival in the Americas. *Science*, *373*(6562). https://www.science.org/content/article/human-footprints-near-ice-age-lake-suggest-surprisingly-early-arrival-americas

Wagner, M. A., & Reynolds, J. D. (2019). Salmon increase forest bird abundance and diversity. *PLOS ONE*, *14*(2), e0210031. https://doi.org/10.1371/journal.pone.0210031

Wagner, M. J., Bladon, K. D., Silins, U., Williams, C. H. S., Martens, A. M., Boon, S., Macdonald, R. J., Stone, M., Emelko, M. B., & Anderson, A. (2014). Catchment-Scale

Stream Temperature Response to Land Disturbance by Wildfire Governed by Surface-Subsurface Energy Exchange and Atmospheric Controls. *Journal of Hydrology*, *517*, 328–338. https://doi.org/10.1016/j.jhydrol.2014.05.006

Waldron, J. W. F., Anderson, S. D., Cawood, P. A., Goodwin, L. B., Hall, J., Jamieson, R. a, Palmer, S. E., Stockmal, G. S., & Williams, P. F. (1998). Evolution of the Appalachian Laurentian margin: Lithoprobe results in western Newfoundland. *Canadian Journal of Earth Sciences*, *35*(11), 1271–1287. https://doi.org/10.1139/e98-053

Walsh, J. E., Shapiro, I., & Shy, T. L. (2005). On the variability and predictability of daily temperatures in the Arctic. *Atmosphere-Ocean*, *43*(3), 213–230. https://doi.org/10.3137/ao.430302

Walsh, K. A., Sanseverino, M., & Higgs, E. (2017). Weather Awareness: On the Lookout for Wildfire in the Canadian Rocky Mountains. *Mountain Research and Development*, *37*(4), 494–501. https://doi.org/10.1659/MRD-JOURNAL-D-16-00048.1

Wang, S., Pan, M., Mu, Q., Shi, X., Mao, J., Bruemmer, C., Jassal, R. S., Krishnan, P., Li, J., & Black, T. A. (2015). Comparing Evapotranspiration from Eddy Covariance Measurements, Water Budgets, Remote Sensing, and Land Surface Models over Canada. *Journal of Hydrometeorology*, *16*(4), 1540–1560. https://doi.org/10.1175/JHM-D-14-0189.1

Warner, B. G., & Asada, T. (2006). Biological diversity of peatlands in Canada. *Aquatic Sciences*, *68*(3), 240–253. https://doi.org/10.1007/s00027-006-0853-2

Warren, S. G. (1982). Optical properties of snow. *Reviews of Geophysics*, *20*(1), 67–89. https://doi.org/10.1029/RG020i001p00067

Way, R. G., Bell, T., & Barrand, N. E. (2014). An Inventory and Topographic Analysis of Glaciers in the Torngat Mountains, Northern Labrador, Canada. *Journal of Glaciology*, *60*(223), 945–956. https://doi.org/10.3189/2014JoG13J195

Wayand, N. E., Marsh, C. B., Shea, J. M., & Pomeroy, J. W. (2018). Globally Scalable Alpine Snow Metrics. *Remote Sensing of Environment*, *213*, 61–72. https://doi.org/10.1016/j.rse.2018.05.012

Weatherhead, E., Gearheard, S., & Barry, R. G. (2010). Changes in weather persistence: Insight from Inuit knowledge. *Global Environmental Change*, *20*(3), 523–528. https://doi.org/10.1016/j.gloenvcha.2010.02.002

Webb, S. (2021, April 18). *Gaspé caribou, the last of herds that once roamed the Maritimes, face extinction | CBC News*. CBC. https://www.cbc.ca/news/canada/new-brunswick/gaspe-caribou-last-herd-1.5991230

Weingartner, R., Barben, M., & Spreafico, M. (2003). Floods in mountain areas—An overview based on examples from Switzerland. *Journal of Hydrology*, *282*(1), 10–24. https://doi.org/10.1016/S0022-1694(03)00249-X

Welch, L. A., Allen, D. M., & Van Meerveld, H. J. I. (2012). Topographic Controls on Deep Groundwater Contributions to Mountain Headwater Streams and Sensitivity to Available Recharge. *Canadian Water Resources Journal*, *37*(4), 349–371. https://doi.org/10.4296/cwrj2011-907

Wheler, B. A., & Flowers, G. E. (2011). Glacier subsurface heat-flux characterizations for energy-balance modelling in the Donjek Range, southwest Yukon, Canada. *Journal of Glaciology*, *57*(201), 121–133.

Wheler, B. A., MacDougall, A. H., Flowers, G. E., Petersen, E. I., Whitfield, P. H., & Kohfeld, K. E. (2014). Effects of temperature forcing provenance and extrapolation on the performance of an empirical glacier-melt model. *Arctic, Antarctic, and Alpine Research*, *46*(2), 379–393.

Whitaker, A., Alila, Y., Beckers, J., & Toews, D. (2002). Evaluating Peak Flow Sensitivity to Clear-Cutting in Different Elevation Bands of a Snowmelt-Dominated Mountainous Catchment. *Water Resources Research*, *38*(9), 1–11. https://doi.org/10.1029/2001WR000514

White, C. F. H., Coops, N. C., Nijland, W., Hilker, T., Nelson, T. A., Wulder, M. A., Nielsen, S. E., & Stenhouse, G. (2014). Characterizing a Decade of Disturbance Events Using Landsat and Modis Satellite Imagery in Western Alberta, Canada for Grizzly Bear Management. *Canadian Journal of Remote Sensing*, *40*(5), 336–347. https://doi.org/10.1080/07038992.2014.987082

White, R., Anderson, S., Booth, J., Braich, G., Draeger, C., Fei, C., Harley, C. D. G., Henderson, S. B., Jakob, M., Lau, C.-A., Admasu, L. M., Narinesignh, V., Rodell, C., Roocroft, E., Weinberger, K., & West, G. (2022). *The unprecedented Pacific Northwest heatwave of June 2021*. UBC. https://doi.org/10.14288/1.0416609

Whitfield, P. H. (1983). Regionalization of water quality in the upper fraser river basin, British Columbia. *Water Research*, *17*(9), 1053–1066. https://doi.org/10.1016/0043-1354(83)90045-3

Whitfield, P. H., Cannon, A. J., & Reynolds, C. J. (2002). Modelling Streamflow in Present and Future Climates: Examples from the Georgia Basin, British Columbia. *Canadian Water Resources Journal*, *27*(4), 427–456. https://doi.org/10.4296/cwrj2704427

Whitfield, P. H., & Pomeroy, J. W. (2016). Changes to Flood Peaks of a Mountain River: Implications for Analysis of the 2013 Flood in the Upper Bow River, Canada. *Hydrological Processes*, *30*(25), 4657–4673. https://doi.org/10.1002/hyp.10957

Williams, C. H. S., Silins, U., Spencer, S. A., Wagner, M. J., Stone, M., & Emelko, M. B. (2019). Net Precipitation in Burned and Unburned Subalpine Forest Stands after Wildfire in the Northern Rocky Mountains. *International Journal of Wildland Fire*, *28*(10), 750–760. https://doi.org/10.1071/WF18181

Williams, H. (1979). Appalachian Orogen in Canada. *Canadian Journal of Earth Sciences*, *16*(3), 792–807.

Williamson, S. N., & Menounos, B. (2021). The influence of forest fires aerosol and air temperature on glacier albedo, western North America. *Remote Sensing of Environment*, *267*, 112732. https://doi.org/10.1016/j.rse.2021.112732

Wilson, N. J., Harris, L. M., Joseph-Rear, A., Beaumont, J., & Satterfield, T. (2019). Water Is Medicine: Reimagining

Water Security through Tr'ondek Hwech'In Relationships to Treated and Traditional Water Sources in Yukon, Canada. *Water, 11*(3). https://doi.org/10.3390/w11030624

Wilson, N. J., Walter, M. T., & Waterhouse, J. (2015). Indigenous Knowledge of Hydrologic Change in the Yukon River Basin: A Case Study of Ruby, Alaska. *Arctic, 68*(1), 93–106.

Winkler, R., Boon, S., Zimonick, B., & Spittlehouse, D. (2014). Snow Accumulation and Ablation Response to Changes in Forest Structure and Snow Surface Albedo after Attack by Mountain Pine Beetle. *Hydrological Processes, 28*(2), 197–209. https://doi.org/10.1002/hyp.9574

Winkler, R., Spittlehouse, D., Boon, S., & Zimonick, B. (2015). Forest Disturbance Effects on Snow and Water Yield in Interior British Columbia. *Hydrology Research, 46*(4), 521–532. https://doi.org/10.2166/nh.2014.016

Winstral, A., Elder, K., & Davis, R. E. (2002). Spatial Snow Modeling of Wind-Redistributed Snow Using Terrain-Based Parameters. *Journal of Hydrometeorology, 3*(5), 524–538. https://doi.org/10.1175/1525-7541(2002)003<0524:SSMOWR>2.0.CO;2

Winter, T. C. (1995). Recent advances in understanding the interaction of groundwater and surface water. *Reviews of Geophysics, 33*(S2), 985–994. https://doi.org/10.1029/95RG00115

Wohl, E. (2013). *Mountain Rivers Revisited*. John Wiley & Sons.

Wong, C., Ballegooyen, K., Ignace, L., Johnson, M. J. (Gùdia), & Swanson, H. (2020). Towards reconciliation: 10 Calls to Action to natural scientists working in Canada. *FACETS, 5*(1), 769–783. https://doi.org/10.1139/facets-2020-0005

Woo, M.-K., Kane, D. L., Carey, S. K., & Yang, D. (2008). Progress in permafrost hydrology in the new millennium. *Permafrost and Periglacial Processes, 19*(2), 237–254. https://doi.org/10.1002/ppp.613

Woo, M.-K., & Thorne, R. (2003). Streamflow in the Mackenzie Basin, Canada. *Arctic, 56*(4), 328–340. https://doi.org/10.14430/arctic630

Woo, M.-K., & Thorne, R. (2006). Snowmelt Contribution to Discharge from a Large Mountainous Catchment in Subarctic Canada. *Hydrological Processes, 20*(10), 2129–2139. https://doi.org/10.1002/hyp.6205

Wood, C., & Smith, D. (2004). Dendroglaciological Evidence for a Neoglacial Advance of the Saskatchewan Glacier, Banff National Park, Canadian Rocky Mountains. *Tree-Ring Research, 60*(1), 59–65. https://doi.org/10.3959/1536-1098-60.1.59

Wood, W. H., Marshall, S. J., Whitehead, T. L., & Fargey, S. E. (2018). Daily Temperature Records from a Mesonet in the Foothills of the Canadian Rocky Mountains, 2005–2010. *Earth System Science Data, 10*(1), 595–607. https://doi.org/10.5194/essd-10-595-2018

Wright, S. N., Thompson, L. M., Olefeldt, D., Connon, R. F., Carpino, O. A., Beel, C. R., & Quinton, W. L. (2022). Thaw-induced impacts on land and water in discontinuous permafrost: A review of the Taiga Plains and Taiga Shield, northwestern Canada. *Earth-Science Reviews, 232*, 104104. https://doi.org/10.1016/j.earscirev.2022.104104

Wrzesien, M. L., Durand, M. T., Pavelsky, T. M., Kapnick, S. B., Zhang, Y., Guo, J., & Shum, C. K. (2018). A New Estimate of North American Mountain Snow Accumulation from Regional Climate Model Simulations. *Geophysical Research Letters, 45*(3), 1423–1432. https://doi.org/10.1002/2017GL076664

Wulder, M. A., Coops, N. C., Roy, D. P., White, J. C., & Hermosilla, T. (2018). Land cover 2.0. *International Journal of Remote Sensing, 39*(12), 4254–4284. https://doi.org/10.1080/01431161.2018.1452075

Wynn, G. (2007). *Canada and Arctic North America: An Environmental History*. ABC-CLIO.

Xiao, D., Deng, L., Kim, D.-G., Huang, C., & Tian, K. (2019). Carbon budgets of wetland ecosystems in China. *Global Change Biology, 25*(6), 2061–2076. https://doi.org/10.1111/gcb.14621

Yannick, L. M. (2020). *Investigating Canada's Deadliest Volcanic Eruption and Mitigating Future Hazards* [Dissertation]. Simon Fraser University/Université Clermont Auvergne.

Yonge, C. J., & Lowe, D. J. (2017). Hydrogeology of the Banff Hot Springs, Banff National Park, Canada: A Karst Perspective. *Cave and Karst Science, 44*(2), 82–93.

Young, G. J., & Ommanney, C. S. L. (1984). Canadian Glacier Hydrology and Mass Balance Studies; A History of Accomplishments and Recommendations for Future Work. *Geografiska Annaler, Series A, 66 A*(3), 169–182. https://doi.org/10.1080/04353676.1984.11880107

Yu, Z., Loisel, J., Brosseau, D. P., Beilman, D. W., & Hunt, S. J. (2010). Global peatland dynamics since the Last Glacial Maximum: GLOBAL PEATLANDS SINCE THE LGM. *Geophysical Research Letters, 37*(13), n/a-n/a. https://doi.org/10.1029/2010GL043584

Yunker, Z. (2022, April 19). *Their Land Was Drowned by a Flood of Hydropower*. The Tyee; The Tyee. https://thetyee.ca/News/2022/04/19/Their-Land-Was-Drowned-By-A-Flood-Of-Hydropower/

Zdanowicz, C. M., Fisher, D. A., Clark, I., & Lacelle, D. (2002). An ice-marginal δ18O record from Barnes Ice Cap, Baffin Island, Canada. *Annals of Glaciology, 35*, 145–149.

Zdanowicz, C., Fisher, D., Bourgeois, J., Demuth, M., Zheng, J., Mayewski, P., Kreutz, K., Osterberg, E., Yalcin, K., Wake, C., Steig, E. J., Froese, D., & Goto-Azuma, K. (2014). Ice Cores from the St. Elias Mountains, Yukon, Canada: Their Significance for Climate, Atmospheric Composition and Volcanism in the North Pacific Region. *Arctic, 67*(1), 35–57. https://doi.org/10.14430/arctic4352

Zedeno, M., Pickering, E., & Lanoe, F. (2021). Oral tradition as emplacement: Ancestral Blackfoot memories of the Rocky Mountain Front. *Journal of Social Archaeology, 21*(3), 306–328. https://doi.org/10.1177/14696053211019837

Zedler, J. B., & Kercher, S. (2005). Wetland Resources: Stater, Trends, Ecosystem Services, and Restorability. *Annual Review of Environment and Resources, 30*(1), 39–74. https://doi.org/10.1146/annurev.energy.30.050504.144248

Zhang, M., & Wei, X. (2014). Alteration of Flow Regimes Caused by Large-Scale Forest Disturbance: A Case Study from a Large Watershed in the Interior of British Columbia, Canada. *Ecohydrology, 7*(2), 544–556. https://doi.org/10.1002/eco.1374

Zhang, T. (2005). Influence of the seasonal snow cover on the ground thermal regime: An overview. *Reviews of Geophysics, 43*(4). https://doi.org/10.1029/2004RG000157

Zolkos, S., & Tank, S. E. (2020). Experimental Evidence That Permafrost Thaw History and Mineral Composition Shape Abiotic Carbon Cycling in Thermokarst-Affected Stream Networks. *Frontiers in Earth Science, 8.* https://doi.org/10.3389/feart.2020.00152

Zolkos, S., Tank, S. E., & Kokelj, S. V. (2018). Mineral Weathering and the Permafrost Carbon-Climate Feedback. *Geophysical Research Letters, 45*(18), 9623–9632. https://doi.org/10.1029/2018GL078748

Mountain Homelands near Pangnirtung (ᐸᖕᓂᖅᑑᖅ) in the Arctic Cordillera, Inuit Nunangat. Photo courtesy of Isaac Demeester, 2019.

CHAPTER 3

Mountains as Homelands

CO-LEAD AUTHORS: Dani Inkpen, Megan Dicker

CONTRIBUTING AUTHORS: Leon Andrew, Dawn Saunders Dahl, Goota Desmarais, Karine Gagné, Gùdia Mary Jane Johnson, Linda Johnson, Pnnal Bernard Jerome, Rosemary Langford, Keara Lightning, Lachlan MacKinnon, Brandy Mayes, Hayden Melting Tallow, Charlotte Mitchell, Tim Patterson, Rachel Reimer, Gabriella Richardson, Daniel Sims, Chris Springer, Yan Tapp, Gabrielle Weasel Head, Nicole J. Wilson, Matthew Wiseman

CHAPTER REVIEW EDITOR: PearlAnn Reichwein

"For the mountain is one and indivisible, and rock, soil, water, and air are no more integral to it than what grows from the soil and breathes the air. All are aspects of one entity, the living mountain."—Shepherd, 1977, p. 48

3.1 Introduction

3.1.1 *Homelands and homes*

Mountains can elicit strong feelings of connection to place (Bernbaum, 1997). People of virtually all backgrounds, from many walks of life, have expressed experiences of profound love and feelings of belonging in mountains; many have found solace and healing in mountains. Scholars steeped in Western philosophical traditions have sought to explain the pull of mountains through such concepts as the sublime, the frontier, and the wilderness (Cronon, 1996; Fletcher et al., 2021). But these historically and culturally bounded concepts, the progeny of European modernity, cannot account for the diversity of ways that people can be at home in the mountains. They are predicated on a division between nature and culture which places things like human-made buildings or art and non-human creations, such as beaver dams,

---

* Due to the CMA's unique approach to engaging with multiple knowledge systems, we suggest that readers review the Introduction prior to reading subsequent chapters.

into distinct ontological categories (or realms of reality), that are not universal. In this chapter, we strive to move beyond these dichotomies in our assessment of what we know, what we don't know, and what we need to know about the ways mountain regions in Canada are cultivated as particular kinds of places and about people's experiences of these places. Taking a relational approach informed by Indigenous scholarship in anthropology, history, science and technology studies, geography, and other disciplines (Chan et al., 2018; Hunt, 2014; Liboiron, 2021; TallBear, 2015; Todd, 2016; Watts, 2013), we contextualise spaces of use within larger cultural landscapes to better understand how "people develop senses of place and attachments to place that motivate, structure, and transform their interactions with the material world" (Zedeño & Bowser, 2009, p. 5).

Mountain regions in the land now called Canada have been Homelands to First Nations, Métis, and Inuit since time immemorial (Sterritt, 2016). These Homelands—with a capital "H"— are more than just homes in beautiful landscapes. Homelands are imbued with a deep sense of belonging to a place, which is grounded in multi-generational interconnected and reciprocal kin relationships among humans, and with non-humans such as mountains, waters, glaciers, animals, plants, and spirits. Connections to land are maintained through practices, language, and

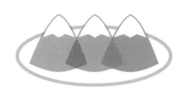

Gùdia Mary Jane Johnson, Lhu'àán Mân Dań, 2022, LC 3.1

Hayden Melting Tallow (Siksika Nation, Blackfoot Confederacy, 2022, LC 3.2

Leon Andrew, Nę K'ə Dene Ts'įlim, 2022, LC 3.3

Pnnal Bernard Jerome, Micmacs of Gesgapegiag, 2022, LC 3.4

stories, and are diverse and specific to community and place. We capitalise 'Land' when referring to its sacred or sentient qualities. However, this enriched sense of the word may not always be clear from context or muddled by the fact that in practice land supports a variety of overlapping uses, sometimes simultaneously. Where uncertain, we have opted for "land" so as not to assume knowledge we do not possess. These uncertainties emphasise the difference between mountain Homelands and mountain homes. They point to opportunities to know more about the specific land practices of individual Indigenous communities. Mountain Homelands, then, are more than just physical geographies, habitats or ecosystems; they are a network of place-based relationships in which mountains actively participate in and shape relationships among beings of different types. These relationships have ethical structures informed by inter-species treaties and agreements (Watts, 2013).

In sharing their thoughts on mountain Homelands, Indigenous Knowledge Holders working with the Canadian Mountain Assessment (CMA) highlighted the diversity and depth of meaning of Homelands. Elder Gùdia Mary Jane Johnson (Lhu'àán Mân Ku Dań) spoke of Homelands as "where you are between your relations, between people," a place for sharing bounty with family that exceeds geographical boundaries (LC 3.1). Hayden Melting Tallow (Siksika Nation, Blackfoot Confederacy) spoke of Homelands as a place where his people have been since time immemorial. He explicitly contrasted this with the homes made by people from away who settle on the land (LC 3.2). Leon Andrew (Nę K'ə Dene Ts'įli) described beautifully the Homelands of the Mountain Dene as being made and sustained by trails carved in the earth by humans and non-human people. "We call it our Homeland," he said, "because of our grandfathers' trails" (LC 3.3). Several Indigenous Knowledge Holders emphasised the relations and responsibilities that undergird the idea of Homelands. Pnnal Bernard Jerome (Micmacs of Gesgapegiag) described Homelands as places of sharing and giving back—places of responsibility and caretaking (LC 3.4). Brandy Mayes (Kwanlin Dün First Nation) stressed the importance of sharing, caring, and being respectful for understanding and cultivating Homelands (LC 3.5). This understanding and cultivation of Homelands involves ongoing learning and receptivity. Whenever you go into mountains, observed Anne York, a Nlaka'pamx Knowledge Holder and author who is not affiliated with the CMA, "You stay there and learn all there is to learn in that place. Next time you go somewhere else and talk to all the plants in that place. You get knowledge and grow strong. K'ek'áwzik is the place our young people went to learn. They might stay up to ten days. Not eating or drinking. Learning on that mountain" (York et al., 1993, p. xvii). To have a Homeland is to be a steward. Yan Tapp (Gespeg First Nation) spoke with moving passion about his Homelands in the Chic-Choc mountains. Encroached upon by private land—"everywhere there are signs"—Homelands, he maintained, are worth fighting for (LC 3.6). Indeed, many Indigenous Peoples in Canada are today fighting on behalf of their mountain Homelands (Moreton-Robinson, 2015).

Settler-colonialism—defined briefly as a set of active relations that aims to destroy or replace Indigenous Peoples and their relations—has dispossessed Indigenous Peoples or separated them from their mountain Homelands in ways that change what is possible on the land. Indigenous Peoples did not historically think of relationships to land in terms of "ownership" or "property" (Liboiron, 2021; Nadasdy, 2002). Relationships based on ideas of ownership—whether through private property or "public" lands such as "crown land" or parks—are key aspects of how colonialism has impacted Indigenous land relations in the mountains. As we shall see, they continue to severely limit how they are able to access and interact with their Homelands (Liboiron, 2021; Yang, 2017). "The power of these colonial systems," observes Knowledge Holder Gabrielle Weasel Head (Kainaiwa First Nation, Blackfoot Confederacy), "is really to instil in us this sense of disempowerment that we can't move forward" (LC 3.7). The historical and ongoing changes to mountains resulting from settler-colonialism are a central concern of our chapter.

When we refer to mountains as home with a lower-case 'h', we gesture toward the many ways that non-Indigenous people have made homes and felt at home in mountains. These, too, are varied and may be long standing and deep, emotional or even spiritual. For our purposes, stories of mountains as home have been largely captured in peer-reviewed literature on place-making in the mountains, in documentary and biographical literatures, in creative expressions like visual art, and in work that seeks to understand the specifics of colonial encounters and change in Canada (Harris, 1996, 2004, 2021). Much of the scholarly work considered here falls under efforts to understand "place-making"; that is, how peoples' understandings and experiences of a place are made through social and material practices, representations, and forms of knowledge (Low & Lawrence-Zúñiga, 2003; Malpas, 2018; Tuan, 2001).

In this chapter, we strive to weave together stories of specific Indigenous knowledge of mountains as Homelands and stories of mountains as homes for non-Indigenous people as they are found in peer-reviewed academic literatures and grey literatures. We have attempted to be as thorough as possible in our assessment of the stories captured in the peer-reviewed literature, but we have been limited by the bounds (both geographical and topical) of our individual areas of expertise, and the limited ability of the systematic review process to capture certain literatures relevant to this chapter.

3.1.2 *Conceptual underpinnings*

This chapter has been influenced by two scholarly approaches: multispecies ethnography and ontology studies. Multispecies ethnography, described by Eduardo Kohn (2013) as an "anthropology beyond the human," examines entanglements among humans and non-humans (Haraway, 2013; Mathur, 2021; Tsing, 2015). Multispecies work challenges ways of thinking that overemphasise human agency and dominance over non-humans. It aims to show how humans are shaped by and are co-evolving with beings other than themselves. This conceptual shift has spread well beyond anthropology, and aligns, if imperfectly, with how some Indigenous communities regard their relationships with the land.

An ontology may be understood as a way of being and knowing the world. Ontology studies take seriously the possibility that we do not all know or occupy the world in the same way. Take, for instance, a foundational case for the genre: the dichotomy between nature and culture. Not all communities adhere to the nature/culture divide central to Western thought (Descola, 2013; Kohn, 2013). While epistemologies

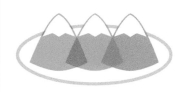

Brandy Mayes, Kwanlin Dün First Nation, 2022, LC 3.5

Yan Tapp, Gespeg First Nation, 2022, LC 3.6

Gabrielle Weasel Head, Kainaiwa First Nation, Blackfoot Confederacy, 2022, LC 3.7

(theories of knowledge) and ontologies (theories of being) are separate branches of Western thought, Indigenous worldviews do not separate the two—conceptualised as onto-epistemologies or Indigenous place-thought (Hunt, 2014; Watts, 2013). The notion of ontology has been mobilised in the context of Indigenous studies in Canada (Kakaliouras, 2012; Nadasdy, 2007; Wilson & Inkster, 2018). However, as Métis scholar Zoe Todd (2016) argues, the ideas at the heart of ontology studies—long present in Indigenous knowledge systems—have often gone unacknowledged by non-Indigenous scholars in the field. Together, multispecies and ontologies studies provide us with ways of thinking beyond a strict nature-culture divide. While we may not always reference them directly, these ideas have shaped our thinking in this chapter.

We have found in our research that the relevant multispecies literature and ontologies studies on Canadian mountain regions is linguistically and geographically limited. References to multispecies work in French language scholarship are scarce. Moreover, most English language scholarship focuses on mountains in western Canada (British Columbia and Alberta) and northern Canada (Yukon and Northwest Territories). We found few studies relevant to the Atlantic Maritime and Boreal Shield, Eastern Subarctic, Arctic Cordillera, and Interior Hills regions. Throughout this chapter, ontology studies have been productive for illustrating and understanding how mountain Homelands bypass and exceed ways of being in the world built on a divide between nature and culture. However, pertinent literature on cultural landscapes, spirits, deities, narratives, and beliefs about or involving mountains in Canada remains limited. What is available focuses on northern and western Canada, and on Indigenous ways of knowing and being in mountains. We believe there is an opportunity to expand both the geographical scope and cultural scope of this body of scholarship to include investigations concerned with Interior, eastern Arctic, subarctic areas, and Maritime mountain regions and with non-Indigenous ontological relationships to mountains understood as one of many ways of perceiving and acting in the world, rather than assumed to be a "given" or "normal" way.

This chapter begins by considering the ways that mountain Homelands are constituted as more than human geographies through stories about the creation of mountains and their features (Sec. 3.2.1). We then consider how mountain Homelands are understood and experienced as places of spirit (Sec. 3.2.2). These two sections help illustrate what we mean when we state that mountain Homelands are more than just landscape—they are lively and spiritual places. We then turn to the formative role that place names play in building and maintaining mountain Homelands (Sec. 3.2.3) before assessing the role archaeology has played in establishing the longevity of mountain Homelands (Sec. 3.3). Multispecies literature on human-animal relations (Sec. 3.4.1) and human-plant relations (Sec. 3.4.2) make up the next two sections, which help establish the groundwork for understanding the historical and ongoing changes in the land wrought by settler-colonialism (Sec. 3.5). This is examined through scholarly work on early forms of colonialism (Sec. 3.5.1), the mobilisation of science (Sec. 3.6.2), and treaties and private land (Sec. 3.5.3). Parks and protected areas have had far-reaching impacts in shaping mountains in Canada (Sec. 3.5.4). We then look at the literature on how recreation (Sec. 3.6) and labour (Sec. 3.7) shape mountain places and the people who use them before turning to that on governance systems as formative forces in mountain regions (Sec. 3.8). The chapter concludes with an assessment of the state of knowledge about Homelands and homes. Briefly, we highlight opportunities for better understanding of mountain homes and Homelands outside of the Boreal Cordillera, Montane Cordillera, and Pacific Maritime regions of western Canada, call for more nuanced studies of Indigenous resistance and perpetuity on mountain Homelands, and encourage more scholarly attention to be paid to intersectional experiences of mountain places that attend to the ways race, gender, and class can shape mountain places and experiences of them.

3.2 Stories of Homelands

3.2.1 *Stories of creation*

Indigenous creation stories can provide insight into the origins of mountains and describe the Land in ways that show it to be more than physical, but rather a place of knowledge, memory, and spirit, and equally home to non-human kin. There are many different creation stories that tell of how mountains came to be and we cannot document them all here. We will confine ourselves to a selection of illustrative examples, inviting readers to look further at Blackfoot (Bastien 8–9) and Ktunaxa creation stories among others.[1]

There is a story told by Ronnie Georgekish (Eastern Cree) about a mountain that was formed and shaped by a cooking pot that a giant dropped on the land after being killed by a Shaman (G. Reid et al., 2020). Dogrib oral traditions from along the Idaa Trail in the Northwest Territories (Interior Hills West mountain region) relate the formative agency of a mountain, Kwe?ehdoo, also known as "blood rock." Kwe?ehdoo is described as an old man with psychic abilities (Andrews & Zoe, 1997). Gille (2012) reports that for Coast Salish Peoples, the rocks, animals, and all non-humans, including mountains, are ancestors whose form was stabilised by a Transformer (beings of mythical time, often half-human, half-animal) named Khaals. Similarly for Cheam Peak, in the southwest Coastal Mountains of the Pacific Maritime region near Chilliwack: the mountain's three peak structure suggests, as the stories tell, that the Transformer petrified a giant woman and her three children there (Gille, 2012). The literature documenting stories such as these illustrate conceptions of mountains as storied, social, spiritual and living Land—much more than scenic landscape or the two-dimensional topography of cartographic maps. Much of this literature was written by non-Indigenous scholars who collaborated with Indigenous Knowledge Holders. The nature of the collaboration was unclear in many cases. The literature focuses on western and northern mountain regions, inviting further studies into creation stories about mountains in eastern regions.

3.2.2 Stories of mountain spirits

Studies of Indigenous understandings of Canadian mountain places describe mountain spirits. This literature further emphasises the ways in which mountain Homelands are more than mere topography. For instance (Heyes, 2011), considers how an Inuit community in northern Quebec believes the Torngat spirit resides in the Torngat mountains and has for over one thousand years. Peter Freuchen, who was part of the Fifth Thule Expedition from 1921–1924, noted the behaviour of "Eskimo [sic] dogs" and how they bark at the mountain spirits (Freuchen 1935:181f as cited in (Laugrand & Oosten, 2002). E. Duchesne and Crépeau (2020, p. 72) and (Duchesne, 2022) describe how the ethnographic literature on Algonquin culture demonstrates how master-entities—beings who control and protect the animals—are organised hierarchically according to different domains. Among the Innu, Papakassiku, the master of the caribou, occupies a similarly pre-eminent position. The master of the caribou lives on a mountain called Atiku-mitshuap (the dwelling of the caribou) in which the caribou are contained as well as the masters of other species. It is from this mountain that the caribou are released and given to the hunters. Mountain spirits are described in the oral histories of many Indigenous traditions, mediating people's relationships with mountain places and offering protection. Elder and Learning Circle participant and Elder Pnnal Bernard Jerome, of the Micmacs of Gesgapegiag, shared a story of the Little People, tricksters and protectors who dwell high on a peak in the Chic-Choc mountains and warn the Micmac People if strangers are coming to their territory (LC 3.8).

In western Canada, too, mountains serve as spiritual places. Chief John Snow tells of the Stoney Nakoda practice of going on a vision quest, a journey into "the rugged mountains, seeking wisdom and divine guidance" (2005, p. 16). People prepared for these journeys in ceremonial lodges on the plains, thereby linking through practice the lowland and highland Homelands of the Stoney Nakoda. Hayden Melting Tallow (Siksika

---

1 See, for instance, legendsofamerica.com/na-blackfootcreation/ and https://www.ktunaxa.org/who-we-are/creation-story/.

Pnnal Bernard Jerome, Micmacs of Gesgapegiag, 2022, LC 3.8

Hayden Melting Tallow, Siksika Nation, Blackfoot Confederacy, 2022, LC 3.9

Gùdia Mary Jane Johnson, Lhu'ààn Mân Ku Dań, 2022, LC 3.10

Nation, Blackfoot Confederacy) spoke poignantly at the CMA Learning Circle about Blackfoot sacred mountain sites. "Waterton Lakes," he said, "those mountains there, are very sacred." He continued, "we've been cut off from there, relegated to the reserve" (LC 3.9) In *The Story of the Blackfoot People: Niitsitapiisinni*, a story is related about the Waterton Lakes area in which a boy named Scabby-Round-Robe was given powers and sacred objects that he kept in Beaver Bundles by Old Man Beaver (The Blackfoot Gallery Committee, 2013, pp. 22–23). Bastien (2004) is another source of information for learning about Blackfoot relations to their mountain Homelands and their understanding of land relations.

It is worth noting that mountains may not be sacred sites for all Indigenous groups who live near them. Even for those for whom mountains are spiritual, it may be that such stories are not appropriate for general circulation. While far from comprehensive, at the very least, those documented in the literature and shared by Indigenous Knowledge Holders reveal mountains as much more than just rocks, water, plants, and animals. While acknowledging that not all stories may be shared in published venues, we believe nonetheless that there is a room for scholarship that goes beyond documenting the spirituality of mountain Homelands and investigates how sacred mountain places have been altered or intersected with other forces in Canadian society. For instance, in Unama'ki (Cape Breton Island, Atlantic Maritime and Boreal Shield region), the mountains are sacred sites for the Mi'kmaq. As

Mackenzie and Dalby (Mackenzie & Dalby, 2003) show, this fuelled opposition to a proposed super-quarry on an island with complex histories of community, nature, and culture. More studies of this kind, which probe the ways sacred sites have been desecrated and may fuel Indigenous resistance, should also be a scholarly focus.

We also note that, aside from important general studies (Bernbaum, 1997, 2006), we found very little scholarly work on the ways that non-Indigenous people experience mountains as spiritual or religious places. Studies of Mary Schäffer and Mary Vaux note the important role that Quaker beliefs played in their experience of the Rocky Mountains and nature (Cavell, 1983; M. G. Jones, 2015; Skidmore, 2017). More generally, Christianity was a prominent feature of Victorians' experiences of nature and what they perceived as wilderness (Berger, 1983). We also note that mountains as spiritual places is a prominent theme in much mountaineering literature (Tabei, 2017). Further, as we will see in Sec. 3.6, there is a grey literature that covers spiritual experiences of mountain professionals. Nevertheless, it seems that critical scholarly work on exactly *how* senses of spirituality or religious practices of non-Indigenous people shape mountain places and how they are experienced in the Canadian context would benefit our understanding of mountains as home.

3.2.3 *Mountain place names*

The stories and names given to mountains by Indigenous Peoples are important for delineating and maintaining Homelands. On the second day of the CMA Learning Circle meeting, Gùdia Mary Jane Johnson (Lhu'ààn Mân Ku Dań) shared songs about her Homeland that showed how knowledge of mountain places in her people's Traditional Territory is embedded in language, story, and song (LC 3.10).

Indigenous place names, as scholars such as Keith Basso (1996) have noted, are more than just nominal labels: they describe places and embed them in rich cultural geographies imbued with history, memory, and the knowledge required to live on the land. For instance, Cruikshank's (1998, 2005, 2007) relating of stories about glaciers and the names of places around the Saint Elias Mountains demonstrates how Southern

Tutchone communities are tied to mountains through their cultural history and stories. Thornton (2019) describes how Tlingit place names form an important element of their social life. They referred to a prominent peak on the BC-Alaska border as Waas'eita Shaa or Yaas'eita Shaa (Mount Saint Elias), meaning "Mountain at the Head of the Icy Bay" (Cruikshank, 1991; Thornton, 1997). The importance of place names is more than just historical. Yaas'eita Shaa's name locates the mountain within a lived-in geography that contains information about the land and thus continually reinforces connections to it. The Tahltan refer to a particular peak as "Stingy Mountain." This designation originates from hunters who report seeing animals on the mountain while others do not; it is stingy because it provides food to only some hunters. McIlwraith (2012) discusses Talhtan meanings of place and connections to the land as reasons for why their hunting camps, at least one of which is on the side of a mountain, cannot be moved.

Based on fieldwork conducted in the Algonquin community of Kitcisakik in the Abitibi-Témiscamingue region of Quebec, Leroux (2003) reports several stories of local summits in oral traditions. One of which refers to Nanipawi Pokwatina, a summit which, Leroux conjectures, corresponds to *Mont Chaudron*/Mount Cheminis. While the mountain does not play an active role in the narrative, which centres on Northern Pike, its name, Nanipawi Pokwatina, which translates as "staying awake," alludes to a key episode in the story. According to Leroux (2003), the episode incorporates important elements of Algonquin filial relations.

The names given to mountain places by First Nations, Métis, and Inuit Peoples in Canada illuminate how meaning is inscribed onto the land through language and living, provide information about how to live well on that land, and articulate the long-standing historical presence of Indigenous Peoples in the mountains. The inscription of non-Indigenous names overtop Homelands with their own typonomies (geographies of names) was and remains a way of asserting colonial presence upon a place through non-Indigenous geographic and historical understandings (Robinson & Slemon, 2015).

There is some documentation and circulation of Indigenous place names for mountain regions in Canada, such as the *Stó:lō-Coast Salish Historical Atlas* (Carlson et al., 2006), which details the 15,000-year history and territory of the Sto:lo, upon which settlers would erect the cities of Vancouver, Chilliwack, and other communities. But this level of detailed historical and geographical knowledge of Indigenous place names is not always achievable. As Fromhold (2010, pp. 1–3) notes in the introduction to *2001 Indian Place Names*, not all traditional place names were known by all Peoples, different tribes knew different names for the same place, or the same name could apply to different places among Peoples who did not have much contact with one another. The use of slang, difference in word use between men and women, and errors of translation when documenting place names bring additional hurdles to collecting this knowledge (Fromhold, 2010).

Indigenous place name knowledge may be successfully gathered and yet still difficult to access. For instance, there is a book about Stoney Nakoda place names for areas around Morley, Eden Valley, and Kananaskis: *Ozade Mnotha Wapta Makochi: Stoney Place Names*, by the Chiniki Research Team and the Stoney Elders for the Chiniki Band Council. This resource, made in the 1980s, is difficult to access. The only copy we know of is held at the Archives of the Whyte Museum of the Canadian Rockies. Yet, it contains knowledge of the land, such as the location of blue soil for painting and decorating (1980, p. 65). The Ktunaxa, Cree, and Blackfoot also have typonomies that cover these mountain regions, of which we learn some from Hart (1999), who states that the Ktunaxa also used ochre from the Paint Pots which they would convert into a red oxide to trade with the Blackfoot (1999, p. 62).[2]

While we recognize that not all place names should be shared, for those names that may be more widely circulated, there remain difficulties in finding and translating knowledge. Nevertheless,

---

2 Note that we treat this text gingerly. Although it contains much historical information, it was written in a style that uses group psychological descriptions such as "particularly aggressive" or "ferocious" to explain the actions of certain Indigenous Peoples, rather than seeking to understand the reasons behind conflicts and rivalries. We are thus careful in our selection of material and do not endorse this as a quality interpretive text.

when Indigenous place names are available to be shared, they can be used effectively on multilingual signage, such as that on the Sea-to-Sky Highway running from Vancouver to Whistler, to remind non-Indigenous people that they are in Indigenous Homelands and to "re-story" the land.

3.2.4 Summary: Stories of Homelands

In stories of how mountains were created, stories of spirits in the mountains, and through place names, we see land revealed as sentient and active, and as part of a social order. Turner and Clifton (2009) note how members of the Gitga'at (Coast Tsimshian) and neighbouring communities believe pointing at a mountain or mountain range shows disrespect and will therefore cause storms and bad weather. Similarly, Nadasdy (2021) discusses how mountains in the Yukon are perceived as sentient beings, part of the natural landscape, and possessing unique personalities. These ideas of mountain sentience and their social significance are discussed in Julie Cruikshank's (2005, 2012) work, where she relates how glaciers and mountains in Southern Tutchone territory are perceived as sentient entities, "shape-shifters of magnificent power" demanding respect, abhorring hubris, who will respond when provoked (2005, p. 69). These stories demonstrate the spirituality, agency, and sentience of non-human mountain denizens such as glaciers, underlying the need for reverence and respect for Homelands.

The already-noted geographical emphasis on the west and northwest characterises much of the literature on these topics, and we observed a difficulty in accessing information that was documented. Given what we found, we judge that there is room for scholarly work that goes beyond documenting and instead investigates how Indigenous stories, place names, and spiritual Lands intersect with colonial structures in specific cases. Such work could be mobilised in Indigenous efforts to protect their lands and lives and promote greater knowledge of complex land relations in mountain regions of Canada (see Sec. 3.4.1).

3.3 Mountain Archaeology and the Longevity of Homelands

Mountains have long been significant features for Indigenous Peoples world-wide (Bernbaum, 2006; Reimer, 2011, 2018; Reinhard & Ceruti, 2010; Ruru, 2004). As described in Sec. 2.1.4, scientific understandings of human migration patterns into North America after the Last Glacial Maximum emphasize the importance of mountain corridors. In the past, mountains were integral to the daily lives of Indigenous Peoples, as travel and trade corridors, areas for procuring resources such as ochre and medicines, and spiritual places (Pitblado, 2017; Reimer, 2011; Todd, 2015). In Canada, the material evidence of this is found archaeologically in the form of short-term habitation sites, lithic scatters (stone tools and the debris from their manufacture), resource processing sites, and, more recently, Ancestral remains and organic material culture (e.g., clothing, bows, arrows, etc.) that typically decays at lower elevations (Dixon et al., 2014; Hebda et al., 2017; Reimer, 2003, 2014, 2018). Despite the richness of the archaeological record in high-elevation places across North America generally, with some exceptions (Fladmark, 1984; Reeves & Dormaar, 1972), it is only since the late 1990s that focus has moved upwards from the lowland areas along coastal shorelines and the lower reaches of river systems where the remains of large ancestral settlements are typically located (Sullivan & Prezzano, 2001). It is only since the late 1990s that archaeological focus has truly moved upwards. This relatively recent emphasis in archaeological research has produced a new sub-discipline—glacial archaeology (Andrews & MacKay, 2012; Dixon et al., 2014; Helwig et al., 2021; Lee, 2012; Pilø et al., 2021; Thomas & MacKay, 2012)—which, in many ways, is a response to a rapidly changing climate causing widespread glacial recession and permafrost thaw, both of which are revealing an ancient human presence previously unrecognised by archaeologists.

Many descendant First Nation Communities' oral histories record their ancestral use of mountains and glaciers (Champagne and Aishihik First Nations et al., 2017; Cruikshank, 2005; Kennedy & Bouchard, 2010; Reimer, 2003; Teit, 1906). Archaeology complements these histories, most commonly through toolstone provenance studies that seek to connect lithic artefacts found at archaeological sites to toolstone sources (Conolloy et al., 2015; Kendall & MacDonald, 2015; Mierendorf & Baldwin, 2015; Reimer, 2014; Rorabaugh & McNabb, 2014). This partnership of Indigenous culture and science was most dramatically demonstrated following the discovery of the frozen remains of a young adult male eroding out of a glacier at approximately 1600 m above sea level in the Tatshenshini-Alsek Provincial Park, British Columbia (Hebda et al., 2017). The individual was given the name Kwäday Dän Ts'ìnchi, a Southern Tutchone phrase meaning "long ago person found." Through various analyses, Kwäday Dän Ts'ìnchi was determined to have spent most of his life on the coast but during his last months had been living inland (Corr et al., n.d.; Dickson et al., 2014; Hebda et al., 2017). He was about 20 years old when he died while travelling from the coast to the interior sometime between CE 1670 and CE 1850 (Richards et al., 2007). Through an agreement with First Nations representatives, a DNA analysis was conducted on Kwäday Dän Ts'ìnchi and more than 200 volunteers from the Champagne and Aishihik First Nations, the results of which showed that he was related through the maternal line to 17 living members of the community (Greer et al., 2017).

The discovery and subsequent analyses of Kwäday Dän Ts'ìnchi exemplify the importance of high-elevation places for Indigenous Peoples of Canada. He connected past and present and anchored his descendants to the high and low places of their Traditional Territories. As alpine glaciers continue to recede, it is certain that more evidence of the deep relationship that Indigenous Peoples had, and continue to have, with high elevation places will come to light and serve to enrich our understanding of mountains in Canada beyond consideration as sites of resource extraction and alpine sports.

Archaeology also provides insights into Indigenous Peoples' long-standing multispecies relationships with mountains in Canada. Reeves (1978) found archaeological evidence of bison killing amongst communities in the southwest Alberta Rocky Mountains between 10,000–8000 years ago, and Zedeño (2017) describes bison hunters and the Rocky Mountains as having a historical partnership. Driver (1982) provides archaeological evidence showing that bighorn sheep were also hunted in the southeastern Rockies around 8500 years ago. Allan (2018) presents evidence of Hummingbird Creek archaeological site's significance as a specialised hunting camp used by the Stoney Nakoda on the eastern slopes

of the Rocky Mountains approximately 2500–1000 years ago. The site was used to plan hunts into areas with known animal presence (Allan, 2018). Archaeological evidence dating back 8000 years ago indicates Indigenous caribou hunting took place in southern Yukon alpine ice patches (Greer & Strand, 2012; Hare et al., 2004). The available archaeological evidence, then, demonstrates vital relationships with animals in mountains in Canada. Animals were killed and consumed to sustain life in mountainous regions. The movements and population fluctuations of animals influenced humans' movements within mountain Homelands and their lowland counterparts, illustrating the power and agency of animals in these long-standing relationships.

As of 2011, there were more than 2000 known archaeological sites in the mountain national parks alone (Langemann, 2011, p. 304). These sites are revealing mountains as cultural crossroads since time immemorial. However, here, as elsewhere, we noticed a tendency for the literature to gravitate westward; archaeology of non-western mountain regions could be better represented. Moreover, as Hayden Melting Tallow (Siksika Nation, Blackfoot Confederacy) reminds us, the value of archaeology is specific. The Blackfoot do not have burial sites in the mountains because they do not bury their dead. "But if there was gravesites, if we dug up Mother Earth and buried our people," he said, "there would be a lot of change, we could claim that" (LC 3.11). While archaeology can aid land claims and access for many, it cannot be the only basis upon which such work is established. Given the state of the literature, we believe there is opportunity for scholarly efforts to improve our understanding of how archaeology in mountain places is conditioned by historical cultural practices, and by land use. Studies that investigate what it is possible to know about

Hayden Melting Tallow, Siksika Nation, Blackfoot Confederacy, 2022, LC 3.11

mountain archaeology, given constraints such as difficult terrain, private land ownership, or by the materials used by specific mountain-dwelling communities would be welcome additions.

3.4 Multispecies Literature

3.4.1 *Human-animal relationships in mountains*

Literature discussing human and animal relationships in mountains in Canada tends to focus on Indigenous Peoples and highlights the importance of animals to how they create, know, and move about their mountain Homelands. Johnson (2010) explains how hunters in mountain regions look for mineral licks, as these are frequented by moose, mountain sheep, goats, caribou, and other species. The caribou is significant to many, but not all, Indigenous communities that call mountains Homelands. Wray and Parlee (2013) note the ways in which the Teel'it Gwich'in hunt and respect caribou living in and near the Richardson and Ogilvie Mountains in Yukon, while Johnson (2010) describes the path and presence of caribou herds in this region. Homelands, according to Indigenous Knowledge Holder Leon Andrew (Nę K'ə Dene Ts'ı̨li), are shaped by the paths traced through them by human and non-human alike. "You mention bear," he said, "they've got their own markings everywhere. And my people always respect that, you know, that's their territory,

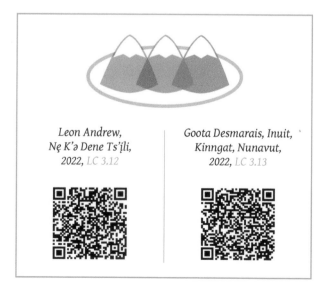

Leon Andrew,
Nę K'ə Dene Ts'ı̨li,
2022, LC 3.12

Goota Desmarais, Inuit,
Kinngat, Nunavut,
2022, LC 3.13

they've got their own Homeland to protect" (LC 3.12).

Relationships with animals are constitutive of Homelands. Goota Desmarais (Inuit, Kinngat, Nunavut), shared her childhood experiences of her summer home in the mountains and the variety of generative relationships she and her community had with the animals on the land: birds that chased her off mountain tops, geese that provided eggs for eating (LC 3.13). The work of Daniel Clément (1995; 2012), based on extensive fieldwork conducted among the Innu of northeastern Québec (*Côte-Nord*), provides information on the relationships between human communities and the local fauna. In the Innu context, animals are prominent in stories and oral narratives, and they are central to how people engage with the environment (Clement, 1995; Clément, 2012). Clément's work showcases Innu knowledge of animals. In particular, the volume "*Le bestiaire innu,*" organised into 20 chapters, each covering a species, reports a rich terminology concerning not only animals, but also their movements, and the component parts of their bodies (Clément, 2012).

Other species are singled out in the literature as culturally important to First Nations, Métis, and Inuit Peoples and illustrative of the ways that Homelands are created and maintained in conjunction with other creatures. Bighorn Sheep (*Ovis canadensis*), for instance, are a critical part of the cultural landscape for the Coast Salish of British Columbia; and the Kluane Peoples in southwest Yukon have extensive knowledge of Dall Sheep (*Ovis dalli dalli*) (Cross, 1996; Nadasdy, 2003). Wolverine (*Gulo gulo*) are described by Dene and Métis trappers in the Northwest Territories as admirable, strong creatures but also as dangerous tricksters and thieves (Bonamy et al., 2020). Johnson (2010) relates a story in which an Elder saved two sisters from a wolverine, and its bones remain buried atop a mountain in the Cassiar region of British Columbia (Montane Cordillera).

Perhaps unsurprisingly, given their importance to many Indigenous cultures and charismatic appeal across non-Indigenous cultures, bears are prominent in the multispecies literature. Entanglements with bears go back generations; Henson et al. (2021) have found correlations among the genetics of grizzly bear populations and Indigenous language groups along the coasts of BC.

Clark and Slocombe (2011) examined the Indigenous terminology, stories, rituals, and practices of respect and reciprocity towards bears in the southwestern Yukon. Spiritual significance can motivate action. For the Ktunaxa First Nation in the Kootenay region, BC, the spirit of the grizzly bear residing in Qat'muk fuelled a fight against the development of a ski resort on the Jumbo Glacier that went to the highest court in the nation ("Ktunaxa and Qat'muk," 2015) (see Sec. 3.5.3). Grizzly bears, D.A. Clark and others (2021) find, are central to the livelihoods and cultural identities of several Indigenous Peoples in British Columbia, including the Haí̓lzaqv (Heiltsuk), Kitasoo/Xai'xais, and Nuxalk First Nations. Relations with polar bears are at the heart of Torngat National Park where Innu guides and bear-monitors are the backbone of the park's tourist industry (Lemelin & Maher, 2009).

Bear-human relationships are also examined in non-Indigenous contexts. Skiers' encounters with grizzly bears in the mountains of British Columbia were studied by Stoddart (2011b). The experiences of Charlie Russell, an Alberta naturalist and wildlife photographer, have been examined as forging relationships with bears that teach trust, love, and respect for others (Bradshaw, 2020). While Charlie's experiences are well-known, those of his then partner, Maureen Enns, are not. Enns also cultivated an intimate, empathetic understanding of mountain grizzlies and produced art that sought to gaze through the "Eyes of the Bear" (D. Thomas & Enns, 1995). This imbalance in the record suggests that there is room for analyses of the ways that gender inflects relations with other animals, and how those relations are remembered or not.

More broadly, human-bear relations may illustrate how multispecies relations can be shaped by economics, media, and conservation. This is suggested in the case of Boo,[3] an orphaned grizzly bear on Kicking Horse Mountain in south-central British Columbia. Boo is both a protected animal who lives in a 8 hectare refuge on the mountain, and a social media star inadvertently advertising for Kicking Horse Mountain Resort. Boo's situation, and the lack of studies we found treating

---

3 https://kickinghorseresort.com/purchase/boo-grizzly-bear/

Yan Tapp, Gespeg First Nation, 2022, LC 3.14

the complexities of human-animal relations in relation to commodification and social media, suggests an opportunity for more studies examining the overlapping and sometimes competing narratives that human-animal relations can take in the mountains.

Charismatic mammals are generally well covered in the multispecies literature. Salmon, although of cultural, spiritual, and economic importance for Indigenous Peoples in both the east and west, including but not only the Ktunaxa, Secwempc, and Mi'kmaq, are less well represented in that body of literature. However, there is a growing literature on the role that Indigenous knowledges and practices ought to play in the management of salmon fisheries (Adams et al., 2021; Atlas et al., 2021; Massey et al., 2021; Taylor III, 1999). We know from Yan Tapp (Gespeg First Nation) that salmon is critical to the Mi'kmaq on the East Coast and ties into land access issues for which the Gespeg First Nation have been fighting for years (LC 3.14). However, we found fewer studies of salmon on the East Coast than the more studied West Coast.

Given our research, we believe that there may be an opportunity to apply a multi-species ethnographic lens (as opposed to, for instance, an ecological or biological lens) to investigate relations among animal species without applying a human versus non-human dichotomy. In many Indigenous traditions, people and animals of ancient times have been understood as belonging to the same domain, rather than relegated to separate ontological categories. For instance, people and animals may be indistinguishable or change between forms, with non-human animals sometimes described as people wearing animal clothing (Brightman, 1993; Hanna & Henry, 1996). Thus, multi-species ethnographies in which humans are distinguished from animals may unnecessarily promote a culture-nature dichotomy which constrains the scope of inquiry.

3.4.2 Human-plant relationships in mountains

The literature describing people-plant interactions in mountains in Canada captures well how knowledge of plants can shape how people move through and shape mountain places. According to Taylor and Pacini-Ketchabaw (2017) and Pacini-Ketchabaw and Taylor (2015), in mountain forests people develop intimate knowledge of plants. Northwestern boreal montane forests (Taiga Cordillera and Boreal Cordillera regions) have been historically and contemporarily important habitats for Indigenous Peoples such as the Dene, Wisuwet'en (Wet'suwet'en) and Gitksan/Gitxsan to collect culturally important botanical specimens for subsistence and medicinal uses (Johnson, 2006, 2008; Joseph et al., 2022; Turner, 1988; Turner et al., 2011; Turner & Clifton, 2009; Uprety et al., 2012). Mountain huckleberries (*Vaccinium membranaceum*) receive special treatment in the literature and are known for their sustenance value year-round (Johnson, 2010; Shelvey & Boyd, 2000; Trusler & Johnson, 2008), and several sources note how Indigenous groups burn huckleberry patches in autumn to improve their production and predictability (Shelvey & Boyd, 2000; Trusler & Johnson, 2008; Turner et al., 2011). One of our authors, Dawn Saunders Dahl, has been developing a seasonal tea walk at the Whyte Museum of the Canadian Rockies that seeks to show how knowledge of plants is a knowledge of land and movement through it. In consultation with Ktunaxa and Stoney Nakoda Elders, she has learned that wolf willow, berries of various hues, including silver and red-orange, and prairie turnips are used for tea and for making jewellery.

Overall, the multispecies literature we considered reveals how relations among humans, animals, and plants create meaningful connections across species that shape how mountain places are experienced and known as Homelands and homes. Generally speaking, there tends to be a northern and western geographical focus, and critical masses of literature around certain species or types, which opens possibilities for geographical and topical extensions by other scholars and knowers.

3.5 Changes to Mountain Homelands

The coming of non-Indigenous people to mountain regions, and their encounters with those who lived there (human and otherwise), catalysed massive rearrangements of relations. Certainly, Indigenous Peoples had always altered their Homelands through daily, seasonal, and non-regular practices, such as prescribed burning. However, the changes brought by the coming of non-Indigenous people modified relationships on new geographical and temporal scales. These rearrangements persist today, though contested by many Indigenous communities. They are discernible in the ways that mountains are represented in science and art, reflected in built environments, engaged within mountain recreation, and often fossilised and reinforced in the legislation governing their use. The effects of these changes and how they have been refused, resisted, and appropriated for their own purposes by First Nations, Métis, and Inuit Peoples throughout the mountain regions of Canada are the concern of the next four sections.

3.5.1 Early colonial presence

Colonialism in Canada did not take a single form. The extractive colonialism of the 16th, 17th, and 18th centuries (e.g., the cod fishery and fur trade) was soon joined by missionary colonialism, and then settler colonialism. Whereas fur traders were primarily focused on the business of the fur trade, and missionaries on "saving souls," settlers arrived seeking land. It is important to remember that the hallmark of settler colonialism was the replacement of Indigenous populations with non-Indigenous ones. How each of these forms of colonialism arrived and how they played out differed across mountain regions. We do not have the expertise or space to describe the details for all mountain regions. However, a brief discussion of early colonial presence in what is now British Columbia can provide a sense of the major forces and players at work. Even within the context of the western mountains of the Boreal Cordillera, Montane Cordillera, and Pacific Maritime regions, colonial influences reached different areas in different ways at different times.

Europeans reached the coast of what is now British Columbia in the late-18th century, almost three hundred years since they had arrived in the east (Harris, 2008, p. 416). They did so by two routes: the Pacific Coast, with early arrivals coming from present-day Russia, Spain, and Britain, and overland as an extension of the fur trade by way of the northern Cordillera and the Peace River. Yet, through the long arm of disease, effects of their presence in eastern North America preceded the actual coming of European individuals. After crossing the Rocky Mountains in 1811, geographer David Thompson met the Ktunaxa who had been subject to at least two smallpox epidemics late in the preceding century; a common experience on the west coast and Haida Gwaii (Harris, 2008, p. 418). Early colonial presence was violent and shaped by the movement of capital dictated by both distant markets and on-the-ground encounters with Indigenous Peoples and the presumed "resources" (Harris, 1996, pp. 32–33, 2008, p. 421). Indigenous people responded to the new economic opportunities and concomitant disruption of trading patterns and alliances. They bargained with newcomers to their advantage and countered aggression with aggression. The mountains and their distance from eastern metropolises (the North West Company and the Hudson's Bay Company, which merged in 1821, were based in Montréal and London respectively) made colonial administration virtually impossible (Harris, 2008, p. 423). For most of the first half of the 19th century, fur traders operated largely beyond the reach of British law (Harris, 1996, p. 34). Only later, with settlement by non-Indigenous peoples, did a locally specialised version of British law emerge.

By 1850, despite the establishment of several colonies of varying size, most people in what would become British Columbia were Indigenous (Harris, 2008, p. 428). Settler incursion did not begin in earnest until after the 1846 Oregon Treaty which settled the southern border with the United States. After this point, European-Indigenous relations became more land-based. Settlers assumed that their notions of private property and British common law applied universally, though there was initially little colonial oversight to enforce it (Harris, 2008, p. 437). In 1858, a gold rush brought miners with experience from the California rush of 1849 into the Fraser Valley, flooding what had been a colonial economy that was diversifying into forestry, mining, and agriculture but still based largely in the fur trade (Mackie, 1997). The virtually unregulated placer mining wreaked havoc on the waterways and hillsides and introduced brutal paramilitaries against Indigenous Peoples who contested the miners' assurance that they were free to extract gold however and wherever they pleased (Harris, 2008, pp. 432–433).

In the context of what would become the colony and later province of British Columbia we can see that early colonial incursions by Europeans and Euro-Canadians were, in part, shaped by the ruggedness of mountain geographies and their distance from eastern centres of colonial administration. Although many populations were lessened by earlier attacks of diseases such as smallpox, First Nations Peoples were numerous in comparison and effectively manoeuvred evolving economic and geopolitical situations. Not everyone did so in the same way or to the same degree, which generated new social and economic practices within Indigenous communities (Harris, 2008, p. 422). Even when settler projects sought inroads to the western ranges, these factors continued to inhibit colonists' goals. Their ideas about what these mountain spaces *ought* to be were resisted by geography and the people who lived there. We might, then, see this as evidence for geographer Cole Harris' assertion that the settler colonial project in Canada has been a "bounded" one in which the geographical reach of settler colonialism has, in fact, been quite limited (Harris, 2021, p. 10).

There is undoubtedly much more literature dealing with the ways that early colonial presence in mountain regions altered the relations that constitute mountain Homelands and generated new mountain homes for non-Indigenous people. Hart (1999, pp. 7–69) contains information about this period for the Rocky Mountains but, as noted above, it is a work that we treat cautiously for its tendency toward casual judgement of individuals and peoples as "ferocious" or "amazing." Additionally, (Murphy & MacLaren, 2007) offers a selection of articles dealing with the fur trade, homesteading, and early colonial exploration and art in the Athabasca River watershed. Detailed studies about specific mountain regions during early colonial incursions were not captured by the systematic review process, and so our engagement with this material has relied on authorial research, but it should be noted that none of our authors are experts in this area. This is an area upon which future iterations of the CMA can productively build; particularly, we note, by considering Indigenous perspectives on this period.

3.5.2 *Science as colonial tool*

Knowledge making was a critical tool in European efforts to exploit and assert control over mountain Homelands. Historians have considered how natural history was a tool of empire through which governments and companies like the Hudson's Bay Company achieved colonial economic and political goals in western mountainous regions (Braun, 2000; Krotz, 2014; Payne, 2009; Schefke, 2008; Zeller, 2009), how scientific surveying shaped mountain spaces in the west (MacLaren, 2005, 2007), and, later on, how science and technology were used to cultivate mountain spaces into industrial spaces that served international markets (Mouat, 1992) and domestic markets through "internal colonialism" (Peyton, 2016; Zeller, 2009). Some scholars have noted how both landscape (Skidmore, 2017) and repeat photography (Inkpen, 2018) were used by colonial knowledge-makers to generate and reinforce ideas about mountains as wildernesses for exploring and investigating with the tools of Western science.

The literature on science as a colonial tool in the mountains, while not overly large, and tending toward the western regions, is detailed and specific and fits with the more general literature on the topic. We note, however, that many studies of scientific activities in mountains, such as botanical collection or glaciology, with a few exceptions (Inkpen, 2018), tend not to examine these practices as tools of colonialism. This may be because much of the work we found was documentary or biographical in nature (Cavell, 1983; Jones, 2015). More comprehensive studies of how scientific activities relied upon and promoted colonial incursions in the mountain regions of

Canada would be welcome additions to the existing literature. As would work that explicitly investigates the roles First Nations, Métis, and Inuit Peoples played in the generation of scientific knowledge, such as the Secwépemc guides who led surveyors like Walter Moberly through their Homelands. Elsewhere, it has been shown that the generation of scientific knowledge in colonial settings was based on knowledge shared by Indigenous Peoples who were themselves experts (Camerini, 1996; Montero Sobrevilla, 2018). There are some studies that touch on this topic in Canadian contexts (Skidmore, 2017; Zeller, 2009). More investigation of this issue in mountain regions in Canada would greatly enhance our knowledge of mountain regions and the history of science.

3.5.3 *Treaties and land access*

Mountain regions in Canada are covered by many different treaties. We have neither the space nor the expertise to delve into the details of every treaty and how it influenced land access and exclusion. Instead, we consider some of the ways that treaties do and do not impact mountain Homelands through a selection of examples.

First Nations, Métis, and Inuit Peoples' Homelands span large overlapping areas encompassing different ecological regions. Historically, this would allow Indigenous Peoples to travel between different sites based on availability of food sources, seasonal weather patterns, and cultural practices (Mason, 2014, p. 41). Different Indigenous Nations could gather for trade, sharing of knowledge and resources, and ceremonies. Nakoda Elder Lenny Poucette is recorded saying:

> Over many generations we had become good friends with the Kootenay [Ktunaxa] and the Cree ... We even had relationships with the Blackfoot too ... who at times were our traditional enemies ... We would learn from each other ... hunt together, share knowledge about the mountains and ... also get together to celebrate our cultural practices ... These interactions were important for many reasons. (Mason, 2014, p. 44)

These relationships among Nations were formed over many generations and are regarded as sacred.

Cree-Blackfoot relations are discussed in an informative webinar on Indigenous knowledges of mountains recorded for Keepers of the Water.[4]

Indigenous Peoples largely viewed the numbered treaties as peace treaties and agreements to share resources in this same tradition, not as a surrender of land (Mason 2014, 28). During the signing of Treaty 7, which covers a geographical area on the southeastern slopes of the Rocky Mountains, the Stoney Nakoda leaders were assured that although they would be allotted reserve lands on what they knew to be their Traditional Territory, they would be able to continue their traditional land uses and ways of life (Mason, 2014; Snow, 2005). Within decades, the pass system would be used to confine them onto the reserves under intensifying surveillance and restrictions. Confinement onto reserves, which operated most acutely in western Canada and the Prairies, separated Indigenous Peoples from accessing Homelands for food and medicines and for ceremonial practices, and hindered communication among Indigenous Nations. The isolation of the reserve system, Gabrielle Weasel Head, Kainaiwa, Blackfoot Confederacy explained, also inflicted deep psychological damage on Indigenous Peoples with lasting consequences for Indigenous ways of knowing and guardianship of the land (LC 3.15).

A variety of tactics, which included forcible removal from the land and the establishment of parks, displaced a network of relations among Indigenous Peoples and non-humans, and it interrupted kinship among Indigenous Nations (Government of Canada, n.d.). Despite the recognition of Indigenous rights to subsistence hunting and fishing in Treaty 7, within decades the use of the pass system, along with the creation of mountain parks and conservation areas, effectively made these subsistence and cultural practices illegal (Mason, 2014). Access to mountain land remains difficult. Elder Hayden Melting Tallow (Siksika Nation, Blackfoot Confederacy), spoke of the pilgrimages the Blackfoot people would make to the mountains for ochre and to the Paint Pots, which for them were ceremonial places, from which they are now cut off, despite it being part of their territory (LC 3.16). Chief John Snow (Stoney Nakoda) relates the challenges that private land ownership posed for the establishment of the Wesley Band (now called Goodstoney) of Stoney Nakoda in the Kootenay Plains—part of their Traditional Territory, but an area that was not covered in Treaty 7, to which they were party (2005, pp. 107–114).

The stories and experiences surrounding Treaty 7 do not hold across all Indigenous mountain communities in Canada. Indigenous Knowledge Holder and CMA author Dr. Daniel Sims (Tsay Keh Dene First Nation) reminds us that not all First Nations are party to treaty agreements (LC 3.17). Of the approximately 200 First Nations in British Columbia, many of whom have mountain Homelands, relatively few have signed historic or modern-day treaties, and about half have yet to show any interest in negotiating one. Even for those who do, there is the example of the Lheidli T'enneh First Nation, in the Rockies and Interior Plateau (Montane Cordillera region), which twice negotiated a modern comprehensive treaty only to reject it when it came to vote in the

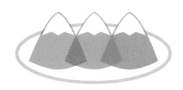

Gabrielle Weasel Head, Kainaiwa First Nation, Blackfoot Confederacy, 2022, LC 3.15

Hayden Melting Tallow, Siksika Nation, Blackfoot Confederacy, 2022, LC 3.16

Daniel Sims, Tsay Keh Dene First Nation, 2022, LC 3.17

---

4   For the webinar, see: https://fb.watch/dG7HWqcPFt/. Please also see Keepers of the Water website https://www.keepersofthewater.ca/.

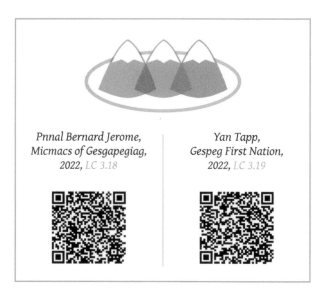

Pnnal Bernard Jerome,
Micmacs of Gesgapegiag,
2022, LC 3.18

Yan Tapp,
Gespeg First Nation,
2022, LC 3.19

community. The Tsilhqot'in Nation, in the Chilcotin Range (Montane Cordillera region), in 1864 were betrayed at a "truce meeting" with the colonial governments against whom they had been waging war, leading to the wrongful hanging of leaders and decades of colonial assault through land grabs, residential schools, the Indian Act, and the abduction of children. In 2016, the Tsilhqot'in Nation achieved legal recognition of their ownership of land in their Traditional Territory. Following this victory, rather than sign a treaty, they negotiated an accord (the *Nenqay Deni Accord*)[5] with the province of British Columbia, which guides their interactions with the province and is renewed and potentially revised every five years. Explicitly not a treaty, the Tsilhqot'in approach to Indigenous-Crown relations has inspired other Nations in the province to pursue similar agreements instead of treaties.

Moreover, we must also bear in mind that existing treaties operate differently across contexts. There are treaties among Indigenous Peoples. For instance, the Buffalo Treaty,[6] signed by 31 Indigenous groups, recognizes the "keystone" role played by buffalo in life ways grounded in "cooperation, kindness, renewal, and sharing amongst and between people." Elder Pnnal Bernard Jerome

---

5 https://www2.gov.bc.ca/assets/gov/environment/ natural-resource-stewardship/consulting-with-first- nations/agreements/other-docs/ nenqay_deni_accord.pdf

6 https://www.buffalotreaty.com/relationships

(Micmacs of Gesgapegiag) reminds us that not all mountain Homelands are covered by treaty agreements that make land claims. The Mi'kmaq of eastern Canada are party to Treaties of Peace and Friendship, which did not mention land. "Homelands," he observed, "would be the unceded lands," and "there are no boundaries where we are at" (LC 3.18). Far more relevant to how they negotiate land access are the barriers erected by private land ownership and bureaucracies set up to protect it. Both he and Yan Tapp (Gespeg First Nation) spoke at length at the Learning Circle of how their communities meet challenges of access and exclusion in seeking to hunt and fish on their Homelands in the Chic-Choc Mountains when "there is private land everywhere" and "consultation" is done in bad faith (LC 3.19).

The impact of private land ownership on mountain Homelands is a vast and under-investigated topic. This may be in part because concepts such as binding written deeds (1677) and their management by the state—the Torrens system (1858)—emerged while European Nations were colonising the world and so have been assumed by many non-Indigenous people as simply "given" (G. Taylor, 2008). Certainly, early colonisers simply assumed that British law applied in lands claimed by the British Crown, irrespective of the laws of the people already living there (Harris, 1996, 2008). While there is considerable literature on the impacts of parks and protected areas (see Sec. 3.5.4), we found that in the systematic literature review private land or private interests came up most frequently in studies of conflicts between "public" lands (like parks) and private uses in the development of mountain parks (Lundgren, 1984; Orr, 2011; P. A. Reichwein, 1995, 2014).

There is an opportunity for studies on the unique, situated, and ongoing effects that private land ownership has on mountain Homelands of First Nations, Métis, and Indigenous Peoples. One notable illustration of such work is at the intersection between commercial ski hills and unceded Indigenous Homelands, as was the case for the Ktunaxa First Nation and Jumbo Glacier Resort (see Sec. 3.4.1). While the Ktunaxa First Nation was able to halt construction of the proposed resort on Qat'muk, other ski hills such as Sun Peaks Resort were pushed through. Sun Peaks (the resort and municipality) was constructed on Skwelkwek'welt, a spiritual and traditional site for the Secwépemc, despite growing concern, protests, and advocacy by the community (Manuel & Derrickson, 2015). These two developments are part of larger, ongoing colonial efforts of land dispossession and the criminalization of Indigenous Peoples who stand in opposition (Gobby et al., 2022; Manuel & Derrickson, 2015). Lisa Cooke (2017) analyses Sun Peaks Resort as "settler-colonial moral terrain" and challenges settler-colonial understandings of "progress" that underpin these developments. Preliminary findings from Dr. Daniel Sims' (Tsay Keh Dene First Nation) ongoing Tri-Council-funded research project "A Forgotten Land: Development in the Finlay-Parsnip Watershed of Northern British Columbia, 1860–1956," indicate that in at least the Finlay-Parsnip watershed this apparent oversight may be an example of narrative forgetting stemming from the perceived failure to establish a settler population in the area (Sims, 2021).

Comprehensive land claim agreements—negotiated after 1973—also shape the governance of mountain regions as they seek to more clearly define Indigenous Peoples' land, resources, and self-government rights. For instance, the 11 Yukon First Nations who completed comprehensive Final and Self Government agreements under the Yukon Umbrella Final Agreement (Yukon Umbrella Final Agreement, 1993) have retained title to approximately 10% of their Traditional Territories ("Settlement Lands") and have the right to shared decision-making (co-management) in the remaining 90%. Kluane National Park, discussed in detail in Sec. 3.5.4, is an example of co-management, but there are many other co-management boards. Co-management in this context has also been the subject of significant critique (e.g., Clark & Joe-Strack, 2017; Nadasdy, 2003; Natcher et al., 2005). Later in this chapter we also discuss the Labrador Inuit Land Claims Agreement (LILCA) (2005) (Section 3.5.4.4).

3.5.4 *Parks and protected areas*

The Rocky Mountain National Park
In 1885, an officially completed Canadian Pacific Railway (CPR) opened up the Rocky Mountain Cordillera to non-Indigenous people to a greater degree than ever before. The railway was a joint project of eastern and European capitalists and the Canadian federal government. It was a po-litical vehicle for linking the disparate parts of the emerging nation and a physical vehicle for altering who had access to and use of the Montane Cordillera and Pacific Maritime regions. One of the most dramatic effects the coming of the railway had on these regions and the subsequent history of land use in the country was the establishment of Canada's first national park.

Rocky Mountains National Park (renamed Banff National Park in 1930, Fig. 3.1) was established in 1886, covering a small area around hot springs near Banff townsite. The hot springs were already used by the Stoney Nakoda for healing and spiritual renewal (Snow, 2005, p. 10), but their "discovery" was nevertheless claimed by two CPR employees, who were swiftly divested of their claim by the railway and the federal government. A national park was established to control access to the springs and surrounding area. Hot springs were very popular, and lucrative, tourist attractions in the late 19th century, and CPR executives sought to profit from tourism as well as money generated from settlers travelling by rail (Hart, 1983).

Much of the early infrastructure in the mountain parks, including hotels and businesses to cater to tourists, was developed under the auspices of the CPR. Ideas of sublime wilderness, rooted in European Enlightenment and Romantic thought, impacted how the first mountain parks were perceived by promoters and their target audiences. From the early stages of construction, the railway hired painters and photographers to document the laying of the tracks, with the understanding that the art produced would portray the process as a heroic endeavour in beautiful wilderness landscapes (Hart, 1983). Under the patronage of the CPR a school of art developed that shaped the way mountains in Canada were perceived for decades to come, often underlining the idea of mountains as wilderness and as scenery. Art continued to play a formative role in producing representations that sculpted notions of what mountains were for and who belonged there, as Reichwein (Reichwein, 2004) and Wall (Reichwein & Wall, 2020) have argued in their histories of the Banff School of Fine Arts. Visuals, including photographs and postcards, continue to promote ideas of mountain parks as wildernesses and homes for charismatic wildlife (Colpitts, 2011; Cronin, 2006, 2011). Yet, landscape art has also

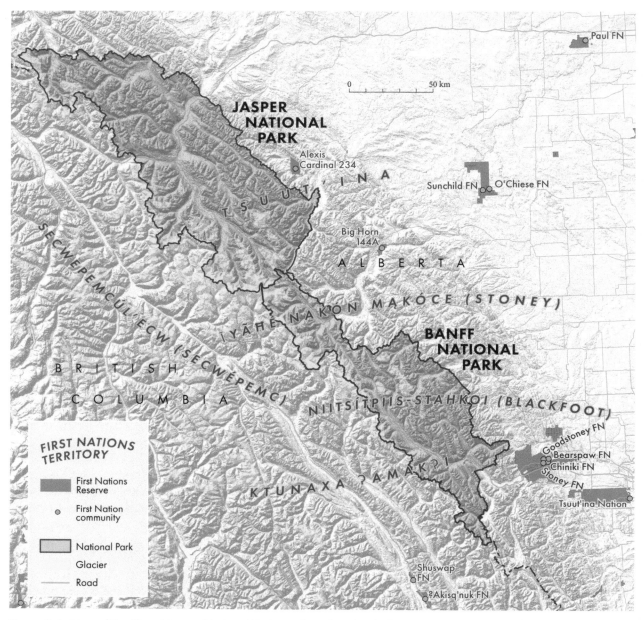

Figure 3.1: Map of Banff and Jasper National Parks and overlapping Indigenous territories. Data from Native-Land.ca; Natural Resources Canada (https://open.canada.ca/data/en/dataset/522b07b9-78e2-4819-b736-ad9208eb1067); U.S. Geological Survey's Center for Earth Resources Observation and Science (https://doi.org///doi.org/10.5066/F7DF6PQ).

been a medium of expression for Indigenous artists such as Sitting Wind-Frank Kaquitts (Stoney Nakoda) (Fig. 3.2), as well as a point of connection between Indigenous people and settlers like Catherine Whyte, founding patron of the Whyte Museum of the Canadian Rockies (Mayberry, 2003, pp. 101–104) (Fig. 3.3).

Science was also a tool used in the forging of the vision of mountain spaces as parks. In the late 19th and early 20th centuries, it was used as a tool for cordoning off mountain spaces (Gardner & Campbell, 2002; Loo, 2006; Reichwein, 2004). For instance, early conservation science, and glacier study, were underwritten by ideas about mountain spaces as unpeopled "wildernesses" and sanctuaries for certain kinds of charismatic large animals like moose, bear, elk, and sheep (Colpitts, 2010; Inkpen, 2018, pp. 21–76; Reichwein & McDermott, 2007). These ideas, legitimised by the science of the day, played a role in how Canada's first national park would be understood and administered.

Indigenous people were not immediately banned from hunting within park boundaries; this came later as non-Indigenous public opinions about wilderness and wildlife changed in the final decade of the 19th century, following the precipitous decline of species like bison and elk across the continent driven predominantly by market hunting pressure. The first wildlife regulations in Canadian national parks were designed to maintain a sporting playground, prioritising trophy hunting over subsistence practices (Mason, 2014, pp. 54–55). In *These Mountains Are Our Sacred Spaces*, Chief John Snow (Stoney Nakoda) explains how non-Indigenous popular sentiment about wildlife pressured the federal government to enact laws in 1893 that banned his people from hunting on the eastern slopes of the southern Rockies: "In 1893 public attitudes and government goals

combined to lead to the first outright, straightforward breaking of the treaty: the Indian Affairs Branch firmly and specifically committed itself to a policy of restricting the hunting of game" (2005, pp. 79–80).

This, coupled with contradictory government policies aimed at rendering Indigenous people "self-sufficient" and confined to reservations, amplified the effects of food shortages, lack of access to health care—both traditional and government provided—and disconnection from traditional practices and territories that were already being experienced by the Stoney Nakoda.

Despite these harsh measures, the Stoney Nakoda and other Indigenous Peoples risked fines and imprisonment to continue to gather, hunt and fish. As one Nakoda elder states, "Even while the governments tried to change how we lived with their rules ... when there were opportunities ... or a need to do so ... many of us continued

Figure 3.2: "Bow Lake," 1969, Sitting Wind (1925–2002), oil on canvas board, 30.5 x 40.4 cm WiS.02.08. Image courtesy of the Whyte Museum of the Canadian Rockies. Gift of Catharine Robb Whyte, O.C., Banff, 1979.

Figure 3.3: "Crowfoot Glacier," 1945–55, Catherine Robb Whyte (1906–1979), oil on canvas. 22.8 x 28.0 cm WyC.01.202. Image courtesy the Whyte Museum of the Canadian Rockies.

to hunt in the mountains like we'd always done" (Mason, 2014, p. 46). Snow (2005, pp. 85–87) describes the history of the Bighorn Reserve on the Kootenay Plains as a place where some Nakoda went so they could continue to hunt and fish in the Eastern Ranges. Mason (2014) documented how the Nakoda strategically built relationships and used involvement in tourism and the Banff Indian Days festival to reassert their culture and presence in the region.

These stories are important reminders that government and colonial institutions do not *determine* life for Indigenous people in the mountains. As long as there has been settler-colonialism, there has been Indigenous resistance and refusal. Given the narrow geographical and temporal scope of the studies we were able to find, we believe that this is an area that needs further investigation.

We note that an event as significant as the Smallboy Camp—set up in the 1960s on the Kootenay Plains by members of the Cree Ermineskin Nation, led by Apitchitchiw (Robert) Smallboy—is little known and virtually undocumented in an otherwise sizable literature on the eastern Rockies. The Smallboy Camp is described in the Keepers of the Water webinar on Indigenous knowledge of the mountains, but it was found nowhere in the scholarly literature we reviewed, despite having given rise to Kisiko Awasis Kiskinahamawin (the Mountain Cree Camp School) on Muskiki Lake, which continues to occupy what is considered provincial land and ran until 2021.[7] That such a significant instance of Indigenous Peoples

7 https://www.facebook.com/keepersofthewater/videos/241248714322362/

THE CANADIAN MOUNTAIN ASSESSMENT

taking back land in the mountains is virtually unmentioned in scholarly literature is a prime example of narrative forgetting and colonial erasure (Wolfe, 2006): a community is conceptually and historically erased as part of the colonial project through the narratives of non-Indigenous peoples which either overwrite or simply fail to acknowledge Indigenous stories.

Cape Breton Highlands National Park

Rocky Mountains Park was but the first of many instances in which the establishment of parks and protected areas entailed the eviction or relocation of communities of people to make way for wildernesses "unimpaired for the enjoyment" of contemporary and future generations (*The National Parks Act*, 1930, Sec. 3.4). Cape Breton Highlands National Park (Fig. 3.4), established in 1936, illustrates this discordant approach to land in the Maritimes. While the Unamaki (Cape Breton) Highlands did not offer the same vertiginous terrain as other mountain parks, the contrast between its heights and the coastal waters invited what Alan MacEachern describes as "the coastal sublime" (MacEachern, 2001, p. 48). Foreshadowing later expropriation campaigns in the Maritimes (Rudin, 2016), the methods employed to achieve this sublimity involved moving whole communities to make way for the importation of unspoilt wilderness.

As Ian McKay has argued, the transformation of the mountainous terrain of northern Unama'ki into the Cape Breton Highlands represented one plank in a broader construction of "tartanist" Nova Scotia; packaging Cape Breton as a quaint, pre-modern isle full of dull-witted but hardworking "Highland folk" (McKay, 1992, p. 24, 1994, p. 9). Yet, the rolling back of modernity faced a variety of stumbling blocks, from the presence of timber lease held by the Oxford Paper Company to settled communities such as Cap Rouge, Pleasant Bay, and Ingonish. In establishing the park, this required state actors to think carefully about which pre-existing communities conformed to the desired pre-modern sublimity and which could be summarily dispensed with. This was emphasised by the decision to expropriate the community of Cap Rouge–an Acadian fishing village–while allowing the ethnically Scottish farming settlement of Pleasant Bay to remain within the boundaries of the Park (MacEachern, 2001, p. 54).

The expropriation of the Acadian community at Cap Rouge and the cessation of expropriation against the ethnic Scots at Pleasant Bay was not only about reorienting the geography along tartanist lines; it was, as Catriona Sandilands reveals, an articulation of hierarchical whiteness in Canadian society. She writes:

> With the Acadians safely elsewhere [...] the fantasy of whiteness as unity was not only sustained in the space of the park but also given added vigour by contemporary naturalising discourses of pristine, untouched wilderness in which CBH's (originating) whiteness could now be planted (Sandilands, 2011, p. 73)

The transformation of mountains in northern Unama'ki during the 1930s was yet another iteration of a much longer history of colonial settlement and transformation that mobilised notions about sublime wilderness in the colonisation of Indigenous mountain Homelands. It also carefully treats the discordances and hierarchies embedded in what is often treated monolithically as "settler colonialism" or "whiteness". This kind of critical attention to detail, with a few notable exceptions (e.g., Reichwein, 2014; Robinson, 2005), is generally absent in the literature we found treating non-Indigenous incursion on mountain Homelands; we believe more of it would be a welcome intellectual contribution.

Kluane National Park and Reserve

The processes involved in establishing national parks evolved over time and played out in subtly different ways in other mountain areas. For instance, Neufield (2011) suggests that the impetus behind Kluane National Park and Reserve (1973) (Fig. 3.5) began as an expression of the "Canadian ideals" of wildlife and wilderness protection, and built upon earlier efforts in the region to cordon off and exploit game, develop mineral extraction, and pursue scientific research in the Homelands of the Champagne and Aishihik First Nations (CAFN), the Kluane First Nation (KFN), and White River First Nation (WRFN), at their expense. He notes, however, that these intentions did not alone determine how the story would go. In 1943, the Kluane Game Sanctuary (KGS) was established in southwest Yukon,

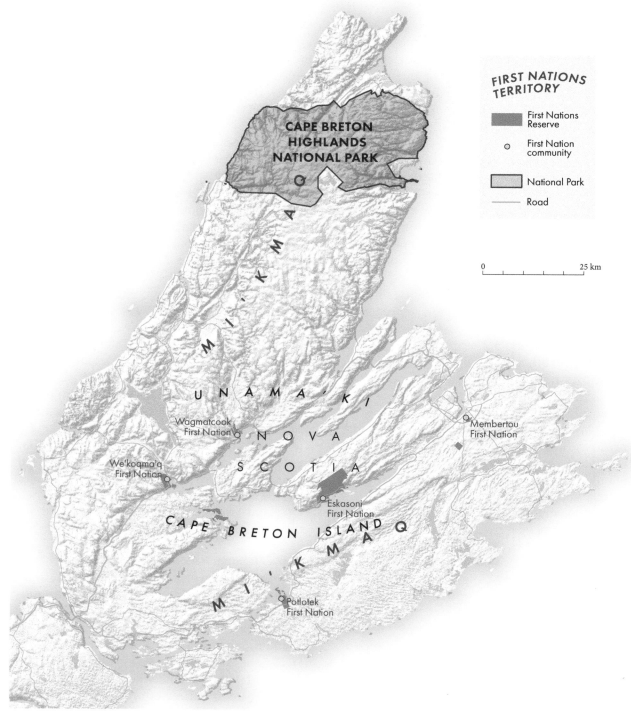

Figure 3.4: Map of Cape Breton Highlands National Park boundaries and overlapping Indigenous territories. Data from Native-Land.ca; Natural Resources Canada (https://open.canada.ca/data/en/dataset/522b07b9-78e2-4819-b736-ad9208eb1067); U.S. Geological Survey's Center for Earth Resources Observation and Science (https://doi.org///doi.org/10.5066/F7DF6PQ).

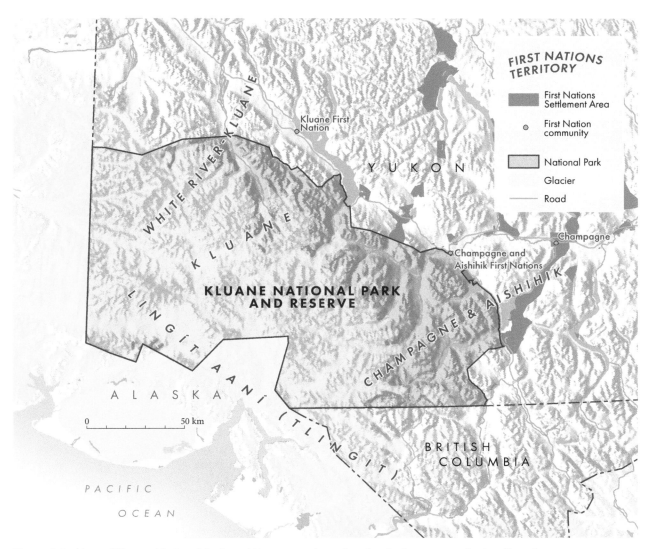

Figure 3.5: Map of Kluane National Park and Reserve and overlapping Indigenous territories. Data from Native-Land.ca; Natural Resources Canada (https://open.canada.ca/data/en/dataset/522b07b9-78e2-4819-b736-ad9208eb1067); U.S. Geological Survey's Center for Earth Resources Observation and Science (https://doi.org///doi.org/10.5066/F7DF6PQ).

restricting these First Nations from accessing the portions of their territories by making it illegal to hunt and trap or otherwise occupy their Homeland (e.g., building cabins) by fining people and confiscating meat and other possessions from those who did harvest in the area (Nadasdy, 2003; Nakoochee, 2018; Zanasi, 2005). In 1973, First Nation organisations, including the Yukon Native Brotherhood and the Council for Yukon Indians, fiercely opposed the creation of a National Park until land claims were settled. As a result, the KGS became the Kluane National Park Reserve. These events, their myriad and

still resonating effects, and their relation to the building of the Alaska Highway, are explored in greater detail in Sec. 3.7.4.

While land claims for Kluane First Nation and White River First Nation—who, to date, do not have settled claims—were not reached prior to the establishment of the National Park, the responsiveness of the federal government to Indigenous land claims marked the beginning of a shift in understandings of parks and protected areas. They were not to be regarded as simply wilderness places to be protected from resource extraction (Neufield, 2011; Roberts, 2023).

Gùdia Mary Jane Johnson, Lhu'ààn Mân Ku Dań, 2022, LC 3.20

Even so, First Nations citizens were displaced from the region for over 50 years as harvesting continued to be banned, according to the Government of Canada's interpretation of the Parks Act (Nakoochee, 2018; Zanasi, 2005). This displacement has significant impacts on First Nation connections to their Homelands, including implications for spiritual and cultural wellbeing, food security, knowledge transmission, and more. Healing First Nation relationships with the park was the focus of initiatives starting in the early 2000s including the "Healing Broken Connections" initiative (2004–2008) which, through partnership between CAFN, KFN and Kluane National Park and Reserve, offered opportunities to reconnect on the land and to determine how Indigenous Knowledge could be used in the co-management of the park (Nakoochee, 2018). Efforts to re-engage with lands inside the park are ongoing, including culture camps, interpretive programs led by Elders, and other joint initiatives. As Elder Gùdia Mary Jane Johnson (Lhu'ààn Mân Ku Dań) told those gathered at the CMA Learning Circle, Parks could learn from the rotational-burning practices that people like her grandfather practised on the land now encompassed in the National Park and Reserve (LC 3.20). (The related topic of the Peel Watershed Planning Commission will be treated in Sec. 3.8)

Torngat Mountains National Park

The case of the Torngat Mountains National Park in Labrador is another illustrative case of the evolution of parks policies and Indigenous rejoinders to national parks in mountain Homelands. The park itself is a symbol and product of Inuit self-determination and resistance. In the 1940s and 1950s, the federal government, the provincial government of Newfoundland and Labrador, and the International Grenfell Association (a group founded by settler Wilfred Grenfell who practised medicine, led religious and social services, and was involved in the removal of Indigenous children to residential schools) evicted northern Labrador Inuit from their Homelands north of Nain (Marcus, 1995).[8] These Homelands covered a 468-kilometre span of coastline, including what is now known as Torngat Mountains National Park. Inuit lived in sod houses and *tupet* (tents) during the summer months and *illuvigait* (not "igloo"—the correct word is "illuvigak") during the winter months. Inuit travelled by *kajak* (not "kayak") in the summer, and by Kimutsik (dog team) during the winter months. They also travelled by foot when need be. Land and sea are often mentioned as one, omitting the distinction between the two. When referring to the land, Inuit could be talking exclusively about the terrestrial land, or the land and sea combined. Inuit from the north were often referred to as "Avanimiut," or people of the north, by Inuit further south. The Avanimiut and their descendents now live in the five Inuit communities of Nain, Hopedale, Makkovik, Postville, and Rigolet. These communities make up the Inuit region of Nunatsiavut. Between the 1970s and the early 2000s, Nunatsiavut Inuit united to create the Labrador Inuit Association (LIA). The work of the LIA included negotiations with the federal government to secure land claims agreements, which would outline and honour Labrador Inuit rights in northern Labrador. Negotiations also led to the legitimating of the Labrador and Inuit Land Claims Agreement (LILCA),[9] signed by Labrador Inuit, the Newfoundland and Labrador provincial government, and Canada in 2005. Torngat Mountains National Reserve then became the Torngat Mountains National Park.

The signing of the agreement initiated the Nunatsiavut Government, the first Inuit self-government in Canada. Chapter 9[10] of the agreement is dedicated to national parks and protected areas, which includes Torngat Mountains National Park, and Inuit Use and Occupancy Rights.

8 https://publications.gc.ca/collections/
   collection_2017/bcp-pco/Z1-1991-1-41-149-eng.pdf
9 https://www.nunatsiavut.com/wp-content/
   uploads/2014/07/Labrador-Inuit-Land-Claims-
   Agreement.pdf
10 https://www.gov.nl.ca/exec/iar/files/ch9.pdf

Labrador Inuit have the right to hunt, travel, harvest, collect stone, and work in the base camp as first priority amongst other things.

It is important to understand that the borders of the park were delineated to serve a political purpose, rather than reflecting meaning in the geography as understood by Labrador Inuit. The creation of these borders did secure and protect the land and sea from extraction and exploitation, which is one of the reasons why Labrador Inuit were supportive of the park. The protection of the park ensures their livelihoods, protection, and sustainability of their Homelands. As Inuit who live in and continue to value the Torngait and surrounding areas, the only legitimate borders are

Note: Readers may note an imbalance in the maps included in this chapter. While there are maps depicting park boundaries and surrounding Indigenous territories for the Rocky Mountain National Parks, Cape Breton Highlands National Park, and Kluane National Park and Reserve, there is no equivalent for the Torngat Mountains. This is because cartographic data for the region and the right to use them must be formally requested from the Nunatsiavut Government, and the CMA did not do so in time to incorporate a map for the Torngat Mountains region. Out of respect for the autonomy of the Nunatsiavut Government over data pertaining to their lands, we did not pursue a map through other data sources. The co-lead authors for the Homelands chapter state this in the spirit of transparency.

determined by seasonal hunting areas and campgrounds. Inuit still hunt seals year-round, either in the open ocean or at seal breathing holes in the ice. Almost all animals are hunted at different times throughout the year depending on migrations. Examples include those of Canada geese, snow geese, caribou, whales, and char and salmon runs. Berry picking is also best after the first frost in the fall, and enough berries are picked to last the year.

One of our authors and Indigenous Knowledge Holders, Megan Dicker (Inuit, Nunatsiavut), shared some of her experience of these mountains as a person whose grandparents were displaced from the region, but who, nevertheless, has a strong connection to the Torngait as her Homelands.

Summary: Parks and protected areas

The scholarly literature treating the role of parks and protected areas in mountain regions is substantial and varied. While the tendency toward studies of western mountain regions is still present, it is far less acute than in other cases. The establishment and characteristics of mountain parks in the north and east have been treated in the peer-reviewed literature, though to a lesser degree than those of the parks in the Montane Cordillera region. We note that the topic of mountain parks has been a relatively fertile place for

---

TORNGAIT: PLACE OF SPIRITS

My relationship to the mountains—the Torngait in the north and the kiglapait to the south—has been forged based on my grandparent's relation to them.

The Inuit of northern Labrador, including my grandparents, were displaced from their home near the Torngait by the provincial government of Newfoundland and Labrador in the late 1950s. This information shaped the way I think about mountains, Homelands, and mountains as Homelands—how can you determine what your Homeland is when your family has been displaced for generations? Despite these experiences, my grandparents and those of their generation haven't stopped returning to their Homelands with their children, grandchildren and now great-grandchildren. Labrador Inuit continue to spend time in the

Torngait and the surrounding area via skidoo during the winter months and via speedboat or longliner during the summer months. People go for the sentimental and heart value, but also to hunt, fish, and harvest.

My first visit to the Torngait was in 2014 (Fig. 3.6). Just south of the Torngat Mountains National Park (TMNP) border lies Hebron, Okak, and Nutaak where my family used to live prior to the relocations. Saglek, Sallikuluk, and Cape Chidley were other well-known communities near the Park and are just as important in this unique story. During my time in the area in 2014 and again in 2016 I had the privilege to go to Hebron, Okak, Ramah, which is within the Park boundaries, and all throughout the Park. I visited my grandparents'

/continued from page 153

Homelands, including the areas where they used to live when they weren't travelling and hunting. I loved travelling throughout and thinking about how they looked at the same mountains, hunted in the same areas, and lived their lives in such a beautiful and abundant place.

I am less familiar with the Kaujamet mountains just south of the park, but I have family members who travel there to fish for char in the winter. We also pass the Kaumajet mountains when travelling to the Park via speedboat during the summer months.

Even though Inuit don't live in the Torngait and the surrounding area permanently anymore, we still consider them to be our ancestral Homelands. We still have a strong connection that (in my opinion) has only been severed by distance. We value, respect, and think of the mountains daily and always wish to be there. We consider ourselves to be lucky and privileged to travel

Megan Dicker, Inuit, Nunatsiavut, 2022, LC 3.21

there—despite our connection to the mountains, it is expensive to travel and stay at the base camp. Fuel itself is expensive, and the supplies and food cost a lot in Nunatsiavut. Only those who can afford the trips tend to go, but our regional government is creating programs that will provide opportunities for us to return to these Homelands. If we are not physically in the mountains, they are always close at heart. (LC 3.21)

Figure 3.6: Collecting driftwood for a fire, Southwest Arm, Torngat Mountains National Park. Photo courtesy of Megan Dicker, 2014.

place-specific studies that consider how changing land use policies impact Indigenous Peoples in diverse ways. Indeed, this topic can be used as an entry point for thinking about how land use practices have changed over time and how they have remained the same. We note, finally, that there seems to be less literature on mountain places designated "protected" but not as parks.

3.6 Recreation

3.6.1 *Place-making through recreation*

Questions about what parks are for have been around as long as parks, and historians have written about how they have been negotiated in mountain regions (Chen & Reichwein, 2016; Reichwein, 1995, 2014). One of the most influential voices in discussions of mountain parks has been that of recreationalists (Reichwein, 2014, p. 3). With the establishment of parks and protected areas, mountain lands became places for a host of recreational activities including mountaineering, climbing, canoeing and kayaking, hiking, skiing, and motorised sports (Steiger et al., 2022). Such pursuits continue to shape how mountain regions in Canada are understood and managed, with impacts for who calls them home and those who call them Homelands and how the land is used (Clayton, 2016; Colpitts, 2011; Héritier, 2003; Heritier, 2010; Kariel & Kariel, 1988; Kulczycki & Halpenny, 2014; Lam, 2016; Lemelin & Maher, 2009; Nepal & Jamal, 2011; Pavelka, 2017, 2019; Toth & Mason, 2021). The popularity of mountain outdoor activities and the diversity of those participating in them is growing rapidly. Efforts are underway to better comprehend recreationists' experiences in the mountains, the evolving relationships they have with high places, and the sense of connection to mountains that recreational activities can engender (e.g., Kulczycki & Halpenny, 2014; Reid & Palechuk, 2017). Diverse and ever-changing ideas about recreation—what types are suitable, who ought to pursue them, and how they ought to be pursued—have shaped mountains into particular kinds of places, both materially and in people's imaginations.

For instance, mountaineering was integral in shaping perceptions of what western mountains in Canada were for and who had access to them. Historian PearlAnn Reichwein has documented how the Alpine Club of Canada (ACC) was instrumental in imagining and forging a nationalist vision of "Canada's mountains" best captured in the words of ACC founders who imagined, "a nation of mountaineers, loving its mountains with a patriot's passion" (Parker, 1907, p. 7). Early ACC top brass regarded western mountains as playgrounds for tourists, as places for scientific research, and spaces for the conservation of wildlife and, later, ecosystems, and opposed them as places for industrial development, Indigenous Peoples, and ostensibly "ethnic" people. Early club policies enabled ACC oligarchy to "blackball" membership applications and thereby police the ethnic and racial demographics of the club and so access to the mountains (Reichwein, 1997; Reichwein, 1995, 2014). Historians have also investigated how ideas about recreation inscribed themselves on lands and communities elsewhere, as in the case of Revelstoke, BC, where ski tourism was promoted during the First World War, largely by immigrants of Scandinavian descent seeking to enliven the local economy through tourism and sport modelled on reminiscences of the "old country" (Clayton, 2016). This heritage remains written on the cultural and physical landscape surrounding Revelstoke, much as the legacy of Swiss mountain guides can be felt in the Canadian Rockies.

In the case of Rocky Mountains Park, the Canadian Pacific Railway aspired to recreate the western mountains as a space for wealthy, white tourists. To this end, they targeted Victorian mountaineers and emphasised the Alpine-like qualities of the Rockies and Selkirks, particularly their large glaciers. They advertised the Canadian Rockies as "50 Switzerlands in 1!" and likened Mount Assiniboine to the Matterhorn. The legacy of this period is written onto the built landscape of many mountain parks in the form of Swiss-influenced architectural styles (Hart, 1983), and into their cultural histories. The CPR hired European-trained mountain guides to live and work at the trackside hotels to assist tourists getting up and down the mountains (Fig. 3.7).

A body of scholarly work is emerging that seeks to understand the experiences of these migrant guides in the mountains of their new homes (Robinson, 2014; Stephen, 2021), and there is a growing body of grey literature (Costa & Scardellato, 2015; Kain, 2014; Sanford, 2001; Scott, 2015;

Figure 3.7: Canadian Pacific guides Edward Feuz and Christian Hasler at Glacier House, 1899. Photo courtesy of the Whyte Museum of the Canadian Rockies, Vaux Family Fonds, V653/NG-584.

Stephen, 2021). There is also work that considers more recent experiences of Japanese mountain workers and guides (Satsuka, 2015). However, there is room for more work in this arena, particularly critical work that investigates immigrant experiences and encounters in mountains understood as Indigenous Homelands. Guide Pat Morrow relates the reminiscences of Shelagh Dehart, granddaughter of Shushway Chief Pierre Kinbasket:

> I was a teenage girl when he came to visit my Auntie Rosalie Kinbasket in Stoddard Creek (directly across the Rocky Mountain

Trench from Wilmer). Rosalie broke many horses for him over the years. He had to have many horses, pack and saddle, that were sure-footed and gentle. He was always talking about horses, brands, horse thieves, medicine, mountains, and stupid climbers, etc. He was a friend of my mother's and when lunchtime would come around well here comes Conrad, always at lunchtime! (Morrow, 2009)

This quote suggests a rich body of stories about mountains as Homelands for Indigenous people and homes for immigrant guides beckoning for more scholarly attention.

3.6.2 Recreation and gender

Critical studies of recreation practices in mountain regions have paid special care to how gender intersects with mountain recreation, particularly mountaineering. Mountaineering has long been regarded as a bastion of heroic, heteronormative masculinity. However, recent scholars have treated this subject with care and nuance, revealing that many forms of masculinity and femininity operate within the worlds of mountain recreation (Deslandes, 2009; Dummit, 2004; Erickson, 2003; Frohlick, 2005; Robinson, 2005; Stoddart, 2011a). There is also a substantial body of historical grey literature that documents the first-hand experiences of women in the mountains. Much of the earlier work focuses on local celebrity figures in the western ranges such as Mary Schäffer, Mary Vaux Walcott, Catherine Whyte, and Phyllis Munday (Beck, 2006; Mayberry, 2003; Reichwein & McDermott, 2007; Skidmore, 2006; Smith, 1989; Squire, 1995) and is documentary or celebratory in nature. It tends to underscore the uniqueness and fortitude of these women navigating both rugged mountains and restrictive gender norms. The sentiments of Mary Vaux Walcott, a Quaker woman from Philadelphia who frequented the Rockies in the years after the CPR was built, is often quoted as representative of this class of women in the mountains:

> Of course golf is a fine game, but can it compare with a day on the trail, or a scramble over the glacier, or even with a quiet day in camp to get things in order for the morrow's

conquests? Somehow when once this wild spirit enters the blood, golf courses and hotel piazzas, be they ever so brilliant, have no charm, and I can hardly wait to be off again. (Mary Vaux to Charles Doolittle Walcott, 1912, quoted in Skidmore (2006, p. xvii))

This quotation underlines her experience of the mountains as a wilderness playground. It was both a rejection and an embrace of contemporary white bourgeois culture which valued both invigorating wilderness and women who stuck to golf. This balancing act can be seen in the visual legacy of these women. Watercolour painting was deemed an appropriated pastime for their demographic, but several, including Vaux and Schäffer, used the medium to enter both mountains and scientific circles, usually the domains of men at this time.

While there is excellent work on gender in mountain recreation, in light of the predominance of grey literature in the area of women's experiences specifically, we believe there is room for more critical, intersectional studies of gender and place making in mountains. Studies that consider the class- and gender-inflected relationships among women and guides, and those that take a more fulsome look at the colonial conditions and implications of white women's finding freedom in mountains in Canada. Colleen Skidmore's recent work is a welcome step in this direction. Her study of Mary Schäffer attends to the ways Schäffer used gender stereotypes of her time to challenge and transgress them through her photographic and written work about her travels in the Canadian Rockies and Japan. In her analysis, Skidmore points to the colonial conditions for Schäffer's work and how it was made possible by her own socio-economic position and background, noting how these make her less of an extraordinary instance and more of a representative of her times (Skidmore, 2017, p. 238). Another notable exception to the general trend in this topic is Schaefer's (2021) recent study which highlights the social injustice and microaggressions that are taking place along gender lines among rock climbers on the Niagara Escarpment in southern Ontario.

We did not find any work dealing with Indigenous women's experiences and knowledge of mountains specifically, though we note the importance of recreational groups and social media platforms such as Indigenous Womxn Climb,[11] which are providing venues for their stories and experiences to be shared and to generate opportunities for mentorship.

We did not find many peer-reviewed studies on how Two-Spirit, Lesbian, Gay, Bisexual, Transgender, Queer, Intersex, plus (2SLGBTQI+) communities (Indigenous or non-Indigenous) engage with mountain places through recreation in the Canadian context. Current research focuses primarily on the intersections of 2SLGBTQI+ communities and rural tourism. For example, Toth and Mason's (2021) work examines the experiences of gay men travelling to rural British Columbia for vacation. The mountains and access to outdoor recreation were indicated by participants as motivations for travel, however, "perceptions of rural homophobia" and safety were identified as potential concerns (Toth & Mason, 2021, p. 86). The convergence of mountains, tourism and the creation of gay spaces is also highlighted through local sporting events, such as Whistler's gay ski week (1992–2012). The annual event utilised the pull of the mountains to bring together gay skiers and snowboarders in events that fostered competition, community, and gay activism (Herbert, 2014). The 2019 avalanche and guiding industry study in Canada amplified the voices of 2SLGBTQI+ people who work in the guiding and avalanche industry. One individual shared, "I am transgender. I am not 'out' to my co-workers. I fear that I would not be treated equally due to the comments and jokes I hear on a daily basis" (Reimer & Eriksen, 2018, p. 158).

In concert with a growth in organisations supporting 2SLGBTQI+ persons' access to mountain space, there are academic and grey literatures that look at 2SLGBTQI+ youth and wilderness experiences (e.g., Litwiller, 2018), but we found none that focus on mountains specifically. Moreover, we found no scholarly work that considers non-binary experiences of mountains for people whose very languages push back against binaries, such as Inuktitut, in which individuals are often referred to as "them" rather than "he" or "she". Queerness, language, and mountain life are interconnected. Identities are influenced by languages and languages are influenced by identities. For individuals residing in mountainous areas, these

_____

11 https://www.indigenouswomxnclimb.com/

languages relate to the environment around them. Pronouns in language indicate binaries, or in some cases, the lack thereof. These distinctions express how gender, sexuality, and identities are viewed, and call attention to the nature of sexuality and gender as fluid and informed by cultural and linguistic norms. This, again, indicates a need for more intersectional studies.

While we have noticed gaps in the scholarly literature treating topics of gender and sexual orientation in studies of recreation in mountains in Canada, we note that artists have contributed to a critical understanding of gender and sexuality in mountain places, offering representations that push us to rethink what, say, a "mountaineer" or "park ranger" might look like. In this regard, Shawna Dempsey and Lorri Millan's 1997 performance art piece, Lesbian National Parks Services[12] and the accompanying handbook, *Junior Lesbian Ranger* were early efforts to make "visible [a] homosexual presence in spaces where concepts of history and biology exclude all but very few" (Dempsey & Millan, n.d.). As detailed in Section 3.7.5, studies of mountain-based professions are another notable area where questions of belonging in mountains have been explored through the lens of gender.

3.6.3 *Race and recreation*

Just as ideas about gender shape who is likely to engage in particular recreational activities and how they do so, so, too, do notions of race and ethnicity. Scholars have considered how ideas about race and ethnicity play out in experiences of mountain recreation outside the context of mountains in Canada (Coleman, 1996; Ortner, 1999). There is some social sciences work that considers race in the mountain-based professions. For instance, in a 2019 study of the avalanche and guiding industry in Canada, 5% of participants identified as black, Indigenous, or people of colour. People who identified as Indigenous reported having higher rates of mental health challenges due to their work environment, and higher rates of suicide-related thoughts than their white peers (Reimer & Eriksen, 2022). This work is joined by

conversations outside of peer-reviewed literature calling for expanding our assumptions about who "belongs" in the outdoors and what adventurers look like (Barr & Mortimer, 2020; Youssef, 2021) and by organisations working toward making mountain recreation more racially inclusive and diverse (e.g., Indigenous Womxn Climb, as well as Inkluskivity, and Colour the Trails).

Based on the systematic review, we found that this is an area that offers opportunities for scholars to contribute to ongoing discussions in the public sphere about the role of race in shaping mountain places and people's experiences of them in the Canadian context. Specifically, intersectional studies that consider how race and mobility (physical and economic) shape who has access to mountain recreation, studies on how invisible racialized labour plays out in mountain regions, and investigations into how recreational practices and cultures are altered and grow from changing racial inclusions would be welcome contributions.

3.7 Labour

3.7.1 *Extraction labour*

With the exception of mountain professionals (guides, avalanche specialists, etc.), our chapter has felt the limitations of our collective expertise acutely on the subject of labour. The ways that labourers in extractive industries, for instance, shaped mountain spaces and carved homes for themselves within these spaces is a topic considered in the work of historical geographers (Gardner, 1986; Harris, 1996, pp. 192–218) but could be expanded upon by historians and other scholars with other disciplinary lenses. Early scholarly work on how labour shapes experiences and perceptions of place often juxtaposed labour to recreation or environmentalism. We have found, based on the literature we located, that historical work on mining industries in mountains tends to focus on disasters (Buckley, 2004; Hinde, 2003). This may contribute to ideas of heroic labour heritage (Arenson, 2007) in mountain places that underlines dualistic thinking about labour and other activities such as recreation, conservation, or traditional Indigenous practices. However, we caution this assessment is based on limited expertise.

---

12 http://www.shawnadempseyandlorrimillan.net/#/alps/

3.7.2 *Incarcerated labour in mountains*

Labour can quite literally make a place. The western mountain parks would not look the way that they do today without a history of forced labour that spanned the first half of the 20th century. During the First World War, "internment camps" at Castle Mountain, Yoho, Cave and Basin, and Jasper put "enemy aliens"—mostly non-combatant men of ethnic heritages from central and southern Europe—to work constructing roads, bridges, and tourist attractions. In Revelstoke, the Scandinavian-descended immigrants who promoted skiing in the area were interned to build a park road (Clayton, 2016). During the Depression, relief camps served similar purposes of providing cheap labour for projects such as the Banff-Jasper Highway. During the Second World War, internment camps were set up for Conscientious Objectors (e.g., Mennonites, Hutterites, Doukhobors, and Jehovah's Witnesses), and for Japanese men evacuated from the West Coast (Waiser, 1995). While these camps within the parks have been well documented in peer-reviewed literature, little has been written about Camp 133 at Ozada, on Morley Flats, just outside the park boundary but within the bounds of Stoney Nakoda Reserves 142, 143, and 144. We have found grey literature that suggests this camp would be a rich topic for investigating cross-cultural encounters and connections during unique historical circumstances. Michael O'Hagan's blog, POWs in Canada,[13] considers some of the visual art produced by prisoners of war depicting tipis flying swastika-emblazoned flags with the front ranges of the Rockies as a backdrop (Fig. 3.8). We see, again, the western mountain parks are well represented in the literature while instances outside their bounds, though interesting for their complex social relations, are less covered in the peer-reviewed work.

---

13 https://powsincanada.ca/2022/03/03/seeing-double-pow-artists-at-camp-133-ozada/

Figure 3.8: "K.G. Lager 133, Ozada Canada," 1943, Richard Schädler. Image courtesy of Michael O'Hagan.

3.7.3 *Military labour*

Beyond the striking and historically significant example of the Alaska Highway (see Sec. 3.7.4), the mountainous landscapes and high-latitude regions of northern British Columbia, the Yukon, and Alaska (Boreal and Taiga Cordillera regions) attracted and enabled a wide array of military activities. During and after the Second World War, military personnel and equipment from southern Canada and the United States were transplanted temporarily and semi-permanently at various northern locales deemed strategic to bolster continental defence. The Soviet-Finnish Winter War of 1939–1940, the Japanese invasion of Aleutian Islands in 1942–1943, and the new reality of total war that encompassed environments as well as troops signalled the military necessity of understanding and preparing for conflict in extreme environments (Lackenbauer & Farish, 2007). In waging the Cold War, military and defence officials in Canada and the United States approached the sub-Arctic and Arctic regions of North America as both a strategic weak point and a natural training ground (Farish, 2010). Geography, terrain, environmental conditions, transportation, and other obstacles to military operations became focal points for research and analysis, as did the challenges of acclimating and acclimatising machines and bodies to the climatic rigours of the continent (Godefroy, 2014).

Within this context, mountain warfare did not receive special attention as an actionable military consideration for officials in Ottawa. The military training exercises that occurred in northern Canada and Alaska at mid-century revealed the important distinction between winter warfare and Arctic warfare, but military officials and strategic planners approached mountain warfare as analogous to jungle combat (Lackenbauer & Kikkert, 2016). The distinct topographical features of the Rocky Mountains (Montane Cordillera region)—wooded ranges, frozen ground, lakes, valleys, and snow—represented an extreme environment which, although challenging, it was believed could be overcome by science, engineering, and human will. Soldiers received training in cold-weather survival, often appropriating and adapting traditional skills from Indigenous guides and knowledge keepers. Skiing, snowshoeing, and ground and celestial navigation were equated with training for operations in mountainous locales, but so, too, was the critical importance of overcoming the human challenges of positioning soldiers in an extreme environment. Some grey literature documents the experiences of soldiers and researchers in 20th-century military-sponsored endeavours (Jackson, 2022). Mountain ranges in North America attracted considerable military activity in the mid-20th century, but the full extent of the human and environmental consequences of that activity remains largely unclear. Isolated studies of specific regiments and individuals who trained in the Canadian Rockies (Reichwein, 2014, pp. 186–195; Smythe, 2013; Taylor, 1994, pp. 301–312) are an invitation to scholars to expand upon their beginnings and the excellent work that focuses on the Arctic and sub-Arctic.

3.7.4 *Built infrastructures*

Built infrastructures shape how land is used and experienced. For instance, see the literature on the ways that infrastructures installed for the 1988 and 2010 Olympic Winter Games can have lasting impacts on mountain places and the ways people engage with them (Kariel & Kariel, 1988; Sant, 2015).

3.7.5 *Mountain professionals*

One of the strongest assessments we can make of how labour operates as a place-making tool is the case of mountain professionals—guides, avalanche technicians, researchers, surveyors, and professional athletes. Two of our authors are mountain professionals and have shared their knowledge of how this group of people know mountains as home.

The morning was crisp on the darkened valley road, the rising sun just illuminating the tops of Hermit range off to the north, winds are barely tracible to us in the valley but seems to be coming from the SSW, yet at upper levels the clouds are wispy towards the east .... The smell of earth from the dew indicates that cooler nights are starting, and it might be a wet walk into our camp.

RECLAIMING DAŃ K'E (THE PEOPLE'S WAY)

Sometimes infrastructures can have effects that are unforeseen or unintended. Beginning in 1942, the construction of the Alaska Highway by the United States military led to a host of short and long-term consequences including several epidemics between 1942–1948, the introduction of new goods and technologies, and short-term meat shortages resulting from overhunting by US military and civilian personnel (Nadasdy, 2003, pp. 32–38). One of our authors, Elder Gùdia Mary Jane Johnson (Lhu'ààn Mân Ku Dań) lived through these changes and shared her knowledge with CMA author Linda Johnson in conversations that took place in September 2022. Together, they prepared the following paragraphs.

During one frenzied year from 1942–43 the U.S. Army Corps of Engineers and a multitude of contractors built the 1000-mile [1600-km] Alaska Highway across the uncharted mountainous regions of northern British Columbia, the Yukon and into Alaska. Many First Nations' men guided the surveyors following their ancestors' foot trails; it followed that much of the original route was built on the First Nations' trails. The gravel road opened the first permanent year-round transportation corridor from southern Canada and the U.S. to these remote areas of North America. First Nations communities, animals, even plant life felt immediate and profound changes from that one Second World War project—bulldozers, trucks, and 11,000 soldiers crowded into temporary camps along the route causing damage to critical habitat, overhunting animals and affecting the food security for both First Nation peoples and animals that depended on those lands for food. Although some northern people gained work opportunities and the state of Alaska was thereby connected to the lower 48, overall it was a very hard time for First Nations families and communities who suffered from epidemic diseases, displacement, and other distressing experiences that had negative consequences long after completion of the highway, the effects of which resonate to this day.

The post-Second World War era brought a flood of newcomers along the new vehicle corridor into Lhù'ààna (the Kluane region): workers to maintain the highway and to construct the parallel telegraph line and eight-inch oil pipeline, then missionaries, and entrepreneurs intent on pursuing fresh prospects. Canadian federal government agents also gained access to vast areas asserting new management regimes that affected all aspects of life for the First Nations people. In response to reports of overhunting, the Yukon government amended the Game Ordinance to limit the sale of meat and hides and introduced trapline registration and regulations. The Yukon and Canadian governments established the Kluane Game Preserve in 1943, banning all First Nations people from large areas west of the highway for hunting, trapping, and fishing. While they still could gather plants for food and medicines, they were banned from practicing their traditions of animal and land conservation that had helped to maintain ecological balance and from being part of the sacred and natural laws in bird, fish, animal, and plant communities existing since time immemorial. The penalties imposed on First Nations people for violations of the newcomers' laws were harsh and ongoing for decades. With only meagre community consultation, the Kluane Game Preserve boundaries were expanded by government with further restrictions imposed after the creation of Kluane National Park and Reserve in 1972.

The newly constructed highway permitted year-round access for government officials to enforce laws requiring all First Nations children to attend school, removing children from their families and home communities to far distant residential schools. Children were forced to cut their hair, speak a different language, wear westernised clothes, and eat a new high calorie, low nutritious diet. All these policies, programs and practices created devastating impacts and massive upheaval for the First Nations Peoples in this mountain region.

Many families were relocated by government agents to land set aside within a different First Nation's Traditional Territory, some became enfranchised and moved to non-Native communities to make a monetary living. This new regime lacked acknowledgement of millennia of First Nations' governance, and instead sought to control every aspect of their lives from birth to death. The removal of children devastated communities, some of which were left without children between the ages of 5 to 18 years of age for decades. The residential school policy is at the root of much of the intergenerational trauma that continues in

/continued from page 161

First Nations communities and has had devastating results such as language loss, loss of cultural practices, fear and shame of ancestral knowledge of their mountain homelands.

In the 1960s through the 1990s the people began to assemble, gaining strength from Dáh Shäw (Our Elders: Nadene—Southern Tutchone—Lhù'ààna dialect) and from the American Indian Movement (AIM) and other civil rights movements around the world. Yukon First Nations reasserted their inherent rights to land and water, they sought to reclaim their Dań Kwanje (the People's words), culture, and Dań K'e (the People's way). The eleven First Nations who negotiated and signed comprehensive Land Claims and Self Government Agreements with Canada and the Yukon governments transformed Yukon society, including the restoration of hunting, fishing, gathering, and trapping rights and co-management regimes for Champagne & Aishihik First Nations, and Kluane First Nations people within the national and territorial parks in each First Nation's Traditional Territory.

As the above paragraphs attest, roads meant to connect also displace and disconnect animals, people and other life from their Homelands. Further developments of infrastructures and modern-day resource extractive industries interact with other forces to influence governmental policies that affect land and water—any and all access has intergenerational impacts. On the second day of the CMA Learning Circle, Gùdia Mary Jane Johnson (Lhù'ààn Mân Ku Dań) explained how after the U.S. Army used the defoliant Agent Orange on the construction of the oil pipeline paralleling the Alaska Highway: "years later we saw many strong, healthy Dashaw—Our Elders suddenly become sick with esophageal and stomach cancers" (LC 3.22). "The loss of Dashaw—Our Elders profoundly affected our communities."

Gùdia Mary Jane Johnson, Lhù'ààn Mân Ku Dań, 2022, LC 3.22

The ruffed wing swallow (*Stelgidopteryx rufkollis*) songs and the all-pervading croak of ravens (*Corvus corax*) are all around, the mosquitoes attack behind our ears and wherever skin is exposed, nonetheless our woollies will be coming off once we get into the sunny avalanche paths of open sections of Arnica (*Arnica cordifolia*) and Mountain Heather (*Phyllodoce empetriformis*) with cool shadows of Alder (*Alnus incana*), Devils Club (*Oplopanax horridus*) small trickling streams. The path is rooted by stands of Hemlock (*Tsuga mertensiana*), Yew (*Taxus brevifolia*), and cedar (*Thuja plicata*) with open rocky in places where ancient rockslides occurred.... Our packs are hardly noticeable except for the odd creaking noise from our hip belts and the slower pace on the steeper hills. Cool air fills our lungs in the shadows, and warm dust coats our throats in the open. As we ascend, the elevation is notable by the sweet smell of Fir (*Abies lasiocarpa*) with pockets of strong sour smell of Valerian (*Valeriana sitchensis*) .... As the snow melts rocks from their peccaries' ledges, we hear rock fall from higher areas across the valley. (Tim Patterson, 1979)

This is a segment from a trip log, detailing minute observations made during a hike into camp and capturing the writer's sense of being embedded in a complex, layered, and dynamic place (Duncan & Agnew, 2014). Mountain professionals develop a strong, often emotionally charged sense of place as they move through the mountains for their work. This connection is built through practice, language, and learning, cultivating strong attachments to mountains as more than a worksite or playground, but intimately as a home (Bachelard et al., 1969).

Exposure to the dangers of moving in environments characterised by snow and ice, exposed terrain, extreme weather, and risk of avalanches or rock falls imbues mountain professionals' sense of home with raw emotional power. Many, especially those working at high elevations have lost colleagues and friends. For some, this adds to their depth of feelings for mountains, as emotionally charged memories further feelings of being at home in the mountains. There is a body of grey literature dealing with how professional and amateur mountain athletes deal with the give and take of mountains (e.g., Roberts, 1968), some of which considers the differential stakes for women and parents (e.g., Mort, 2022; Tabei, 2017), but, with the exception of recent films (Mortimer & Rosen, 2021; Mosher, 2021), we found none that did so for mountains in Canada. We judge this to be a worthwhile topic for further scholarly investigation.

Deep senses of place and feelings of being at home in the mountains develop through practices of hiking, skiing, climbing, and working among mountains over days, months, and years, they develop a layering of experience. Professionals must understand and familiarise themselves with the characteristics and qualities of mountain landscapes, as is evident from the above excerpt. In the process of doing so, they become intimately connected with the places they frequent. Such practices orient mountain professionals to dwell in mountains as places of experience and meaning—what Edward Casey identifies as 'thick places' (2001)—rather than experience them as venues merely for exploration and consumption.

This process is further developed through language. Mountain professionals typically speak about their experiences subjectively, informed by years of experience. This is best seen in morning briefings where weather, snow, or route conditions are outlined and discussed with reference to knowledge of past circumstances of particular places. Their stories are situated in the landscape (Basso, 1996). Anthropologists have examined how matrices of stories extend and deepen experiences of place (Cruikshank, 1998). Frequent use of anecdotes, metaphors, and jokes in mountain professionals' narratives demonstrates the lived experience of their knowledge. This is captured well in Métis mountaineer and guide Barry Blanchard's *The Calling: A Life Rocked by Mountains* (2014). Blanchard's stories reveal a deep, intimate knowledge of mountains.

The acquisition and transmission of knowledge of place plays a formative role, in conjunction with movement through mountain spaces, in developing professionals' intimate relation to mountain places. Mountain professionals are, by necessity,

students of mountains. Knowledge of snowpack, terrain features, ecology, and weather is necessary for successful forays into the mountains. The knowledge acquired through observation, practice, and experience are among the gifts mountain professionals receive from working and being in the mountains. For guides, avalanche specialists, professional athletes, and the like who make their living out of moving through mountains, their montane homes are places of layered meaning and identification.

With the proliferation of adventure travel and social media, more people are coming to the mountains. The increase in popularity of mountain activities is both a blessing and a curse for mountain professionals and their communities. Those seeking mountain experiences will look to hire professionals and thereby support the guiding industry, and they will unknowingly rely on the services of avalanche specialists, researchers, and others to ensure they stay safe. While the mountains have been commodified since at least the advent of railway tourism, the increased volume of traffic and the greater commodification of experiences in the mountains impact mountain denizens and the landscapes themselves (Taylor, 2007; Zezulka-Mailloux, 2007). These changes can alter the relationship between mountain professionals and the places they work, sometimes challenging the sense of home they find within the mountains.

Although our understanding of these topics is informed by first-hand author experiences, we note that there is little peer-reviewed social sciences literature on the topic of mountain professionals' experiences of place in Canadian mountain regions. Notable exceptions are recent, generally critical, studies concerning gender in mountain professions. Women comprise approximately 10–15% of the Canadian guiding and avalanche industry workforce. A 2019 study amongst industry associations found that gender discrimination affects 1 in 2 female guides, and that this is primarily centred on perceptions of their competence as compared to male peers (Reimer & Eriksen, 2022). Guiding and avalanche work, it seems, carries with it colonial legacies of mountains as White cis-male spaces. This becomes apparent in perceptions within the profession (and likely also without). One study participant shared, "As a White male, I am the sought after 'ideal' of a guide and I am treated as such"; and another, "if you are not White male, you'd better be ultra-competent and strong" (p. 157). Lived experiences of gender discrimination in the guiding industry, from higher to lower frequency, centred on: 1) competence; 2) motherhood; 3) traditional gender roles; and 4) hostile, sexualized work environments. The 2019 study also found that 1 in 3 women in the profession experienced sexual harassment, and of those, 30% experienced unwanted touching or further violation. Of those harassing experiences, 60% were instigated by fellow guides and co-workers (Reimer & Eriksen, 2022, p. 158). Critical examination of the effects of this on the felt sense of belonging and safety for women in the mountains is an emerging area of research. It seems to us that there is room for work along these lines that carefully considers the specificity of context, including how gender, class, language, and race influence how mountain professionals experience and work in mountain spaces.

3.8 Governance in Contemporary Mountain Spaces

3.8.1 *Mountains as borderlands*

Mountains have long been regarded as natural borders and states have used them to support territorial claims (Debarbieux & Rudaz, 2015; Hansen, 2013). Certainly, mountains can act as barriers. Daniel Sims (Tsay Keh Dene First Nation), observed during the CMA Learning Circle that the mountains surrounding his community are part of the reason why they enjoy greater access and governance over their Traditional Territory (LC 3.23). Geographer Cole Harris made an analogous point about the efficacy of mountain

Daniel Sims, Tsay Keh Dene First Nation, 2022, LC 3.23

geographies as blockades to colonial law (Harris, 2008) (see Sec. 3.6.1). Scholarly work considering mountains and national borders in the Canadian context tends to be natural scientific and bureaucratic in orientation, often concerned with megafauna migration across international boundaries (Jones, 2010; Proctor et al., 2012, 2015, 2018), and international water treaties such as the Columbia River Treaty (Cosens, 2012; Hirsch, 2020). Academic work investigating mountains in Canada as boundaries assumed, made, and maintained appears to be lacking. The related topic of mountain warfare—its impacts on people and places, and how mountains shape practices of war—is also explored for other mountain regions (Kemkar, 2006), but we have found nothing on this topic in the Canadian context.

3.8.2 *Indigenous governance in mountain places*

Mountain regions—like all other regions in North America—are characterised by complex, long-standing, political relationships between Indigenous Peoples and their Traditional Territories and with settler-colonial states and governance systems, including treaties, imposed land ownership arrangements in contexts where they were alien, and much more. This section explores these relationships through engaging with Indigenous governance or the many ways that Indigenous Peoples have governed themselves and continue to do so despite the profound impacts of historic and ongoing colonialism. We found that there is minimal literature explicitly about Indigenous governance of mountain regions. We find there are two main reasons for this. First, the literature about Indigenous Peoples in mountain spaces often fails to acknowledge that Indigenous ways of knowledge and being expressed through oral history and practice also contain knowledge about governance and law (Todd, 2016; Whyte, 2017). We understand this misrecognition or overlooking of the existence of Indigenous governance and law to be a form of settler-colonial violence, grounded in ontological difference, that has tremendous implications for the ability of Indigenous Peoples to maintain their collective continuance (Todd, 2016; Whyte, 2017). Second, when there is literature on Indigenous governance relevant to mountain spaces, it often simply occurs in mountain spaces rather than being explicitly about governance of uniquely mountainous spaces and relations. While it is beyond the scope of this review to examine all literature on Indigenous governance in mountain spaces, below we present several examples.

The 15-year Peel Watershed Regional Land Use Planning process in Yukon is a story of environmental protection, Indigenous governance, and conservation in a mountain region (Section adapted from Wilson, 2020; see also Staples et al., 2013). The Peel Watershed Planning Commission developed a plan in 2011 (through a 7-year co-management process outlined in Chapter 11 of the Yukon Final Agreements). The recommended plan did not meet the Yukon government's expectation due to the high degree of protected lands (80% protected). Rather than making recommendations to the plan developed by the Commission, the Yukon Government developed their own plan including new land use designations and reduced protected areas (71% open for mineral exploration and 29% protected lands). The Yukon Government's decision was the subject of legal action by three First Nations (First Nation of Nacho Nyak Dun, Tr'ondëk Hwëch'in, and Gwich'in Tribal Council), along with the Yukon Chapter-Canadian Parks and Wilderness Society and Yukon Conservation Society including a series of court cases between 2014 and 2017 that went all the way to the Supreme Court of Canada. In 2014, the Yukon Supreme Court ruled in their favour stating that the Yukon Government's actions did not reflect reconciliation as fundamental to the "spirit and intent" of modern land claim agreements (*The First Nation of Nacho Nyak Dun v. Yukon*, 2014). The Yukon Government appealed this decision, and in 2015 the Yukon Court of Appeal partially reversed the Yukon Supreme Court's decision (*The First Nation of Nacho Nyak Dun v. Yukon*, 2015). First Nations appealed this second decision and the Supreme Court ruled in favour of the First Nations sending the parties back to the point in the process where "Yukon can approve, reject, or modify the Final Recommended Plan" (*First Nation of Nacho Nyak Dun v. Yukon, 2017 SCC 58*, 2017).

While the Peel trial was about interpreting how the land use planning process in Yukon is laid out,

it has broad implications for Indigenous-State reconciliation in Canada. It makes clear that modern land claims, which create a framework for shared governance between First Nations and settler-colonial governments, should not be interpreted in a narrow legalistic manner. Instead, the case affirms that reconciliation is fundamental to the implementation of modern land claims including provisions for co-management, which are legally binding and the "Crown" must act honourably in their implementation (Langlois & Truesdale, 2015a, 2015b). This means that settler-colonial governments have a responsibility to interpret the terms of land claims agreements generously and with the intent to achieve reconciliation. The final approved plan was completed in 2019 (Peel Watershed Planning Commission, 2019).

Indigenous Peoples in mountain places are also working hard to revitalise their Indigenous law and governance systems. Examples can be found through the work of the Relaw ("Revitalizing Indigenous law") program with West Coast Environmental Law. For instance, since 2017, the Taku River Tlingit, whose Traditional Territory is located in northern British Columbia (Boreal Cordillera) have been working to revitalise their governance system as a "living law that can and should be taught, learned and used every day" (West Coast Environmental Law, 2022a). They have documented their process in a video.[14] Similarly, the sməlqmíx, the syilx people of the Similkameen Valley in southern British Columbia (Montane Cordillera), issued a declaration stating the nʔaysnúlaʔxw snxaʔcnitkw (Ashnola Watershed in its entirety) as an Indigenous Protected and Conserved Area (IPCA) (West Coast Environmental Law, 2022b).

3.9 Conclusion

As the stories recounted and assessed in this chapter demonstrate, mountain homes and Homelands are places of complex, layered histories, evolving and competing practices and representations, and wells of cultural and spiritual meaning for Indigenous and non-Indigenous people.

---

14 https://www.youtube.com/watch?v=IvCOtp0MpFk

*Gùdia Mary Jane Johnson, Lhù'àn
Mân Ku Dań, 2022, LC 3.24*

Yet, to have mountains as a Homeland is different from having one's home in the mountains. In closing the meeting of the Canadian Mountain Assessment Learning Circle, Elder Gùdia Mary Jane Johnson (Lhu'àn Mân Ku Dań) reflected on the fact that:

We came from different mountain regions on the land. We came from the St. Elias, where I come from; the Rockies, down in this area; the Mountain Dene mountains; the mountains in interior British Columbia; the Chic-Choc mountains in Quebec; a little bit of the Torngat mountains in Labrador. So, we're really from all places. (LC 3.24)

In light of this geographical and cultural diversity of mountain Homelands, we have endeavoured to be careful and specific in our thinking and our words. At the same time, Gùdia Mary Jane reminds us that the "one thing that has brought us all together is that we all come from the land" (LC 3.24). Illustrating this similarity, Learning Circle Indigenous Knowledge Holders repeatedly commented on how many of them face similar pressures and threats to their Homelands and access to these lands, a topic that will be treated at greater length in Chapter 5: Mountains Under Pressure.

Despite all that we have learned from in preparing this chapter, there are numerous gaps in the topics and regions we were able to assess given the limitations of author expertise and time constraints (Table 3.1). The state of knowledge for these areas and issues remains uncertain.

Overall, we have found that the literature on mountain Homelands and homes gravitates toward the west, with mountain regions in Alberta, British Columbia, and the Yukon accounting for the bulk of the material.

We found that there is a decent amount of English-language literature on multispecies relations, but that French-language scholarship is more limited. The multispecies literature tends to focus on Indigenous relations with animals and plants; we note that with the exception of a few well-known studies (e.g., Cruikshank, 2005), there are few concerned with relations to beings other than plants and animals. With the possible exception of the case of bears, studies concerned with non-Indigenous peoples' multispecies relationships with non-humans are an area to which scholars could productively contribute, as are the ways that mountains can serve as religious or spiritual places for non-Indigenous peoples in Canadian contexts.

While we know quite a lot about the ways that settler colonial infrastructures, ideas, representations, and practices shaped mountain regions in the West, in particular the Rocky Mountains,

Table 3.1: Examples of topics not assessed in this chapter

Non-Indigenous religious and spiritual experiences of mountains in Canada

The multispecies relations around salmon in the Atlantic Maritime and Boreal Shield Region

2SLGBTQI+ experiences of mountains outside the context of recreation

The role of tourism in shaping mountain homes and Homelands

The specifics of early colonial incursion for each mountain region in Canada

The role of heritage preservation in shaping mountain parks & protected areas

The specific histories and analysis of the governance for each mountain park & protected area

Extraction labour as a form of place making in mountains

The role of lobbyists of various kinds (industrial, environmentalist) in shaping mountain places

Scholarship relevant for place-making in Arctic Cordillera, Interior Hills North, Interior Hills West, and Interior Hills Central regions

Specifics of literatures for mountain place-making in Atlantic Maritime and Boreal Shield, and Eastern Subarctic regions we deem that there is more to be known about how these were established and continue to operate in other mountain regions. The impacts and workings of systems of private land is another area where we noticed an opportunity for greater scholarly engagement. We believe that more studies that carefully treat such systems as diverse and changing over time, with an eye to their ontological implications for how land is known, used, and experienced, would be especially welcome for our understanding of mountain Homelands and homes.

We note that one important virtue of studies that investigate non-Indigenous peoples' multispecies and spiritual relations in mountains, as well as those that examine the precise, ongoing workings of settler colonialism is that such work can reveal non-Indigenous and colonial ways of knowing and doing as one type among many, rather than as "natural", "normal", or "default".

Based on our assessment of the role recreation plays in the shaping of mountains as home and its impact on mountains as Homelands, we conclude that the following areas are subjects about which we need to know more: how various forms of recreation in addition to skiing and mountaineering have shaped mountains in Canada and their demographics; how recreational practices differ across mountain regions in Canada; intersectional experiences of mountain places through recreation; how race, specifically, intersects with recreation in the context of mountains, and how tourist experiences can impact governance of mountain spaces through advocacy groups and lobbying. We also noted an opportunity in the literature to study the impacts and alterations which commodification and increased visitor traffic have on mountain homes and Homelands, a topic taken up in greater detail in Chapter 5.

The topic of governance, both Indigenous and non-Indigenous, in Canadian mountain regions is a weak point in our assessment due to the composition of our author group. We agree much more can be surveyed and known about how legal and political systems shape mountain homes and Homelands for all their denizens, human and non-human.

Finally, we note that while there is literature on the ways that Indigenous Peoples in Canada were dispossessed or barred from their mountain Homelands, there are fewer documented stories detailing resistance, refusal, and co-opting of colonial structures for the purpose of re-establishing and maintaining connection to mountain Homelands. We know these stories exist because we heard them from our colleagues at the CMA Learning Circle, and we have tried to highlight them where we could. However, this lack of understanding seems symptomatic of a more general feature of the literature. Topics exploring how Indigenous Peoples cultivate and maintain mountain Homelands are generally treated in isolation from those considering how non-Indigenous people are at home in mountains, except when the stories are ones of hegemony and dispossession. We are uncertain to what extent this may be an artefact of the framing we have used in this chapter. Still, our framing seems unable to fully account for this observed separation. It seems, then, that there is an opportunity, even a need, for studies that weave together, in fulsome ways, the multiple, interconnected, and ever-evolving stories of mountain Homelands and homes.

Glossary

Indigenous Epistemologies and Ontologies: Indigenous Peoples, and their ways of knowing and being, have been suppressed and marginalised through colonialism both historically and in an ongoing manner. In spite of this, Kim TallBear (Sisseton Wahpeton Oyate) reminds us, "[I]ndigenous peoples have never forgotten that non-humans are agential beings engaged in social relations that profoundly shape human lives" (TallBear, 2015, p. 234). Yet, Western knowledge systems are limited in their capacity to account fully for Indigenous worldviews (Hunt, 2014; Z. C. Todd, 2016; Watts, 2013). Consequently, Indigenous ontologies are frequently seen as cultural perceptions that occupy the realm of "myth" or "belief." There is a need to take Indigenous Peoples' ontological assumptions literally rather than symbolically (Hunt, 2014; Nadasdy, 2007) and by doing so to take seriously the possibility and politics of multiple worlds that include an active role for non-human relations such as plants, animals, rocks, glaciers, water, and more. Sarah Hunt (Kwagiulth, of the Kwakwaka'wakw Nation) points out that to move beyond the limits of Western knowledge we must centre Indigenous Knowledge Holders including the "work of Indigenous thinkers (scholars, Elders, community leaders, activists, community members) [which] contain a wealth of place-specific practices for understanding how categories of being are made possible within diverse Indigenous cultures" (Hunt, 2014, p. 27). Much of this, we believe, has not been captured in our assessment.

Indigenous Governance: Indigenous governance refers to the many ways that Indigenous Peoples have governed themselves and continue to do so despite the profound impacts of historic and ongoing settler-colonialism on their "collective continuance," including ways of life, health, and culture (Barker, 2011; Borrows, 2002; Coulthard, 2014; Ladner, 2017; Napoleon, 2013; Simpson, 2014; Whyte, 2017). Indigenous governance starts from the assumption that all Indigenous Peoples "had self-complete, non-state systems of social ordering that were successful enough for them to continue as societies for tens of thousands of years" (Napoleon & Friedland, 2014, p. 3). While disrupted by historic and ongoing colonialism, knowledge of these systems persists in practice and oral traditions (Borrows, 2002; Napoleon, 2013). Indigenous Peoples are working to revitalise their legal and governance systems and to assert their self-determination within and outside of processes of state-based recognition (Coulthard, 2014). While Indigenous ontologies and epistemologies are often misidentified as just being about relationships to the environment or cultural understandings, Indigenous governance scholarship and practice reminds us that they are complete systems that also contain knowledge about governance and law (Todd, 2016; Whyte, 2017).

Ontology and Epistemology: Ontologies are ways of being and epistemologies are ways of knowing. Ontologies are systems of identification and classification that define the boundaries between things in the world (Descola, 2013). By way of analogy, if the world is a room, an ontology is a description of the furniture in it, and how they are arranged in relationships to one another. There are different ways to furnish rooms and different ways to arrange their placements, so, too, are there different ontologies or models of the world. In other words, ontologies can be thought of as the basic conceptual underpinnings of the meaning, purpose, and identity of a thing and where it belongs in the larger social order of relations, obligations, and origin (Descola, 2013). Epistemologies are accounts about what knowledge is, how it is obtained, and what features make it valid or invalid.

Settler-Colonialism: Settler-Colonialism is a form of colonialism in which colonisers dispossess Indigenous Peoples of their land for settlement and resource development. Both colonialism and settler-colonialism are based on domination by an external power, only settler-colonialism seeks to replace Indigenous Peoples with a settler society (Wolfe, 2006). Settler-colonial scholars define colonialism as a "structure, not an event" (Kauanui, 2016; Wolfe, 2006). We define colonialism, and resistance to colonialism, as "a living, quotidian, and ever present moment that actors can interact with and interrupt. It is not an event, not even a structure, but a milieu or active set of relations that we can push on, move around in, and redo from moment to moment" (Barker, 2011; King, 2019, p. 40). Defining colonialism as a set of active relations, we understand colonialism as something that attempts to destroy or replace Indigenous relations. This negotiation and dispossession are ongoing. In this way, we understand colonialism as something that attempts to destroy or replace Indigenous relations with colonial relations. While different sets of relations are not necessarily mutually exclusive, colonial relations based on "property" and "ownership" seek to replace or dispossess Indigenous Peoples of their Homelands in a way that seeks to destroy Indigenous land relations and resistance to colonialism. While dispossession is often initially carried out by physical force, diverse technologies maintain this dispossession (e.g., maps, laws, and numbers) (Harris, 2004). In other words, settler-colonialism is a set of technologies of "alienation, separation, conversion of land into property and of people into targets of subjection" (Yang, 2017). All forms of dispossession are legitimated, justified, and reinforced through ideology and discourse about identity (Harris, 2004).

References

Adams, M. S., Connors, B., Levi, T., Shaw, D., Walkus, J., Rogers, S., & Darimont, C. (2021). Local Values and Data Empower Culturally Guided Ecosystem-Based Fisheries Management of the Wuikinuxv Bear-Salmon-Human System. *Marine and Coastal Fisheries*, 13(4), 362–378.

Allan, T. E. (2018). *The Hummingbird Creek archaeological site: An ancient hunting camp in Alberta's central Rockies, Canada*. [Master's thesis, University of British Columbia]. https://doi.org/10.14288/1.0365751

Andrews, T. D., & MacKay, G. (2012). The Archaeology and Paleoecology of Alpine Ice Patches: A global perspective. *Arctic*, 65(5), iii–vi.

Andrews, T. D., & Zoe, J. B. (1997). The Idaa Trail: Archaeology and the Dogrib Cultural Landscape, Northwest Territories, Canada. In G. P. Nicholas & T. D. Andrews, *At the Crossroads: Archaeology and First Peoples in Canada* (pp. 160–177). Archaeology Press.

Arenson, A. (2007). Anglo-Saxonism in the Yukon: The Klondike Nugget and American-British Relations in the Two Wests, 1898–1901. *Pacific Historical Review, 76*(3), 373–403.

Atlas, W., Ban, N. C., Moore, J. W., Tuohy, A., Greening, S., Reid, A. J., Morven, N., White, E., Housty, W. G., Housty, J. A., Service, C. N., Greba, L., Harrison, S., Sharpe, C., Butts, K. I. R., Shepert, W. M., Sweeney-Bergen, E., Macintyre, D., Sloat, M. R., & Connors, K. (2021). Indigenous Systems of Management for Culturally and Ecologically Resilient Pacific Salmon (Oncorhynchus spp.) Fisheries. *Bioscience, 71*(2), 186–204.

Bachelard, G., Jolas, M., & Bachelard, G. (1969). *The poetics of space.* Beacon Press.

Barker, J. (2011). Why 'Settler Colonialism' Isn't Exactly Right. *Tequila Sovereign, 13.*

Barr, Z., & Mortimer, P. (Directors). (2020). *Black Ice.*

Basso, K. (1996). *Wisdom Sits in Places: Landscape and Language among the Western Apache.* University of New Mexico Press.

Bastien, B. (2004). *Blackfoot Ways of Knowing: The Worldview of the Siksikaitsitapi.* University of Calgary Press.

Beck, J. S. (2006). *No Ordinary Woman: The Story of Mary Schäffer Warren.* Rocky Mountain Books.

Berger, C. (1983). *Science, God, and Nature in Victorian Canada.* University of Toronto Press.

Bernbaum, E. (1997). *Sacred Mountains of the World.* University of California Press.

Bernbaum, E. (2006). Sacred Mountains: Themes and Teachings. *Mountain Research & Development, 26*(4), 304–309.

Blanchard, B. (2014). *The Calling: A Life Rocked by Mountains.* Patagonia.

Bonamy, M., Herrmann, T. M., & Harbicht, A. B. (2020). 'I think it is the toughest animal in the North': Human-wolverine interactions among hunters and trappers in the Canadian Northwest Territories. *Polar Geography, 43*(1), 1–24. https://doi.org/10.1080/1088937X.2019.1685020

Borrows, J. (2002). *Recovering Canada: The Resurgence of Indigenous Law.* University of Toronto Press, Scholarly Publishing Division.

Bradshaw, G. A. (2020). *Talking with Bears: Conversations with Charlie Russell.* Rocky Mountain Books Ltd.

Braun, B. (2000). Producing Vertical Territory: Geology and Governmentality in Late Victorian Canada. *Ecumene, 7*(1), 7–46.

Brightman, R. (1993). *Grateful Prey: Rock Cree Human-Animal Relationships.* University of California Press.

Buckley, K. (2004). *Danger, Death and Disaster in the Crowsnest Pass Minces, 1902-1928.* University of Calgary Press.

Camerini, J. (1996). Wallace in the Field. *Osiris, 11*, 44–65.

Carlson, K. T., Schaepe, D. M., Smith, D. A., McHalsie, A. "Sonny," Rhodes, L., & Duffield, C. (2006). *A Stó:lō-Coast Salish Historical Atlas.* Douglas & McIntyre.

Cavell, E. (1983). *Legacy in Ice: The Vaux Family and the Canadian Alps.* Whyte Foundation.

Champagne and Aishihik First Nations, Greer, S., Gaunt, S., Strand, D., Joe, S., Fingland, J., Chambers, R., Adamson, J., Charlie, W., Jackson, M., & Smith, J. (2017). Traditional Stories of Glacier Travel. In R. Hebda, S. Greer, & A. Mackie (Eds.), *Kwädąy Dän Ts'ìnchį: Teachings from Long Ago Person Found* (pp. 419–435). Royal BC Museum.

Chan, K. M. A., Gould, R. K., & Pascual, U. (2018). Editorial overview: Relational values: What are they, and what's the fuss about? *Current Opinion in Environmental Sustainability, 35*, A1–A7.

Chen, Q., & Reichwein, P. A. (2016). The Village Lake Louise Controversy: Ski Resort Planning, Civil Activism, and the Environmental Politics of Banff National Park, 1964–1979. *Sport History Review, 47*(1), 90–110. https://doi.org/10.1123/shr.2015-0015

Chiniki Research Team, & Stoney Elders for Chiniki Band Council. (1980). *Ozade Mnotha Wapta Makochi: Stoney Place Names.*

Clark, D. A., & Slocombe, D. S. (2011). Grizzly Bear conservation in the Foothills Model Forest: Appraisal of a collaborative ecosystem management effort. *Policy Sciences, 44*(1), 1–11. https://doi.org/10.1007/s11077-010-9118-y

Clark, D., Artelle, K., Darimont, C., Housty, W., Tallio, C., Neasloss, D., Schmidt, A., Wiget, A., & Turner, N. (2021). Grizzly and polar bears as nonconsumptive cultural keystone species. *FACETS, 6*(1), 379–393. https://doi.org/10.1139/facets-2020-0089

Clark, D., & Joe-Strack, J. (2017). Keeping the "co" in the co-management of Northern resources. *Northern Public Affairs, 5*(1), 71–74.

Clayton, J. (2016). National Playground Both in Summer and Winter: Civic Groups, Ethnic Organizations, and Tourism Promotion in Revelstoke, BC, 1890–1920. *Social History, 49*(99), 389–408.

Clement, D. (1995). *La zoologie des Montagnais.* Peeters Publishers.

Clément, D. (2012). *Le bestiaire innu: Les quadrupèdes.* Presses de l'Université Laval.

Coleman, A. G. (1996). The unbearable whiteness of skiing. *Pacific Historical Review, 65*(4), 583–614.

Colpitts, G. (2010). *Game in the Garden: A human history of wildlife in western Canada to 1940.* UBC Press.

Colpitts, G. (2011). Films, Tourists, and Bears in the National Parks: Managing Park Use and the Problematic "Highway Bum" Bear in the 1970s. In *A Century of Parks Canada, 1911-2011* (pp. 153–178). University of Calgary Press.

Conolloy, T., Skinner, C., & Baxter, P. (2015). Ancient Trade Routes for Obsidian Cliffs and Newberry Volcano Toolstone in the Pacific Northwest. In T. Oxbun & R. Adams (Eds.), *Toolstone Geography of the Pacific Northwest* (pp. 180–192). Archaeology Press.

Cooke, L. (2017). Carving "turns" and unsettling the ground under our feet (and skis): A reading of Sun Peaks Resort as a settler colonial moral terrain. *Tourist Studies, 17*(1), 36–53.

Corr, L., Richards, M., Jim, S., Ambrose, S., Mackie, A., Beattie, O., & Evershed, R. (n.d.). Probing Dietary Change of the Kwäday Dän Ts'ìnchį Individual, an Ancient Glacier Body from British Columbia: I. Complimentary Use of Marine Lipid Biomarker and Carbon Isotope Signatures as Novel Indicators of a Marine Diet. *Journal of Archaeological Science, 35*(8), 2102–2110.

Cosens, B. (Ed.). (2012). *The Columbia River Treat Revisited: Transboundary River Governance in the Face of Uncertainty.* Oregon State University Press.

Costa, E., & Scardellato, G. (2015). *Lawrence Grassi: From Piedmont to the Rocky Mountains.* University of Toronto Press.

Coulthard, G. S. (2014). *Red Skin, White Masks: Rejecting the Colonial Politics of Recognition.* University of Minnesota Press.

Cronin, J. K. (2006). The Bears Are Plentiful and Frequently Good Camera Subjects: Postcards and the Framing of Interspecies Encounters in the Canadian Rockies. *Mosaic—A Journal for the Interdisciplinary Study of Literature, 39*(4), 77–92.

Cronin, J. K. (2011). *Manufacturing National Park Nature: Photography, Ecology, and the Wilderness Industry of Jasper.* UBC Press.

Cronon, W. (1996). The Trouble with Wilderness; Or Getting Back to the Wrong Nature. *Environmental History, 1*(1), 1–28.

Cross, M. P. (1996). *Bighorn sheep and the Salish world view: A cultural approach to the landscape.* [Master's thesis, University of Montana]. ProQuest Dissertations Publishing.

Cruikshank, J. (1991). *Life Lived like a Story: Life Stories of Three Yukon Native Elders.* UBC Press.

Cruikshank, J. (1998). *The social life of stories: Narrative and knowledge in the Yukon Territory.* UBC Press.

Cruikshank, J. (2005). *Do Glaciers Listen?: Local knowledge, colonial encounters, and social imagination.* UBC Press.

Cruikshank, J. (2007). Melting Glaciers and Emerging Histories in the Saint Elias Mountains. In *Indigenous Experience Today.* Berg.

Cruikshank, J. (2012). Are Glaciers 'Good to Think With'? Recognising Indigenous Environmental Knowledge 1. *Anthropological Forum, 22*(3), 239–250. https://doi.org/10.1080/00664677.2012.707972

Debarbieux, B., & Rudaz, G. (2015). *The Mountain: A Political History from the Enlightenment to the Present.* University of Chicago Press.

Dempsey, S., & Millan, L. (n.d.). *Lesbian National Parks and Services.* Shawna Dempsey and Lorri Millan, Performance Artists. Retrieved 22 July 2022, from http://www.shawnadempseyandlorrimillan.net/#/alps/

Descola, P. (2013). *Beyond nature and culture.* University of Chicago Press.

Deslandes, P. R. (2009). Curing Mind and Body in the Heart of the Canadian Rockies: Empire, Sexual Scandal and the Reclamation of Masculinity, 1880s–1920s. *Gender & History, 21*(2), 358–379.

Dickson, J., Richards, M., Hebda, R., Mudie, P., Beattie, O., Ramsay, S., Turner, N., Leighton, B., Webster, J., Hobischak, N., Anderson, G., Troffe, P., & Wigen, R. (2014). Kwäday Dän Ts'ìnchį, the First Ancient Body of a Man from a North American Glacier: Reconstructing His Last Days by Intestinal and Biomolecular Analyses. *The Holocene, 14*(4), 481–486.

Dixon, D., Boon, S., & Silins, U. (2014). Watershed-Scale Controls on Snow Accumulation in a Small Montane Watershed, Southwestern Alberta, Canada. *Hydrological Processes, 28*(3), 1294–1306. https://doi.org/10.1002/hyp.9667

Dixon, J., Callanan, M., Hafner, A., & Hare, P. G. (2014). The Emergence of Glacial Archaeology. *Journal of Glacial Archaeology, 1*(1), 1–9.

Driver, J. C. (1982). Early Prehistoric Killing of Bighorn Sheep in the Southeastern Canadian Rockies. *Plains Anthropologist, 27*(98), 265–271. https://doi.org/10.1080/2052546.1982.11909108

Duchesne, E. (2022). Le respect des animaux et la fluidité des catégories humaines et animales dans la cosmologie innue. In *"Parle à la terre, et elle t'instruira": Les religions et l'écologie* (pp. 67–87). Presses de l'Université Laval.

Duchesne, É., & Crépeau, R. (2020). Manitu et entités-maîtres: Pouvoir et juridicité chez les Premières Nations algonquiennes. *Recherches amérindiennes au Québec, 50*(3), 67–78. https://doi.org/10.7202/1088576ar

Dummit, C. (2004). Risk on the Rocks: Modernity, Manhood and Mountaineering in Postwar British Columbia. *BC Studies, 141*(Spring), 3–29.

Duncan, J. S., & Agnew, J. A. (Eds.). (2014). *The Power of Place: Bringing Together Geographical and Sociological Imaginations.* Routledge.

Edward S. Casey. (2001). Between Geography and Philosophy: What does it mean to be in the place-world? *Annals of the Association of American Geographers, 91*(4), 683–693.

Erickson, B. (2003). The Colonial Climbs of Mount Trudeau: Thinking masculinity through the homosocial. *TOPIA: Canadian Journal of Cultural Studies, 9*, 67–82.

Farish, M. (2010). Creating Cold War Climates: The Laboratories of American Globalism. In J. R. McNeil & C. R. Unger, *Environmental Histories of the Cold War* (pp. 51–83). Cambridge University Press.

First Nation of Nacho Nyak Dun v. Yukon, 2017 SCC 58, (Supreme Court of Canada 1 December 2017). https://scc-csc.lexum.com/scc-csc/scc-csc/en/item/16890/index.do?r=AAAAAQAEbnlhawE

Fladmark, K. R. (1984). Mountain of Glass: Archaeology of the Mount Edziza Obsidian Source, British Columbia, Canada. *World Archaeology, 16*(2), 139–156. https://doi.org/10.1080/00438243.1984.9979924

Fletcher, M.-S., Hamilton, R., Dressler, W., & Palmer, L. (2021). Indigenous knowledge and the shackles of wilderness. *Proceedings of the National Academy of Sciences, 118*(40), e2022218118. https://doi.org/10.1073/pnas.2022218118

Frohlick, S. (2005). That Playfulness of White Masculinity: Mediating Masculinities and Adventure at Mountain Film Festivals. *Tourist Studies, 5*(2), 175–193. https://doi.org/10.1177/1468797605066926

Fromhold, J. (2010). *2001 Indian Place Names of the West: Western Canadian History Reference Bibliography.* Self-published.

Gardner, J. (1986). Snow as a Resource and Hazard in Early-20th-Century Mining, Selkirk Mountains, British Columbia. *Canadian Geographer-Geographe Canadien, 30*(3), 217–228. https://doi.org/10.1111/j.1541-0064.1986.tb01050.x

Gardner, J., & Campbell, J. M. (2002). A century of research in Banff and surrounding National Parks. In S. Bondrup-Nielsen, N. Munro, G. Nelson, J. H. M. Willison, T. B. Herman, & P. F. J. Eagles, *Managing Protected Areas in a Changing World: Proceedings of the Fourth International Conference on Science and Management of Protected Areas, 14–19 May 2000* (pp. 234–243). Science and Management of Protected Areas Association.

Gille, B. (2012). De l'écologie symbolique à l'écologie politique. Anthropologie des controverses environnementales chez les Salish côtiers. *Tracés. Revue de Sciences humaines, 22*, Article 22. https://doi.org/10.4000/traces.5442

Gobby, J., Temper, L., Burke, M., & von Ellenrieder, N. (2022). Resistance as governance: Transformative strategies forged on the frontlines of extractivism in Canada. *The Extractive Industries and Society, 9*, 100919. https://doi.org/10.1016/j.exis.2021.100919

Godefroy, A. B. (2014). *In Peace Prepared: Innovation and Adaptation in Canada's Cold War Army.* UBC Press.

Government of Canada. (n.d.). *Indigenous connections* [National Parks site]. Jasper National Park. Retrieved 4 December 2022, from https://parks.canada.ca/pn-np/ab/jasper/autochtones-indigenous

Greer, S., Mooder, K., & Strand, D. (2017). The Kwädąy Dän Ts'ìnchį Community DNA Study. In R. Hebda, S. Greer, & A. Mackie (Eds.), *Kwädąy Dän Ts'ìnchį: Teachings from Long Ago Person Found* (pp. 375–382). Royal BC Museum.

Greer, S., & Strand, D. (2012). Cultural Landscapes, Past and Present, and the South Yukon Ice Patches. *Arctic, 65*(1), 136–152.

Hanna, D., & Henry, M. (1996). *Our tellings: Interior salish stories of the Nlha7kapmx people.* UBC Press.

Hansen, P. (2013). *The Summits of Modern Man: Mountaineering after the Enlightenment.* Harvard University Press.

Haraway, D. J. (2013). When Species Meet: Introductions. In *When Species Meet* (pp. 3–44). U of Minnesota Press.

Hare, P. G., Greer, S., Gotthardt, R., Farnell, R., Bowyer, V., Schweger, C., & Strand, D. (2004). Ethnographic and Archaeological Investigations of Alpine Ice Patches in Southwest Yukon, Canada. *Arctic, 57*(3), 260–272.

Harris, C. (1996). *The Resettlement of British Columbia: Essays on Colonialism and Geographical Change.* UBC Press.

Harris, C. (2004). How Did Colonialism Dispossess? Comments from an Edge of Empire. *Annals of the Association of American Geographers, 94*(1), 165–182. https://doi.org/10.1111/j.1467-8306.2004.09401009.x

Harris, C. (2008). *The Reluctant Land: Society, Space, and Environment in Canada before Confederation.* UBC Press.

Harris, C. (2021). *A Bounded Land: Reflections on Settler Colonialism in Canada.* UBC Press.

Hart, E. J. (1983). *The Selling of Canada: The CPR and the Beginnings of Canadian Tourism.* Altitude Publishing.

Hart, E. J. (1999). *The Place of Bows: Exploring the Heritage of the Banff-Bow Valley, Part I.* EJH Literary Enterprises Limited.

Hebda, R., Greer, S., & Mackie, A. (Eds.). (2017). *Kwädąy Dän Ts'ìnchį: Teachings from Long Ago Person Found.* Royal BC Museum.

Helwig, K., Poulin, Monahan, V., & Thomas, C. (2021). Ancient Throwing Dart Reveals First Archaeological Evidence of Castoreum. *Journal of Archaeological Science: Reports, 37*(1), 102949.

Henson, L., Balkenhol, N., Gustas, R., Adams, M., Walkus, J., Housty, W. G., Stronen, A. V., Moody, J., Service, C., Reece, D., vonHoldt, B. M., McKechnie, I., Koop, B. F., & Darimont, C. T. (2021). Convergent geographic patterns between grizzly bear population genetic structure and Indigenous language groups in coastal British Columbia, Canada. *Ecology and Society, 26*(3), 7.

Herbert, C. D. (2014). Out on the Slopes: Activism, Identity, and Money in Whistler's Gay Ski Week, 1992–2012. *BC Studies: The British Columbian Quarterly, 181*, 105–126. https://doi.org/10.14288/BCS.V0I181.184356

Héritier, S. (2003). Tourisme et activités récréatives dans les parcs nationaux des montagnes de l'Ouest canadien: Impacts et enjeux spatiaux (Parcs nationaux Banff, Jasper, Yoho, Kootenay, Lacs Waterton, Mount Revelstoke et des Glaciers) / Recreative activities and tourism in Canada's Rockies National parks: spatial issues and impacts (Banff, Jasper, Yoho, Kootenay, Waterton Lakes, Mount Revelstoke and Glacier National Parks). *Annales de Géographie, 112*(629), 23–46.

Heritier, S. (2010). Public Participation and Environmental Management in Mountain National Parks: Anglo-Saxon Perspectives. *Revue de geographie alpine-Journal of Alpine Research, 98*(44200), 160–178.

Heyes, S. (2011). *Recovering and Celebrating Inuit Knowledge through Design: The Making of a Virtual Storytelling Space.* 11.

Hinde, J. R. (2003). *When Coal was King: Ladysmith and the Coal-Mining Industry on Vancouver Island.* UBC Press.

Hirsch, S. L. (2020). *Anticipating Future Environments: Climate Change, Adaptive Restoration, and the Columbia River Basin.* University of Washington Press.

Hunt, S. (2014). Ontologies of Indigeneity: The politics of embodying a concept. *Cultural Geographies, 21*(1), 27–32. https://doi.org/10.1177/1474474013500226

Inkpen, D. K. (2018). *Frozen Icons: The science and politics of repeat glacier photographs, 1887-2010*. Harvard University Press.

Jackson, C. I. (2022). *Has Anyone Read Lake Hazen?* University of Alberta Press.

Johnson, L. M. (2006). Gitksan medicinal plants-cultural choice and efficacy. *Journal of Ethnobiology and Ethnomedicine, 2*(1), 29. https://doi.org/10.1186/1746-4269-2-29

Johnson, L. M. (2008). Plants and habitats—A consideration of Dene ethnoecology in northwestern Canada. This paper was submitted for the Special Issue on Ethnobotany, inspired by the Ethnobotany symposium organized by Alain Cuerrier, Montréal Botanical garden, and held in Montréal at the 2006 annual meeting of the Canadian Botanical Association/l'Association botanique du Canada. *Botany, 86*(2), 146–156. https://doi.org/10.1139/B07-126

Johnson, L. M. (2010). *Trail of Story, Traveller's Path: Reflections on Ethnoecology and Landscape*. Athabasca University Press.

Jones, K. (2010). From Big Bad Wolf to Ecological Hero: Canis Lupus and the Culture(s) of Nature in the American-Canadian West. *American Review of Canadian Studies, 40*(3), 338–350. https://doi.org/10.1080/02722011.2010.496902

Jones, M. G. (2015). *The Life and Times of Mary Vaux Walcott*. Schiffer Publishing.

Joseph, L., Cuerrier, A., & Mathews, D. (2022). Shifting narratives, recognizing resilience: New anti-oppressive and decolonial approaches to ethnobotanical research with Indigenous communities in Canada. *Botany, 100*(2), 65–81. https://doi.org/10.1139/cjb-2021-0111

Kain, C. (2014). *Letters from a Wandering Mountain Guide, 1906-1933*. University of Alberta Press.

Kakaliouras, A. M. (2012). An anthropology of repatriation: Contemporary physical anthropological and Native American ontologies of practice. *Current Anthropology, 53*(S5), S210–S221.

Kariel, H. G., & Kariel, P. E. (1988). Tourist Developments in the Kananaskis Valley Area, Alberta, Canada, and the Impact of the 1988 Winter Olympic Games. *Mountain Research & Development, 8*(1), 44206. https://doi.org/10.2307/3673401

Kauanui, J. K. (2016). "A Structure, Not an Event": Settler Colonialism and Enduring Indigeneity. *Lateral, 5*(1). https://doi.org/10.25158/L5.1.7

Kemkar, N. A. (2006). An Environmental Peacemaking: Ending Conflict Between India and Pakistan on the Siachen Glacier through the Creation of a Transboundary Peace Park. *Stanford Environmental Law Journal, 25*(1), 1–56.

Kendall, H., & MacDonald, B. L. (2015). Chert Artifact-Materila Correlation at Keatley Creek using Geochemical Techniques. In T. Oxbun & R. Adams (Eds.), *Toolstone Geography of the Pacific Northwest* (pp. 49–61). Archaeology Press.

Kennedy, D., & Bouchard, R. (2010). *The Lil'wat World of Charlie Mack*. Talonbooks.

King, T. L. (2019). *The Black shoals: Offshore formations of Black and Native studies*. Duke University Press.

Kohn, E. (2013). *How Forests Think: Toward an Anthropology Beyond the Human*. University of California Press.

Krotz, S. W. (2014). A Poetics of Simpson Pass: Natural History and Place-Making in Rocky Mountains Park. *Studies in Canadian Literature/Études en littérature canadienne, 39*(1), 57–76. https://doi.org/10.7202/1062355ar

Ktunaxa and Qat'muk. (2015, July 28). *Jumbo Wild*. https://keepitwild.ca/ktunaxa-and-qatmuk/

Kulczycki, C., & Halpenny, E. A. (2014). Sport Cycling Tourists: Setting Preferences, Appraisals and Attachments. *Journal of Sport and Tourism, 19*(2), 169–197. https://doi.org/10.1080/14775085.2015.1070741

Labrador Inuit Land Claims Agreement, (2005). https://www.aadnc-aandc.gc.ca/DAM/DAM-INTER-HQ/STAGING/texte-text/al_ldc_ccl_fagr_labi_labi_1307037470583_eng.pdf

Lackenbauer, P. W., & Farish, M. (2007). The Cold War on Canadian Soil: Militarizing a Northern Environment. *Environmental History, 12*(4), 902–950.

Lackenbauer, P. W., & Kikkert, P. (2016). *Lessons in Arctic Operation: The Canadian Army Experience: 1945-1956*.

Ladner, K. L. (2017). Taking the Field: 50 Years of Indigenous Politics in the CJPS. *Canadian Journal of Political Science, 50*(1), 163. https://doi.org/10.1017/S0008423917000257

Lam, E. (2016). Rails, Trails, Roads and Lodgings: Networks of Mobility and the Touristic Development of the "Canadian Pacific Rockies," 1885–1930. In *Moving Natures: Mobility and Environment in Canadian History* (pp. 290–313). University of Calgary Press.

Langemann, E. G. (2011). Archaeology in the Rocky Mountain National Parks: Uncovering an 11, 000-Year-Long-Story. In C. E. Campbell (Ed.), *A Century of Parks Canada, 1911-2011* (pp. 303–331). University of Calgary Press.

Langlois, J., & Truesdale, C. (2015a). *Yukon Court of Appeal kills Yukon's Peel Watershed plan, but parties sent back to the drawing board—JFK Law—Canada*. JFK Law. https://jfklaw.ca/yukon-court-of-appeal-kills-yukons-peel-watershed-plan-but-parties-sent-back-to-the-drawing-board/

Langlois, J., & Truesdale, C. (2015b, January 16). Yukon court overturns government land use plan for the Peel Watershed. *JFK Law*. http://www.jfklaw.ca/yukon-court-overturns-government-land-use-plan-for-the-peel-watershed/

Laugrand, F., & Oosten, J. (2002). Quviasukvik. The celebration of an Inuit winter feast in the central Arctic. *Journal de La Société Des Américanistes, 88*(88), 203–225. https://doi.org/10.4000/jsa.2772

Lee, C. M. (2012). Withering Snow and Ice in the Mid-latitudes: A new archaeological and paleobiological record for the Rocky Mountain region. *Arctic, 65*(5), 165–177.

Lemelin, H., & Maher, P. (2009). Of the Torngats: Human-Polar Bear Interactions in the Torngat Mountains National Park, Newfoundland and Labrador, Canada. *Human Dimensions of Wildlife, 14*(2), 152–155. https://doi.org/10.1080/10871200802688532

Leroux, J. (2003). *Cosmologie, mythologie et récit historique dans la tradition orale des Algonquins de Kitciaskik* [Doctoral dissertation, Université de Montreal]. file:///Users/gabbyrichardson/Downloads/Leroux_Jacques_2003_these%20(3).pdf

Liboiron, M. (2021). *Pollution Is Colonialism.* Duke University Press.

Litwiller, F. (2018). "You can see their minds grow": Identity Development of LGBTQ Youth at a Residential Wilderness Camp. *Leisure/ Loisir, 42*, 347–361.

Loo, T. (2006). *States of Nature: Conserving Canada's wildlife in the twentieth century.* UBC Press.

Low, S. M., & Lawrence-Zúñiga, D. (Eds.). (2003). *The anthropology of space and place: Locating culture.* Blackwell Publishing.

Lundgren, J. (1984). Mont St. Hilaire—A Recreational Resource and Its Use (Quebec). *Park News, 20*(1), 44387.

MacEachern, A. (2001). *Natural Selections: National Parks in Atlantic Canada, 1935-1970.* McGill-Queen's University Press.

Mackenzie, A. F. D., & Dalby, S. (2003). Moving Mountains: Community and Resistance in the Isle of Harris, Scotland, and Cape Breton, Canada. *Antipode, 35*(2), 309–333. https://doi.org/10.1111/1467-8330.00325

Mackie, R. S. (1997). *Trading Beyond the Mountains: The British Fur Trade on the Pacific, 1793-1843.* UBC Press.

MacLaren, I. S. (2005). *Mapper of Mountains: M.P. Bridgland in the Canadian Rockies, 1902-1930.* University of Alberta Press.

MacLaren, I. S. (Ed.). (2007). *Culturing Wilderness in Jasper National Park: Studies in two centuries of the human history in the Upper Athabasca.* University of Alberta Press.

Malpas, J. (2018). *Place and experience: A philosophical topography* (Second edition). Routledge.

Manuel, A., & Derrickson, G. C. R. M. (2015). *Unsettling Canada: A National Wake-Up Call.* Between the Lines. https://ebookcentral.proquest.com/lib/ualberta/reader.action?docID=4789771

Marcus, A. R. (1995). *Inuit Relocation Policies in Canada and other Circumpolar Countries, 1925-60.* Government of Canada.

Mason, C. W. (2014). *Spirits of the Rockies: Reasserting an Indigenous Presence in Banff National Park.* University of Toronto Press.

Massey, C. D., Vayro, J., & Mason, C. W. (2021). Conservation Values and Actor Networks that Shape the Adams River Salmon Run in Tsútswecw Provincial Park, British Columbia. *Society & Natural Resources, 34*(9).

Mathur, N. (2021). *Crooked Cats: Beastly Encounters in the nthropocene.* University of Chicago Press.

https://press.uchicago.edu/ucp/books/book/chicago/C/bo85902176.html

Mayberry, K. (2003). *Romance in the Rockies: The Life and Adventures of Catherine and Peter Whyte.* Altitude Publishing.

McIlwraith, T. (2012). Indigenous Hunting Camps Can't Be Moved. *The Northern Review, 36*(3), 97–126.

McKay, I. (1992). Tartanism Triumphant: The Construction of Scottishness in Nova Scotia, 1933-1954. *Acadiensis, 21*(2), 5–47.

McKay, I. (1994). *The Quest of the Folk: Antimodernism and Cultural Selection in Twentieth Century Nova Scotia.* McGill-Queen's University Press.

Mierendorf, R., & Baldwin, K. (2015). Toolstone Geography in the Northern Cascades of Washington and Adjacent Areas. In T. Oxbun & R. Adams (Eds.), *Toolstone Geography of the Pacific Northwest,.* Archaeology Press.

Montero Sobrevilla. (2018). Indigenous naturalists. In H. A. Curry, N. Jardine, J. A. Secord, & E. C. Spary (Eds.), *Worlds of Natural History* (pp. 112–130). Cambridge University Press.

Moreton-Robinson, A. (2015). *White Possessive: Property, Power, and Indigenous Sovereignty.* University of Minnesota Press.

Morrow, P. (2009). Foreword. In *Where the Clouds Can Go* (pp. xiii–xvii). Rocky Mountain Books.

Mort, H. (2022). *A Line Above the Sky: A story of climbing and motherhood.* Ebury Publishing.

Mortimer, P., & Rosen, N. (Directors). (2021). *The Alpinist.*

Mosher, H. (Director). (2021). *Not Alone.*

Mouat, J. (1992). "The Assistance of Science and Capital": The Role of Technology in Establishing B.C.'s Hard Rock Mining Industry, 1876–1906. *Scientia Canadensis, 16*(2), 165–192.

Murphy, P. J., & MacLaren, I. S. (2007). Homesteading the Athabasca Valley to 1910. In *Culturing Wilderness in Jasper National Park: Studies in Two Centuries of Human History in the Upper Athabasca Watershed* (pp. 123–153). University of Alberta Press.

Nadasdy, P. (2002). "Property" and Aboriginal Land Claims in the Canadian Subarctic: Some Theoretical Considerations. *American Anthropologist, 104*(1), 247–261.

Nadasdy, P. (2003). *Hunters and Bureaucrats: Power, Knowledge, and Aboriginal-state Relations in the Southwest Yukon.* UBC Press.

Nadasdy, P. (2007). The Gift in the Animal: The Ontology of Hunting and Human-Animal Sociality. *American Ethnologist, 34*(1), 25–43.

Nadasdy, P. (2021). How many worlds are there? *American Ethnologist, 48*(4), 357–369. https://doi.org/10.1111/amet.13046

Nakoochee, R. (2018). *Reconnection with Asi Kéyi: Healing Broken Connections' Implications for Ecological Integrity in Canadian National Parks* [Doctoral dissertation]. University of Guelph.

Napoleon, V. (2013). Thinking About Indigenous Legal Orders. In R. Provost & C. Sheppard (Eds.), *Dialogues on*

Human Rights and Legal Pluralism (Vol. 17, pp. 229–245). Springer. http://link.springer.com/chapter/10.1007/978-94-007-4710-4_11

Napoleon, V., & Friedland, H. (2014). Indigenous Legal Traditions: Roots to Renaissance. In M. D. Dubber & T. Hörnle (Eds.), *The Oxford Handbook of Criminal Law*. Oxford University Press.

Natcher, D. C., Davis, S., & Hickey, C. G. (2005). Co-Management: Managing Relationships, Not Resources. *Human Organization, 64*(3), 240–250.

Nepal, S. K., & Jamal, T. B. (2011). Resort-Induced Changes in Small Mountain Communities in British Columbia, Canada. *Mountain Research and Development, 31*(2), 89–101. https://doi.org/10.1659/MRD-JOURNAL-D-10-00095.1

Neufield, D. (2011). Kluane National Park 1923–76: Modernity and Pluralism. In C. Campbell (Ed.), *A Century of Parks Canada 1911–2011* (pp. 235–272). University of Calgary Press.

Orr, S. K. (2011). The Private Sector on Public Land: Policy Implications of a Swot Analysis of Banff National Park. *Journal of Natural Resources Policy Research, 3*(4), 341–354. https://doi.org/10.1080/19390459.2011.607959

Ortner, S. (1999). *Life and Death on Mount Everest: Sherpas and Himalayan Mountaineering*. Princeton University Press.

Pacini-Ketchabaw, V., & Taylor, A. (2015). Unsettling Pedagogies Through Common World Encounters: Grappling with (Post)Colonial Legacies in Canadian Forests and Australian Bushlands. In V. Pacini-Ketchabaw & A. Taylor (Eds.), *Unsettling the Colonial Places and Spaces of Early Childhood Education* (pp. 43–62). Routledge.

Parker, E. (1907). The Alpine Club of Canada. *Canadian Alpine Journal, 1*, 7.

Pavelka, J. (2017). Are They Having Fun Yet? Leisure Management Within Amenity Migration. *World Leisure Journal, 59*(1), 21–38. https://doi.org/10.1080/16078055.2016.1277610

Pavelka, J. (2019). *Crowding and Congestion in Banff Alberta Canada*. TTRA Canada 2019 Conference.

Payne, M. (2009). The Fur Trade on the Upper Athabasca River, 1810–1910. In *Culturing Wilderness in Jasper National Park: Studies in two centuries of human history in the Upper Athabasca* (pp. 1–40). University of Alberta Press.

Peel Watershed Planning Commission. (2019). *Peel Watershed Regional Land Use Plan*. https://yukon.ca/sites/yukon.ca/files/emr/emr-peel-watershed-regional-land-use-plan_0.pdf

Peyton, J. (1016). *Unbuilt Environments: Tracing Postwar Development in Northwestern British Columbia*. UBC Press.

Pilø, L., Finstad, E., Wammer, E. U., Post-Melbye, J., Rømer, A. H., Andersen, Ø. R., & Barrett, J. (2021). On a Mountain High: Finding and Documenting Glacial Archaeological Sites During the Anthropocene. *Journal of Field Archaeology, 47*(3), 149–163.

Pitblado, B. (2017). The Role of the Rocky Mountains in the Peopling of North America. *Quaternary International, 461*(15 December), 54–79.

Proctor, M. F., Kasworm, W. F., Annis, K. M., Machutchon, A. G., Teisberg, J. E., Radandt, T. G., & Servheen, C. (2018). Conservation of Threatened Canada-USA Trans-Border Grizzly Bears Linked to Comprehensive Conflict Reduction. *Human-Wildlife Interactions, 12*(3), 348–372.

Proctor, M. F., Nielsen, S. E., Kasworm, W. F., Servheen, C., Radandt, T. G., Machutchon, A. G., & Boyce, M. S. (2015). Grizzly Bear Connectivity Mapping in the Canada-United States Trans-Border Region. *Journal of Wildlife Management, 79*(4), 544–558. https://doi.org/10.1002/jwmg.862

Proctor, M. F., Paetkau, D., Mclellan, B. N., Stenhouse, G. B., Kendall, K. C., Mace, R. D., Kasworm, W. F., Servheen, C., Lausen, C. L., Gibeau, M. L., Wakkinen, W. L., Haroldson, M. A., Mowat, G., Apps, C. D., Ciarniello, L. M., Barclay, R. M. R., Boyce, M. S., Schwartz, C. C., & Strobeck, C. (2012). Population Fragmentation and Inter-Ecosystem Movements of Grizzly Bears in Western Canada and the Northern United States. *Wildlife Monographs, 180*(8), 1–46. https://doi.org/10.1002/wmon.6

Reeves, B. O. K. (1978). Bison Killing in the Southwestern Alberta Rockies. *Plains Anthropologist, 23*(82), 63–78.

Reeves, B. O. K., & Dormaar, J. F. (1972). A Partial Holocene Pedological and Archaeological Record from the Southern Alberta Rocky Mountains. *Arctic and Alpine Research, 4*(4), 325–336.

Reichwein, P. (1997). *Beyond the visionary mountains: The Alpine Club of Canada and the Canadian National Park idea, 1906 to 1969*. [Doctoral dissertation], Carleton University.

Reichwein, P. (2004). Holiday at the Banff School of Fine Arts: The cinematic production of culture, nature, and nation in the Canadian Rockies, 1945–1952. *Journal of Canadian Studies-Revue D'Études Canadiennes, 39*(1), 49–73.

Reichwein, P. A. (1995). "Hands off our National Parks": The Alpine Club of Canada Hydro-development Controversies in the Canadian Rockies, 1922–1930. *Journal of the Canadian Historical Review, 6*(1), 129–155.

Reichwein, P. A. (2014). *Climber's Paradise: Making Canada's Mountain Parks, 1906–1974*. University of Alberta Press.

Reichwein, P. A., & Wall, K. (2020). *Uplift: Visual Culture at the Banff School of Fine Arts*. UBC Press.

Reichwein, P., & McDermott, L. (2007). Opening the Secret Garden: Mary Schäffer, Jasper Park Conservation and the Survey of Maligne Lake, 1911. In I. S. MacLaren (Ed.), *Culturing Wilderness in Jasper National Park: Studies in Two Centuries of Human History in the Upper Athabasca River Watershed*. University of Alberta Press.

Reid, G., Sieber, R., & Blackned, S. (2020). Visions of time in geospatial ontologies from Indigenous peoples: A case study with the Eastern Cree in Northern Quebec. *International Journal of Geographical Information Science, 34*(12), 2335–2360. https://doi.org/10.1080/13658816.2020.1795176

Reid, R., & Palechuk, T. (2017). Place Relationships in a Wilderness Setting: An Analysis of Two Mountaineering Camps in the Canadian Rocky Mountains. *Leisure/Loisir, 41*(2), 185–204. https://doi.org/10.1080/14927713.2017.1353435

Reimer, R., & Eriksen, C. (2018). The wildfire within: Gender, leadership and wildland fire culture. *International Journal of Wildland Fire*, 27(11), 715. https://doi.org/10.1071/WF17150

Reimer, R., & Eriksen, C. (2022). Leadership in Mountain and Wildland Professions in Canada. In A. J. Fletcher & M. G. Reed (Eds.), *Gender and the Social Dimensions of Climate Change* (pp. 149–167). Routledge.

Reimer, R. (Yumks). (2003). Alpine Archaeology and Oral Traditions of the Squamish. In R. Carlson (Ed.), *Archaeology of Coastal British Columbia: Essays in honour of Professor Philip M. Hobler* (pp. 45–59). Archaeology Press.

Reimer, R. (Yumks). (2011). *The Mountains and Rocks are Forever: Lithics and Landscapes of Skwxwú7mesh Uxwumixw Territory*. McMaster University.

Reimer, R. (Yumks). (2014). The Nch'kay (Mount Garibaldi) Obsidian Source and its Local to Regional Archaeological Distribution. *International Association for Obsidian Studies Bulletin*, 50, 10–17.

Reimer, R. (Yumks). (2018). The Social Importance of Volcanic Peaks for the Indigenous Peoples of British Columbia. *Journal of Northwest Anthropology*, 52(1), 4–35.

Reinhard, J., & Ceruti, M. C. (2010). *Inca Rituals and Sacred Mountains: A Study of the World's Highest Archaeological Sites*. Cotsen Institute of Archaeology Press.

Richards, M., Greer, S., Corr, L., Beattie, O., Mackie, A., Evershed, R., von Finster, A., & Southon, J. (2007). Radiocarbon Dating and Dietary Stable Isotope Analysis of Kwäday Dän Ts'ìnchí. *American Antiquity*, 72(4), 719–733.

Roberts, D. (1968). *The Mountain of my Fear*. Vanguard Press.

Roberts, P. (2023). Walter Wood and the Legacies of Science and Alpinism in the St Elias Mountains. In M. Armiero, R. Biasillo, & S. Morosini (Eds.), *Rethinking Geographical Explorations in Extreme Environments: From the Arctic to Mountaintops*. Routledge.

Robinson, Z. (2005). Storming the Heights: Canadian Frontier Nationalism and the Making of Manhood in the Conquest of Mount Robson, 1906–13. *International Journal of the History of Sport*, 22, 425–435.

Robinson, Z. (2014). Introduction. In *Conrad Kain: Letters from a Wandering Mountain Guide* (pp. xxi–xxxvii). University of Alberta Press.

Robinson, Z., & Slemon, S. (2015). The Shining Mountains. *Alpinist Magazine*, 50, 115–124.

Rorabaugh, A., & McNabb, C. (2014). A Geospatial Analysis of Toolstone Acquisition and Use: A Preliminary Investigation of Material Quality and Access Over 4,000 Years in the Salish Sea. *Canadian Journal of Archaeology*, 38(2), 371–393.

Rudin, R. (2016). *Kouchibouguac: Removal, Resistance, and Remembrance at a Canadian National Park*. University of Toronto Press.

Ruru, J. (2004). Indigenous Peoples' Ownership and Management of Mountains: The Aotearoa/New Zealand Experience. *Indigenous Law Journal*, 3, 111–137.

Sandilands, C. A. H. (2011). Cap Rouge Remembered: Whiteness, Scenery, and Memory in Cape Breton Highlands National Park. In A. Baldwin, L. Cameron, & A. Kobayashi, *Rethinking the Great White North: Race, Nature, and the Historical Geographies of Whiteness in Canada* (pp. 62–82). UBC Press.

Sanford, R. (Ed.). (2001). *A Mountain Life: The Stories and Photographs of Bruno Engler*. Alpine Club of Canada.

Sant, S.-L. (2015). *Conceptualizing Olympic Legacy: The Case of Vancouver 2010*. University of Alberta.

Satsuka, S. (2015). *Nature in Translation: Japanese Tourism Encounters in the Canadian Rockies*. Duke University Press.

Schaefer, B. (2021). *Rock climbing on the Niagara Escarpment: Emerging entanglements of care at the crag* [Masters thesis, University of Guelph]. https://atrium.lib.uoguelph.ca/xmlui/handle/10214/26442

Schefke, B. (2008). The Hudson's Bay Company as a Context for Science in the Columbia Department. *Scientia Canadensis*, 31(1–2), 67–84.

Scott, C. (2015). *Deep Powder and Steep Rock: The Life of Mountain Guide Hans Gmoser*. Rocky Mountain Books.

Shelvey, B., & Boyd, R. (2000). Indians, Fire, and the Land in the Pacific Northwest. *The Western Historical Quarterly*, 31(2), 225. https://doi.org/10.2307/970071

Shepherd, N. (1977). *The Living Mountain*. Aberdeen University Press.

Simpson, A. (2014). *Mohawk Interruptus: Political Life Across the Borders of Settler States*. Duke University Press.

Sims, D. (2021, May 8). *Eastern Farmers in Tsek'ehne Wilderness*. BC Studies Conference.

Skidmore, C. (2006). *This Wild Spirit: Women in the Rocky Mountains of Canada*. University of Alberta Press.

Skidmore, C. (2017). *Searching for Mary Schaeffer; Women Wilderness Photography*. University of Alberta Press.

Smith, C. (1989). *Off the Beaten Track: Women Adventurers and Mountaineers in Western Canada*. Coyote Books.

Smythe, T. (2013). *My Father Frank: The Forgotten Alpinist*. Mountaineers Books.

Snow, J. (2005). *These Mountains are Our Sacred Places: The Story of the Stoney People*. Fifth House.

Squire, S. J. (1995). In the Steps of Genteel Ladies: Women Tourists in the Canadian Rockies, 1885–1939. *Canadian Geographer / Le géographe canadien*, 39(1), 44242. https://doi.org/10.1111/j.1541-0064.1995.tb00396.x

Staples, K., Chávez-Ortiz, M., Barrett, M. J., & Clark, D. (2013). Fixing Land Use Planning in the Yukon Before It Really Breaks: A Case Study of the Peel Watershed. *Northern Review*, 37. http://journals.sfu.ca/nr/index.php/nr/article/view/278

Steiger, R., N. Knowles, K. Pöll, M. Rutty. (2022). Impacts of Climate Change on Mountain Tourism: A Review. *Journal of Sustainable Tourism*, 1–34. 10.1080/09669582.2022.2112204

Stephen, D. L. (2021). *Edward Feuz Jr.: A Story of Enchantment*. Rocky Mountain Books.

Sterritt, N. (2016). *Mapping My Way Home: A Gitxsan History*. Creekstone Press.

Stoddart, M. C. J. (2011a). Constructing Masculinized Sportscapes: Skiing, Gender and Nature in British Columbia, Canada. *International Review for the Sociology of Sport*, *46*(1), 108–124. https://doi.org/10.1177/1012690210373541

Stoddart, M. C. J. (2011b). Grizzlies and Gondolas: Animals and the Meaning of Skiing Landscapes in British Columbia, Canada. *Nature + Culture*, *6*(1), 41–63. https://doi.org/10.3167/nc.2011.060103

Sullivan, L. P., & Prezzano, S. C. (2001). *Archaeology of the Appalachian Highlands*. University of Tennessee Press.

Tabei, J. (2017). *Honouring High Places: The Mountain Life of Junko Tabei* (Y. Hiraki & R. Holtved, Trans.). Rocky Mountain Books.

TallBear, K. (2015). An Indigenous Reflection on Working Beyond the Human/Not Human. *GLQ: A Journal of Lesbian and Gay Studies*, *21*(2), 230–235.

Taylor, A., & Pacini-Ketchabaw, V. (2017). Kids, raccoons, and roos: Awkward encounters and mixed affects. *Children's Geographies*, *15*(2), 131–145. https://doi.org/10.1080/14733285.2016.1199849

Taylor, C. J. (2007). The Changing Habitat of Jasper Tourism. In I. S. MacLaren (Ed.), *Culturing Wilderness in Jasper National Park: Two Centuries of Human History in the Upper Athabasca Watershed* (pp. 199–231). University of Alberta Press.

Taylor, G. (2008). *The Law of the Land: The Advent of the Torrens System in Canada*. The Osgoode Society for Canadian Legal History by University of Toronto Press.

Taylor III, J. E. (1999). *Making Salmon: An Environmental History of the Northwest Fisheries Crisis*. University of Washington Press.

Taylor, W. C. (1994). *Highland Soldiers: The Story of a Mountain Regiment*. Coyote Books.

Teit, J. (1906). *The Lillooet Indians* (Vol. 2). AMS Press.

The Blackfoot Gallery Committee. (2013). *The Story of the Blackfoot People: Niitsitapiisinni*. Firefly Books.

The First Nation of Nacho Nyak Dun v. Yukon, YKCA 18 (Yukon Supreme Court 2015).

The First Nation of Nacho Nyak Dun v. Yukon, YKSC 69 (Yukon Supreme Court 2014).

The National Parks Act, no. Statues of Canada, 20–21, Government of Canada (1930). http://parkscanadahistory.com/publications/national-parks-act-1930.htm

Thomas, A., & MacKay, G. (2012). The Archaeology and Paleoecology of Alpine Ice Patches: A Global perspective. *Arctic*, *65*(1), iii–vi.

Thomas, D., & Enns, M. (1995). *Grizzly Kingdom: An Artist's Encounter*. Brush Education.

Thornton, T. F. (1997). Know your place: The organization of Tlingit geographic knowledge. *Ethnology*, *10*(1), 295–307.

Tim Patterson. (1979). *Hiking Log Book*.

Todd, L. (2015). Chapter 5—A Record of Overwhelming Complexity: High Elevation Archaeology in Northwestern Wyoming. *Plains Anthropologist*, *60*(236), 355–374.

Todd, Z. C. (2016). An Indigenous Feminist's Take on the Ontological Turn: 'Ontology' Is Just Another Word for Colonialism. *Journal of Historical Sociology*, *29*(1), 4–22. https://doi.org/10.1111/johs.12124

Toth, S. J., & Mason, C. W. (2021). "Out" in the Countryside: Gay Tourist Perspectives on Rural Travel in British Columbia, Canada. *Journal of Rural and Community Development*, *16*(3), 84–107. https://journals.brandonu.ca/jrcd/article/view/2052

Trusler, S., & Johnson, L. M. (2008). "Berry Patch" as a Kind of Place—The Ethnoecology of Black Huckleberry in Northwestern Canada. *Human Ecology*, *36*(4), 553–568. https://doi.org/10.1007/s10745-008-9176-3

Tsing, A. L. (2015). *The Mushroom at the End of the World: On the Possibility of Life in Capitalist Ruins*. Princeton University Press. https://doi.org/10.1515/9781400873548

Tuan, Y.-F. (2001). *Space and Place: The Perspective of Experience*. University of Minnesota Press.

Turner, N. J. (1988). "The Importance of a Rose": Evaluating the Cultural Significance of Plants in Thompson and Lillooet Interior Salish. *American Anthropologist*, *90*(2), 272–290.

Turner, N. J., & Clifton, H. (2009). "It's so different today": Climate change and indigenous lifeways in British Columbia, Canada. *Global Environmental Change*, *19*(2), 180–190. https://doi.org/10.1016/j.gloenvcha.2009.01.005

Turner, N. J., Deur, D., & Mellott, C. R. (2011). Up on the Mountain: Ethnobotanical Importance of Montane Sites in Pacific Coastal North America. *Journal of Ethnobiology*, *31*(1), 4–43. https://doi.org/10.2993/0278-0771-31.1.4

Uprety, Y., Asselin, H., Dhakal, A., & Julien, N. (2012). Traditional use of medicinal plants in the boreal forest of Canada: Review and perspectives. *Journal of Ethnobiology and Ethnomedicine*, *8*(1), 7. https://doi.org/10.1186/1746-4269-8-7

Waiser, B. (1995). *Park Prisoners: The Untold Story of Western Canada's National Parks, 1915-1946*. Fifth House.

Watts, V. (2013). Indigenous place-thought and agency amongst humans and non humans (First Woman and Sky Woman go on a European world tour!). *Decolonization: Indigeneity, Education & Society*, *2*(1), 20–34.

West Coast Environmental Law. (2022a). *New video: Taku River Tlingit First Nation's Journey to Revitalize its Indigenous Laws*. West Coast Environmental Law. https://www.wcel.org/blog/new-video-taku-river-tlingit-first-nations-journey-revitalize-its-indigenous-laws

West Coast Environmental Law. (2022b). *nʔaysnúlaʔxw iʔ kłluxwnwixwmntət: The Declaration of the Ashnola Protected and Conserved Area*. West Coast Environmental Law. https://www.wcel.org/blog/naysnulaxw-i-klluxwnwixwmntt-declaration-ashnola-protected-and-conserved-area

Whyte, K. (2017). What do indigenous knowledges do for indigenous peoples? *Forthcoming in Keepers of the Green*

World: Traditional Ecological Knowledge and Sustainability, Edited by Melissa K. Nelson and Dan Shilling.

Wilson, N. J. (2020). Querying Water Co-Governance: Yukon First Nations and Water Governance in the Context of Modern Land Claim Agreements. *Water Alternatives, 13*(1), 93–118.

Wilson, N. J., & Inkster, J. (2018). Respecting water: Indigenous water governance, ontologies, and the politics of kinship on the ground. *Environment and Planning E: Nature and Space, 1*(4), 516–538. https://doi.org/10.1177/2514848618789378

Wolfe, P. (2006). Settler colonialism and the elimination of the native. *Journal of Genocide Research, 8*(4), 387–409. https://doi.org/10.1080/14623520601056240

Wray, K., & Parlee, B. (2013). Ways We Respect Caribou: Teetł'it Gwich'in Rules. *Arctic, 66*(1), 68–78.

Wyllie De Echeverria, V. R., & Thornton, T. F. (2019). Using Traditional Ecological Knowledge to Understand and Adapt to Climate and Biodiversity Change on the Pacific Coast of North America. *Ambio, 48*(12), 1447–1469. https://doi.org/10.1007/s13280-019-01218-6

Yang, K. W. (2017). *A Third University is Possible.* University of Minnesota Press.

York, A., Arnett, C., & Daly, R. (1993). *They write their dream on the rock forever: Rock writings of the Stein River Valley of British Columbia* (1. print). Talonbooks.

Youssef, A. (2021, August 21). "Purpose and power": Meet 10 BIPOC adventurers challenging ideals of who belongs in the outdoors. *The Narwhal.* https://thenarwhal.ca/bipoc-outdoor-adventure/

Yukon Umbrella Final Agreement, (1993). http://www.ainc-inac.gc.ca/al/ldc/ccl/fagr/ykn/umb/umb-eng.asp

Zanasi, L. (2005). *Economic History of the Kluane Region: Background Paper# 3, Kluane National Park and Reserve Economic Impact Study.*

Zedeño, M. N. (2017). Bison hunters and the Rocky Mountains: An evolving partnership. *Quaternary International, 461*, 80–101. https://doi.org/10.1016/j.quaint.2017.06.043

Zedeño, M. N., & Bowser, B. J. (2009). The Archaeology of Meaningful Places. In M. N. Zedeño & B. J. Bowser (Eds.), *The Archaeology of Meaningful Places* (pp. 1–14). University of Utah Press.

Zeller, S. (2009). *Inventing Canada: Early Victorian Science and the Idea of a Transcontinental Nation.* McGill-Queen's University Press.

Zezulka-Mailloux, G. (2007). Laying the Tracks for Tourism. In I. S. MacLaren (Ed.), *Culturing Wilderness in Jasper National Park: Two centuries of Human History in the Upper Athabasca Watershed* (pp. 233–259). University of Alberta Press.

Receiving gifts of the mountains, Vermilion Lakes, Banff National Park. Photo courtesy of Paul Zizka, 2017.

CHAPTER 4

Gifts of the Mountains

CO-LEAD AUTHORS: Brenda Parlee, Wanda Pascal

CONTRIBUTING AUTHORS: Ashley-Anne Churchill, Goota Desmarais, Megan Dicker, Erika Gavenus, Jiaao Guo, Nina Hewitt, Eric Higgs, Pnnal Bernard Jerome, Patricia Joe, Gùdia Mary Jane Johnson, Stephen Johnston, Sydney Lancaster, Keara Lightning, Brandy Mayes, Graham McDowell, Tim Patterson, Sophie Pheasant, Brooklyn Rushton, María Elisa Sánchez, Niiyokamigaabaw Deondre Smiles, Tonya Smith, Lauren Somers, Madison Stevens, Daniel Sims, Hayden Melting Tallow, Gabrielle Weasel Head, Nicole J. Wilson, Kristine Wray

CHAPTER REVIEW EDITOR: Thomas McIlwraith

"Your care and celebration will carry on into the next generations so that the gifts are reciprocal—you give the gift and you accept the gift"—Elder Gùdia Mary Jane Johnson, Lhu'ààn Mân Ku Dań (LC 4.1)

4.1 Introduction

4.1.1 *Gifts and benefits*

Mountain regions in Canada offer important contributions to the wellbeing of human communities. As an alternative to the conventional language of resources or ecosystem services, this chapter conceptualises these contributions as 'gifts of the mountains'. This focus on 'gifts' suggests a relationship built on reciprocity, in which benefits flow from mountains to people and people give back to the mountains through care and stewardship. In speaking about gifts of the mountains we aim to acknowledge and foreground First Nations, Métis, and Inuit worldviews, which often emphasise deep reciprocal relations with mountainous places and the physical resources,

spiritual importance, and cultural identity they provide. That is, the worldviews of those who have occupied mountain regions and neighbouring areas in lands now referred to as Canada since time immemorial, and are among those who currently live in mountain areas. However, we also emphasise that many non-Indigenous individuals and communities are connected to mountains in both tangible and intangible ways, including economic, cultural, spiritual, and emotional connections. Ultimately, the framing of this chapter is premised on the idea that people and mountains exist in relationships and is rooted in the recognition that the land, water, and wildlife are gifts that require reciprocal care and stewardship for current and future generations.

Gùdia Mary Jane Johnson, Lhu'ààn Mân Ku Dań, 2022, LC 4.1

---

* *Due to the CMA's unique approach to engaging with multiple knowledge systems, we suggest that readers review the Introduction prior to reading subsequent chapters.*

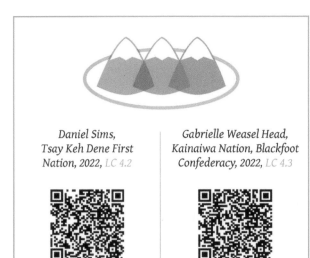

*Daniel Sims,
Tsay Keh Dene First
Nation, 2022, LC 4.2*

*Gabrielle Weasel Head,
Kainaiwa Nation, Blackfoot
Confederacy, 2022, LC 4.3*

Our framing of gifts is something that 'has been written about and communicated previously; for example, some anthropologists citing west coast and northern communities talk about how mountain environments give of themselves willingly with the promise of stewardship and care in return (Nadasdy, 2007). Reciprocal connections are also evident in Indigenous teachings such as those of "Netukulimk", which is a way of life in which Mi'kmaw take what is needed to support physical and emotional well-being while assuming responsibilities to do so without jeopardising the integrity, diversity, or productivity of the environment (The Confederacy of Mainland Mi'kmaq, 2014). Likewise, participants in the Canadian Mountain Assessment (CMA) Learning Circle spoke eloquently about the kinds of gifts provided by mountains: water, plants, foods such as berries and meat, medicines, peacefulness and serenity, room to play, as well as non-renewable resources for trade, tools, and other materials needed for everyday life. In exchange, as Daniel Sims, Tsay Keh Dene First Nation, notes, mountains expect respect (LC 4.2). Respect implies care and proper treatment on the part of users of mountain places—a kind of moral obligation (Ignace & Ignace, 2020, pp. 142–143)—and Indigenous oral histories from many parts of Canada describe the harms that befall disrespectful users of mountains, their environments, and the non-human kin that live in these places (e.g., Brightman, 1993; Cruikshank, 2005a).

In assessing the state of gifts of the mountains in Canada, this chapter also includes consideration of the products derived from mountains for the benefit of regional and global economies, including consumer benefits. This includes mineral extraction, the harvesting of timber, hydroelectric development, and commercial fishing of rivers, lakes, and oceans. We also call attention to how these benefits from mountains are not always respected in the spirit of reciprocity, with an understanding that a reciprocal model premised on kinship relations with the land and its non-human kin is often incongruent with predominant modes of resource extraction and consumerism (see, e.g., McIlwraith 2012). Indeed, as Gabrielle Weasel Head, Kainaiwa, Blackfoot Confederacy explained, this consumer paradigm has resulted in widespread abuse of the gifts of the mountains and disregard for the principles of respect and reciprocity (LC 4.3). Furthermore, Indigenous Peoples are among those who have historically borne greater costs and experienced fewer benefits from the extractive activities undertaken in mountain areas in Canada.

Many kinds of gifts have been lost or degraded as a result of the pressures of colonisation, resource development, climate change, and other forms of environmental change. These stresses that present as ecological losses (e.g., species extirpations), hazards (e.g., flooding, forest fires) or circumstances of poor health (e.g., due to bioaccumulation of contaminants) have socio-economic, cultural, spiritual, and health implications for both Indigenous and non-Indigenous communities. These dynamics are discussed in greater depth in Chapter 5.

Some mountain gifts, although degraded, are being restored or recovered (Hobbs & Cramer, 2008). Indigenous Peoples are playing a leadership role in many of these restoration initiatives, including those described as ecocultural restoration. "Ecocultural restoration explicitly includes humans as active participants in restored landscapes through recovering ecosystem structure, composition, processes, and function, along with traditional, time-tested, ecologically appropriate and sustainable Indigenous cultural practices that helped shape ecosystems" (Martinez, 2018, p. 170). This is not only healing of the land; it also involves the restoration of values and uses of mountain environments that have been and continue to be marginalised, such as those of Indigenous Peoples, the original stewards of mountains in the lands now referred to as Canada.

Many predominantly non-Indigenous communities are also working to cultivate more sustainable relations with mountain areas and the myriad benefits they provide, including progressive human-wildlife coexistence programs and climate actions initiatives in towns such as Canmore and Banff, Alberta, in the Montane Cordillera region. Despite some positive developments and opportunities, the preponderance of unsustainable uses of mountain environments and increasing pressures from climate change and other anthropogenic stressors presents growing challenges for those who depend on gifts of the mountains (Adler et al., 2022; Fast, 2014; Nitschke, 2008).

This chapter begins by describing some of the immaterial and intangible gifts that mountains provide to the health and wellbeing of individuals and communities, including gifts related to feelings of well-being, spiritual beliefs, healing activities and outcomes, art, and teachings (Sec. 4.2–4.4). These intangibles, commonly overlooked in standard accounting or valuation, can frame or inform the physical relationships and benefits people receive from mountains (Satterfield et al., 2013; Studley, 2012).

We then turn to other kinds of physical gifts of the mountains, including provision of food and medicines to humans through relationships with plant, fungi, and animal species (Sec. 4.5). Gifts of water from the mountains, including glaciers, snow, and freshwater are crucial to the well-being of mountain communities and flow downstream to the benefit of a large proportion of the population of Canada (Sec. 4.6). The direction of human movement in mountain environments often flows in reverse, from lowlands to highlands, bringing people into the mountains for tourism and recreation activities. This delivers important economic benefits to mountain communities (Sec. 4.7). Economically, mountains are also sources of materials and energy for much of Canada, in the form of timber and other gifts of the forests, rocks and minerals, and sources of energy (Sec. 4.8).

We also consider the many ways in which mountains protect people, both from natural hazards and from the consequences of our own activities, including by providing gifts such as carbon sequestration and biodiversity conservation, disaster resilience and sanctuary, and sites of resurgence, particularly for Indigenous Peoples. The chapter concludes with our assessment of the state of knowledge about mountains and the gifts they provide (Sec. 4.9).

4.2 Gifts of Identity and Wellbeing

4.2.1 *Emotional and physical wellbeing of mountain communities*

Mountain environments and regions are strongly interconnected with the spiritual and cultural identities of both Indigenous and non-Indigenous peoples, as the previous chapter on Mountains as Homelands has detailed. The concept of cultural landscape is often used to consider how cultural identities and practices are interwoven with physical mountain environments (Baird, 2013; Prosper, 2007). These strong interconnections, although largely intangible (felt rather than seen), are nurtured in ceremonies such as feasts and potlatches, water ceremonies, pilgrimages, and in day-to-day practices such as harvesting, travel, and "being" on the land (Cuerrier et al., 2015; Prosper, 2007). As noted in Chapter 3 (Sec. 3.2), mountains are often places where creation occurred and where spirits are encountered. They engender strong connections to physical and cultural landscapes. Gwich'in elder Elizabeth Wright from Tetlit Zheh (Fort McPherson) described her feelings of well-being and security that come from living in the mountains and being surrounded by food resources and family members.

> I like living here, [...] I like my backyard that I could just make a fire anytime I want and you can't do that in Inuvik, [...] and it's quiet, I like it quiet [...] anybody can get on a skidoo and go, you know and—then you can get into your truck and drive up the mountains! You could just, you see something different every time you go up there. I just love that drive, you can go to 8 Miles and get fish, I mean even if you have no food in Inuvik, who are you gonna phone? You know I can go to my brothers and get caribou meat, you know,

I could probably visit any of these houses and ask for bannock and somebody will have bannock (Luig, 2015, p. 256).

Similarly, during the Learning Circle, Brandy Mayes of Kwanlin Dün First Nation described her appreciation for being able to live near the mountains in her own Traditional Territory, and the ways in which going into the mountains to walk, sit quietly, pray, gather berries and medicine, or simply be present have supported her own physical, spiritual, and emotional wellbeing: "call it your playground, your spiritual place." "I feel like the mountains give you gifts sometimes in ways that you don't understand that they give you gifts, until later you can look back and reflect on what that gift was" (LC 4.4).

Many other people, and not only Indigenous Peoples, have strong personal and cultural connections associated with mountains, which nourish the wellbeing and identities of these communities. Mountains in Canada have mentally, emotionally, and physically inspired people from across many cultures in search of opportunities for adventure, living with nature, or a sense of identity in mountain places. This includes people seeking and pursuing active lifestyles such as mountain climbing, skiing, or hiking (see Sec. 4.7). Spending time in mountainous settings is therapeutic and can elicit demonstrable physical, emotional, and spiritual benefits. Many contemporary lifestyle trends have led individuals and communities to seek the healing power of nature in mountainous regions, and even to seek refuge, asylum, and redemption in these places. It is common to hear people of all backgrounds speak of a 'connection' to mountain places.

As early as the 18th and 19th centuries, these settings were believed to have the "power to cure the human psyche while simultaneously pro-

viding redemption" (Osama, 2019). Mountains as therapeutic landscapes provide diverse benefits to those who imagine them, dwell within their shadows and peaks, or visit them from time to time (Gastaldo et al., 2004). Acknowledging how healing processes are grounded in places, Gastaldo et al. (2004) observe that therapeutic landscapes are a kind of 'landscape of the mind', constituted by individuals through a web of emotions and social relations that include real and imagined sites and actors that live within them (Gastaldo et al., 2004, p. 170). For example, the Canadian Alpine Club "urged Canadians to become mountain climbers so that they might stand face to face with Infinitude and learn spiritual truths which would be otherwise denied them" (Altmeyer, 1976, p. 31). These landscapes of the mind are among the push-pull factors that drive tourism and immigration to mountain regions, given their connection to people's identities and imaginations. Indeed, the memories of such places can evoke strong connections to place and, by extension, shape mental health. Notably, ideas about the importance of time spent in natural areas implies that there are areas that are less natural (e.g., urban environments), and this points to the social and cultural constructions inherent in these worldviews (Gastaldo et al., 2004; Locke, 2006).

For many, mountains in Canada, particularly the Rocky Mountains in western Canada, within the Montane Cordillera region, hold particular symbolic and imaginative power. These mountains are associated with Canadian identity, embedded in historical and colonial stereotypes and icons. For instance, Moraine Lake and the Valley of the Ten Peaks graced the Canadian $20 bill for many years. Such iconography has been a source of unity for settlers in the building and marketing of the colonial state. As the previous chapter on Mountains as Homelands has articulated, mountain narratives have helped newcomers to Canada to make homes and find a sense of belonging and wellbeing in the mountains, in part by dispossessing and delegitimizing the presence of Indigenous Peoples. This history has been problematic for those who have suffered from the associated cultural erasure, including separation from the mountain gifts that have sustained First Nations, Métis, and Inuit cultures since time immemorial (Francis, 1992).

The promotion of such Canadian stereotypes has fostered dichotomies of belonging and not-belonging that influenced many sectors of the economy and socio-political institutions. A clear case in point is Banff National Park. Linnard notes:

> Banff National Park is most commonly and powerfully represented as a place intended for wealthy tourists to experience leisure and for "all Canadians" to encounter "the essence of Canada," representations that emphasise transience, leisure, safety and abstract notions of nature and nation. These institutional narratives of place validate management decisions that alienate residents and motivate them to assert special claims to belonging that distinguish between the local who belongs and those who are out of place (Linnard, 2015, p. 1).

Among these institutional narratives is the Canadian Pacific Railway, which made mountain landscapes accessible in real and imagined ways. Although celebrated in Canadian non-Indigenous history, railroad landscapes are sites and sources of trauma for others including Indigenous Peoples (Binnema & Niemi, 2006) and Chinese railway workers (Chan, 2008):

> The Chinese workers first came here for the railway, and they were forgotten people in many ways, because they didn't have a name, because they came in such huge numbers, because they were virtually indentured labour, like slaves, and they died in great numbers as well. But they contributed an enormous amount to the building of this country. Without the railway, you wouldn't have this country of Canada. (Li, 2000, p. 158, cited in Chan, 2008)

Many others are often made invisible in mountain lifestyle stereotypes, but nonetheless have important connections; those with physical and mental disabilities are however, becoming more visible and included through "nature interventions."

> Whether during single day trips, weekend or week-long, these nature interventions provided adaptive experiences such as hiking in the foothills regions or the high alpine regions of the Rocky Mountains, canoeing or kayaking. Adapted equipment, such as the Trail Rider, a single-tyre wheelchair designed to allow individuals living with physical disabilities to explore the outdoors assisted by 2–6 volunteers or 'sherpas', facilitated inclusion of all (Jakubec et al., 2016).

On the whole, it is important to recognize the many ways in which mountains have featured in the identities and cultures of different communities and to acknowledge the diversity as well as conflict between different kinds of intangible connections of people to mountain environments, and how the identities of some social groups may be well represented, valued, and protected in narratives of mountains, whereas the identities and connections of others are poorly represented. These incongruencies are not only visible in popular culture but also translate into decisions about resource use and management, with implications for human wellbeing.

4.3 Gifts of Art

4.3.1 *Mountains as sites of creative inspiration and dialogue*

The scale and grandeur of mountain environments has also been an ongoing source of inspiration and content for many of the most recognized artists in Canada. Imagery of mountains and mountain environments captured by artists has contributed to (and been utilised in the manufacture of) Canada as an idea in popular culture and for political ends (Anderson, 2007, p. 246). The art-historical view of Canadian painting within the country's visual culture from the 1920s to the 1980s often reinforced this association of wilderness landscape and national identity (Stanworth, 2013, p. 69).

Some of the most iconic and well recognized work of this nature has been produced by the artists known as the Group of Seven. Their work was related to the rise of middle-class tourism across the country; for example, when Lawren Harris and A. Y. Jackson embarked on a painting trip to Jasper in 1924, hiking and packhorse trips were already an important part of tourism and promotional literature for the area (Jessup, 2002, p. 155).

Though each member forged his own unique style, as a group, these painters tended toward expressions of the "Euro-Canadian wilderness sublime" (Bordo, 2007, p. 332) in work capturing landscapes, including mountain subjects. Many works of the Group of Seven represent "wilderness" as space devoid of human intervention, occupation, or even passing presence. As Jonathan Bordo notes, "Euro-Canadian wilderness as a system of representation—an ethos—will be marked by this absence" (Bordo, 2007, p. 332). As such, these works both erase Indigenous presence and territory, and set the landscape represented as something entirely apart from human life—something to be observed and preserved, rather than dynamic environments full of life with which one would have an ongoing relationship. In this sense, the landscapes of the Group of Seven manifest the social construction of 'wilderness' as part of a persistent national iconography of "Canadianness" (Stanworth, 2013, pp. 68; 86) which could be harnessed to both nationalist pride and the claiming of vast territories as uniquely "Canadian" lands within settler-colonial borders.

The impact of the Group of Seven's work on the popular imagination in Canada and internationally cannot be underestimated (Cole, 2007, p. 129; Lord, 2007, p. 121; Reid, 2007, pp. 101–102). Notions of the sublime in landscape and of the separation of humanity from the "wild" aspects of nature have informed settler politics, economics, and leisure activities in mountain environments for generations. As Candace Hopkins and Lucia Sandromán note:

> Landscape is not a neutral phenomenon, but a device framed by the particular perspective from which it is seen. There is nothing stable about this familiar subject, and there is a difference between the spaces we inhabit and the natural environment, and a difference between the experience of the land that constitutes a place and "place" as a site of memory and affection (Hopkins & Sandromán, 2014, p. 35).

The perspective as captured so effectively by the Group of Seven has its roots in European conceptions of human relationships to land and resources, and indeed to the conception of what constitutes civilization as it stands in opposition to wilderness (Payne, 2007, p. 160). The dichotomy set up in this understanding of human relationships to mountain spaces (and any other environment) has had profound real-world impacts: from urban planning and resource development, to the shaping of property laws and ideas of land 'ownership', to the recognition of Traditional Territories and lifeways, including access and use of mountain places for food, travel, medicines, and income (Colpitts & Devine, 2017, pp. 2–4; 7; Payne, 2007, pp. 153–156).

Contemporary artists, both Indigenous and non-Indigenous, have also drawn inspiration from the mountains in the creation of their work, but often to very different effect than the Group of Seven. Indeed, contemporary artists may take their cues in making work from a desire to express concern or critique popular (settler) perceptions of mountain environments as untouched wilderness, devoid of Indigenous history, or as sites impacted by resource extraction. Here, we offer a few examples of the range of creative expression inspired by relationships with—and created within—mountain environments.

Alana Bartol is a multidisciplinary settler artist based in Calgary Alberta.[1] She has created several inter-related bodies of work since 2020, examining mining in the Eastern Slopes of the Rockies and its ongoing impact on the environment. *To Dig Holes and Pierce Mountains, Hag's Taper,* and *Coal Futures* all address the lasting impacts of coal mining in the Crowsnest Pass. A residency and exhibition titled *Processes of Remediation: art, relationships, nature* at the University of Lethbridge in 2021 brought these works together.

Rebecca Belmore is an internationally recognized multidisciplinary artist and member of the Lac Seul First Nation (Anishinaabe). She has dedicated her practice to speaking difficult truths to government and settler society regarding the treatment of Indigenous Peoples and the erasure of their stories. In 1991, Belmore sketched out and built *Ayum-ee-aawach Oomama-mowan: Speaking to Their Mother,* a 1.8 m wide, 2.1 m long conical megaphone she created to speak to the land (Fig. 4.1). As the Banff Centre describes it,

---

1 A Tour of Alana Bartol's Processes of Remediation: art, relationships, nature: https://www.youtube.com/watch?v=sXLrQaWzpUA

Figure 4.1: Rebecca Belmore *Ayum-ee-aawach Oomama-mowan: Speaking to Their Mother* (1991). Gathering, Johnson Lake, Banff National Park, Banff, Alberta, 26 July 2008. Photo: Sarah Ciurysek Presented by the Walter Phillips Gallery as part of the exhibition 'Bureau de Change,' 12 July–29 September 2008. Courtesy of Walter Phillips Gallery, Banff Centre for Arts and Creativity. Purchased with the support of the York Wilson Endowment Award, administered by the Canada Council for the Arts Accession #P08 0001 S.

Before Belmore first spoke into the megaphone, the sculpture was carried through the woods and assembled in a meadow near Johnson Lake in the Bow Valley [in Banff National Park]. Her words echoed through the mountains and, she hoped, reached Mother Earth.

The piece was a response to the Oka Crisis of 1990—a protest against a proposed golf course on Mohawk territory in Quebec. But after its 1991 debut at the *Between Views and Points of View* exhibition at our Walter Phillips Gallery, it was used to address the land at political demonstrations from coast to coast (Frizzell, 2016).

While created in the Rockies, this work also travelled across the country, as a symbol and call to expression:

Stopping at reserves and significant sites, Belmore encouraged the local community to address the land through her megaphone in their own language. The piece is well travelled, having spoken to a clear-cut forest, Indigenous land claims, and even making it as far as Parliament Hill (Frizzell, 2016).

Belmore's relationships with the land and with other-than-human beings permeate her work to create calls for justice for Indigenous Peoples and to reflect on the violence that permeates settler-colonialism as a system. Her work can be seen as a "powerful testimony to art as a process of concretizing acts of remembering and resistance" (Tuer, 2007, p. 338).

Braiding knowledges has been a conceptual tool used in the CMA; this powerful visual metaphor embodies the desire both to recognize and elevate multiple ways of knowing and understanding human relationships to the land, and to mountains specifically (see Section 1.2.3). It seems fitting, then, to turn to the work of Megan Musseau as a third example of the kind of work that is being created to interrogate the interrelationships of traditional and contemporary Indigenous knowledges, and forms of knowledge transmission, that rely on an understanding of dynamic reciprocity with the land. Musseau is an L'nu woman, artist, and dancer from Elmastukwek, Ktaqmkuk territory (Bay of Islands, Newfoundland). She nourishes an interdisciplinary arts practice by working with customary art forms and new media, such as basketry, beadwork, land-based performance, video, and installation (Musseau, n.d.). She has exhibited and completed land-based performances across the country, including at the Banff Centre (Musseau, n.d.). Musseau's endurance performance, "when they poison the bogs we will still braid sweetgrass," was created on Sacred Buffalo Guardian Mountain (Banff, AB) in 2017. In this work, the artist braids neon flagging tape in the landscape, a reference both to logging and other types of resource extraction, and the traditions of land-based learning and use of natural materials in L'nu traditional practices.

A similar work, Me'ki'tetmek na Maqmikewminen, was created in collaboration with drummer Jennie Duval in Duntara, Newfoundland, for the 2019 Bonavista Bienniale; as the curator's discussion of the work notes,

> Each component of the work draws on a community of nurturing Indigenous women, emphasising collective agency and culminating in an offering that reciprocates the generosity of the land. The embodied knowledge of Musseau's action, her rigorous commitment to the process of communal shared learning, and the transmission of knowledge through art and language, is in generous relationship to Ktaqmkuk—acting in defiance of settler-colonial systems, and in the process, actively decolonizing (Hills, 2019).

These are but a few examples of the historical and contemporary ways in which mountain locales have fostered creativity. It would be worthwhile to investigate the connections between mountains and the gifts of art and creativity in a fully developed, systematic and inclusive way. It is possible that such a study could foster nuanced conversations about the capacity for creative work to encourage better conversations between Indigenous and non-Indigenous individuals and communities regarding the sharing of the many gifts which mountain environments provide. Likewise, such work may have the potential to support a deeper, more reciprocal and respectful approach to these environments among a broad population.

4.3.2 *Mountains as sites of art institutions and programs*

Mountain environments have long served settler populations as places of retreat and creative rejuvenation, often associated with urban tourists seeking an "untainted" environment (Jessup, 2002, pp. 146–147; Fig. 4.2). Banff National Park has been associated with the creation of a national identity and the idea of "Canadianness" especially in the aftermath of the First World War (Anderson, 2007, pp. 245–246), and so became a strategic choice for the location of a school of the arts (Reichwein, 2005, pp. 50–52; 55; Reichwein & Wall, 2017, pp. 203–205). The original Banff Centre for Continuing Education was founded in 1933 as a summer school through the University of Alberta. In time the school became autonomous, and the programs were expanded to include painting and other fine arts disciplines; Donald Cameron, the director from 1936–1966, was instrumental in the crafting of the image of the school and its environment, in concert with marketing efforts by the National Film Board and Banff National Park (Reichwein, 2005, pp. 57–58).

The representation of the Banff School and the national park surrounding it can be seen as evolving over time to suit the needs of governments in relation to the purpose or utility of mountain spaces. It served to define a national identity focussed on the prosperity and mobility that positioned creative leisure time as a sign of national success but which also commodified the flora, fauna, and other natural features, reinforcing stereotypes of 'wilderness' and 'nature' as both restorative and inspiring (Cronin, 2006, pp. 78–81; Reichwein & Wall, 2017, pp. 206–207; Saari, 2015,

Figure 4.2: Holidays in Canada Poster by Canadian Pacific, 1925, by Leonard Richmond. Marc Choko collection. Library and Archives Canada, e000009456.

pp. 405–406). Today, the internationally recognized Banff Centre for Arts and Creativity offers themed and self-directed residencies in contemporary fine art practices, curatorial research and writing, music, and performance. Additionally, the school's mandate has expanded to include executive leadership programming, retreats, academic conferences, performing arts, and the world-renowned Banff Mountain Book and Film Festival. Its administrative and curatorial branch includes Indigenous-specific arts residencies, programming and leadership training.[2]

Banff Centre's vision statement includes the aim:

> To experience the power of the mountains, particularly our home on Sacred Buffalo Guardian Mountain, supported by talented

employees and thought leaders, to envision and to create, and be in relationship with our environment and each other.

This statement and associated programs are indicative of an evolution in thinking with respect to the Centre's relationship with overlapping communities and its environment. The expanded Indigenous leadership and programming are also positive steps toward working in a more expanded and reciprocal way. This shift may foster deeper relationships and respectful communication between settler and Indigenous communities more broadly over time.

Other artist residency opportunities have become available in mountain environments in western Canada and elsewhere. The participation of Parks Canada in most of these residencies provides an overarching connection between this varied group of residencies; this ongoing association of mountain parks with creative and recreational opportunities has informed Parks Canada's marketing and policies for decades. Examples of these residencies include the Gushul Residency Program in Blairmore, Alberta which operates out of the Gushul Studio and Cottage, owned by the University of Lethbridge and the Caribou Artists' Cabin Program within Mount Revelstoke National Park. Gros Morne Summer Music has also offered music and performance programming in the setting of Gros Morne National Park since 2003.[3]

4.4 Gifts of Teaching and Pedagogy

Mountain landscapes elicit storytelling practices that are central means of both spiritual and socio-cultural learning amongst Indigenous Peoples who are connected to mountain regions (Cruikshank, 2005; Isaac, 2016; Solomon, 2022), and increasingly recognized as salient pedagogical contexts in Western education (Landrum et al., 2019). Mountains have inspired teachings around spiritual and metaphysical beings and realms. As one example, metaphysical entities such as "Bigfoot" of the Canadian Rockies, figure in current discourse around education as illustrated by a teaching-oriented session, "Teaching with Bigfoot" scheduled for the 2023 American Association

2 https://www.youtube.com/watch?v=sL9yKVeYZ BQ&t=156s

3 https://www.gmsm.ca/about-gmsm

of Geographers annual meeting, and related Special Issue of The Geography Teacher (Education Specialty Group, AAG 2022). Indigenous Peoples, of course, also have long traditions of honouring metaphysical and spiritual mountain beings.

This section of the CMA highlights the gifts of mountains to current pedagogy at Canadian teaching institutions, as well as with respect to Indigenous teachings. Beginning with Indigenous approaches to mountain teachings, the section then explores the traditions of scientific and arts-based pedagogies in institutional settings.

Indigenous ways of teaching and learning in mountains have sustained First Nations, Métis, and Inuit peoples for millennia, guiding their traditions, land stewardship and cultures (Solomon, 2022). We may draw insights specifically about education from some examples and approaches in which Indigenous knowledges are shared and embedded in learning and practices of First Nations, Métis, and Inuit Peoples of mountain regions in the land now known as Canada. These resources reflect approaches to learning and pedagogy that flow from a connection to mountains, some of which we highlight below. (For a longer discussion of these and other approaches, see Chapter 3 and Sec. 1.2)

The physicality of mountains provides other kinds of learning opportunities related to ecosystem health. Mountains might be viewed as natural laboratories that can demonstrate the effects of orogeny on landforms and of elevation on water, ice (Church, 2010; Ives & Barry, 1974; Owens & Slaymaker, 2004), and biota (Turner et al., 2003). The effects of global changes such as climate warming are often highly visible in mountains, from glacier retreat to species range shifts (Parrott et al., 2022; Tito et al., 2020). Mountains can thus serve as early warning systems and as foci for understanding environmental changes.

Mountains instruct observers and visitors in the physicality of the environments (Fig. 4.3). Ecosystem patterns, for example, are influenced by elevation and its interplay with ruggedness and local relief, slope aspect, and moisture-bearing winds. In British Columbia, better illumination on south-facing aspects leads to drought tolerant plant communities more than on north-facing aspects, and this pattern of community composition changes with distance from the coast as snow depth and snowpacks decrease. Learners can engage with diverse and contrasting geographies, given integral connections between mountains and lowlands peoples and environments (see Sec.

Figure 4.3. One of two glaciology huts constructed in the 1970s to house researchers in Sentinel Bay, Garibaldi Provincial Park. Photo courtesy of Nina Hewitt, 2022.

2.6). In the Pacific Maritime region, for example, are the homelands of many distinctive First Nations groups (e.g., Doyle-Yamaguchi & Smith, 2022; Kew, 2010; Reimer, 2003) who speak a notable diversity of languages (Gessner et al., 2018), each of which holds distinct teachings grounded in relationships with mountain landscapes (see Chapter 1, Fig. 1.3). Both the mountains themselves and the people who know them, offer opportunities and challenges that enrich learning experiences about complex biophysical and socio-ecological environments.

4.4.1 Storytelling and narrative

Oral traditions have been key to knowledge production and sharing in many Indigenous cultures in what has come to be known as Canada since time immemorial. These oral knowledge traditions include diverse kinds of story and narrative (Cruikshank, 2005), many of which include observations of the natural world, teachings embedded in local knowledge and which are meant to be passed on to future generations (Isaac, 2016). As Learning Circle participant Gùdia Mary Jane Johnson (Lhù àán Ku Dań) described, songs and stories are set in places and mountains are central to many of those storied places (LC 4.5). 'Welila'ogwa Irene Isaac, a Kwakwaka'wakw (Kwakiutl) writer and educator, notes how "Indigenous stories," in her community "influence young people to become knowledgeable and responsible citizens." (Isaac, 2016).

Through story, mountains have fostered rich narratives that have sustained Indigenous Peoples and cultures over generations. Among the Kwakwaka'wakw, stories specified seasonal timings for harvesting materials from montane populations of Western redcedar, related to tree elevation on the mountain (Kwakwaka'wakw educator, Aitken, Emily [Gwixsisalas], 2016). In *Do*

Gùdia Mary Jane Johnson, Lhu'àán Mân Ku Dań, 2022, LC 4.5

Glaciers listen? Local knowledge, Colonial Encounters and Social Imagination, anthropologist Julie Cruikshank writes about the role of narrative among the Tlingit peoples of the Mount Saint Elias ranges, Alaska and northern British Columbia, who shared stories, grounded in the community, to educate citizens about appropriate behaviour around mountain glaciers (Cruikshank, 2005). Cooking grease, for instance, such as frying bacon or traditional, fatty foods like moose, was discouraged near glaciers because it was believed to trigger surges and endanger community safety. Cruikshank suggests possible interpretations for these beliefs, but notes that it is the method of sharing around storytelling, and what the stories say about local meaning and the construction of knowledge, that matters (and see Simpson, 2014). Importantly, stories often convey local protocols that recognize reciprocity between nature and culture. This contrasts with the approach taken by European visitors to the region, beginning in the 18th century, who followed "Enlightenment" values popular in their society. They strove to separate nature from culture and treated glaciers as inanimate objects to be measured and characterised with recently developed instrumentation (Cruikshank, 2005, p. 10). Enlightenment values prevailed and persisted in schools established within the Canadian settler state and defined modes of scientific inquiry, discrediting local knowledge systems, until recently.

In addition to stories, Indigenous knowledges are also represented in pictographs and petroglyphs (rock art) throughout mountainous areas in Canada, including numerous sites in British Columbia in the Pacific Maritime region, and throughout the Canadian Arctic (Vastokas, 2012), that signify a broad tradition of recorded knowledge on less well-preserved materials like wood, fibre, hide and bone. Among the mountains and lowlands along the Fraser River delta and BC Gulf Islands (Pacific Maritime), the Marpole culture produced a "plentiful variety of stone and bone carvings in the shape of ceremonial bowls, effigies and utensils that are distinct forerunners of the style and iconography of historic west coast native art" from ca. 500 BCE to 500 CE (*Norval Morrisseau—Rock Art*, 2006). Pictographs and Petroglyphs are known to have provided material sites and imaginaries for Indigenous teaching and learning. For example, rock writings in the Stein

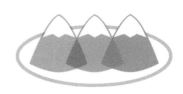

Hayden Melting Tallow, Siksika Nation, Blackfoot Confederacy, 2022, LC 4.6

Leon Andrew, Nę K'ə Dene Ts'ı̨lı, 2022, LC 4.7

Pnnal Bernard Jerome, Micmacs of Gesgapegiag, 2022, LC 4.8

River Valley reflect the animation of the natural world. They are associated with places of power and have been likened to writings (York et al., 1993). Artistics traditions within storytelling are recognized today through a writing competition for Indigenous youth (aged 14–29) that includes a program for those who "prefer to work through painting, drawing and photography" (Indigenous Arts and Stories, Historica Canada, 2023).[4]

4.4.2 *Sacredness*

Attitudes of respect and sacredness are common, and metaphysical beings appear in teachings with specific reference to mountain spaces. For example, the glacier-fed Ts'il?os (Chilko) Lake (referred to above) is considered a living ancestor by the traditional land holders, the Tsilhqot'in Nation (Mack, 2022). Elders who participated in the Learning Circle explained that sacred teachings of mountains are often held in songs. Elder Gùdia Mary Jane Johnson, Lhù ààn Ku Dań, shared songs which identify mountain places of her grandfather's land and Traditional Territory, including streams and valleys and the stories that took place there (LC 4.5). In the Blackfoot way, as Hayden Melting Tallow, Siksika, Blackfoot Confederacy, explained, sacred songs link mountain place names and Medicines, such as Paahtómahksikimi (Waterton Lakes), where the sacred beaver bundles originated, and Nínaiistáko, Chief Mountain (Fig. 4.4). These songs of mountain places, the "highlights of our territory," he explains, tell the People where they are from (LC 4.6). Leon Andrew, an Elder of the Nę K'ə Dene Tsį̨li Nation, shared that the Mountain Dene People also hold the mountains as sacred in their songs, from songs to share joy in nature and being in the mountains to documenting oral history (LC 4.7).

The Ktunaxa Nation believe that a grizzly bear spirit goes to dance during the winter months along the Jumbo Pass and Horseshoe Glacier, BC, within their traditional lands in the East Kootenays. The spiritual and cultural significance of such legacies has been trivialised in settler-colonial discourses, as may be illustrated by events surrounding settler-colonial plans for a slated development, the "Jumbo Glacier ski resort" (Low & de Kleer, 2022) in which the spirit bear's importance was questioned and downplayed, prompting this reaction from one Ktunaxa citizen: "We are the ones that have to prove our rights to the land. It's ridiculous, right? If we say that a space ... or place is sacred within the boundaries of our territory, then just accept that. Four hundred generations of existence here and you are going to question me about the sacredness of a place?" (in conversation with the production team of the documentary film *Jumbo Wild*, Bullfrog Films (2015), at 32:40 mins).

4.4.3 *Land-based learning and healing*

Just as practices of learning are grounded on and from the land itself (Simpson, 2014), mountains themselves, and the many animal, plant, and supernatural beings therein, hold essential teachings which emerge

---

4 http://www.our-story.ca/. Also https://twitter.com/IndigArtStories

Figure 4.4: View over Paahtómahksikimi (Waterton Lake), known to the Siksikaitsitapi (Blackfoot Nations) as a sacred site in the mountains, where the People were originally gifted the beaver bundle, an important source of Blackfoot knowledge and identity. The townsite of Waterton Park is now situated on the shore of the lake, serving as the headquarters for Waterton Lakes National Park (established in 1895), which receives around 500,000 visitors per year. Photo courtesy of Madison Stevens, 2022.

through different kinds of relationships and experience. During the CMA Learning Circle, Elder Pnnal Bernard of the Micmacs of Gesgapegiag described some of the teachings provided by mountain spirits, including the Little People, guardians of the Micmac from the high peaks, and spirits who dwell in the foothills. These leaders offer moral lessons about collaboration, good intentions, and well-being (LC 4.8).

Reconnecting with the Land and its teachings is essential to heal the community of decades of colonial dispossession. Tsilhqot'in Nation member Trevor Mack (2022) discusses the importance of mountain spaces in the healing and remembering among his community, particularly their youth. Mack presents a video of community Elder, Gilbert Solomon, filmed on location at Ts'il?os (Chilko) lake, in which Solomon says "You see the beautiful, powerful mountains here? ... Mountain itself is healing you.... Mountain is very important—they keep giving us water... So we come down here to this island to help people—to help wake you up...." (Solomon, 2022). Mack then recounts a "trip to Sacred Mountain" and Ts'il?os lake to educate youth through journey. He says "... along that trip, song was created, and every single day we got to learn the language ... every new day." They brought with them "knowledge carriers who knew the stories of Ts'il?os... and of the Land," as well as plant "medicine carriers," all of whom helped to contextualise the experience within the community's traditions. Through this experience, they were able to "honour supernatural beings, and in that process, heal our communities." (Mack, 2022)

Cultures of stewarding the land and its inhabitants are central to many North American Indigenous mountain cultures, such as those around the Nass River of the mountainous region of Northern British Columbia, on the border between the Montane Cordillera and Boreal Cordillera regions (Reid et al., 2021), and are embedded into their teachings, through storytelling. Among the Kwakwaka'wakw Peoples of the coastal areas and neighbouring mountains of northeastern Vancouver Island and mainland British Columbia, "It was story that educated us about conservation and it was conservation that guided the story. There was little impact on the natural environment because the stories passed down from generation to generation teach us to 'take only what you need.' For the lessons, the students took care not to collect too many plants and displayed gratitude to the plants and animals for providing them with food" (Isaac, 2016, unpaginated). Significantly, where stewardship and care for the mountains and the plant medicines they provide are concerned, Keara Lightning, Nehiyaw, Samson Cree First Nation, reminds us that relationships with the mountains and those plants matter (LC 4.9).

Keara Long Lightning, Nehiyaw, Samson Cree First Nation, 2022, LC 4.9

These lessons and attitudes speak to the rich cultural legacies of teaching and learning produced by Indigenous Peoples through their intimate connections with mountain places. Such lessons and attitudes are distinct from Western ways of knowing in an educational context (Ahenakew, 2016; Battiste & Youngblood Henderson, 2009) and are grounded in experiences on the land (Simpson, 2014). It is possible, however, that these approaches could be meaningfully brought into conversation with Western, settler-colonial education systems to inform more holistic, place-based and respect-centred approaches to teaching and inform understandings of decolonial perspectives and land stewardship.

4.4.4 Challenges to Indigenous-led teaching and learning in Canada

Indigenous Peoples' abilities to pass on ways of knowing within their own communities, let alone be enabled to shape settler-colonial educational systems, have been severely disrupted by the continuing processes of colonisation and dispossession, from the intergenerational impacts of residential schools, to the ongoing systemic racism, exclusion, and inequity in the educational system (Graham, 2010; Isaac, 2016; United Nations Department of Economic and Social Affairs, Indigenous Peoples, 2017). In Canadian settler-colonial schools, Indigenous teachings have been either absent from or seriously misrepresented (Battiste, 2000, 2002; Snively & Williams, 2016), a pattern of exclusion and erasure (Ahenakew, 2016) that has left impoverished common understandings of mountain peoples and environments. Moreover, the situation in Canada echoes experiences of mountain peoples around the world, from the Andes, to the Himalayas, to the Caucasus, and beyond, who have been excluded and marginalised, often in exchange for lowland security; and who face growing challenges associated with patterns of global change (Grover et al., 2015; IRIN, 2012; Price, 2013). Thus, while mountains have wonderful gifts to offer knowledge and education, this must be considered in light of ongoing legacies of dispossession.

In Canadian educational settings, the situation is changing slowly in response to the UN Declaration on the Rights of Indigenous Peoples (UN General Assembly 2007, Articles 14.1 and

15.1),[5] the recommendations from the Permanent Forum on Indigenous Issues, Education (UNPFII no date), and Canada's Truth and Reconciliation Commission (TRC) (2015) Calls to Action. Jurisdictions are actively working to align curriculum and learning materials with these calls, for example, in primary and secondary schools, with Indigenous Education Resources provided by the BC Government, e.g., a series of learning modules entitled Continuing Our Learning Journey (Government of British Columbia, n.d.); and for higher education institutions, with the development of Indigenous strategic plans, teaching funds and resources,[6] and renewed investments in hiring, units, and programs dedicated to advancing Indigenous studies.[7]

Nevertheless, Indigenous teaching and learning in mountain education faces numerous ongoing challenges at non-Indigenous institutions. First, methods of Indigenous teachings and local knowledge sharing are difficult to reconcile with classroom-based Western education systems, being lived, rather than written, as in Western systems (Simpson, 2014; Wong et al., 2020).

Second, incorporation of teachings into curriculum risks misappropriation of knowledge and culture unless it is Indigenous-led; that is, driven by Indigenous Peoples. But this in turn creates a risk of overburdening Indigenous teachers and learners who are expected to do most of this work (Daigle, 2019). Daigle offers some solutions to these problems, including investing in permanent, paid positions for Elders and other Indigenous Knowledge Holders, and asking non-Indigenous educators to do the work of learning about colonial systems to address its legacies in the classroom. However, institutions will no doubt continue to struggle with these challenges, even with such investments.

Finally, and perhaps most importantly, simply embedding decolonial perspectives into classrooms, creating spaces for Indigenous students and faculty, and acknowledging past harms alone will fail to achieve meaningful change. Gaudry and Lorenz note that current reconciliatory practice at post-secondary institutions often revolve around minimally impactful "Indigenous inclusion," whereas the goal should be a move requiring the academy "to fundamentally reorient knowledge production based on balanced power relations between Indigenous peoples and Canadians...." (Gaudry & Lorenz, 2018, p. 226). This is necessary to move Canadian higher education beyond a "Spectacle of Reconciliation" and toward reckoning with colonialism as ongoing process enabled by institutional "reconciliatory rhetoric" that treats it as an historical relic (Coulthard, 2014; Daigle, 2019). Education must move beyond assimilation and integration of Indigenous knowledges within settler-colonial systems (Ahenakew, 2016; Battiste & Henderson, 2009), and toward Indigenous educational self-determination (Coulthard, 2014; Nadasdy, 1999).

4.5 Gifts of Foods and Medicines

The mountain regions of Canada support a rich diversity of peoples, plants, animals, waters, and practices woven together within food and medicinal systems. For Indigenous Peoples in Canada, mountains have long traditions as harvesting sites. Trips into the mountains or time at mountain camps often involve the harvesting and managing of multiple foods and medicines. For example, Goota Desmarais, Inuit, Kinnegat, Nunavut offers an introduction to the importance of mountains as providers of gifts of food and medicine to her People (LC 4.10). Despite ecological shifts, socio-political barriers to access, and changing diets, foods and medicines from mountains remain central to nourishing people (Kuhnlein et al., 2006). Goota also explained her community's ongoing tradition of gathering to

---

5 UNDRIP Article 14.1 states: "Indigenous peoples have the right to establish and control their educational systems and institutions providing education in their own languages, in a manner appropriate to their cultural methods of teaching and learning." Article 15.1 states: "Indigenous peoples have the right to the dignity and diversity of their cultures, traditions, histories and aspirations which shall be appropriately reflected in education." And see: https://www.un.org/development/desa/indigenouspeoples/mandated-areas1/education.html

6 See, e.g., University of British Columbia, Centre for Teaching and Learning, Indigenous Initiatives https://indigenousinitiatives.ctlt.ubc.ca/

7 See, e.g., University of Victoria: Indigenous Studies Program https://www.uvic.ca/humanities/indigenous/index.php; at UBC: First Nations and Indigenous Studies Department https://fnis.arts.ubc.ca/ and Institute for Critical Indigenous Studies https://cis.arts.ubc.ca/people/

Goota Desmarais, Inuit, Kinngat, Nunavut, 2022, LC 4.10 and LC 4.11

Pnnal Bernard Jerome, Micmacs of Gesgapegiag, 2022, LC 4.12

share a picnic at the base of the ᑮᖕᒥᖅ, qaqqaq (mountain), while they wait to harvest ducks and geese as they fly overhead. She reflected on the joy of these gatherings, illustrating that these kinds of harvesting experiences in the mountains offer gifts beyond the physical sustenance provided by the harvest, providing space to share knowledge and connect as families and communities (LC 4.11).

4.5.1 *Plants, Fungi, and Medicinal Species*

Numerous plant species in mountain regions provide gifts of food and medicine to many people, including First Nations, Métis, and Inuit Peoples (Fig. 4.5). Plant-based foods in general, though often overlooked in accounts of peoples who hunt and fish extensively (Oberndorfer et al., 2017), provide crucial sources of energy from carbohydrates along with essential vitamins, minerals, and dietary fibre (Turner et al., 2000; Tushingham et al., 2021). Plants can also provide a more consistently accessible source of food during times of fish and game scarcity (Turner et al., 2000). In regions like the Eastern Subarctic, where mountain plants might not directly contribute as much to human diets, they can still be central to practices of fishing and hunting (Oberndorfer et al., 2017). For peoples of the Montane Cordillera, the edible bulbs of yellow avalanche lilies (*Erythronium grandiflorum*) and camas are harvested in large quantities primarily from montane regions (Cross, 1996; Turner et al., 2000). Berries and fruits are also abundant plant-based foods found across mountain regions. For the Gitksan and Wet'suwet'en peoples of the Pacific Maritime region, black huckleberries are the central plant resource of their seasonal round, being harvested in large quantities for eating, trading, and sharing during feasts (Trusler & Johnson, 2008).

In the Atlantic Maritime and Boreal Shield regions, bakeapples (*Rubus chamaemorus*), also known cloudberries remain central to social customs and economic exchange among the community of Charlottetown, Labrador (Karst & Turner, 2011), recently renamed NunatuKavummiut. While some plant-based foods occur at particular sites and elevations of mountains (Karst & Turner, 2011), others can be found at multiple points along the slopes, providing opportunities to extend harvesting seasons by travelling upward through space (Turner, 2014). Sharing his own experiences of growing up in the Micmac territory of Gesgapegiag, Elder Pnnal Bernard Jerome described the way steep mountain slopes offer diverse gifts of food and medicine in close proximity, from sugar maple (*Acer saccharum*) to medicinal plants. These gifts, traditionally known and stewarded by women, are reciprocated with offerings of tobacco and ceremonies (LC 4.12). Gitksan and Wet'suwet'en maintained black huckleberry (*Gaylussacia baccata*) patches at various elevations and locations, possibly as a buffer against conditions, such as drought or late frosts, that might differ across elevations (Trusler & Johnson, 2008). In these ways, harvesting and cultivating plant foods along the slopes of mountains can provide greater flexibility in the seasonal round and resilience to shocks.

Maintaining the abundance and quality of these plant-based foods requires concerted effort and specific knowledge. Mary Thomas,

Figure 4.5: Huckleberries (*Vaccinium spp.*) growing along Munro Lake in Pinecone Burke Provincial Park, ancestral lands of Coast Salish-speaking peoples. Photo courtesy of Erika Gavenus, 2020.

Secwépemc, shares that the lower portion of lily bulbs were removed and replanted, and regular tilling, weeding, and repropagating likely contributed to the productivity of the lilies (Turner et al., 2000). Interruptions to regular root harvesting, along with the compaction of soil caused by grazing cattle, have left previously productive areas devoid of harvestable roots (Turner et al., 2000). Controlled burns were used to promote the growth of multiple root vegetables and to keep shrubs from inundating meadows (Turner et al., 2000). Gitksan and Wet'suwet'en also used periodic burning of the landscape to maintain the presence and productivity of black huckleberries (Trusler & Johnson, 2008). The precise timing of the burning varied among groups, and Trusler and Johnson suggest the timing was likely specific to sites as well (2008). With the restrictions on berry patch burning imposed by the BC forest service, many of the higher elevation black huckleberry patches of the Gitksan and Wet'suwet'en have been overtaken by more fire sensitive shrubs (Trusler & Johnson, 2008). Among the Métis of southeast Labrador pickers know not to pull the bakeapple stalks out from the ground and some follow the practice of picking all berries that are ripe—not "picking through" for the largest, there are concerns that interruptions to being on the land may cause loss of collective knowledge and social protocols among younger generations (Karst & Turner, 2011).

The nutritional value of medicinal plants, fungi, and berries has been assessed in some regions through case study research as in northern Canada and British Columbia; in addition to providing necessary daily nutrients, they are protective against many kinds of chronic illnesses including Type II diabetes (Kuhnlein, 1989;

Keara Long Lightning, Nehiyaw, Samson Cree First Nation, 2022, LC 4.13

Wanda Pascal, Teetl'it Gwich'in, 2022, LC 4.14

Kuhnlein et al., 2004; Kuhnlein & Chan, 2000). Less is known about their value and use in other mountain regions.

Indigenous oral histories, practices of harvesting (gathering) and uses of plants as medicine has been well documented, particularly in British Columbia (Peacock & Turner, 2000; Turner, 1984, 1988, 2020). In northern Canada, in the Richardson Mountains of the Boreal Cordillera, for example, there is also a growing number of examples of ethnobotanical knowledge of Gwich'in and Sahtú communities. Ethnobotanical studies, by the Gwich'in Social and Cultural Institute and related research celebrates the complexity of knowledge about plants of the *dthaa* (Tetli't Gwich'in name for the Richardson Mountains) (Andre & Fehr, 2001; Parlee & Berkes, 2006).

Uprety and colleagues found that medicinal plants are found throughout boreal forests in Canada (Uprety et al., 2012). While the most prolific and widespread plants were listed most frequently as having medicinal properties, other plants used as medicine are highly specific to locations and elevations (Uprety et al., 2012), as explained by Elder Pnnal Bernard Jerome, Micmacs of Gesgapegiag (LC 4.12). In many cases, the locations, relationships, and harvesting practices are imperative to the medicinal qualities and guarded from public sharing (Uprety et al., 2012). Cuerrier et al. (2019) found through their work with Inuit living in Kangiqsualujjuaq, Nunavik, and Nain, Nunatsiavut, within the Eastern Subarctic mountain region, that less than half of the identified medicinal plants are used in both communities, and that there is often low specificity in medicinal plant uses—specific plants are used for multiple purposes, and multiple plants are used for a single ailment.

While discussions of foods and medicines can be highly focused on physical health (e.g., the precise micronutrients and chemicals contributing to healing and nourishment; Fig. 4.6), foods and medicines gifted by mountains support people in other ways (Turner, 2014). Appreciating how mountains nourish and heal beyond the physical gifts of food and medicines is an ongoing space for learning. Keara Lightning, Nehiyaw, Samson Cree First Nation, describes relationships with mountains, and others, themselves as healing (LC 4.13); and Wanda Pascal, Teetl'it Gwich'in, shares that the activity of picking berries and being on the land relieved pain and healed an injury (LC 4.14). Oberndorfer et al. (2017) explain: "The value and utility of plants is at the systems level, in how plants function as one of many strands that connect people to fish, birds, soils, berries, and other people, as well as to aesthetics, memory, emotion, and cultural values." Similarly, Norton et al. (2021) learn through their work within the self-governing Inuit region of Nunatsiavut that in relationship with people, plants fill multiple roles. They are used as indicators of seasonal change, offer markers of memories and histories, reflect customary laws, support being on the land and living off the land, and provide a means for practising and renewing shared values.

The value and practices of harvesting plants, fungi, and berries to Indigenous Peoples have been little documented in academic research (see, however, Armstrong et al., 2018, 2022); this gap is in part attributable to gender biases in anthropology and other disciplines that value male knowledge practices and have been chronically preoccupied with larger species (Díaz-Reviriego et al., 2016; Kuhnlein, 2017; Parlee & Berkes, 2006; Parlee et al., 2018). It is a significant concern in many regions that Indigenous Knowledge related to the use of medicinal plants has been eroded in Canada due to the impacts of colonisation. Agriculture, forestry, mining, urbanisation and tourism have significantly impacted the capacity for Indigenous women to continue to harvest berries and plants to contribute to their communities' health and livelihood.

Table 4.1: Teetl'it Gwich'in Names for Berries valued in the Gwich'in Region (Richardson Mountains and Mackenzie Delta). Adapted from Andre & Fehr (2001); nB. L. Parlee (2006).

Gwich'in	Common English	Latin
Natl'at	Cranberry	Vaccinium vitis-idaea
Jak na	Bog blueberry	Vaccinium uliginosum
Nakal	Cloudberry	Rubus chamaemorus
Nichih	Rosehips	Rosa acicularis
Ts'iivii ch'ok	Juniper berries	Juniperus communis
Deetree jak	Black currant	Ribes hudsoniaum
Nee'uu	Red currant	Ribes triste
Shis jak	Red bearberry	Arctostaphylos rubra
Dineech'uh	Crowberry	Empetrum nigrum

Figure 4.6: Rosehips (*Rosa spp.*), a common addition to medicinal teas, ripening upon the Chilcotin Plateau, Tŝilhqot'in Nen and Dakelh Territory. Photo courtesy of Erika Gavenus, 2021.

Much of the land in British Columbia, including Pacific Maritime and Montane Cordillera mountain regions, does not fall under the ownership, control or management of First Nations but is considered Crown land; approximately 94% of the province's land is designated as provincial Crown land, 1% is "federal Crown land," and the remaining 5% is private land (Hamilton, 2012, p. 6; Kamieniecki, 2000). First Nations in British Columbia and in many parts of Canada are afforded rights to harvest plants, fungi and berries on public or Crown land for their personal use but have limited opportunity to develop them for commercial use. "Explicit rights to harvest, manage, and charge fees for NTFPs on public land have only been granted by the provincial government to those who hold a Community Forest Agreement or First Nations Woodland Licence. Private forest landowners have rights to all forest resources on their lands and some large forest companies manage access to NTFPs on these lands" (Hamilton, 2012, p. 5).

The resurgence and recovery of knowledge is happening in numerous areas as a result of research partnerships, entrepreneurship, forest management protections (e.g., Indigenous protected areas and parks) as well as various kinds of biodiversity conservation initiatives in mountain regions. Indigenous management practices based on decades of knowledge and practices are particularly valuable in this resurgence (Berkes & Turner, 2006; Gavin et al., 2018). Cultural burning, or the use of fire to shape mountain landscapes, has been used by many Indigenous groups in mountains to support the production of berries and other plants (Hoffman et al., 2022; Ignace et al., 2017). This practice has been widespread in many parts of British Columbia including mountain regions. The vegetation communities of the Skeena and Bulldey Valleys around Hazelton for example, have been shaped by cultural burning. It is estimated that the Gitskan and Wet'suwet'en peoples have been using cultural burning for at least 1000 years (pre-European contact) to influence productivity of key plants. The principal berry species managed by burning were black huckleberry (*Vaccinium membranaceum Dougl.*) and low-bush blueberry (*V. caespitosum Michz.*). Soapberries (*Shepherdia canadensis (L.) Nutt.*) may also have been managed by burning at least in some

locations. The other main function of burning was to clear areas around village sites (Gottesfeld, 1994).

This is true in other regions further west towards the coast. As described by the late Lil'wat elder Baptiste Ritchie from the Stl'atl'imx region of British Columbia: "They [the Stl'atl'imx, Lil'wat or Lilloeet] burned them [the hills] so that they would get good crops there. They told others who went there, 'Do the same at your place, do the same at your place.' Their hills were just like a garden" (Peacock & Turner, 2000, p. 133).

There is potential for many Indigenous and other communities to develop local economies from the harvesting, processing, and marketing of plants for food and medicines. In their assessment of factors relating to successful commercial development of chanterelle harvesting on northern Vancouver Island within the Pacific Maritime region, Ehlers and Hobby (2010) note potential trade-offs between further developing mushroom harvesting and the interests of the timber industry—namely the age at which trees are harvested Most chanterelle harvesting takes place on land that has been designated as Crown Land, which, as discussed above, has implications for who has the authority to regulate how the harvesting happens, and potentially expands.

Informed by examples internationally, there is widespread concern in Canada about intellectual property rights associated with medicinal plants and the potential impact that commercialization of the resources could have on the sustainability of various species and the practices and uses of local people (Tsing, 2015). Elder Gùdia Mary Jane Johnson, Lhu'ààn Mân Ku Dań, shared concerns about the commodification of these traditional foods and medicines. She described the escalating fervour to harvest lucrative morel mushrooms, which each year brings people from all over the world to recently burned sites in the mountains of her territory to search for morels. She explained that members of her community are careful about guarding their knowledge of mushroom foraging places, sharing the harvest but avoiding sharing harvest locations with outsiders in particular. "There's economic value," she explained, "but there are other values that are equal or of more value than the economic values that are usually tagged on to anything on the land"

(LC 4.15). Seasonal closures of commercial harvesting of huckleberry in parts of the Kootenay, within the Montane Cordillera, began in 2017 due to concerns raised by the Ktunaxa Nation, and others, that the harvest was harming bears (Government of British Columbia, 2022). One anonymous reviewer offered this as an example of how precarious the gifts of the mountains can be "if not managed with sustainability and holistic benefits in mind."

In describing foods as gifts from the landscape, Enrique Salmón notes the importance of how such gifts are received and practices of reciprocity (Salmón, 2012). Such reciprocity can take the form of offerings, which are often foods and medicines themselves (Andrews et al., 2012; Uprety et al., 2012). Controlled burning and returning bones can maintain the cycling of nutrients, just as salmon returning to their spawning grounds bring influxes of marine-based nutrients to mountain forests (Haskell, 2018; Hocking & Reynolds, 2011; Louis, 2021; Wagner & Reynolds, 2019). Gabrielle Weasel Head, Kainaiwa Nation, Blackfoot Confederacy, shared that guardianship of mountains and the responsible use of gifts are also required (LC 4.16). In these ways, along with many others, receiving gifts from the mountains comes with responsibilities to the mountains.

4.5.2 *Wildlife*

Wild species, including wild animals, are among those gifts that contribute significantly to the well-being of communities in Canada (Nadasdy, 2007). While some animals use high mountain areas as their permanent homes, others are visitors to mountains, moving into highland areas along their migrations or during specific seasons. Mountains provide these animals with respite from heat, plants for foraging, and safety from predators. They are a source of food security and economic livelihood to many peoples. For example, within the Taiga Cordillera the mountain woodland caribou move to higher elevations of the Selwyn Mountains in summer for calving season (Andrews et al., 2012). Caribou meat is a staple food and trade item for the Shuta Got'ine, or Mountain Dene, and hunters take advantage of mountain ice patches as reliable places to find caribou seeking refuge from heat and insects (Andrews et al., 2012). Smaller game, such as ground squirrels and grouse, are also harvested during the same trips and used as food (Andrews et al., 2012). Goota Desmarais, Inuit, Kinnegat, Nunavut, shared that waterfowl and eggs are also harvested from mountain areas (LC 4.17).

Within the Montane Cordillera mountain region, the Salish had camps from which bighorn sheep were hunted, and along the Rocky Mountain Front the Blackfoot hunted bighorn sheep in the winter (Zedeno et al., 2021). In the southwestern Canadian Rockies region, the Ktunaxa hunted mountain herds of bison, who moved into alpine areas during the summers (Reeves, 1978) (Fig. 4.7). Place names and archaeological records suggest that the physical features of the mountains were often used to facilitate successful hunts—driving caribou up against cliffs or bison into depressions left by ice (Andrews et al., 2012; Reeves, 1978). Among the Iskut First Nation within the Boreal Cordillera region, McIlwraith finds moose hunting to be "the central activity of life" with tasks—camping,

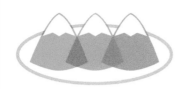

Gùdia Mary Jane Johnson, Lhu'ààn Mân Ku Dań, 2022, LC 4.15

Gabrielle Weasel Head, Kainaiwa Nation, Blackfoot Confederacy, 2022, LC 4.16

Goota Desmarais, Inuit, Kinngat, Nunavut, 2022, LC 4.17

Gùdia Mary Jane Johnson, Lhu'ààn Mân Ku Dań, 2022, LC 4.18

cutting and drying meat, feasting—undertaken with "passion and vigour" (McIlwraith, 2008, p. 125).

While practices and protocols for hunting continue, many of these wildlife populations have declined significantly in the last fifty to a hundred years, for multiple and interrelated reasons including development, deforestation, and additional hunting pressures (Andrews et al., 2012; Oetelaar, 2014). Elder Gùdia Mary Jane Johnson, Lhu'ààn Mân Ku Dań described her Nation's observations of and responses to declines in Dall Sheep populations, explaining the value of Elders in the herd and her Nation's efforts to lobby the Yukon Government to reduce trophy hunting as a contributing factor to population decline (LC 4.18). People can also find it harder to fit hunting trips into schedules that are increasingly determined by seasonal and full-time wage work (McIlwraith, 2008).

Numerous studies have revealed the significant nutritional contribution of wild species when harvested; moose, elk, mountain caribou are among those species important in the Rocky Mountains and foothills regions. In the mountains of northern Canada (e.g., Yukon, Northwest Territories and Nunavut) where access to market food alternatives is very limited, traditional and country food are fundamental to food security (Kuhnlein et al., 2004). Many sources of wild meat are also critical to health; Inuit and First Nations who consume higher levels of wild meat and other traditional foods in their diets report greater levels of well-being and evidence lower levels of chronic illness (e.g., heart disease and Type II diabetes) when compared to those more dependent

Figure 4.7: Plains bison (*Bison bison*), also known as buffalo, have been vital to the cultures and lifeways of Nations living along the Rocky Mountain Front since time immemorial. Photo courtesy of Madison Stevens, 2019.

THE CANADIAN MOUNTAIN ASSESSMENT

THE MAN WHO TURNED INTO A CARIBOU

Indigenous Peoples have well developed knowledge systems that reflect generations of living on the land; this knowledge includes well developed insights about wildlife ecology in mountain regions. This close relationship is deeply embedded in oral histories that detail the kinship between people and animals. One good example is the story from the Tetlit Gwich'in elder about a person becoming a caribou.

Story: The Man Who Turned into a Caribou
There was a man whose medicine was the caribou and he went and hunted the caribou. Suddenly, as he was shooting at the last of the caribou going by, the men in the group saw that there was no man. They ran along after him to see what happened. They found his clothes on the ground and an extra caribou running away. The men were very confused and upset about this, but there was nothing they could do. The next year they went to the same spot, where there was a caribou crossing, and again they saw the caribou. But one caribou did not follow the others. He turned back into the lake and swam towards an island. One man took a canoe and went after him. Now this man who went after the caribou was the father of the man who had disappeared the year before. When the man got to the island, to his amazement he heard the caribou calling to him saying, "Father, father don't shoot me! I'm going to swim to the shore and when I get to the shore, throw a stone at me." The man, who was startled and rather alarmed by this, returned in his canoe to the shore. The caribou swam after him and when the caribou got to the shore, the man threw a stone at it. Lo and behold! The caribou turned back into his son again, and stood there, naked and shivering on the beach (Benson & Department of Cultural Heritage, Gwich'in Tribal Council, 2019, p. 4).

on non-wild meats (Kuhnlein et al., 2004; Willows, 2005). "The Inuit dietary survey conducted by the Centre for Indigenous Peoples, Nutrition and the Environment demonstrated that days with country food provided more protein and micronutrients than days without country food, and that carbohydrate intake, particularly refined carbohydrates, increased on days without country food" (Egeland et al., 2009, p. 12). However, wild meat is not a universal solution, given the cost of the tools, fuel, and other resources required; many women, including single mothers, are particularly excluded from access to wild meat in many regions. In one study, Inuit (up to 45% within age groups) reported that they could not afford to go hunting or fishing (Lambden et al., 2006).

Country foods are expensive to acquire relative to store-bought foods, with gear being a large investment. The high cost of equipment is not only a limitation, but often means that acquiring country foods is not profitable, potentially costing the hunter more money than purchasing equivalent foods at the store. This cost discrepancy is made worse by the fact that store-bought foods receive federal subsidies divided among national taxpayers, while country foods costs fall only on the individual hunter, or immediate family. (Hoover et al., 2016)

Many iconic wild species also feature prominently in Indigenous cultures and spiritual well-being. The Spirit Bear (*Ursus americana*) is among those species of significance to Indigenous Peoples in the mountain regions of British Columbia. "People in Haíl˜zaqv territory live and harvest food resources among grizzly bears, indeed sharing salmon, berries, and other foods with them. The grizzly bear is present in ceremony through masks, songs, dances, issuing reminders as an enforcer for Haíl˜zaqv people to conduct themselves respectfully" (Clark et al., 2021)." Threats on the Spirit Bear associated with Pacific salmon declines, and forest ecosystem loss as well as trophy hunting) have echoing impacts in the Haíl˜zaqv and other communities.

Gwich'in and Sahtu hunters have documented the cycles of Porcupine and Bluenose caribou population change, triggers of caribou stress and poor health, and good management practices for caribou in the Richardson and Mackenzie Mountains (Parlee & Caine, 2018). Similar to forest ecosystem management and the recovery of intact forests, there is growing evidence that the leadership of Indigenous Peoples is key to ensuring the sustainability of wildlife (Schuster et al., 2019). Some key examples include the mountain caribou in British Columbia (Lamb et al., 2022) and grizzly bear in the eastern slopes of the Rocky Mountains.

4.5.3 *Fisheries*

Among the wildlife supported by mountains, fish from alpine lakes to coastal regions benefit from the aquatic habitats, food and nutrients, and spawning grounds provided by mountains (Fig. 4.8). These fish, in turn, support fisheries that are central to livelihoods, identities, and continuance of many communities across Canada (Armstrong & William, 2015; Ommer & Coasts Under Stress Research Project Team, 2007)

Figure 4.8: The Bella Coola River flows through Nuxalk Territory from the coastal mountains to the North Bentinck Arm. Salmon travel the river to return to their spawning grounds, and the river once supported large returns of eulachon. The surrounding mountains, including Nusatsum Mountain in the photo, play a central role in the health of the river and the fish who travel along it. Photo courtesy of Erika Gavenus, 2021.

THE CANADIAN MOUNTAIN ASSESSMENT

Fish of the mountains, including species like cutthroat trout (*Oncorhynchus clarkii*) and char (*Salvelinus spp.*), whitefishes (*Coregoninae spp.*), and burbot (*Lota lota*), often find refugia in cold, clear waters of mountain streams and alpine lakes (Sinnatamby et al., 2020). Some trout, like westslope cutthroat (*Oncorhynchus clarkii lewisi*), Athabascan rainbow (*Onchorhynchus mykiss spp.*), and bull (*Salvelinus confluentus*) also rely on groundwater seeps for overwintering in mountain regions (Sinnatamby et al., 2020). Mountain fish can be an important part of harvesting trips. Megan Dicker, an Inuit woman from Nunatsiavut, describes the importance of returning to the Torngat Mountains for hunting and fishing for Inuit who have grown up in southern communities following relocation:

> There is still such a strong connection there for people of my generation who go there [Torngat Mountains]. People still go there every year to hunt and to fish and to just go. Just to be. Go just to be there, to spend time there. They have those camps all along the way from our communities north to the tip of Labrador where people go camp. Most people go in the summer months by boat, but people have also been going by skidoo on the ice this spring. So even though nobody lives there permanently anymore, people still go back. It's like a pilgrimage. Something that they need. Something that was taken from them. (LC 4.19)

Within the academic literature, much of the focus on mountain fishing considers angling or recreational fishing. In particular, the stocking of mountain lakes with fish preferred by anglers has received significant attention for the cascading ecological effects of such introductions (Parker et al., 2001; Pearon & Goater, 2008; Weidman et al., 2011). This research focus has generated considerable insights into the complexity of alpine aquatic systems (Heinle et al., 2021; Macdonald et al., 2014; Paul & Post, 2001). Jeanson and colleagues (2021) have also offered insights into the social complexity of these same systems. The revealed complexity has complicated efforts, thus far, to make more generalised predictions about how cumulative impacts—such as shifting temperatures, pressure from anglers, or removal of

Megan Dicker, Inuit, Nunatsiavut, 2022, LC 4.19

Brandy Mayes, Kwanlin Dün First Nation, 2022, LC 4.20

introduced species—are likely to affect fish of the mountains and the relationships we have with them (Ripley et al., 2005; Sinnatamby et al., 2020).

Mountains also offer gifts to fishes of the lowlands, including marine species such as herring (*Clupea pallasii*), and anadromous species such as eulachon (*Thaleichthys pacificus*) and salmon (*Oncorhynchus spp.*) which spawn in estuaries and lower reaches of rivers originating in coastal mountains (COSEWIC, 2013; Moody, 2008). Bodaly et al. (1984) similarly note the connection between mountain activities and pike and walleye in Northern Manitoba. For many of these fish, the freshwater and nutrients that flow from mountains, snowpack, and glaciers are critical to their survival and successful spawning (Pitman et al., 2020). At the same time sediment loading (Pentz & Kostaschuk, 1999), shifting flows and timing (Rand et al., 2006), and contaminants from mountain activities (Reid et al., 2021) can pose significant risks to these lowland fish and associated fisheries. Brandy Mayes, Kwanlin Dün First Nation, explains the detrimental effects of historically unprecedented flooding on salmon populations in her Nation's Traditional Territory (LC 4.20). Contamination of fish in mountains is also documented and is an area of concern for restoration of mountain fish populations (Orr et al., 2012; Rudolph et al., 2008). Attending to these multiple pressures, across landscapes and at times jurisdictions, remains a space for significant learning. Tulloch et al. (2022) offer one approach for bringing terrestrial and marine pressures together in assessing risks for Pacific salmon and herring. How such

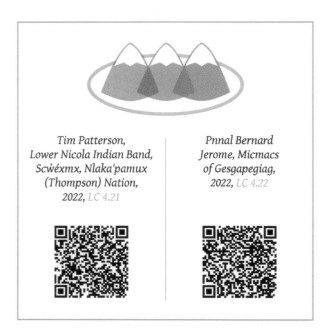

Tim Patterson,
Lower Nicola Indian Band,
Scw̓éxmx, Nlaka'pamux
(Thompson) Nation,
2022, LC 4.21

Pnnal Bernard
Jerome, Micmacs
of Gesgapegiag,
2022, LC 4.22

assessments can inform decisions within fisheries management and land use deserves further attention and conversation.

Finally, there are the fish which travel between the highlands and lowlands. Tim Patterson, Lower Nicola Indian Band, Scw̓éxmx, Nlaka'pamux (Thompson) Nation, noted that some lowland fish, particularly eulachon in the Pacific Maritime region, make this journey following harvest, with extensive networks of 'grease trails' shaping mountains and relationships among First Nations (LC 4.21). Other fish, most notably Atlantic salmon (*Salmo salar*) and Pacific salmon (*Oncorhynchus spp.*), make the long journey from sea to mountainous spawning habitats where they have a tremendous effect on those systems, as Brandy Mayes (Kwanlin Dün First Nation) described:

> In our world, salmon feed everything. Not us, not just us. They feed the land, they feed the bears, and everything that survives on salmon. Between the birds that live on the land, and the squirrels, and the trees, and everything. (LC 4.20)

While there is increasing attention in the reviewed academic literature to the multiple ways that salmon, and other anadromous fish, nourish and shape mountain spaces (Hassan et al., 2008; Hocking & Reynolds, 2011; Wagner & Reynolds, 2019), Gende et al. (2002) along with Levi et al. (2012) note that the implications of dramatically

reduced salmon returns on mountain systems have received limited attention in academic literature. Yet, these changes are widely observed by those who live alongside and depend on salmon, on both Pacific and Atlantic coasts. Elder Pnnal Bernard Jerome, Micmacs of Gesgapegiag, described protracted activism by Micmac communities to protect declining Atlantic salmon habitat and place limits on the recreational sport fishing industry, returning the salmon to Micmac stewardship (LC 4.22). Likewise, sharing observations from Kwanlin Dün territory, Brandy Mayes (Kwanlin Dün First Nation) says:

> We're looking at all of these different ways that climate change and the environment is changing from one species [salmon], from the warming of the weather. And, now we are at: "What are we going to do? What is it going to do? What is going to happen?" We already know culturally, the impacts. We always went to salmon camp. Not only was it just about eating better food and a healthy diet and having that food come through every year. It was about your social aspects of salmon camp: what you taught and the stories were passed down to your children and that family connection. And knowing, when you've all gathered together, what was happening up and down the river. Coming together in ceremony and meeting. You look at that species, by not having it coming back every year in the abundance that it was—we used to take tens of thousands before the dam went in, and then we were still at five thousand, twelve hundred. We're at two hundred salmon a year coming back, and counting only nineteen redds. If you guys know what nineteen redds are, it's the spawning, where they lay their eggs. Nineteen. Last year we had five. That's only that many salmon that are spawning, and what's going to survive out of that to make it back? To make it back to the ocean and come back and then keep feeding everything along the way? (LC 4.20)

In the Pacific Maritime region, the Wuikinuxv Nation in collaboration with academic researchers and fisheries scientists have shared an ecosystem-based management approach for fishing activities that centres the needs of bears alongside the needs of humans (Adams et al., 2021). Principles of fisheries governance that have been shared by Indigenous Peoples across Canada (Atlas et al., 2021; A. J. Reid et al., 2021, 2022; M. Reid et al., 2022) often highlight the importance of managing marine or lower-river fishing activities with regard to sharing with humans and non-humans upriver. However, such principles remain largely absent in approaches to fisheries governance that have long privileged single-species management (M. Reid et al., 2022) and potentially hindered by gaps in Western science's understanding of how anadromous fish influence the productivity of mountain systems (Gende et al., 2002).

Broadly, the reviewed academic literature primarily casts the use of foods and medicines from mountains as practices of the past, with a focus on practices of Indigenous Peoples. Notably absent from the reviewed academic literature is reference to local knowledge and practices held by non-Indigenous multi-generational populations. The approach of the CMA, therefore, does not necessarily represent what is known about foods and medicines of the mountains among these populations if it falls outside of academic literature. Scholars and practitioners within the movement of Indigenous food sovereignty have rightfully criticised the over-emphasis and intellectual curiosity with Indigenous food practices of the past that too often occurs alongside the under-scrutiny of the colonial processes that interrupted such practices and the discounting of contemporary efforts to renew them (Coté, 2016). In general, there seems to be a gap in the literature with regard to the foods and medicines currently given by mountains, the food practices that take people into the mountains, and how those foods and practices might be expected to change looking forward. The knowledge shared during the Learning Circles included more references to current practices and gifts. In cases wherein sharing such information aligns with the responsibilities of mountain stewardship and respectful relationships, there is much to be learned with regard to the continued gifts of foods and medicines.

4.6 Gifts of Water

Mountains, sometimes referred to as the world's 'water towers', are recognized globally as import-

ant sources of freshwater (Viviroli et al., 2007). This is because mountains receive more precipitation than surrounding lowlands, experience less evapotranspiration due to lower temperatures and less vegetation, and store water as snow and ice from which summer meltwater subsidises dry-season streamflow (Barnett et al., 2005; Viviroli et al., 2003). Mountain water resources are critical for both mountain populations and those who live hundreds or even thousands of kilometres downstream (Immerzeel et al., 2020; Viviroli et al., 2020).

4.6.1 *Gifts of freshwater*

In Canada, many communities and industries rely on water resources derived from mountains. From the perspective of water demand relative to local supply, this is particularly true in southwestern Canada, e.g., in semi-arid areas such as the Okanagan Valley and the southern Canadian Prairies (Mitchell et al., 2021). But water from mountains matters in myriad ways across mountain systems. For example, Patricia Joe of Kwanlin Dün First Nation described the connection between the mountains, the Yukon River, and its people:

> We come from the Yukon River, the biggest artery in the Yukon, and it connects us to all the communities. But we would not be river people if it wasn't for the mountain people. It's the mountains that made the river.
> (LC 4.23)

The Montane Cordillera region is an often-cited example of an important mountain water tower in western Canada. The apex of the Columbia Icefield in the Canadian Rockies represents a rare hydrological "triple point," with meltwaters from the Icefield flowing west to the Pacific, east to the

Patricia Joe, Kwanlin Dün First Nation, 2022, LC 4.23

Atlantic, via Hudson Bay, and north to the Arctic, via the Athabasca and Mackenzie River systems. Waters from this icefield reach five of Canada's thirteen provinces and territories, where they play an essential role in ecological, municipal, agricultural, and industrial water resources. The westward-flowing Columbia River system is also a critical hydrological artery for the U.S. Pacific Northwest, with much of its flow derived from mountain headwaters in Canada. These headwaters are sacred and are imbued with cultural value for numerous Indigenous populations of western North America (e.g., Atlas et al., 2021; Awume et al., 2020).

The Columbia Icefield is a signature feature of the Canadian Rockies, but glaciers and snowfields along the entire expanse of the continental divide serve as the wellspring for much of western North

America's water supply. Runoff from the eastern slopes of the Rocky Mountains (Fig. 4.9) contributes disproportionately to the flow in the Bow, North Saskatchewan, Athabasca, and Peace River systems, flows which are heavily drawn upon for agriculture and industry (e.g., Demuth & Pietroniro, 2003; Schindler & Donahue, 2006; Marshall et al., 2011; Toth et al., 2009). A recent study compiled municipal water sources in Alberta and found that 232 of 567 communities rely on snow- and glacier-fed rivers from the Rocky Mountains (Anderson & Radic, 2020).

Similarly, the western slopes of the Rockies and several other ranges within the Montane Cordillera and Pacific Maritime regions are critical sources of water to downstream communities and hydroelectric facilities. Immerzeel et al. (2020) ranked global mountain basins in terms of their

Figure 4.9: The Athabasca River flowing from mountain water towers in the Canadian Rockies, Alberta. Photo courtesy of Graham McDowell, 2016.

THE CANADIAN MOUNTAIN ASSESSMENT

importance to water supply. They conclude that the Fraser River basin, which spans the Pacific Maritime and Montane Cordillera regions, is the most important mountain water tower in North America, based on the extensive mountain water resources in this region's hydrological system (Supply Index) and the high demand for that water (Demand Index). The Columbia River Basin was assessed as the second most critical mountain water tower. The Columbia River is the most heavily dammed river system on earth, and hydroelectric dams in the Canadian portion of the Columbia provide 58% of British Columbia's electricity (BC Hydro, n.d.).

Water is much more than simply a material substance. Water holds complex meanings and values for all human communities (Strang, 2004) and hydrosocial relations with mountain waters are diverse and complex. In Canada, mountain water is valued for environmental, spiritual, cultural, economic and political reasons including tourism (Romeo et al., 2021), habitat for fish (Turner & Clifton, 2009) and a source of drinking water (Anderson & Radic, 2020) or water for various industrial uses including agriculture and mining (Laidlaw, 2018; Schindler & Donahue, 2006).

Much of the literature on human-water relationships in mountain regions in Canada focuses on Indigenous knowledges and relationships with water, often understood as a living entity (Wilson & Inkster, 2018). While focusing on Tlingit and northern Athapaskan peoples' relationships with glaciers in the St. Elias Mountains (Pacific Maritime and Boreal Cordillera), Cruikshank highlights the place of water in local traditions as well as the central role of human-water-glacier relationships in everyday life (Cruikshank, 2005). Nancy Turner and Elder Helen Clifton (Gitga'at (Coast Tsimshian) Nation of Hartley Bay, BC) (Pacific Maritime) discuss human-water relationships as they share Secwépemc elder Mary Thomas's recollection of "her own mother breaking off stems of swamp gooseberry (*Ribes lacustre*) during a summer drought, dipping these in the water of a mountain creek and invoking rain" (Turner & Clifton, 2009, p. 183). Research with Stellat'en First Nation (Montane Cordillera) also indicates concerns about the impacts of climate change on water and fish (Sanderson et al., 2015).

Parlee and Martin (2016) review existing documentation of Indigenous knowledge of the Peel River Watershed (Taiga Cordillera), a sub-watershed of the Mackenzie River Watershed highlight the importance of water to the Teetl'it Gwich'in, Vuntut Gwich'in, Tr'ondëk Hwëch'in and Northern Tutchone. They discuss the value of the rivers in the Peel watershed as transportation corridors and the fish in the rivers as important to the food security of families who utilised the area. Furthermore, they document changes in water quality and levels (e.g., riverbank erosion, fluctuating water levels) and concerns about the impacts of development and climate change on the watershed and the fish that rely on it. Finally, Wilson, Tr'ondek Hwech'In Elder Angie Joseph-Rear, and others (Wilson et al., 2019) discuss the importance of mountain water sources (traditional drinking water sources) near Tombstone Territorial Park in Yukon (Taiga Cordillera) for the spiritual, cultural, and physical health of the Tr'ondek Hwech'In.

The complexity of hydrosocial relations means that climate change has cascading socio-cultural, political, and ecological implications for human communities. For instance, mountain communities that rely on glacially fed rivers for municipal drinking water supplies are potentially vulnerable to reduced streamflow resulting from deglaciation (e.g., in Alberta; Anderson & Radic, 2020). Climate impacts on the snowpack mountains within the Capilano and Seymour watersheds that supply water to Metro Vancouver are also of concern for long-term planning (Mood & Smith, 2021). While Canada has been noted to suffer from the "myth of abundance" (Sprague, 2007), these examples illustrate the importance of paying attention to the implications of water scarcity for mountain communities and those outside mountain regions that rely on these water sources.

Water governance is also an important topic related to hydrosocial relationships. There is limited literature on water governance in mountain regions in Canada. Challenges in water governance may prevent the protection of water. For instance, weak governance is at the heart of Canada's water problems including significant jurisdictional overlap and conflict (Bakker, 2011). Furthermore, Indigenous Peoples have inherent water rights, authorities, and responsibilities to water (Craft, 2017; McGregor, 2014), and yet are frequently excluded or marginalised within colonial water governance frameworks in Canada including specific examples from mountain regions (Arsenault et al., 2018; Simms et al., 2016; Wilson, 2020). Indigenous Peoples are also articulating approaches to water governance—rooted in their Indigenous governance systems that centre water as a living entity (Wilson & Inkster, 2018). These issues are not specific to mountain regions; however, future literature should consider the specificities of governance in these regions.

4.6.2 *Gifts of wetlands*

Wetlands provide a variety of gifts or ecosystem services: water quality improvement, flood risk mitigation, water retention, support for biodiversity, and carbon management (Zedler & Kercher, 2005). They are key stops for migratory species, they host specialised species adapted to living in very specific conditions, and they provide for landscape heterogeneity. In mountains in Canada, wetlands have been described as acting as kidneys for the Earth (Bai et al., 2013), playing a critical role in cleaning water of excessive nutrients and polluting chemicals. Wetlands in the mountains are also important flood risk mitigators, as seen in Westbrook et al. (2020), who describe the 2013 flood in Kananaskis region of southern Alberta, in the Montane Cordillera. Wetlands retain runoff water, allowing for a slower release of water through time and buffering the input to downstream areas.

Wetlands also comprise key wildlife habitat in mountain regions. They provide habitat for moose and elk calving, as well as beaver, which are landscape architects and have shaped much of the low- and mid-elevation wetlands in the mountains in Southern Alberta (Morrison et al., 2014). Wetlands are also a stop for migratory species for resting, drinking water, and feeding as well as nesting areas for birds. By providing landscape heterogeneity these ecosystems allow for protection of habitat-specific species, and can act as a natural barrier to break up homogeneity in landscapes, particularly above the treeline. If undrained and well conserved, wetlands act as natural fire breaks and refuges for communities during wildfires, which are becoming more common. Wetlands may potentially act as climate refugia as species ranges shift by buffering temperature swings (Stralberg et al., 2020).

Wetlands can also capture large amounts of carbon, demonstrating the resilience of mountain environments. Studies of the carbon accumulation rates in peatlands in the mountain regions of Canada are scant; however, it has been shown that despite lower carbon content, long-term carbon accumulation rates of mountain peatlands may be similar to that of boreal lowland peatlands as the peat is usually denser (Cooper et al., 2012). Peat in the Rocky Mountains started to accumulate after the last glaciation, and the ages range from 3800 to 12,000 years ago (Cooper et al., 2012; Gardner & Jones, 1985; Mercer, 2018). The estimated average depth of peat in the Canadian Rocky Mountains is 50–100 cm (Mercer, 2018; Tarnocai et al., 2011). The mean long-term accumulation rates for peatlands in the foothills of the Canadian Rockies are estimated to be about 25 gC m^{-2} yr^{-1}, which are similar to carbon storage rates of peatlands in Colorado (Chimner & Cooper, 2003; Wickland et al., 2001; Yu et al., 2003). Further inventorying and carbon accounting of peatlands in the mountain regions of Canada are needed to understand their carbon sequestration capabilities.

Anthropogenic impacts including climate change are affecting and will continue to alter important functions of wetlands and specifically peatlands in sensitive world regions like mountains. Current and predicted changes to mountain wetland ecosystems are discussed in Chapter 5, Sec. 5.10.3.

4.7 Gift of Mountain Spaces and Terrain for Tourism and Recreation Activities

4.7.1 *Nature and adventure tourism economies*

Mountain regions across the world are popular for tourism and recreation activities, as mountains hold rich socio-ecological diversity and inspiring landscapes that create opportunities for reflection and adventure (Romeo et al., 2021). The same holds true for mountain regions across Canada (Mitchell et al., 2021), which have grown in popularity with rising visitation numbers (IUCN, 2020). Mountains in Canada have drawn people from across many cultures seeking opportunities for physical adventure and an escape from everyday life (Fig. 4.10). Mountain-based tourism and recreation activities in Canada include, but are not limited to, sight-seeing, hiking, mountaineering (e.g., rock climbing, ice climbing, alpine climbing, ski mountaineering, via ferrata), skiing (e.g., backcountry, alpine, cross country, kite-assisted), water-based activities (e.g., swimming, paddleboarding, canoeing, kayaking, rafting, sailing), biking (road and mountain), camping, fishing and hunting, and mechanised recreation (e.g., snowmobiles, all-terrain vehicles/quads, helicopters, snowcats for skiing), which occur across different seasons depending on conditions.

Today this is a multi-million dollar industry in Canada in places such as the Rocky Mountains of western Canada and the associated "adventure culture" economy (e.g., clothing, retreats, artwork) is worth many more million dollars per annum. In Canada, over half of national park visits occur in the seven so-called mountain parks (Banff, Jasper, Mount Revelstoke, Glacier, Yoho, Kootenay, and Waterton Lakes) annually, and in a pre-COVID-19 era, $1.48 billion was generated annually from tourism activities in Alberta's Rocky Mountains alone (Alberta Government, 2012). Tourism and recreation activities in mountain regions across Canada emerged with the establishment of Rocky Mountain National Park in 1886 as the introduction of railways brought elite European and North American travellers to Banff's hot springs (Draper, 2000). Since then, tourism and recreation development has been steady across mountain regions in Canada, with many communities transitioning away from economies based on mining and forestry, towards those based on tourism and recreation (Héritier, 2003; Nepal & Jamal, 2011).

With the increase in tourism and recreation opportunities in mountain regions across Canada, many urbanites have flocked to mountain

Figure 4.10: Mount Rundle and Sacred Buffalo Guardian Mountain (foreground) in Banff National Park, a popular destination in the Montane Cordillera region. Photo courtesy of Graham McDowell, 2022.

communities in pursuit of leisure and recreation lifestyles that cannot be found in urban environments (Pavelka, 2017). As with any transition, there are social and ecological trade-offs associated with moving towards a tourism-dependent economy, which is further discussed in Chapter 5. However, a holistic understanding of the economic, social, and environmental implications of mountain-based tourism and recreation across mountain regions in Canada, particularly in Northern and Eastern mountain ranges, is still lacking, and too little is known about how tourism revenues flow back to local communities.

Beyond the economic importance of tourism and recreation in mountain regions, tourism and recreation activities provide diverse benefits to people. Earlier work by Bratton et al. (1979) examines the reason why people are drawn to the sport of mountaineering in Canada and found that people participate in mountaineering activities for a social outlet, health and fitness, excitement, relaxation, competitive and non-competitive achievement, and the love of nature. Further, it is recognized that participating in tourism and recreation activities in nature can enhance pro-environmental behaviour and stewardship behaviours by strengthening the relationship between humans and nature, as seen in recreational fishermen in British Columbia (Jeanson et al., 2021).

In essence, tourism and recreation activities in mountain regions provide humans with a gift of reconnecting with the natural world through movement and play. In Canada, beliefs and behaviours during recreational activities are driven by each individual person's experience in nature

Figure 4.11: Backcountry skiers ascending a slope above Lake McArthur in Yoho National Park. Photo courtesy of Madison Stevens, 2023.

THE CANADIAN MOUNTAIN ASSESSMENT

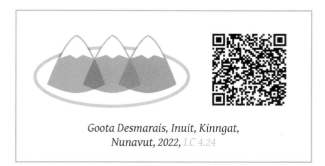

Goota Desmarais, Inuit, Kinngat, Nunavut, 2022, LC 4.24

and can be influenced by the species with which they interact and the habitats they use for recreation (Jeanson et al., 2021; Stoddart, 2011). For example, trail users in Banff, Jasper, Kootenay, and Yoho national parks (Fig. 4.11) were likely to support the closure of a particular area for conservation efforts, such as for a female bear with cubs (Elmeligi et al., 2021). Yet, the mountains are not equally accessible and do not provide tourism and recreation gifts to everyone, as Goota Desmarais (Inuit, Kinngat, Nunavut), stated, "only the rich could use the mountains, you need a vehicle and you need money to buy passes" (LC 4.24).

4.7.2 Challenges and drawbacks of mountain recreation

Important aspects of the history of tourism and recreation activities in Canada require more focused consideration, including the sometimes extractive history and characteristics of tourism and recreation in mountain regions across Canada, as well as the ways in which the benefits of tourism and recreation are often experienced in unequal ways. The mountain adventure economy has been described as prioritising the values of white, wealthy tourists with disproportionate benefits being captured by corporations who market mountain lifestyles to Canadian and global markets. Other social groups, including Indigenous Peoples who have long histories and connections to mountain environments, have seen little economic benefit and often experienced harm. This occurs when adventure activities conflict in time and place with Indigenous Peoples' access or uses, or physically impact or degrade places of cultural value and importance.

Importantly, the establishment of formal protected areas in Canada, such as National and Provincial Parks, for conservation and tourism

purposes has led to the displacement and exclusion of Indigenous Peoples from their homelands (Binnema & Niemi, 2006), contributing to current and historical marginalization of Indigenous knowledges and ways of living. For example, with the "discovery" of the Cave and Basin Hot Springs by Canadian Pacific Railway surveyors, the Banff Springs Reserve was created in 1885, later extended to Lake Minnewanka in 1887, and further expanded in 1902, creating barriers for Indigenous Peoples to access traditional hunting grounds and restricting the right to hunt for subsistence purposes (Binnema & Niemi, 2006). With the further establishment of National Parks for tourism and conservation purposes, such as Banff National Park, came further exclusion of Indigenous ways of knowing and interacting with the natural landscape, pushing Indigenous Peoples to reserves and away from their homelands in the mountains (Binnema & Niemi, 2006).

More recent protected area developments have aimed to work in partnership with local Indigenous groups to ensure connection and culture is upheld. This was seen with the recent development of Torngat Mountains National Park (Inuktitut: Tongait KakKasuangita SilakKijapvinga) located on the homelands of Inuit Peoples, which was developed in partnership with Inuit members of Nunatsiavut and Nunavik who have traditionally used the land for hunting and gathering (Maher & Lemelin, 2011). While Torngat Mountains National Park is currently co-managed between Parks Canada and the Inuit communities of Nunatsiavut and Nunavik, it is important to recognize that Inuit members in Labrador were historically dispossessed and relocated from their traditional harvesting areas within the current park boundaries, and as such "the park should be viewed as a tremendous gift from the people of Nunatsiavut to Canada" (Maher & Lemelin, 2011).

Since the 1980s, there has been a growing effort towards healing the impacts of historic conservation efforts, with the need to reshape and develop new kinds of protected areas in ways that improve representation and equity of benefits for Indigenous Peoples. Co-management agreements, ranging from advisory roles to shared governance and consensus-based decision-making have developed in some mountain regions such as those in the Yukon Territory. Although less common in southern regions such as Alberta and

British Columbia, commitments of the federal government to meet global Aichi Targets (e.g., Target 1) for biodiversity conservation have catalysed a movement towards Indigenous Protected and Conserved Areas (IPCAs) (Zurba et al., 2019). IPCAs are lands and waters where Indigenous governments have the primary role in protecting and conserving ecosystems through Indigenous laws, governance and knowledge systems. Culture and language are the heart and soul of an IPCA. IPCAs vary in terms of their governance and management objectives (Zurba et al., 2019).

The exclusion of Indigenous Peoples is not the only cost that tourism and recreation development has on mountains in Canada. Recreation and tourism development and activity impacts both human (i.e., local communities) and non-human animal populations (i.e., flora and fauna) in mountain regions in Canada through disturbance and displacement (Gaudreau, 1990; Ladle et al., 2019; St-Louis et al., 2013), which is further discussed in Chapter 5. Some key examples of this conflict exist in respect of recreational versus subsistence hunting and fishing (Binnema & Niemi, 2006; Colton, 2005; Mason et al., 2022), recreational vehicle use (e.g., off-roading, mudding) (Kadykalo, 2022; Kershaw, 2008; Liddle, 1997; Pigeon et al., 2016; Yarmoloy, 1986), as well as less extractive activities (e.g., trail riding), that by virtue of a human presence may indirectly and directly fragment wildlife habitats and create problems of human-wildlife conflict (Geng, 2021; Loosen et al., 2023; Thornton & Quinn, 2009).

Participating in mountain-based tourism and recreation activities also involves people engaging with significant risk, which can be fatal given the circumstances of exposure to mountain hazards. For example, 1088 incidents and 1377 fatalities were reported in the Alpine Club of Canada's search and rescue database from 1970–2005, with 92% of incidents occurring in mountain regions in British Columbia and Alberta (Curran-Sills & Karahalios, 2015; Wild, 2008). This database shows that hiking and mountaineering result in more than half of all casualties that yield any type of morbidity, whereas mountaineering, skiing, ski mountaineering, or snowboarding account for almost two thirds of all fatalities (Curran-Sills & Karahalios, 2015). However, further research is needed to assess how mountain towns and communities are dealing with the impact of these

natural hazards. For example, with increased tourism, especially by visitors who are not particularly experienced with outdoor safety and travel, it is important to assess how to properly educate and conduct preventative intervention to avoid an increased number of search and rescue efforts, which can tax the funds and resources of small mountain communities.

While there has been some research trying to capture the intricacies of tourism and recreation as gifts in mountain regions across Canada, there is a lack of geographic diversity in the literature. To date, much of the tourism literature, based on a review by McDowell and Hanly (2022), is spatially concentrated in the Montane Cordillera and Pacific Maritime regions within Canada, with only a small body of literature published in other mountain regions. While there are still many research gaps in the Montane Cordillera and Pacific Maritime regions, attention should also be focused on the other mountain regions to increase knowledge on the social, environmental, and economic impacts of tourism and recreation, both positive and negative. Further, more attention should be given to examining how we can transition tourism and recreation economies away from extractive practices that commodify the gift of space and terrain towards reciprocal practices with the mountains and mountain communities.

4.8 Gifts and Benefits of Forests, Materials, and Energy Sources

This section focuses specifically on the material benefits provided by mountains. This includes a summary of the different kinds of reciprocal relationships of benefit and stewardship that exist between Indigenous Peoples and forests and energy resources. Forests, like water resources, can be exploited for commercial benefits, feeding urban and global markets. As such, the idea of gifts and gifting, particularly in which people and mountains exist in a reciprocal relationship of care, is uncomfortably suited to a discussion of energy and materials (e.g., forests and minerals) extracted from mountain environments. Yet these materials are also part of ongoing reciprocal relations and meanings for Indigenous Peoples, and offer more-than-material gifts to some non-Indigenous communities through traditions of sustainable use and harvest. The practice of community forestry can be sustainable and not extractive, but this is not typical of Western economic systems, where the gifts and benefits tend to leave the community.

Recognizing the multiple ways in which these materials are used and managed, this chapter posits that mountains provide for different peoples in ways that reflect different engagements with mountains and different views of the environment in economic practices. In this subsection, then, the notion of gifts is complicated by the observation that for many people mountains provide benefits in the form of commodities, energies, and employment. This section shows some of the benefits that emerge from mountain environments for many, though not all, people in Canada. In doing so, we recognize that talking about gifts and benefits is often a narrow distinction which depends on the perspective from which one views the topic in question. We thus call for further critical attention to how large-scale resource extraction is sometimes incongruent with the principles of cultural, social, ecological, and economic sustainability.

4.8.1 *Forests*

Mountain forests are composed of trees and plants that grow in unique assemblages and physiological growth patterns, much different than those found at lower elevations. Mountain forests contain distinct ecological zones which present challenging conditions for the growth of trees, including harsh climates, strong winds, and unique and variable hydrological conditions (see also Chapter 2). In some areas within mountain forests, hardy trees show their ability to adapt on the edge of life itself. It is here, for example, that trees demonstrate the phenomenon of *krummholz*, trees with stunted growth patterns shaped by the harsh conditions of persistent mountain winds and freezing temperatures. Due to their extent and composition, mountain forests can be significant centres of above-ground carbon storage. For example, the mountain-focused analysis of Mitchell et al. (2021) reveals that the Pacific Maritime, Montane Cordillera, and Interior Hills Central regions all have above-ground carbon storage well in excess of the average above-ground carbon storage of non-mountainous areas

of Canada (5.5, 4.5, and 3.4 times the national average, respectively).

Forested landscapes at different altitudes are understood, used, and managed to maximise the diversity of benefits of those ecosystems; as described by Turner et al. (2003), the diversity of forest resources which can be found at different altitudes is reflected in the social organisation of Indigenous Peoples. These ecological edges are described by Turner et al. as:

> Ecological edges can be understood as places where one habitat type changes to another, which are at the same time zones of specialised habitat with unique biological species. They can also be realised temporally as periods of time where one stage gives way to another. Ecological edges, in other words, are both places in and of themselves, as well as markers for the transition from one type of ecosystem to another, or from one phase to another within a single ecosystem. Thus, mixed habitat patches and zones where different successional stages abut one another can be areas of unique ecological diversity and interchange. (Turner et al., 2003, p. 456)

The uses of these ecological edges are intertwined with cultural institutions such as spiritual ceremony. The seasonal sharing of these resources, for example, from different mountain forest habitats in different ways, within and across different communities, is a fundamental dimension of the Coast Salish potlatch (Turner et al., 2003).

Within mountain forests are trees with special qualities that have been prized for thousands of years, first by Indigenous Peoples and later by settlers and within global economies (Fig. 4.12). Some notable examples in British Columbia include: yellow cedar (*Chamaecyparis nootkatensis*), prized for its tight grain and resistance to decay, making it an excellent material for building; whitebark pine (*Pinus albicaulis*), a tree that is struggling at the brink of extinction across its range that plays an important role in supporting birds and small mammals with its pinenuts, particularly Clark's nutcracker (*Nucifraga columbiana*); subalpine fir (*Abies lasiocarpa*); and mountain hemlock (*Tsuga mertensiana*) (Laroque & Smith, 2005). In subalpine

Figure 4.12: Forest on the Traditional Territory of the Lil'wat and Squamish Nations, near present-day Whistler, BC. Photo courtesy of Madison Stevens, 2018.

forests, just below the alpine treeline, tree island regeneration occurs. Here, trees regenerate in 'island' formations, with older trees providing cover from the snow and supporting early season snowmelt, helping to create the conditions necessary for seedlings to persist and regenerate (Brett & Klinka, 1998). While the unique conditions of mountain forests make them fragile and slow to recover after disturbances (Brett & Klinka, 1998), these forests have long been cared for by Indigenous Peoples across Canada.

Traditional uses of trees by Indigenous Peoples in mountains across Canada are numerous and diverse. In eastern Canada for example, the forests of the Gaspé and Laurentians have long supported the livelihoods of diverse peoples including the Mi'kmaq. Mi'kmaq peoples use trees to construct the poles in order to fish. Black ash (*Fraxinus nigra*) is the type of tree that has been most commonly used, but is now also very scarce throughout Mi'kma'ki. "[An elder] leaves behind tobacco as an offering of respect to the Earth. The trees are then used to make spears in order to catch the fish" (Graham, 2015, p. 36).

One of the most prominent trees honoured by Indigenous Peoples of western Canada is yellow cedar, which is known by many, including the Nuu-chah-nulth Nations (a collective name for the people "all-along-the-mountains" of the western coast of Vancouver Island), to be a Tree of Life (Earnshaw, 2016). Due to its close grain patterns and resistance to rot and decay, yellow cedar is the preferred wood for crafting many items, including shelter, subsistence tools, clothing, ceremonial regalia, and art (Earnshaw, 2016). Yellow cedar wood is sought for carving by many Indigenous artists, and also valued for its bark and roots, which are used for many purposes including crafting baskets and clothing as well as ropes and twines by various Indigenous Peoples. Yellow cedar is also important ceremonially, as for example, the boughs are dried and ground to make a smudge.

Yellow cedar is just one of the many trees valued for each part by Indigenous Peoples; and within traditional Indigenous healthcare systems each tree and plant has a purpose and a role in healthcare for human and non-human beings. Some trees in mountain areas, like Sitka spruce (*Picea sitchensis*) for example, provide buds with medicinal properties that are prepared as teas and decoctions used for both preventative and curative health and healing (Lílwat Nation, 2017). Other trees like Balsam fir (*Abies balsamea*) contain medicinal pitch (sap), which is used as both an external and internal medicine amongst various Indigenous Nations. Growing amongst alpine trees are numerous medicinal plants and fungi. For example, in Lil'wat Nation, more than 100 species growing in mountains were noted by Indigenous herbalists as having important medicinal qualities (Lílwat Nation, 2017).

Industrial forestry

As Indigenous lands in Canada began to swell with incoming colonists, many of whom supported the government's violent land grabs starting from the 18th century in the east, forest resources were one of the major drives for the expansion of colonial empires. Under Canada's model of federalism, the constitutional division of powers dictates that the Provinces and Territories are responsible for regulations and permitting on forest lands. Licences and ownership to log across Canada have often been done with willful ignorance of Indigenous Peoples' ownership of their lands, following the colonial doctrine of *terra nullius* ('empty land'), which has significant implications in Canadian laws to this day (Borrows, 2015). The development of Canada's forestry sector is closely entangled with the steady erosion of Indigenous

Peoples' rights within their territories, through instances such as the creation of 'Indian Reserves' under the *Indian Act*, the traumatic removal of Indigenous children from their lands as part of the Residential School System and the Sixties Scoop, in parallel with the creation of logging rights to Indigenous territories (Smith & Bulkan, 2021).

Forestry regulations and property rights differ across provincial and territorial lines in Canada, with each province featuring distinct histories of how the logging industry came to be in its early days. For example, British Columbia's forest tenure system dates back to the 1865 *Land Ordinance Act*, which was the first piece of legislation enabling companies to do logging on public lands without alienating the land from provincial ownership (the 'Crown') (FLNRORD, 2019). Forestry companies operating in British Columbia and elsewhere where lands are publicly held, are granted legal rights to log in the form of concession licences. In British Columbia, these rights are granted in exchange for taxes in the form of stumpage (a complex and graduated fee) and 'royalties' (*ad valorem* taxes), a system which has been in place since the 1884 *Timber Act* (FLNRORD, 2019). Throughout the 1900s, logging in Canada became increasingly regulated, with logging concessions that are either volume-based, providing companies with a fixed volume of timber to log from an area shared with other licensees, or area-based, which is a more secure concession type wherein companies are given more responsibilities in exchange for long-term rights to a fixed area of forest to log (Rajala, 1998).

As technologies for logging improved, the development of oligopolistic forestry industries across Canada followed in lockstep the investments in capital-intensive mills during the 20th century. In British Columbia, Ben Parfitt (2005; 2007; 2010) has documented the steady erosion of regulatory control in the forestry sector, documenting how powerful lobbying and consolidated ownership by forestry companies led to the erosion of monitoring compliance with forest laws and regulations. In other provinces, powerful companies like J.D. Irving Ltd. control a significant amount of the logging rights in New Brunswick (Mullally & MacDonald, 2017). In British Columbia and elsewhere, natural resources sectors have experienced ongoing risk to legal tenures to resources due to outstanding Aboriginal title, with activities of the forestry industry being contested by Indigenous Peoples and local communities whose rights have been often disregarded by those in control of logging in their homelands (Brody, 1981; Hayter, 2004; Natcher, 2009; Pasternak, 2017).

Various levels of government have largely failed to implement protection for Aboriginal rights, which include the rights to fishing, hunting, trapping, and gathering, in a way that is satisfying for many Indigenous Peoples (Smith & Bulkan, 2021). Moreover, Canada's forest resource peripheries have become increasingly dependent on global markets for forest products (Hayter, 2004; Hayter & Barnes, 2012). British Columbia's forest industry, for example, is heavily export-oriented, sending huge volumes of unprocessed timber for processing elsewhere. Exports from British Columbia forests increased in value from $36 billion CDN in 2014 to 47 billion in 2018 (Bautista, 2020). As such, global markets increasingly dictate the activities of local mills and logging (Hayter & Barnes, 2012). In complex and intersecting ways, then, commercial forestry, and acts of reforestation, reflect a capitalist reciprocity rather than a gift exchange. Extraction of forest products provides jobs and materials for sale—provisions from mountain environments—on which a forest economy supports communities.

Community forestry

As the global climate crisis becomes more immediate, a partial response to some of the challenges for conventional logging in Canada has emerged in the form of community forests. Community forestry is one way that forest-dependent communities in the mountain areas of Canada are striving to have more of a say over the logging practices happening in their homelands. Community forestry is one way to protect the gifts that montane forests provide as unique contributors to the wellbeing of networks of relations. Community forestry has emerged following a history of the Canadian forestry industry bringing fewer benefits for people that live near forests. The purpose of many community forestry initiatives across Canada is to restore and strengthen the relationships that people have with the gifts of the forest, including protecting aspects of forests that have been disregarded and/or diminished by industrial forestry practices.

Community forestry across mountain areas takes on many different forms, due to the different governance regimes of forestry in each of Canada's provinces and territories. However, the common thread of community forests is to create more benefits from forestry for local communities. Benefits may include increasing the capture of monetary benefits by local communities, increasing participation in the stewardship of forests, or enhancing ecological stewardship. Within community forest arrangements, the gifts of forests may be enhanced through means such as: increasing the ability of Indigenous Peoples to practise collective cultural stewardship; maintaining access to culturally important sites, places of spiritual importance and burial grounds; increasing the ability for community members to have a say about when are where logging happens; enhancing protection for forest foods, medicines, game, wildlife habitat and biodiversity; maintaining access for recreation; protection for community watersheds and sources of drinking water; and enhancing protective aspects of forests and mitigating the risk of forest fires and disease outbreaks. Community foresters select which objectives are the most important to them in the management of their forest, and pursue processes based on meeting these objectives. Community forestry stakeholders include both rights holders, who are Indigenous Peoples with longstanding ancestral connections with their territory, and stakeholders, who are people who may also have long standing connections with mountain forests but are not Indigenous and thus rarely have ancestral connections to place dating back more than a few generations (Bulkan et al., 2022). Both Indigenous Peoples and local communities have been engaging with community forests to protect their mountain forests, creating varied experiences and outcomes.

The creation of community forests involves legal aspects of forestry governance. The first consideration for community forest proponents is to determine who will be involved in the community forest, and where the community forest will be located. In Canada, 91.4% of the forests are held as public Crown Land, with ownership claimed by the provincial governments (Lawler & Bullock, 2017). The provinces issue permissions for logging in the form of area-based and volume-based concession licences, which vary from province

COMMUNITY FORESTS ON UNCEDED TERRITORY: LIL'WAT NATION'S SPE'LKÚMTN COMMUNITY FOREST IN BRITISH COLUMBIA

In British Columbia (Pacific Maritime region), most Indigenous Peoples deny the provincial government claims on their territories, saying that their rights have never been ceded through treaty. Across other parts of Canada, historical treaties exist and, yet, the fulfilment of treaty obligations by Canadian and provincial governments remains an ongoing concern and challenge (Asch 2014). In many places, various levels of government deny the legal claims of Indigenous Peoples to their territories, which has led to a series of court cases in the Supreme Courts of Canada and Provinces that have clarified who has a responsibility to uphold Aboriginal title rights in decisions made about Indigenous Peoples' territories, including decisions about the issuing of tenures and logging (Gunter, 2022). While the progression of Indigenous Peoples' rights proceeds slowly within the court system, some Indigenous Nations have chosen to participate in the forestry sector as community forest licence holders to seek immediate involvement in how forests are being stewarded (Smith & Bulkan, 2021).

Indigenous Peoples have been closely involved with the creation of community forests in British Columbia in particular, where they have long been excluded from involvement in and benefits from the forestry sector on their territories. Approximately half of the community forest arrangements in the province involve a partnership between Indigenous Peoples and local communities who co-inhabit areas and work together to meet shared goals (BCCFA, 2022). One such example is the Spe'lkúmtn Community Forest in Lil'wat Nation Territory, Pemberton, BC, which is a partnership between the Lil'wat Nation and the Municipality of Pemberton. Through co-managing forests around the local villages, the newly created Spe'lkúmtn Community Forest will practise forest fire mitigation through thinning forest stands, protect the botanical resources of Lil'wat Nation, including food and medicinal plants and fungi, and cultural trails and sites alongside recreational values for multiple forest users. Though the community forest managers must ensure the long-term economic profitability of the association to continue to exist through time, they are also focusing on enhancing non-market values from the forest to bolster their social licence to operate and support amongst Lilwat7u'l (Lil'wat Nation members) and non-Indigenous locals.

to province. Many of the forest licences across Canada have been held by large forestry companies for decades, and so one challenge for community foresters is to find volumes of wood fibre that are available for including in their licence areas (Gunter, 2022). Another challenge is to involve each of the affected rights holders and stakeholders, which is a task that requires working across a variety of forest values held by diverse individuals and groups (Doyle-Yamaguchi & Smith, 2022).

Community forests compete with large forestry companies that were consolidated during the 1900s, and thus face economic pressures to meet bottom line business objectives while also maintaining environmental and social objectives (Rajala, 2006). For many community forests, the only mills in proximity are owned by big forestry conglomerates (labelled the 'Majors'), and thus the benefits of wood processing cannot be easily captured by the community forest licensees themselves (BCCFA, 2022; Smith & Bulkan, 2021). There are few economic incentives available for community forests to protect non-timber values, and protecting and enhancing the gifts of the forests often comes at an economic cost to community forest operators (Gunter, 2022; Smith & Bulkan, 2021). Moreover, because community forests are unique to place and community, they risk falling into the 'local trap', where assumptions are made that local communities are best positioned to manage their local forests, when in fact they may not have the capacity or will to do so (Duinker & MacLellan, 2017).

Yet, community forests in mountain regions have demonstrated success in redistributing the benefits from forestry to local communities. For example, in 2019, $16 million was redistributed from respondents to a British Columbia community forest survey to local community groups, supporting initiatives such as community infrastructure, youth groups, or reinvestment of profits back into the forest via ecosystem restoration (Gunter, 2022). In British Columbia, community forests are also found to produce 76% more jobs per cubic metre of wood cut than industry average, be more proactive in mitigating climate change and wildfire risk, and facilitate partnerships between Indigenous and non-Indigenous communities (BCCFA, 2022). While British Columbia is a national leader in community forestry, other provinces including Quebec, Nova Scotia, and New Brunswick have also demonstrated interest in establishing community forest programs (Bouthillier et al., 2022; Duinker & MacLellan, 2017; Fortier et al., 2013).

While community forests mature beyond the early phase of development, there is a need to assess common experiences across ecological zones, and to consider, for example, how montane regions across Canada may feature similar or diverse experiences based on their unique conditions. To date, there is no research comparing experiences of community forests in mountain regions of Canada.

4.8.2 *Minerals and hydrocarbons*

Beneath the forest roots holding mountain slopes in place, the very bedrock of the mountains has provided important material and spiritual contributions to First Nations, Métis, and Inuit Peoples since time immemorial, from caves that serve as sacred sites, to carving stones, to the rocks used for making tools. Even placenames can reflect the rocks and minerals which make up the mountains. Learning Circle participant Sophie Pheasant, Anishinaabe, offered a story about the name of an Anishinaabe community in the La Cloche mountain range called Wawaskinaga (Birch Island), in reference to the mountain range that shines in the sunlight because of the quartz faces of its peaks (LC 4.25). Similarly, Elder Pnnal Bernard Jerome, Micmacs of Gesgapegiag, shared a story about a place called Pipestone Mountain, where the gathering of stone for making pipes (known as catlinite in Western science) is a sacred process carefully stewarded by Micmac Elders with the knowledge and permission to pass on these protocols for respectful use (LC 4.26).

Within the context of industrial economies, people also derive from mountain places economically significant natural industrial (non-metallic)

and metallic mineral and rock resources, and hydrocarbon-based (fossil fuel) energy resources. Excluding fossil fuels, the entire Canadian mining industry produced goods valued at approximately $47 Billion in 2021 (Natural Resources Canada (NRC); Prospectors & Developers Association of Canada (PDAC)), of which >30% was attributable to mines located within the Cordilleran mountain regions alone. Here we review these natural 'gifts', covering only the most economically significant, and describe the links between deposit types and the geological processes responsible for the development of mountain regions in Canada. We follow with a brief look at energy and mineral deposits which may gain economic significance in the near future.

We also consider how the extraction of these gifts can impact other values and meanings embodied in the landscape. Sophie Pheasant's story of Wawaskinaga (above) illustrates this well: one of the quartz peaks which gave the community its name no longer exists because of the mining activities undertaken to extract the rock and minerals of the mountain top, which fundamentally affects the community's identity and sense of place. In her own home on Manitoulin Island, the industrial extraction of limestone also shows the risks of extracting resources which are fundamentally non-renewable, "it's not something we can grow back," and the tradeoffs between using these resources and being able to receive and benefit from other gifts of the mountains, such as habitat for caribou and other wildlife.

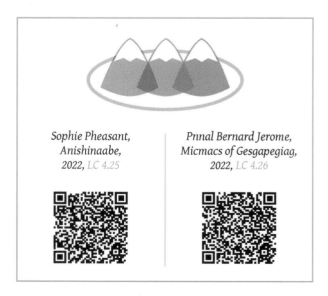

| *Sophie Pheasant, Anishinaabe, 2022, LC 4.25* | *Pnnal Bernard Jerome, Micmacs of Gesgapegiag, 2022, LC 4.26* |

4.8.3 *Sedimentary deposits and quarries*

Industrial mineral resources include minerals that are not sources of metals, fuel, or gemstones. They include chemical and biogenic sedimentary rocks, evaporites, terrigenous clastic rocks including various clays, and a number of other elements and rocks. Sand and gravel constitute the most common industrial materials mined from our mountainous regions. Although most widely used in construction, and specifically in concrete production, sand and gravel uses are almost infinite and include drainage, road beds, filtration systems, glass and fibreglass, and hydraulic fracking in oil and gas production. Much of our sand and gravel are products of glacial processes. Because of their topographic relief and high elevation, glaciers and glaciation-related sand and gravel deposits are particularly common in the high-elevation mountainous regions of Canada. Canadian sand and gravel production is worth $2.3 billion dollars annually, of which more than a third is sourced from mountains in Canada.

Another required component of cement and concrete is limestone. During the Paleozoic, 300 to 540 Ma, North America lay far to the south within the tropics (Irving, 1977) and was commonly covered by shallow tropical seas characterised by coral reefs and lime mud deposits that lithified into and are now preserved as thick limestone and dolomite sequences. Mountain building processes resulted in the exhumation and exposure of these sequences within the Cordilleran mountain regions of western Canada and the southeastern half of the Atlantic Maritime and Boreal Shield mountain region (i.e. Appalachians) where they are now mined for the manufacturing of cement, but also for building stone, aggregate, soil conditioning, and the neutralisation of chemical and industrial waste.

Numerous other industrial minerals are either exposed within mountain regions or are attributable to the processes responsible for the development of the mountains. Examples include Bentonite and other 'swelling' clays which originate as volcanic ash erupted from volcanoes that were present during the formation of the Cordilleran mountain regions of western Canada and the southeastern half of the Atlantic Maritime and Boreal Shield region; and Evaporites (Gypsum and salt) that crystallised out of the shallow and

Pnnal Bernard Jerome, Micmacs of Gesgapegiag, 2022, LC 4.27

occasionally ephemeral tropical seas that used to cover the continent and which were subsequently deformed and exposed for mining during orogeny. Certain volcanic rocks have also been valued for their importance as materials for sweat lodges since time immemorial, as Elder Pnnal Bernard Jerome (Micmacs of Gesgapegiag) explains. These perforated lava rocks are considered sacred in Micmac culture, because they come from the belly of Mother Earth, and release that spirit to the People in the process of conducting a sweat lodge (LC 4.27).

The geological processes responsible for the formation of mountains give rise to several types of carving stones that have long been valued by Indigenous Peoples. Rocks that are easy to carve, durable, and heat resistant are invaluable for use in cooking, heating, and for use as lamps. Such carving stones have also long been used in carvings as a means of recording and passing along Indigenous knowledges, particularly among the Inuit (Beauregard et al., 2012; Rathwell & Armitage, 2016). The most common carving stones are serpentinite and soapstone (talc schist) that most formed through the metamorphism of ultramafic rocks (peridotite) and, more rarely, dolomite. Most elaborate carvings are restricted to soapstone (>80% talc). Small carving stone quarries are found throughout the Arctic Cordillera with notable, high-quality carving stone quarries in Markham Bay (southern Baffin Island) and Qikiqtarjuaq (east coast southern Baffin). Industrial soapstone and serpentinite quarries are present in the Appalachian mountains of Quebec. Haida argillite is a black carving stone unique to the west coast and to the Haida Nation. Quarried on Haida Gwaii, it consists of weakly metamorphosed dark grey to black shale and is attributable to the tectonic process that gave rise to the Cordilleran mountain systems. Like soapstone and serpentinite, Haida argillite carvings

Megan Dicker, Inuit, Nunatsiavut, 2022, LC 4.28

record cultural knowledge as well as being used to depict family crests (Barbeau, 1957).

Stones like chert have also provided important material contributions to First Nations, Métis, and Inuit Peoples for use in making tools and as trade items. Learning Circle participant Megan Dicker, Inuit, Nunatsiavut, explained that the Torngat mountains of Northern Labrador are the source of Ramah Chert, a stone highly valued by flintknappers which was used locally to make arrowheads and other implements and also traded around the world as an important component of both ancient and modern economies (LC 4.28).

4.8.4 *Metallic mineral deposits*

Metallic minerals (those that contain and can be processed to provide one or more metals, excluding the iron-containing metals and alloys), are common within mountain regions in Canada and include both base metals—Copper (Cu), Lead (Pb), Tin-Tungsten (Sn-W), and Zinc (Zn)—and precious metals—Gold (Au) and Silver (Ag). Metalliferous deposits characterise: continental margins, forming during rifting and ocean formation; oceanic crust, most commonly forming adjacent to the spreading ridges along which oceanic lithosphere is formed; volcanic arcs, where they result from the interaction of igneous intrusions and explosive volcanoes with groundwater; and active collisional orogens, where they are products of crustal metamorphism and deformation.

Both the Cordilleran mountain regions of western Canada and the Atlantic Maritime and Boreal Shield region orogens developed on pre-existing rifted continental margins, characterised by rift and passive margin-related Sedimentary Exhalitive (SedEx) mineral deposits (Goodfellow & Lyndon, 2007). Examples of these large volume,

sedimentary-hosted, Pb-Zn-Ag deposits include the 1.4 Ga Sullivan deposit of southeastern British Columbia, the Paleozoic Faro deposit of Yukon, and Mississippian-age 'Windsor' deposits in Nova Scotia.

Slivers of oceanic lithosphere are commonly trapped and preserved within orogenic belts during ocean closure. The most common oceanic mineral deposits found within these oceanic slivers are volcanogenic massive sulphide (VMS) deposits. We now recognize that such Cu, Zn, (minor Pb), Ag, and Au-rich VMS deposits, which originate at oceanic spreading ridges as 'Black Smokers', are present along the length of the Cordilleran mountain regions of western Canada and the Atlantic Maritime and Boreal Shield region orogens, but the Bathurst deposit of New Brunswick (van Staal et al., 2003) is by far the largest and most economically important such deposit.

The most economically important 'volcanic arc deposits' are the large volume, low-grade 'Porphyry' deposits that are spatially and genetically associated with granitoid intrusions. These Cu (minor Mo, Au, Ag, Sn-W) deposits characterise the Cordilleran mountain regions of western Canada and the Atlantic Maritime and Boreal Shield region orogens, but they are particularly well-developed in central British Columbia (McMillan et al., 1995). Only 20% of known Canadian deposits have been mined, in part because of the socio-economic and environmental costs associated with such deposits: they require large, open-pit mines and result in significant piles of acidic tailings that require long-term management.

Lode gold deposits occur in both volcanic arcs and collisional orogens. Deposits include orogenic shear zone and fault-hosted, intrusion-related and epithermal volcano-hosted deposits (Nelson & Colpron, 2007). 80% of Canada's gold production comes from the Canadian Shield, but important deposits characterise both the Atlantic Maritime and Boreal Shield orogen and Cordilleran mountain regions of western Canada. Epithermal deposits are largely restricted to the younger and less deeply eroded western Cordilleran mountain regions. Given the history of exploitation during the gold rush era, and its connection to settlement and dispossession of Indigenous Peoples, deposits of gold and other valuable minerals known to Indigenous communities may be closely guarded

Daniel Sims, Tsay Keh Dene First Nation, 2022, LC 4.29

secrets. Daniel Sims, Tsay Keh Dene First Nation, shared (without disclosing detail or locations) that his community holds knowledge of such deposits within the mountains of their Traditional Territory, and maintains unspoken agreements to prevent this knowledge from ending up in the hands of entities who might seek to extract profit. In this tradition, the offering expected for extracting gold is not tobacco (commonly offered to reciprocate gifts of harvest), but blood (LC 4.29).

4.8.5 *Fossil fuels deposits*

Energy (fossil fuel) deposits, including oil, natural gas, and sedimentary coal deposits, are commonly found in mountain regions and originate from the same geological processes responsible for mountain formation. More than 80% of Canadian coal is associated with the Cordilleran mountain regions of western Canada and the southeastern portion of the Atlantic Maritime and Boreal Shield mountain region. Thickening of the crust during collisional orogenesis results in the development of fringing 'foreland' basins. Slow subsidence of these swampy basins provides an ideal setting for the burial, preservation, and thermal maturation of organic material, giving rise to thick and continuous coal seams. Numerous mountain communities in western Canada had their origins in coal mining, including Canmore, Grand Cache, Beaver Mines, many communities in the East Kootenays of British Columbia, and the ghost town of Bankhead, outside of Banff.

Coal deposits along the margins of orogenic belts are typically less thermally mature and are mined primarily for electricity production, accounting for 47% of Canada's coal production. Coal deposits located closer to the interior of an orogen are typically more thermally mature

'metallurgical' coal used in the production of steel and account for 53% of production. Thermal coal used in Canadian energy production decreased ~50% between 2008 and 2018 and is to be phased out entirely by 2030. 95% of Canada's metallurgical coal is exported.

The burial, heating, and thermal maturation of organic-rich marine shales during ocean closure and collisional orogenesis liberates liquid and gaseous hydrocarbons. The elevated topography of mountainous orogens results in a hydrostatic head that promotes fluid flow, entraining hydrocarbons and driving them out toward the fringing foreland basins where they collect in structural and stratigraphic traps. Hence, the large amounts of oil and natural gas found in northern Alberta and northeastern BC are direct products of the growth of the Cordilleran orogen, including the enormous oil sand deposits of northeastern Alberta.

4.8.6 *Renewable energy*

There are also established and emerging renewable energy development opportunities in mountain regions in Canada; gifts of hydropower, wind, solar, and geothermal energy as well as other renewables (e.g. wood pellets) (Jessop et al., 1991; Majorowicz & Grasby, 2021). Renewables have been highlighted as essential alternatives to fossil fuels and represent an opportunity for communities, particularly those in western Canada, to reduce their carbon footprint.

Hydroelectric power has long been associated with mountain areas in Canada, and remains the most significant source of renewable energy provided by mountains. This gift is particularly important in the provinces of British Columbia and Quebec, where hydroelectricity is the dominant source of energy in the electricity grids. Alberta also generates significant hydroelectricity, but it makes up less than 10% of the provincial electricity supply. However hydropower developments are associated with habitat destruction (Barbarossa et al., 2020; Reid et al., 2019) and the alteration or loss of mountain homelands (Randell, 2022). Emissions of methane, a potent greenhouse gas, can also result from the decomposition of organic materials retained in reservoirs (Deemer et al., 2016; St. Louis et al., 2000). The distribution of existing hydropower infrastructure across Canada can be examined using the Canadian Hydropower Interactive Map.

Wind energy is also produced in the vicinity of mountainous areas in Canada, particularly in areas that funnel prevailing or katabatic winds. At present, the most significant mountain-related wind development is found along the southeastern edge of the Montane Cordillera region, east of Crowsnest Pass, see the Canadian Wind Turbine Interactive Map. Solar potential in mountain areas is thought to be less important than adjacent lowlands, and accordingly mountain areas in Canada currently see little in the way of large-scale solar installations. Likewise, while mountain geology can produce geothermal hotspots (e.g., Sulphur Mountain in Banff National Park), the production of geothermal energy in mountain areas is currently limited due to the distributed nature of the resource and difficulties associated with extraction (B. Hayes, personal communication, 24 October 2022).

Notwithstanding extensive hydroelectricity generation, the relatively paucity of clean energy projects in mountain areas could change significantly in the years ahead, as the clean energy transition unfolds (Canadian Energy Regulator, 2021). Communities such as Squamish, BC, are illustrative of the kinds of clean energy trends that could be seen in other mountain communities in the years ahead, including a growing focus on clean energy generation as well as the scaling of carbon capture and storage and other mitigation technologies.

Renewables are essential for addressing the climate crisis and are largely supported by the public in Canada (Donald et al., 2022). However, some communities and landowners continue to have reservations about clean energy development, with aesthetic concerns, political views, and employment in the non-renewable energy sector influencing opposition (Sherren et al., 2019). As well, biodiversity conservation advocates and Indigenous Peoples have in some cases protested the development of hydroelectric dams, due to their proximate impacts on the wellbeing of mountain communities and ecosystems and the flooding of traditional lands (Bakker & Hendriks 2019). Such tensions and tradeoffs warrant further research in mountains in Canada.

4.9 Conclusions

This chapter offers examples of the gifts and benefits provided by mountains to individual and community users. The examples in this chapter remind us that we know a great deal about the health benefits that come from spending time in the mountains. For Indigenous Peoples, the ongoing connections to Lands and the food, medicines, and waters are numerous, profound, and complex. We also understand that people who recreate in the mountains gain health benefits from doing so. We know much about different approaches to teaching in the mountains. Some teachings and pedagogical practices are embedded in the principles of land-based education; other approaches, including field schools, encourage the study of the sciences and the arts situated in place. We also have a good understanding of the ways in which colonial practices have alienated Indigenous Peoples from their Lands. There is, likewise, a direct relationship between the colonial practices of alienation from Lands and the extractive processes that are used to derive commercial benefits from the energy and material resources of the mountains.

Mountain environments also contain features that help in ecosystem restoration. Some of these features, like wetlands and forests, help all of us by storing carbon and slowing climate change. Other features help mountain environments overcome the damage created by human activities. These are the natural regenerative actions that come with the passage of time.

In this chapter, we also looked at both the regenerative power of mountain environments and their resilience in the face of the rapid pace of human action. We observed further that mountains offer the gift of sanctuary for many Indigenous Peoples. In the Sahtú region of present-day Northwest Territories (Taiga Cordillera region), for example, Saoyú-ʔehdacho has long been considered a place of refuge with material as well as spiritual value. It was designated a national historic site of Canada in 1997. "Its cultural values, expressed through the interrelationship between the landscape, oral histories, graves and cultural resources, such as trails and cabins, help to explain and contribute to an understanding of the origin, spiritual values, lifestyle, and land-use

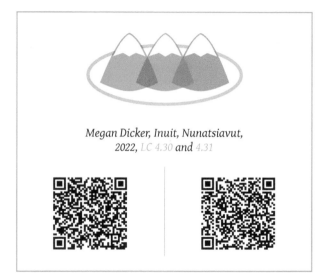

Megan Dicker, Inuit, Nunatsiavut, 2022, LC 4.30 *and* 4.31

of the Sahtu Dene" (Parks Canada, 2019). Megan Dicker, Inuit, Nunatsiavut, shared a story during the CMA Learning Circle about the role of mountains as places of sanctuary, providing protection and safe harbour (LC 4.30).

This chapter has also raised important questions of equity, reciprocity, and sustainability. As illustrated, the ways in which people manage and value the gifts of the mountains differ considerably, from forms of engagement grounded in reciprocity and sustainable use to highly unsustainable levels of extraction for short-term gain. Certainly, then, their use can engender tensions and tradeoffs among different values, systems, and groups. For example, access to mountain spaces for snowmobiling may exclude Indigenous hunters, while the sacredness of a mountain meadow may discourage or prevent ski touring. In thinking about gifts, it is therefore critical to consider circumstances where the benefits accrued by one group result in costs or the exclusion of others. Such considerations are also important when thinking about the distributional effects of increasing pressures on mountains, the focus of the next chapter.

Despite what we have learned through this chapter, there are notable gaps in our assessment efforts (Table 4.2). More work is needed to clarify what is known about these and other topics relevant to our understanding of gifts of the mountains.

We conclude this chapter where it began—by calling attention to the importance of reciprocal relations with mountainous places. Ultimately, as summarised by Learning Circle participant Megan Dicker, Inuit, Nunatsiavut, if you take care of the mountains, they will do the same for you (LC 4.31).

Table 4.2: Examples of topics not thoroughly assessed in this chapter

Renewable Energy, including geothermal energy
Last chance tourism and the intersections of environmental change and recreation
Equity issues with recreation in mountain spaces, including access issues
Gifts of mountain freshwater ecosystems
Parks and protected areas

Glossary

Benefit: A benefit is understood as something given or provided by a mountain environment where the receiver is not necessarily obligated to return the gift. In other words, a benefit is received or taken for the use or advantage of the person who receives it. A benefit might be the wood extracted from a forest by logging or the ore miners dig out of a mine. In this chapter, the idea of gifts is complemented by the idea of benefits.

Community forestry: The term community forestry refers to a model of forest management in which decisions about a given forest area are led and implemented by local communities, at local scales. While approaches vary among communities, typically, community forests are managed to support a range of benefits, including but not limited to the provision of timber and non-timber forest products, including: medicinal plants; recreational, spiritual, and/or aesthetic values; and protection of habitat for wildlife.

Gift: A gift is understood as something given or provided within a reciprocal relationship. A gift might be food in the form of a hunted animal, received in exchange for respect shown to the animal and the place in which it is harvested. In this chapter, the idea of benefits is complemented by the idea of gifts.

Hydrosocial: Hydrosocial relationships refer to the complex relationships between humans and water that go beyond understanding water as simply a material substance or H_2O. The hydrosocial cycle emphasises water's different physical forms and cultural meanings and the processes through which water and society are co-produced. Linton and Budds describe the hydrosocial cycle, as "the process by which alterations or manipulation of water flows and quality affect social relations and structure, which, in turn, affect further alteration of water" (Linton & Budds, 2014, p. 175).

Non-timber forest products (NTFP): Non-timber forest products (NTFPs) are the diverse biological goods beyond timber which derive from forest ecosystems. These include medicinal plants and wild foods (plant, animal, and fungi); grasses, shrubs, barks, and other fibres used for building and materials; and more. NTFPs may be cultivated directly by humans (e.g., maple plantations), harvested in wild forest ecosystems without deliberate intervention, or stewarded and encouraged by practices such as cultural burning that support healthy populations of valued species.

Water Governance: Water governance is the set of regulatory processes, mechanisms, and institutions through which political actors influence environmental decisions, actions, and outcomes (Bakker, 2003).

References

Adams, M. S., Connors, B., Levi, T., Shaw, D., Walkus, J., Rogers, S., & Darimont, C. (2021). Local Values and Data Empower Culturally Guided Ecosystem-Based Fisheries Management of the Wuikinuxv Bear-Salmon-Human System. *Marine and Coastal Fisheries, 13*(4), 362–378.

Adler, C., Wester, P., Bhatt, I., Huggel, C., Insarov, G., Morecroft, M., Muccione, V., Prakash, A., Alcántara-Ayala, I., Allen, S., Bader, M., Bigler, S., Camac, J., Chakraborty, R., Sanchez, A., Cuvi, N., Drenkhan, F., Hussain, A., Maharjan, A., & Werners, S. (2022). IPCC WGII Sixth Assessment Report Cross-Chapter Paper 5: Mountains. In H.-O. Pörtner, D. C. Roberts, M. Tignor, E. Poloczanska, K. Mintenbeck, A. Alegría, M. Craig, S. Langsdorf, V. Löschke, A. Möller, A. Okem, & B. Rama (Eds.), *Climate Change 2022: Impacts, Adaptation and Vulnerability. Contribution of Working Group II to the Sixth Assessment Report of the Intergovernmental Panel on Climate Change* (pp. 2273–2318). Cambridge University Press. doi:10.1017/9781009325844.022

Ahenakew, C. (2016). Grafting Indigenous Ways of Knowing Onto Non-Indigenous Ways of Being: The (Underestimated) Challenges of a Decolonial Imagination. *International Review of Qualitative Research, 9*(3), 323–340. https://doi.org/10.1525/irqr.2016.9.3.323

Aitken, Emily [Gwixsisalas]. (2016). Seasonal Wheel: The Kwakwaka'Wakw Ebb and Flow of Life. In G. Snively & W. L. Williams (Eds.), *Knowing Home: Braiding Indigenous Science with Western Science* (pp. 165–170). University of Victoria Press. https://ecampusontario.pressbooks.pub/knowinghome/chapter/chapter-10/

Alberta Government. (2012). *Tourism Works for Alberta: The Economic Impact of Tourism in Alberta 2012.* Tourism Research and Innovation Branch, Alberta Tourism, Parks and Recreation. https://open.alberta.ca/dataset/0f815981-c329-4133-b651-3fef3cb18a0c/resource/3047a7d9-de8a-4e60-b18d-439fb6576796/download/2012-economic-impact-tourism-alberta-2012.pdf

Altmeyer, G. (1976). Three ideas of nature in Canada, 1893–1914. *Journal of Canadian Studies, 11*(3), 21–36.

Anderson, B. (2007). Staging Antimodernism in the Age of High Capitalist Nationalism. In J. O'Brian & P. White (Eds.), *Beyond Wilderness: The Group of Seven, Canadian Identity, and Contemporary Art* (pp. 245–246). McGill-Queen's University Press.

Anderson, S., & Radic, V. (2020). Identification of local water resource vulnerability to rapid deglaciation in Alberta. *Nature Climate Change 10*, 933–938. https://doi.org/10.1038/s41558-020-0863-4

Andre, A., & Fehr, A. (2001). *Gwich'in Ethnobotany: Plants Used by the Gwich'in for Food, Medicine, Shelter and Tools.* Gwich'in Social and Cultural Institute and Aurora Research Institute.

Andrews, T. D., Mackay, G., Andrew, L., Stephenson, W., Barker, A., Alix, C., & Tulita, S. E. (2012). Alpine Ice Patches and Shuhtagot'Ine Land Use in the Mackenzie and Selwyn Mountains, Northwest Territories, Canada. *Arctic, 65*(5), 22–42. https://doi.org/10.14430/arctic4183

Armstrong, C. G., Dixon, W. M., & Turner, N. J. (2018). Management and traditional production of beaked hazelnut (k'áp'xw-az', Corylus cornuta; Betulaceae). *Human Ecology, 46*, 547–559. https://doi.org/10.1007/s10745-018-0015-x

Armstrong, C. G., Earnshaw, J., & McAlvay, A. C. (2022). Coupled archaeological and ecological analyses reveal ancient cultivation and land-use in Nuchatlaht (Nuu-chah-nulth) territories in the Pacific Northwest. *Journal of Archaeological Science, 143*(105611). https://doi.org/10.1016/j.jas.2022.105611

Armstrong, J., & William, G. (Eds.). (2015). *River of Salmon Peoples.* Theytus Books.

Arsenault, R., Diver, S., McGregor, D., Witham, A., & Bourassa, C. (2018). Shifting the Framework of Canadian Water Governance through Indigenous Research Methods: Acknowledging the Past with an Eye on the Future. *Water, 10*(1), 49. https://doi.org/10.3390/w10010049

Asch, Michael. 2014. *On Being Here to Stay: Treaties and Aboriginal Rights in Canada*. Toronto: University of Toronto Press.

Atlas, W., Ban, N. C., Moore, J. W., Tuohy, A., Greening, S., Reid, A. J., Morven, N., White, E., Housty, W. G., Housty, J. A., Service, C. N., Greba, L., Harrison, S., Sharpe, C., Butts, K. I. R., Shepert, W. M., Sweeney-Bergen, E., Macintyre, D., Sloat, M. R., & Connors, K. (2021). Indigenous Systems of Management for Culturally and Ecologically Resilient Pacific Salmon (Oncorhynchus spp.) Fisheries. *Bioscience*, 71(2), 186–204.

Awume O, Patrick R, Baijius W. (2020) Indigenous Perspectives on Water Security in Saskatchewan, Canada. Water; 12(3):810. https://doi.org/10.3390/w12030810

Bai, J., Cui, B., Cao, H., Li, A., & Zhang, B. (2013). Wetland Degradation and Ecological Restoration. *The Scientific World Journal*, 2013, e523632. https://doi.org/10.1155/2013/523632

Baird, M. F. (2013). 'The breath of the mountain is my heart': indigenous cultural landscapes and the politics of heritage. *International Journal of Heritage Studies*, 19(4), 327–340.

Bakker, K. (2003). *Good governance in restructuring water supply: A handbook*. Federation of Canadian Municipalities. http://www.ww7b.org/userfile/file/good_governance_WaterSupply.pdf

Bakker, K. (2011). *Eau Canada: The Future of Canada's Water*. UBC Press.

Bakker K, Hendriks R. Contested Knowledges in Hydroelectric Project Assessment: The Case of Canada's Site C Project. *Water*. 2019; 11(3):406. https://doi.org/10.3390/w11030406

Barbarossa, V., Schmitt, R. J. P., Huijbregts, M. A. J., Zarfl, C., King, H., & Schipper, A. M. (2020). Impacts of current and future large dams on the geographic range connectivity of freshwater fish worldwide. *Proceedings of the National Academy of Sciences*, 117(7), 3648–3655. https://doi.org/10.1073/pnas.1912776117

Barbeau, M. (1957). *Haida Carvers in Argillite*. National Museum of Canada, Bulletin No. 139.

Barnett, T. P., Adam, J. C., & Lettenmaier, D. P. (2005). Potential impacts of a warming climate on water availability in snow-dominated regions. *Nature*, 438(7066), 303–309. https://doi.org/10.1038/nature04141

Battiste, M. (2000). Maintaining Aboriginal identity, language, and culture in modern society. In M. Battiste (Ed.), *Reclaiming Indigenous voice and vision* (pp. 192–208). UBC Press.

Battiste, M. (2002). *Indigenous knowledge and pedagogy in First Nations education: A literature review with recommendations*. National Working Group on Education and the Minister of Indian Affairs, Indian and Northern Affairs Canada (INAC). http://www.afn.ca/uploads/files/education/24._2002_oct_marie_battiste_indigenousknowledgeandpedagogy_lit_review_for_min_working_group.pdf

Battiste, M., & Youngblood Henderson, J. (Sa'ke'j). (2009). Naturalizing Indigenous Knowledge in Eurocentric Education. *Canadian Journal of Native Education*, 32(1), 5–18. https://doi.org/10.14288/CJNE.V32I1.196482

Bautista, L. (2020). *2019 Economic State of British Columbia's Forest Sector* (pp. 1–25). Ministry of Forests, Lands, Natural Resource Operations and Rural Development.

BC Hydro. (n.d.). *Columbia Region*. https://www.bchydro.com/energy-in-bc/operations/our-facilities/columbia.html

BCCFA. (2022). *Community Forest Indicators 2022: Measuring the Benefits of Community Forestry*. British Columbia Community Forest Association. https://bccfa.ca/wp-content/uploads/2022/10/BCCFA-Indicators-2022-final-web-1.pdf

Beauregard, M., Ell, J., Pikor, R., & Ham, L. (2012). Nunavut carving stone deposit evaluation program (2010–2013): Third year results. *Summary of Activities*, 151–162.

Benson, K., & Department of Cultural Heritage, Gwich'in Tribal Council. (2019). *Gwich'in Knowledge of Porcupine caribou: State of Current Knowledge and Gaps Assessment*. Department of Cultural Heritage, Gwich'in Tribal Council. https://thelastgreatherd.com/wp-content/uploads/2020/06/GTC-current-knowledge-and-gaps-assessment.pdf

Berkes, F., & Turner, N. J. (2006). Knowledge, learning and the evolution of conservation practice for social-ecological system resilience. *Human Ecology*, 34(4), 479–494.

Binnema, T., & Niemi, M. (2006). Let the Line Be Drawn Now': Wilderness, Conservation, and the Exclusion of Aboriginal People from Banff National Park in Canada. *Environmental History*, 11(4), 724–750. https://doi.org/10.1093/envhis/11.4.724

Bodaly, R. A., Hecky, R. E., & Fudge, R. J. P. (1984). Increases in Fish Mercury Levels in Lakes Flooded by the Churchill River Diversion, Northern Manitoba. *Canadian Journal of Fisheries and Aquatic Sciences*, 41(4), 682–691. https://doi.org/10.1139/f84-079

Bordo, J. (2007). Jack Pine: Wilderness Sublime or the Erasure of the Aboriginal Presence from the Landscape. In J. O'Brian & P. White (Eds.), *Beyond Wilderness: The Group of Seven, Canadian Identity, and Contemporary Art* (pp. 331–334). McGill-Queen's University Press.

Borrows, J. (2015). The durability of terra nullius: Tsilhqot'in nation v. British columbia. *UBCL Rev.*, 48, 701.

Bouthillier, L., Chiasson, G., & Beaulieu, H. (2022). The difficult art of carving space(s) for community forestry in the Quebec regime. In J. Bulkan, J. Palmer, A.M. Larson, & M. Hobley (Eds.), *Routledge Handbook of Community Forestry*. (1st ed.). Routledge. https://doi.org/10.4324/9780367488710

Bratton, R. D., Kinnear, G., & Koroluk, G. (1979). Why Man Climbs Mountains. *International Review for the Sociology of Sport*, 14(2), 23–36. https://doi.org/10.1177/101269027901400202

Brett, R., & Klinka, K. (1998). A Transition from Gap to Tree-Island Regeneration Patterns in the Subalpine Forest of South-Coastal British Columbia. *Canadian Journal of Forest Research-Revue Canadienne De Recherche Forestière, 28*(12), 1825–1831. https://doi.org/10.1139/cjfr-28-12-1825

Brightman, R. (1993). *Grateful Prey: Rock Cree Human-Animal Relationships.* University of California Press.

Brody, H. (1981). *Maps and dreams: Indians and the British Columbia frontier.* Waveland PressInc.

Bulkan, J., Palmer, J., Larson, A. M., & Hobley, M. (2022). Old World and New World collision. In J. Bulkan, J. Palmer, A. M. Larson, & M. Hobley, *Routledge Handbook of Community Forestry* (1st ed., pp. 141–145). Routledge. https://doi.org/10.4324/9780367488710-12

Canadian Energy Regulator. (2021). *Canada's Energy Future 2021.* Government of Canada.

Chan, J. (2008). Who Built the Canadian Pacific Railway? Chinese Workers from Hoisan. *Canadian Folk Music Bulletin, 42*(1), 14–21.

Chimner, R. A., & Cooper, D. J. (2003). *Carbon dynamics of pristine and hydrologically modified fens in the southern Rocky Mountains, 81*(5), 477–491. https://doi.org/10.1139/B03-043

Church, M. (2010). The trajectory of geomorphology. *Progress in Physical Geography: Earth and Environment, 34*(3), 265–286. https://doi.org/10.1177/0309133310363992

Clark, D., Artelle, K., Darimont, C., Housty, W., Tallio, C., Neasloss, D., Schmidt, A., Wiget, A., & Turner, N. (2021). Grizzly and polar bears as nonconsumptive cultural keystone species. *FACETS, 6*(1), 379–393. https://doi.org/10.1139/facets-2020-0089

Cole, D. (2007). Artists, Patrons, and Public: An Enquiry into the Success of the Group of Seven. In J. O'Brian & P. White (Eds.), *Beyond Wilderness: The Group of Seven, Canadian Identity, and Contemporary Art* (pp. 129–133). McGill-Queen's University Press.

Colpitts, G., & Devine, H. (2017). Introduction: Migration and Transformation in the Canadian West. In G. Colpitts & H. Devine (Eds.), *Finding Directions West: Readings that Locate and Dislocate Western Canada's Past* (1st ed., pp. 1–18). University of Calgary Press. https://doi.org/10.2307/j.ctv64h781

Colton, J. W. (2005). Indigenous tourism development in northern Canada: Beyond economic incentives. *The Canadian Journal of Native Studies, 25*(1), 185–206.

Cooper, D. J., Chimner, R. A., & Merritt, D. M. (2012). Western Mountain Wetlands. In *Wetland Habitats of North America* (pp. 313–328). University of California Press. https://doi.org/10.1525/9780520951419-024

COSEWIC. (2013). *COSEWIC Assessment and Status Report on the Eulachon, Nass/Skeena population, Thaleichthys pacificus in Canada* (pp. xi + 18 pp.). https://wildlife-species.canada.ca/species-risk-registry/virtual_sara/files/cosewic/sr_eulakane_eulachon_nass-skeena_1213_e.pdf

Coté, C. (2016). "Indigenizing" Food Sovereignty. Revitalizing Indigenous Food Practices and Ecological Knowledges in Canada and the United States. *Humanities, 5*(57). https://doi.org/10.3390/h5030057

Coulthard, G. S. (2014). *Red Skin, White Masks: Rejecting the Colonial Politics of Recognition.* University of Minnesota Press.

Craft, A. (2017). Giving and receiving life from Anishinaabe nibi inaakonigewin (our water law) research. In J. Thorpe, S. Rutherford, & L. A. Sandberg (Eds.), *Methodological Challenges in Nature-Culture and Environmental History Research* (pp. 105–119). Routledge.

Cronin, J. K. (2006). The Bears Are Plentiful and Frequently Good Camera Subjects: Postcards and the Framing of Interspecies Encounters in the Canadian Rockies. *Mosaic—A Journal for the Interdisciplinary Study of Literature, 39*(4), 77–92.

Cross, M. P. (1996). *Bighorn sheep and the Salish world view: A cultural approach to the landscape.* [Master's thesis, University of Montana]. ProQuest Dissertations Publishing.

Cruikshank, J. (2005). *Do Glaciers Listen?: Local Knowledge, Colonial Encounters, and Social Imagination.* UBC Press.

Cuerrier, A., Clark, C., & Norton, C. H. (2019). Inuit plant use in the eastern Subarctic: Comparative ethnobotany in Kangiqsualujjuaq, Nunavik, and in Nain, Nunatsiavut. *Botany, 97,* 272–282. https://doi.org/dx.doi.org/10.1139/cjb-2018-0195

Cuerrier, A., Turner, N. J., Gomes, T. C., Garibaldi, A., & Downing, A. (2015). Cultural keystone places: conservation and restoration in cultural landscapes. *Journal of Ethnobiology, 35*(3), 427–448.

Curran-Sills, G. M., & Karahalios, A. (2015). Epidemiological Trends in Search and Rescue Incidents Documented by the Alpine Club of Canada from 1970 to 2005. *Wilderness & Environmental Medicine, 26*(4), 536–543. https://doi.org/10.1016/j.wem.2015.07.001

Daigle, M. (2019). The spectacle of reconciliation: On (the) unsettling responsibilities to Indigenous peoples in the academy. *Society and Space, 37*(4), 703–721. https://doi.org/10.1177/0263775818824342

Deemer, B. R., Harrison, J. A., Li, S., Beaulieu, J. J., DelSontro, T., Barros, N., Bezerra-Neto, J. F., Powers, S. M., dos Santos, M. A., & Vonk, J. A. (2016). Greenhouse Gas Emissions from Reservoir Water Surfaces: A New Global Synthesis. *BioScience, 66*(11), 949–964. https://doi.org/10.1093/biosci/biw117

Demuth, M. N., & Pietroniro, A. (2003). The impact of climate change on the glaciers of the Canadian Rocky Mountain eastern slopes and implications for water resource-related adaptation in the Canadian prairies "Phase I "—Headwaters of the North Saskatchewan River Basin. *Holocene, 4322,* 96.

Díaz-Reviriego, I., González-Segura, L., Fernández-Llamazares, Á., Howard, P. L., Molina, J. L., & Reyes-García, V. (2016). Social organization influences the exchange and species richness of medicinal plants in Amazonian homegardens. *Ecology and Society, 21*(1).

Donald, J., Axsen, J., Shaw, K., & Robertson, B. (2022). Sun, wind or water? Public support for large-scale renewable energy development in Canada. *Journal of Environmental Policy & Planning, 24*(2), 175–193, DOI: 10.1080/1523908X.2021.2000375

Doyle-Yamaguchi, E., & Smith, T. (2022). Following the Líl̓wat pathway towards reciprocal and relational forest research in Líl̓wat Indigenous Territory, British Columbia, Canada. In J. Bulkan, J. Palmer, A. M. Larson, & M. Hobley (Eds.), *Routledge Handbook of Community Forestry*. Routledge.

Draper, D. (2000). Toward Sustainable Mountain Communities: Balancing Tourism Development and Environmental Protection in Banff and Banff National Park, Canada. *AMBIO: A Journal of the Human Environment, 29*(7), 408–415. https://doi.org/10.1579/0044-7447-29.7.408

Duinker, P., & MacLellan, L. (2017). The local trap and community forest policy in Nova Scotia: Pitfalls and promise. In R. Bullock, G. Broad, & L. Palmer (Eds.), *Growing Community Forests*. University of Manitoba Press.

Earnshaw, J. T. K. (2016). *Cultural forests of the Southern Nuu-chah-nulth: Historical ecology and salvage archaeology on Vancouver Island's West Coast* [Master's thesis, University of Victoria]. https://dspace.library.uvic.ca/handle/1828/7291

Egeland, G. M., Charbonneau-Roberts, G., Kuluguqtuq, J., Kilabuk, J., Okalik, L., Soueida, R., & Kuhnlein, H. V. (2009). Back to the future: Using traditional food and knowledge to promote a healthy future among Inuit. *Indigenous Peoples' Food Systems*, 9–22.

Ehlers, T., & Hobby, T. (2010). The chanterelle mushroom harvest on northern Vancouver Island, British Columbia: Factors relating to successful commercial development. *BC Journal of Ecosystems and Management, 11*(1 & 2), 72–83.

Elmeligi, S., Nevin, O. T., Taylor, J., & Convery, I. (2021). Visitor attitudes and expectations of grizzly bear management in the Canadian Rocky Mountain National Parks. *Journal of Outdoor Recreation and Tourism, 36*(100444), nan. https://doi.org/10.1016/j.jort.2021.100444

Fast, T. (2014). Stapled to the front door: Neoliberal extractivism in Canada. *Studies in Political Economy, 94*(1), 31–60.

Films, B. (2015). Jumbo Wild. *Documentary Film. Patagonia, Sweetgrass Productions.* http://www.bullfrogfilms.com/catalog/jwild.html

FLNRORD. (2019). *FLNRORD Research Program Annual Report: Fiscal Year 2019/20* (p. 32). British Columbia Ministry of Forests, Lands, Natural Resource Operations and Rural Development. https://www2.gov.bc.ca/assets/gov/environment/research-monitoring-and-reporting/research/research-program/flnrod_research_group_annual_report_2019-2020.pdf

Fortier, J., Truax, B., Gagnon, D., & Lambert, F. (2013). Root biomass and soil carbon distribution in hybrid poplar riparian buffers, herbaceous riparian buffers and natural riparian woodlots on farmland. *SpringerPlus, 2*(1), 539. https://doi.org/10.1186/2193-1801-2-539

Francis, D. (1992). *The Imaginary Indian: The Image of the Indian in Canadian Culture*. Arsenal Pulp Press.

Frizzell, S. (2016, May 25). *Creative Voices: 1991—Rebecca Belmore Gave the Voiceless a Megaphone*. Banff Centre for Arts and Creativity. https://www.banffcentre.ca/articles/creative-voices-1991-rebecca-belmore-gave-voiceless-megaphone

Gardner, J. S., & Jones, N. K. (1985). Evidence for a Neoglacial Advance of the Boundary Glacier, Banff National Park, Alberta. *Canadian Journal of Earth Sciences, 22*(11), 1753–1755. https://doi.org/10.1139/e85-185

Gastaldo, D., Andrews, G. J., & Khanlou, N. (2004). Therapeutic landscapes of the mind: Theorizing some intersections between health geography, health promotion and immigration studies. *Critical Public Health, 14*(2), 157–176. https://doi.org/10.1080/09581590410001725409

Gaudreau, L. (1990). Environmental Impacts of Recreation on Natural Areas and Living Resources. *Loisir et Société / Society and Leisure, 13*(2), 297–324. https://doi.org/10.1080/07053436.1990.10715356

Gaudry, A., & Lorenz, D. (2018). Indigenization as inclusion, reconciliation, and decolonization: Navigating the different visions for indigenizing the Canadian Academy. *AlterNative: An International Journal of Indigenous Peoples, 14*(3), 218–227.

Gavin, M. C., McCarter, J., Berkes, F., Mead, A. T. P., Sterling, E. J., Tang, R., & Turner, N. J. (2018). Effective Biodiversity Conservation Requires Dynamic, Pluralistic, Partnership-Based Approaches. *Sustainability, 10*(6), Article 6. https://doi.org/10.3390/su10061846

Gende, S. M., Edwards, R. T., Willson, M. F., & Wipfli, M. S. (2002). Pacific Salmon in Aquatic and Terrestrial Ecosystems: Pacific salmon subsidize freshwater and terrestrial ecosystems through several pathways, which generates unique management and conservation issues but also provides valuable research opportunities. *BioScience, 52*(10), 917–928. https://doi.org/10.1641/0006-3568(2002)052[0917:PSIAAT]2.0.CO;2

Geng, D. (2021). *Managing national park visitor experience and visitor-wildlife coexistence: a case study of Banff National Park* [Doctoral dissertation, University of British Columbia].

Gessner, S., Herbert, T., & Parker, A. (2018). *Recognizing the Diversity of BC's First Nations Languages* (pp. 273–289). First Peoples' Cultural Council. http://www.tandfonline.com/doi/abs/10.1080/09500782.2011.577218

Goodfellow, W., & Lyndon, L. (2007). *GEOSCAN Search Results: Fastlink.* https://geoscan.nrcan.gc.ca/starweb/geoscan/servlet.starweb?path=geoscan/fulle.web&search1=R=328384

Gottesfeld, L. M. J. (1994). Aboriginal burning for vegetation management in northwest British Columbia. *Human Ecology, 22*(2), 171–188. https://doi.org/10.1007/BF02169038

Government of British Columbia. (2022). *Huckleberry harvesting* [Government]. Government of British Columbia. https://www2.gov.bc.ca/gov/content/industry/crown-land-water/crown-land/crown-land-uses/huckleberry-harvesting

Government of British Columbia. (n.d.). *Indigenous education resources | Building Student Success—B.C. Curriculum.* Retrieved January 19, 2023, from https://curriculum.gov.bc.ca/curriculum/indigenous-education-resources#learning-journey

Graham, B. (2015). *Talking Trees-Sustainable Narratives of the Logging and Forestry Industries in Nova Scotia and New Brunswick and their Relationships with Mi'kmaq Peoples* [Honours Thesis, Dalhousie University]. https://dalspace.library.dal.ca/bitstream/handle/10222/56643/Bridget%20Graham-SUST4900Honours.pdf?sequence=1

Graham, L. (2010). Reconciling Collective and Individual Rights: Indigenous Education and International Human Rights Law. *UCLA Journal of International Law and Foreign Affairs 15*(1), 83–109. https://ssrn.com/abstract=1680605

Grover, V., Borsdorf, A., Breuste, J., Tiwari, P., & Frangetto, F. (2015). *Impact of Global Changes on Mountains: Responses and Adaptation.* Responses and Adaptation, CRC Press. https://www.routledge.com/Impact-of-Global-Changes-on-Mountains-Responses-and-Adaptation/Grover-Borsdorf-Breuste-Tiwari-Frangetto/p/book/9780367377908

Gunter, J. (2022). Community forestry in British Columbia, Canada: History, successes, and challenges. In J. Bulkan, J. Palmer, A. M. Larson, & M. Hobley (Eds.), *Routledge Handbook of Community Forestry.* Routledge.

Hamilton, E. (2012). Non-Timber Forest Products in British Columbia: Management Framework and Current Practices. *Journal of Ecosystems and Management, 13*(2).

Haskell, C. A. (2018). From salmon to shad: Shifting sources of marine-derived nutrients in the Columbia River Basin. *Ecology of Freshwater Fish, 27*(1), 310–322. https://doi.org/10.1111/eff.12348

Hassan, M. A., Gottesfeld, A. S., Montgomery, D. R., Tunnicliffe, J. F., Clarke, G. K. C., Wynn, G., Jones-Cox, H., Poirier, R., Macisaac, E., Herunter, H., & Macdonald, S. J. (2008). Salmon-Driven Bed Load Transport and Bed Morphology in Mountain Streams. *Geophysical Research Letters, 35*(4). https://doi.org/10.1029/2007GL032997

Hayes, B. (2022, October 24). [Personal communication].

Hayter, R. (2004). 'Requiem for a "local" champion: Globalization, British Columbia's forest economy and MacMillan Bloedel'". In A. A. Lehtinen, J. Donner-Amnell, & B. Saether (Eds.), *Politics of Forests: Northern Forest-Industrial Regimes in the Age of Globalization.* Routledge.

Hayter, R., & Barnes, T. J. (2012). Neoliberalization and Its Geographic Limits: Comparative Reflections from Forest Peripheries in the Global North. *Economic Geography, 88*(2), 197–221.

Heinle, K. B., Eby, L. A., Muhlfeld, C. C., Steed, A., Jones, L., D'Angelo, V., Whiteley, A. R., & Hebblewhite, M. (2021). Influence of water temperature and biotic interactions on the distribution of westslope cutthroat trout (Oncorhynchus clarkia lewisi) in a population stronghold under climate change. *Canadian Journal of Fisheries and Aquatic Sciences, 78.0*(4), 444–456. https://doi.org/10.1139/cjfas-2020-0099

Héritier, S. (2003). Tourisme et activités récréatives dans les parcs nationaux des montagnes de l'Ouest canadien: Impacts et enjeux spatiaux (Parcs nationaux Banff, Jasper, Yoho, Kootenay, Lacs Waterton, Mount Revelstoke et des Glaciers) / Recreative activities and tourism in Canada's Rockies National parks: spatial issues and impacts (Banff, Jasper, Yoho, Kootenay, Waterton Lakes, Mount Revelstoke and Glacier National Parks). *Annales de Géographie, 112*(629), 23–46.

Hills, M. (2019). *Me'ki'tetmek na Maqmikewminen.* Meagan Musseau. https://meaganmusseau.com/Me-ki-tetmek-na-Maqmikewminen

Historica Canada. (2023). *Indigenous Arts and Stories.* http://www.our-story.ca/

Hobbs, R. J., & Cramer, V. A. (2008). Restoration ecology: interventionist approaches for restoring and maintaining ecosystem function in the face of rapid environmental change. *Annual Review of Environment and Resources, 33*(1), 39–61.

Hocking, M. D., & Reynolds, J. D. (2011). Impacts of Salmon on Riparian Plant Diversity. *Science, 331*(6024), 1609–1612. https://doi.org/10.1126/science.1201079

Hoffman, K. M., Christianson, A. C., Dickson-Hoyle, S., Copes-Gerbitz, K., Nikolakis, W., Diabo, D. A., McLeod, R., Michell, H. J., Mamun, A. A., & Zahara, A. (2022). The right to burn: Barriers and opportunities for Indigenous-led fire stewardship in Canada. *FACETS, 7*(1), 464–481.

Hoover, C., Ostertag, S., Hornby, C., Parker, C., Hansen-Craik, K., Loseto, L., & Pearce, T. (2016). The continued importance of hunting for future Inuit food security. *Solutions, 7*(4), 40–50.

Hopkins, C., & Sandromán, L. (2014). Invented Landscapes. In J. Dees, I. Hofmann, C. Hopkins, & L. Sandromán, *Unsettled Landscapes* (pp. 35–48). SITE Santa Fe.

Ignace, M., & Ignace, C. R. E. (2020). A Place Called Pípsell: An Indigenous Cultural Keystone Place, Mining, and Séwepemc Law. In N. J. Turner (Ed.), *Plants, Peoples, and Places: The Roles of Ethnobotany and Ethnoecology in Indigenous Peoples' Land Rights in Canada and Beyond* (pp. 131–150). McGill-Queen's University Press.

Ignace, M., Ignace, R. E., & Turner, N. J. (2017). Re Secwépemcúlecws-kucw: How We Look(ed) after Our Land. In M. Ignace & R. E. Ignace (Eds.), *Secwépemc*

People, Land, and Laws: Yerḵ7 re Stsq'ey's-kucw (pp. 145–219). McGill-Queen's University Press/Shuswap Nation Tribal Council.

Immerzeel, W. W., Lutz, A. F., Andrade, M., Bahl, A., Biemans, H., Bolch, T., Hyde, S., Brumby, S., Davies, B. J., Elmore, A. C., Emmer, A., Feng, M., Fernández, A., Haritashya, U., Kargel, J. S., Koppes, M., Kraaijenbrink, P. D. A., Kulkarni, A. V., Mayewski, P. A., ... Baillie, J. E. M. (2020). Importance and vulnerability of the world's water towers. *Nature, 577*(7790), 364–369. https://doi.org/10.1038/s41586-019-1822-y

IRIN. (2012, May 8). *Nepal: Mountain dwellers "neglected."* https://www.refworld.org/docid/4fad057d2.html

Irving, E. (1977). Drift of the major continental blocks since the Devonian. *Nature, 270*(5635), Article 5635. https://doi.org/10.1038/270304a0

Isaac, I. 'Welila'ogwa. (2016). Chapter 14—Storytelling is our Textbook and Curriculum Guide. In G. Snively & W.L. Williams (Eds.), *Knowing Home: Braiding Indigenous Science with Western Science, Book 1 G* (pp. 211–232). University of Victoria Press. https://ecampusontario.pressbooks.pub/knowinghome/chapter/chapter-5/

IUCN. (2020). *Canadian Rocky Mountain Parks: 2020 Conservation Outlook Assessment.* IUCN World Heritage Outlook. https://worldheritageoutlook.iucn.org/

Ives, J. D., & Barry, R. G. (Eds.). (1974). *Arctic and Alpine Environments* (1st ed.). https://doi.org/10.4324/9780429330827

Jakubec, S. L., Carruthers Den Hoed, D., Ray, H., & Krishnamurthy, A. (2016). Mental well-being and quality-of-life benefits of inclusion in nature for adults with disabilities and their caregivers. *Landscape Research, 41*(6), 616–627.

Jeanson, A. L., Cooke, S. J., Danylchuk, A. J., & Young, N. (2021). Drivers of pro-environmental behaviours among outdoor recreationists: The case of a recreational fishery in Western Canada. *Journal of Environmental Management, 289.0*(0401664, du5), 112366. https://doi.org/10.1016/j.jenvman.2021.112366

Jessop, A. M., Ghomshei, M. M., & Drury, M. J. (1991). Geothermal Energy in Canada. *Gemics, 20*(44322), 369–385. https://doi.org/10.1016/0375-6505(91)90027-S

Jessup, L. (2002). The Group of Seven and the Tourist Landscape in Western Canada, or the More Things Change .... *Journal of Canadian Studies, 37*(1), 144–179. https://doi.org/10.3138/jcs.37.1.144

Kadykalo, A. N. (2022). *Evaluating evidence-informed decision-making in the management and conservation of British Columbia's fish and wildlife resources* [Doctoral dissertation, Carleton University].

Kamieniecki, S. (2000). Testing Alternative Theories of Agenda Setting: Forest Policy Change in British Columbia, Canada. *Policy Studies Journal, 28*(1), 176–189. https://doi.org/10.1111/j.1541-0072.2000.tb02022.x

Karst, A. L., & Turner, N. J. (2011). Local Ecological Knowledge and Importance of Bakeapple (Rubus chamaemorus L.) in a Southeast Labrador Métis Community. *Ethnobiology Letter, 2*, 6–18.

Kershaw, R. (2008). *Exploring the Castle: Discovering the backbone of the world in southern Alberta.* Rocky Mountain Books Ltd.

Kew, M. (2010). Northwest Coast Indigenous Peoples in Canada. In *The Canadian Encyclopedia.* Historica Canada. Article Published November, 17.

Kuhnlein, H., Erasmus, B., Creed-Kanashiro, H., Englberger, L., Okeke, C., Turner, N., Allen, L., & Bhattacharjee, L. (2006). Indigenous peoples' food systems for health: Finding interventions that work. *Public Health Nutrition, 9*(8), 1013–1019. https://doi.org/10.1017/PHN2006987

Kuhnlein, H. V. (1989). Nutrient values in indigenous wild berries used by the Nuxalk people of Bella Coola, British Columbia. *Journal of Food Composition and Analysis, 2*(1), 28–36.

Kuhnlein, H. V. (2017). Gender roles, food system biodiversity, and food security in Indigenous Peoples' communities. *Maternal & Child Nutrition, 13*, e12529.

Kuhnlein, H. V., & Chan, H. M. (2000). Environment and contaminants in traditional food systems of northern indigenous peoples. *Annual Review of Nutrition, 20*, 595–626.

Kuhnlein, H. V., Receveur, O., Soueida, R., & Egeland, G. M. (2004). Arctic Indigenous Peoples Experience the Nutrition Transition with Changing Dietary Patterns and Obesity. *The Journal of Nutrition, 134*(6), 1447–1453. https://doi.org/10.1093/jn/134.6.1447

Ladle, A., Avgar, T., Wheatley, M., Stenhouse, G. B., Nielsen, S. E., & Boyce, M. S. (2019). Grizzly Bear Response to Spatio-Temporal Variability in Human Recreational Activity. *Journal of Applied Ecology, 56*(2), 375–386. https://doi.org/10.1111/1365-2664.13277

Laidlaw, D. K. (2018). Indigenous water rights & global warming in Alberta. In J. Ellis (Ed.), *Water Rites: Reimagining Water in the West* (pp. 64–83). University of Calgary Press.

Lamb, C., Willson, R., Richter, C., Owens-Beck, N., Napoleon, J., Muir, B., McNay, R. S., Lavis, E., Hebblewhite, M., Giguere, L., Dokkie, T., Boutin, S., & Ford, A. T. (2022). Indigenous-Led Conservation: Pathways to Recovery for the Nearly Extirpated Klinse-Za Mountain Caribou. *Ecological Applications 32*(5). https://doi.org/10.1002/eap.2581

Lambden, J., Receveur, O., Marshall, J., & Kuhnlein, H. (2006). Traditional and market food access in Arctic Canada is affected by economic factors. *International Journal of Circumpolar Health, 65*(4), 331–340. https://doi.org/10.3402/ijch.v65i4.18117

Landrum, R. E., Brakke, K., & McCarthy, M. A. (2019). The pedagogical power of storytelling. *Scholarship of Teaching and Learning in Psychology, 5*(3), 247–253.

Laroque, C. P., & Smith, D. J. (2005). Predicted short-term radial-growth changes of trees based on past climate on Vancouver Island, British Columbia. *Dendrochrono-*

logia, *22*(3), 163–168. https://doi.org/10.1016/j.dendro.2005.04.003

Lawler, J. H., & Bullock, R. C. L. (2017). A Case for Indigenous Community Forestry. *Journal of Forestry, 115*(2), 117–125. https://doi.org/10.5849/jof.16-038

Levi, T., Darimont, C. T., Macduffee, M., Mangel, M., Paquet, P., & Wilmers, C. C. (2012). Using Grizzly Bears to Assess Harvest-Ecosystem Tradeoffs in Salmon Fisheries. *Plos Biol, 10*(4), e1001303. https://doi.org/10.1371/journal.pbio.1001303

Li, J. N. (2000). *Canadian Steel, Chinese Grit.* Paxlink Communications, Inc.

Liddle, M. (1997). *Recreation ecology: the ecological impact of outdoor recreation and ecotourism.* Chapman & Hall Ltd.

Lílwat Nation. (2017). *I Wa7 Cát'nem: Celebration: Lílwat Nation Annual Report 2017* (pp. 1–60). https://lilwat.ca/wp-content/uploads/2015/03/Lilwat-Nation-AR17.pdf

Linnard, A. J. (2015). *Justice on the Rocks: (Re)writing People and Place in Banff National Park.* https://yorkspace.library.yorku.ca/xmlui/handle/10315/34788

Linton, J., & Budds, J. (2014). The hydrosocial cycle: Defining and mobilizing a relational-dialectical approach to water. *Geoforum, 57,* 170–180.

Locke, H. (2006). The spiritual dimension of moving to the mountains. In L. A. G. Moss (Ed.), *The Amenity Migrants: Seeking and Sustaining Mountains and their Cultures* (pp. 26–34). CABI.

Loosen, A., Capdevila, T. V., Pigeon, K., Wright, P., & Jacob, A. L. (2023). Understanding the role of traditional and user-created recreation data in the cumulative footprint of recreation. *Journal of Outdoor Recreation and Tourism,* 100615.

Lord, B. (2007). The Group of Seven: A National Landscape Art. In J. O'Brian & P. White (Eds.), *Beyond Wilderness: The Group of Seven, Canadian Identity, and Contemporary Art* (pp. 115–122). McGill-Queen's University Press.

Louis, S. (2021). Sensory access at sxxnitk: Blockages, fluidities and futures. *Journal of Environmental Media, 2*(1), 9.1–9.16. https://doi.org/10.1386/jem_00057_1

Low, J., & de Kleer, L. (2022). The disregard of First Nations' Concerns: Analyzing the environmental assessment of Jumbo Glacier resor. *Trailsix, 16,* 73–83.

Luig, T. (2015). *Ontological Security, Movement, and Wellbeing: Teetł'it Gwich'in Experiences of Life Transformations.* University of Alberta.

Macdonald, R. J., Boon, S., Byrne, J. M., Robinson, M. D., & Rasmussen, J. B. (2014). Potential Future Climate Effects on Mountain Hydrology, Stream Temperature, and Native Salmonid Life History. *Canadian Journal of Fisheries and Aquatic Sciences, 71*(2), 189–202. https://doi.org/10.1139/cjfas-2013-0221

Mack, T. (Director). (2022). *Video clip, "Trevor Mack" and "Trip to Sacred Mountain" with Tsilhqot'in member, Trevor Mack] In "Towards Legal Recognition for Non-Human Relations, Webinar 2: Supernatural Beings and Sacred Places."* https://allard.ubc.ca/about-us/events-calendar/towards-legal-recognition-non-human-relations-webinar-2-supernatural-beings-and-sacred-places

Maher, P. T., & Lemelin, R. H. (2011). Northern Exposure: Opportunities and Challenges for Tourism Development in Torngat Mountains National Park, Labrador, Canada. *Polar Record, 47*(240), 40–45. https://doi.org/10.1017/S0032247409990581

Majorowicz, J., & Grasby, S. E. (2021). Deep Geothermal Heating Potential for the Communities of the Western Canadian Sedimentary Basin. *Energies, 14*(3), Article 3. https://doi.org/10.3390/en14030706

Marshall, S. J., White, E., Demuth, M. N., Bolch, T., Wheate, R., Menounos, B., Beedle, M. J., & Shea, J. M. (2011). Glacier Water Resources on the Eastern Slopes of the Canadian Rocky Mountains. *Canadian Water Resources Journal, 36*(2), 109–134. https://doi.org/10.4296/cwrj3602823

Martinez, D. (2018). Redefining sustainability through kincentric ecology: Reclaiming Indigenous lands, knowledge, and ethics. In M. Nelson & D. Shilling (Eds.), *Traditional ecological knowledge* (pp. 139–174). Cambridge University Press.

Mason, C. W., Carr, A., Vandermale, E., Snow, B., & Philipp, L. (2022). Rethinking the Role of Indigenous Knowledge in Sustainable Mountain Development and Protected Area Management in Canada and Aotearoa/New Zealand. *Mountain Research and Development, 42*(4), A1-A9.

McDowell, G., & Hanly, K. (2022). The state of mountain research in Canada. *Journal of Mountain Science, 19*(10), 3013–3025. https://doi.org/10.1007/s11629-022-7569-1

McGregor, D. (2014). Traditional Knowledge and Water Governance: The ethic of responsibility. *AlterNative: An International Journal of Indigenous Peoples, 10*(5), 493–507. https://doi.org/10.1177/117718011401000505

McIlwraith, T. (2008). "The Bloody Moose Got up and Took off": Talking Carefully about Food Animals in a Northern Athabaskan Village. *Anthropological Linguistics, 50*(2), 125–147.

McIlwraith, T. (2012). A Camp is a Home and Other Reasons Why Indigenous Hunting Camps Can't Be Moved Out of the Way of Resource Developments. *Northern Review, 36*(2), 97–126.

McMillan, W., Thompson, J., Hart, C., & Johnston, S. (1995). Regional geological and tectonic setting of porphyry deposits in British Columbia and Yukon Territory. *Metallurgy and Petroleum, SV 46.*

Mercer, J. J. (2018). *Insights into mountain wetland resilience to climate change: An evaluation of the hydrological processes contributing to the hydrodynamics of alpine wetlands in the Canadian Rocky Mountains* [Master's thesis, University of Saskatchewan]. https://doi.org/10.13140/RG.2.2.12825.47205

Mitchell, M. G. E., Schuster, R., Jacob, A. L., Hanna, D. E. L., Dallaire, C. O., Raudsepp-Hearne, C., Bennett, E. M., Lehner, B., & Chan, K. M. A. (2021). Identifying key ecosystem service providing areas to inform national-scale conservation planning. *Environmental Research Letters, 16*(1), 014038. https://doi.org/10.1088/1748-9326/abc121

Mood, B. J., & Smith, D. J. (2021). A multi-century July-August streamflow reconstruction of Metro Vancouver's water supply contribution from the Capilano and Seymour watersheds in southwestern British Columbia, Canada. *Canadian Water Resources Journal, 46*(3), 121–138. https://doi.org/10.1080/07011784.2021.1931458

Moody, Megan. (2008). *Eulachon past and present* [Master's thesis, University of British Columbia]. http://nuxalk.net/media/eulachon_moody.pdf

Morrison, A., Westbrook, C. J., & Bedard-Haughn, A. (2014). Distribution of Canadian Rocky Mountain Wetlands Impacted by Beaver. *Wetlands, 35*(1), 95–104. https://doi.org/10.1007/s13157-014-0595-1

Mullally, S., & MacDonald, K. (2017). Call the Doctor? Understanding Health Service Trends in New Brunswick, Part I, 1918–1950. *Journal of New Brunswick Studies / Revue d'études sur le Nouveau-Brunswick, 8.* https://journals-lib-unb-ca.ezproxy.library.ubc.ca/index.php/JNBS/article/view/25879

Musseau, M. (n.d.). *Biography.* Meagan Musseau. Retrieved December 22, 2022, from https://meaganmusseau.com/Biography

Nadasdy, P. (1999). The Politics of Tek: Power and the "Integration" of Knowledge. *Arctic Anthropology, 36*(1/2), 1–18.

Nadasdy, P. (2007). The Gift in the Animal: The Ontology of Hunting and Human-Animal Sociality. *American Ethnologist, 34*(1), 25–43.

Natcher, D. C. (2009). Subsistence and the Social Economy of Canada's Aboriginal North. *Northern Review, 30*, Article 30.

Nelson, J., & Colpron, M. (2007). Tectonics and metallogeny of the British Columbia, Yukon and Alaskan Cordillera, 1.8 Ga to the present. In: Mineral Deposits of Canada: A Synthesis of Major Deposit-Types, District Metallogeny, the Evolution of Geological Provinces, and Exploration Methods,. *GAC Special Publication, 5.* https://data.geology.gov.yk.ca/Reference/81666#InfoTab

Nepal, S. K., & Jamal, T. B. (2011). Resort-Induced Changes in Small Mountain Communities in British Columbia, Canada. *Mountain Research and Development, 31*(2), 89–101. https://doi.org/10.1659/MRD-JOURNAL-D-10-00095.1

Nitschke, C. R. (2008). The cumulative effects of resource development on biodiversity and ecological integrity in the Peace-Moberly region of Northeast British Columbia, Canada. *Biodiversity and Conservation, 17*(7), 1715–1740.

Norval Morrisseau—Rock Art. (2006, 2011). Native Art in Canada: An Elder's Stories About Ojibwa Art and Culture. https://www.native-art-in-canada.com/rock-art.html

Norton, C. H., Cuerrier, A., & Hermanutz, L. (2021). People and Plants in Nunatsiavut (Labrador, Canada): Examining Plants as a Foundational Aspect of Culture in the Subarctic. *Economic Botany, 75*(3), 287–301.

Oberndorfer, E., Winters, N., Gear, C., Ljubicic, G., & Lundholm, J. (2017). Plants in a "Sea of Relationships": Networks of Plants and Fishing in Makkovik, Nunatsiavut (Labrador, Canada). *Journal of Ethnobiology, 37*(3), 458–477. https://doi.org/10.2993/0278-0771-37.3.458

Oetelaar, G. A. (2014). Worldviews and human–animal relations: Critical perspectives on bison–human relations among the Euro-Canadians and Blackfoot. *Critique of Anthropology, 34*(1), 94–112. https://doi.org/10.1177/0308275X13510187

Ommer, R. E., & Coasts Under Stress Research Project Team. (2007). *Coasts Under Stress: Restructuring and social-ecological health.* McGill-Queen's University Press.

Orr, P. L., Wiramanaden, C. I. E., Paine, M. D., Franklin, W., & Fraser, C. (2012). Food Chain Model Based on Field Data to Predict Westslope Cutthroat Trout (Oncorhynchus Clarkii Lewisi) Ovary Selenium Concentrations from Water Selenium Concentrations in the Elk Valley, British Columbia. *Environmental Toxicology and Chemistry, 31*(3), 672–680. https://doi.org/10.1002/etc.1730

Osama, M. (2019). Asylum: A Place of Refuge. *Marwah Osama: Architecture & Design.* https://www.marwahosama.com/asylum

Owens, P., & Slaymaker, O. (2004). *Mountain Geomorphology* (1st ed.). Routledge. https://doi.org/10.4324/9780203764824

Parfitt, B. (2005). *Getting More from our Forests: Ten Proposals for Building Stability in BC's Forestry Communities.* Canadian Centre Policy Alternatives.

Parfitt, B. (2007). *True partners.* desLibris. https://policycommons.net/artifacts/1215317/true-partners/1768416/

Parfitt, B. (2010). Managing BC's forests for a cooler planet: Carbon storage, sustainable jobs and conservation. *Managing BC's Forests for a Cooler Planet: Carbon Storage, Sustainable Jobs and Conservation.* https://davidsuzuki.org/science-learning-centre-article/executive-summary-managing-bcs-forests-cooler-planet-carbon-storage-sustainable-jobs-conservation/

Parker, B., Schindler, D., Donald, D., & Anderson, R. (2001). The Effects of Stocking and Removal of a Nonnative Salmonid on the Plankton of an Alpine Lake. *Ecosystems, 4*(4), 334–345. https://doi.org/10.1007/s10021-001-0015-2

Parks Canada. (2019). "Saoyú-?ehdacho National Historic Site of Canada." Canada's Historic Places. Accessed 29 July 2023: https://www.historicplaces.ca/en/rep-reg/place-lieu.aspx?id=13033

Parlee, B., & Berkes, F. (2006). Indigenous knowledge of ecological variability and commons management: A case study on berry harvesting from Northern Canada. *Human Ecology, 34*(4), 515–528.

Parlee, B. L. (2006). *Dealing with ecological variability and change: Perspectives from the Denesoline and the Gwich'in of northern Canada* [Doctoral dissertation, The University of Manitoba].

Parlee, B. L., & Caine, K. J. (2018). *When the caribou do not come: Indigenous knowledge and adaptive management in the Western Arctic*. UBC Press.

Parlee, B. L., Sandlos, J., & Natcher, D. C. (2018). Undermining subsistence: Barren-ground caribou in a "tragedy of open access." *Science Advances, 4*(2), e1701611.

Parlee, B., & Martin, C. (2016). *Literature Review: Local and Traditional Knowledge in the Peel River Watershed*. Tracking Change Project.

Parrott, L., Robinson, Z., & Hik, D. (Eds.). (2022). *State of the Mountains Report* (Vol. 5). Alpine Club of Canada.

Pasternak, S. (2017). *Grounded authority: The Algonquins of Barriere Lake against the state*. University of Minnesota Press.

Paul, A., & Post, J. (2001). Spatial Distribution of Native and Nonnative Salmonids in Streams of the Eastern Slopes of the Canadian Rocky Mountains. *Transactions of the American Fisheries Society, 130*(3), 417–430. https://doi.org/10.1577/1548-8659(2001)130<0417:SDONAN>2.0.CO;2

Pavelka, J. (2017). Are They Having Fun Yet? Leisure Management Within Amenity Migration. *World Leisure Journal, 59*(1), 21–38. https://doi.org/10.1080/16078055.2016.1277610

Payne, C. (2007). How Shall We Use These Gifts? In J. O'Brian & P. White (Eds.), *Beyond Wilderness: The Group of Seven, Canadian Identity, and Contemporary Art* (pp. 153–160). McGill-Queen's University Press.

Peacock, S. L., & Turner, N. J. (2000). "Just Like a Garden": Traditional Resource Management and Biodiversity Conservation on the Interior Plateau of British Columbia. In *Biodiversity and Native America* (pp. 133–179). University of Oklahoma Press.

Pearon, K. J., & Goater, C. P. (2008). Distribution of Long-Toed Salamanders and Introduced Trout in High- and Low-Elevation Wetlands in Southwestern Alberta, Canada. *Ecoscience, 15*(4), 453–459. https://doi.org/10.2980/15-4-3127

Pentz, S., & Kostaschuk, R. (1999). Effect of placer mining on suspended sediment in reaches of sensitive fish habitat. *Environmental Geology, 37*(1), 78–89.

Pigeon, K. E., Anderson, M., MacNearney, D., Cranston, J., Stenhouse, G., & Finnegan, L. (2016). Toward the restoration of caribou habitat: understanding factors associated with human motorized use of legacy seismic lines. *Environmental management, 58*(5), 821–832.

Pitman, K. J., Moore, J. W., Sloat, M. R., Beaudreau, A. H., Bidlack, A. L., Brenner, R. E., Hood, E. W., Pess, G. R., Mantua, N. J., Milner, A. M., Radić, V., Reeves, G. H., Schindler, D. E., & Whited, D. C. (2020). Glacier Retreat and Pacific Salmon. *BioScience, 70*(3), 220–236. https://doi.org/10.1093/biosci/biaa015

Price, M. F. (Ed.). (2013). *Mountain geography: Physical and human dimensions*. University of California Press.

Prosper, L. (2007). Wherein lies the heritage value? Rethinking the heritage value of cultural landscapes from an Aboriginal perspective. *The George Wright Forum 24*(2), 117–124.

Rajala, J. (1998). *Bringing back the white pine*. J. Rajala.

Rajala, R. (2006). *Up-coast: Forests and industry on British Columbia's north coast, 1870-2005*. Royal BC Museum.

Rand, P. S., Hinch, S. G., Morrison, J., Foreman, M. G. G., MacNutt, M. J., Macdonald, J. S., Healey, M. C., Farrell, A. P., & Higgs, D. A. (2006). Effects of River Discharge, Temperature, and Future Climates on Energetics and Mortality of Adult Migrating Fraser River Sockeye Salmon. *Transactions of the American Fisheries Society, 135*(3), 655–667. https://doi.org/10.1577/T05-023.1

Randell, H. (2022). The challenges of dam-induced displacement: Reducing risks and rethinking hydropower. *One Earth, 5*(8), 849–852. https://doi.org/10.1016/j.oneear.2022.07.002

Rathwell, K. J., & Armitage, D. (2016). Art and artistic processes bridge knowledge systems about social-ecological change: An empirical examination with Inuit artists from Nunavut, Canada. *Ecology and Society, 21*(2), art21. https://doi.org/10.5751/ES-08369-210221

Reeves, B. O. K. (1978). Bison Killing in the Southwestern Alberta Rockies. *Plains Anthropologist, 23*(82), 63–78.

Reichwein, P. (2005). Holiday at the Banff School of Fine Arts: The Cinematic Production of Culture, Nature, and Nation in the Canadian Rockies, 1945–1952. *Journal of Canadian Studies, 39*(1), 49–73. https://doi.org/10.1353/jcs.2006.0010

Reichwein, P., & Wall, K. (2017). Mountain Capitalists, Space, and Modernity at the Banff School of Fine Arts. In G. Colpitts & H. Devine (Eds.), *Finding Directions West: Readings that Locate and Dislocate Western Canada's Past* (pp. 203–232). University of Calgary Press. https://doi.org/10.2307/j.ctv64h781

Reid, A. J., Carlson, A. K., Creed, I. F., Eliason, E. J., Gell, P. A., Johnson, P. T. J., Kidd, K. A., MacCormack, T. J., Olden, J. D., Ormerod, S. J., Smol, J. P., Taylor, W. W., Tockner, K., Vermaire, J. C., Dudgeon, D., & Cooke, S. J. (2019). Emerging threats and persistent conservation challenges for freshwater biodiversity. *Biological Reviews, 94*(3), 849–873. https://doi.org/10.1111/brv.12480

Reid, A. J., Eckert, L. E., Lane, J.-F., Young, N., Hinch, S. G., Darimont, C. T., Cooke, S. J., Ban, N. C., & Marshall, A. (2021). "Two-Eyed Seeing": An Indigenous framework to transform fisheries research and management. *Fish and Fisheries, 22*(2), 243–261. https://doi.org/10.1111/faf.12516

Reid, A. J., Young, N., Hinch, S. G., & Cooke, S. J. (2022). Learning from Indigenous knowledge holders on the state and future of wild Pacific salmon. *FACETS, 7*, 718–740. https://doi.org/10.1139/facets-2021-0089

Reid, D. (2007). Introduction to the Group of Seven. In J. O'Brian & P. White (Eds.), *Beyond Wilderness: The Group of Seven, Canadian Identity, and Contemporary Art* (pp. 101–107). McGill-Queen's University Press.

Reid, M., Collins, M. L., Hall, S. R. J., Mason, E., McGee, G., & Frid, A. (2022). Protecting our coast for everyone's future: Indigenous and scientific knowledge support marine spatial protections proposed by Central Coast

First Nations in Pacific Canada. *People & Nature, 4*, 1052–1070. https://doi.org/10.1002/pan3.10380

Reimer, R. (Yumks). (2003). Alpine Archaeology and Oral Traditions of the Squamish. In R. Carlson (Ed.), *Archaeology of Coastal British Columbia: Essays in honour of Professor Philip M. Hobler* (pp. 45–59). Archaeology Press.

Ripley, T., Scrimgeour, G., & Boyce, M. (2005). Bull Trout (Salvelinus Confluentus) Occurrence and Abundance Influenced by Cumulative Industrial Developments in a Canadian Boreal Forest Watershed. *Canadian Journal of Fisheries and Aquatic Sciences, 62*(11), 2431–2442. https://doi.org/10.1139/F05-150

Romeo R., Russo, L., Parisi F., Notarianni M., Manuelli S., Carvao S., & UNWTO. (2021). *Mountain tourism—Towards a more sustainable path*. FAO, the World Tourism Organization (UNWTO),. https://doi.org/10.4060/cb7884en

Rudolph, B.-L., Andreller, I., & Kennedy, C. J. (2008). Reproductive Success, Early Life Stage Development, and Survival of Westslope Cutthroat Trout (*Oncorhynchus clarki lewisi*) Exposed to Elevated Selenium in an Area of Active Coal Mining. *Environmental Science & Technology, 42*(8), 3109–3114. https://doi.org/10.1021/es072034d

Saari, P. J. (2015). Marketing Nature: The Canadian National Parks Branch and Constructing the Portrayal of National Parks in Promotional Brochures, 1936–1970. *Environment and History, 21*(3), 401–446. https://doi.org/10.3197/096734015X14345369355863

Salmón, E. (2012). *Eating the Landscape*. The University of Arizona Press.

Sanderson, D., Picketts, I. M., Déry, S. J., Fell, B., Baker, S., Lee-Johnson, E., & Auger, M. (2015). Climate change and water at Stellat'en First Nation, British Columbia, Canada: Insights from western science and traditional knowledge. *The Canadian Geographer / Le Géographe Canadien, 59*(2), 136–150. https://doi.org/10.1111/cag.12142

Satterfield, T., Gregory, R., Klain, S., Roberts, M., & Chan, K. M. (2013). Culture, intangibles and metrics in environmental management. *Journal of environmental management, 117*, 103–114.

Schindler, D. W., & Donahue, W. F. (2006). An impending water crisis in Canada's western prairie provinces. *Proceedings of the National Academy of Sciences, 103*(19), 7210–7216. https://doi.org/10.1073/pnas.0601568103

Schuster, R., Germain, R. R., Bennett, J. R., Reo, N. J., & Arcese, P. (2019). Vertebrate biodiversity on indigenous-managed lands in Australia, Brazil, and Canada equals that in protected areas. *Environmental Science & Policy, 101*, 1–6. https://doi.org/10.1016/j.envsci.2019.07.002

Sherren, K., Parkins, J.R., Owen, T., Terashima, M. (2019). Does noticing energy infrastructure influence public support for energy development? Evidence from a national survey in Canada, Energy Research & Social Science, 51: 176–186. DOI:10.1016/j.erss.2019.01.014.

Simms, R., Harris, L., Joe, N., & Bakker, K. (2016). Navigating the tensions in collaborative watershed governance: Water governance and Indigenous communities in British Columbia, Canada. *Geoforum, 73*, 6–16. https://doi.org/10.1016/j.geoforum.2016.04.005

Simpson, A. (2014). *Mohawk Interruptus: Political Life Across the Borders of Settler States*. Duke University Press.

Sinnatamby, R. N., Cantin, A., & Post, J. R. (2020). Threats to At-Risk Salmonids of the Canadian Rocky Mountain Region. *Ecology of Freshwater Fish, 29*(3), 477–494. https://doi.org/10.1111/eff.12531

Smith, T., & Bulkan, J. (2021). A 'New Relationship'? Reflections on British Columbia's 2003 Forest Revitalization Plan from the perspective of the Líl̓wat First Nation. *Land Use Policy, 105*, 105345. https://doi.org/10.1016/j.landusepol.2021.105345

Snively, E. (2016). Chapter 5—Representations of Indigenous Science in Textbooks, Curriculum Resources, and Government Documents. In G. Snively & W.L. Williams (Eds.), *Knowing Home: Braiding Indigenous Science with Western Science Book One* (pp. 73–85). University of Victoria Press. https://ecampusontario.pressbooks.pub/knowinghome/chapter/chapter-5/

Solomon, G. (2022). Video clip with Tsilhqot'in Nation Elder, Gilbert Solomon speaking about mountains in spiritual recovery and learning in the Ts'il?os (Chilko) River region. In "Towards Legal Recognition for Non-Human Relations, Webinar 2: Supernatural Beings and Sacred Places". *Centre for Law and the Environment*. https://allard.ubc.ca/about-us/events-calendar/towards-legal-recognition-non-human-relations-webinar-2-supernatural-beings-and-sacred-places

Sprague, J. B. (2007). Great wet north? Canada's myth of water abundance. In K. Bakker (Ed.), *Eau Canada: The future of Canada's water.* (pp. 23–36). UBC Press.

St. Louis, V. L., Kelly, C. A., Duchemin, É., Rudd, J. W. M., & Rosenberg, D. M. (2000). Reservoir Surfaces as Sources of Greenhouse Gases to the Atmosphere: A Global Estimate. *BioScience, 50*(9), 766. https://doi.org/10.1641/0006-3568(2000)050[0766:RSASOG]2.0.CO;2

Stanworth, K. (2013). Revisioning the "Culture of Nature" in Canadian Visual Culture Studies: John Russell and An/Other Case of Modern Art. *Journal of Canadian Studies, 47*(3), 67–92.

St-Louis, A., Hamel, S., Mainguy, J., & Cote, S. D. (2013). Factors Influencing the Reaction of Mountain Goats Towards All-Terrain Vehicles. *Journal of Wildlife Management, 77*(3), 599–605. https://doi.org/10.1002/jwmg.488

Stoddart, M. C. J. (2011). Grizzlies and Gondolas: Animals and the Meaning of Skiing Landscapes in British Columbia, Canada. *Nature + Culture, 6*(1), 41–63. https://doi.org/10.3167/nc.2011.060103

Stralberg, D., Arseneault, D., Baltzer, J. L., Barber, Q. E., Bayne, E. M., Boulanger, Y., Brown, C. D., Cooke, H. A., Devito, K., Edwards, J., Estevo, C. A., Flynn, N., Frelich, L. E., Hogg, E. H., Johnston, M., Logan, T., Matsuoka, S. M., Moore, P., Morelli, T. L., … Whitman, E. (2020). Climate-change refugia in boreal North America: What, where, and for how long? *Frontiers in Ecology and the Environment, 18*(5), 261–270. https://doi.org/10.1002/fee.2188

Strang, V. (2004). *The meaning of water.* Berg.

Studley, J. (2012). Uncovering the intangible values of earth care: Using cognition to reveal the eco-spiritual domains and sacred values of the peoples of eastern Kham. In B. Verschuuren, R. Wild, J. McNeely, & G. Oviedo (Eds.), *Sacred natural sites: Conserving Nature and Culture* (pp. 107–118). Earthscan.

Tarnocai, C., Kettles, I. M., & Lacelle, B. (2011). *Peatlands of Canada* (No. 6561). https://doi.org/10.4095/288786

The Confederacy of Mainland Mi'kmaq. (2014). *Mission & Netukulimk—Mi'kmaw Conservation Group.* https://mikmawconservation.ca/mission-netukulimk/

Thornton, C., & Quinn, M. S. (2009). Coexisting with cougars: public perceptions, attitudes, and awareness of cougars on the urban-rural fringe of Calgary, Alberta, Canada. *Human-Wildlife Conflicts, 3*(2), 282–295.

Tito, R., Vasconcelos, H. L., & Feeley, K. J. (2020). Mountain Ecosystems as Natural Laboratories for Climate Change Experiments. *Frontiers in Forests and Global Change, 3*(38). https://doi.org/10.3389/ffgc.2020.00038

Toth, B., Corkal, D. R., Sauchyn, D., Van Der Kamr, G., & Pietroniro, E. (2009). The Natural Characteristics of the South Saskatchewan, River Basin: Climate, Geography and Hydrology. *Prairie Forum, 34*(1), 95–127.

Trusler, S., & Johnson, L. M. (2008). "Berry Patch" as a Kind of Place—The Ethnoecology of Black Huckleberry in Northwestern Canada. *Human Ecology, 36*(4), 553–568. https://doi.org/10.1007/s10745-008-9176-3

Tsing, A. L. (2015). *The Mushroom at the End of the World: On the Possibility of Life in Capitalist Ruins.* Princeton University Press. https://doi.org/10.1515/9781400873548

Tuer, D. (2007). Performing Memory: The Art of Storytelling in the Work of Rebecca Belmore. In J. O'Brian & P. White (Eds.), *Beyond Wilderness: The Group of Seven, Canadian Identity, and Contemporary Art* (pp. 338–340). McGill-Queen's University Press.

Tulloch, V. J. D., Adams, M. S., Martin, T. G., Tulloch, A. I. T., Martone, R., Avery-Gomm, S., & Murray, C. C. (2022). Accounting for direct and indirect cumulative effects of anthropogenic pressures on salmon- and herring-linked land and ocean ecosystems. *Philosophical Transactions B, 377*(20210130). https://doi.org/10.1098/rstb.2021.0130

Turner, N. J. (1984). Counter-irritant and other medicinal uses of plants in Ranunculaceae by native peoples in British Columbia and neighbouring areas. *Journal of Ethnopharmacology, 11*(2), 181–201.

Turner, N. J. (1988). "The Importance of a Rose": Evaluating the Cultural Significance of Plants in Thompson and Lillooet Interior Salish. *American Anthropologist, 90*(2), 272–290.

Turner, N. J. (2014). *Ancient Pathways, Ancestral Knowledge: Ethnobotany and Ecological Wisdom of Indigenous Peoples of Northwestern North America.* McGill-Queen's University Press.

Turner, N. J. (2020). *Plants, Peoples, and Places: The Roles of Ethnobotany and Ethnoecology in Indigenous Peoples' Land Rights in Canada and Beyond.* McGill-Queen's University Press.

Turner, N. J., & Clifton, H. (2009). "It's so different today": Climate change and indigenous lifeways in British Columbia, Canada. *Global Environmental Change, 19*(2), 180–190. https://doi.org/10.1016/j.gloenvcha.2009.01.005

Turner, N. J., Davidson-Hunt, I. J., & O'Flaherty, M. (2003). Living on the edge: Ecological and cultural edges as sources of diversity for social—Ecological resilience. *Human Ecology, 31*(3), 439–461.

Turner, N. J., Ignace, M. B., & Ignace, R. (2000). Traditional Ecological Knowledge and Wisdom of Aboriginal Peoples in British Columbia. *Ecological Applications, 10*(5), 1275–1287. https://doi.org/10.1890/1051-0761(2000)010[1275:TEKAWO]2.0.CO;2

Tushingham, S., Barton, L., & Bettinger, R. L. (2021). How ancestral subsistence strategies solve salmon starvation and the "protein problem" of Pacific Rim resources. *American Journal of Physical Anthropology, 175*, 741–761. https://doi.org/10.1002/ajpa.24281

United Nations Department of Economic and Social Affairs, Indigenous Peoples. (2017). *UN Permanent Forum on Indigenous Issues.* https://www.un.org/development/desa/indigenouspeoples/mandated-areas1/education/recs-education.html

Uprety, Y., Asselin, H., Dhakal, A., & Julien, N. (2012). Traditional use of medicinal plants in the boreal forest of Canada: Review and perspectives. *Journal of Ethnobiology and Ethnomedicine, 8*(1), 7. https://doi.org/10.1186/1746-4269-8-7

van Staal, C., Wilson, R., Rogers, N., Fyffe, L., Langton, J., McCutcheon, S., McNicoll, V., & Ravenhurst, C. (2003). Geology and Tectonic History of the Bathurst Supergroup, Bathurst Mining Camp, and Its Relationships to Coeval Rocks in Southwestern New Brunswick and Adjacent Maine—A Synthesis. In W. Goodfellow, S. McCutcheon, & J. Peter (Eds.), *Massive Sulfide Deposits of the Bathurst Mining Camp, New Brunswick, and Northern Maine* (Vol. 11). Society of Exploration Geophysicists.

Vastokas. (2012). Pictographs and Petroglyphs. *The Canadian Encyclopedia.* https://www.thecanadianencyclopedia.ca/en/article/pictographs-and-petroglyphs#

Viviroli, D., Dürr, H. H., Messerli, B., Meybeck, M., & Weingartner, R. (2007). Mountains of the world, water towers for humanity: Typology, mapping, and global significance: Mountains as Water Towers for Humanity. *Water Resources Research, 43*(7). https://doi.org/10.1029/2006WR005653

Viviroli, D., Kummu, M., Meybeck, M., Kallio, M., & Wada, Y. (2020). Increasing dependence of lowland populations on mountain water resources. *Nature Sustainability, 3*(11), 917–928. https://doi.org/10.1038/s41893-020-0559-9

Viviroli, D., Weingartner, R., & Messerli, B. (2003). Assessing the Hydrological Significance of the World's

Mountains. *Source: Mountain Research and Development Mountain Research and Development, 2302300322*(23). http://www.bioone.org/doi/full/10.1659/0276-4741% 282003%29023%5B0032%3AATHSOT

Wagner, M. A., & Reynolds, J. D. (2019). Salmon increase forest bird abundance and diversity. *PLOS ONE, 14*(2), e0210031. https://doi.org/10.1371/journal.pone. 0210031

Weidman, R. P., Schindler, D. W., & Vinebrooke, R. D. (2011). Pelagic Food Web Interactions Among Benthic Invertebrates and Trout in Mountain Lakes. *Freshwater Biology, 56*(6), 1081–1094. https://doi.org/10.1111/ j.1365-2427.2010.02552.x

Westbrook, C. J., Ronnquist, A., & Bedard-Haughn, A. (2020). Hydrological functioning of a beaver dam sequence and regional dam persistence during an extreme rainstorm. *Hydrological Processes, 34*(18), 3726–3737. https://doi.org/10.1002/hyp.13828

Wickland, K. P., Striegl, R. G., Mast, M. A., & Clow, D. W. (2001). Carbon gas exchange at a southern Rocky Mountain wetland, 1996–1998. *Global Biogeochemical Cycles, 15*(2), 321–335. https://doi.org/10.1029/ 2000GB001325

Wild, F. J. (2008). Epidemiology of Mountain Search and Rescue Operations in Banff, Yoho, and Kootenay National Parks, 2003–06. *Wilderness & Environmental Medicine, 19*(4), 245–251. https://doi.org/10.1580/ 07-WEME-OR-141.1

Willows, N. D. (2005). Overweight in Aboriginal Children: Prevalence, Implications, and Solutions. *International Journal of Indigenous Health, 2*(1), 76–86.

Wilson, N. J. (2020). Querying Water Co-Governance: Yukon First Nations and Water Governance in the Context of Modern Land Claim Agreements. *Water Alternatives, 13*(1), 93–118.

Wilson, N. J., Harris, L. M., Joseph-Rear, A., Beaumont, J., & Satterfield, T. (2019). Water Is Medicine: Reimagining Water Security Through Tr'ondek Hwech'In Relationships to Treated and Traditional Water Sources in Yukon, Canada. *Water, 11*(3). https://doi. org/10.3390/w11030624

Wilson, N. J., & Inkster, J. (2018). Respecting water: Indigenous water governance, ontologies, and the politics of kinship on the ground. *Environment and Planning E: Nature and Space, 1*(4), 516–538. https://doi.org/ 10.1177/2514848618789378

Wong, C., Ballegooyen, K., Ignace, L., Johnson, M. J. (Gùdia), & Swanson, H. (2020). Towards reconciliation: 10 Calls to Action to natural scientists working in Canada. *FACETS, 5*(1), 769–783. https://doi.org/10.1139/facets-2020-0005

Yarmoloy, C. P. (1986). *The impact of off-highway recreation vehicles on big game: management implications for Alberta's eastern slopes* [Master's thesis, University of Calgary].

York, A., Arnett, C., & Daly, R. (1993). *They write their dream on the rock forever: Rock writings of the Stein River Valley of British Columbia* (1. print). Talonbooks.

Yu, Z., Vitt, D. V., Campbell, I. D., & Apps, M. J. (2003). *Understanding Holocene peat accumulation pattern of continental fens in western Canada. 81*, 267–282. https://doi.org/10.1139/B03-016

Zedeno, M., Pickering, E., & Lanoe, F. (2021). Oral tradition as emplacement: Ancestral Blackfoot memories of the Rocky Mountain Front. *Journal of Social Archaeology, 21*(3), 306–328. https://doi.org/10.1177/ 1469605321101983

Zedler, J. B., & Kercher, S. (2005). Wetland Resources: Status, Trends, Ecosystem Services, and Restorability. *Annual Review of Environment and Resources, 30*(1), 39–74. https://doi.org/10.1146/annurev.energy.30.050504. 144248

Zurba, M., Beazley, K. F., English, E., & Buchmann-Duck, J. (2019). Indigenous Protected and Conserved Areas (IPCAs), Aichi Target 11 and Canada's Pathway to Target 1: Focusing Conservation on Reconciliation. *Land, 8*(1), 10. https://doi.org/10.3390/land8010010

1900

2012

Retreat of the Kaskawulsh Glacier in Kluane National Park and Reserve between 1900 (J.J. McArthur, courtesy of Library and Archives Canada) and 2012 (courtesy of Mountain Legacy Project, https://explore.mountainlegacy.ca/stations/show/2321).

CHAPTER 5

Mountains Under Pressure

CO-LEAD AUTHORS: Michele Koppes, Niiyokamigaabaw Deondre Smiles

CONTRIBUTING AUTHORS: Leon Andrew, Caroline Aubry-Wake, Ashley-Anne Churchill, Dawn Saunders Dahl, Stephan Gruber, Jiaao Guo, Katherine Hanly, Pnnal Bernard Jerome, Patricia Joe, Gùdia Mary Jane Johnson, Stephen Johnston, Knut Kitching, Keara Lightning, Christopher Marsh, Shawn Marshall, Brandy Mayes, Graham McDowell, Wanda Pascal, Tim Patterson, Lauren Rethoret, María Elisa Sánchez, Richard Schuster, Joseph Shea, Daniel Sims, Lauren Somers, Karson Sudlow, Hayden Melting Tallow, Yan Tapp, Andrew Trant, Gabrielle Weasel Head, Sonia Wesche

CHAPTER REVIEW EDITOR: Stephen Chignell

5.1 Introduction

Mountains in Canada are subject to an array of direct and indirect pressures from human activity and environmental change. The Intergovernmental Panel on Biodiversity and Ecosystem Services (IPBES) biodiversity assessment discusses these pressures as 'drivers of change', and these drivers are broadly relevant to mountain systems and peoples (Díaz et al., 2019). Pressures such as climate change, land-use development, and the increasing demand for tourism and recreation are tied to the "great acceleration" of increasing human population and activity since 1950 (Steffen et al., 2015). Each pressure drives biophysical, socio-political, cultural, and ecological responses, with effects that vary from region to region, and which may be experienced far beyond mountain areas. These primary pressures are ultimately all driven by human activity, but they interact with natural systems to create secondary pressures such as changes in hydrology or ecology that can compromise the quality of life in mountain environments (e.g., impacts on water quality, health,

Due to the CMA's unique approach to engaging with multiple knowledge systems, we suggest that readers review the Introduction prior to reading subsequent chapters.

or food security), representing existential threats to the sustainability of the mountain environments, livelihoods, and gifts of the mountains discussed in Chapters 2 to 4 of this book.

Many pressures, such as land management and governance practices, represent long-standing drivers of change, especially for Indigenous communities. Obvious examples include resource development (e.g., mining, forestry), establishment of infrastructure (e.g., roads, railways, pipelines, towns, ski areas), and land claims (e.g., the establishment of National Parks, which changed access to and 'ownership' of the mountains). Biocultural relationships, socio-ecological values, and socio-economic and political privilege/marginalisation underpin differentiated experiences of these drivers and their associated effects.

Pressures are often interactive and compounding, which can lead to cascading socio-ecological effects, including impacts on community health and wellbeing. Anthropogenic and climatic pressures on mountain landscapes can interact with each other in a complex manner, including in cumulative, synergistic, or additive ways; they also vary in their spatial and temporal scales, making understanding of how they interact essential for adaptation planning. Mitigating further anthropogenic disturbance requires identifying the patterns of change in these environmental and social pressures and their cumulative effects, and forecasting their impacts into the future (Hirsh-Pearson, 2022).

This chapter focuses on historical and future changes in mountains in Canada from 1950 to 2100, including the anthropogenic drivers of these changes, current and emerging impacts and vulnerabilities, as well as responses to attendant challenges (and opportunities) in mountain systems. Historical changes and future projections for drivers of change are discussed in Sec. 5.2 to 5.6. Sec. 5.7 to 5.11 assess the effects of these pressures on physical, ecological, and socio-cultural systems, including consideration of the vulnerability, resilience, and adaptation within these systems.

5.2 Climate Change: Historical Trends and Future Projections

Mountain systems are sensitive to the cumulative effects of climate change. Contemporary climate change includes both natural forcing and anthropogenic components, and these can be difficult to separate. Cooler temperatures during the main phase of the Little Ice Age from the 17th to 19th centuries have been attributed to solar variability and the cooling effects of frequent volcanic activity (Brönnimann et al., 2019). Natural climate forcings such as volcanic events and sunspot cycles are associated with interannual to decadal variability, with fluctuations in radiative balance

that can impact biophysical and socio-cultural systems but which often 'balance out' over multi-decadal timescales. Other natural forcings, such as variations in the Earth's orbit around the Sun, act on millennial timescales and influence the Quaternary and Holocene evolution of climate, glaciation, and ecosystems, but with negligible changes over the timescale of focus here, 1950 to 2100.

Natural processes continue to influence the climate, and the cooling effects of volcanic events are well-known in oral histories. As Elder Gùdia Mary Jane Johnson, Lhu'ààn Mân Ku Dań shared, the Kluane hold stories of the time when the volcano erupted and the ash spread across the Yukon, the time when there were two winters and no summer (LC 5.1).

Most aspects of natural, built, and socio-cultural environments are vulnerable to climate change, but glaciers provide an intuitive and visible indicator that naturally integrates short-term fluctuations ('weather') to provide a clear signal of the cumulative impacts of climate change. The Little Ice Age was characterised by widespread glacier advance, with cool summers in the Little Ice Age also affecting harvests and growing conditions across much of the world. The onset of glacier retreat coming out of the Little Ice Age was largely associated with natural climate forcing, but accelerated and intensified glacier retreat since the 1970s is almost entirely due to anthropogenic climate forcing from the buildup of carbon dioxide and methane in the atmosphere (Marzeion et al., 2014). The accumulation of these greenhouse gases represents a direct and steadily increasing warming influence that is also affecting the hydrological cycle and circulation patterns in the ocean and atmosphere. The IPCC (2021) notes that there has been no significant solar variation over the period 1950 to present, and that anthropogenic forcing from greenhouse gases is now much stronger than natural forcing of the climate system.

The pressures of climate change on cryospheric, hydrological, and ecological systems, food security, wildfire, extreme weather, mountain hazards, built infrastructure, mountain recreation, and ways of life produce cascading impacts in mountain regions. As Brandy Mayes, Kwanlin Dün First Nation, explained, increased heat and

Gùdia Mary Jane Johnson, Lhu'ààn Mân Ku Dań, 2022, LC 5.1

Brandy Mayes, Kwanlin Dün First Nation, 2022, LC 5.2

precipitation due to climate change affects the salmon, which feed the land, the bears, the trees, and which are felt in the salmon camps (LC 5.2).

Weather patterns and climate normals—the average weather over 30 years or more—are changing across Canada and the world, but mountain environments are sensitive to a range of particular climate change processes and considerations, as discussed in Chapter 2. This includes basic questions of whether warming varies with elevation, as well as questions of how climate change is impacting physical features (e.g., glaciers, hazards), ecological niches, and socio-cultural activities that are specific to high elevations. The following sections assess historical trends and future climate change projections specific to major mountain regions in Canada.

5.2.1 *Historical temperature trends*

Numerous research studies provide multi-year meteorological records from high-elevation and alpine sites in mountain regions in Canada (e.g., Marshall, 2014; Pradhananga et al., 2020; Rasouli et al., 2019). At some sites these records extend long enough to estimate a climate normal, but they do not have the duration, continuity, or homogeneity to support detection and analysis of climate change trends. Where multi-decadal records from mountain regions are available, they typically correspond to low elevations (e.g., valley-bottom or coastal sites), such as in the analysis of Whitfield (2014) in the Kananaskis Valley (ca. 1400 m).

Data from alpine environments or higher elevations, above about 1600 m, are mostly collected through short-term research studies or may be available as seasonal records (e.g., from Parks warden stations, ski areas, or fire lookouts). Such observations are also concentrated in populated areas. Given the limited extent of multi-decadal station data, it is difficult to assess climate change trends in mountain regions in Canada or their variation with elevation. Hindcasts from numerical weather prediction models, known as climate reanalyses, offer insight into regional- to national-scale climate patterns and their historical variability. Climate reanalyses use available observational constraints to drive numerical weather models in 'retrospective' mode, essentially using the atmospheric physics and coupled surface-atmospheric processes embedded within the model, constrained by available data, to provide a detailed reconstruction of past climate.

Historical climate trends in mountain regions in Canada are assessed based on the ERA5 climate reanalysis for the period 1950–2020. This climate reanalysis, from the European Centre for Medium-Range Weather Forecasting (ECMWF), provides hourly climate reconstructions from 1950 to present, with a longitude-latitude resolution of 0.25°C (Hersbach et al., 2020). Because this has complete spatial and temporal coverage, it is valuable for assessing decadal-scale climate change trends in mountain and northern regions, where station data is generally sparse.

Average temperatures increased in all of the mountain regions in Canada from 1950 to 2020, with warming rates from 0.06 to 0.34°C per decade (Table 5.1). Western Canada has seen the greatest temperature increases, with the Pacific Maritime and Boreal Cordillera regions warming at roughly twice the national average. Temperature increases in eastern Canada are comparatively modest, and are below the national average. This is consistent with the broad national picture documented in Bush & Lemmen (2019), where trends are based on station records. Overall, western mountain regions in Canada have warmed at rates exceeding the national average, but this is not true of the eastern or high Arctic mountain regions in Canada.

Contrasting seasonal patterns are embedded within the overall warming trend. Nationally, winter warming is more than twice the rate of summer warming, 0.28°C vs. 0.13°C per decade. Winter warming is pronounced in northwestern Canada, with rates exceeding 0.6°C per decade in the Boreal and Taiga Cordillera. In contrast, the Atlantic Maritime and Eastern Subarctic regions experienced modest winter cooling over the period 1950–2020. The overall pattern of temperature trends is consistent with a climatological shift in the jet stream. This shift has led to stronger and more persistent ridges over western Canada and a trough over eastern Canada, associated with northerly (cold) air advection. Decadal-scale trends in atmospheric circulation show signs of persistence in this setup, which accompanies a more 'wavy' jet stream (i.e., meridional flow with strong ridge and trough structures,

Table 5.1: Historical climate trends of major mountain regions in Canada, calculated from the ERA5 global climate reanalysis. Trends dT/dt and dP/dt are calculated from a linear regression over the period 1950–2021, expressed as rate of change per decade. Changes ΔT and ΔP refer to differences in the mean values from 1991–2020 relative to 1951–1980. Bold values highlight large departures from the average Canadian trends.

Climate Trends and Changes (1950–2020), Canadian Mountain Regions								
	dT/dt (°C dec^{-1})			ΔT (°C)	dP/dt (% dec^{-1})			ΔP (%)
Mountain Regions	DJF	JJA	ann	ann	DJF	JJA	ann	ann
Pacific Maritime	0.36	**0.56**	**0.35**	1.49	1.6	**3.7**	0.4	1.6
Montane Cordillera	0.38	0.23	0.26	1.08	**-3.9**	2.1	-0.2	-2.3
Boreal Cordillera	**0.67**	0.20	0.31	1.31	1.6	1.8	**1.9**	6.6
Taiga Cordillera	**0.62**	0.13	0.25	1.14	2.2	-0.2	0.7	2.9
Atlantic Maritime	0.06	0.12	0.07	0.41	1.8	0.7	0.0	0.5
Eastern Subarctic	-0.06	0.14	0.06	0.46	-2.6	-1.9	**-1.3**	-5.4
Arctic Cordillera	0.01	0.22	0.11	0.53	-2.3	**3.5**	**1.9**	9.1
All of Canada	0.28	0.13	0.17	0.74	-0.6	0.6	0.6	2.5

vs. zonal flow). This kind of shift as a response to Arctic warming and sea ice loss has been widely discussed in the literature (Cohen et al., 2014; Francis & Vavrus, 2012, 2015).

Warmer summer temperatures are being experienced in all mountain regions in Canada, with trends equal to or exceeding the national average. Warming in the Pacific Maritime region stands out in particular, with a rate of 0.56°C per decade, which is four times the national average. The Montane and Arctic Cordillera regions are also experiencing strong summer warming, and a range of processes that include albedo feedbacks from declining snow and ice cover (Pepin et al., 2015) and increased atmospheric moisture and downwelling longwave radiation (Williamson et al., 2020) may contribute to the amplified mountain warming.

Elevation-dependent warming
Numerous studies suggest that high elevation mountain regions may be highly sensitive to climate change, a phenomenon known as elevation-dependent warming (EDW; Diaz & Bradley, 1997; Hock et al., 2019; Pepin et al., 2015; Rangwala & Miller, 2012). Climate model studies generally find a systematic increase in warming with elevation in future climate projections (Giorgi et al., 1997; Kotlarski et al., 2012; Palazzi et al., 2019). Pepin and Lundquist (2008) observe that climate change may vary systematically with elevation, but this does not necessarily mean that highest elevations are warming the most. Hence, EDW can be more

subtle and complicated than just amplified warming at higher elevations.

Elevation-dependent warming also needs to be considered in the broader context of elevation-dependent climate change (EDCC), as other meteorological variables, energy fluxes, and surface conditions have strong gradients with altitude, and can be expected to respond nonlinearly to climate change. Several climate change feedbacks vary with elevation, such as albedo declines due to reduced snow and glacier cover, the effects of aerosols, changes in cloud cover, and increases in atmospheric humidity and diabatic heating (i.e., heat release from condensation). Increased humidity drives an increase in incoming longwave radiation and also reduces surface fluxes of evaporation and sublimation at high elevations, and their associated cooling influences. Changes in aerosols, clouds, and atmospheric humidity vary with elevation, and not all of these effects will lead to increased climate sensitivity at high elevations.

There is observational evidence for EDW in some parts of the world, although limited long-term in situ data are being collected to evaluate this at high elevations in most mountain regions, including those in Canada. Where data are available, observational evidence for EDW in the world's mountain regions is mixed (Hock et al., 2019), although several studies document a strong EDW signal in winter months and for minimum temperatures (Beniston & Rebetez, 1996; Pepin et al., 2015; Sharma & Dery, 2016). This argues for

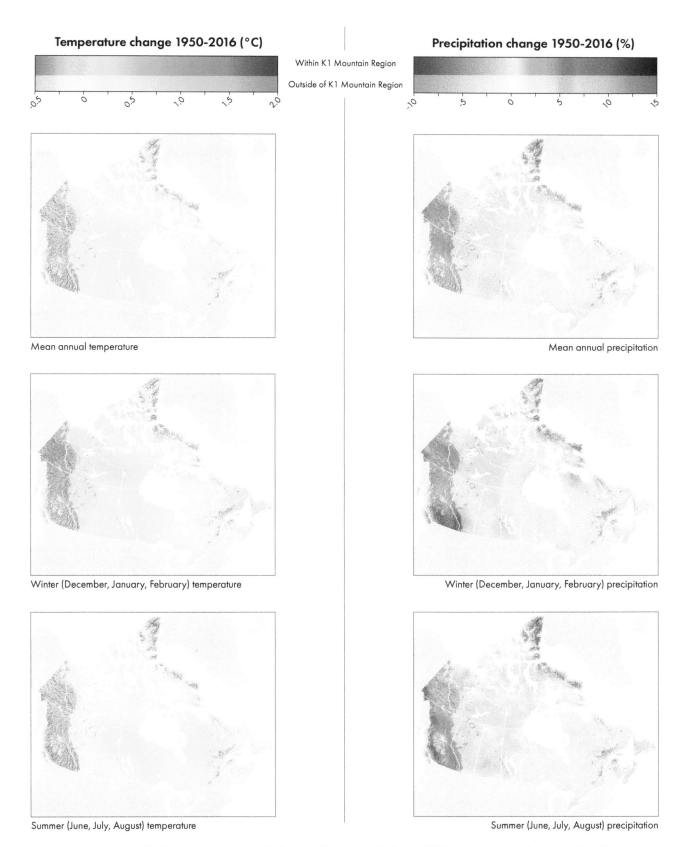

Temperature change 1950-2016 (°C)

Within K1 Mountain Region

Outside of K1 Mountain Region

-0.5 0 0.5 1.0 1.5 2.0

Mean annual temperature

Winter (December, January, February) temperature

Summer (June, July, August) temperature

Precipitation change 1950-2016 (%)

-10 -5 0 5 10 15

Mean annual precipitation

Winter (December, January, February) precipitation

Summer (June, July, August) precipitation

Fig. 5.1: Temperature (left) and precipitation (right) trends in Canada in the ERA5 climate reanalysis, 1950 to 2016, expressed as degrees C of temperature change and % change in precipitation per decade. The top, middle, and bottom rows show the mean annual, winter (December, January, February), and summer (June, July, August) trends. Data from Hersbach et al., 2023.

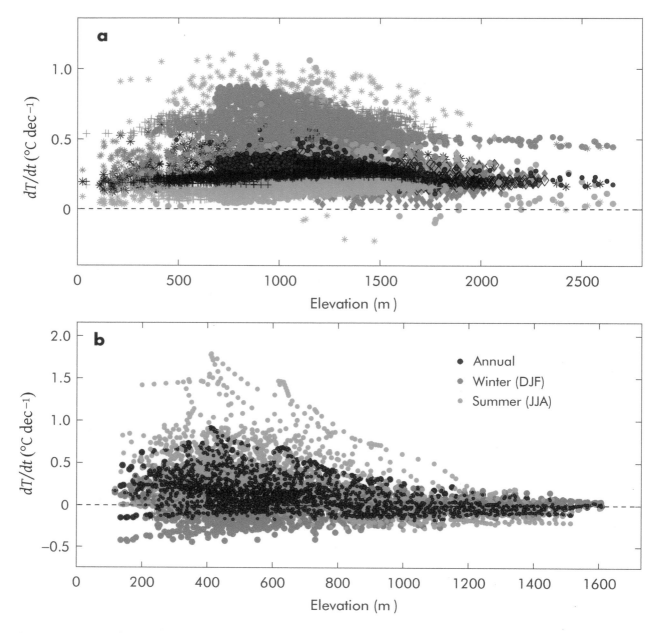

Figure 5.2: Rates of decadal temperature change from 1950–2021 as a function of elevation for each of the ERA5 grid cells in mountain regions of (a) western and (b) eastern Canada. Black, blue, and red symbols are for mean annual, winter, and summer temperatures, respectively. The various symbols in (a) refer to specific mountain regions: Pacific Maritime (asterisks), Montane Cordillera (circles), Boreal Cordillera (diamonds), and Taiga Cordillera (plus signs).

the influence of free-atmosphere conditions such as humidity changes (Williamson et al., 2020) rather than the influence of albedo feedbacks, as albedo effects should be strongest during summer and for maximum temperatures. Pepin and Lundquist (2008) report maximum warming in the elevation band near 0°C, where feedbacks from reduced snow and ice cover or other effects may be accentuated. At higher elevations, it is

often cold enough that snow and ice cover are not yet strongly affected by climate change; precipitation still falls as snow, not rain, and seasonal snow cover at high elevations may not (yet) be declining.

The extent to which EDW is occurring within Canada is unclear, and the dearth of high-elevation observational data makes it difficult to assess this. Sharma and Déry (2016) analyse temperature trends from 1950–2010 using interpolated climate station records in the Cariboo Mountains of British Columbia (Montane Cordillera). They report higher rates of warming in this region than the regional and national average, with a statistically-significant trend for the increase of minimum temperature with elevation but the opposite relation for maximum temperatures (i.e., muted warming at higher elevations). The analysis is mostly restricted to elevations below 2000 m, as there are insufficient station records to assess temperature trends above this elevation. Based on climate reanalyses, Williamson et al. (2020) report amplified warming at high elevations in the St. Elias Mountains, Yukon (Boreal Cordillera). This was attributed to increases in humidity and incoming longwave radiation above ~2000 m, also reported by Ochwat et al. (2021). We are not aware of other assessments of EDW in mountain regions in Canada.

There is no systematic pattern with elevation for the ERA5 temperature trends in Canada (Figure 5.2). All mountain regions in Canada are warming (Table 5.1), but only three of the seven major regions (Pacific Maritime, Atlantic Maritime, and Taiga Cordillera) show statistically significant increases in annual warming rates with elevation, from +0.06 to +0.12°C decade^{-1} km^{-1}. Distance from the ocean may be a factor here, as temperature changes are moderated in low-elevation coastal environments. Three other mountain regions in Canada see *less* warming at higher elevations (Montane Cordillera, Boreal Cordillera, and Arctic Cordillera). Temperature changes in the Arctic Cordillera decline with elevation, with a gradient of -0.23°C decade^{-1} km^{-1} (Figure 5.2b). The strongest decline in warming rates with elevation in the Arctic Cordillera is in the summer months, with an altitudinal gradient of -0.48°C decade^{-1} km^{-1}. This may be due to the strong relation between Arctic warming and sea ice loss, which is felt most strongly at sea level; the climate change signal is muted at higher elevations on Arctic icefields.

The strongest EDW signal in Canada is in the summer months and the maximum warming rate is at low- to mid-elevations, roughly 500–1200 m in western Canada and 300–600 m in eastern Canada. This may reflect elevations near the 0°C isotherm and with the strongest changes in snow and ice cover, as observed by (Pepin & Lundquist,

2008). Future warming trends may deviate from this pattern, if the strongest band of warming follows the 0°C isotherm or the summer snowline to higher elevations in the coming decades. It should also be restated that climate reanalyses and most climate models do not resolve the mountain-specific atmospheric and surface processes that may underlie EDCC. There is an acute need for increased high-elevation observations to test the EDW hypothesis in Canada and to fully understand what climate change means for alpine environments (Hik & Williamson, 2019).

5.2.2 *Historical precipitation trends*

Weather station data show mixed precipitation changes across Canada in recent decades, and this is also true of the mountain regions in Canada (Fig. 5.1). Northern Canada has gotten wetter, with observed precipitation increases of 20–50% from 1948–2016 (Bush and Lemmen, 2019). This is reflected in the observations of Brandy Mayes of the Kwanlin Dün First Nation, who notes the increasing unpredictability of precipitation regimes in Yukon Territory (LC 5.3). The magnitude and sign of historical precipitation changes in most of southern Canada are more equivocal, with modest drying in some locations but recent annual precipitation totals within 10% of 20th-century baseline values.

Within the ERA5 climatology, historical precipitation trends also show a complex regional and seasonal picture. Overall, precipitation in Canada increased by 0.4% per decade from 1950–2021, with a decline in winter precipitation (0.8% per decade) offset by increases in precipitation in the spring, summer, and autumn. The Arctic Cordillera is the only Canadian mountain region to follow this overall pattern, with strong increases in summer and annual precipitation (+3.5 and +1.8% per decade, respectively), along with drying

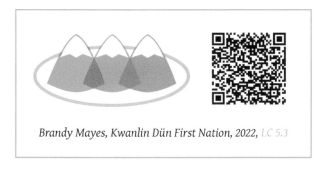

Brandy Mayes, Kwanlin Dün First Nation, 2022, LC 5.3

in the winter season (-2.2% per decade). These are among the strongest precipitation signals in the country. In the Pacific Maritime, Montane Cordillera, and Eastern Subarctic mountain regions, both winter and annual precipitation declined over the historical period. In contrast, the Boreal and Taiga Cordillera regions in northwestern Canada are exceptions to this overall trend, with increased winter precipitation of +1.1 to +1.5% per decade. Summer precipitation changes are regionally variable, but most mountain regions in Canada have seen increased summer precipitation.

It is important to recognize the need to monitor and model surface evaporation rates and soil moisture levels within these considerations, as increased evapotranspiration in a warmer climate can offset increases in precipitation and lead to drier conditions overall. This is difficult to infer or estimate from climate reanalyses, without specific resolution of the mountain environments. This analysis also cannot separate rainfall and snowfall, without sufficient definition of the mountain topography. However, declines in winter precipitation are projected in several of the mountain regions of Canada, at rates of up to -4% per decade. Combined with winter warming, this would lead to reduced winter snowpacks (Sec. 2.3.4). This is echoed in the comments of Elder Gùdia Mary Jane Johnson, Lhu'àùn Mân Ku Dań, who discussed the shifting seasons and the increasing unpredictability of the snow and ice seasons (LC 5.4).

5.2.3 *Caveats and research gaps*

The ERA5 climate reanalysis used here has a longitude-latitude resolution of 0.25 degrees (Hersbach et al., 2020). Over Canada, this translates to ~28 km in latitude by ~5 to 20 km in longitude, with finer coverage in northern Canada. At this resolution, reanalyses do not resolve detailed mountain weather and climate processes. Nor will they capture details of precipitation and snowpack distribution in the mountains, alpine ecological, hydrological, or cryospheric conditions, or atmospheric processes such as cold air drainage or the phase of precipitation in the mountains. However, climate reanalyses provide a good representation of regional-scale historical temperature and precipitation trends in different mountain regions in Canada. This is valuable in the context of the CMA, as long-term climate conditions in mountain regions in Canada are not well-observed or documented. Targeted high-resolution modelling studies are needed to construct mountain meteorological and climate change processes in more depth, including a detailed assessment of EDCC. The effects of changing wind and circulation patterns on precipitation trends also require further exploration.

5.2.4 *Future climate projections*

Recent reports of the Intergovernmental Panel on Climate Change (IPCC, 2021; 2022) present global climate change scenarios for an ensemble of global climate models and for different assumptions about future emissions, known as 'shared socio-economic pathways' (SSPs) (Riahi et al., 2017). Model projections were coordinated and compiled through the sixth international Coupled Model Intercomparison Project exercise, known as CMIP6.

Sobie et al. (2021) assess the CMIP6 archive for the ensemble of climate model projections over Canada, illustrated in Fig. 5.3 and demonstrating the wide range of potential climate futures in Canada. There are differences between the climate models, but the dominant factor is the future emissions trajectory. SSP1 describes a scenario for global cooperation and emissions reductions similar to what has been pledged in the Paris Agreement (i.e., achieving net-zero emissions by mid-century), while SSP5 is the opposite scenario, representing a world with intensive ongoing development, limited global cooperation, and minimal adoption of climate mitigation policies, giving continued increases in greenhouse gas emissions. This is essentially our current trajectory, although effective implementation

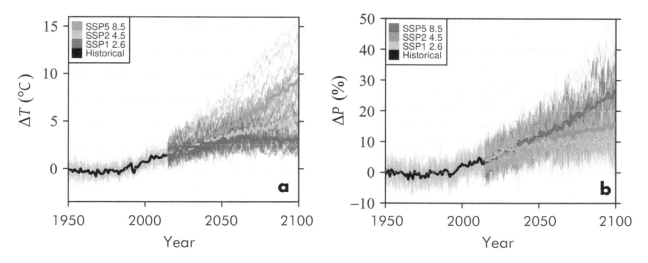

Figure 5.3: Projected (a) temperature and (b) precipitation changes over Canada to 2100 from the suite of CMIP6 climate models for scenarios SSP1-2.6, SSP2-4.5 and SSP5-8.5, after Sobie et al. (2021). Each line indicates individual model results, with the colours indicating the SSP scenario and the heavy lines showing the mean of all models for each SSP scenario.

of current global emissions reductions pledges would deflect us from this scenario and set the world on a course closer to SSP2.

The Canada-wide projections in Fig. 5.3 indicate a warmer, wetter country, overall, although temperature and precipitation changes in future decades depend a great deal on the emissions trajectory. There is ongoing climate change in the next two decades with all scenarios, due to inertia in the climate system and the time required for large-scale emissions reductions (i.e., through the necessary transformation of energy and transportation systems). For SSP1, where emissions are aggressively reduced and the buildup of greenhouse gases in the atmosphere is eliminated by mid-century, the climate system stabilises and average warming over Canada reaches about 2.5°C, accompanied by a 10% increase in annual precipitation over Canada. For SSP2 and SSP5, climate change continues through the century but there are radical differences in the national average by the year 2100, depending on how much global greenhouse gas emissions can be reigned in. For SSP2, Canada warms by about 5°C by 2100, with a 15% increase in average precipitation, while SSP5 projections indicate a mean warming of almost 10°C, with a ~25% increase in annual precipitation. There is considerable spread in the model forecasts for 2100, associated with the climate sensitivity of different global climate models. This means that forecasts for 2100 are highly

uncertain; climate change in Canada might be moderate relative to the ensemble mean forecast, but changes in Canada could also be even more severe.

Detailed future climate change projections over Canada were analysed in the 2019 Canada's Changing Climate report (Bush & Lemmen, 2019) and show the same essential picture of a warmer, wetter Canada in future decades, but there are important regional differences. CMIP6 projections for end-of-century from the most recent version of the Canadian climate model, CanESM5 (Swart et al., 2019) are shown in Fig. 5.4 to 5.6.

Table 5.2 compiles projected future temperature and precipitation conditions over the major mountain regions in Canada for the period 2071–2100. Results are presented for the CMIP6 simulations from CanESM5 for scenarios SSP1, SSP2, and SSP5, based on the gridded climate model data that intersects each mountain region. Results are also shown for the full Canadian land mass. All regions are expected to experience significant warming by end-of-century, with warming trends of 0.3–0.5°C per decade for SSP1 and 0.9–1.6°C per decade for SSP5. As is well documented elsewhere (e.g., Bush & Lemmen, 2019), the northern regions of Canada experience the most acute warming; the Arctic Cordillera, Eastern Subarctic, and Taiga Cordillera all see annual mean temperature increases that exceed the national average. Warming is most dramatic in the winter months

Table 5.2: Projections of future climate conditions for the different mountain regions in Canada. Calculated from the CMIP6 simulations of the CanESM5 Earth system climate model, based on the mean of 10 simulations (i.e., a 10-member ensemble) for the historical period (1850–2014) and future projections (2015–2100) from the SSP1-2.6, SSP2-4.5, and SSP5-8.5 emissions scenarios. The baseline climatology is from 1971–2000 and the SSP projections are the means for the period 2071–2100. Trends are calculated from 2000–2100, expressed as decadal rates of change, and winter (DJF), summer (JJA) and mean annual values are denoted w, s, and a. Bold values highlight large departures from the average Canadian trends.

Projected Temperature and Precipitation Conditions, 2071–2100: CanESMS-CMIPS

Mountain Region	Annual Temperature (°C)				Temperature Trends, 2000–2100 (°C dec⁻¹) SSP1-2.6			SSP2-4.5			SSP5-8.5		
	Ref	SSP1	SSP2	SSP5	w	s	a	w	s	a	w	s	a
Pacific Maritime	2.7	6.2	7.6	10.5	0.3	0.3	0.3	0.5	0.5	0.5	0.9	1.0	0.9
Montane Cordillera	0.4	4.0	5.5	9.0	0.3	0.3	0.3	0.5	0.5	0.5	0.9	1.1	0.9
Boreal Cordillera	-5.1	-1.4	0.4	4.0	0.3	0.3	0.3	0.6	0.5	0.6	1.2	1.0	1.1
Taiga Cordillera	-7.8	-3.3	-0.9	3.6	0.5	0.3	0.3	1.0	0.5	0.7	1.8	0.9	1.3
Atlantic Maritime	0.2	4.9	6.9	10.7	0.5	0.3	0.3	0.8	0.5	0.6	1.4	1.0	1.2
Eastern Subarctic	-6.5	-0.3	2.2	6.6	0.7	0.3	0.4	1.1	0.6	0.8	1.8	1.2	1.4
Arctic Cordillera	-21.1	-13.6	-10.6	-5.7	0.8	0.2	0.5	**1.5**	0.3	0.9	**2.7**	0.6	1.6
All of Canada	-2.2	2.6	4.8	8.9	0.5	0.3	0.4	0.9	0.5	0.7	1.6	1.0	1.2

Mountain Region	Annual Temperature (m)				Precipitation Trends, 2000–2100 (% dec⁻¹) SSP1-2.6			SSP2-4.5			SSP5-8.5		
	Ref	SSP1	SSP2	SSP5	w	s	a	w	s	a	w	s	a
Pacific Maritime	1.72	1.92	1.97	2.11	1.3	0.8	1.2	1.6	**0.5**	1.6	2.7	-1.7	2.6
Montane Cordillera	0.99	1.18	1.23	1.33	1.5	1.9	1.9	2.3	1.9	2.5	3.6	1.6	3.7
Boreal Cordillera	0.86	1.06	1.15	1.35	1.6	2.2	1.9	2.5	3.1	3.1	4.7	4.1	5.3
Taiga Cordillera	0.48	0.62	0.68	0.82	1.9	2.2	2.2	3.4	3.2	3.7	5.4	4.9	6.2
Atlantic Maritime	1.21	1.42	1.46	1.52	1.5	1.0	1.3	3.0	**0.8**	1.7	5.4	**0.0**	2.3
Eastern Subarctic	0.85	1.09	1.15	1.25	2.4	1.3	1.7	3.8	2.0	2.8	6.3	1.6	3.9
Arctic Cordillera	0.27	0.39	0.44	0.58	**4.1**	2.3	2.5	**7.1**	**3.7**	**4.4**	**13.6**	**7.2**	**8.5**
All of Canada	0.69	0.81	0.86	0.96	1.7	1.3	1.5	3.3	1.8	2.5	5.9	2.9	4.3

in northern and eastern Canada, particularly for the Arctic Cordillera, but this is not the case for lower latitudes in southwestern Canada, where summer warming rates exceed the winter warming. Fig. 5.4 plots the projected century-scale temperature increases for each mountain region and the two end-member scenarios, SSP1 and SSP5. Fig. 5.6 illustrates the projected warming by 2050 within each mountain region of Canada.

Projected precipitation changes in each mountain region also have some systematic regional and seasonal structure. Mean annual precipitation changes generally scale with the amount of warming, and as a percentage are greatest in the Arctic Cordillera (Table 5.2 and Fig. 5.5, 5.6). The high rates of warming and wetting in the high Arctic are associated with a number of climate processes, including extensive sea ice loss in the high-emissions scenarios. Winter precipitation increases are greatest in all mountain regions, from 1–4% per decade for SSP1 and 3–14% per decade for SSP5. This bodes well for potential increases in winter snowpack in the mountains, although there is a trade-off against warming, which will cause a greater fraction of precipitation to fall as rain rather than snow at lower elevations (DeBeer et al., 2021; Mortezapour et al., 2022). This may increase the intensity of rain-on-snow driven flooding but projected frequency of rain-on-snow events is highly location-dependent (López-Moreno et al., 2021). Increases in high-elevation snowpack can be expected in most regions, though lower latitudes in the Pacific and Atlantic Maritime regions, where winters are relatively mild, may see increased winter rainfall rather than snow accumulation at high elevations.

Summer precipitation also increases across mountain regions in Canada in most of the future

Predicted temperature change (°C)

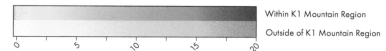

Within K1 Mountain Region

Outside of K1 Mountain Region

SSP1-2.6   **SSP5-8.5**

Mean annual temperature change

Mean annual temperature change

Winter (December, January, February) temperature change

Winter (December, January, February) temperature change

Summer (June, July, August) temperature change

Summer (June, July, August) temperature change

Figure 5.4: Projected temperature changes in 2050 relative to the reference period 1971–2000 for scenarios SSP1-2.6 (left) and SSP5-8.5 (right). Top, middle, and lower panels show the mean annual, winter (December, January, February), and summer (June, July, August) temperature anomalies, respectively, calculated from the mean CanESM5 temperature projections for the period 2036–2065. Data from Swart et al., 2019, 2019a, 2019b.

Within K1 Mountain Region

Outside of K1 Mountain Region

-50 -25 0 25 50 75 100 125

SSP1-2.6

SSP5-8.5

Mean annual precipitation

Mean annual precipitation

Winter (December, January, February) precipitation

Winter (December, January, February) precipitation

Summer (June, July, August) precipitation

Summer (June, July, August) precipitation

Figure 5.5: Projected precipitation changes (%) in 2050 relative to the reference period 1971–2000 for scenarios SSP1-2.6 (left) and SSP5-8.5 (right). Top, middle, and lower panels show the mean annual, winter (December, January, February), and summer (June, July, August) precipitation anomalies, respectively, calculated from the mean CanESM5 precipitation projections for the period 2036–2065. Data from Swart et al., 2019, 2019a, 2019b.

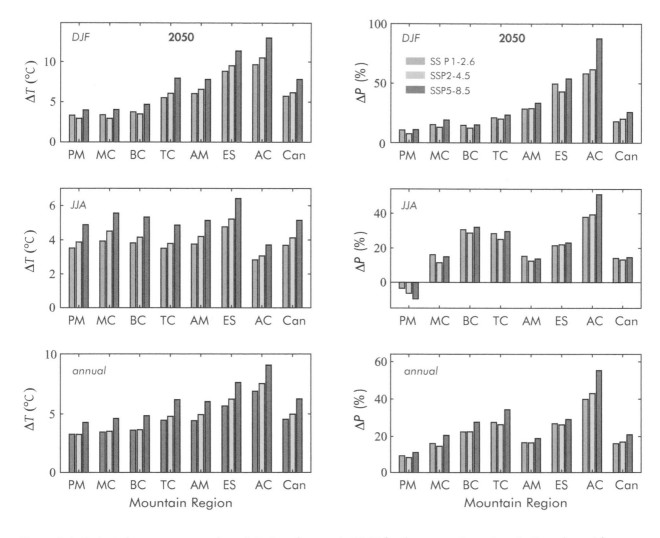

Figure 5.6: Projected temperature and precipitation changes in 2050 for the mountain regions in Canada and for all of Canada (Can) for future climate scenarios SSP1-2.6, SSP2-4.5, and SSP5-8.5 (Riahi et al., 2017). Anomalies are calculated from average conditions over the period 2036–2065 relative to the 1971–2000 baseline climatology. Simulations are from the CanESM5 model of the Canadian Centre for Climate Modelling and Analysis. Data from Swart et al., 2019.

climate change scenarios, although summer precipitation trends are weaker than the winter and annual values (Table 5.2). Scenario SSP5 is a notable exception, with summer precipitation projected to decline in the Pacific and Atlantic Maritime regions. Both of these coastal regions are projected to see a shift to warmer and drier summers, accompanied by modelled decreases in summer cloud cover. This weather setup is associated with greater wildfire risk, heat stress on lakes, rivers, and ecosystems, and high rates of glacier mass loss (e.g., WMO, 2022).

Climate change scenarios have been examined over specific mountain regions in Canada in

several previous analyses, most commonly within investigations of future changes in snow, glaciers, or hydrological systems (Clarke et al., 2015; Islam et al., 2017; Mortezapour et al., 2022). Future climate scenarios in the Montane Cordillera region have received the most attention (e.g., Murdock et al., 2013). The prediction of warmer, wetter conditions in future decades is unanimous in the published literature, but changes in precipitation vary geographically and seasonally. Drier summers are projected in southwestern Canada in many studies (Bush & Lemmen, 2019; Murdock et al., 2013), which would negatively impact the ecology, wildfire risk, stream and lake temperatures, freshwater availability, alpine snowpack, and glacier melt rates in mountains of the Pacific Maritime and Montane Cordillera regions.

5.2.5 *Caveats and research gaps*

The climate models used for these future scenarios do not resolve the mountain topography, so they cannot explicitly capture the detailed meteorological or climatological processes or elevation-dependent considerations that need to be understood for climate change impact assessment or adaptation activities in mountain regions. This is a clear gap in future climate change scenarios. Regional climate models help to bridge this gap and provide improved representation of precipitation patterns in mountain regions, but most regional climate modelling studies to date in Canada have resolutions of 10s of km, which do not explicitly resolve mountain slope or alpine processes (e.g., Murdock et al., 2013; Perroud et al., 2019). This makes it difficult to directly assess considerations such as local orographic precipitation processes, the rain-to-snow transition, snow avalanche hazards, or alpine ecological, hydrological, and glaciological processes as a function of elevation.

As an example, climate models generally predict increases in high-elevation precipitation in a warmer climate, but it is difficult to resolve changes in the snowline (rain to snow transition) and to predict the impacts on snow accumulation at upper elevations. There is broad consensus that snow accumulation and snow cover will decline at low elevations in the mountains, but numerous modelling studies project increases in snow accumulation at high elevations (e.g., Schnorbus et al., 2014; Shannon et al., 2019). There is limited direct data to assess this for the historical period. There is a chance that high-elevation snow accumulation has been increasing, or could increase in future decades, although such a trend is not evident for recent climate change in hydrological and glacier mass balance studies in the Montane Cordillera (Islam et al., 2017; Pradhananga & Pomeroy, 2022). High-elevation snow and precipitation observations are needed to assess this in the different mountain regions in Canada.

The overall structure of EDCC is highly uncertain in mountain regions in Canada. There is a narrative that warming is amplified in global mountain regions and at high elevations (e.g., Beniston et al., 1997; Palazzi et al., 2019; Toledo et al., 2022), but this is not well-documented in Canada (see Sec. 5.2.1). The influences of continentality, latitude, and regional climate change trends may dominate the elevation dependency in Canada, e.g., Arctic amplification in association with sea ice loss and increasing humidity; strong warming in western Canada in association with Pacific warming and changes in atmospheric circulation (Bush & Lemmen, 2019). Within a given mountain range, however, there are theoretical reasons to anticipate an elevation dependency as well (Pepin et al., 2015; Rangwala & Miller, 2012). Changes in snow, ice, and vegetation cover, atmospheric humidity, cloud conditions, and atmospheric lapse rates all influence surface climate conditions differently as a function of elevation, and these interactions need to be better understood to inform climate downscaling strategies and construction of high-resolution climate scenarios in alpine regions in Canada.

Additional studies of future climate projections in mountain regions in Canada should also consider ensembles of climate models. We restrict the analysis to the Canadian climate model here, CanESM5, with results based on the average of multiple realisations, but a rigorous analysis is needed to consider multiple climate models and to assess the skill of different models over the historical period in different regions of Canada.

5.3 Land Cover and Land Use Pressures

Development of land and waterways for industrial, agricultural, energy production, and municipal needs represents a significant anthropogenic pressure in some of the mountain regions in Canada, with direct impacts on ecosystems, hydrology, Indigenous lands and ways of life, and sacred cultural sites. Land use changes are introduced by a wide array of human activities, including clearing of land for industry (e.g., mines, quarries, forestry, oil and gas production), conversion to agriculture, horticulture and pastoralism; development and expansion of urban communities and transportation networks including road, rail, and human-use trails and; supporting infrastructure such as water treatment plants and landfills. The plentiful water supply and steep slopes in mountain areas are supportive of hydroelectric power generation, but hydroelectric facilities can have a large landscape footprint when they involve dams and flooding of the land to create reservoirs. These economic development activities and encroaching infrastructure all disrupt the biophysical environment, with particular concerns around natural hazards, habitat fragmentation, and loss of connectivity. They may also disrupt and displace existing human activities, relationships, and values in the landscape, with consequences for social, cultural, and economic life, especially in Arctic regions (Povoroznyuk et al., 2022). This has been steadily documented through history, both by Indigenous knowledge sources and scientific studies.

5.3.1 Changes in land cover

Mountain regions in Canada are covered by a wide range of surface types (see Chapter 2). Changes in land cover occur through both natural and human pressures (Hermosilla et al., 2018; Lambin & Geist, 2008), and can occur over both short (daily) and long (decadal) timescales. Deforestation or wildfire, for example, are two mechanisms for rapid land cover changes. Perennial snow cover and afforestation represent two slower mechanisms for land cover change. Changes in land cover have profound impacts on biodiversity and ecology (Sala et al., 2000), but also affect global and regional climate (Feddema et al., 2005; Mahmood et al., 2014) and hydrology (Matheussen et al., 2000; Quinton et al., 2019; VanShaar et al., 2002).

Rapid land cover changes have been observed in the Torngat Mountains (Davis et al., 2021b), where shrub-covered terrain has expanded over the past 30 years. A Canada-wide land cover change analysis for the period 2000–2011 found decreases in needle-leaf forests and attributed this to wildfires and the mountain pine beetle outbreak in the Montane Cordillera (Pouliot et al., 2014). To our knowledge, no studies to date have focused specifically and comprehensively on land-cover change in the mountain regions in Canada.

We use the annual land cover classification derived for all of the forested regions in Canada (Hermosilla et al., 2018, 2022) to examine land cover change in CMA mountain regions (Fig. 5.7)

between 1985 and 2019. Regions with little or no forest cover, including the Arctic Cordillera, Interior Hills North, Eastern Subarctic, and Taiga Cordillera, are not included in this analysis, as the dataset only covers forested regions. For the remaining regions, striking patterns of land cover change emerge.

The area of perennial snow and ice declined in nearly all regions, by 24 to 78%. This change reflects the declines in mountain glaciers and snowpacks described in Sec. 5.7. The only region to see an increase in snow and ice over this period was the Atlantic Maritime and Boreal Shield—and it is unclear if this is due to a small sample size, or the availability and timing of imagery used in the classification. Areas with extensive snow and ice coverage such as the Montane Cordillera and Pacific Maritime saw corresponding increases in rock and barren terrain, as deglaciation exposes barren alpine landscapes. The remaining mountain regions saw decreases in barren terrain, and this is most likely a result of forest expansion. All mountain regions saw increases in the area of broadleaf forests (+14% to +141%), and with the exception of Interior Hills Central region, all mountain regions saw substantial increases in the area of mixedwood forests (+41% to +422%). The magnitude of some of these increases may be due to small sample sizes, but they clearly indicate the need for further research on land cover changes in mountain regions in Canada.

5.3.2 Changes in land use

The three major land uses in Canada can be categorised as 'Cities and Farms', 'Shared Lands', and 'Large Wild Areas' (Fig. 5.8). This classification follows a global framework of land use classification (Locke et al., 2019). Cities and Farms represent the areas across Canada and its mountains with the highest level of land use and cover modification compared to historical baseline conditions. Those are the parts of the country that have the highest pressure from human settlement and agriculture (Coristine et al., 2018). The mountain ecosystems in that land use class have seen the highest level of modification and have seen extensive biodiversity loss. The 'Shared Lands' category is dominated by resource extraction uses such as forestry. The impact on biodiversity in these areas is less pronounced than in the 'Cities and

Percentage change in landcover types from 1985 to 2019

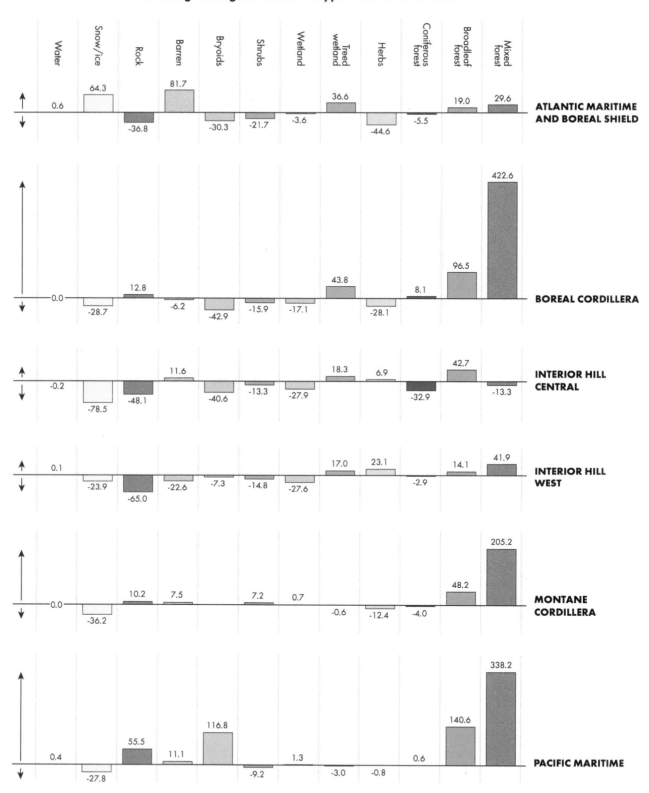

Figure 5.7: Percentage change in land cover types from 1985 to 2019 for six different mountain regions in Canada, as a percentage of the area in 1985. Columns are coloured according to the land cover type. Analysis based on the land cover dataset of Hermosilla et al., 2022.

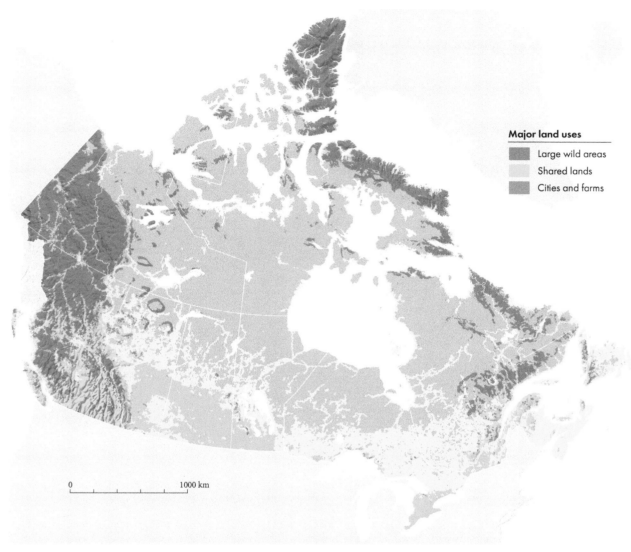

Figure 5.8: Map of major land uses across Canada. Bolded colours represent mountain regions. Data from Locke et al., 2019.

Farms' category, but still present. The mountains of this category are largely impacted by forestry operations related to access corridors, roads, and timber removal.

As a result of human modification, only about 40% of remaining forests have high ecosystem integrity globally (Grantham et al., 2020), with values only slightly higher in Canada. The least impacted and modified areas in Canada and its mountains can be found primarily in the North in the 'Large Wild Areas' part of the country. Mountain ecosystems and functions are least affected by direct human pressures in these parts of the country, but indirect impacts related to climate change and the proliferation of invasive species

are having a large effect on that part of Canada due to the high latitudes generally facing greater changes than other parts of the country (Sec. 5.2). 'Large Wild Areas' in northern Canada as well as the Rocky Mountains represent some of the largest areas of forest with high integrity globally (Grantham et al., 2020).

A recent study on anthropogenic pressures across Canada (Hirsh-Pearson et al., 2022) concluded that some of the most ecologically intact areas of the country can be found in northern mountain regions, where 95% of the area has been classified as ecologically intact. In the southern montane regions, roughly 66% of the area is still

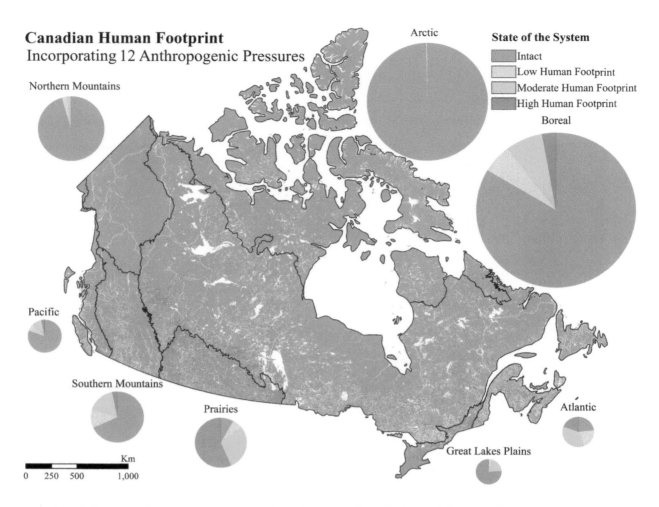

Canadian Human Footprint
Incorporating 12 Anthropogenic Pressures

Northern Mountains

Arctic

State of the System
- Intact
- Low Human Footprint
- Moderate Human Footprint
- High Human Footprint

Boreal

Pacific

Southern Mountains

Prairies

Atlantic

Great Lakes Plains

Km
0   250   500   1,000

Figure 5.9: Anthropogenic stressors and human footprint across Canada in 2016 (from Hirsh-Pearson, 2022).

ecologically intact (Fig. 5.9). For this work, individual anthropogenic pressures such as roads, crop land, and population density are combined into a human footprint metric that is meant to represent the cumulative anthropogenic pressure across Canada as well as globally (Venter et al., 2016). The highest anthropogenic pressures in Canada are roads (see also Poley et al., 2022), crop land, and population density. Forestry, built environments and pasture lands contribute to the pressure values as well, but each of them contributes less than 10% to the human footprint scores generated for Canada. Combining anthropogenic pressures data with information on climate change impacts would further help us in assessing the health of our mountain ecosystems.

To the best of our knowledge, there are no specific future land use and land cover change predictions available for the entire country that would help us predict potential future pressures

on mountain ecosystems in Canada. There are some efforts available, however, to quantify land use risk at a global scale in the form of global land systems analysis (Kehoe et al., 2017; van Asselen & Verburg, 2012). Those efforts are not specific to mountain ecosystems and primarily focus on agricultural development (Kehoe et al., 2017). This kind of information can be of use for planning protected areas for biodiversity conservation into the future (Schuster et al., 2022), however, we would ideally want Canada-specific information on predicted future land use and land cover in order to best estimate the associated impacts on mountain ecosystems.

5.3.3 Demographic changes

There is no dedicated approach to understanding demographic changes specifically in mountain regions in Canada, although broad demographic traits and recent trends can be found in census surveys conducted across the country. The delineation of mountain boundaries using geomorphological standards rarely matches enumeration units from census surveys (e.g., the K1 definition of Kapos et al., 2000; McDowell & Guo, 2021), although assumptions can be made about demographic traits in the mountain regions of Canada from census data outside of these defined mountain boundaries.

Global gridded population datasets such as from the Center for International Earth Science Information Network (CIESIN) can also provide a starting point for looking at broad demographic trends in the mountain regions of Canada. We use the gridded population dataset from CIESIN (2018) to observe long-term population changes in mountainous areas. As Table 5.3 below shows, population increases within the mountains in Canada are generally slower than the national average rate of increase from 2000 to 2020. The three major mountain regions with relatively large human settlements (Atlantic Maritime and Boreal Shield, Montane Cordillera, and Pacific Maritime) all experienced below national average population increases over the past two decades. Notably, migration out of the Interior Hills Central mountain region since 2000 was close to 7%, a significant loss of inhabitants in the region.

To explore more recent demographic change in the mountains, we used a similar approach with federal census data from Statistics Canada (2022) from 2016 and 2021, selecting census subdivisions (municipalities) where >50% of the jurisdictional area overlapped with K1 mountain boundaries (McDowell & Guo, 2021). We find that the Pacific Maritime and Montane Cordillera in the west, and the Atlantic Maritime and Boreal Shield mountain regions in the east, demonstrate significant variability in population change, with some municipalities within the mountainous census subdivisions experiencing population decreases of up to 20% and others increases of >15% from 2016 to 2021. Overall, municipalities in these mountain regions experienced an average population growth of 7.2% from 2016 to 2021, slightly higher than the national average growth rate of 5.2%. Gender ratios (expressed as the number of males per 100 females) do not show any significant change from 2016 to 2021 (99.2 to 99.7). However, males are over-represented in mountain regions in Canada relative to the national average, with national gender ratios of 96.5 in 2016 and 97.1 in 2021.

5.4 Resource Development Pressures

5.4.1 *Resource extraction and development*

Resource extraction activities such as mining, oil and gas development, and logging all involve land-use changes (Sec. 5.3), which can be highly visible in mountain regions. Mining scars and clear-cuts often persist for decades in mountain environments, where soil development and reforestation can be slow. These directly alter

Table 5.3: Approximate population count by major mountain regions, clipped to the CMA's 10 mountain regions using the CIESIN global gridded population dataset for the years 2000 and 2020. Note: population numbers do not necessarily account for socio-cultural significance or human presence on the landscape.

Major Mountain Regions	2000 population	2020 population	Percent change in population 2000–2020
Arctic Cordillera	190	253	33.3%
Eastern Subarctic	606	622	2.7%
Atlantic Maritime and Boreal Shield	161,891	183,537	13.4%
Boreal Cordillera	33,402	45,734	36.9%
Interior Hills Central	4922	4596	-6.6%
Interior Hills North	4	5	30.8%
Interior Hills West	16,591	22,110	33.3%
Montane Cordillera	848,967	1,020,490	20.2%
Pacific Maritime	38,441	49,861	29.7%
Taiga Cordillera	132	201	52.2%
Total mountain population	1,105,146	1,327,409	20.1%
National estimate	29,591,177	37,309,968	26.1%

ecological and hydrological function, causing habitat loss and changes in habitat connectivity. In addition, many resource extraction pressures do not necessarily involve land-use changes, including hunting and fishing, harvesting of herbs, berries, and medicines, and water extraction or diversion for industry, communities, or energy production. Unsustainable hunting, fishing, and harvesting activities can represent a significant pressure on ecosystems and biodiversity.

Most water extraction and use in mountain regions is non-consumptive (e.g., municipal water supplies or run-of-river hydroelectric projects), although water quality and temperature is altered as the water is used, treated, and returned to the rivers. Where water is diverted to reservoirs, there will be increased heating and evaporative losses, also affecting the downstream water supply. There can also be consumptive water use by irrigation and industry, affecting both water quantity and quality. For instance, where water is diverted to snow-making activities in ski areas, most of the water remains within the catchment and returns to the system. However, this can introduce chemicals into the environment and may represent a transfer between streamflow and groundwater recharge, which can in turn impact base flows or rivers or aquifer levels. Moreover, substantial energy is required for the snow-making itself, which feeds back on natural systems through increasing demand for power.

The extractive nature of resource development has invasive and colonial elements that go beyond just land-use changes. Local and remote human activities can act as sources of pollution that compromise soil, air, and water quality in mountain regions. Learning Circle participants, including Elder Gùdia Mary Jane Johnson, Lhu'ààn Mân Ku Daǹ, expressed concern that resource extraction activities can also introduce toxic chemicals to the soils, air, and water (LC 5.5).

Gùdia Mary Jane Johnson, Lhu'ààn Mân Ku Daǹ, 2022, LC 5.5

Many aspects of pollution in mountains in Canada are similar to broader concerns in Canada and globally, but there are also several mountain-specific concerns (McCune et al., 2019). Wildfire smoke has increasingly negative impacts on air quality, felt strongly in many mountain regions due to their proximity to forest cover and the way that high elevations intersect air flows (e.g., Yao et al., 2020). Persistent organic pollutants that have been banned in Canada since the 1980s, such as polychlorinated biphenyls (PCBs) and Dichlorodiphenyltrichloroethane (DDT), continue to melt out of old glacier ice in the Canadian Rockies (Blais et al., 2001). As described in Mountain Environments, these legacy contaminants are being released to alpine streams in low but measurable quantities. Deposition in mountain environments contains other far-travelled pollutants as well, such as heavy metals from upstream industrial activity (e.g., smelters). Mining activity and oil and gas development can also produce toxic tailings that contaminate soils and enter the hydrological system. As an example, high concentrations of selenium released through coal mining activities are well documented in western Canada and internationally, with negative impacts on water quality and aquatic ecosystems (Orr et al., 2006; Rudolph et al., 2008).

5.4.2 *Logging pressures*

Resource development and extraction such as mining and logging activities have cascading implications for the economies, cultures, and health of mountain communities across Canada, especially of Indigenous People. The impacts from the loss of intact forest are described by Watson et al. (2018) as "Fragmentation and degradation of the forest make a traditional lifestyle no longer tenable, pushing indigenous peoples off their land, and driving people to adopt production systems that are incompatible with the maintenance of intact forests. As traditional forest peoples become increasingly sedentary and connected to urban markets, gender roles, diets and cultural values also change. These changes in the lifestyles of indigenous and traditional peoples create greater dependence on urban markets for provisioning, which can lead to effects that erode their cultural identities. Indeed, for many indigenous forest peoples their cultural sense of self is inextricably linked to intact forests."

Degradation and loss of intact forests in mountain regions in Canada is significant due to logging and climate change. These pressures are also interrelated with the socio-political institutions including land tenure, land use planning and forest management that date back many decades if not hundreds of years. Forest management systems in eastern Canada, for example, are based on centuries of colonial and neo-colonial relationships with forest ecosystems and forest peoples including Indigenous Peoples. Mi'kmaq for example, have been legally excluded from pursuing forest-based livelihoods including logging as a result of Supreme Court decisions such as *R. v. Marshall, R. v. Bernard*:

> *The Supreme Court ruled that Mi'kmaq people should not be allowed to utilise the timber resources on Crown land in New Brunswick and Nova Scotia because they had not done so in 1760–61. Logging was not perceived to be a traditional occupation or need of the Mi'kmaq people, unlike fishing. Fishing was thought to be a traditional need and way of subsistence for those living along the coast or on the water* (Graham, 2015, p. 2).

These kinds of decisions, which assume Indigenous Peoples' cultures and livelihoods are static and frozen in time (e.g., 1760), have been highly contested.

Loss of forest resources due to widespread logging in eastern Canada and elsewhere has had significant ecological impacts in mountains. One example is the fate of the white cedar, as described by Campbell and Laroque "to allow naturally occurring eastern white cedar to disappear from the Nova Scotian landscape would be to allow a piece of living natural history to fall to the wayside, removing a significant cultural icon that connects us to the past" (Leddy, 2013).

One solution to this emerging problem of forest ecosystem degradation and associated impacts on biodiversity, livelihoods, and cultures involves the support of the leadership of Indigenous Peoples, including the respect for Indigenous title, knowledges and forest management practices (Berkes & Davidson-Hunt, 2006; Watson et al., 2018). "Although comprehensive global analyses are lacking, some regional data reveal the remarkable contribution of stewardship by forest peoples to sustaining high-integrity forest systems, often in the face of substantial pressures to liquidate forest timber or mineral resources" (Watson et al., 2018).

There is generally limited development in the Arctic mountain ranges of northeastern Canada, but impacts from developments in the western Arctic and subarctic regions are more significant and comparatively better described. The mountains of Yukon Territory are sites of significant forestry and mining activity, with a long history of developments and plans to continue this pattern. Resource development in these mountain spaces follows a similar pattern to other sites further south in Canada, with sites in higher terrain accessed by a network of roads which act as conduits for impacts, magnifying any point specific impacts in the mountains and acting as a potential barrier for wildlife and a conduit for human traffic and disturbance (Coffin, 2007; Trombulak & Frissell, 2000).

Resource development in the Yukon mountains is also noteworthy for a strong history of, and potential for, both downstream and upstream impacts (Webster et al., 2015). Wanda Pascal of the Teetl'it Gwich'in Nation (a Learning Circle participant) noted how the placement of a fibre optic cable to a mine in the Richardson Mountains increases the potential for natural hazards to disrupt communications links in the mountains (LC 5.6). Mountain spaces can be particularly high-consequence environments for resource development due to the potential for impact pathways to carry downstream effects into other lower elevation ecosystems. Whether due to increased runoff due to deforestation, or increased sedimentation in valley bottom rivers, downstream effects have been noted in relation to historic Yukon mines (Pentz & Kostaschuk, 1999).

Wanda Pascal, Teetl'it Gwich'in, 2022, LC 5.6

5.4.3 *Mining and fossil fuel pressures*

Mining and fossil fuel production result in significant pressures affecting mountain environments and the communities associated with and downstream of mines. British Columbia alone has 173 mines that have produced over 300,000 tonnes of ore, including 21 operating mines (Bellringer, 2016; Office of the Auditor General of British Columbia, 2022). Most of these mine sites have associated pollution concerns. Water contamination is the most common threat presented by mountain-region mines. Acid mine drainage is a concern at more than a third of mountain mine sites, and remediation is expensive. It is estimated that mitigating acid mine drainage at the Tulsequah Chief mine in northwestern British Columbia will alone cost $60 million (British Columbia Ministry of Energy, Mines and Petroleum Resources). Selenium pollution of watershed systems is a common product of coal mining. Reproductive failures and deformities of fish in the Elk River valley watershed of southeastern British Columbia are attributed to Selenium sourced in waste rock dumps from the Teck Sparwood coal mine (Bellringer, 2016). And as was spectacularly demonstrated by the 2014 mine tailings pond collapse at the Mount Polley mine, instability and collapse of tailings piles and ponds is an ever-present problem (Bellringer, 2016). The Mount Polley tailings pond collapse spilt 24 million cubic metres of mine waste into Quesnel Lake in the Montane Cordillera. Watershed pollution is not the only risk. For example, the abandoned Thetford asbestos mines in the Maritime mountain region south of Quebec City, which closed in 2011, are responsible for asbestos contamination of the surrounding communities exceeding government limits and are associated with significantly increased risks of cancer (Belleville, 2011).

Oil and natural gas production also present significant pressures for mountain regions. Oil and gas pipelines cut across mountains, valleys, rivers, and permafrost, disrupting animal migration routes and providing access to once pristine wilderness areas. While spills are not common, even small spills can be locally devastating. Canadian pipelines leak about 1000 barrels per year (Canada Energy Regulator statistics). Gas and oil leakage from abandoned wells is a significant problem, especially for Alberta. Hydraulic fracturing (fracking), the practice of injecting fluids at high pressure into 'tight' oil-bearing strata risks pollution of groundwater and aquifers, and has resulted in the triggering of earthquakes (induced seismicity). Above all, fossil fuels are the prime contributor to global warming as their combustion releases CO_2, a potent greenhouse gas, into the atmosphere.

5.4.4 *Invasive species*

Like pollution, invasive species pose a broad challenge to ecosystem health, but there are several specific considerations in mountain regions. Invasive and non-native species of plants and animals can be deliberately or accidentally introduced into mountain environments through recreational or industrial activities, where they may proliferate at the expense of native species and ecosystem functioning. For instance, the spread of spotted knapweed has altered plant community composition and arthropod health in grasslands of the montane west (Foster et al., 2021), and eastern brook trout introduced to mountain lakes have successfully out-competed the endangered westslope cutthroat trout, leading to genetic hybridization of native species and reducing alpine fish biodiversity (Pacas & Taylor, 2015; Schindler & Parker, 2002). Elder Hayden Melting Tallow, Siksika Nation (Blackfoot Confederacy), discussed such changes in the composition of species affect the web of kinship relationships that form the backbone of Blackfoot ways of knowing, threatening their sacred relatives (LC 5.7).

Mountain pine beetle, although native to western Canada, has heavily impacted many mountain regions of Canada, killing wide swaths of mature forest in regions east and north of its native range. Elder Gùdia Mary Jane Johnson, Lhu'ààn Mân Ku Dań described the effects of the spruce bark beetle on the forests of the Yukon (LC 5.8). Whirling disease is a parasite affecting salmonid fish populations that was discovered in Johnston Lake in Banff National Park in 2016, and has since spread to other freshwater sites in the Alberta foothills (Veillard & James, 2020). Like the spread of mountain pine beetle, whirling disease is enabled by warming temperatures (Nehring & Walker, 1996), though it also requires a vector, and is often associated with tourism and visitation.

5.5 Growing Pressures from Mountain Tourism and Recreation

Pressures from increasing tourism and recreation visitation and the attendant increase in supporting infrastructure (e.g., transportation networks to create access) represent another significant anthropogenic pressure in mountain regions, particularly those near urban population centres in southern Canada. Elder Gùdia Mary Jane Johnson, Lhu'ààn Mân Ku Dań, explained how these activities have significant impacts on her Nation's Traditional Territory (LC 5.9).

Mountain tourism and recreation can also involve significant disturbance and displacement through land use and land cover changes, particularly in the case of ski areas and golf courses, resulting in landscape fragmentation, slope erosion, and loss of habitat connectivity (Ladle et al., 2019; St. Louis et al., 2013). Mountain tourism and recreation also drives increased vehicle congestion and costs of living for nearby communities, resulting in increased threats to human health and wellbeing. These impacts can extend to non-human animals as well, such as concerns regarding the impact of increased traffic on polar bears in the case of the Torngat Mountains National Park (Maher & Lemelin, 2011). Protection of infrastructure to service tourism and recreation activities has resulted in changes in forest fire and flood control management practices, altering species composition and threats from hazards. As Elder Gùdia Mary Jane Johnson, Lhu'ààn Mân Ku Dań explained, these alterations to fire management regimes carried out in part to shape visitors' experiences in parks, including in Kluane National Park on her Nation's Traditional Territory, displaced longstanding Indigenous practices of care for the landscape (LC 5.10).

Further, mountain recreation and tourism can contribute to a loss of sense of place and the erosion of associated place attachment through increased competition for resources, such as recreational areas, and displacement of local people by 'amenity migrants' (Lemelin et al., 2012; Maher & Lemelin, 2011). For Indigenous Peoples, these experiences represent the ongoing effects of colonial displacement from many mountain areas. Access to mountain recreation opportunities—particularly in parks and protected areas—is widely known to be inequitable, and Indigenous Peoples on whose territories these activities take place frequently experience barriers to accessing these places. Dawn Saunders Dahl, Métis (Red River Ojibwe), described the experience of working with Stoney Nakoda youth who felt alienated from the parks other visitors enjoyed (LC 5.11).

As the population of Canadian mountain communities grows and the number of people seeking adventure tourism experiences increases, the popularity of mountain-focused recreation activities is also on the rise. Though the sparse availability of data makes this change difficult to quantify, especially at wide geographic scales, limited studies and datasets demonstrate a significant shift. For example, Parks Canada reports a 28% increase in visitation at the seven mountain parks between 2010 and 2020 (Parks Canada Agency, 2021) and Helicat Canada—the group that represents commercial helicopter and snowcat skiing operations—reported a 20% increase in skier days between 2013–15 and 2016–18

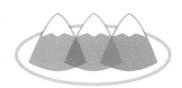

Hayden Melting Tallow, Siksika Nation, Blackfoot Confederacy, 2022, LC 5.7

Gùdia Mary Jane Johnson, Lhu'ààn Mân Ku Dań, 2022, LC 5.8, LC 5.9, LC 5.10

Dawn Saunders Dahl, Métis (Red River Ojibwe), 2022, LC 5.11

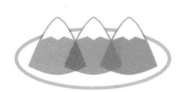

Dawn Saunders Dahl, Métis (Red River Ojibwe), 2022, LC 5.12

(Helicat Canada, 2019). The increasing popularity of nature-focused recreation and tourism has impacts on both natural environments and human mountain community dynamics.

Gaudreau (1990) explains that ecosystems are vulnerable to many negative effects caused by recreation, including habitat modification, wildlife disturbance, and the introduction of new or invasive species, and Burgin & Hardiman (2012) contend that a paradigm shift is required to better reflect ecological priorities in outdoor recreation management. While there are data gaps related to specific species, a general finding that recreation disturbs many forms of wildlife is well documented, especially motorised recreation in the mountain west. For example, snowmobiling displaces mountain caribou from suitable habitat and has been a factor in their population decline (Seip et al., 2007). Mountain goats are also sensitive to motorised recreation, with one study showing that they are "moderately to strongly disturbed" by all-terrain vehicles (ATVs) nearly half the time (St-Louis et al., 2013). Non-motorized recreation can also be problematic, with Voyer et al. (2003) demonstrating that hiker activity disturbs pikas, causing them to initiate antipredator behaviour which reduces foraging time. Mountain caribou were also shown to be sensitive to non-motorized backcountry skiing in Gaspesie National Park in Quebec (Lesmerises et al., 2018).

Certain forms of recreation (hunting, fishing) have more direct impacts on populations. Wildlife managers are sometimes challenged to sustainably manage fish and wildlife populations with recreational value in the absence of quality data, a finding Lofroth and Ott (2007) confirmed for wolverines, which have experienced unsustainable harvests in some population units in British Columbia. A legacy of stocking in mountain lakes has also affected alpine ecosystems, as exemplified by in Banff National Park, where historic stocking practices displaced now at-risk native species (bull trout, westslope cutthroat trout) with other species (brook trout, rainbow trout) considered more desirable to anglers at the time (Schindler, 2000). Studies from other non-Canadian jurisdictions also detail the challenges faced by managers when confronting this legacy (Chiapella et al., 2018). The impacts of this legacy are felt downstream as well, highlighted by the words shared by Hayden Melting Tallow of the Siksika Nation (Blackfoot Confederacy) and Dawn Saunders Dahl, Métis of the Red River Ojibway people, regarding the introduction of non-native fish species to improve angling for recreators (LC 5.7, LC 5.12).

Fishing and hunting can, however, also be a tool for conservation, with multiple studies documenting the results of attempts—some successful and some not—to manage certain wildlife populations through selective harvest of others. For example, Paul et al. (2003) describe efforts to selectively harvest brook trout in favour of restoring native cutthroat trout in a Rocky Mountain stream, while Serrouya et al. (2017) evaluate the efficacy of moose harvest as a means of reducing wolf populations and therefore improving mountain caribou survival in southeastern British Columbia. In addition, hunting and angling associations have played a substantial role in funding and advocating for wildlife conservation, with several examples from the mountains of western Canada detailed in Heffelfinger et al. (2013).

With regards to ecosystem impacts, limited attention is being paid to the impacts of recreational activities on the physical environment, such as ecological degradation associated with hiking and human-use trails (Nepal & Way, 2007) and the shift away from 'low-impact relaxation holidays' towards adventure tourism vacations (e.g., ATV tours), which have greater impacts on sensitive alpine ecosystems (Burgin & Hardiman, 2012). This relatively limited body of research reveals important gaps in our understanding, some of which include waste generation (e.g., McConnell, 1991; Nepal, 2016), impacts on biodiversity (e.g., Geneletti & Dawa, 2009; Lynn & Brown, 2003; Stevens, 2003; Tolvanen & Kangas, 2016), and the impacts on habitat of alpine species (e.g., Immitzer et al., 2014).

While academic literature on this topic is limited, the impacts of mountain recreation in

Canada have been acutely observed and felt by many Indigenous Peoples. Elder Gùdia Mary Jane Johnson, Lhu'ààn Mân Ku Dań, shared her observations regarding the impacts of activities such as rafting, mountain biking, and fly fishing on the natural environment (LC 5.13). Given that visitation to mountain regions in Canada is on the rise, the lack of literature at the nexus of tourism, visitation, and the natural environment represents an important gap. A gap that is highlighted by tourists' expectations and the level of acceptable change they are willing to endure, particularly in relation to environmental degradation (Needham et al., 2004, 2011).

Mountain communities are also experiencing the effects of a growing interest in mountain-based recreation. Destination management and marketing organisations have, in some circumstances, been so successful that their role is shifting to a focus on preserving the nature of the community and experience, rather than simply attracting visitors. Mountain communities are confronted with different phenomena related to visitors or newcomers. Some are experiencing high levels of nature-based tourism, even 'overtourism' which contributes to lower levels of visitor satisfaction while hiking and mountain biking (Kohlhardt et al., 2018; Needham et al., 2011), and in some cases this has led to conflict between users, particularly on multi-use trails (Neumann & Mason, 2019). Other communities are host to high rates of second home ownership (Mcnicol & Glorioso, 2014), and still others are hubs for 'amenity migration' (Gripton, 2009), which sees the movement of mobile workers or retirees to areas with outstanding recreational or environmental qualities (Chipeniuk, 2004). There is a growing body of literature on the challenging effects of short-term rentals on housing markets, and while there are few studies focused on Canadian mountain communities (e.g., Petit et al., 2022), studies from other jurisdictions provide useful evidence for this issue (e.g., Combs, et al., 2020).

Recreation and tourism have been actively promoted by mountain communities in recent decades as a strategy through which to facilitate an economic transition away from declining resource industries like forestry. Residents of many areas acknowledge the importance of tourism to the vitality of the community (Nepal, 2008; Perehudoff & Rethoret, 2021). However, the growing number of people coming to communities to experience their recreational assets brings challenges. Nepal and Jamal (2011) detail some of the common issues faced by emerging 'resort communities', including local concerns about economic leakage (i.e., through amenity developers hiring non-local crews), "enclavic" developments that happen on the outskirts of town and therefore draw visitors away from downtown, and specific planning challenges. Kelly and Williams (2007) describe one such challenge in their analysis of water supply in Whistler, British Columbia, where the high water demands of visitors, especially in the peak summer tourism season when natural water supplies in mountain communities are often at their lowest, has required development of innovative solutions. These challenges are also evident in Indigenous communities, where tourism-related development has encroached on both access to and use of ancestral lands evident in the story shared by Keara Lightning of the Nehiyaw, Samson Cree First Nation (LC 5.14).

Most literature to date focuses on recreation and tourism impacts on mountain communities, which generally emerges from western communities like Whistler, Banff/Canmore, and interior British Columbia resort communities like Revelstoke and Rossland. These works collectively point to a need for mountain communities to improve planning capacity, including bolstering available datasets, in order to better understand and respond to the challenges posed by increasing rates of nature-based tourism and recreation.

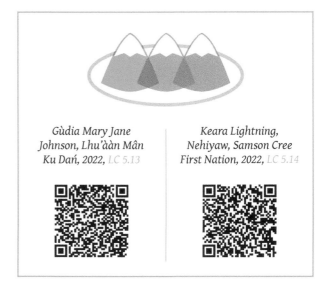

| *Gùdia Mary Jane Johnson, Lhu'ààn Mân Ku Dań, 2022, LC 5.13* | *Keara Lightning, Nehiyaw, Samson Cree First Nation, 2022, LC 5.14* |

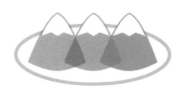

Dawn Saunders Dahl, Métis (Red River Ojibwe), 2022, LC 5.15

Yan Tapp, Gaspeg First Nation, 2022, LC 5.16, 5.17

Gabrielle Weasel Head, Kainaiwa Nation, Blackfoot Confederacy, 2022, LC 5.18

Hayden Melting Tallow, Siksika Nation, Blackfoot Confederacy, 2022, LC 5.19

5.6 Changes in the Governance of Mountain Spaces

Legal and jurisdictional decisions over 'ownership' of the mountains have a strong impact on development, access, and the availability of these spaces for Indigenous traditional cultural or recreational practices. The establishment of the mountain National Parks in Alberta, British Columbia, and later in Yukon Territory displaced some of these Indigenous practices, including hunting and fishing rights. Governance of the national parks regions and development of settler infrastructure in these regions (e.g., towns, ski areas) have direct impacts on the gifts of the mountains (Fig. 5.10). As Dawn Saunders Dahl (Métis, Red River Ojibwe) explained, the parks have long excluded Indigenous Peoples in the Canadian Rockies around Banff and Jasper National Parks (Montane Cordillera) from accessing the places where governance is passed down from generation to generation, disrupting their systems of governance (LC 5.15). As Yan Tapp, Gaspeg First Nation explained, these same tensions exist in eastern Canada with respect to private ownership, land management, and access to traditional lands (LC 5.16, LC 5.17).

A major component of Indigenous/settler relations in much of Canada, in particular surrounding governance of land, is based on treaties. Mountain environments in Canada (with the exception of much of British Columbia) are within the territories of many treaties, including the major numbered treaties (e.g., Treaties 6, 7, 8, and 11 cover much of the Canadian Rockies). The treaties made provisions for co-existence of Indigenous Peoples and settlers upon the ceded territories. Per the spirit of these documents, Indigenous consultation and co-governance surrounding land and environment (or governance in unceded territories) must be adhered to and upheld, in keeping with key tenets of the UN Declaration of the Rights of Indigenous Peoples (UNDRIP, 2007). As provinces and the federal government adjudicate land claims, and as modern day treaties are negotiated and renegotiated with First Nations, Métis, and Inuit governments across Canada, governance of mountain landscapes is shifting and evolving.

As discussed in Mountains as Homelands, colonialism brought non-Indigenous populations to Canadian mountain regions, which generated and continues to exert pressures in new ways—especially in the areas of governance, consultation, and overall viewpoints on *who* the mountains are for—or more specifically, who has the right and responsibility to guide the trajectory that mountain environments take in an era of environmental change. Learning Circle participants—including members of the Blackfoot Confederacy Gabrielle Weasel Head (Kainaiwa Nation) and Elder Hayden Melting Tallow (Siksika Nation)—spoke extensively about the pervasive and ongoing effects of colonial dispossession, settlement, and extraction in mountain spaces. By actively excluding and suppressing Indigenous governance and stewardship, they explained, the colonial model of land management resulted in fragmentation of the landscape, disrupted kinship relationships among people and other-than-human beings, and initiated a pattern of unsustainable extraction which continues to obstruct opportunities for a livable future for future generations in mountain places (LC 5.18, LC 5.19).

Figure 5.10: A sequence of historical and repeat photographs from the Mountain Legacy Project (MLP) collections (http://explore.mountainlegacy.ca/) overlooking the town of Jasper from The Whistlers in Jasper National Park shows significant changes in land cover associated with the establishment of the Park and changes in governance. The original photograph (M.P. Bridgland, Dominion Land Surveyor) from 1915 (top) depicts a patchy mosaic of mixed-age coniferous stands (A), and the early development of the town of Jasper (B). Small-scale farmsteads were established in the Athabasca Valley in the 19th century by Métis peoples, who were evicted from the Park after it was established in 1907; while not visible in these images there are legacies of these pre-Park activities on the landscape today (C). The first repeat photograph taken in 1998 by MLP crews (middle) shows much of the pre-existing patchwork has been replaced by dense, maturing coniferous stands (D), and the treeline ecotone has moved upslope (E). The town expanded well beyond its 1915 outline. The subsequent repeat photograph also taken by MLP crews in 2022 (bottom) shows the pervasive effects of a new disturbance, mountain pine beetle, as indicated by the red-grey hue of dead pine stands (F). To mitigate increased fire risk, recent mechanical thinning projects have reintroduced some of the patchwork on the bench above the townsite (G).

Daniel Sims, Tsay Keh Dene First Nation, 2022, LC 5.20

The UN Declaration of the Rights of Indigenous Peoples (UNDRIP) recognizes that Indigenous Peoples have a right to meaningful consultation and input into activities that occur in mountain environments, in both political-/socio-cultural spheres and economic spheres (UNDRIP, 2007). Indigenous Nations' abilities to exercise these rights are complicated by the persistence in legal proceedings of colonial definitions of territorial boundaries and governing authorities, which are often incongruent with Indigenous laws and governance of their Traditional Territories in place since time immemorial (LC 5.20). It is clear from the literature that there has been increasing engagement with Indigenous consultation surrounding mountain and mountain-adjacent environments, such as the Columbia River basin (Cohen & Norman, 2018; Cosens, 2012; Mouat, 2016; Sandford et al., 2014); landmark legal cases asserting Indigenous rights to territories and resources have considerably advanced the presence of Indigenous definitions of place in the context of Canadian law (Borrows, 1999, 2015; Christie, 2005; Rosenberg & Woodward, 2015); and the proliferation of Indigenous Protected and Conserved Areas (IPCAs) represents growing recognition of Indigenous stewardship rights (Plotkin, 2018; Zurba et al., 2019). Yet, the literature surrounding

COMMUNITY-LED RECREATION PLANNING IN SOUTHEAST BRITISH COLUMBIA

In British Columbia, use of public lands—which cover 94% of the area of the province—has traditionally been governed through a series of regional-scale resource management plans. These plans were intended to set a strategic direction for use of the resources that surround mountain communities and drive their economies (Government of British Columbia, n.d.-a). Two decades have elapsed since many of these plans were completed, and the land management context has changed substantially. The provincial government is modernising its approach to land use planning in order to reflect current drivers of land management, including a commitment to reconciliation with Indigenous Peoples (Government of British Columbia, n.d.-b). However, while the government works to develop this process and repair foundational government-to-government relationships with Indigenous Nations, land use pressures persist, leaving many communities seeking venues through which to take a more active role in setting a course toward a desirable future.

Many such examples centre on use of public lands for recreation and adventure tourism. The Columbia Valley Recreation Planning Initiative is bringing local and Indigenous communities, the provincial government, recreation groups, and land users together to develop a Recreation Strategy for public lands in the region. As a first step in the process, the groups collaborated to create a set of land use principles and ground rules that would guide plan development. The Shuswap Trails Alliance (and associated Regional Trails Roundtable and Trails Working Group) serves as a strategic meeting point for the various organisations involved in implementing a regional Trails Strategy. The strategy was developed in 2006 to unify various trail plans through a common focus on sustainability, inclusion, and health (Fraser Basin Council, 2019). The strategy was championed by the Secwepemc Nation, which continues to serve as lead government partner of the initiative, ensuring that regional trail work upholds their traditional values while also respecting their rights and title (Nadeau & Rethoret, 2021).

Multiple other examples exist, some of which were analysed by Nadeau and Rethoret (Nadeau & Rethoret, 2021) in an attempt to identify pathways and best practices for communities looking to engage in similar planning initiatives. Some of the best practices that emerged included developing meaningful partnerships with Indigenous governments, involving settler governments early in the process, ensuring public interests are well-understood and incorporated, and securing adequate funding to both develop and implement the plan.

mountains in Canada still displays a lack of engagement about the idea of what meaningful co-governance of mountain environments in Canada would look like. Absent this, as Gabrielle Weasel Head (Kainaiwa Nation, Blackfoot Confederacy) suggests, the consequences could be dire for Indigenous sovereignty in mountain environments (LC 5.18).

Indigenous/settler conflicts and pressures are not the only socio-cultural pressures that occur in mountainous areas in Canada. The possibilities for other sorts of friction points, including tensions between locals and outside companies/actors also exist, such as questions surrounding mining, tourism, and other forms of economic development which occur in mountain environments. While the literature here is more robust and does a better job at outlining these potential conflicts, there is also a marked bias in the literature towards examples in western Canada versus other mountainous areas in the country (Chipeniuk, 2005; Hudson & Miller, 2005; Jamal & Getz, 1999; Needham & Rollins, 2005; Nepal, 2008; Nepal & Jamal, 2011; Neumann & Mason, 2019; Sadler, 1983; Saremba & Gill, 1991). While this points towards key conflicts that are occurring in the West, such an emphasis also indicates consequential shortcomings in consideration of Indigenous/settler conflicts over economic-development pathways in other mountainous regions in Canada.

Emerging Threats and Impacts on Mountain Systems

"Mountains are like people, they are always changing"
—Tim Patterson, Lower Nicola Indian Band, Scw̓éxmx, Nlaka'pamux (Thompson) Nation (LC 5.21)

The different pressures that are acting on mountain regions in Canada have a compounding in-

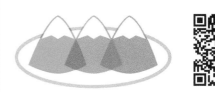

Tim Patterson, Lower Nicola Indian Band, Scw̓éxmx, Nlaka'pamux (Thompson) Nation Confederacy, 2022, LC 5.21

fluence on a wide range of physical, ecological, and social systems. Sec. 5.7 to 5.11 elaborate on the changes that are documented within each of these systems and the cascading stresses and threats associated with these changes.

5.7 Threats and Impacts from a Changing Cryosphere

5.7.1 *Changes in snowpack*

Snow cover change is typically diagnosed from *in situ* observations (Vionnet et al., 2021) and gridded blends of observations, analysis, and remote sensed products (Mudryk et al., 2018). As trends vary with elevation, estimated trends from coarse-resolution products can be more uncertain in alpine regions than in others. Changes in air temperature and precipitation (Sec. 5.3) have had profound global impacts on the snow cover processes of high mountain catchments (Hock et al., 2019), and the majority of snow cover changes observed in the mountain regions of Canada have been reported in the high-mountain Cordillera and Pacific Maritime ranges (DeBeer et al., 2021). During the past several decades, western Canada has had a widespread reduction in spatial and temporal extents of snow cover, decreases in snow depth, and shorter snow-covered periods by 1 to 2 months, generally due to earlier spring melt (Brown et al., 2020; DeBeer et al., 2021; Mudryk et al., 2018; Musselman et al., 2021). In the Boreal Cordillera, spring snow cover declines were observed at elevations up to and above 5000 m a.s.l. (Williamson et al., 2018). As the seasonal change in melt and accumulation occurs, there is evidence that the seasonal distinction between accumulation and ablation is increasingly blurred (Musselman et al., 2021).

In the Atlantic region, no trends have been detected for snow-cover changes in the mountains of the Gaspesie Peninsula (Fortin & Hetu, 2014), but a south-north gradient of decreased maximum snow accumulations and spring snow cover duration was found in southern Quebec (Atlantic and Boreal Shield), with increases in maximum snow and spring duration in northern Quebec (Eastern Subarctic) (Brown, 2010). Satellite data and ground observations point towards decreasing snow cover durations and maximum snow depths in the Arctic Cordillera (Brown et al., 2021), especially for maritime locations (Callaghan et al., 2011).

Warmer temperatures are a dominant cause of the snow cover extent decrease (Brown & Robinson, 2011). Increased air temperatures can enhance snowmelt due to an increase in available energy. Under continued warming, there is an increased likelihood of mid-winter melts (Musselman et al., 2017). Midwinter melt can cause ice growth at the snow-soil interface of seasonally or permanently frozen soil and impact runoff processes (Sec. 2.4; Marsh & Woo, 1984). However, a shift to earlier melt periods also means snowmelt occurs with lower available melt energy (López-Moreno et al., 2013; Marsh et al., 2012; Pavlovskii et al., 2019). Counterintuitively, this then manifests as slower snowmelt (Musselman et al., 2017; Pomeroy et al., 2015).

Warmer temperatures also affect the phase of precipitation, and the transition from snow to rain drives significant changes in streamflow (Musselman et al., 2018). These transitions are particularly sensitive during warm air precipitation (near 0°C) (Harder & Pomeroy, 2014; Jennings et al., 2018; Mekis et al., 2020) and at lower elevations (Shea et al., 2021) with substantial spatial variability in the sensitivity of these transitions (Jennings et al., 2018). Widespread warming will increase rain-on-snow events at mid- to high-elevation areas that are still covered by snow in the spring (Corripio & López-Moreno, 2017; McCabe et al., 2007; Musselman et al., 2018).

Warmer temperatures can also affect the redistribution of snow. Warmer, wetter, and older snow is less susceptible to blowing snow transport (Li & Pomeroy, 1997) and therefore reduced sublimation loss and transport. In a study in the Montane Cordillera, Pomeroy et al. (2015) found that a warming of 5°C reduced blowing snow transport by up to 50%, and decreased sublimation by 30%. The change in snow cover distribution then impacts the rate and timing of ablation (Debeer & Pomeroy, 2017). The impact of warming snow covers on avalanche formation remains an open question (Strapazzon et al., 2021). However, there is evidence for decreased mid-winter low-elevation avalanches and an increase, even in mid-winter, in the occurrence of wet-snow avalanches (Strapazzon et al., 2021). Elder Gùdia Mary Jane Johnson, Lhu'ààn Mân Ku Dań, also described an increase in sloughing activity as a

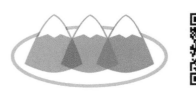

Gùdia Mary Jane Johnson, Lhu'ààn Mân Ku Dań, 2022, LC 5.22

consequence of climate change and melting permafrost, which presents significant hazards for people travelling on the landscape (LC 5.22).

Warmer and wetter snow intercepted in the forest canopy is more likely to quickly unload and fall to the ground as the retention of intercepted snow is highly temperature dependent (Ellis et al., 2010; Lundquist et al., 2021) despite snowfall interception efficiency being generally insensitive to air temperature (Hedstrom & Pomeroy, 1998). Snow that is intercepted by the forest canopy is prone to high sublimation rates (Pomeroy et al., 1998). However, the phase of this unloading is somewhat unclear, and may be from meltwater in the canopy (i.e., liquid) or solid snow/ice cover (Lundquist et al., 2021). Increases in air temperature can result in snowmelt under the canopy to become more long-wave radiation dominated (Lundquist et al., 2013).

Patches of late-lying or perennial snow and ice are used by caribou for seeking relief from flies and for cooling during warm summer days (Ion & Kershaw, 1989). Correspondingly, their reduction and disappearance can influence animal behaviour. Alpine perennial snow patches, small ice bodies without significant movement, are subject to permafrost conditions and can therefore preserve organic materials for thousands of years (Andrews & MacKay, 2012). A marked reduction in snow- and ice-patch area has been found in Canada and Europe (Farnell et al., 2004; Ødegård et al., 2017), both leading to the exposure of valuable archeological artefacts and to fears about their accelerated loss.

Projected changes in snow regime in the Montane Cordillera have been synthesised by DeBeer et al. (2021). Over the coming decades, climate warming will result in a shift of precipitation from snow to rain, especially noticeable during shoulder seasons, at lower elevations, and in southern regions, as well as more frequent rain-on-snow events, warmer and wetter snow, more mid-winter rainfall and melt events, and earlier spring melt and snow cover depletion. Future snow regimes are expected to see similar shifts for the Pacific Maritime region, with earlier onset of snowmelt and a shift towards rain-dominated regimes especially noticeable for lower elevations (Islam et al., 2017; Schnorbus et al., 2014; Sobie & Murdock, 2022). Recent change and projected future change varies strongly with elevation, so projected changes in snow storage dynamics have a large spatial variation. Spatial and elevation gradients in precipitation and snowpack and how they will change are not well quantified.

The Arctic as a whole is expected to see declines in snow cover (5–10%/decade) and maximum snow accumulations (10% per decade) by 2050 (Mudryk et al., 2018). Mountain regions of eastern Canada (Eastern Subarctic and Atlantic Maritime and Boreal Shield) are also expected to see declines in snow cover duration and maximum snow accumulations, with greater impacts near the coast (McCrary et al., 2022).

Trends in snow-cover extent, duration, and SWE observed across Canadian mid-latitudes in recent decades are expected to continue and possibly speed up in the coming decades (Aygün et al., 2020). The projected future trends depend on the climate scenarios and climate model used, the snow modelling scheme used, and the study area. Despite the predominant signal of an overall predicted decrease in snow regime metrics across mid-latitude cold regions, some studies have projected asymmetric changes in SWE depending on the current temperature regime. For example, while an overall decrease in SWE is projected for three river basins in British Columbia, with the largest reductions found in the Campbell River basin where cold seasons temperatures are already close to the freezing level, SWE is projected to increase at higher elevations in the Upper Columbia River basin, as precipitation increases while cold-season temperatures remain below freezing (Schnorbus et al., 2014). However, projections of future precipitation and phase partitioning are uncertain at local scales due to the uncertainty associated with EDW, the lack of high-elevation data to assess precipitation in climate models, and the high spatio-temporal variability in precipitation. This limits our capacity to assess future changes in SWE. Sensitivity

analysis, where a possible change in precipitation and temperature is applied to current weather to simulate future conditions, can provide insight as to how snow regimes may change in response to climate change (Rasouli et al., 2015).

5.7.2 Changes to glaciers

Multiple studies have estimated rates of past and current glacier area and volume change in mountain ranges in Canada. These include global assessments (Hugonnet et al., 2021; Pfeffer et al., 2014) to regional studies (Bolch et al., 2009; Menounos et al., 2019) and to specific mountain ranges such as the Canadian Rockies (Henoch, 1971; Tennant et al., 2012; Tennant & Menounos, 2013, DeBeer and Sharpe, 2007), the Torngats (Barrand et al., 2017; Way et al., 2014, 2015), the Cariboos (Beedle et al., 2015), the St. Elias Mountains (Clague & Evans, 1993; Flowers et al., 2014), the Canadian Arctic Archipelago (Dowdeswell et al., 2007; Thomson et al., 2011), and southern Baffin Island (Svoboda & Paul, 2009). There are also visual comparisons from repeat photography that help illustrate the change (Sansaverino et al., 2016).

Overall, there is large agreement that glaciers in Canada are shrinking and losing area, volume, and mass (Gardner et al., 2013; Hugonnet et al., 2021; Schiefer et al., 2007; Wouters et al., 2019), and that rates of glacier thinning and area change are accelerating. Long-term mass balance estimates from models and observation data show sustained mass loss since the 1960s in Arctic Canada (Noël et al., 2018; Sharp et al., 2011), the Pacific Cordillera and Montane Cordillera (Menounos et al., 2019; Moore & Demuth, 2001; Pradhananga et al., 2021; Shea et al., 2013), and the Boreal Cordillera (Barrand & Sharp, 2010; Chesnokova et al., 2020). Comparisons between individual approaches and studies are challenging as the time periods and study regions are rarely consistent.

Rates of glacier mass change, calculated from repeat digital elevation models derived from spaceborne remote sensing, have been published for all mountain glaciers using the common period 2000–2019 (Hugonnet et al., 2021). Here, we extract the average rate of glacier mass change over the period 2000–2019 for all glaciers in the individual mountain regions, and calculate regional averages (Fig. 5.11).

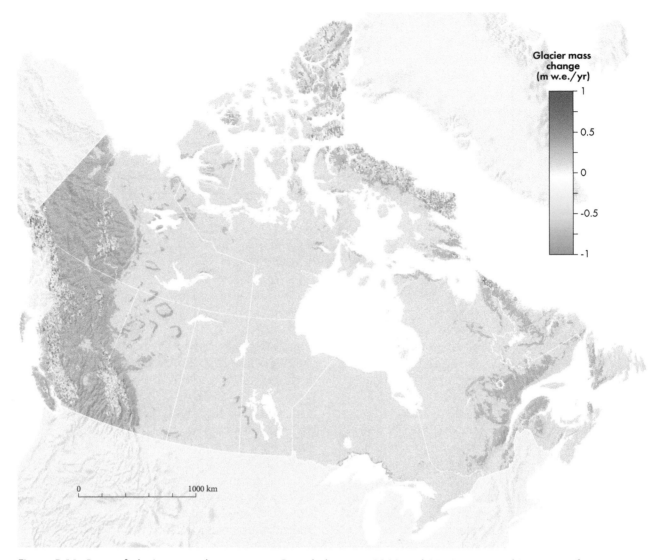

Figure 5.11: Rates of glacier mass change across Canada between 2000 and 2019, expressed in metres of water equivalent. Each dot represents an individual glacier. Data from Huggonet et al., 2021.

Average rates of glacier mass change (expressed as metres of water equivalent [m w.e.]) in mountain ranges in Canada are consistently negative, and vary between -0.36 and -0.56 m w.e. yr^{-1}. Also known as specific mass balance, these rates can be thought of as the average annual thinning (when negative) or thickening (when positive) over the glacier area. The highest average thinning rates in Canada are found in the Eastern Subarctic, Boreal Cordillera, and Montane Cordillera regions. The rates of mass change in Canada for the period 2000–2019 are less negative than those observed in Alaska, Iceland, New Zealand, and Central Europe, but more negative than in Central Asia and the Russian Arctic (Hugonnet et al., 2021).

The specific mass balance differs from the total mass balance or mass change, which is calculated from the specific mass balance times the glacier area. Due to its extensive glacierized area, the Arctic Cordillera experienced the greatest mass loss in Canada over the last two decades. From 2000–2019, glaciers in Canada lost ~2.2 million cubic kilometres of ice, for a total mass loss of ~1900 GT, which is enough to raise global average sea level by 5 mm.

As the current total glaciated area in western Canada is greater than what was present

7000–8000 years ago at the peak of deglaciation (Briner et al., 2016; Menounos et al., 2009), glacier changes today reveal landscapes and cultural practices frozen in time. An 8000-year history of caribou harvesting on Thandlat mountain, for instance, was recently exposed in the southern Tutchone territory of Kluane National Park due to glacier retreat (Cruickshank, 2005).

Projections of future glacier change in Canada are limited. In a regional simulation of glacier retreat across western Canada, Clarke et al. (2015) found that by 2100, glaciers of the western Canadian Cordillera will experience ~70% (RCP2.6) to ~95% (RCP8.5) reductions of both area and volume, relative to 2005 values. Only a few glaciers are predicted to remain in the Interior and Rocky Mountain regions by the end of the 21st century. For example, Haig Glacier, located on the eastern slopes of the Canadian Rockies, is estimated to completely disappear by 2080 (Adhikari & Marshall, 2013). South of the Canadian Rockies, glaciers of the Blackfoot-Jackson Basin of Glacier National Park, in Montana, are expected to completely disappear by 2030 (Hall & Fagre, 2003). On the other hand, coastal maritime glaciers, in particular those in the northwestern Coast Mountains of British Columbia, are predicted to survive but in a diminished state (Clarke et al., 2015). Estimates of glacier mass loss by 2050 are not sensitive to the climate scenario used in the simulation, but the extent of glacier retreat in the second half of this century depends on the magnitude of ongoing climate change.

There are no comparable studies for the glacierized regions of other mountain ranges in Canada, but estimates can be obtained from global studies. For example, Shannon et al. (2019) assessed global glacier volume change relative to 2011 conditions under the RCP8.5 climate change scenario. Within their global scenario, they project a complete (100%) retreat of glaciers in western Canada and a decline of 47 ± 3% for glaciers and ice caps in Arctic Canada, with the survival of these ice masses linked to an increase in snowfall relative to the present day. Estimates for these regions are consistent with global studies from Huss & Hock (2018) and Radic & Hock (2014).

While these large-scale studies of glacier evolution over the upcoming decades provide a consistent overview of glacier behaviour, they do not include local phenomena and various glaciological and climate processes that could either accelerate or slow down the retreat of individual glaciers, which limits their usefulness for local, basin-specific adaptation. Large-scale models often employ simplified melt models, for instance, rather than a full description of surface energy balance processes. Effects of katabatic winds, changing cloud cover, snow avalanching and redistribution, and many other local processes are complex and are not resolved at large scales, so are commonly neglected.

As a specific example, realistic representations of glacier albedo and its evolution over space and time are rarely included in models. Wildfire activity can lead to the deposition of soot on the glacier surface, and increase surface melt through a reduction in surface albedo (Aubry-Wake et al., 2022; Keegan et al., 2014; Marshall & Miller, 2020). Williamson & Menounos (2021) show that mountain glacier albedo is declining across North America, and the decline is correlated not only with rising temperature but also with the deposition of soot from wildfires. Aubry-Wake et al. (2022) found that glacier albedo at Athabasca Glacier in the Canadian Rockies gradually decreased after the onset of regional wildfires, and remained low for two years. Forest fire occurrence in western North America is increasing, in part due to warmer spring and summer temperatures and earlier snowmelt (Gillett, 2004; Westerling et al., 2006), and future fire activity under climate change scenarios is projected to increase extreme fire danger (Abatzoglou et al., 2019; Bedia et al., 2014; Stocks et al., 2003). Understanding the linkage between wildfire activity and glacier melt will be important to improve predictions of glacier melt.

Alpine glacier terminus collapses are also becoming a common sight on glaciers, and are attributed to the collapse of subglacial channels in combination with ice thinning and reductions in ice flux (Egli et al., 2021; Stocker-Waldhuber et al., 2017). Large blocks of ice are lost during such collapses, but this calving process is rarely accounted for in mass balance estimates of alpine glaciers. While most reports of these processes are in the Alps, similar features have been observed in western Canada. A related phenomenon that has been studied for Alberta's Columbia

Glacier is glacier detachment (Rippin et al., 2020). Glacier detachment and subsequent fragmentation lead to loss of ice supply to lower reaches of the glacier, which can then become stagnant. The remnants of the glacier tongue then waste away over a period of years to decades. This process seems to be underway for other glaciers of the Columbia Icefield as well.

Where the lower glacier is heavily debris-covered, it can be insulated from the sun and warm air, allowing the remnant ice to persist much longer. Many glacierized regions in Canada feature relict/buried ice or ice-cored moraines of this type, which are slowly melting and subsiding but may well outlive the main glacier that used to nourish them. Wenkchemna Glacier, behind Moraine Lake in the Canadian Rockies, is a good example of this kind of feature (Gardner, 1987), but buried ice and ice-cored moraines are widespread (e.g., Hayashi, 2020; Langston et al., 2011). These types of buried ice at the edge of the glacier can lead to instability and mass wasting in the marginal area of the glacier, as observed for Boundary Glacier (Mattson & Gardner, 1991).

Glacier retreat opens new terrain for proglacial development, a change already occurring globally (Shugar et al., 2020). A proglacial lake appeared in 2006 at Peyto Glacier in the Canadian Rockies, and has continuously expanded in concert with ongoing glacier retreat (Pradhananga et al., 2021). New proglacial lake development as glaciers retreat were also observed by Geertsema and Clague (2005) at the Tulsequah Glacier in northwestern British Columbia. The presence of proglacial lakes can impact glacier retreat by increasing ice volume loss through calving. There has been an increase in the number of studies examining the response of lake-calving glaciers to climate change, but limited studies focus on Canadian glaciers (Chernos et al., 2016). Overall, a combination of growing proglacial lakes and thinning glaciers is likely to enhance calving rates and accelerate glacier retreat. Proglacial or subglacial lake development is also linked to hazards such as glacier lake outburst floods (Clague & Evans, 1997).

Glaciers are also spaces of human connectivity and identity, with particular historical significance for Indigenous communities in the montane west and north (Cruikshank, 2005b). Many human systems such as agriculture, fisheries, hydropower, potable water, recreation, spirituality, and demo-

graphy adjacent to and beyond the glacierized regions of the mountains in Canada are impacted as glaciers progress towards near-complete disappearance (Carey et al., 2017; Drenkhan et al., 2022; Milner et al., 2017). In addition to threatening water resources by decreasing streamflow in summer, glacier retreat increases the risk of natural hazards affecting mountain communities, especially glacial lake outburst floods (Frey et al., 2010). Glacier retreat also impacts biochemical processes in alpine lakes and streams (Milner et al., 2017). As agents of erosions, glaciers deliver sediments and nutrients downstream (Hood et al., 2015; Hudson & Ferguson, 1999). They also help to maintain cooler temperatures in glacier-fed lakes and streams, supporting aquatic ecosystems and fish habitat that are adapted to these conditions (Lencioni et al., 2015; Milner et al., 2001). Glaciers, as hotspots of mountain recreation and tourism, provide opportunities for visitors to the mountains to engage with the consequences of anthropogenic climate change. As they continue to retreat, so too do these educational and engagement opportunities.

5.7.3 *Changes in permafrost*

"In the north we have permafrost. It's melting at a rate that we can't even keep monitors in it without them starting to sink away."—Brandy Mayes, Kwanlin Dün First Nation, Yukon (Boreal Cordillera) (LC 5.23).

Permafrost in Canada is warming and thawing (Biskaborn et al., 2019; Derksen et al., 2018), though few long-term borehole temperature records exist in mountains, and there, even fewer above the valley floors, to quantify the rate of warming (Gray et al., 2017). As Elder Mary Jane Johnson, Lhu'ààn Mân Ku Dań First Nation, and Brandy Mayes, Kwanlin Dün First Nation stated, Indigenous Knowledge Holders are keenly aware

Brandy Mayes, Kwanlin Dün First Nation, 2022, LC 5.23

of ongoing permafrost thaw, which has serious consequences for buildings, roads, and infrastructure, in addition to the increased risk of mass movements in the mountains (LC 5.24, LC 5.25). Wanda Pascal of the Teetl'it Gwich'in Nation also highlighted the implications of mountain permafrost thaw and other climate change-related hazards for the safety of using traditional trails in mountain areas, describing a large sinkhole she and her grandson encountered while travelling in her Traditional Territory (LC 5.26).

Because air temperature is the major driver of permafrost change, most permafrost in mountains in Canada will undergo warming during and beyond the 21st century, with stronger consequences expected for higher greenhouse gas emission scenarios (Hock et al., 2019). Permafrost warming is usually accompanied by permafrost thaw, the loss of some or all of the ice in a volume of ground. For example, when the active layer, which freezes and thaws seasonally, thickens, some part of the underlying permafrost will thaw during summer. This may lead to a lowering of the ground surface, or to landslides. Alternatively, if temperatures many metres deep gradually approach 0°C, the proportions of ice and water present in soil change. Less ice and more water in the soil reduce its mechanical stability and make it more permeable for water. As a consequence, a location can be underlain by thawing permafrost for a long time while impacts arising from the gradual loss of ice in the ground develop and persist. This can include impacts on ecosystems, water quality, geohazards, and livelihoods. Some are easily visible, such as the retrogressive thaw slumps of the Peel plateau (Kokelj et al., 2021), whereas many others, such as impacts on food security (Calmels et al., 2015) are gradual and often hidden from view.

Permafrost in mountains, its changes, and related impacts have been observed and studied in more detail in the European Alps and in the Scandes. While climate, geology and human interaction with the land are different in Europe, some inference about permafrost change in mountains in Canada, and its consequences, can be made based on this research (similar to the inference in Gruber et al. (2017). Permafrost thaw will affect sediment budgets and geohazards, hydrology, water quality, and ecosystems. The specific character and diversity of impacts and the pathways connecting climate to permafrost to physical impacts to impacts on people in Canada (for example as reduced food security and health) are important gaps in research.

Anticipating future impacts often relies, in part, on computer simulations. While coarse-scale Earth-system model simulations agree on a global reduction of permafrost extent and volume (Fox-Kemper, 2021) with further climate change, the regional and topographic patterns of these changes in mountains can only be understood with high-resolution simulations that are not currently available for mountains in Canada, except in few limited studies (e.g., Bonnaventure & Lewkowicz, 2011; Way et al., 2018). Methods for simulating permafrost change in mountains exist and their application in Canada is underway (Sec. 2.3.3).

The very sparse monitoring, the lack of simulation products for informing the assessment of (future) hazard regimes related to permafrost, and the near absence of research that explicitly considers how mountain topography affects permafrost and its change are important

Gùdia Mary Jane Johnson, Lhu'ààn Mân Ku Dań, 2022, LC 5.24

Brandy Mayes, Kwanlin Dün First Nation, 2022, LC 5.25

Wanda Pascal, Teetl'it Gwich'in, 2022, LC 5.26

gaps in knowledge about permafrost in mountains in Canada. In a 2014 workshop (Gruber et al., 2015), experts from diverse fields in science and engineering found that little was known about permafrost in the mountains of Canada and that research and public perception in Canada were biased towards lowland areas. Likely, this is due to the concentration of infrastructure and settlements in valleys or in gentle terrain, and to easier access on gentle slopes. It is, therefore, not surprising that in much of the literature cited in this assessment, research on permafrost in mountains in Canada does not investigate the influence of mountain topography on permafrost. As a consequence, our ability to understand permafrost environments in mountains in Canada, and to anticipate their future changes is severely limited.

5.8 Threats and Impacts from Changing Water Resources

5.8.1 *Changes in water supply*

Hydrological change in the mountains of Canada has been studied on multiple time scales. Over centuries to a few millennia, hydrological changes are recorded in the sediments of mountain lakes and valleys (Desloges & Gilbert, 1998; Desloges & Gilbert, 1995; Heideman et al., 2018; Menounos & Clague, 2008; Schiefer et al., 2011; Wilkie & Clague, 2009; Wolfe et al., 2011), and in tree rings (Fleming & Sauchyn, 2013; Hart et al., 2010a, 2010b; Mood & Smith, 2021; Sauchyn et al., 2015). Sediment cores from Lake Athabasca indicate that the last several hundred years have been a period of relatively high water availability in the Montane and Boreal Cordilleras, subsidised by glacier retreat since the end of the Little Ice Age around 150 years ago. Lake levels 2000–5000 years ago may have been 2–4 m lower than present (Wolfe et al., 2011). Paleoclimate reconstructions from tree-rings in the Oldman and South Saskatchewan watersheds indicate that droughts in the montane Cordillera had similar frequency but greater severity in the pre-instrumental period (before we measured precipitation and streamflow) back to 1400 years before present (Axelson et al., 2009). A tree ring reconstruction for two rivers near metro Vancouver in the Pacific Maritime mountain region found that more multi-year low-flow

conditions occurred recently (1992 to present) than the pre-instrument reconstruction period from 1711–1992 (Mood & Smith, 2021). The Pacific Decadal Oscillation has a marked influence on these long-term hydrological proxy records (Hart et al., 2010b).

Over recent decades, the volume and timing of water flowing down from the mountains in Canada has changed as the climate changes. Rood et al. (2005) found decreasing annual streamflows in the southern Canadian Rockies over the last century. However, these changes are not applied equally over the year. While late summer streamflows were declining, winter streamflow was found to be increasing due to more frequent rain or snowmelt events. The hydrological changes experienced in individual mountain regions depend on the basin characteristics, and whether they are dominated by glacial melt or snow.

In mountains where glaciers are present, long-term trends in streamflow are often tied to the concept of "peak water." As glaciers retreat, they initially produce more meltwater, causing a gradual increase in streamflow. As glaciers continue to retreat, they cross an area threshold, which results in an overall decrease in glacier melt contribution to streamflow. This decrease is expected to be especially noticeable in late summer flow, when glacier melt contributions are at the highest but other sources of water, such as rainfall and snowmelt, are reduced (Clarke et al., 2015). The point at which a glacier switches from increasing to decreasing melt contribution is termed "peak water," and this signal helps assess how glacier contribution to streamflow is evolving over time.

Multiple studies have observed decreasing trends in streamflow from glacierized watersheds in central and southern British Columbia and in southwestern Alberta which implies that peak water has passed in this region (Bliss et al., 2014; Casassa et al., 2009; Demuth et al., 2008; Rood et al., 2005; Stahl et al., 2008; Stahl & Moore, 2006). However, conflicting evidence highlights the complexity of these systems. For example, both Clarke et al. (2015) and Moore et al. (2020) predicted a peak water for the Columbia River headwaters near 2020, and Moyer et al. (2016) suggested that Bridge Glacier was near or at peak water, contradicting the decreasing trend observed in southern Alberta and British Columbia.

Similarly, Naz et al. (2014) did not identify a significant trend in annual or summer glacier melt for the Bow River above Banff from 1891–2007.

A few studies have sought to project future streamflow conditions in glacial watersheds using hydrological models. Chernos et al. (2020) estimated that peak water would occur mid-21st century, along with a decrease of up to 58% in late summer streamflow by 2100 for the Upper Athabasca River basin. Marshall et al. (2011) provided an estimate of future glacier contribution to streamflow on the eastern side of the Canadian Rockies using a statistical analysis of past conditions, finding a near disappearance of glacier volume by the end-of-the-century and a strong reduction in late summer flow. As glacier melt helps to buffer streamflow variability, both at the inter-annual, seasonal scale and at the event scale, the predicted glacier retreat will leave downstream environments more vulnerable to hot and dry periods (Fig. 5.12).

While many studies observe and/or project declining late summer streamflow in glaciated mountains in Canada, these trends become harder to detect—or may even show contradictory changes—in smaller catchments. This is because streamflow is controlled by more than just glacier change, and multiple processes and interactions occur within a watershed that can enhance or diminish observable changes in streamflow.

Hydrological changes are also occurring in snow-dominated mountain watersheds, with and without glaciers. DeBeer et al. (2016) conducted a review of hydrological changes for the interior of western Canada, within the Montane Cordillera. They found statistically significant declines in annual flows for smaller river basins, including those draining the eastern slopes of the southern Canadian Rockies. However, they do not distinguish between mountain and prairie landscapes in their synthesis. Furthermore, the timing of peak snowmelt runoff is shifting earlier in the year (Aygün et al., 2020a; DeBeer et al., 2016; Zhang et al., 2001). The magnitude of peak runoff either shows no significant trend or a negative trend, typically attributed to decreased snow accumulation due to a shift from snow to rain. This is supported by (Cunderlik & Ouarda, 2009), who find that annual peak flows are constant or declining in much of western Canada. Additionally, some natural hydrographs are exhibiting a decline in late summer flows, and an increase in winter flows (Rood et al., 2008; Zhang et al., 2001), attributed to lower melt contributions in late summer and increased winter streamflow from increased winter rainfall and snowmelt.

Downstream effects from Arctic mountain regions are also impacting northern communities. Mountains are drivers of weather, the sources of rivers and sediment, and create aquatic en-

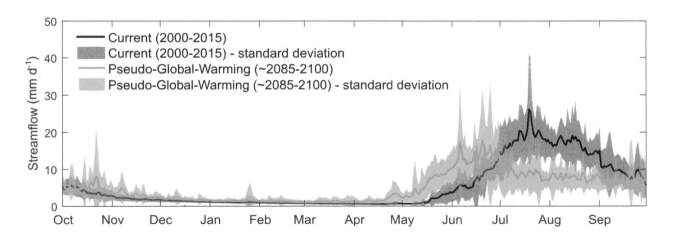

Figure 5.12: Change in simulated streamflow in the Peyto Glacier Research basin, for heavily glacier-covered (50% in 2005) and near complete glacier retreat (3% glacier-cover in for the 2085–2100 period) under an RCP 8.5 scenario. Adapted from Aubry-Wake et al., 2023.

vironments that support cold-water ecological habitats. While in some of the mountains of Arctic Canada the human footprint is limited, changes occurring in the mountains do affect downstream communities and aquatic ecosystems. Changes to snowpacks and glaciology across the mountains of Baffin Island, and other islands in the Eastern Arctic may alter char fisheries in low-elevation coastal rivers and streams, with consequences for the livelihoods of Inuit communities who fish there.

Although hydrological research in the Montane Cordillera has established that groundwater is an important, sometimes dominant, contributor to low-flows (e.g., Hayashi, 2020) and references therein; see Chapter 2), there is little information on how groundwater storage and discharge are *changing* across the mountains in Canada. The drivers of mountain surface hydrological change have implications for groundwater dynamics too. In particular, groundwater recharge may be changing as snowmelt occurs earlier in the year, and higher temperatures cause increased evapotranspiration. In colder/higher mountains, changes in glacier melt and permafrost are likely to alter groundwater dynamics (Somers & McKenzie, 2020). One of the only Canadian studies on this topic found slightly declining late-summer groundwater levels in British Columbia observation wells over 20–30 years of observation (Allen et al., 2014). This presents a substantial research gap in our understanding of mountain water resources in canada and improved observation well coverage would be an asset to advancing our understanding.

Observed changes in flood or drought frequency are difficult to establish due to their infrequent occurrence and typically poor quality data (Whitfield, 2012). For the Bow River at Banff, a well-studied and long-term mountain hydrometric station, Whitfield & Pomeroy (2016) found a significant negative trend for all floods over the last 100 years. However, when distinguishing between generation processes (either rain on snow or snowmelt), no trends were detected. Increasing extreme precipitation and flooding events are expected in western mountain regions in Canada as the atmosphere continues to warm (Pacific Climate Impacts Consortium, 2021). Landscape changes can compound climate-driven changes in flooding intensity. For example, catchments

Brandy Mayes, Kwanlin Dün First Nation, 2022, LC 5.27

disturbed by wildfire experience significantly higher peak flows than undisturbed catchments in the eastern Rocky Mountains (Mahat et al., 2016). Learning Circle participant Brandy Mayes (Kwanlin Dün First Nation) described experiencing higher flood frequency and intensity in the Yukon River Basin:

> In the last couple of years, Whitehorse and the Yukon has had more snow and rain than we've ever had. And we used to be a very dry climate. And they figure it's because the oceans are warming and creating more precipitation in our environment because it flows through this whole valley. This year, some areas are 180% more snow than ever historically recorded. And we're all preparing for floods—big time. We got flooded last year, in some areas really badly and this year they figure it's going to be worse [....] We'd call that part of climate change and how it's affecting our environment."
> (LC 5.27)

The trends observed in glacier-free, snow-dominated basins are expected to continue in the coming decades, with earlier snowmelt and higher winter flows. These shifts will be more pronounced in regions near the freezing temperature than in very cold regions (Aygün et al., 2020; Barnett et al., 2005; Rasouli et al., 2019; Stewart et al., 2004). This means that low elevation mountain basins are more susceptible to climate change. The predicted change in magnitude of peak snowmelt streamflow is not consistent across studies, due to the high sensitivity to the winter precipitation phase under a warmer climate (Minville et al., 2008; Wang et al., 2016). Snowmelt rates are also expected to change. In the "slower snowmelt in a warmer world" hypothesis, Musselman et al. (2017) suggested that shallower snowpack will

A'ÄY CHÙ' (SLIMS RIVER) DIVERSION, KLUANE NATIONAL PARK AND RESERVE, YUKON TERRITORY

Glacier retreat is one of the most visual manifestations of global climate change, with well-documented impacts on water supply in mountain areas. In Kluane National Park and Reserve, Yukon Territory, the retreat of Kaskawulsh Glacier has led to an even more profound impact on glacial runoff: water diversion to an entirely different drainage system (Clague & Shugar, 2023).

Kaskawulsh Glacier is one of the largest glacier systems in Canada, spanning a total area of about 1095 km² (Foy et al., 2011). A vast accumulation area in the St. Elias Icefields feeds several tributary glaciers which converge to create the main trunk of the Kaskawulsh, which is about 70 km in length. Like most glaciers in Canada, the Kaskawulsh has been thinning and receding, and in May 2016, retreat of the Kaskawulsh terminus passed a drainage divide and resulted in an episodic shift in meltwater routing from a northward direction, via A'äy Chù—the Slims River—to a southern drainage route into the Alsek River system. A'äy Chù feeds Lhù'àan Mân' (Kluane Lake) and the Yukon River system, so this drainage reorganisation means that the vast amount of meltwater running off from the Kaskawulsh system is now routed to the North Pacific Ocean south of Dry Bay, Alaska, rather than the Bering Sea (Shugar et al., 2017).

This water piracy event has hydrological and ecological impacts that are still evolving (McKnight et al., 2021). The level of Lhù'àan Mân', Yukon's largest lake, has dropped by more than 2 m and A'äy Chù is largely dried up. In combination with decades of fine silt and sediment deposition from the glacier runoff in this valley, this aridification and exposed sediments along the lake shore have created a large reservoir of readily-mobilised dust. The region experiences persistent, often gusty, katabatic winds from the St. Elias Icefields which are channelled down A'äy Chù, generating frequent dust storms with significant air-quality impacts on the southern shores of Lhù'àan Mân' (Bachelder et al., 2020).

Changes in the level of Lhù'àan Mân', reduced inflow, and greater wind-blown sediment are having impacts on lake ecology and access to the lake for fishing activities. There are also direct impacts of dust storms on air quality and visibility for residents of Kluane First Nation (e.g., Figure 5.13), as described by Elder Mary Jane Johnson, Lhù'àan Mân Ku Dań First Nation (LC 5.28).

Gùdia Mary Jane Johnson, Lhu'ààn Mân Ku Dań, 2022, LC 5.28

Figure 5.13: A dust storm at the A'äy Chù (Slims River) inflow to Lhù'àan Mân' (Kluane Lake) in August 2018. Photo by Gertrudius, CC-BY-SA 4.0.

melt earlier and more slowly compared to deeper and later-lying snowpacks. This is due to declining snow-covered areas and a snowmelt season shifting toward earlier periods with lower available energy. No consistent signal is expected for summer streamflow in snow-dominated basins: increased evapotranspiration could result in a decrease in summer flows, but increased precipitation could also lead to an increase in flow.

These predicted changes are exemplified by the snow-dominated Saint Charles River basin with headwaters in the hills of Charlevoix, QC, studied by Cochand et al. (2019). In the basin, winter stream discharges are predicted to increase by about 80, 120, and 150% for low, medium and high emission scenarios due to warmer winters, leading to more liquid precipitation and more snowmelt, for the 2071 to 2100 period compared to 1970–2000 period. The summer stream discharges were predicted to fall by about 10, 15, and 20% due to earlier snow-melt runoff and an increase in evapotranspiration. The annual mean stream discharge showed little change. Additionally, intense rain events on frozen ground could cause more frequent high winter flows in the future.

Similar changes were discussed by Rasouli et al. (2019) in a study of the hydrological response to climate change in three mountain basins in the mountain west. They projected an increased rainfall fraction of precipitation, and a hydrological regime shifting towards rainfall dominated, with the largest shifts in basins that are currently warmer. Annual streamflow did not change despite an increase in precipitation, as reductions in snow sublimation and increased evapotranspiration offset the changes in precipitation.

In addition to retreating glaciers, shifting precipitation phase and volume, increasing temperatures and evapotranspiration, the mountain landscape is also evolving. Changing land cover complicates the predictions of how water will be stored and flow in the upcoming decades. For example, the growth of proglacial lakes as glaciers retreat increases water storage in the basin, potentially increases evaporation, and influences the streamflow temperature (Bird et al., 2022). Vegetation colonisation of recently deglaciated areas also changes the hydrological functioning of the basin by increasing evapotranspiration (Carnahan et al., 2019). The primary succession and

soil development in the proglacial environment has been well-studied, with multiple case studies in varied glacierized environments (Burga et al., 2010; Glausen & Tanner, 2019; Jones & Henry, 2003; Schumann et al., 2016).

Trends in mountain streamflow are the integration of many interacting hydrological processes which can obscure the basin response to climate change. For example, Harder et al. (2015) found no trends in streamflow in the Marmot Research Basin between the 1970s and 2010s, in southern Alberta. This lack of change in streamflow occurred despite substantial changes in the basin forest cover due to large cut block or small forest gap clearing and increasing air temperature, and a shift in precipitation patterns and decreasing snow accumulation at lower elevation in the basin, despite ongoing changes in both land cover and climate in the region.

Understanding of hydrological change in the mountains in Canada has advanced in recent years, but remains limited by the short time series available with which to conduct trend analysis. These short records make it difficult to distinguish long-term trends, such as those linked to anthropogenic change, from natural variability linked to phenomena like the pacific decadal oscillation. Another general gap in streamflow change assessment is the lack of studies outside of western Canada. However, some studies may have been missed in our assessment if they do not explicitly refer to mountains. This is even more pronounced when considering other mountain regions in Canada, such as the Atlantic Maritime and Boreal Shield, where hydrological assessments might include mountain regions but not explicitly characterise their study area as mountains (e.g., Assani et al., 2021). Finally, we have very limited information of past or future changes in mountain groundwater dynamics across Canada as available observation wells have shorter time series available than surface water gauging stations.

5.8.2 *Water quality*

For many, mountain streams evoke a sense of pure, cold flowing waters, setting a standard for freshwater quality (i.e., the phrase "as clear as a mountain stream"). Those that travel in the mountains know that glacial runoff that is routed through subglacial environments is another thing entirely, commonly running brown (i.e., highly turbid) due to a high suspended sediment load. Given time for the silt and clay to settle out, these waters do develop into clear mountain streams, joining snowmelt, rainfall runoff, and groundwater springs to supply resplendent alpine lakes and ultimately flow downhill to feed most of the major river systems of Canada.

Moreover, glaciers and permafrost are potentially important sources of contaminants to alpine streams, rivers and lakes as glaciers melt and permafrost thaws. Glacial meltwaters, in particular, have been shown to dramatically increase fluxes of mercury and persistent organic pollutants to downstream lakes, observations consistent across the Montane Cordillera (Blais et al., 2001; Blais et al., 2001; Lafreniere et al., 2006), Boreal Cordillera (Zdanowicz et al., 2018), and Arctic Cordillera regions (MacInnis et al., 2019; St. Pierre et al., 2019; Sun et al., 2020). Considerably less is known about the potential for mobilisation of contaminants by permafrost thaw to waterways, but its impact is likely heterogeneous across mountain environments, with some areas experiencing high concentrations of largely particle-bound contaminants with thaw (e.g., St. Pierre et al., 2018) while others may experience little to no impact.

In addition to their role as 'water towers', mountain waters are a source of *cold* water that is essential to the aquatic ecosystems and fish habitat in mountain and downstream environments (Isaak et al., 2010; Richter & Kolmes, 2005; Wehrly et al., 2007), including essential salmon spawning areas in eastern and western Canada (e.g., Moore et al., 2013). Stream temperature is a critical factor for aquatic ecological health, including influences on aquatic biodiversity, the distribution of species, nutrient turnover, dissolved oxygen levels, and metabolic activity (Demars et al., 2011; Isaak et al., 2015; Moore et al., 2013). Snow and glacier melt are a source of 'ice water' that helps to maintain lower stream temperatures and support aquatic habitat, buffering the effects of climate warming (Isaak et al., 2015, 2016). This source of cold water is diminishing as mountain snow and ice recede from the landscape and as snowmelt runoff shifts to earlier in the summer, leading to warmer maximum stream temperatures in July and August (Isaak et al., 2016; Moore et al., 2013).

Stream temperature is not routinely or systematically monitored in mountain regions in Canada, so there is limited understanding of the seasonal and altitudinal evolution of temperatures and how these are changing as a consequence of atmospheric warming, reduced glacier inputs, and changing seasonality of snow melt. Moore et al. (2013) describe a statistical model to estimate maximum stream temperatures in British Columbia, with percentage of glacier cover in a catchment included as one of the variables. This builds on well-developed observation networks and statistical models for stream temperature in the U.S. Pacific Northwest, including several contributions specific to mountain streams (e.g., Isaak et al., 2017). Other applications in western Canada include statistical stream temperature modelling of Daigle et al. (2010) in the Okanagan. These efforts relate the seasonal temperature evolution to air temperature and a range of empirical environmental influences.

MacDonald et al. (2014) measured and modelled two summers of temperature data for Star Creek, a forested mountain-slope setting on the eastern slopes of the Rockies, and discussed the importance of groundwater inputs in maintaining low water temperatures. Roesky and Hayashi (2022) discuss the complexity of generalisations for a groundwater-fed stream in a different setting on the eastern slopes of the Rockies. Groundwater inputs at this site are sourced from a seasonal alpine lake, and summer warming of lake waters leads to the transmission of relatively warm water through the groundwater system. This indicates that alpine lake hydrological inputs and thermal conditions need to be considered along with glacier, snowmelt, rainfall, and groundwater inputs in modelling of stream temperatures.

These studies provide insights into empirical and process-based models of stream temperature in alpine environments, though such models and the observations to inform and constrain the models are restricted to a small number of research studies, primarily in the Montane Cordillera. Systematic monitoring of these alpine hydrological systems at select sites is needed to advance understanding and support of water resources and fisheries managers, and further investment in process-based models is likely needed, given the rapidly changing climate, cryosphere, and hydrological conditions in these catchments.

Hayden Melting Tallow, Siksika Nation,
Blackfoot Confederacy, 2022, LC 5.29

These changes can undermine statistical models that are based on historical conditions. As noted in other chapters of the CMA, primary research studies are also needed in eastern and northern Canada, especially involving the integrated impacts of climate, hydrological, and ecological changes and site-specific stressors.

Intensive, exploitative human activities have had profound impacts on water quality in the mountains. Dam construction for hydropower generation or water resource management is one of the most dramatic manifestations of this. Dam construction necessitates the building of access roads and the dam itself, clear cutting and slashing/burning, as well as the flooding of surrounding areas during reservoir creation, all of which can influence water quality. During the construction phase, these activities are associated with increased soil erosion and leaching of nutrients and carbon into lake environments (Kelly et al., 1980). Longer term impacts of dams on water quality in Canada have included reduced fish production due to drastic water level fluctuations (Stockner et al., 2005), and the enhanced production of greenhouse gases and neurotoxic methylmercury in flooded soils (Kelly et al., 1997) with the subsequent bioaccumulation of methylmercury through reservoir food webs (Bodaly et al., 1984; Hall et al., 2005).

5.9 Risks and Vulnerability from Changing Mountain Hazards

The mountain regions in Canada are subject to a host of natural hazards, including earthquakes, landslides, avalanches, floods, debris flows, storms and extreme precipitation events, wildfires, epidemics, heatwaves and cold temperatures, which have caused injury, death, damage and destruction. People have inhabited the mountains since time immemorial, living with and anticipating the dangers posed by natural hazards (Cruikshank, 2001). For example, Hayden Melting Tallow (Siksika Nation, Blackfoot Confederacy) speaks of the Piikani being aware that the mountains were shaking, and anticipating the Frank Slide (LC 5.29). Today, growing numbers of people are inhabiting, travelling through, and visiting mountain regions, increasing exposure to the increasingly volatile dynamics of mountain environments (Hock et al., 2019). Likewise, proximate human pressures such as mining, forestry, and infrastructure development are degrading mountain environments and, consequently, intensifying the frequency and magnitude of natural hazards (e.g., Gardner & Dekens, 2007, Hetu et al., 2015, Roberts et al. 2004). This tight coupling between environmental and social dynamics is at the heart of vulnerability research (Adger 2007), although such research per se is still limited in the context of rapidly changing mountain systems in Canada.

The magnitude and frequency of landslides, avalanches, floods and wildfires have predominantly increased due to climate change, deforestation/logging practices, and mining (e.g., Geertsema et al., 2006; Germain et al., 2005, 2011; Guthrie et al., 2010; Roberts et al., 2004). For instance, the high mountains of western Canada and high latitudes of northern Canada are experiencing some of the greatest warming rates on Earth and are some of the most sensitive areas to climate change, in part because ecosystems and natural processes in these areas are intimately linked to changes in the cryosphere. Evidence is mounting that warming will further reduce permafrost and snow and ice cover in high mountains (Huss et al., 2017), which in turn destabilises many slopes due to glacier debuttressing, alpine permafrost thaw and displacement, changes in rainfall regimes, the formation and sudden drainage of glacier- and moraine-dammed lakes, avalanches and glacier surges (Chiarle et al., 2021; Clague & Shugar, 2023; Sobie, 2020). This unravelling of slopes alters water and sediment delivery to and transport by streams, with impacts on subalpine and alpine ecosystems.

Large landslides and debris flows in western Canada in particular appear to be on the increase (Cloutier et al., 2016; Evans & Clague, 1994; Geertsema et al., 2006; Huggel et al., 2012), especially in recently deglaciated terrain (Holm et al., 2004; Deline et al. 2021) and regions of permafrost thaw.

As Lhu'ààn Mân Dań Elder Gùdia Mary Jane Johnson shared in the CMA Learning Circle, "you could see where the mountainside had come down, and that's happened in all kinds of areas where I live because of the melting permafrost" (LC 5.30). Brandy Mayes, Kwanlin Dün First Nation, also spoke of the effects of melting permafrost on critical infrastructure, with sinkholes appearing in the access road to the airport (LC 5.31).

The frequency and magnitude of avalanches in the eastern and western mountain regions also appear to be on the increase, in part due to expanding logging, transportation, and pipeline infrastructure in mountain regions, in addition to changing snowpacks (Anderson & Mcclung, 2012; Clarke & McClung, 1999; Germain et al., 2009, 2011; Fortin & Hetu, 2009). Mining and related activities in the mountains also destroy much of the natural forest cover, leading to an increase in the extent of avalanches and mass movements (Sinickas et al., 2016). Moreover, the frequency of extreme and fluctuating meteorological events, such as droughts, heatwaves, wildfire, and extreme precipitation events is increasing. Such events can also compound, resulting in increased vulnerability to major flood events, such as those experienced in the Bow Valley, Alberta in June 2013 and southwestern British Columbia in November 2021. The latter was associated with atmospheric rivers that advected warm, humid air masses from the subtropical Pacific to southern BC, leading to heavy orographic rainfall when the air masses were forced upwards by the Coast Mountains.

Although documentation of such dynamics in mountain systems in Canada is relatively limited to date in the peer-reviewed literature, observed and expected increases in mountain hazards calls attention to the importance of research capable of identifying, and informing responses to address, the root causes of vulnerability. In most cases, this will involve close collaboration with local and Indigenous communities, including studies initiated/conducted by those at the frontlines of mountain hazards (and other pressures affecting people in and adjacent to mountain areas). Here, well developed literature related to social vulnerability (e.g., Adger, 2006; Turner et al., 2003; Ribot, 2011), risk (e.g., Simpson et al., 2021), and resilience (e.g., Berkes et al., 2003; Folke et al., 2010) could be instructive, particularly such work that has been carried out in other mountain regions worldwide (e.g., Carey et al., 2012; Ford et al., 2013; Huggel et al., 2020, McDowell et al., 2021a) .

5.10 Threats and Impacts on Ecosystems

5.10.1 *Changes in treeline and shrubification*

A significant amount of attention has been given to understanding how treelines have changed over the past century (Harsch et al., 2009), and more specifically, over the last few decades when the impacts associated with climate change have been more pronounced. Treeline position is controlled by a number of different factors, including herbivory, snow, and temperature, with soil temperature postulated to be the most significant predictor of treeline position (Körner & Paulsen, 2004). The advance of treeline higher up mountains requires the production of viable seed, uphill dispersal, germination and establishment. The expectation with climate change is that the upper limit of where trees can survive, and ultimately establish, will increase as warming continues.

An advance of treeline has occurred in the MacKenzie Mountains of the Taiga Cordillera mountain region (Mamet & Kershaw, 2012), in the Kluane Region of southwest Yukon (e.g., Danby & Hik, 2007; Dearborn & Danby, 2020), and in the Pacific Maritime mountain region on Vancouver Island (Jackson et al., 2016). In the Montane Cordillera mountain region, treeline advance has occurred across the Rocky Mountains (e.g.,

Trant et al., 2020; Davis et al., 2020). In the Eastern Subarctic mountain region, treeline advance has occurred in the Mealy Mountains (Simms & Ward, 2013; Trant & Hermanutz, 2014). However, there are also examples where treeline advance has not occurred, including in the Atlantic Maritime and Boreal Shield mountain region where treelines in Gaspesie show densification but not advance (Dumais et al., 2014), perhaps due to the short duration of snow cover (Renard et al., 2016). While treeline advance has been documented in the Montane Cordillera mountain region, variability and limitations of more extensive advance may be limited to soil quality and availability beyond the current location of treeline as well as geomorphic and topographic processes (Davis et al., 2018; Macias-Fauria & Johnson, 2013). Other reasons for observed limitations in treeline advance include seed predation, competition with existing vegetation, and the presence (or absence) of disturbance events, such as fire.

In addition to changes in treelines, the density of trees has also increased across many mountain regions of Canada. This increase in density can take different forms including the encroachment of trees into previous open areas and the infilling of open canopy forests. Infilling of trees in the forest-alpine-tundra transition over the past century, and in many cases, over the past few decades, has occurred in the Rocky Mountains (Montane Cordillera mountain region) (Davis et al., 2020; Stockdale et al., 2019; Trant et al., 2020), on Vancouver Island (Pacific Maritime mountain region; (Jackson et al., 2016), MacKenzie Mountains (Taiga Cordillera mountain region; Mamet & Kershaw, 2012), in Gaspésie (Atlantic Maritime and Boreal Shield mountain region; Bailey et al., 2015), and in the Mealy Mountains of Labrador (Eastern Subarctic mountain region; Trant & Hermanutz, 2014). There are also reports of krummholz (<2 m in height) changing to trees (>2 m in height) in the Rocky Mountains (Montane Cordillera mountain region (Trant et al., 2020), a phenomenon attributed to changes in winter wind and snow transport, not just more favourable growing season temperatures, that allow for this shift to occur (Maher et al., 2020). The causal relationship between winter snow and ice damage leading to stem mortality, and in many cases krummholz with multiple leaders, has been documented in

Mont Mégantic, QC (Atlantic Maritime and Boreal Shield mountain region; Lemieux & Filion, 2004).

There are many ecosystem consequences related to treeline and shrub advance, with implications on alpine-tundra species. As forest and woody shrub species' ranges expand higher in elevation, there is limited area for the alpine-tundra species to expand into, as land area decreases with elevation. For the Pacific Maritime mountain region, and parts of the Montane Cordillera and Boreal Cordillera mountain regions, alpine-tundra habitat is predicted to decrease by approximately 97% by 2065, based on shifts in biogeoclimatic zones (Hamann & Wang, 2006). Thus, the fate of many alpine-tundra species is precarious. An example of this occurred in Glacier National Park (Montana, just south of the Montane Cordillera mountain region) where four of seven alpine-tundra plant species declined significantly over a 13-year period at the lower edge of their range (Lesica & McCune, 2004). While the majority of discussion, up to this point, has revolved around vegetation, the resulting changes to habitat have important implications for most animals using these areas. For example, in Torngat Mountains National Park (Eastern Subarctic mountain region), there have been increased sightings of boreal bird species, as the habitat and climate become hospitable to more southern species (Whitaker, 2017). Elder Gùdia-Mary Jane Johnson (Lhu'ààn Mân Ku Dań), explains how greening of the mountains in Kluane National Park is affecting the range of bighorn sheep, and how the proliferation of grasses are impacting the abilities of gophers (Arctic ground squirrels) to avoid predation (LC 5.32).

In northern mountain regions (Boreal Cordillera, Taiga Cordillera, Arctic Cordillera, Interior Hills North, Eastern Subarctic), where shrubs are the dominant woody vegetation at lower eleva-

Gùdia Mary Jane Johnson, Lhu'ààn Mân Ku Dań, 2022, LC 5.32

tions, changes in shrub abundance and cover—termed 'shrubification'—are an important driver of mountain ecosystems. Similar to the changes in trees observed south of the latitudinal treeline, shrub density and biomass often decreases with elevation. For example, in Torngat Mountains National Park (Eastern Subarctic mountain region), shrubification was most noticeable in low elevation riparian areas, with less changes observed at higher elevation (Davis et al., 2021a). This pattern has also been seen in the Arctic Cordillera and Taiga Cordillera mountains regions.

Positive aspects of shrubification include increased above and below ground carbon storage and potential increase in summer forage for caribou. However, increased shrubification has other consequences for alpine-tundra ecosystems, including increased snow depths around taller shrubs, decreased albedo, soil nutrient dynamics, and changes in quality and quantity of light reaching the surface as canopy closure increases (Myers-Smith et al., 2015). Increased shade from shrub canopies alters the moisture regime and the competition dynamics of nearby plant and animal communities. For example, observations from across the Arctic (including many locations within the Arctic Cordillera, Taiga Cordillera and Eastern Subarctic mountain regions) show decreased lichen and moss abundance as shrub height increased (Elmendorf et al., 2012). These changes in mountain vegetation are being detected across scales from plot level observations to regional analyses using remotely-sensed data products, such as Normalised Difference Vegetation Index (NDVI) and also across Knowledges, specifically Inuit Qaujimajatuqangit (Inuit Traditional Knowledge).

Changes in alpine-tundra related to shrubification have important consequences for northerners. Inuit Knowledge in Nunatsiavut (Eastern Subarctic mountain region) has documented increased shrub growth (Siegwart Collier, 2020) with important implications around travel safety. There are also increased travel risks for northerners as shrubification creates better hiding places for polar bears and complicates summer and winter travel. There is also a lot of attention being paid to the changes that shrubification has on access to foods. Inuit *Qaujimajatuqangit* (Knowledge) on changes to berry quality and

quantity has been extensively documented across the Arctic Cordillera and Eastern Subarctic mountain regions (Boulanger-Lapointe et al., 2020). Using ecological experiments and approaches, increased shade under shrub canopies can decrease the amount and quality of berry plants that are an important cultural food for people across Iniut Nunangat (Boulanger-Lapointe et al., 2020).

5.10.2 *Changes in stream ecosystems*

Rapid glacier loss has altered mountain stream ecosystems. Mountain streams historically fed by cold, turbid, and rapid glacial meltwater are transitioning to warmer, clearer, and slower states as glaciers disappear (Brahney et al., 2021). This shift towards more benign streams could promote the upstream colonisation of species previously intolerant of harsh mountain glacial waters. For example, Brahney et al. (2021) found that benthic algal communities were more diverse in streams within catchments less influenced by glaciers in the Montane and Pacific Cordillera. However, while the upstream recruitment of species should benefit general mountain stream biodiversity, increased colonisation could also result in loss of highly specialised species adapted to glacial meltwater (Cauvy-Fraunié & Dangles, 2019). Increased biomonitoring of aquatic ecosystems across mountain regions in Canada is needed to better understand the rate of specialised meltwater diversity loss and upstream colonisation as glaciers continue to disappear.

A consequence of species colonisation into mountain streams is the potential for biotic invasion. Nuisance and invasive species, previously constricted to lowland aquatic environments because of overly harsh headwaters, could move into mountain streams as they become warmer and clearer. Indeed, nuisance algae species have begun to bloom in mountain streams with declining glacial meltwater inputs in the Montane Cordillera (Brahney et al., 2021). The diatom *Didymosphenia geminata*, while native to North America, can form pervasive blooms in clear, cold-water streams with low phosphorus concentrations (Bothwell et al., 2014; Brahney et al., 2021). Also known as rock snot, these blooms can clog potential macroinvertebrate and fish habitat while also producing an unattractive odour and appearance (Brahney et al., 2021). As glaciers disappear, subsequently lowering phosphorus availability, mountain streams could become increasingly susceptible to these blooms with potential consequences for higher trophic levels (Brahney et al., 2021).

Similarly, glacier ice loss could raise mountain stream temperatures beyond the physiological tolerances of species adapted to cold waters. In the Pacific Cordillera, glacial meltwater inputs cool important Pacific salmon migratory pathways, keeping waters below the thermal threshold of most salmon species (Pitman & Moore, 2021). As glaciers disappear, warmer waters thermally stress migrating salmon, potentially harming their reproductive success (Pitman & Moore, 2021). Bull and westslope cutthroat trout also rely on mountain snow and ice to provide cold water habitat (Heinle et al., 2021). The loss of cold-water inputs could constrict the range of these already at-risk species to headwater streams with poorer prey quality (Heinle et al., 2021). Further monitoring of headwater streams is needed to better quantify thermal habitat loss and its consequences for mountain fishes as stream temperatures continue to warm.

Historic introductions of non-native species further challenge mountain aquatic biodiversity. Many alpine lakes in the Montane Cordillera were stocked with non-native trout species, such as brook and brown trout, in the 20th century to provide recreational fishing opportunities (Donald, 1987). An unintended consequence of these introductions is hybridization and competition between exotic and native salmonids, mainly bull, westslope cutthroat, and rainbow trout (Sinnatamby et al., 2020). These native species are now listed as Threatened or of Special concern, depending on the population, by the Committee on the Status of Endangered Wildlife in Canada (Sinnatamby et al., 2020). As warming streams further constrict bull and westslope cutthroat trout habitat upstream, these native species will likely become increasingly stressed with ongoing climate change (Heinle et al., 2021).

5.10.3 *Changes in mountain wetlands*

As mentioned in Gifts of the Mountains, wetlands provide unique ecosystem services to various species. Wetlands are resilient ecosystems, however much like other ecosystems in the mountain regions, they are suffering the consequences of anthropogenic climate change and intervention. Moreover, most of the literature on the pressures on wetlands has focused on lowland regions. The future of mountain wetlands is uncertain. Given climate change and other anthropogenic pressures, changes in sensitive factors such as soil-water balance and biodiversity are unclear and are likely to vary across elevations. Predicting what will happen with mountain wetlands in future decades is therefore difficult, especially as climate change is likely to affect mountain ecosystems disproportionately, and the extent to which mountain wetlands are or will be affected by land use change is unknown.

According to the Global Peatland Assessment, agriculture is the main activity degrading peatlands in North America, followed by the petroleum industry in Canada (UNEP, 2022). The water drainage of wetlands has consequences at biological level as well as chemical. Aside from the destruction of the surface vegetation, drainage of peat is implemented for mining, peat harvesting for horticultural use, agriculture and road construction (Wildlife Conservation Society Canada, 2021). Drained peat promotes the oxygenation process, thus emitting carbon dioxide into the atmosphere which will otherwise be captured under waterlogged conditions. Wetland drainage can also leave wetlands vulnerable to wildfires, formerly a reprieve from fire, could turn into fuel (Turetsky et al., 2011).

Many wetlands in the mid and high elevation areas might not be targeted for agriculture or peat harvesting due to the rough topography and remote location, however, there are plenty of wetlands in the intermountain valleys that are being affected by the mining industry (BC Mining Law Reform, 2021). Several mining projects are well underway, or scheduled to start in the future in sensitive wetland areas with contaminated waste plans that may not protect wetlands or inadequate reclamation plans (BC Mining Law Reform, 2021). Mining affects wetlands by degrading the soil and water quality which has a cascade effect from microbial to larger animal and plant communities (Garris et al., 2018; Orr et al., 2006b). Peat harvesting in the mountains is uncommon, however, and in British Columbia specifically has reduced significantly since its peak at the start of the 20th century (Demwell, 2019; North American Wetlands Conservation Council Committee, 2001). Flooding of wetlands for reservoir creation for hydroelectricity production is also a threat through vegetation loss, and greenhouse gas emissions due to methane release (Harris et al., 2022).

How climate change will affect wetland carbon storage largely depends on the extent to which these wetlands have been modified by humans through land-use changes (Petrescu et al., 2015). Small changes in the delicate balance between long-term climatic conditions, short-term weather events, ecology, hydrology, soil biochemistry, and geomorphology can cause large shifts in the carbon dynamics of wetland ecosystems (Page & Baird, 2016), and in peatlands these changes can reverse the sign of net carbon fluxes, from uptake to emission.

Degradation due to anthropogenic activities are affecting the peatlands' carbon storage capabilities. Greenhouse gas emissions from degraded peatlands in Canada and the United States are estimated to equal 89 Mt CO_2eq yr^{-1} (UNEP, 2022). Without a better sense of the extent of mountain peatlands, their storage capacity, and conservation state, we do not know how much of those emissions mountain peatlands might be contributing to global carbon sources and sinks.

The predicted response of wetlands to climatic change will vary across different wetland types: rain-fed wetlands might maintain structure and function, while wetlands that rely on snow and groundwater inputs will likely be more sensitive to climate change (Wu & Roulet, 2014). Changes in snow cover affect the plant and microbial community during the growing season, influencing biochemistry as changes in water table dynamics due to drought do (Bombonato & Gerdol, 2012; Coletti et al., 2013; Robroek et al., 2013; Wu et al., 2020). Sphagnum moss dominated wetlands, however, have been shown to control their local water table, remaining moist under regional drought (Kettridge & Waddington, 2014). Which has led some scientists to suggest that those wetlands may serve as climate change refugia in the future (Stralberg et al., 2020). Information about how wetlands in the mountains will be affected by

changes in snow cover, rain patterns, and evaporation rates is scant.

Warming of other mountain regions and consequent glacier melt has shown to increase the mean wetland area, as evidenced in the Bolivian Cordillera Real, where warming and glacier melt has been ongoing for the last 30 years (Dangles et al., 2017). Wetland cover showed high inter-annual variability which was correlated to precipitation intensities. Peat formation, or paludification, might require a long—thousands of years—and steady input of water to these areas, however. It is highly probable that multiple basin areas below glaciers have been or will transform to seasonal wetland areas in mountainous areas of Canada.

Peatland restoration and conservation is currently being introduced as a nature-based solution in global climate policy debates, as a viable way for countries to reduce emissions as part of their climate commitments. More attention should therefore be paid to these ecosystems, particularly in mountain regions where "Arctic and Montane Wetlands are being marked at particular risk from climate change with profound consequences for wetland ecosystem services" (Convention on Wetlands, 2021). Canada is one of the few countries that has mentioned peatlands as part of their Nationally Determined Contributions; however, Canada is missing key information on wetland ecosystems in mountain areas, namely inventorying and carbon accounting (FAO, 2022).

5.10.4 *Changes in wildlife, human, and more-than-human relations*

Research studies of the northern mountains in Canada have focused primarily on the physical environment, tracking cryospheric and hydrological changes. Caribou populations are an exception to this, with numerous studies examining current and historical caribou habitat and dynamics in Yukon Territory and Nunatsiavut (e.g., Andrews et al., 2012; Belanger et al., 2019; Hegel et al., 2010, 2012; Macander et al., 2020). In the mountains of the Yukon, consistently expanding programs of resource extraction threaten the integrity of critical habitat for caribou (e.g., McKay et al, 2021), and as a result impact the ability of a variety of Indigenous communities including the Inuvialuit,

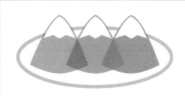

Leon Andrew, Nę K'ə Dene Ts'įlı, 2022, LC 5.33

Daniel Sims, Tsay Keh Dene First Nation, 2022, LC 5.34

Pnnal Bernard Jerome, Micmacs of Gesgapegiag, 2022, LC 5.35

Gwich'in, Trondek Hwech'in, Dene and others to harvest caribou during the critical winter period when travel by skidoo into the higher ground is possible. Hunters from the Inuvialuit communities of the Mackenzie Delta have pursued caribou, wolf, grizzly and other species in the Richardson Range, while the Vuntut Gwich'in and Trondek Hwech'in have used the southern areas of the Richardson Range, the Ogilvie, Wernecke, and Dawson Ranges, for hunting and gathering valued resources.

Elder Leon Andrew of the Nę K'ə Dene Ts'įlı Nation told a story from his homelands in the Mackenzie Mountains of the relocation of culturally important species such as beavers and moose across their Traditional Territory as a result of climate change, making it challenging to rely on Indigenous knowledges of where animals move in the landscape (LC 5.33). Some understand these changes as resulting, at least in part, from a lack of adherence to expectations of reciprocal relationships with the land. Daniel Sims, Tsay Keh Dene First Nation, shared a story to explain that the failure to show respect for mountain environments could lead to the mountains getting their revenge on people, by taking the animals away. "...If we don't share the proper respect to the animals, the animals will get their revenge. It could be them disappearing, it could also be them just getting their revenge in that sense" (LC 5.34).

For the small non-Indigenous population of the boreal and mountain ecosystems of northwestern and Arctic Canada, the mountains exist primarily as sites of resource extraction, including oil, gas, coal, minerals and timber. These activities are largely currently confined to the mountains of British Columbia and the Yukon, where mining and forestry are the primary activities. With greater industrial activity in these regions, comes increased linear disturbance (in the form of roads and transmission lines) and thus increased barriers to animal movement and increased human access and disturbance (Apps et al., 2013; Johnson et al., 2015; Seip, 1992; Wittmer et al., 2007)). Habitat disturbance resulting from resource extraction causes declines in woodland caribou populations in particular through disturbance-mediated apparent competition (Wittmer et al., 2013), whereby disturbance creates favourable conditions for predators (wolves, wolverines) that prey on caribou (Lamb et al., 2022; McNay et al., 2022; Serrouya et al., 2021)

Wildlife populations and wildlife-human relations are also changing considerably in other regions of Canada. Elder Bernard Jerome, Micmacs of Gesgapegiag, observed that caribou populations in the Chic-Choc (Appalachian) Mountains began to decline around 1935, dropping to less than 50 animals in the herd, due to losses of habitat and extractive activities (e.g., copper mining, oil exploration) in the mountains (LC 5.35).

5.11 Impacts on Socio-Cultural Systems

Mountain environments are complex and dynamic social-ecological and social-cultural systems that face a web of pressures and management challenges. Literature addressing the patterns of livelihood, health and wellbeing, and subsistence use of the mountains of Canada remains scarce, especially studies of the impacts of changing pressures on mountains on the livelihoods and knowledge systems of the many First Nations, Métis, and Inuit communities of these regions.

5.11.1 *Threats to Indigenous livelihoods and knowledge systems*

Mountain communities, most especially Indigenous communities, have been impacted via reduced access to traditional resources, cultural practices, and food and water security, all of which have long-standing and multifaceted effects on individual and community health and wellbeing. In a trend observed among Indigenous communities across Arctic and Subarctic Canada, for example, the rising costs of fuel and equipment are enforcing a pattern of wage labour to support harvesting, which is limiting the time that is available to some participants to fulfil their own subsistence needs (Laidler et al., 2009; Natcher, 2009; Wenzel, 2013). This changing quantum of available time is playing out against a backdrop of changing local environmental conditions as a result of anthropogenic climate change, as well as the challenges of maintaining, transferring and using Indigenous ecological knowledge (Ford et al., 2016; Pearce et al., 2011). All these factors are acting to alter patterns of land use, and fundamentally altering the role that mountains across Canada are playing in the livelihoods of Indigenous communities, most especially those in the North (e.g., Ford et al., 2015).

Additionally, the severing of Indigenous knowledges from spaces such as mountains means that knowledge on how to contend with the pressures that mountain environments inherently present to its inhabitants—knowledge on how to contend with avalanches, flash floods, landslides, sea ice loss etc. are lost or are not able to be transferred effectively between groups, presenting new hazards to inhabitants of these spaces—increasing the risk for negative outcomes for all (Gearheard et al., 2006; Pearce et al., 2011; Whyte, 2016); Learning Circle participants, including Patricia Joe (Kwanlin Dün First Nation) and Wanda Pascal (Teetl'it Gwich'in Nation) reflected on the importance of Indigenous knowledges in learning to adapt to changing environmental conditions (LC 5.36, LC 5.37). The question is often asked, "What can we do/what could we have done to prepare for these pressures?", and it is also too often answered by Indigenous communities, 'We have the answer, but we are not given a platform to share it' (Whyte, 2016).

Changes in governance of mountain spaces extend to who has the right and responsibility to create knowledge about mountain systems, what this knowledge looks like, and how it is produced. As Gabrielle Weasel Head, Kainaiwa Nation, Blackfoot Confederacy, explains, colonial erasure of Indigenous communities as distinct Peoples obscures the root causes of the changes occurring in mountain systems and beyond. The violent and destructive changes imposed on Indigenous Peoples have affected Indigenous Nations in many different ways, and addressing questions of how places are known requires elevating place-based ways of knowing, embedded in language, and defining concepts such as sustainability, wellbeing, and resilience (LC 5.38). These experiences take place within a broader context of socio-cultural change occurring in Canada (e.g., The Truth and Reconciliation Commission's 94 Calls to Action), with increasing efforts to decolonize, pluralize, and democratise the environmental sciences and related fields (Liboiron, 2021; Wong et al., 2020).

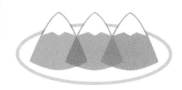

Patricia Joe, Kwanlin Dün First Nation, 2022, LC 5.36

Wanda Pascal, Teetl'it Gwich'in, 2022, LC 5.37

Gabrielle Weasel Head, Kainaiwa Nation, Blackfoot Confederacy, 2022, LC 5.38

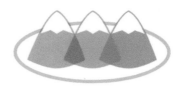

Pnnal Bernard Jerome, Micmacs of Gesgapegiag, 2022, LC 5.39

Yan Tapp, Gespeg First Nation, 2022, LC 5.40

Pnnal Bernard Jerome, Micmacs of Gesgapegiag, 2022, LC 5.41

Yan Tapp, Gespeg First Nation, 2022, LC 5.42

MOUNTAINS OF THE GASPE PENINSULA: THE COMPLEX INTERACTION BETWEEN RECREATION, CONSERVATION, AND FIRST NATION LAND ACCESS

The mountains of the Gaspe Peninsula showcase the intersecting pressures and tensions between conservation, recreational development and Indigenous access and stewardship of Traditional Territory. The mountains of the Gaspé Peninsula, in south-eastern Quebec, can be grouped under three mountains ranges: the McGerrigle mountains, the Mont Albert massif and the Chic-Chocs Range. The name Chic-Chocs comes from the Mi'kmaq word, sigsôg, meaning "impenetrable barrier" or "rocky mountains." The area is the traditional land of the Gespe'gewa'gi, the seventh District of the Mi'gma'gi that includes two on-reserve Mi'kmaq communities (Gesgapegiag and Listuguj) and one off-reserve.

Long cold winters and a short, but warm growing season characterise the region, permitting the development of a dense boreal forest cover, except on the steepest slopes. Despite reported mean annual snowfall exceeding 6 m on the highest summit of the Chic-Choc range (1268 m), winter snowpack on the summits is extremely thin, due to the strong prevailing northwesterly winds redistributing snow to the krumholz and boreal forest below the summits (Davesne et al., 2017; Fortin & Hetu, 2014). The thin snow cover on the alpine summit sustains permafrost on the summit and the development of patterned ground (French & Bjornson, 2008; Gray et al., 2009, 2017). No clear evidence of changes in temperature, snow depth, or snow density could be found in the study area over the last four decades (Fortin & Hétu, 2009; Fortin & Hetu, 2014). This snow-dominated climate and steep terrain also result in high avalanche hazards, threatening roads and other infrastructure (Dubé et al., 2004; Germain et al., 2005, 2009).

The combination of climate and elevation gradient creates a unique landscape with a high diversity of habitat and species, with alpine and arctic tundra vegetation. The endemic vascular flora and lichens found in the Chic-Chocs have led to the hypothesis that these mountains were nuntakas, or ice-free, during the maximum extent of the Wisconsin glaciation (McMullin & Dorin, 2016). The Chic-Chocs are a refuge for many species, many of which typically occur in the Arctic and the western mountains of North America (McMullin & Dorin, 2016). This unique vegetation supports the last herd of caribou south of the St. Lawrence River. This population has been in constant decline since the end of the 19th century, and has been the focus of multiple studies (Frenette et al., 2020; Nadeau Fortin et al., 2016; Turgeon et al., 2018).

The Chic-Choc and McGerrigle mountains are also at the headwaters of important rivers crossing the territory. The rivers in the area are also fisheries, with many of them supporting Atlantic salmon habitat (Kim & Lapointe, 2011). To protect the unique ecosystems of the Gaspe peninsula mountains, the Gaspesie National Park provincial park was created in 1937. Additionally, land outside of the provincial park boundary falls within a varied system of protected land, from wildlife and ecosystem reserves with various restricted access and activities. The Parc de la Gaspesie is a prime tourism destination for outdoor recreationalists across the province and draws high visitation rates during the summer, supporting the economy of the remote region, while supporting conservation efforts within the park. Elder Bernard Jerome, Micmacs of Gesgapegiag, described how Mi'kmaq communities in the region spoke up to protect declining populations of Atlantic salmon by protecting habitat and advocating for a temporary moratorium on recreational sport fishing in the region, after which populations rebounded, and now support a healthy recreational fishing economy (LC 5.39).

The Chic-Chocs and McGerrigle mountains, both within and in the surrounding area of the provincial park, are key recreation areas for the surrounding towns and cities. In winter, it is a hub for ski touring. To increase participant safety of this recreational activity, an avalanche forecasting centre, Avalanche Quebec, was founded in 1999. It is the only avalanche forecasting system east of the Canadian Rockies. In addition, multiple guided ski touring operations have since developed in private, leased public lands or within the provincial park boundaries. Through adventure tourism, the revitalization of towns in this remote region has been fostered. For example, Murdochville, a copper mine and smelter, that closed in 1999, has seen redevelopment in recent year linked with ski tourism, and is now a well-developed ski destination for Quebec residents.

These different uses of the territory, the homeland of First Nations, the protection of natural ecosystems with conservation effort, and tourism revitalising a remote region, are individually all beneficial endeavours. However, the interaction between these three uses leads to tensions. For example, in wintertime, tensions arise between the different users and goals of the park, with concern for caribou habitat conservation and ski touring access. In winter 2022, two popular ski touring areas were closed as the caribou herd moved in the area, reducing access to recreation. This increasing conservation effort and privatisation of the land has significant consequences for the local First Nations, who are seeing access to their traditional land for community hunting and fishing reduced. These tensions results in confrontations between the government officials enforcing the conservation rules on crown land, the local landowners, and the Indigenous Peoples, as shared by Yan Tapp, a member of the local Gaspeg First Nation, who spoke of restricted river access for fishing and the lack of communication and difficult interactions between private landowners, game wardens and First Nation members (LC 5.40) and Elder Pnnal Bernard Jerome, who described historical restrictions on hunting and fishing rights (LC 5.41).

There is a lack of communication between the conservation and recreation policy decision-making and the access to the land that exists for the Mi'kmaq People. The tensions regarding land access were also re-surfacing during the Covid pandemic when visitation numbers in the Gaspésie region increased due to the suspension of international and inter-provincial travel. In response to the overwhelming numbers of visitors, many recreation facilities were closed to prevent the degradation of the sites. These restrictions also applied to local people, such as members of the Gaspeg First Nation, who had been using these sites and showing good stewardship. Yan Tapp discussed the rise of tourism due to Covid and subsequent land restrictions, highlighting their impacts on his community's ability to access important places in their Traditional Territory for activities like hunting and fishing (LC 5.42).

The mountains of the Gaspe Peninsula highlight the complexities in assessing mountain systems across Canada based on language and peer-reviewed literature only. Many reports and assessments of conservation efforts in the region are in French, making them more difficult to find and integrate in large, English-based assessments such as this current effort. Multiple sources of information to understand the intersecting pressures occurring in the mountains of the Gaspe Peninsula also occur in non-peer reviewed publications. Not including French language or grey literature, such as government reports, would indicate a limited understanding of this landscape, when in fact, a reasonable volume of work has been completed in the region.

5.11.2 *Threats to community health and wellbeing*

There is limited literature concerning community health and wellbeing specifically within a mountain context in Canada. Of the relatively few health-related publications that are explicitly set in a Canadian mountain context, the majority focus on health and safety of those undertaking mountain-based recreational activities (e.g., Boyd et al., 2009; Curran-Sills & Karahalios, 2015; Strapazzon et al., 2021) or the impacts of wildfire on air quality in mountain valleys (e.g., Yao et al., 2020). Among these, several studies focus on the dynamics of health and injury around specific recreational activities (e.g., climbing, mountain biking, snowblading, skiing, snowboarding) (Ashwell et al., 2012; Bratton et al., 1979; Bridges et al., 2003; Cameron et al., 2011; Needham et al., 2004) while others discuss hazards and health outcomes related to avalanche survival, and search and rescue incidents (Boyd et al., 2009; Curran-Sills & Karahalios, 2015; Strapazzon et al., 2021; Wild, 2008).

Additionally, there are certain topic areas where a cohesive mountain literature is lacking, but which are more broadly applicable. For example, there is a growing literature on negative mental health impacts (e.g., reduced well-being, trauma, anxiety, depression, suicide and substance use) related to acute and chronic experiences of disaster (e.g., wildfires, floods) and climate change, and there is strong likelihood that these will increase in the future in mountain regions, as elsewhere (Bratu et al., 2022; Cunsolo & Ellis, 2018; Obradovich et al., 2018).

5.11.3 *Threats to mountain tourism and recreation*

As discussed in the Mountains as Homelands chapter, mountains are host to recreational pursuits that contribute to mountain cultures and drive many Canadian mountain economies. More and more people want to visit mountains. This fact is made evident by the popularity of outdoor culture, through National Geographic and Lonely Planet, and online platforms like YouTube or Instagram. With greater numbers seeking mountain experiences and thus the materials and infrastructure to access these experiences, the unique requirements for mountain travel have led to the proliferation of goods and services for outdoor recreational pursuits.

However, these fragile environments are subject to intense climatologic and anthropogenic pressures, the cumulative impacts of which

Gùdia Mary Jane Johnson, Lhu'ààn Mân Dań, 2022, LC 5.43

Dawn Saunders Dahl, Métis (Red River Ojibway), 2022, LC 5.44

threaten the very conditions upon which the mountain tourism industry was built, as Learning Circle participants Elder Gùdia Mary Jane Johnson, Lhu'ààn Mân Ku Dań, and Dawn Saunders Dahl (Métis, Red River Ojibwe) described (LC 5.43, LC 5.44).

While the literature on the physical impacts of climate change in mountainous environments is well-established (Hock et al., 2019), studies examining the implications of this change on mountain tourism and recreation in Canada are lacking. Of the existing literature, an overwhelming proportion has focused on the ski resort industry, primarily in Eastern Canada (Scott et al., 2003, 2019), and suggests that due to warmer temperatures and shifting hydrological regimes, ski season length will likely decrease, potentially limiting operations to the degree that some resorts will no longer be viable (Steiger et al., 2022).

Beyond impacts to the ski resort industry, the direct impacts of climate change on mountain tourism and recreation in Canada is relatively under-studied. There is limited literature exploring the impacts of glacial retreat and permafrost thaw on mountain tourism and recreation, a consequential gap given the growing global body of literature which highlights increases in natural hazards (rockfall, slope instabilities, emergence of proglacial streams and lakes) occurring in these environments (Deline et al., 2021; Mourey et al., 2019; Purdie & Kerr, 2018; Ritter et al., 2012; Watson & King, 2018), and the recent decision to dismantle the iconic Abbot Hut due to safety concerns related to cryospheric degradation (Hik et al., 2022). The impacts of changing ecosystems on mountain tourism has received similarly little attention. For example, despite modelling projections that suggest forest fires could increase in frequency and magnitude throughout mountainous regions in Canada (Global Climate and Health Alliance, 2021), the impacts on tourism and recreation in these areas appears to have been under-studied both in terms of the short term (Hystada & Keller, 2006) and long-term impacts (Hystad & Keller, 2008).

Even less understood in the Canadian context are adaptations to, and opportunities that arise, as a result of climate change. The most studied adaptations stem from the ski resort industry, where advances in snowmaking has allowed resorts to overcome shorter and more variable ski seasons, and the development of summer tourism opportunities such as chairlift-assisted mountain biking and hiking (e.g., Gilani et al., 2018; Needham et al., 2004) has provided alternative revenue streams. Globally, this topic has been comparatively better studied, revealing a range of adaptation strategies the mountain tourism and recreation industry have employed, including the use of geotextile blankets to slow glacier retreat by increasing albedo (e.g., Huss et al., 2021), the installation of ladders to maintain iconic climbing routes and access to alpine huts (e.g., Mourey & Ravanel, 2017), and the introduction of boat tours on large pro-glacial lakes (Purdie et al., 2020).

Climate-related change has been demonstrated to impact visitation in mountain tourism destinations. For example, a study in the Canadian Rocky Mountain Region projected that because of warmer weather visitation would increase up to 36% by 2050, but would decrease by 2080 due to significant environmental change (Scott et al., 2007), such as a reduction in perceived aesthetics (Groulx et al., 2019; Weber et al., 2019). However, change in landscape aesthetics, particularly glacier retreat, has also been identified as a key factor motivating tourists. 'Last chance tourism', the idea that visitors are attracted to destinations threatened by climate change because their visit represents a unique opportunity to experience a place before they disappear, is an important phenomenon prompting tourists to visit to the Athabasca Glacier in the Canadian Rockies (Groulx et al., 2019).

While visitation appears to be increasingly studied in the Canadian context, a great deal of uncertainty persists due to a lack of understanding regarding the relationship between visitation and the impact of climate-related change on shifts in seasonality (Hoy et al., 2016), hazards (Frank, 2000), environmental conditions required for specific tourism activities (e.g., Pickering et al., 2010), and cultural loss (Hock et al., 2019). The dearth of such research constrains the ability of mountain communities, planners, and local organisations to anticipate changes in visitation and inhibits their ability to develop plans capable of securing desirable and sustainable futures. For example, the majority of visits to Canadian national parks are to the country's mountain parks with approximately $1.48 billion generated annually from tourism activities in the communities of Canmore, Banff, and Jasper alone (Alberta Government, 2012). Thus, the potential economic impacts associated with climate change and mountain tourism are substantial (Gössling & Hall, 2017), but are under-studied in Canada.

5.12 Adaptation to Changing Pressures

Adaptation refers to response to challenges and opportunities associated with changing environmental and social conditions, and is often associated with responses to climate change (Smit et al., 1999). While there is limited evidence of a cohesive body of literature on climate change adaptation in mountain regions in Canada, global scale systematic review work shows that adaptation is indeed occurring in many mountain regions globally (McDowell et al., 2019) (note that this differs considerably from the Canadian Arctic, where adaptation has been widely documented, see: Ford et al., 2014). Documented adaptations in mountain areas are commonly implemented in response to cryospheric and hydrological changes, increased hazards, warming temperatures, and changing seasonality combined with non-climatic stimuli such as new or expanding economic activity (e.g., tourism, mining, energy generation) (McDowell et al., 2019). Notwithstanding emerging evidence of significant adaptation efforts in mountain areas globally (again, not well reported/documented in Canada), evidence of shortcomings in these adaptations relative to the nature of current and projected socio-ecological changes in mountain areas as well as core tenets of keystone global agreements (e.g., Paris Agreement; Sustainable Development Goals) is spurring concern (McDowell et al. 2021b). For example, a recent scoping review by Aylward et al. (2022) highlights literature gaps related to climate-mental health adaptation strategies and future mental health risks. Accordingly, there has been a recent push to better recognize and include mental health as a dimension of both climate change impacts and adaptation assessments (Harper et al., 2022; Hayes & Poland, 2018).

In mountain regions, as elsewhere, Indigenous Peoples and communities have long histories of responding to environmental variation and change, and are known to exhibit significant resilience in this context (Ford et al., 2020). As such, rural communities have much to contribute to adaptation policy and decision-making (AMAP, 2017). Local-scale adaptation is place-based and commonly draws on local and Indigenous knowledge, and historical experience with responding to variability and change. A study of 11 Indigenous communities in the Pacific Northwest (whose territories are both coastal and mountainous) highlight how communities are adapting to broader climatic changes, as well as to changing access and availability of resources, harvesting and processing techniques, knowledge systems, and co-management processes (Wyllie De Echeverria & Thornton, 2019). Recognizing the impacts of changing biodiversity and provisioning ecosystem services to Indigenous livelihoods, the authors promote a Cultural Keystone Indicator Species approach, which focuses on "critical species of both cultural importance and perceptual salience in relation to environmental change" (Wyllie De Echeverria & Thornton, 2019, p. 1449), as a framework for embedding Indigenous knowledges in climate and adaptation research in a way that is holistic, meaningful and empowering.

In another study with four coastal British Columbia First Nations, despite colonisation and industrial fishing pressures which restricted Indigenous management rights and stewardship capacity, evidence shows that core stewardship strategies and teachings around important cultural species remains intact, offering a foundation for reinvigorating local governance practices to support cultural and biological conservation (Eckert et al., 2018). Evidence from other communities highlights certain enablers of adaptation, including strong Indigenous culture and knowledge systems, locally-tailored climate education, collaborative decision-making, and mainstream-

KLUANE FIRST NATION ADAPTIVE FOOD SECURITY STRATEGY

"I remember my dad and my mom always had meat in their fish frame. [...] We can remember people coming and just cutting meat off and my mom and dad would just sit back. [...] I said, 'Dad, why are you letting everybody take meat from your fish frame?' He said, 'I'm not worried because the more I give, the more I get back.'" —Kluane First Nation, 2014, p. 24

In southwest Yukon, in response to observed changes on the land and recognized impacts on traditional food systems, Kluane First Nation (KFN) developed a community food security strategy in 2014. Recognizing both the strong connection between KFN citizens and the land, and the threat of climate and landscape change not only to the natural environment, but also to the survival of First Nations as a people, the strategy emphasises the importance of protecting KFN homelands, waters and resources to build a healthy and sustainable food system for the future.

Participants highlighted many activities that are already taking place to strengthen food security in the community, and recommended action items in several areas. To protect the Traditional Territory in the face of climate change, participants encouraged both conservation and the monitoring of key areas and of impacts on culturally important species. Strengthening cultural practices was a key theme, specifically related to community-wide sharing and trading of traditional foods, community-organised harvesting and food distribution, and the application of ancient wildlife conservation methods. Relatedly, improving engagement with outfitting concessions and improving processes to procure donated meat were deemed priorities. A focus on youth empowerment was also deemed essential, including opportunities for youth to engage in cultural activities and to learn from Elders and Knowledge Holders. Participants also supported the promotion of healthy eating including a wider range of traditional foods within a mixed food system. Improving local food production was also supported, including recommendations to support home and community gardening and greenhouse growing, as well as broader agricultural production, including raising animals for food. Complementarily, a community store and storage facility were proposed, to improve food access. Finally, participants recognized the importance of periodic community celebrations and get-togethers as opportunities to come together and share cultural activities, and engage children and youth.

This adaptive food security strategy is one example of a grassroots community effort to adapt to a changing environment and set a positive path forward for the future.

ing climate adaptation into existing programs (Gauer et al., 2021).

While local-scale autonomous adaptation appears to be especially important in mountain regions, municipalities and higher-level governments are also instituting adaptation plans to provide a framework for decision-making and action. Mountain communities are often disproportionately susceptible to the impacts of climate change due to their isolation, tendency toward resource-based economies, and political under-representation (e.g., McDowell & Koppes, 2017). Their reliance on vulnerable mountain gifts and benefits (see Chapter 4), such as the supply and storage of fresh water (Aggarwal et al., 2021) or provision of the assets that fuel tourism-based economies (Knowles, 2019; Scott & McBoyle, 2007), is also a factor.

There is a small but growing body of peer-reviewed literature related to community-scale adaptation in Canadian mountain regions, as well as evidence stemming directly from local adaptation plans and projects. Reports from the *Canada in a Changing Climate* platform review adaptation progress across the various regions of Canada, including mountain regions. Stories from the North tell of the experience developing Yukon's first adaptation plan in Dawson City (Government of Canada, 2021). The plan was created as part of a project that brought together three municipalities in the interest of building adaptive capacity. Similar regional projects have happened elsewhere in mountain regions in Canada—for example a project in the Columbia Basin in British Columbia assembled nine local governments to assess adaptation progress and build skills and knowledge related to identified gaps (Nadeau & Rethoret, 2021). These examples, rooted in their specific mountain geographies and climates, demonstrate the value of place-based approaches to adaptation. The critical role of place-specific information in successful climate action points to a need to expand documentation of community risks, responses, and adaptation experiences in many geographies across Canada.

As detailed in McDowell et al. (2021b), there are significant gaps between known adaptation needs and actual adaptation actions in mountain regions, and there are pervasive issues constraining progress. At an institutional level, a study of four North American regions (some of which are mountainous) identified both barriers and opportunities to adaptation actions. Barriers included a lack of political support and financial resources, as well as challenges in translating knowledge of complex, interacting factors into management actions. Opportunities were identified when collaboration, funding and strong leadership were present (Lonsdale et al., 2017). These findings align with the broader, non-mountain-specific body of knowledge on community climate adaptation planning in Canada (see e.g., Burch, 2010; Dale et al., 2020; Vogel et al., 2020). Lessons from the growing literature on rural climate adaptation (see e.g., Drolet & Sampson, 2017; Vodden & Cunsolo, 2021) are relevant to mountain regions, given that many mountain communities are rural and share some similar adaptation challenges (e.g., small tax bases, demographic changes) and opportunities (e.g., high amounts of local and/or Indigenous knowledges, high rates of community participation).

The management of complex social-ecological systems through periods of change, which can be conceptualised as a form of adaptation (McDowell et al., 2016), is challenging, and tensions and conflicts can often emerge due to differing representations and relationships between diverse stakeholder/rights-holder groups with mountain environments. In this context, different forms of co-management (collaborative management) and/or scenario planning (AMAP, 2017) are commonly used to bring stakeholder and rights-holder groups together to share their visions, priorities and decision-making power in an effort to achieve more holistic and effective management outcomes (Clark & Joe-Strack, 2017; Cruickshank et al., 2019; Danby et al., 2003; Staples & Natcher, 2017). Some such arrangements have been institutionalised as a result of modern land claim agreements, ensuring Indigenous representation in decision-making regarding environmental resource management on their Traditional Territories. While these regimes are imperfect and often critiqued, it is important to recognize that they are in a process of maturation, and that significant gains have been achieved (Clark & Joe-Strack, 2017). In the Yukon context, Staples & Natcher (2017) highlight the important role of gender in such processes, recognizing the importance of women's participation in achieving a positive institutional culture and holistic decision-making, while noting that women and men experience barriers to participation in distinct ways. The vignette on Kluane First Nation above highlights the potential for First Nations to increase their influence on co-management decisions by using food security as a lens through which to re-frame resource issues (Cruickshank et al., 2019).

Despite the efforts and successes noted above, the relatively limited extent of adaptation research and initiatives in the mountain areas of Canada calls attention to the need for increased efforts to study and collaboratively work towards enhanced adaptation action in mountain systems in the country. Here, relatively well developed adaptation research and initiatives from other mountain areas globally (see McDowell et al., 2019)—including engagement with co-development, the political economy of adaptation, community-based adaptation, ecosystem-based adaptation, maladaptation, and adaptation gaps and limits—could prove instructive. However, we also see tremendous opportunity for researchers and communities in Canada to stimulate meaningful innovation in adaptation theory and practice by way of novel insights from the Canadian mountain context.

5.13 Conclusions

The climatic and anthropogenic pressures on mountains in Canada and the resulting threats and impacts described in this chapter are both interconnected and increasing, raising important concerns around the future governance and sustainability of mountain regions. Threats to mountain ecosystems and communities vary considerably across mountain regions in Canada, and are unevenly distributed within and among each region, as well as among downstream communities. The impacts of the pressures of climate change, land use change, and resource development on mountain landscapes described in Mountain Environments (Chapter 2), their political, cultural and spiritual significance elucidated in Mountains as Homelands (Chapter 3), and their contributions to human communities covered in Gifts of the Mountains (Chapter 4), are all increasing as the population in Canada grows and the cascading effects of climate change become more extreme. These pressures are also becoming increasingly entangled, requiring adaptation

efforts to consider the interdependencies and tradeoffs among various biophysical and socio-cultural systems.

Mountains are often conceptualised as the water towers of the world, supplying a substantial part of ecological and anthropogenic water demand. The effects of ongoing climate change on water supply and water quality due to glacier and snowpack decline in mountain areas in Canada will only intensify over the coming decades. Changes to ice, snow, and water in the mountains will exert increasing pressures on humans and ecosystems via increasing risks to natural hazards, changes in water resources, and increasing transport and deposition of contaminants. The pathways connecting climate change to changing snowpacks, freshwater supply, and the impacts on people in the mountains and downstream regions are important gaps in our understanding, as are the lack of systematic observational data and simulation products for informing hazard assessment and adaptation.

Colonialism brought non-Indigenous populations to mountain regions in Canada, which generated and continues to exert pressures in new ways. This is especially true in the areas of governance, consultation, and overall viewpoints on *who* the mountains are for—or, more specifically—who has the right and responsibility to guide the trajectories of mountain systems in an era of rapid and profound environmental change. These questions also extend to who has the right and responsibility to create knowledge about mountain systems, what this knowledge looks like, and how it is produced and communicated.

While there is a limited body of literature focused on community health and wellbeing in the context of mountain regions in Canada, there is growing awareness of the negative mental health impacts related to experiences of natural disasters and climate change (Aylward et al., 2022), which are likely to increase in mountains in the future. Of the few health-related publications that are explicitly set in a Canadian mountain context, the majority focus on health and safety of those undertaking mountain-based tourism and recreational activities. Indeed, mountains are host to recreational pursuits that contribute to mountain cultures and drive many mountain economies in Canada. As climate change and land use change continues to impact mountain environments, information on how socio-cultural and economic systems are responding and adapting will be key. Given that visitation to mountain regions in Canada is on the rise, the lack of literature at the nexus of tourism, visitation, community health and wellbeing, and the natural environment represents an important gap.

Overall, the pressures facing mountains in Canada—namely those of climate change, land use change, resource extraction, development, tourism and recreation demands, and governance of mountain spaces—need to be considered together in evaluating the combined and cumulative impacts of these multiple stressors on the mountain systems of Canada, and in devising and assessing the associated adaptive responses. This is especially needed for local, community-scale adaptation plans and projects, which are commonly implemented in response to climatic drivers combined with non-climatic stressors such as new or expanding economic activity (McDowell et al., 2019). Future research seeking to understand these connections will benefit not only from additional data and monitoring, but also from greater attention to, and better inclusion of, community members and context-dependent cultural information, which has to date has been largely overlooked in favour of modelling approaches that seek to find generalizable patterns. This will require further cross-training and cross-pollination among academic and government researchers and decision-makers engaged in adaptation and mitigation planning, as well as continued engagement with mountain communities, most especially Indigenous communities.

This assessment is not comprehensive, and numerous aspects of mountain pressures were not thoroughly assessed given gaps in author expertise and time constraints (Table 5.4).

Notwithstanding these gaps in our assessment, the CMA found that the existing literature on the changing pressures in mountains gravitates toward the mountains of the west. The Pacific Maritime, Montane Cordillera and Boreal Cor-

Table 5.4: Examples of topics not thoroughly assessed in this chapter

Paleo-environments and natural forcings that have driven past changes in mountain regions over timescales of centuries to millennia.
Stresses on mountain ecosystems associated with climate, cryosphere, and hydrological change, and associated implications for biodiversity and ecological integrity.
Changing mountain hazards and extreme weather in mountain regions in Canada associated with climate change.
Recent remote sensing and modelling tools that are creating new capacity to monitor mountain environments, including early warning systems for mountain hazards.
Patterns of migration and population pressures in different mountain regions of Canada.
Initiatives/policies and funding mechanisms to reduce vulnerability and support adaptation in mountain communities.
Recent changes in the governance structures of protected areas and other lands, which show promise for increasing self-determination and sustainable land use practices.

dillera regions account for the bulk of research and scholarship on mountain environmental and socio-ecological change, and pressures unique to eastern and Arctic Canada, as well as interior mountain regions, require greater attention. The knowledge gaps described in each section of this chapter are key areas for future research, but one overall priority is the need for more interdisciplinary and transdisciplinary studies in mountain regions in Canada, particularly with respect to questions about the interconnected aspects of pressures, threats, vulnerabilities, and adaptations in mountain regions in Canada. Such efforts, at the intersection of Indigenous knowledges and natural, social, and health sciences, are needed if we are to successfully navigate the rapid and compounding changes affecting mountain systems in Canada.

Glossary

Ablation: Processes by which snow or ice are removed, inclusive of melting, sublimation, wind erosion, and mechanical losses such as calving of icebergs or mass loss through avalanches.

Accumulation: Processes by which snow or ice are added to a system, including precipitation, condensation/deposition, wind deposition, and mass deposited through avalanches.

Albedo: The reflectivity of a surface in the solar (shortwave) radiation spectrum, calculated from the ratio of the reflected vs. incoming solar radiation.

Bioaccumulation: The gradual accumulation of chemicals or contaminants within a living organism, often magnified through the food chain.

CanESM5: The Canadian global climate (Earth system) model used for the CMIP6 future climate change projections; CanESM is developed and run by the Canadian Centre for Climate Modelling and Analysis, a research group within Environment and Climate Change Canada.

Clear-cut: A previously forested area where most trees have been harvested and removed, leaving bare ground or stumps.

Climate downscaling: The process of interpolating climate data or climate model output to finer scales where it may better represent local processes and conditions.; this includes a wide range of statistical methods and dynamical (physics/model-based) approaches.

CMIP: Coupled Model Intercomparison Project—an international project that invites the global climate modelling community to perform simulations of historical and future climate change under specified and standardised boundary conditions, allowing an intercomparison of model projections under different climate forcing and emissions scenarios. These results feed into the IPCC analyses and the most recent exercise was CMIP6, feeding the IPCC 6th Assessment.

Downwelling longwave radiation: Infrared radiation emitted from the sky (primarily from clouds and from greenhouse gases) towards the Earth surface.

Elevation-Dependent Warming (EDW): Systematic differences in the rate of warming at different elevations in association with climate change. This is often assumed to mean higher rates of warming at higher elevations, but the relation is more complex than that; there may be no altitudinal pattern, or the greatest degree of warming may be at lower elevations. The research community is now considering this concept more generally as elevation-dependent climate change (EDCC), inclusive of other meteorological variables.

Empirical- and process-based models: Empirical models are statistically based, grounded in observations with a statistical relation that essentially describes a fit to the data. Process-based models are rooted in a physical/mathematical description of the system, typically following principles of conservation of mass, momentum, and energy. These are intrinsically more transferable between sites, but are often limited by an incomplete understanding or representation of the physics at the relevant scales (i.e., by the intrinsic complexity of nature).

Evapotranspiration: Water loss through a combination of evaporation (e.g., for soil or surface water) and transpiration (e.g., vapour loss through plant stomata).

Forcing(s): Drivers of change to a system, typically referring to external agents. For instance, climate forcings include solar radiation (i.e., changes in solar irradiance), volcanic influences (e.g., releases of sulphate aerosols, which have a cooling effect), anthropogenic drivers (greenhouse gas emissions), and many other forcings.

Glacier terminus: The lowest point of a glacier. Glacier ice flows to this point from higher elevations, as ablation exceeds accumulation at lower elevations in glacial systems.

Hydrograph: A graph depicting the discharge of water with time within a river system. This can be over a short period (e.g., a storm hydrograph) or over a year (an annual hydrograph).

Hydrological catchment: The area of land from which water flows into a river, lake, or reservoir.

In situ: Direct observations or measurements from ground control sites, in contrast with remotely sensed or modelled estimates of ground conditions.

IPCC: Intergovernmental Panel on Climate Change

Isotherm: Points with a common temperature, which can be illustrated by a line or surface on 2D or 3D representations of the terrain.

Invasive species: Organisms that are not native to a particular region. They may be benign but this term is usually used for intrusive species that disturb the regional ecosystem dynamics.

Katabatic winds: Downslope winds associated with drainage of air from high-elevation plateaus, where cold air masses create dense air (a thermal high pressure) that drives the cold-air drainage. These are common on large icefields, but are not restricted to glacier environments.

Proglacial lake: Water body adjacent to a glacier terminus, often occupying a basin created through glacial erosion which becomes exposed when the glacier retreats. These are often dammed by glacier moraines. Glacier lake outburst floods usually involve proglacial lakes.

Radiative balance: The net solar (shortwave) and infrared (longwave) radiation balance at a point or averaged over the planet. This includes incoming minus reflected solar radiation and the incoming infrared radiation from the sky/clouds minus outgoing infrared radiation emitted from the surface. Radiation balance is usually positive by day and negative overnight.

Snow cover: The spatial extent or area of snow on the ground.

Snow water equivalent (SWE): The thickness of a water layer one would produce by melting all of the snow at a given location. This essentially converts from the average density of the snowpack to the density of water, to represent the volume of water within the snowpack.

Snowpack: The amount of snow on the ground, expressed through its depth (in cm or m) or its snow-water equivalence.

SSPs: Shared socio-economic pathways: Greenhouse gas emissions scenarios for the 21st century based on various assumptions about global population growth, economic development, and the carbon intensity of the world's energy, transportation, and agricultural systems.

Sublimation: Phase change of snow or ice to water vapour.

References

Abatzoglou, J. T., Williams, A. P., & Barbero, R. (2019). Global Emergence of Anthropogenic Climate Change in Fire Weather Indices. *Geophysical Research Letters*, 46(1), 326–336. https://doi.org/10.1029/2018GL080959

Adger, W.N. (2006) Vulnerability. *Global Environmental Change* 16(3), 268–281.

Adhikari, S., & Marshall, S. J. (2013). Influence of High-Order Mechanics on Simulation of Glacier Response to Climate Change: Insights from Haig Glacier, Canadian Rocky Mountains. *Cryosphere*, 7(5), 1527–1541. https://doi.org/10.5194/tc-7-1527-2013

Aggarwal, A., Frey, H., McDowell, G., Drenkhan, F., Nüsser, M., Racoviteanu, A., & Hoelzle, M. (2021). Adaptation to climate change induced water stress in major glacierized mountain regions. *Climate and Development*, 14(7), 1–13. https://doi.org/10.1080/17565529.2021.1971059

Alberta Government. (2012). *Tourism Works for Alberta: The Economic Impact of Tourism in Alberta 2012.* Tourism Research and Innovation Branch, Alberta Tourism, Parks and Recreation. https://open.alberta.ca/dataset/0f815981-c329-4133-b651-3fef3cb18a0c/resource/3047a7d9-de8a-4e60-b18d-439fb6576796/download/2012-economic-impact-tourism-alberta-2012.pdf

Allen, D. M., Stahl, K., Whitfield, P. H., & Moore, R. D. (2014). Trends in groundwater levels in British Columbia. *Canadian Water Resources Journal / Revue Canadienne Des Ressources Hydriques*, 39(1), 15–31. https://doi.org/10.1080/07011784.2014.885677

AMAP. (2017). *Adaptation actions for a changing Arctic: Perspectives from the Bering-Chukchi-Beaufort Region.* Arctic Monitoring and Assessment Programme. http://edepot.wur.nl/455075

Anderson, G., & Mcclung, D. (2012). Snow Avalanche Penetration into Mature Forest from Timber-Harvested Terrain. *Canadian Geotechnical Journal*, 49(4), 477–484. https://doi.org/10.1139/T2012-018

Andrews, T. D., & MacKay, G. (2012). The Archaeology and Paleoecology of Alpine Ice Patches: A global perspective. *Arctic*, 65(5), iii–vi.

Apps, C. D., Mclellan, B. N., Kinley, T. A., Serrouya, R., Seip, D. R., & Wittmer, H. U. (2013). Spatial Factors Related to Mortality and Population Decline of Endangered Mountain Caribou. *Journal of Wildlife Management*, 77(7), 1409–1419. https://doi.org/10.1002/jwmg.601

Ashwell, Z., Mckay, M. P., Brubacher, J. R., & Gareau, A. (2012). The Epidemiology of Mountain Bike Park Injuries at the Whistler Bike Park, British Columbia (BC), Canada. *Wilderness & Environmental Medicine*, 23(2), 140–145. https://doi.org/10.1016/j.wem.2012.02.002

Assani, A. A., Zeroual, A., Roy, A., & Kinnard, C. (2021). Impacts of Agricultural Areas on Spatio-Temporal Variability of Daily Minimum Extreme Flows during the Transitional Seasons (Spring and Fall) in Southern Quebec. *Water*, 13(24), Article 24. https://doi.org/10.3390/w13243487

Aubry-Wake, C., Bertoncini, A., & Pomeroy, J. W. (2022). Fire and Ice: The Impact of Wildfire-Affected Albedo and Irradiance on Glacier Melt. *Earth's Future*, 10(4), e2022EF002685. https://doi.org/10.1029/2022EF002685

Axelson, J. N., Sauchyn, D. J., & Barichivich, J. (2009). New Reconstructions of Streamflow Variability in the South Saskatchewan River Basin from a Network of Tree Ring Chronologies, Alberta, Canada. *Water Resources Research*, 45(9). https://doi.org/10.1029/2008WR007639

Aygün, O., Kinnard, C., & Campeau, S. (2020). Impacts of climate change on the hydrology of northern midlatitude cold regions. *Progress in Physical Geography: Earth and Environment*, 44(3), 338–375. https://doi.org/10.1177/0309133319878123

Aylward, B., Cunsolo, A., Vriezen, R., & Harper, S. L. (2022). Climate change is impacting mental health in North America: A systematic scoping review of the hazards, exposures, vulnerabilities, risks and responses. *International Review of Psychiatry*, 34(1), 34–50. https://doi.org/10.1080/09540261.2022.2029368

Bachelder, J., Cadieux, M., Liu-Kang, C., Lambert, P., Filoche, A., Galhardi, J. A., Hadioui, M., Chaput, A., Bastien-Thibault, M.-P., Wilkinson, K. J., King, J., & Hayes, P. L. (2020). Chemical and microphysical properties of wind-blown dust near an actively retreating glacier in Yukon, Canada. *Aerosol Science and Technology*, 54(1), 2–20. https://doi.org/10.1080/02786826.2019.1676394

Bailey, S. W., Hoy, J., & Cogbill, C. V. (2015). Vascular Flora and Geoecology of Mont de la Table, Gaspesie, Quebec. *Rhodora*, *117*(969), 1–40. https://doi.org/10.3119/14-07

Barnett, T. P., Adam, J. C., & Lettenmaier, D. P. (2005). Potential impacts of a warming climate on water availability in snow-dominated regions. *Nature*, *438*(7066), 303–309. https://doi.org/10.1038/nature04141

Barrand, N. E., & Sharp, M. J. (2010). Sustained Rapid Shrinkage of Yukon Glaciers since the 1957–1958 International Geophysical Year. *Geophysical Research Letters*, *37*(7). https://doi.org/10.1029/2009GL042030

Barrand, N. E., Way, R. G., Bell, T., & Sharp, M. J. (2017). Recent Changes in Area and Thickness of Torngat Mountain Glaciers (Northern Labrador, Canada). *Cryosphere*, *11*(1), 157–168. https://doi.org/10.5194/tc-11-157-2017

BC Mining Law Reform. (2021). *Dirty Dozen 2021: B.C's top polluting and risky mines*. BC Mining Law Reform. https://reformbcmining.ca/wp-content/uploads/2021/05/BCMLR-Dirty-Dozen-2021-report-web.pdf

Bedia, J., Herrera, S., Camia, A., Moreno, J. M., & Gutiérrez, J. M. (2014). Forest fire danger projections in the Mediterranean using ENSEMBLES regional climate change scenarios. *Climatic Change*, *122*(1–2), 185–199. https://doi.org/10.1007/s10584-013-1005-z

Beedle, M. J., Menounos, B., & Wheate, R. (2015). Glacier Change in the Cariboo Mountains, British Columbia, Canada (1952–2005). *Cryosphere*, *9*(1), 65–80. https://doi.org/10.5194/tc-9-65-2015

Belanger, E., Leblond, M., & Cote, S. D. (2019). Habitat Selection and Population Trends of the Torngat Mountains Caribou Herd. *Journal of Wildlife Management*, *83*(2), 379–392. https://doi.org/10.1002/jwmg.21583

Belleville, M.-H. B.-D. (2011). *Presence of asbestos fibres in indoor and outdoor air in the city of Thetford Mines: Estimation of lung cancer and mesothelioma risks—Summary*. https://policycommons.net/artifacts/2053100/presence-of-asbestos-fibres-in-indoor-and-outdoor-air-in-the-city-of-thetford-mines/2806191/

Bellringer, C. (2016). An audit of compliance and enforcement of the mining sector. *Auditor General for the Province of British Columbia*.

Beniston, M., Diaz, H. F., & Bradley, R. S. (1997). Climatic change at high elevation sites: An overview. *Climatic Change*, *36*(3), 233–251. https://doi.org/10.1023/A:1005380714349

Beniston, M., & Rebetez, M. (1996). Regional behavior of minimum temperatures in Switzerland for the period 1979–1993. *Theoretical and Applied Climatology*, *53*(4), 231–243. https://doi.org/10.1007/BF00871739

Berkes, F., Colding, J., Folke, C. (2003) *Navigating social-ecological systems: building resilience for complexity and change*. Cambridge University Press. https://doi.org/10.1017/CBO9780511541957

Berkes, F., & Davidson-Hunt, I. J. (2006). Biodiversity, traditional management systems, and cultural landscapes: Examples from the boreal forest of Canada. *International Social Science Journal*, *58*(187), 35–47. https://doi.org/10.1111/j.1468-2451.2006.00605.x

Bird, L. A., Moyer, A. N., Moore, R. D., & Koppes, M. N. (2022). Hydrology and thermal regime of an ice-contact proglacial lake: Implications for stream temperature and lake evaporation. *Hydrological Processes*, *36*(4), e14566. https://doi.org/10.1002/hyp.14566

Biskaborn, B. K., Smith, S. L., Noetzli, J., Matthes, H., Vieira, G., Streletskiy, D. A., Schoeneich, P., Romanovsky, V. E., Lewkowicz, A. G., Abramov, A., Allard, M., Boike, J., Cable, W. L., Christiansen, H. H., Delaloye, R., Diekmann, B., Drozdov, D., Etzelmüller, B., Grosse, G., … Lantuit, H. (2019). Permafrost is warming at a global scale. *Nature Communications*, *10*(1), Article 1. https://doi.org/10.1038/s41467-018-08240-4

Blais, J. M., Schindler, D. W., Muir, D. C., Sharp, M., Donald, D., Lafreniere, M., Braekevelt, E., & Strachan, W. M. (2001). Melting Glaciers: A Major Source of Persistent Organochlorines to Subalpine Bow Lake in Banff National Park, Canada. *Ambio*, *30*(7), 410–415.

Blais, J., Schindler, D., Sharp, M., Braekevelt, E., Lafreniere, M., Mcdonald, K., Muir, D., & Strachan, W. (2001). Fluxes of Semivolatile Organochlorine Compounds in Bow Lake, a High-Altitude, Glacier-Fed, Subalpine Lake in the Canadian Rocky Mountains. *Limnology and Oceanography*, *46*(8), 2019–2031. https://doi.org/10.4319/lo.2001.46.8.2019

Bliss, A., Hock, R., & Radic, V. (2014). Global Response of Glacier Runoff to Twenty-First Century Climate Change. *Journal of Geophysical Research-Earth Surface*, *119*(4), 717–730. https://doi.org/10.1002/2013JF002931

Bodaly, R. A., Hecky, R. E., & Fudge, R. J. P. (1984). Increases in Fish Mercury Levels in Lakes Flooded by the Churchill River Diversion, Northern Manitoba. *Canadian Journal of Fisheries and Aquatic Sciences*, *41*(4), 682–691. https://doi.org/10.1139/f84-079

Bolch, T., Menounos, B., & Wheate, R. (2009). Landsat-Based Inventory of Glaciers in Western Canada, 1985–2005. *Remote Sensing of Environment*, *114*(1), 127–137. https://doi.org/10.1016/j.rse.2009.08.015

Bombonato, L., & Gerdol, R. (2012). Manipulating snow cover in an alpine bog: Effects on ecosystem respiration and nutrient content in soil and microbes. *Climatic Change*, *114*(2), 261–272. https://doi.org/10.1007/s10584-012-0405-9

Bonnaventure, P. P., & Lewkowicz, A. G. (2011). Modelling Climate Change Effects on the Spatial Distribution of Mountain Permafrost at Three Sites in Northwest Canada. *Climatic Change*, *105*(44198), 293–312. https://doi.org/10.1007/s10584-010-9818-5

Borrows, J. (1999). Sovereignty's Alchemy: An Analysis of Delgamuukw v. British Columbia. *Osgoode Hall Law Journal*, *37*(3), 537–596.

Borrows, J. (2015). The durability of terra nullius: Tsilhqot'in nation v. British columbia. *University of British Columbia Law Review*, *48*(3), 701.

Bothwell, M. L., Taylor, B. W., & Kilroy, C. (2014). The Didymo story: The role of low dissolved phosphorus in the formation of Didymosphenia geminata blooms. *Diatom Research, 29*(3), 229–236. https://doi.org/10.1080/0269249X.2014.889041

Boulanger-Lapointe, N., Henry, G. H. R., Lévesque, E., Cuerrier, A., Desrosiers, S., Gérin-Lajoie, J., Hermanutz, L., & Siegwart Collier, L. (2020). Climate and environmental drivers of berry productivity from the forest-tundra ecotone to the high Arctic in Canada. *Arctic Science, 6*(4), 529–544. https://doi.org/10.1139/AS-2019-0018

Boyd, J., Haegeli, P., Abu-Laban, R. B., Shuster, M., & Butt, J. C. (2009). Patterns of Death Among Avalanche Fatalities: A 21-Year Review. *Canadian Medical Association Journal, 180*(5), 507–512. https://doi.org/10.1503/cmaj.081327

Brahney, J., Bothwell, M. L., Capito, L., Gray, C. A., Null, S. E., Menounos, B., & Curtis, P. J. (2021). Glacier recession alters stream water quality characteristics facilitating bloom formation in the benthic diatom Didymosphenia geminata. *Science of the Total Environment, 764*, nan. https://doi.org/10.1016/j.scitotenv.2020.142856

Bratton, R. D., Kinnear, G., & Koroluk, G. (1979). Why Man Climbs Mountains. *International Review for the Sociology of Sport, 14*(2), 23–36. https://doi.org/10.1177/101269027901400202

Bratu, A., Card, K. G., Closson, K., Aran, N., Marshall, C., Clayton, S., Gislason, M. K., Samji, H., Martin, G., Lem, M., Logie, C. H., Takaro, T. K., & Hogg, R. S. (2022). The 2021 Western North American heat dome increased climate change anxiety among British Columbians: Results from a natural experiment. *The Journal of Climate Change and Health, 6*, 100116. https://doi.org/10.1016/j.joclim.2022.100116

Bridges, E. J., Rouah, F., & Johnston, K. M. (2003). Snowblading Injuries in Eastern Canada. *British Journal of Sports Medicine, 37*(6), 511–515. https://doi.org/10.1136/bjsm.37.6.511

Briner, J. P., McKay, N. P., Axford, Y., Bennike, O., Bradley, R. S., de Vernal, A., Fisher, D., Francus, P., Fréchette, B., Gajewski, K., Jennings, A., Kaufman, D. S., Miller, G., Rouston, C., & Wagner, B. (2016). Holocene climate change in Arctic Canada and Greenland. *Quaternary Science Reviews, 147*, 340–364. https://doi.org/10.1016/j.quascirev.2016.02.010

Brönnimann, S., Franke, J., Nussbaumer, S. U., Zumbühl, H. J., Steiner, D., Trachsel, M., Hegerl, G. C., Schurer, A., Worni, M., Malik, A., Flückiger, J., & Raible, C. C. (2019). Last phase of the Little Ice Age forced by volcanic eruptions. *Nature Geoscience, 12*(8), Article 8. https://doi.org/10.1038/s41561-019-0402-y

Brown, R. D. (2010). Analysis of snow cover variability and change in Québec, 1948–2005. *Hydrological Processes, 24*(14), 1929–1954. https://doi.org/10.1002/hyp.7565

Brown, R. D., & Robinson, D. A. (2011). Northern Hemisphere spring snow cover variability and change over 1922–2010 including an assessment of uncertainty. *The Cryosphere, 5*(1), 219–229. https://doi.org/10.5194/tc-5-219-2011

Brown, R. D., Smith, C., Derksen, C., & Mudryk, L. (2021). Canadian In Situ Snow Cover Trends for 1955–2017 Including an Assessment of the Impact of Automation. *Atmosphere-Ocean, 59*(2), 77–92. https://doi.org/10.1080/07055900.2021.1911781

Brown, R., Marsh, P., Déry, S., & Yang, D. (2020). Snow Cover—Observations, Processes, Changes, and Impacts on Northern Hydrology. In D. Yang & D.L. Kane (Eds.), *Arctic Hydrology, Permafrost and Ecosystems* (pp. 61–99). Springer. https://doi.org/10.1007/978-3-030-50930-9_3

Burch, S. (2010). Transforming barriers into enablers of action on climate change: Insights from three municipal case studies in British Columbia, Canada. *Global Environmental Change, 20*(2), 287–297. https://doi.org/10.1016/j.gloenvcha.2009.11.009

Burga, C. A., Krüsi, B., Egli, M., Wernli, M., Elsener, S., Ziefle, M., Fischer, T., & Mavris, C. (2010). Plant succession and soil development on the foreland of the Morteratsch glacier (Pontresina, Switzerland): Straight forward or chaotic? *Flora: Morphology, Distribution, Functional Ecology of Plants, 205*(9), 561–576. https://doi.org/10.1016/j.flora.2009.10.001

Burgin, S., & Hardiman, N. (2012). Extreme Sports in Natural Areas: Looming Disaster or a Catalyst for a Paradigm Shift in Land Use Planning? *Journal of Environmental Planning and Management, 55*(7), 921–940. https://doi.org/10.1080/09640568.2011.634228

Bush, E., & Lemmen, D. (2019). *Canada's Changing Climate Report* (pp. 444). Government of Canada. https://changingclimate.ca/CCCR2019/

Callaghan, T. V., Johansson, M., Brown, R. D., Groisman, P. Ya., Labba, N., Radionov, V., Barry, R. G., Bulygina, O. N., Essery, R. L. H., Frolov, D. M., Golubev, V. N., Grenfell, T. C., Petrushina, M. N., Razuvaev, V. N., Robinson, D. A., Romanov, P., Shindell, D., Shmakin, A. B., Sokratov, S. A., ... Yang, D. (2011). The Changing Face of Arctic Snow Cover: A Synthesis of Observed and Projected Changes. *AMBIO, 40*(1), 17–31. https://doi.org/10.1007/s13280-011-0212-y

Calmels, F., Laurent, C., & Brown, R. (2015). *How Permafrost Thaw May Impact Food Security of Jean Marie River First Nation, NWT.* 68th Canadian geotechnical conference and 7th Canadian Permafrost Conference, Quebec City, Canada.

Cameron, C., Ghosh, S., & Eaton, S. L. (2011). Facilitating communities in designing and using their own community health impact assessment tool. *Environmental Impact Assessment Review, 31*(4), 433–437. https://doi.org/10.1016/j.eiar.2010.03.001

Carey, M., Huggel, C., Bury, J. et al. (2012). An integrated socio-environmental framework for glacier hazard management and climate change adaptation: lessons from Lake 513, Cordillera Blanca, Peru. *Climatic Change 112*(3–4), 733–767. https://doi.org/10.1007/s10584-011-0249-8

Carey, M., Molden, O. C., Rasmussen, M. B., Jackson, M., Nolin, A. W., & Mark, B. G. (2017). Impacts of Glacier Recession and Declining Meltwater on Mountain Societies. *Annals of the American Association of Geographers*, *107*(2), 350–359. https://doi.org/10.1080/24694452.2016.1243039

Carnahan, E., Amundson, J. M., & Hood, E. (2019). Impact of glacier loss and vegetation succession on annual basin runoff. *Hydrol. Earth Syst. Sci, 23*, 1667–1681. https://doi.org/10.5194/hess-23-1667-2019

Casassa, G., Lopez, P., Pouyaud, B., & Escobar, F. (2009). Detection of Changes in Glacial Run-Off in Alpine Basins: Examples from North America, the Alps, Central Asia and the Andes. *Hydrological Processes*, *23*(1), 31–41. https://doi.org/10.1002/hyp.7194

Cauvy-Frauniée, S., & Dangles, O. (2019). A global synthesis of biodiversity responses to glacier retreat. *Nature Ecology & Evolution*, *3*(12), 1675–1685. https://doi.org/10.1038/s41559-019-1042-8

Chernos, M., Koppes, M., & Moore, R. D. (2016). Ablation from Calving and Surface Melt at Lake-Terminating Bridge Glacier, British Columbia, 1984–2013. *Cryosphere*, *10*(1), 87–102. https://doi.org/10.5194/tc-10-87-2016

Chernos, M., Macdonald, R. J., Nemeth, M. W., & Craig, J. R. (2020). Current and Future Projections of Glacier Contribution to Streamflow in the Upper Athabasca River Basin. *Canadian Water Resources Journal*, *45*(4), 324–344. https://doi.org/10.1080/07011784.2020.1815587

Chesnokova, A., Baraër, M., Laperrière-Robillard, T., & Huh, K. (2020). Linking Mountain Glacier Retreat and Hydrological Changes in Southwestern Yukon. *Water Resources Research*, *56*(1). https://doi.org/10.1029/2019WR025706

Chiapella, A. M., Nielsen-Pincus, M., & Strecker, A. L. (2018). Public Perceptions of Mountain Lake Fisheries Management in National Parks. *Journal of Environmental Management*, *226*, 169–179. https://doi.org/10.1016/j.jenvman.2018.08.040

Chiarle, M., Geertsema, M., Mortara, G., & Clague, J. (2021). Relations between climate change and mass movement: Perspectives from the Canadian Cordillera and the European Alps. *Global and Planetary Change*, *202*, 103499. https://doi.org/10.1016/j.gloplacha.2021.103499

Chipeniuk, R. (2004). Planning for Amenity Migration in Canada—Current Capacities of Interior British Columbian Mountain Communities. *Mountain Research and Development*, *24*(4), 327–335. https://doi.org/10.1659/0276-4741(2004)024[0327:PFAMIC]2.0.CO;2

Chipeniuk, R. (2005). Planning for the Advent of Large Resorts: Current Capacities of Interior British Columbian Mountain Communities. *Environments*, *33*(2), 57–69.

Christie, G. (2005). A colonial reading of recent jurisprudence: Sparrow, Delgamuukw and Haida Nation. *Windsor Yearbook of Access to Justice*, *23*(1).

Clague, J., & Evans, S. (1993). Historic Retreat of Grand Pacific and Melbern Glaciers, Saint Elias Mountains, Canada—An Analog for Decay of the Cordilleran Ice-Sheet at the End of the Pleistocene. *Journal of Glaciology*, *39*(133), 619–624. https://doi.org/10.1017/S0022143000016518

Clague, J., & Evans, S. (1997). The 1994 Jokulhlaup at Farrow Creek, British Columbia, Canada. *Geomorphology*, *19*(44198), 77–87. https://doi.org/10.1016/S0169-555X(96)00052-9

Clague, J. J., & Shugar, D. H. (2023). Impacts of Loss of Cryosphere in the High Mountains of Northwest North America. *Quaternary*, *6*(1), Article 1. https://doi.org/10.3390/quat6010001

Clark, D., & Joe-Strack, J. (2017). Keeping the "co" in the co-management of Northern resources. *Northern Public Affairs*, *5*(1), 71–74. http://www.northernpublicaffairs.ca/index/wp-content/uploads/2017/04/npa_5_1_april_2017.pdf#page=71

Clarke, G. K. C., Jarosch, A. H., Anslow, F. S., Radic, V., & Menounos, B. (2015). Projected Deglaciation of Western Canada in the Twenty-First Century. *Nature Geoscience*, *8*(5), 372–377. https://doi.org/10.1038/NGEO2407

Clarke, J., & Mcclung, D. (1999). Full-Depth Avalanche Occurrences Caused by Snow Gliding, Coquihalla, British Columbia, Canada. *Journal of Glaciology*, *45*(151), 539–546. https://doi.org/10.3189/S0022143000001404

Cloutier, C., Locat, J., Geertsema, M., Jakob, M., & Schnorbus, M. (2016). Potential impacts of climate change on landslides occurrence in Canada. In K. Ho, S. Lacasse, & L. Picarelli (Eds.), *Slope Safety Preparedness for Impact of Climate Change* (pp. 71–104). CRC Press. https://doi.org/10.1201/9781315387789-3

Cochand, F., Therrien, R., & Lemieux, J. M. (2019). Integrated Hydrological Modeling of Climate Change Impacts in a Snow-Influenced Catchment. *Groundwater*, *57*(1), 3–20. https://doi.org/10.1111/gwat.12848

Coffin, A. W. (2007). From roadkill to road ecology: A review of the ecological effects of roads. *Journal of Transport Geography*, *15*(5), 396–406.

Cohen, A., & Norman, E. S. (2018). Renegotiating the Columbia River Treaty: Transboundary Governance and Indigenous Rights. *Global Environmental Politics*, *18*(4), 4–24. https://doi.org/10.1162/glep_a_00477

Cohen, J., Screen, J. A., Furtado, J. C., Barlow, M., Whittleston, D., Coumou, D., Francis, J., Dethloff, K., Entekhabi, D., Overland, J., & Jones, J. (2014). Recent Arctic amplification and extreme mid-latitude weather. *Nature Geoscience*, *7*(9), Article 9. https://doi.org/10.1038/ngeo2234

Coletti, J. Z., Hinz, C., Vogwill, R., & Hipsey, M. R. (2013). Hydrological controls on carbon metabolism in wetlands. *Ecological Modelling*, *249*, 3–18. https://doi.org/10.1016/j.ecolmodel.2012.07.010

Combs, J., Kerrigan, D., & Wachsmuth, D. (2020). Short-term rentals in Canada: Uneven growth, uneven impacts. *Canadian Journal of Urban Research*, *29*(1), 119–134. https://www.jstor.org/stable/26929901

Convention on Wetlands. (2021). *Global Wetland Outlook: Special Edition 2021*. Secretariat of the Convention on Wetlands. https://www.global-wetland-outlook.ramsar.org/

Coristine, L. E., Jacob, A. L., Schuster, R., Otto, S. P., Baron, N. E., Bennett, N. J., Bittick, S. J., Dey, C., Favaro, B., Ford, A., Nowlan, L., Orihel, D., Palen, W. J., Polfus, J. L., Shiffman, D. S., Venter, O., & Woodley, S. (2018). Informing Canada's commitment to biodiversity conservation: A science-based framework to help guide protected areas designation through Target 1 and beyond. *FACETS*, 3(1), 531–562. https://doi.org/10.1139/facets-2017-0102

Corripio, J., & López-Moreno, J. (2017). Analysis and Predictability of the Hydrological Response of Mountain Catchments to Heavy Rain on Snow Events: A Case Study in the Spanish Pyrenees. *Hydrology*, 4(2), 20. https://doi.org/10.3390/hydrology4020020

Cosens, B. (Ed.). (2012). *The Columbia River Treaty Revisited: Transboundary River Governance in the Face of Uncertainty*. Oregon State University Press.

Cruickshank, A., Notten, G., Wesche, S., Ballegooyen, K., & Pope, G. (2019). Co-management of Traditional Foods: Opportunities and Limitations for Food Security in Northern First Nation Communities. *Arctic*, 72(4), 360–380. https://doi.org/10.14430/arctic69363

Cruikshank, J. (2001). Glaciers and Climate Change: Perspectives from oral tradition. *Arctic*, 54(4), 377–393.

Cruikshank, J. (2005). *Do Glaciers Listen?: Local Knowledge, Colonial Encounters, and Social Imagination*. UBC Press.

Cunderlik, J. M., & Ouarda, T. B. M. J. (2009). Trends in the timing and magnitude of floods in Canada. *Journal of Hydrology*, 375(3), 471–480. https://doi.org/10.1016/j.jhydrol.2009.06.050

Cunsolo, A., & Ellis, N. R. (2018). Ecological grief as a mental health response to climate change-related loss. *Nature Climate Change*, 8(4), Article 4. https://doi.org/10.1038/s41558-018-0092-2

Curran-Sills, G. M., & Karahalios, A. (2015). Epidemiological Trends in Search and Rescue Incidents Documented by the Alpine Club of Canada from 1970 to 2005. *Wilderness & Environmental Medicine*, 26(4), 536–543. https://doi.org/10.1016/j.wem.2015.07.001

Daigle, A., St-Hilaire, A., Peters, D., & Baird, D. (2010). Multivariate Modelling of Water Temperature in the Okanagan Watershed. *Canadian Water Resources Journal*, 35(3), 237–258. https://doi.org/10.4296/cwrj3503237

Dale, A., Robinson, J., King, L., Burch, S., Newell, R., Shaw, A., & Jost, F. (2020). Meeting the climate change challenge: Local government climate action in British Columbia, Canada. *Climate Policy*, 20(7), 866–880. https://doi.org/10.1080/14693062.2019.1651244

Danby, R., Hik, D., Slocombe, D., & Williams, A. (2003). Science and the St Elias: An Evolving Framework for Sustainability in North America's Highest Mountains. *Geographical Journal*, 169(3), 191–204. https://doi.org/10.1111/1475-4959.00084

Danby, R. K., & Hik, D. S. (2007). Variability, Contingency and Rapid Change in Recent Subarctic Alpine Tree Line Dynamics. *Journal of Ecology*, 95(2), 352–363. https://doi.org/10.1111/j.1365-2745.2006.01200.x

Dangles, O., Rabatel, A., Kraemer, M., Zeballos, G., Soruco, A., Jacobsen, D., & Anthelme, F. (2017). Ecosystem sentinels for climate change? Evidence of wetland cover changes over the last 30 years in the tropical Andes. *PLOS ONE*, 12(5), e0175814. https://doi.org/10.1371/journal.pone.0175814

Davesne, G., Fortier, D., Domine, F., & Gray, J. T. (2017). Wind-Driven Snow Conditions Control the Occurrence of Contemporary Marginal Mountain Permafrost in the Chic-Choc Mountains, South-Eastern Canada: A Case Study from Mont Jacques-Cartier. *Cryosphere*, 11(3), 1351–1370. https://doi.org/10.5194/tc-11-1351-2017

Davis, E. L., Hager, H. A., & Gedalof, Z. (2018). Soil Properties as Constraints to Seedling Regeneration Beyond Alpine Treelines in the Canadian Rocky Mountains. *Arctic Antarctic and Alpine Research*, 50(1). https://doi.org/10.1080/15230430.2017.1415625

Davis, E. L., Brown, R., Daniels, L., Kavanagh, T., & Gedalof, Z. (2020). Regional Variability in the Response of Alpine Treelines to Climate Change. *Climatic Change*, 162(3), 1365–1384. https://doi.org/10.1007/s10584-020-02743-0

Davis, E., Trant, A., Hermanutz, L., Way, R. G., Lewkowicz, A. G., Siegwart Collier, L., Cuerrier, A., & Whitaker, D. (2021a). Plant–Environment Interactions in the Low Arctic Torngat Mountains of Labrador. *Ecosystems*, 24(5), 1038–1058. https://doi.org/10.1007/s10021-020-00577-6

Davis, E. L., Trant, A. J., Way, R. G., Hermanutz, L., & Whitaker, D. (2021b). Rapid ecosystem change at the southern limit of the Canadian Arctic, Torngat Mountains National Park. *Remote Sensing*, 13.0 (11), 2085. https://doi.org/10.3390/rs13112085

Dearborn, K. D., & Danby, R. K. (2020). Spatial Analysis of Forest-Tundra Ecotones Reveals the Influence of Topography and Vegetation on Alpine Treeline Patterns in the Subarctic. *Annals of the American Association of Geographers*, 110(1), 18–35. https://doi.org/10.1080/24694452.2019.1616530

Debeer, C. M., & Pomeroy, J. W. (2017). Influence of Snowpack and Melt Energy Heterogeneity on Snow Cover Depletion and Snowmelt Runoff Simulation in a Cold Mountain Environment. *Journal of Hydrology*, 553, 199–213. https://doi.org/10.1016/j.jhydrol.2017.07.051

DeBeer, C. M., Wheater, H. S., Carey, S. K., & Chun, K. P. (2016). Recent climatic, cryospheric, and hydrological changes over the interior of western Canada: A review and synthesis. *Hydrology and Earth System Sciences*, 20(4), 1573–1598. https://doi.org/10.5194/hess-20-1573-2016

DeBeer, C. M., Wheater, H. S., Pomeroy, J. W., Barr, A. G., Baltzer, J. L., Johnstone, J. F., Turetsky, M. R., Stewart, R. E., Hayashi, M., van der Kamp, G., Marshall, S., Campbell, E., Marsh, P., Carey, S. K., Quinton, W. L., Li,

Y., Razavi, S., Berg, A., McDonnell, J. J., ... Pietroniro, A. (2021). Summary and synthesis of Changing Cold Regions Network (CCRN) research in the interior of western Canada—Part 2: Future change in cryosphere, vegetation, and hydrology. *Hydrology and Earth System Sciences*, 25(4), 1849–1882. https://doi.org/10.5194/hess-25-1849-2021

Deline, P., Gruber, S., Amann, F., Bodin, X., Delaloye, R., Failletaz, J., Fischer, L., Geertsema, M., Giardino, M., Hasler, A., Kirkbride, M., Krautblatter, M., Magnin, F., McColl, S., Ravanel, L., Schoeneich, P., & Weber, S. (2021). Chapter 15—Ice loss from glaciers and permafrost and related slope instability in high-mountain regions. In W. Haeberli & C. Whiteman (Eds.), *Snow and Ice-Related Hazards, Risks, and Disasters (Second Edition)* (pp. 501–540). Elsevier. https://doi.org/10.1016/B978-0-12-817129-5.00015-9

Demars, B. O. L., Russell Manson, J., Ólafsson, J. S., Gíslason, G. M., Gudmundsdóttir, R., Woodward, G., Reiss, J., Pichler, D. E., Rasmussen, J. J., & Friberg, N. (2011). Temperature and the metabolic balance of streams: Temperature and the metabolic balance of streams. *Freshwater Biology*, 56(6), 1106–1121. https://doi.org/10.1111/j.1365-2427.2010.02554.x

Demuth, M., Pinard, V., Pietroniro, A., Luckman, B., Hopkinson, C., Dornes, P., & Comeau, L. (2008). Recent and past-century variations in the glacier resources of the Canadian Rocky Mountains: Nelson River system. *Terra Glacialis*, 26.

Demwell, N. (2019, January 20). *North Delta history: The local peat plant* [News]. Surrey Now-Leader. https://www.surreynowleader.com/community/north-delta-history-the-local-peat-plant/

Desloges, J., & Gilbert, R. (1998). Sedimentation in Chilko Lake: A Record of the Geomorphic Environment of the Eastern Coast Mountains of British Columbia, Canada. *Geomorphology*, 25(44198), 75–91. https://doi.org/10.1016/S0169-555X(98)00039-7

Desloges, J. R., & Gilbert, R. (1995). The Sedimentary Record of Moose Lake: Implications for Glacier Activity in the Mount Robson Area, British Columbia. *Canadian Journal of Earth Sciences*, 32(1), 65–78. https://doi.org/10.1139/e95-007

Diaz, H. F., & Bradley, R. S. (1997). Temperature Variations During the Last Century at High Elevation Sites. In H. F. Diaz, M. Beniston, & R. S. Bradley (Eds.), *Climatic Change at High Elevation Sites* (pp. 21–47). Springer Netherlands. https://doi.org/10.1007/978-94-015-8905-5_2

Díaz, S., Settele, J., & Brondizio, E. S. (2019). *Summary for policymakers of the global assessment report on biodiversity and ecosystem services of the Intergovernmental Science-Policy Platform on Biodiversity and Ecosystem Services* (pp. 39). Intergovernmental Science-Policy Platform on Biodiversity and Ecosystem Services. https://www.ipbes.net/sites/default/files/downloads/spm_unedited_advance_for_posting_htn.pdf

Donald, D. B. (1987). Assessment of the Outcome of Eight Decades of Trout Stocking in the Mountain National Parks, Canada. *North American Journal of Fisheries Management*, 7(4), 545–553. https://doi.org/10.1577/1548-8659(1987)7[545:AOTOOE]2.0.CO;2

Dowdeswell, E. K., Dowdeswell, J. A., & Cawkwell, F. (2007). On the Glaciers of Bylot Island, Nunavut, Arctic Canada. *Arctic Antarctic and Alpine Research*, 39(3), 402–411. https://doi.org/10.1657/1523-0430(05-123)[DOWDESWELL]2.0.CO;2

Drenkhan, F., Buytaert, W., Mackay, J. D., Barrand, N. E., Hannah, D. M., & Huggel, C. (2022). Looking beyond glaciers to understand mountain water security. *Nature Sustainability*, 1–9. https://doi.org/10.1038/s41893-022-00996-4

Drolet, J. L., & Sampson, T. (2017). Addressing climate change from a social development approach: Small cities and rural communities' adaptation and response to climate change in British Columbia, Canada. *International Social Work*, 60(1), 61–73. https://doi.org/10.1177/0020872814539984

Dubé, S., Filion, L., & Hétu, B. (2004). Tree-ring reconstruction of high-magnitude snow avalanches in the northern Gaspé Peninsula, Québec, Canada. *Arctic, Antarctic, and Alpine Research*, 36(4), 555–564. https://doi.org/10.1657/1523-0430(2004)036[0555:TROHSA]2.0.CO;2

Dumais, C., Ropars, P., Denis, M.-P., Dufour-Tremblay, G., & Boudreau, S. (2014). Are Low Altitude Alpine Tundra Ecosystems Under Threat? A Case Study from the Parc National de la Gaspesie, Quebec. *Environmental Research Letters*, 9(9), 1–10. https://doi.org/10.1088/1748-9326/9/9/094001

Eckert, L. E., Ban, N. C., Tallio, S.-C., & Turner, N. (2018). Linking marine conservation and Indigenous cultural revitalization: First Nations free themselves from externally imposed social-ecological traps. *Ecology and Society*, 23(4), art23. https://doi.org/10.5751/ES-10417-230423

Egli, P. E., Belotti, B., Ouvry, B., Irving, J., & Lane, S. N. (2021). Subglacial Channels, Climate Warming, and Increasing Frequency of Alpine Glacier Snout Collapse. *Geophysical Research Letters*, 48(21), e2021GL096031. https://doi.org/10.1029/2021GL096031

Ellis, C., Pomeroy, J. W., Brown, T., & MacDonald, J. (2010). Simulation of snow accumulation and melt in needleleaf forest environments. *Hydrology and Earth System Sciences*, 14(6), 925–940. https://doi.org/10.5194/hess-14-925-2010

Elmendorf, S. C., Henry, G. H. R., Hollister, R. D., Björk, R. G., Boulanger-Lapointe, N., Cooper, E. J., Cornelissen, J. H. C., Day, T. A., Dorrepaal, E., Elumeeva, T. G., Gill, M., Gould, W. A., Harte, J., Hik, D. S., Hofgaard, A., Johnson, D. R., Johnstone, J. F., Jónsdóttir, I. S., Jorgenson, J. C., ... Wipf, S. (2012). Plot-scale evidence of tundra vegetation change and links to recent summer warming.

Nature Climate Change, 2(6), Article 6. https://doi.org/10.1038/nclimate1465

Evans, S. G., & Clague, J. J. (1994). Recent climatic change and catastrophic geomorphic processes in mountain environments. *Geomorphology, 10*(1–4), 107–128. https://doi.org/10.1016/0169-555X(94)90011-6

FAO. (2022). *Peatlands and climate planning.* FAO. https://doi.org/10.4060/cc2895en

Farnell, R., Hare, P. G., Blake, E., Bowyer, V., Schweger, C., Greer, S., & Gotthardt, R. (2004). Multidisciplinary Investigations of Alpine Ice Patches in Southwest Yukon, Canada: Paleoenvironmental and Paleobiological Investigations. *Arctic, 57*(3), 247–259.

Feddema, J. J., Oleson, K. W., Bonan, G. B., Mearns, L. O., Buja, L. E., Meehl, G. A., & Washington, W. M. (2005). The Importance of Land-Cover Change in Simulating Future Climates. *Science, 310*(5754), 1674–1678. https://doi.org/10.1126/science.1118160

Fleming, S. W., & Sauchyn, D. J. (2013). Availability, Volatility, Stability, and Teleconnectivity Changes in Prairie Water Supply from Canadian Rocky Mountain Sources over the Last Millennium. *Water Resources Research, 49*(1), 64–74. https://doi.org/10.1029/2012WR012831

Flowers, G. E., Copland, L., & Schoof, C. G. (2014). Contemporary Glacier Processes and Global Change: Recent Observations from Kaskawulsh Glacier and the Donjek Range, St. Elias Mountains. *Arctic, 67*(1), 22–34. https://doi.org/10.14430/arctic4356

Folke, C., Carpenter, S.R., Walker, B., Scheffer, M., Chapin, T., Rockstrom, J. (2010) Resilience thinking: integrating resilience, adaptability and transformability. *Ecology and Society 15*(4), 20.

Ford, J., McDowell, G., Shirley, J., et al. (2013) The dynamic multi-scale nature of climate change vulnerability: An Inuit harvesting example. *Annals of the American Association of Geographers, 103*(5), 1193–1211.

Ford, J., McDowell, G. Jones, J. (2014) The state of climate change adaptation in the Arctic. *Environmental Research Letters, 9*(10), 104005–104014.

Ford, J. D., McDowell, G., & Pearce, T. (2015). The adaptation challenge in the Arctic. *Nature Climate Change, 5*(12), Article 12. https://doi.org/10.1038/nclimate2723

Ford, J., King, N., Galappaththi, E., Pearce, T., McDowell, G., Harper, S. (2020) The Resilience of Indigenous Peoples to Environmental Change. *One Earth, 2*(6), 532–543. https://doi.org/10.1016/j.oneear.2020.05.014

Ford, J. D., Stephenson, E., Cunsolo Willox, A., Edge, V., Farahbakhsh, K., Furgal, C., Harper, S., Chatwood, S., Mauro, I., Pearce, T., Austin, S., Bunce, A., Bussalleu, A., Diaz, J., Finner, K., Gordon, A., Huet, C., Kitching, K., Lardeau, M.-P., McDowell, G., McDonald, D., Nakoneczny, L. Sherman, M. (2016). Community-based adaptation research in the Canadian Arctic. *WIREs Climate Change, 7*(2), 175–191. https://doi.org/10.1002/wcc.376

Fortin, G., & Hétu, B. (2009). Variabilité de l'épaisseur, de l'équivalent en eau et de la densité de la neige dans les Monts Chic-Chocs en Gaspésie (1980–2009). *Actes du colloque de l'Association internationale de climatologie, Rennes, France*, 227–232.

Fortin, G., & Hetu, B. (2014). Estimating Winter Trends in Climatic Variables in the Chic-Chocs Mountains, Canada (1970–2009). *International Journal of Climatology, 34*(10), 3078–3088. https://doi.org/10.1002/joc.3895

Foster, J. G., Gervan, C. A., Coghill, M. G., & Fraser, L. H. (2021). Are arthropod communities in grassland ecosystems affected by the abundance of an invasive plant? *Oecologia, 196*(1), 1–12. https://doi.org/10.1007/s00442-020-04833-3

Fox-Kemper, B. (2021). *Ocean, cryosphere and sea level change. 2021*, U13B-09.

Foy, N., Copland, L., Zdanowicz, C., Demuth, M., & Hopkinson, C. (2011). Recent Volume and Area Changes of Kaskawulsh Glacier, Yukon, Canada. *Journal of Glaciology, 57*(203), 515–525. https://doi.org/10.3189/002214311796905596

Francis, J. A., & Vavrus, S. J. (2012). Evidence linking Arctic amplification to extreme weather in mid-latitudes. *Geophysical Research Letters, 39*(6). https://doi.org/10.1029/2012GL051000

Francis, J. A., & Vavrus, S. J. (2015). Evidence for a wavier jet stream in response to rapid Arctic warming. *Environmental Research Letters, 10*(1), 014005. https://doi.org/10.1088/1748-9326/10/1/014005

Franke, M. A. (2000). Wildlife: The Fittest Survive. In M.A. Franke, *Yellowstone in the afterglow: Lessons from the fires* (1st ed.). Yellowstone Center for Resources, Yellowstone National Park.

Fraser Basin Council. (2019). *Shuswap Regional Trails Strategy.* https://shuswaptrails.com/userfiles/file/Shuswap_Regional_Trails_strategy_UPDATES_2019.pdf

French, H. M., & Bjornson, J. (2008). Mountain-Top Detritus and Patterned Ground in the Gaspésie Mountains, Quebec, Canada. *Geographia Polonica, 81*(1), 29–39.

Frenette, J., Pelletier, F., & St-Laurent, M. H. (2020). Linking habitat, predators and alternative prey to explain recruitment variations of an endangered caribou population. *Global Ecology and Conservation, 22*, e00920. https://doi.org/10.1016/j.gecco.2020.e00920

Frey, H., Haeberli, W., Linsbauer, A., Huggel, C., & Paul, F. (2010). A multi-level strategy for anticipating future glacier lake formation and associated hazard potentials. *Natural Hazards and Earth System Science, 10*(2), 339–352. https://doi.org/10.5194/nhess-10-339-2010

Gardner, A. S., Moholdt, G., Cogley, J. G., Wouters, B., Arendt, A. A., Wahr, J., Berthier, E., Hock, R., Pfeffer, W. T., Kaser, G., Ligtenberg, S. R. M., Bolch, T., Sharp, M. J., Hagen, J. O., van den Broeke, M. R., & Paul, F. (2013). A Reconciled Estimate of Glacier Contributions to Sea Level Rise: 2003 to 2009. *Science, 340*(6134), 852–857. https://doi.org/10.1126/science.1234532

Gardner, J. (1987). Evidence for Headwall Weathering Zones, Boundary Glacier, Canadian Rocky-Mountains.

Journal of Glaciology, 33(113), 60–67. https://doi.org/10.3189/S0022143000005359

Gardner, J. S., & Dekens, J. (2007). Mountain Hazards and the Resilience of Social-Ecological Systems: Lessons Learned in India and Canada. *Natural Hazards, 41*(2), 317–336. https://doi.org/10.1007/s11069-006-9038-5

Garris, H. W., Baldwin, S. A., Taylor, J., Gurr, D. B., Denesiuk, D. R., Van Hamme, J. D., & Fraser, L. H. (2018). Short-term microbial effects of a large-scale mine-tailing storage facility collapse on the local natural environment. *PLOS ONE, 13*(4), e0196032. https://doi.org/10.1371/journal.pone.0196032

Gaudreau, L. (1990). Environmental Impacts of Recreation on Natural Areas and Living Resources. *Loisir et Société / Society and Leisure, 13*(2), 297–324. https://doi.org/10.1080/07053436.1990.10715356

Gauer, V. H., Schaepe, D. M., & Welch, J. R. (2021). Supporting indigenous adaptation in a changing climate: Insights from the stó:Lō research and resource management centre (British Columbia) and the fort apache heritage foundation (Arizona). *Elementa, 9*(1), nan. https://doi.org/10.1525/elementa.2020.00164

Gearheard, S., Matumeak, W., Angutikjuaq, I., Maslanik, J., Huntington, H. P., Leavitt, J., Kagak, D. M., Tigullaraq, G., & Barry, R. G. (2006). "It's Not that Simple": A Collaborative Comparison of Sea Ice Environments, Their Uses, Observed Changes, and Adaptations in Barrow, Alaska, USA, and Clyde River, Nunavut, Canada. *AMBIO: A Journal of the Human Environment, 35*(4), 203–211. https://doi.org/10.1579/0044-7447(2006)35[203:INTSAC]2.0.CO;2

Geertsema, M., & Clague, J. (2005). Jokulhlaups at Tulsequah Glacier, Northwestern British Columbia, Canada. *Holocene, 15*(2), 310–316. https://doi.org/10.1191/0959683605hl812rr

Geertsema, M., Clague, J., Schwab, J., & Evans, S. (2006). An Overview of Recent Large Catastrophic Landslides in Northern British Columbia, Canada. *Engineering Geology, 83*(44199), 120–143. https://doi.org/10.1016/j.enggeo.2005.06.028

Geneletti, D., & Dawa, D. (2009). Environmental impact assessment of mountain tourism in developing regions: A study in Ladakh, Indian Himalaya. *Environmental Impact Assessment Review, 29*(4), 229–242. https://doi.org/10.1016/j.eiar.2009.01.003

Germain, D., Filion, L., & Hetu, B. (2005). Snow Avalanche Activity After Fire and Logging Disturbances, Northern Gaspe Peninsula, Quebec, Canada. *Canadian Journal of Earth Sciences, 42*(12), 2103–2116. https://doi.org/10.1139/E05-087

Germain, D., Filion, L., & Hetu, B. (2009). Snow Avalanche Regime and Climatic Conditions in the Chic-Choc Range, Eastern Canada. *Climatic Change, 92*(44198), 141–167. https://doi.org/10.1007/s10584-008-9439-4

Gilani, H. R., Innes, J. L., & De Grave, A. (2018). The Effects of Seasonal Business Diversification of British Columbia Ski Resorts on Forest Management. *Journal of Outdoor Recreation and Tourism-Research Planning and Management, 23*, 51–58. https://doi.org/10.1016/j.jort.2018.07.005

Gillett, N. P. (2004). Detecting the effect of climate change on Canadian forest fires. *Geophysical Research Letters, 31*(18), L18211. https://doi.org/10.1029/2004GL020876

Giorgi, F., Hurrell, J. W., Marinucci, M. R., & Beniston, M. (1997). Elevation Dependency of the Surface Climate Change Signal: A Model Study. *Journal of Climate, 10*(2), 288–296. https://doi.org/10.1175/1520-0442(1997)010<0288:EDOTSC>2.0.CO;2

Glausen, T. G., & Tanner, L. H. (2019). Successional trends and processes on a glacial foreland in Southern Iceland studied by repeated species counts. *Ecological Processes, 8*(1), 11. https://doi.org/10.1186/s13717-019-0165-9

Global Climate and Health Alliance. (2021). *The Limits of Livability: The emerging threat of smoke impacts on health from forest fires and climate change.* https://climateandhealthalliance.org/wp-content/uploads/2021/06/limits_liability_country-report_bushfires-canada_EN_final.pdf

Gössling, S., & Hall, C. M. (Eds.). (2017). *Tourism and global environmental change: Ecological, social, economic and political interrelationships.* Routledge.

Government of British Columbia. (n.d.-a). Land Use Plans & Legal Direction By Region. *Government of BC*. Retrieved 20 July 2022, from https://www2.gov.bc.ca/gov/content/industry/crown-land-water/land-use-planning/regions

Government of British Columbia. (n.d.-b). Modernizing Land Use Planning. *Provincial Land Use Planning*. Retrieved July 20, 2022, from https://landuseplanning.gov.bc.ca/modernizing

Government of Canada. (2021). Dawson City Climate Change Adaptation Project. *Canada in a Changing Climate: Map of Adaptation Actions.* https://changingclimate.ca/case-study/dawson-climate-change-adaptation-project-dcap/

Graham, B. (2015). *Talking Trees-Sustainable Narratives of the Logging and Forestry Industries in Nova Scotia and New Brunswick and their Relationships with Mi'kmaq Peoples* [Honours thesis, Dalhousie University]. https://dalspace-library-dal-ca.ezproxy.library.ubc.ca//handle/10222/56643

Grantham, H. S., Duncan, A., Evans, T. D., Jones, K. R., Beyer, H. L., Schuster, R., Walston, J., Ray, J. C., Robinson, J. G., Callow, M., Clements, T., Costa, H. M., Degemmis, A., Elsen, P. R., Ervin, J., Franco, P., Goldman, E., Goetz, S., Hansen, A., … Watson, J. E. M. (2020). Anthropogenic Modification of Forests Means Only 40% of Remaining Forests Have High Ecosystem Integrity. *Nature Communications, 11*(1), 5978–6010. https://doi.org/10.1038/s41467-020-19493-3

Gray, J., Davesne, G., Fortier, D., & Godin, E. (2017). The Thermal Regime of Mountain Permafrost at the Summit of Mont Jacques-Cartier in the Gaspé Peninsula, Québec, Canada: A 37 Year Record of Fluctuations showing an Overall Warming Trend. *Permafrost and Periglacial Processes*, *28*(1), 266–274. https://doi.org/10.1002/ppp.1903

Gray, J., Godin, É., Masse, J., & Fortier, D. (2009). Trois décennies d'observation des fluctuations du régime thermique du pergélisol dans le parc national de la Gaspésie. *Le Naturaliste Canadien*, *133*(3), 69–77. https://www.researchgate.net/publication/268512758

Gripton, S. V. (2009). The Effects of Amenity Migration on the Resort Municipality of Whistler and Its Surrounding Environs. *Environments*, *37*(1), 59–81.

Groulx, M., Boluk, K., Lemieux, C. J., & Dawson, J. (2019). Place stewardship among last chance tourists. *Annals of Tourism Research*, *75*, 202–212. https://doi.org/10.1016/j.annals.2019.01.008

Gruber, S., Burn, C. R., Arenson, L., Geertsema, M., Harris, S., Smith, S. L., Bonnaventure, P., & Benkert, B. (2015). Permafrost in mountainous regions of Canada. *Proceedings of GeoQuebec 2015*. GeoQuebec, September 20–23, 2015, Quebec, Canada.

Gruber, S., Fleiner, R., Guegan, E., Panday, P., Schmid, M.-O., Stumm, D., Wester, P., Zhang, Y., & Zhao, L. (2017). Review article: Inferring permafrost and permafrost thaw in the mountains of the Hindu Kush Himalaya region. *The Cryosphere*, *11*(1), 81–99. https://doi.org/10.5194/tc-11-81-2017

Guthrie, R. H., Mitchell, S. J., Lanquaye-Opoku, N., & Evans, S. G. (2010). Extreme Weather and Landslide Initiation in Coastal British Columbia. *Quarterly Journal of Engineering Geology and Hydrogeology*, *43*(4), 417–428. https://doi.org/10.1144/1470-9236/08-119

Hall, B. D., Louis, V. L. St., Rolfhus, K. R., Bodaly, R. A., Beaty, K. G., Paterson, M. J., & Cherewyk, K. A. P. (2005). Impacts of Reservoir Creation on the Biogeochemical Cycling of Methyl Mercury and Total Mercury in Boreal Upland Forests. *Ecosystems*, *8*(3), 248–266. https://doi.org/10.1007/s10021-003-0094-3

Hall, M. H. P., & Fagre, D. B. (2003). Modeled Climate-Induced Glacier Change in Glacier National Park, 1850–2100. *BioScience*, *53*(2), 131–140. https://doi.org/10.1641/0006-3568(2003)053[0131:MCIGCI]2.0.CO;2

Hamann, A., & Wang, T. (2006). Potential Effects of Climate Change on Ecosystem and Tree Species Distribution in British Columbia. *Ecology*, *87*(11), 2773–2786. https://doi.org/10.1890/0012-9658(2006)87[2773:PEOCCO]2.0.CO;2

Harder, P., & Pomeroy, J. W. (2014). Hydrological Model Uncertainty due to Precipitation-Phase Partitioning Methods. *Hydrological Processes*, *28*(14), 4311–4327. https://doi.org/10.1002/hyp.10214

Harder, P., Pomeroy, J. W., & Westbrook, C. J. (2015). Hydrological Resilience of a Canadian Rockies Headwaters Basin Subject to Changing Climate, Extreme Weather, and Forest Management. *Hydrological Processes*, *29*(18), 3905–3924. https://doi.org/10.1002/hyp.10596

Harper, S. L., Cunsolo, A., & Clayton, S. (2022). Including mental health as part of climate change impacts and adaptation assessment: A critical advance in IPCC AR6. *PLOS Climate*, *1*(5), e0000033. https://doi.org/10.1371/journal.pclm.0000033

Harris, L. I., Richardson, K., Bona, K. A., Davidson, S. J., Finkelstein, S. A., Garneau, M., McLaughlin, J., Nwaishi, F., Olefeldt, D., Packalen, M., Roulet, N. T., Southee, F. M., Strack, M., Webster, K. L., Wilkinson, S. L., & Ray, J. C. (2022). The essential carbon service provided by northern peatlands. *Frontiers in Ecology and the Environment*, *20*(4), 222–230. https://doi.org/10.1002/fee.2437

Harsch, M. A., Hulme, P. E., McGlone, M. S., & Duncan, R. P. (2009). Are treelines advancing? A global meta-analysis of treeline response to climate warming. *Ecology Letters*, *12*(10), 1040–1049. https://doi.org/10.1111/j.1461-0248.2009.01355.x

Hart, S. J., Clague, J. J., & Smith, D. J. (2010a). Dendrogeomorphic Reconstruction of Little Ice Age Paraglacial Activity in the Vicinity of the Homathko Icefield, British Columbia Coast Mountains, Canada. *Geomorphology*, *121* (44259), 197–205. https://doi.org/10.1016/j.geomorph.2010.04.011

Hart, S. J., Smith, D. J., & Clague, J. J. (2010b). A Multi-Species Dendroclimatic Reconstruction of Chilko River Streamflow, British Columbia, Canada. *Hydrological Processes*, *24* (19), 2752–2761. https://doi.org/10.1002/hyp.7674

Hayashi, M. (2020). Alpine Hydrogeology: The Critical Role of Groundwater in Sourcing the Headwaters of the World. *Groundwater*, *58*(4), 498–510. https://doi.org/10.1111/gwat.12965

Hayes, K., & Poland, B. (2018). Addressing Mental Health in a Changing Climate: Incorporating Mental Health Indicators into Climate Change and Health Vulnerability and Adaptation Assessments. *International Journal of Environmental Research and Public Health*, *15*(9), 1806. https://doi.org/10.3390/ijerph15091806

Hedstrom, N. R., & Pomeroy, J. W. (1998). Measurements and modelling of snow interception in the boreal forest. *Hydrological Processes*, *12*(10–11), 1611–1625. https://doi.org/10.1002/(sici)1099-1085(199808/09)12:10/11<1611::aid-hyp684>3.0.co;2-4

Heffelfinger, J., Geist, V., & Wishart, W. (2013). The role of hunting in North American wildlife conservation. *International Journal of Environmental Studies*, *70*(3), 399–413.

Hegel, T. M., Mysterud, A., Huettmann, F., & Stenseth, N. C. (2010). Interacting Effect of Wolves and Climate on Recruitment in a Northern Mountain Caribou Population. *Oikos*, *119*(9), 1453–1461. https://doi.org/10.1111/j.1600-0706.2010.18358.x

Hegel, T. M., Verbyla, D., Huettmann, F., & Barboza, P. S. (2012). Spatial Synchrony of Recruitment in Mountain-Dwelling Woodland Caribou. *Population Ecology*, *54*(1), 19–30. https://doi.org/10.1007/s10144-011-0275-4

Heideman, M., Menounos, B., & Clague, J. J. (2018). A Multi-Century Estimate of Suspended Sediment Yield from Lillooet Lake, Southern Coast Mountains, Canada. *Canadian Journal of Earth Sciences*, *55*(1), 18–32. https://doi.org/10.1139/cjes-2017-0025

Heinle, K. B., Eby, L. A., Muhlfeld, C. C., Steed, A., Jones, L., D'Angelo, V., Whiteley, A. R., & Hebblewhite, M. (2021). Influence of water temperature and biotic interactions on the distribution of westslope cutthroat trout (Oncorhynchus clarkia lewisi) in a population stronghold under climate change. *Canadian Journal of Fisheries and Aquatic Sciences, 78.0*(4), 444–456. https://doi.org/10.1139/cjfas-2020-0099

Helicat Canada. (2019). *Elevating adventure: A Three Year Update on the Economic Impact of Helicopter and Snowcat Skiing in British Columbia.* https://www.helicat.org/socio-economic

Henoch, W. E. S. (1971). Estimate of Glaciers Secular (1948–1966) Volumetric Change and Its Contribution to the Discharge in the Upper North Saskatchewan River Basin. *Journal of Hydrology, 12*(2), 145–160. https://doi.org/10.1016/0022-1694(71)90106-5

Hermosilla, T., Wulder, M. A., White, J. C., & Coops, N. C. (2022). Land cover classification in an era of big and open data: Optimizing localized implementation and training data selection to improve mapping outcomes. *Remote Sensing of Environment, 268*, 112780. https://doi.org/10.1016/j.rse.2021.112780

Hermosilla, T., Wulder, M. A., White, J. C., Coops, N. C., & Hobart, G. W. (2018). Disturbance-Informed Annual Land Cover Classification Maps of Canada's Forested Ecosystems for a 29-Year Landsat Time Series. *Canadian Journal of Remote Sensing, 44*(1), 67–87. https://doi.org/10.1080/07038992.2018.1437719

Hersbach, H., Bell, B., Berrisford, P., Hirahara, S., Horányi, A., Muñoz-Sabater, J., Nicolas, J., Peubey, C., Radu, R., Schepers, D., Simmons, A., Soci, C., Abdalla, S., Abellan, X., Balsamo, G., Bechtold, P., Biavati, G., Bidlot, J., Bonavita, M., ... Thépaut, J.-N. (2020). The ERA5 global reanalysis. *Quarterly Journal of the Royal Meteorological Society, 146*(730), 1999–2049. https://doi.org/10.1002/qj.3803

Hetu, B., Fortin, G., & Brown, K. (2015). Winter Climate, Land Settlement and Avalanche Dynamics in Southern Quebec: An Analysis from the Known Accidents Since 1825. *Canadian Journal of Earth Sciences, 52*(5), 307–321. https://doi.org/10.1139/cjes-2014-0205

Hik, D., Robinson, Z., & Slemon, S. (2022, July 4). The Abbot Pass hut, an iconic mountain refuge, is dismantled—Due to climate change. *Canadian Geographic.* https://canadiangeographic.ca/articles/the-abbot-pass-hut-an-iconic-mountain-refuge-is-dismantled-due-to-climate-change/

Hik, D. S., & Williamson, S. N. (2019). Need for mountain weather stations climbs. *Science, 366*(6469), 1083–1083. https://doi.org/10.1126/science.aaz7450

Hirsh-Pearson, K., Johnson, C.J., Schuster, R., Wheat, R.D., & Venter, O. (2022). Canada's human footprint reveals large intact areas juxtaposed against areas under immense anthropogenic pressure. *Facets (Ottawa), 7*, 398–419. https://doi.org/10.1139/facets-2021-0063

Hock, R., Rasul, G., Adler, C., Cáceres, B., Gruber, S., Hirabayashi, Y., Jackson, M., Kääb, A., Kang, S., Kutuzov, S., Milner, A., Molau, U., Morin, S., Orlove, B., & H. Steltzer. (2019). High Mountain Areas. In N. M. W. H.-O. Pörtner, D.C. Roberts, V. Masson-Delmotte, P. Zhai, M. Tignor, E. Poloczanska, K. Mintenbeck, A. Alegría, M. Nicolai, A. Okem, J. Petzold, B. Rama (Ed.), *IPCC Special Report on the Ocean and Cryosphere in a Changing Climate [H.-O.]* (pp. 131–202). Cambridge University Press. https://doi.org/10.1017/9781009157964.004

Holm, K., Bovis, M., & Jakob, M. (2004). The Landslide Response of Alpine Basins to Post-Little Ice Age Glacial Thinning and Retreat in Southwestern British Columbia. *Geomorphology, 57*(44259), 201–216. https://doi.org/10.1016/S0169-555X(03)00103-X

Hood, E., Battin, T. J., Fellman, J., O'Neel, S., & Spencer, R. G. M. (2015). Storage and release of organic carbon from glaciers and ice sheets. *Nature Geoscience, 8*(2), 91–96. https://doi.org/10.1038/ngeo2331

Hoy, A., Katel, O., Thapa, P., Dendup, N., & Matschullat, J. (2016). Climatic changes and their impact on socio-economic sectors in the Bhutan Himalayas: An implementation strategy. *Regional Environmental Change, 16*(5), 1401–1415. https://doi.org/10.1007/s10113-015-0868-0

Hudson, A. J., & Ferguson, R. I. (1999). Fluvial suspended sediment transport from cold and warm-based glaciers in Svalbard. *Earth Surface Processes and Landforms, 24*(11), 957–974. https://doi.org/10.1002/(SICI)1096-9837(199910)24:11<957::AID-ESP19>3.0.CO;2-J

Hudson, S., & Miller, G. (2005). The Responsible Marketing of Tourism: The Case of Canadian Mountain Holidays. *Tourism Management, 26*(2), 133–142. https://doi.org/10.1016/j.tourman.2003.06.005

Huggel, C., Carey, M., Emmer, A., Frey, H., Walker-Crawford, N., and Wallimann-Helmer, I. (2020) Anthropogenic climate change and glacier lake outburst flood risk: local and global drivers and responsibilities for the case of lake Palcacocha, Peru. *Nat. Hazards Earth Syst. Sci., 20*, 2175–2193, https://doi.org/10.5194/nhess-20-2175-2020

Huggel, C., Clague, J. J., & Korup, O. (2012). Is climate change responsible for changing landslide activity in high mountains?: Climate Change and Landslides in High Mountains. *Earth Surface Processes and Landforms, 37*(1), 77–91. https://doi.org/10.1002/esp.2223

Hugonnet, R., McNabb, R., Berthier, E., Menounos, B., Nuth, C., Girod, L., Farinotti, D., Huss, M., Dussaillant, I., Brun, F., & Kääb, A. (2021). Accelerated global glacier mass loss in the early twenty-first century. *Nature, 592*(7856), 726–731. https://doi.org/10.1038/s41586-021-03436-z

Huss, M., Bookhagen, B., Huggel, C., Jacobsen, D., Bradley, R. S. S., Clague, J. J. J., Vuille, M., Buytaert, W., Cayan, D. R. R., Greenwood, G., Mark, B. G. G., Milner, A. M. M., Weingartner, R., & Winder, M. (2017). Toward mountains without permanent snow and ice. *Earth's Future*, 5(5), 418–435. https://doi.org/10.1002/2016EF000514

Huss, M., & Hock, R. (2015). A new model for global glacier change and sea-level rise. *Frontiers in Earth Science*, 3, 54. https://doi.org/10.3389/FEART.2015.00054/BIBTEX

Hystad, P. W., & Keller, P. C. (2008). Towards a destination tourism disaster management framework: Long-term lessons from a forest fire disaster. *Tourism Management*, 29(1), 151–162. https://doi.org/10.1016/j.tourman.2007.02.017

Hystada, P., & Keller, P. (2006). Disaster Management: Kelowna Tourism Industry's Preparedness, Impact and Response to a 2003 Major Forest Fire. *Journal of Hospitality and Tourism Management*, 13(1), 44–58. https://doi.org/10.1375/jhtm.13.1.44

Immitzer, M., Nopp-Mayr, U., & Zohmann, M. (2014). Effects of habitat quality and hiking trails on the occurrence of Black Grouse (Tetrao tetrix L.) at the northern fringe of alpine distribution in Austria. *Journal of Ornithology*, 155(1), 173–181. https://doi.org/10.1007/s10336-013-0999-3

Ion, P. G., & Kershaw, G. P. (1989). The Selection of Snowpatches as Relief Habitat by Woodland Caribou (Rangifer Tarandus Caribou), Macmillan Pass, Selwyn/Mackenzie Mountains, N.W.T., Canada. *Arctic & Alpine Research*, 21(2), 203–211. https://doi.org/10.2307/1551633

IPCC. (2021). *IPCC, 2021: Climate Change 2021: The Physical Science Basis. Contribution of Working Group I to the Sixth Assessment Report of the Intergovernmental Panel on Climate Change* [Masson-Delmotte, V. et al. (Eds.)]. Cambridge University Press. Doi:10.1017/9781009157896.

IPCC. (2022). *IPCC, 2022: Climate Change 2022: Impacts, Adaptation, and Vulnerability. Contribution of Working Group II to the Sixth Assessment Report of the Intergovernmental Panel on Climate Change* [H.-O. Pörtner et al. (Eds.)]. Cambridge University Press.

Isaak, D. J., Luce, C. H., Rieman, B. E., Nagel, D. E., Peterson, E. E., Horan, D. L., Parkes, S., & Chandler, G. L. (2010). Effects of climate change and wildfire on stream temperatures and salmonid thermal habitat in a mountain river network. *Ecological Applications*, 20(5), 1350–1371. https://doi.org/10.1890/09-0822.1

Isaak, D. J., Wenger, S. J., Peterson, E. E., Ver Hoef, J. M., Nagel, D. E., Luce, C. H., Hostetler, S. W., Dunham, J. B., Roper, B. B., Wollrab, S. P., Chandler, G. L., Horan, D. L., & Parkes-Payne, S. (2017). The NorWeST Summer Stream Temperature Model and Scenarios for the Western U.S.: A Crowd-Sourced Database and New Geospatial Tools Foster a User Community and Predict Broad Climate Warming of Rivers and Streams. *Water Resources Research*, 53(11), 9181–9205. https://doi.org/10.1002/2017WR020969

Isaak, D. J., Young, M. K., Luce, C. H., Hostetler, S. W., Wenger, S. J., Peterson, E. E., Ver Hoef, J. M., Groce, M. C., Horan, D. L., & Nagel, D. E. (2016). Slow climate velocities of mountain streams portend their role as

refugia for cold-water biodiversity. *Proceedings of the National Academy of Sciences*, 113(16), 4374–4379. https://doi.org/10.1073/pnas.1522429113

Isaak, D. J., Young, M. K., Nagel, D. E., Horan, D. L., & Groce, M. C. (2015). The cold-water climate shield: Delineating refugia for preserving salmonid fishes through the 21st century. *Global Change Biology*, 21(7), 2540–2553. https://doi.org/10.1111/gcb.12879

Islam, S. U., Dery, S. J., & Werner, A. T. (2017). Future Climate Change Impacts on Snow and Water Resources of the Fraser River Basin, British Columbia. *Journal of Hydrometeorology*, 18(2), 473–496. https://doi.org/10.1175/JHM-D-16-0012.1

Jackson, M. M., Topp, E., Gergel, S. E., Martin, K., Pirotti, F., & Sitzia, T. (2016). Expansion of Subalpine Woody Vegetation over 40 Years on Vancouver Island, British Columbia, Canada. *Canadian Journal of Forest Research*, 46(3), 437–443. https://doi.org/10.1139/cjfr-2015-0186

Jamal, T., & Getz, D. (1999). Community Roundtables for Tourism-Related Conflicts: The Dialectics of Consensus and Process Structures. *Journal of Sustainable Tourism*, 7(44259), 290–313. https://doi.org/10.1080/09669589908667341

Jennings, K. S., Winchell, T. S., Livneh, B., & Molotch, N. P. (2018). Spatial variation of the rain–snow temperature threshold across the Northern Hemisphere. *Nature Communications*, 9(1), 1148. https://doi.org/10.1038/s41467-018-03629-7

Johnson, C. J., Ehlers, L. P. W., & Seip, D. R. (2015). Witnessing Extinction—Cumulative Impacts Across Landscapes and the Future Loss of an Evolutionarily Significant Unit of Woodland Caribou in Canada. *Biological Conservation*, 186, 176–186. https://doi.org/10.1016/j.biocon.2015.03.012

Jones, G. A., & Henry, G. H. R. (2003). Primary plant succession on recently deglaciated terrain in the Canadian High Arctic. *Journal of Biogeography*, 30(2), 277–296. https://doi.org/10.1046/j.1365-2699.2003.00818.x

Kapos, V. (2000). UNEP-WCMC Web Site: Mountains and Mountain Forests. *Mountain Research and Development*, 20(4), 378–378. https://doi.org/10.1659/0276-4741(2000)020[0378:UWWSMA]2.0.CO;2

Keegan, K. M., Albert, M. R., McConnell, J. R., & Baker, I. (2014). Climate change and forest fires synergistically drive widespread melt events of the Greenland Ice Sheet. *Proceedings of the National Academy of Sciences of the United States of America*, 111(22), 7964–7967. https://doi.org/10.1073/pnas.1405397111

Kehoe, L., Romero-Muñoz, A., Polaina, E., Estes, L., Kreft, H., & Kuemmerle, T. (2017). Biodiversity at risk under future cropland expansion and intensification. *Nature Ecology & Evolution*, 1(8), Article 8. https://doi.org/10.1038/s41559-017-0234-3

Kelly, C. A., Rudd, J. W. M., Bodaly, R. A., Roulet, N. P., St.Louis, V. L., Heyes, A., Moore, T. R., Schiff, S., Aravena, R., Scott, K. J., Dyck, B., Harris, R., Warner, B., & Edwards,

G. (1997). Increases in Fluxes of Greenhouse Gases and Methyl Mercury following Flooding of an Experimental Reservoir. *Environmental Science & Technology, 31*(5), 1334–1344. https://doi.org/10.1021/es9604931

Kelly, D. M., Underwood, J. K., & Thirumurthi, D. (1980). Impact of construction of a hydroelectric project on the water quality of five lakes in Nova Scotia. *Canadian Journal of Civil Engineering, 7*(1), 173–184. https://doi.org/10.1139/l80-016

Kelly, J., & Williams, P. (2007). Tourism Destination Water Management Strategies: An Eco-Efficiency Modelling Approach. *Leisure/ Loisir, 31*(2), 427–452. https://doi.org/10.1080/14927713.2007.9651390

Kettridge, N., & Waddington, J. M. (2014). Towards quantifying the negative feedback regulation of peatland evaporation to drought: Quantifying the negative feedback regulation of peatland evaporation. *Hydrological Processes, 28*(11), 3728–3740. https://doi.org/10.1002/hyp.9898

Kim, M., & Lapointe, M. (2011). Regional variability in Atlantic salmon (Salmo salar) riverscapes: A simple landscape ecology model explaining the large variability in size of salmon runs across Gaspé watersheds, Canada. *Ecology of Freshwater Fish, 20*(1), 144–156. https://doi.org/10.1111/j.1600-0633.2010.00471.x

Kluane First Nation. (2014). *Nourishing Our Future: An Adaptive Food Security Strategy to Ensure the Cultural and Physical Well-Being of the Kluane First Nation Against the Impacts of Climate Change in the Yukon* (pp. 43).

Knowles, N. L. B. (2019). Can the North American ski industry attain climate resiliency? A modified Delphi survey on transformations towards sustainable tourism. *Journal of Sustainable Tourism, 27*(3), 380–397. https://doi.org/10.1080/09669582.2019.1585440

Kohlhardt, R., Honey-Rosés, J., Fernandez Lozada, S., Haider, W., & Stevens, M. (2018). Is this trail too crowded? A choice experiment to evaluate tradeoffs and preferences of park visitors in Garibaldi Park, British Columbia. *Journal of Environmental Planning and Management, 61*(1), 1–24. https://doi.org/10.1080/09640568.2017.1284047

Kokelj, S. V., Kokoszka, J., Sluijs, J. van der, Rudy, A. C. A., Tunnicliffe, J., Shakil, S., Tank, S. E., & Zolkos, S. (2021). Thaw-driven mass wasting couples slopes with downstream systems, and effects propagate through Arctic drainage networks. *The Cryosphere, 15*(7), 3059–3081. https://doi.org/10.5194/tc-15-3059-2021

Körner, C., & Paulsen, J. (2004). A world-wide study of high altitude treeline temperatures. *Journal of Biogeography, 31*(5), 713–732. https://doi.org/10.1111/j.1365-2699.2003.01043.x

Kotlarski, S., Bosshard, T., Lüthi, D., Pall, P., & Schär, C. (2012). Elevation gradients of European climate change in the regional climate model COSMO-CLM. *Climatic Change, 112*(2), 189–215. https://doi.org/10.1007/s10584-011-0195-5

Ladle, A., Avgar, T., Wheatley, M., Stenhouse, G. B., Nielsen, S. E., & Boyce, M. S. (2019). Grizzly Bear Response to Spatio-Temporal Variability in Human Recreational Activity. *Journal of Applied Ecology, 56*(2), 375–386. https://doi.org/10.1111/1365-2664.13277

Lafreniere, M. J., Blais, J. M., Sharp, M. J., & Schindler, D. W. (2006). Organochlorine Pesticide and Polychlorinated Biphenyl Concentrations in Snow, Snowmelt, and Runoff at Bow Lake, Alberta. *Environmental Science & Technology, 40*(16), 4909–4915. https://doi.org/10.1021/es060237g

Laidler, G. J., Ford, J. D., Gough, W. A., Ikummaq, T., Gagnon, A. S., Kowal, S., Qrunnut, K., & Irngaut, C. (2009). Travelling and hunting in a changing Arctic: Assessing Inuit vulnerability to sea ice change in Igloolik, Nunavut. *Climatic Change, 94*(3–4), 363–397. https://doi.org/10.1007/s10584-008-9512-z

Lamb, C., Willson, R., Richter, C., Owens-Beck, N., Napoleon, J., Muir, B., McNay, R. S., Lavis, E., Hebblewhite, M., Giguere, L., Dokkie, T., Boutin, S., & Ford, A. T. (2022). Indigenous-Led Conservation: Pathways to Recovery for the Nearly Extirpated Klinse-Za Mountain Caribou. *Ecological Applications.* https://doi.org/10.1002/eap.2581

Lambin, E., & Geist, H. (Eds.). (2008). *Land-Use and Land-Cover Change: Local Processes and Global Impacts.* Springer.

Langston, G., Bentley, L. R., Hayashi, M., Mcclymont, A., & Pidlisecky, A. (2011). Internal Structure and Hydrological Functions of an Alpine Proglacial Moraine. *Hydrological Processes, 25*(19), 2967–2982. https://doi.org/10.1002/hyp.8144

Leddy, L. C. (2013). Land & Sea: Environmental History in Atlantic Canada. *American Review of Canadian Studies, 43*(4), 532–534. https://doi.org/10.1080/02722011.2013.859358

Lemelin, R. H., Dawson, J., Johnston, M. E., Stewart, E. J., & Mattina, C. (2012). Resilience, belonging, and tourism in Nain, Nunatsiavut. *Études Inuit Studies, 36*(2), 35–58. Scopus. https://doi.org/10.7202/1015977ar

Lemieux, C., & Filion, L. (2004). Tree-Ring Evidence for a Combined Influence of Defoliators and Extreme Climatic Events in the Dynamics of a High-Altitude Balsam Fir Forest, Mount Megantic, Southern Quebec. *Canadian Journal of Forest Research, 34*(7), 1436–1443. https://doi.org/10.1139/X04-025

Lencioni, V., Jousson, O., Guella, G., & Bernabò, P. (2015). Cold adaptive potential of chironomids overwintering in a glacial stream. *Physiological Entomology, 40*(1), 43–53. https://doi.org/10.1111/phen.12084

Lesica, P., & McCune, B. (2004). Decline of arctic-alpine plants at the southern margin of their range following a decade of climatic warming. *Journal of Vegetation Science, 15*(5), 679–690. https://doi.org/10.1111/j.1654-1103.2004.tb02310.x

Lesmerises, F., Dery, F., Johnson, C. J., & St-Laurent, M.-H. (2018). Spatiotemporal Response of Mountain Caribou to the Intensity of Backcountry Skiing. *Biological Conservation, 217*, 149–156. https://doi.org/10.1016/j.biocon.2017.10.030

Li, L., & Pomeroy, J. W. (1997). Probability of occurrence of blowing snow. *Journal of Geophysical Research: Atmospheres, 102*(D18), 21955–21964. https://doi.org/10.1029/97jd01522

Liboiron, M. (2021). *Pollution Is Colonialism*. Duke University Press.

Locke, H., Ellis, E. C., Venter, O., Schuster, R., Ma, K., Shen, X., Woodley, S., Kingston, N., Bhola, N., Strassburg, B. B. N., Paulsch, A., Williams, B., & Watson, J. E. M. (2019). Three global conditions for biodiversity conservation and sustainable use: An implementation framework. *National Science Review, 6*(6), 1080–1082. https://doi.org/10.1093/nsr/nwz136

Lofroth, E. C., & Ott, P. K. (2007). Assessment of the Sustainability of Wolverine Harvest in British Columbia, Canada. *Journal of Wildlife Management, 71*(7), 2193–2200. https://doi.org/10.2193/2007-095

Lonsdale, W. R., Kretser, H. E., Chetkiewicz, C.-L. B., & Cross, M. S. (2017). Similarities and Differences in Barriers and Opportunities Affecting Climate Change Adaptation Action in Four North American Landscapes. *Environmental Management, 60*(6), 1076–1089. https://doi.org/10.1007/s00267-017-0933-1

López-Moreno, J. I., Pomeroy, J. W., Morán-Tejeda, E., Revuelto, J., Navarro-Serrano, F. M., Vidaller, I., & Alonso-González, E. (2021). Changes in the frequency of global high mountain rain-on-snow events due to climate warming. *Environmental Research Letters, 16*(9), 094021. https://doi.org/10.1088/1748-9326/ac0dde

López-Moreno, J. I., Pomeroy, J. W., Revuelto, J., & Vicente-Serrano, S. M. (2013). Response of snow processes to climate change: Spatial variability in a small basin in the Spanish Pyrenees. *Hydrological Processes, 27*(18), 2637–2650. https://doi.org/10.1002/hyp.9408

Lundquist, J. D., Dickerson-Lange, S. E., Lutz, J. A., & Cristea, N. C. (2013). Lower forest density enhances snow retention in regions with warmer winters: A global framework developed from plot-scale observations and modeling. *Water Resources Research, 49*(10), 6356–6370. https://doi.org/10.1002/wrcr.20504

Lundquist, J. D., Dickerson-Lange, S., Gutmann, E., Jonas, T., Lumbrazo, C., & Reynolds, D. (2021). Snow interception modeling: Isolated observations have led to many land surface models lacking appropriate temperature sensitivities. *Hydrological Processes 35*(7). https://doi.org/10.1002/hyp.14274

Lynn, N. A., & Brown, R. D. (2003). Effects of recreational use impacts on hiking experiences in natural areas. *Landscape and Urban Planning, 64*(1–2), 77–87. https://doi.org/10.1016/S0169-2046(02)00202-5

Macander, M. J., Palm, E. C., Frost, G. V., Herriges, J. D., Nelson, P. R., Roland, C., Russell, K. L. M., Suitor, M. J., Bentzen, T. W., Joly, K., Goetz, S. J., & Hebblewhite, M. (2020). Lichen Cover Mapping for Caribou Ranges in Interior Alaska and Yukon. *Environmental Research Letters, 15*(5). https://doi.org/10.1088/1748-9326/ab6d38

Macias-Fauria, M., & Johnson, E. A. (2013). Warming-Induced Upslope Advance of Subalpine Forest Is Severely Limited by Geomorphic Processes. *Proceedings of the National Academy of Sciences U.S.A, 110*(20), 8117–8122. https://doi.org/10.1073/pnas.1221278110

MacInnis, J. J., Lehnherr, I., Muir, D. C. G., St. Pierre, K. A., St. Louis, V. L., Spencer, C., & De Silva, A. O. (2019). Fate and Transport of Perfluoroalkyl Substances from Snowpacks into a Lake in the High Arctic of Canada. *Environmental Science & Technology, 53*(18), 10753–10762. https://doi.org/10.1021/acs.est.9b03372

Mahat, V., Silins, U., & Anderson, A. (2016). Effects of Wildfire on the Catchment Hydrology in Southwest Alberta. *Catena, 147*, 51–60. https://doi.org/10.1016/j.catena.2016.06.040

Maher, C. T., Nelson, C. R., & Larson, A. J. (2020). Winter damage is more important than summer temperature for maintaining the krummholz growth form above alpine treeline. *Journal of Ecology, 108*(3), 1074–1087. https://doi.org/10.1111/1365-2745.13315

Maher, P. T., & Lemelin, R. H. (2011). Northern Exposure: Opportunities and Challenges for Tourism Development in Torngat Mountains National Park, Labrador, Canada. *Polar Record, 47*(240), 40–45. https://doi.org/10.1017/S0032247409990581

Mahmood, R., Pielke Sr., R. A., Hubbard, K. G., Niyogi, D., Dirmeyer, P. A., McAlpine, C., Carleton, A. M., Hale, R., Gameda, S., Beltrán-Przekurat, A., Baker, B., McNider, R., Legates, D. R., Shepherd, M., Du, J., Blanken, P. D., Frauenfeld, O. W., Nair, U. s., & Fall, S. (2014). Land cover changes and their biogeophysical effects on climate. *International Journal of Climatology, 34*(4), 929–953. https://doi.org/10.1002/joc.3736

Mamet, S. D., & Kershaw, G. P. (2012). Subarctic and Alpine Tree Line Dynamics during the Last 400 Years in North-Western and Central Canada. *Journal of Biogeography, 39*(5), 855–868. https://doi.org/10.1111/j.1365-2699.2011.02642.x

Marsh, C. B., Pomeroy, J. W., & Spiteri, R. J. (2012). Implications of Mountain Shading on Calculating Energy for Snowmelt Using Unstructured Triangular Meshes. *Hydrological Processes, 26*(12), 1767–1778. https://doi.org/10.1002/hyp.9329

Marsh, P., & Woo, M. (1984). Wetting front advance and freezing of meltwater within a snow cover: 1. Observations in the Canadian Arctic. *Water Resources Research, 20*(12), 1853 1864. https://doi.org/10.1029/wr020i012p01853

Marshall, S. J. (2014). Meltwater run-off from Haig Glacier, Canadian Rocky Mountains, 2002–2013. *Hydrology and Earth System Sciences, 18*(12), 5181–5200. https://doi.org/10.5194/hess-18-5181-2014

Marshall, S. J., & Miller, K. (2020). Seasonal and Interannual Variability of Melt-Season Albedo at Haig Glacier,

Canadian Rocky Mountains. *The Cryosphere, 14*(10), 3249–3267. https://doi.org/10.5194/tc-14-3249-2020

Marshall, S. J., White, E. C., Demuth, M. N., Bolch, T., Wheate, R., Menounos, B., Beedle, M. J., & Shea, J. M. (2011). Glacier Water Resources on the Eastern Slopes of the Canadian Rocky Mountains. *Canadian Water Resources Journal, 36*(2), 109–133. https://doi.org/10.4296/cwrj3602823

Marzeion, B., Cogley, J. G., Richter, K., & Parkes, D. (2014). Attribution of global glacier mass loss to anthropogenic and natural causes. *Science, 345*(6199), 919–921. https://doi.org/10.1126/science.1254702

Matheussen, B., Kirschbaum, R. L., Goodman, I. A., O'Donnell, G. M., & Lettenmaier, D. P. (2000). Effects of land cover change on streamflow in the interior Columbia River Basin (USA and Canada). *Hydrological Processes, 14*(5), 867–885. https://doi.org/10.1002/(SICI)1099-1085(20000415)14:5<867::AID-HYP975>3.0.CO;2-5

Mattson, L. E., & Gardner, J. S. (1991). Mass Wasting on Valley-Side Ice-Cored Moraines, Boundary Glacier, Alberta, Canada. *Geografiska Annaler: Series A, Physical Geography, 73*(3–4), 123–128. https://doi.org/10.1080/04353676.1991.11880337

McCabe, G. J., Clark, M. P., & Hay, L. E. (2007). Rain-on-Snow Events in the Western United States. *Bulletin of the American Meteorological Society, 88*(3), 319–328. https://doi.org/10.1175/bams-88-3-319

McConnell, R. M. (1991). Solving Environmental Problems Caused by Adventure Travel in Developing Countries: The Everest Environmental Expedition. *Mountain Research and Development, 11*(4), 359. https://doi.org/10.2307/3673719

McCrary, R. R., Mearns, L. O., Hughes, M., Biner, S., & Bukovsky, M. S. (2022). Projections of North American snow from NA-CORDEX and their uncertainties, with a focus on model resolution. *Climatic Change, 170*(3), 20. https://doi.org/10.1007/s10584-021-03294-8

McCune, J. L., Colla, S. R., Coristine, L. E., Davy, C. M., Flockhart, D. T. T., Schuster, R., & Orihel, D. M. (2019). Are we accurately estimating the potential role of pollution in the decline of species at risk in Canada? *FACETS, 4*(1), 598–614. https://doi.org/10.1139/facets-2019-0025

McDowell, G., & Guo, J. (2021). A Nationally Coherent Characterization and Quantification of Mountain Systems in Canada. *Mountain Research and Development, 41*(2), R21–R31. https://doi.org/10.1659/MRD-JOURNAL-D-20-00071.1

McDowell, G., Huggel, C., Frey, H., Wang, F. M., Cramer, K., & Ricciardi, V. (2019). Adaptation action and research in glaciated mountain systems: Are they enough to meet the challenge of climate change? *Global Environmental Change, 54*, 19–30. https://doi.org/10.1016/j.gloenvcha.2018.10.012

McDowell, G., & Koppes, M. (2017). Robust Adaptation Research in High Mountains: Integrating the Scientific, Social, and Ecological Dimensions of Glacio-Hydrological Change. *Water, 9*(10), 739. https://doi.org/10.3390/w9100739

McDowell, G., Koppes, M., Harris, L., Chan, K. M., Price, M. F., Lama, D. G., Jiménez, G. (2021a). Lived experiences of 'peak water' in the high mountains of Nepal and Peru. *Climate and Development, 14*(3), 268–281. https://doi.org/10.1080/17565529.2021.1913085

McDowell, G., Stephenson, E., Ford, J. (2016). Adaptation, Adaptation Science, and the Status of Adaptation in Mountain Regions. In Salzmann, N., Huggel, C., Nussbaumer, S., Ziervogel, G. (eds) Climate Change Adaptation Strategies—An Upstream-downstream Perspective. Springer, Cham. https://doi.org/10.1007/978-3-319-40773-9_2

McDowell, G., Stevens, M., Lesnikowski, A., Huggel, C., Harden, A., DiBella, J., Morecroft, M., Kumar, P., Joe, E. T., Bhatt, I. D., & the Global Adaptation Mapping Initiative. (2021b). Closing the Adaptation Gap in Mountains. *Mountain Research and Development, 41*(3), A1. https://doi.org/10.1659/MRD-JOURNAL-D-21-00033.1

McKay, T. L., Pigeon, K. E., Larsen, T. A., & Finnegan, L. A. (2021). Close encounters of the fatal kind: Landscape features associated with central mountain caribou mortalities. *Ecology and Evolution, 11.0*(5), 2234–2248. https://doi.org/10.1002/ece3.7190

McKnight, E. A., Swanson, H., Brahney, J., & Hik, D. S. (2021). The physical and chemical limnology of Yukon's largest lake, Lhù'àan Mân' (Kluane Lake), prior to the 2016 'A'äy Chù' diversion. *Arctic Science, 7*(3), 655–678. https://doi.org/10.1139/as-2020-0012

McMullin, R. T., & Dorin, B. C. (2016). The Chic-Choc Mountains are the last southern refuge for Arctic lichens in eastern North America. *Arctic Science, 2*(4), 183–193. https://doi.org/10.1139/as-2015-0024

McNay, R. S., Lamb, C. T., Giguere, L., Williams, S. H., Martin, H., Sutherland, G. D., & Hebblewhite, M. (2022). Demographic responses of nearly extirpated endangered mountain caribou to recovery actions in Central British Columbia. *Ecological Applications, 32*(5). https://doi.org/10.1002/eap.2580

Mcnicol, B. J., & Glorioso, R. S. (2014). Second Home Leisure Landscapes and Retirement in the Canadian Rocky Mountain Community of Canmore, Alberta. *Annals of Leisure Research, 17*(1), 27–49. https://doi.org/10.1080/11745398.2014.885845

Mekis, E., Stewart, R. E., Theriault, J. M., Kochtubajda, B., Bonsal, B. R., & Liu, Z. (2020). Near-0 °C surface temperature and precipitation type patterns across Canada. *Hydrology and Earth System Sciences, 24*(4), 1741–1761. https://doi.org/10.5194/hess-24-1741-2020

Menounos, B., & Clague, J. J. (2008). Reconstructing Hydro-Climatic Events and Glacier Fluctuations Over the Past Millennium from Annually Laminated Sediments of Cheakamus Lake, Southern Coast Mountains, British Columbia, Canada. *Quaternary Science Reviews, 27*(44385), 701–713. https://doi.org/10.1016/j.quascirev.2008.01.007

Menounos, B., Hugonnet, R., Shean, D., Gardner, A., Howat, I., Berthier, E., Pelto, B., Tennant, C., Shea, J., Noh, M.-J., Brun, F., & Dehecq, A. (2019). Heterogeneous Changes in Western North American Glaciers Linked to Decadal Variability in Zonal Wind Strength. *Geophysical Research Letters*, 46(1), 200–209. https://doi.org/10.1029/2018GL080942

Menounos, B., Osborn, G., Clague, J. J., & Luckman, B. H. (2009). Latest Pleistocene and Holocene Glacier Fluctuations in Western Canada. *Quaternary Science Reviews*, 28(21–22), 2049–2074. https://doi.org/10.1016/j.quascirev.2008.10.018

Milner, A. M., Brittain, J. E., Castella, E., & Petts, G. E. (2001). Trends of macroinvertebrate community structure in glacier-fed rivers in relation to environmental conditions: A synthesis. *Freshwater Biology*, 46(12), 1833–1847. https://doi.org/10.1046/j.1365-2427.2001.00861.x

Milner, A. M., Khamis, K., Battin, T. J., Brittain, J. E., Barrand, N. E., Füreder, L., Cauvy-Fraunié, S., Gíslason, G. M., Jacobsen, D., Hannah, D. M., Hodson, A. J., Hood, E., Lencioni, V., Ólafsson, J. S., Robinson, C. T., Tranter, M., & Brown, L. E. (2017). Glacier shrinkage driving global changes in downstream systems. *Proceedings of the National Academy of Sciences of the United States of America*, 114(37), 9770–9778. https://doi.org/10.1073/pnas.1619807114

Minville, M., Brissette, F., & Leconte, R. (2008). Uncertainty of the impact of climate change on the hydrology of a nordic watershed. *Journal of Hydrology*, 358(1–2), 70–83. https://doi.org/10.1016/J.JHYDROL.2008.05.033

Mood, B. J., & Smith, D. J. (2021). A multi-century July-August streamflow reconstruction of Metro Vancouver's water supply contribution from the Capilano and Seymour watersheds in southwestern British Columbia, Canada. *Canadian Water Resources Journal*, 46(3), 121–138. https://doi.org/10.1080/07011784.2021.1931458

Moore, R. D., Nelitz, M., & Parkinson, E. (2013). Empirical modelling of maximum weekly average stream temperature in British Columbia, Canada, to support assessment of fish habitat suitability. *Canadian Water Resources Journal*, 38(2), 135–147. https://doi.org/10.1080/07011784.2013.794992

Moore, R. D., Pelto, B., Menounos, B., & Hutchinson, D. (2020). Detecting the Effects of Sustained Glacier Wastage on Streamflow in Variably Glacierized Catchments. *Frontiers in Earth Science*, 8. https://www.frontiersin.org/articles/10.3389/feart.2020.00136

Moore, R., & Demuth, M. (2001). Mass Balance and Streamflow Variability at Place Glacier, Canada, in Relation to Recent Climate Fluctuations. *Hydrological Processes*, 15(18), 3473–3486. https://doi.org/10.1002/hyp.1030

Mortezapour, M., Menounos, B., Jackson, P. L., & Erler, A. R. (2022). Future Snow Changes over the Columbia Mountains, Canada, using a Distributed Snow Model. *Climatic Change*, 172(1–2), 6. https://doi.org/10.1007/s10584-022-03360-9

Mouat, J. (2016). Engineering a Treaty: The Negotiation of the Columbia River Treaty of 1961/1964. In L. Heasley & D. Macfarlane (Eds.), *Border Flows: A Century of the Canadian-American Water Relationship* (pp. 169–203). University of Calgary Press.

Mourey, J., Marcuzzi, M., Ravanel, L., & Pallandre, F. (2019). Effects of climate change on high Alpine mountain environments: Evolution of mountaineering routes in the Mont Blanc massif (Western Alps) over half a century. *Arctic, Antarctic, and Alpine Research*, 51(1), 176–189. https://doi.org/10.1080/15230430.2019.1612216

Mourey, J., & Ravanel, L. (2017). Evolution of Access Routes to High Mountain Refuges of the Mer de Glace Basin (Mont Blanc Massif, France): An Example of Adapting to Climate Change Effects in the Alpine High Mountains. *Revue de Géographie Alpine*, 105-4. https://doi.org/10.4000/rga.3790

Moyer, A. N., Moore, R. D., & Koppes, M. N. (2016). Streamflow Response to the Rapid Retreat of a Lake-Calving Glacier. *Hydrological Processes*, 30(20), 3650–3665. https://doi.org/10.1002/hyp.10890

Mudryk, L. R., Derksen, C., Howell, S., Laliberté, F., Thackeray, C., Sospedra-Alfonso, R., Vionnet, V., Kushner, P. J., & Brown, R. (2018). Canadian snow and sea ice: Historical trends and projections. *The Cryosphere*, 12(4), 1157–1176. https://doi.org/10.5194/tc-12-1157-2018

Murdock, T. Q., Sobie, S. R., Zwiers, F. W., & Eckstrand, H. D. (2013). Climate Change and Extremes in the Canadian Columbia Basin. *Atmosphere-Ocean*, 51(4), 456–469. https://doi.org/10.1080/07055900.2013.816932

Musselman, K. N., Addor, N., Vano, J. A., & Molotch, N. P. (2021). Winter melt trends portend widespread declines in snow water resources. *Nature Climate Change*, 11(5), 418–424. https://doi.org/10.1038/s41558-021-01014-9

Musselman, K. N., Clark, M. P., Liu, C., Ikeda, K., & Rasmussen, R. (2017). Slower snowmelt in a warmer world. *Nature Climate Change*, 7(3), 214–219. https://doi.org/10.1038/nclimate3225

Musselman, K. N., Lehner, F., Ikeda, K., Clark, M. P., Prein, A. F., Liu, C., Barlage, M., & Rasmussen, R. (2018). Projected Increases and Shifts in Rain-on-Snow Flood Risk over Western North America. *Nature Climate Change*, 8(9), 808–812. https://doi.org/10.1038/s41558-018-0236-4

Myers-Smith, I. H., Elmendorf, S. C., Beck, P. S. A., Wilmking, M., Hallinger, M., Blok, D., Tape, K. D., Rayback, S. A., Macias-Fauria, M., Forbes, B. C., Speed, J. D. M., Boulanger-Lapointe, N., Rixen, C., Lévesque, E., Schmidt, N. M., Baittinger, C., Trant, A. J., Hermanutz, L., Collier, L. S., … Vellend, M. (2015). Climate sensitivity of shrub growth across the tundra biome. *Nature Climate Change*, 5(9), 887–891. https://doi.org/10.1038/nclimate2697

Nadeau Fortin, M. A., Sirois, L., & St-Laurent, M. H. (2016). Extensive forest management contributes to maintain suitable habitat characteristics for the endangered Atlantic-Gaspésie caribou. *Canadian Journal of Forest Research*, 46(7), 933–942. https://doi.org/10.1139/cjfr-2016-0038

Nadeau, M., & Rethoret, L. (2021). *Community-Led Land Use Management and Planning*. Columbia Basin Rural Development Institute at Selkirk College. https://sc.arcabc.ca/islandora/object/sc%3A5384

Natcher, D. C. (2009). Subsistence and the Social Economy of Canada's Aboriginal North. *Northern Review*, 30, Article 30.

Naz, B. S., Frans, C. D., Clarke, G. K. C., Burns, P., & Lettenmaier, D. P. (2014). Modeling the effect of glacier recession on streamflow response using a coupled glacio-hydrological model. *Hydrology and Earth System Sciences*, 18(2), 787–802. https://doi.org/10.5194/hess-18-787-2014

Needham, M. D., Rollins, R. B., Ceurvorst, R. L., Wood, C. J. B., Grimm, K. E., & Dearden, P. (2011). Motivations and Normative Evaluations of Summer Visitors at an Alpine Ski Area. *Journal of Travel Research*, 50(6), 669–684. https://doi.org/10.1177/0047287510382298

Needham, M. D., Wood, C. J. B., & Rollins, R. B. (2004). Understanding Summer Visitors and Their Experience at the Whistler Mountain Ski Area, Canada. *Mountain Research and Development*, 24(3), 234–242. https://doi.org/10.1659/0276-4741(2004)024[0234:USVATE]2.0.CO;2

Needham, M., & Rollins, R. (2005). Interest Group Standards for Recreation and Tourism Impacts at Ski Areas in the Summer. *Tourism Management*, 26(1), 44209. https://doi.org/10.1016/j.tourman.2003.08.015

Nehring, R. B., & Walker, P. G. (1996). Whirling disease in the wild. *A Fresh Approach to Stock Assessment*, 21(6), 28.

Nepal, S. (2016). Tourism and change in Nepal's Mt Everest region. In H. Richins & J. Hull (Eds.), *Mountain tourism: Experiences, communities, environments and sustainable futures*. CABI.

Nepal, S. K. (2008). Residents' Attitudes to Tourism in Central British Columbia, Canada. *Tourism Geographies*, 10(1), 42–65. https://doi.org/10.1080/14616680701825123

Nepal, S. K., & Jamal, T. B. (2011). Resort-Induced Changes in Small Mountain Communities in British Columbia, Canada. *Mountain Research and Development*, 31(2), 89–101. https://doi.org/10.1659/MRD-JOURNAL-D-10-00095.1

Nepal, S. K., & Way, P. (2007). Characterizing and Comparing Backcountry Trail Conditions in Mount Robson Provincial Park, Canada. *Ambio*, 36(5), 394–400. https://doi.org/10.1579/0044-7447(2007)36[394:CACBTC]2.0.CO;2

Neumann, P., & Mason, C. W. (2019). Managing Land Use Conflict Among Recreational Trail Users: A Sustainability Study of Cross-Country Skiers and Fat Bikers. *Journal of Outdoor Recreation and Tourism-Research Planning and Management*, 28(SI). https://doi.org/10.1016/j.jort.2019.04.002

Noël, B., van de Berg, W. J., Lhermitte, S., Wouters, B., Schaffer, N., & van den Broeke, M. R. (2018). Six Decades of Glacial Mass Loss in the Canadian Arctic Archipelago. *Journal of Geophysical Research: Earth Surface*, 123(6), 1430–1449. https://doi.org/10.1029/2017JF004304

North American Wetlands Conservation Council Committee. (2001). *Canadian Peat Harvesting and the Environment* (No. 2001–1). North American Wetlands Conservation Council Committee. https://nawcc.wetlandnetwork.ca/Can%20Peat%20Harvesting%202001-1.pdf

Obradovich, N., Migliorini, R., Paulus, M. P., & Rahwan, I. (2018). Empirical evidence of mental health risks posed by climate change. *Proceedings of the National Academy of Sciences*, 115(43), 10953–10958. https://doi.org/10.1073/pnas.1801528115

Ochwat, N. E., Marshall, S. J., Moorman, B. J., Criscitiello, A. S., & Copland, L. (2021). Evolution of the firn pack of Kaskawulsh Glacier, Yukon: Meltwater effects, densification, and the development of a perennial firn aquifer. *Cryosphere*, 15(4), 2021–2040. https://doi.org/10.5194/tc-15-2021-2021

Office of the Auditor General of British Columbia. (2022). *Annual Report of the Chief Inspector of Mines 2021/2022* (p. 35). https://www2.gov.bc.ca/assets/gov/farming-natural-resources-and-industry/mineral-exploration-mining/documents/directives-alerts-incidents/chief-inspector-s-report-page/21-22_cim_annual_report.pdf

Orr, P. L., Guiguer, K. R., & Russel, C. K. (2006). Food chain transfer of selenium in lentic and lotic habitats of a western Canadian watershed. *Ecotoxicology and Environmental Safety*, 63(2), 175–188. https://doi.org/10.1016/j.ecoenv.2005.09.004

Pacific Climate Impacts Consortium. (2021). *Pacific Climate Impacts Consortium November 2021 Updates*. https://pacificclimate.org/sites/default/files/publications/PCIC_Update_Nov-2021.pdf

Pacas C. & Taylor, M. K. (2015). Nonchemical eradication of an introduced trout from a headwater complex in Banff National Park, Canada. *North American Journal of Fisheries Management*, 35 (4), 748–754.

Page, S. E., & Baird, A. J. (2016). Peatlands and Global Change: Response and Resilience. *Annual Review of Environment and Resources*, 41(1), 35–57. https://doi.org/10.1146/annurev-environ-110615-085520

Palazzi, E., Mortarini, L., Terzago, S., & von Hardenberg, J. (2019). Elevation-dependent warming in global climate model simulations at high spatial resolution. *Climate Dynamics*, 52(5), 2685–2702. https://doi.org/10.1007/s00382-018-4287-z

Parks Canada Agency, G. of C. (2021, January 21). *Parks Canada attendance 2019-20*. https://www.pc.gc.ca/en/docs/pc/attend

Paul, A., Post, J., & Stelfox, J. (2003). Can Anglers Influence the Abundance of Native and Nonnative Salmonids in a Stream from the Canadian Rocky Mountains? *North American Journal of Fisheries Management*, 23(1), 109–119. https://doi.org/10.1577/1548-8675(2003)023<0109:CAITAO>2.0.CO;2

Pavlovskii, I., Hayashi, M., & Itenfisu, D. (2019). Midwinter melts in the Canadian prairies: Energy balance and hydrological effects. *Hydrology and Earth System Sciences*, 23(4), 1867–1883. https://doi.org/10.5194/hess-23-1867-2019

Pearce, T., Wright, H., Notaina, R., Kudlak, A., Smit, B., Ford, J., & Furgal, C. (2011). Transmission of Environmental Knowledge and Land Skills among Inuit Men in Ulukhaktok, Northwest Territories, Canada. *Human Ecology*, 39(3), 271–288. https://doi.org/10.1007/s10745-011-9403-1

Pentz, S., & Kostaschuk, R. (1999). Effect of placer mining on suspended sediment in reaches of sensitive fish habitat. *Environmental Geology*, 37(1), 78–89.

Pepin, N., Bradley, R. S., Diaz, H. F., Baraer, M., Caceres, E. B., Forsythe, N., Fowler, H., Greenwood, G., Hashmi, M. Z., Liu, X. D., Miller, J. R., Ning, L., Ohmura, A., Palazzi, E., Rangwala, I., Schöner, W., Severskiy, I., Shahgedanova, M., Wang, M. B., ... Mountain Research Initiative EDW Working Group. (2015). Elevation-dependent warming in mountain regions of the world. *Nature Climate Change*, 5(5), Article 5. https://doi.org/10.1038/nclimate2563

Pepin, N. C., & Lundquist, J. D. (2008). Temperature trends at high elevations: Patterns across the globe. *Geophysical Research Letters*, 35(14). https://doi.org/10.1029/2008GL034026

Perehudoff, L., & Rethoret, L. (2021). *Tourism in the Kootenay Rockies Region During COVID-19: Assessing Resident Sentiment*. Selkirk College. https://www.krtourism.ca/wp-content/uploads/2021/04/2021-01_KRT_Assessing_Resident_Sentiment.pdf

Perroud, M., Fasel, M., & Marshall, S. J. (2019). Development and Testing of a Subgrid Glacier Mass Balance Model for Nesting in the Canadian Regional Climate Model. *Climate Dynamics*, 53(44259), 1453–1476. https://doi.org/10.1007/s00382-019-04676-6

Petit, G., Cameron, A., Khanal, M., & Tedds, L. M. (2022). *A Comparative Analysis of Short-Term Rental Regulations in Six Alberta Municipalities* [Munich Personal RePEc Archive Paper]. University of Calgary.

Petrescu, A. M. R., Lohila, A., Tuovinen, J.-P., Baldocchi, D. D., Desai, A. R., Roulet, N. T., Vesala, T., Dolman, A. J., Oechel, W. C., Marcolla, B., Friborg, T., Rinne, J., Matthes, J. H., Merbold, L., Meijide, A., Kiely, G., Sottocornola, M., Sachs, T., Zona, D., ... Cescatti, A. (2015). The uncertain climate footprint of wetlands under human pressure. *Proceedings of the National Academy of Sciences*, 112(15), 4594–4599. https://doi.org/10.1073/pnas.1416267112

Pfeffer, W. T., Arendt, A. A., Bliss, A., Bolch, T., Cogley, J. G., Gardner, A. S., Hagen, J.-O., Hock, R., Kaser, G., Kienholz, C., Miles, E. S., Moholdt, G., Mölg, N., Paul, F., Radić, V., Rastner, P., Raup, B. H., Rich, J., Sharp, M. J., & Consortium, T. R. (2014). The Randolph Glacier Inventory: A globally complete inventory of glaciers. *Journal of Glaciology*, 60(221), 537–552. https://doi.org/10.3189/2014JoG13J176

Pickering, C. M., Castley, J. G., & Burtt, M. (2010). Skiing Less Often in a Warmer World: Attitudes of Tourists to Climate Change in an Australian Ski Resort. *Geographical Research*, 48(2), 137–147. https://doi.org/10.1111/j.1745-5871.2009.00614.x

Pitman, K. J., & Moore, J. W. (2021). The role of large, glaciated tributaries in cooling an important Pacific salmon migration corridor: A study of the Babine River. *Environmental Biology of Fishes*, 104(10), 1263–1277. https://doi.org/10.1007/s10641-021-01152-1

Plotkin, R. (2018). *Tribal Parks and Indigenous Protected and Conserved Areas: Lessons Learned from B.C. Examples*. David Suzuki Foundation. https://apps.uqo.ca/LoginSigparb/LoginPourRessources.aspx?url=http://www.deslibris.ca/ID/10097616

Poley, L. G., Schuster, R., Smith, W., & Ray, J. C. (2022). Identifying differences in roadless areas in Canada based on global, national, and regional road datasets. *Conservation Science and Practice*, 4(4), e12656. https://doi.org/10.1111/csp2.12656

Pomeroy, J. W., Fang, X., & Rasouli, K. (2015). Sensitivity of snow processes to warming in the Canadian Rockies. *Proceedings of the 72nd Eastern Snow Conference*, 9–11.

Pomeroy, J. W., Parviainen, J., Hedstrom, N., & Gray, D. M. (1998). Coupled modelling of forest snow interception and sublimation. *Hydrological Processes*, 12(15), 2317–2337. https://doi.org/10.1002/(sici)1099-1085(199812)12:15<2317::aid-hyp799>3.0.co;2-x

Pouliot, D., Latifovic, R., Zabcic, N., Guindon, L., & Olthof, I. (2014). Development and assessment of a 250m spatial resolution MODIS annual land cover time series (2000–2011) for the forest region of Canada derived from change-based updating. *Remote Sensing of Environment*, 140, 731–743. https://doi.org/10.1016/j.rse.2013.10.004

Povoroznyuk, O., Vincent, W. F., Schweitzer, P., Laptander, R., Bennett, M., Calmels, F., Sergeev, D., Arp, C., Forbes, B. C., Roy-Léveillée, P., & Walker, D. A. (2022). Arctic roads and railways: Social and environmental consequences of transport infrastructure in the circumpolar North. *Arctic Science*, 9(2), 297–330. https://doi.org/10.1139/as-2021-0033

Pradhananga, D., Pomeroy, J., Aubry-Wake, C., Munro, D., Shea, J., Demuth, M., Kirat, N., Menounos, B., & Mukherjee, K. (2021). Hydrometeorological, glaciological and geospatial research data from the Peyto Glacier Research Basin in the Canadian Rockies. *Earth System Science Data*, 13(6), 2875–2894. https://doi.org/10.5194/essd-13-2875-2021

Pradhananga, D., & Pomeroy, J. W. (2022). Recent hydrological response of glaciers in the Canadian Rockies to changing climate and glacier configuration. *Hydrology and Earth System Sciences*, 26(10), 2605–2616. https://doi.org/10.5194/hess-26-2605-2022

Pradhananga, D., Pomeroy, J. W., Aubry-Wake, C., Munro, D. S., Shea, J. M., Demuth, M. N., Kirat, N. H., Menounos, B., & Mukherjee, K. (2020). *Hydrometeorological, glaciological and geospatial research data from the Peyto Glacier Research Basin in the Canadian Rockies*. Federated Research Data Repository (FRDR). https://doi.org/10.20383/101.0259

Purdie, H., Hutton, J. H., Stewart, E., & Espiner, S. (2020). Implications of a changing alpine environment for geotourism: A case study from Aoraki/Mount Cook, New Zealand. *Journal of Outdoor Recreation and Tourism*, 29, 100235. https://doi.org/10.1016/j.jort.2019.100235

Purdie, H., & Kerr, T. (2018). Aoraki Mount Cook: Environmental Change on an Iconic Mountaineering Route. *Mountain Research and Development, 38*(4), 364. https://doi.org/10.1659/MRD-JOURNAL-D-18-00042.1

Quinton, W., Berg, A., Braverman, M., Carpino, O., Chasmer, L., Connon, R., Craig, J., Devoie, É., Hayashi, M., Haynes, K., Olefeldt, D., Pietroniro, A., Rezanezhad, F., Schincariol, R., & Sonnentag, O. (2019). A synthesis of three decades of hydrological research at Scotty Creek, NWT, Canada. *Hydrology and Earth System Sciences, 23*(4), 2015–2039. https://doi.org/10.5194/hess-23-2015-2019

Radic, V., & Hock, R. (2014). Glaciers in the Earth's Hydrological Cycle: Assessments of Glacier Mass and Runoff Changes on Global and Regional Scales. *Surveys in Geophysics, 35*(3), 813–837. https://doi.org/10.1007/s10712-013-9262-y

Rangwala, I., & Miller, J. R. (2012). Climate change in mountains: A review of elevation-dependent warming and its possible causes. *Climatic Change, 114*(3), 527–547. https://doi.org/10.1007/s10584-012-0419-3

Rasouli, K., Pomeroy, J. W., Janowicz, J. R., Williams, T. J., & Carey, S. K. (2019). A Long-Term Hydrometeorological Dataset (1993–2014) of a Northern Mountain Basin: Wolf Creek Research Basin, Yukon Territory, Canada. *Earth System Science Data, 11*(1), 89–100. https://doi.org/10.5194/essd-11-89-2019

Rasouli, K., Pomeroy, J. W., & Marks, D. G. (2015). Snowpack Sensitivity to Perturbed Climate in a Cool Mid-Latitude Mountain Catchment. *Hydrological Processes, 29*(18), 3925–3940. https://doi.org/10.1002/hyp.10587

Rasouli, K., Pomeroy, J. W., & Whitfield, P. H. (2019). Hydrological Responses of Headwater Basins to Monthly Perturbed Climate in the North American Cordillera. *Journal of Hydrometeorology, 20*(5), 863–882. https://doi.org/10.1175/JHM-D-18-0166.1

Renard, S. M., Mcintire, E. J. B., & Fajardo, A. (2016). Winter Conditions—Not Summer Temperature—Influence Establishment of Seedlings at White Spruce Alpine Treeline in Eastern Quebec. *Journal of Vegetation Science, 27*(1), 29–39. https://doi.org/10.1111/jvs.12347

Riahi, K., van Vuuren, D. P., Kriegler, E., Edmonds, J., O'Neill, B. C., Fujimori, S., Bauer, N., Calvin, K., Dellink, R., Fricko, O., Lutz, W., Popp, A., Cuaresma, J. C., Kc, S., Leimbach, M., Jiang, L., Kram, T., Rao, S., Emmerling, J., … Tavoni, M. (2017). The Shared Socioeconomic Pathways and their energy, land use, and greenhouse gas emissions implications: An overview. *Global Environmental Change, 42*, 153–168. https://doi.org/10.1016/j.gloenvcha.2016.05.009

Ribot, J. (2011) Vulnerability before adaptation: Toward transformative climate action. *Global Environmental Change 21*(4), 1160–1162. https://doi.org/10.1016/j.gloenvcha.2011.07.008

Richter, A., & Kolmes, S. A. (2005). Maximum Temperature Limits for Chinook, Coho, and Chum Salmon, and Steelhead Trout in the Pacific Northwest. *Reviews in Fisheries Science, 13*(1), 23–49. https://doi.org/10.1080/10641260590885861

Rippin, D. M., Sharp, M., Van Wychen, W., & Zubot, D. (2020). Detachment of Icefield Outlet Glaciers: Catastrophic Thinning and Retreat of the Columbia Glacier (Canada). *Earth Surface Processes and Landforms, 45*(2), 459–472. https://doi.org/10.1002/esp.4746

Ritter, F., Fiebig, M., & Muhar, A. (2012). Impacts of Global Warming on Mountaineering: A Classification of Phenomena Affecting the Alpine Trail Network. *Mountain Research and Development, 32*(1), 4–15. https://doi.org/10.1659/MRD-JOURNAL-D-11-00036.1

Roberts, B., Ward, B., & Rollerson, T. (2004). A Comparison of Landslide Rates Following Helicopter and Conventional Cable-Based Clear-Cut Logging Operations in the Southwest Coast Mountains of British Columbia. *Geomorphology, 61*(44259), 337–346. https://doi.org/10.1016/j.geomorph.2004.01.007

Robroek, B. J. M., Heijboer, A., Jassey, V. E. J., Hefting, M. M., Rouwenhorst, T. G., Buttler, A., & Bragazza, L. (2013). Snow cover manipulation effects on microbial community structure and soil chemistry in a mountain bog. *Plant and Soil, 369*(1–2), 151–164. https://doi.org/10.1007/s11104-012-1547-2

Roesky, B., & Hayashi, M. (2022). Effects of lake-groundwater interaction on the thermal regime of a sub-alpine headwater stream. *Hydrological Processes, 36*(2). https://doi.org/10.1002/hyp.14501

Rood, S. B., Pan, J., Gill, K. M., Franks, C. G., Samuelson, G. M., & Shepherd, A. (2008). Declining Summer Flows of Rocky Mountain Rivers: Changing Seasonal Hydrology and Probable Impacts on Floodplain Forests. *Journal of Hydrology, 349*(44259), 397–410. https://doi.org/10.1016/j.jhydrol.2007.11.012

Rood, S., Samuelson, G., Weber, J., & Wywrot, K. (2005). Twentieth-Century Decline in Streamflows from the Hydrographic Apex of North America. *Journal of Hydrology, 306*(44200), 215–233. https://doi.org/10.1016/j.jhydrol.2004.09.010

Rosenberg, D. M., & Woodward, J. (2015, October). The Tsilhqot'in case: The recognition and affirmation of aboriginal title in Canada. *University of British Columbia Law Review, 48*(3), 934–970.

Rudolph, B.-L., Andreller, I., & Kennedy, C. J. (2008). Reproductive Success, Early Life Stage Development, and Survival of Westslope Cutthroat Trout (*Oncorhynchus clarki lewisi*) Exposed to Elevated Selenium in an Area of Active Coal Mining. *Environmental Science & Technology, 42*(8), 3109–3114. https://doi.org/10.1021/es072034d

Sadler, B. (1983). Ski-Area Development in the Canadian Rockies: Past Lessons, Future Prospects (Alberta). *Western Geographical Series, 21*, 309–330.

Sala, O. E., Stuart Chapin, F., III, Armesto, J. J., Berlow, E., Bloomfield, J., Dirzo, R., Huber-Sanwald, E., Huenneke, L. F., Jackson, R. B., Kinzig, A., Leemans, R., Lodge, D. M., Mooney, H. A., Oesterheld, M., Poff, N. L., Sykes, M. T., Walker, B. H., Walker, M., & Wall, D. H. (2000). Global Biodiversity Scenarios for the Year 2100. *Science, 287*(5459), 1770–1774. https://doi.org/10.1126/science.287.5459.1770

Sandford, R. W., Harford, D., & O'Riordan, J. (2014). *The Columbia River Treaty: A Primer*. Rocky Mountain Books.

Sanseverino, M. E., Whitney, M. J., & Higgs, E. S. (2016). Exploring Landscape Change in Mountain Environments with the Mountain Legacy Online Image Analysis Toolkit. *Mountain Research and Development*, 36(4), 407–416. https://doi.org/10.1659/MRD-JOURNAL-D-16-00038.1

Saremba, J., & Gill, A. (1991). Value Conflicts in Mountain Park Settings. *Annals of Tourism Research*, 18(3), 455–472. https://doi.org/10.1016/0160-7383(91)90052-D

Sauchyn, D., Vanstone, J., St Jacques, J.-M., & Sauchyn, R. (2015). Dendrohydrology in Canada's Western Interior and Applications to Water Resource Management. *Journal of Hydrology*, 529(2), 548–558. https://doi.org/10.1016/j.jhydrol.2014.11.049

Schiefer, E., Gilbert, R., & Hassan, M. A. (2011). A Lake Sediment-Based Proxy of Floods in the Rocky Mountain Front Ranges, Canada. *Journal of Paleolimnology*, 45(2), 137–149. https://doi.org/10.1007/s10933-010-9485-6

Schiefer, E., Menounos, B., & Wheate, R. (2007). Recent Volume Loss of British Columbian Glaciers, Canada. *Geophysical Research Letters*, 34(16). https://doi.org/10.1029/2007GL030780

Schindler, D. (2000). Aquatic Problems Caused by Human Activities in Banff National Park, Alberta, Canada. *Ambio*, 29(7), 401–407. https://doi.org/10.1639/0044-7447(2000)029[0401:APCBHA]2.0.CO;2

Schindler, D.W. & Parker, B. R. (2002). Biological pollutants: alien fishes in mountain lakes. *Water, Air, and Soil Pollution: Focus*, 2 (2): 379–397, doi:10.1023/A:1020187532485.

Schnorbus, M., Werner, A., & Bennett, K. (2014). Impacts of climate change in three hydrologic regimes in British Columbia, Canada. *Hydrological Processes*, 28(3), 1170–1189. https://doi.org/10.1002/hyp.9661

Schumann, K., Gewolf, S., & Tackenberg, O. (2016). Factors affecting primary succession of glacier foreland vegetation in the European Alps. *Alpine Botany*, 126(2), 105–117. https://doi.org/10.1007/s00035-016-0166-6

Schuster, R., Buxton, R., Hanson, J. O., Binley, A. D., Pittman, J., Tulloch, V., Sorte, F. A. L., Roehrdanz, P. R., Verburg, P. H., Rodewald, A. D., Wilson, S., Possingham, H. P., & Bennett, J. R. (2022). Protected area planning to conserve biodiversity in an uncertain future. *Conservation Biology*, 37(3), 1–9. https://doi.org/10.1101/2022.11.18.517054

Scott, D., Jones, B., & Konopek, J. (2007). Implications of Climate and Environmental Change for Nature-Based Tourism in the Canadian Rocky Mountains: A Case Study of Waterton Lakes National Park. *Tourism Management*, 28(2), 570–579. https://doi.org/10.1016/j.tourman.2006.04.020

Scott, D., & McBoyle, G. (2007). Climate change adaptation in the ski industry. *Mitigation and Adaptation Strategies for Global Change*, 12(8), 1411–1431. https://doi.org/10.1007/s11027-006-9071-4

Scott, D., McBoyle, G., & Mills, B. (2003). Climate change and the skiing industry in southern Ontario (Canada): Exploring the importance of snowmaking as a technical adaptation. *Climate Research*, 23, 171–181. https://doi.org/10.3354/cr023171

Scott, D., Steiger, R., Rutty, M., Pons, M., & Johnson, P. (2019). The Differential Futures of Ski Tourism in Ontario (Canada) Under Climate Change: The Limits of Snowmaking Adaptation. *Current Issues in Tourism*, 22(11), 1327–1342. https://doi.org/10.1080/13683500.2017.1401984

Seip, D. R. (1992). Factors Limiting Woodland Caribou Populations and Their Interrelationships with Wolves and Moose in Southeastern British Columbia. *Canadian Journal of Zoology*, 70(8), 1494–1503. https://doi.org/10.1139/z92-206

Seip, Dale. R., Johnson, C. J., & Watts, G. S. (2007). Displacement of Mountain Caribou from Winter Habitat by Snowmobiles. *Journal of Wildlife Management*, 71(5), 1539–1544. https://doi.org/10.2193/2006-387

Serrouya, R., Dickie, M., Lamb, C., van Oort, H., Kelly, A. P., DeMars, C., McLoughlin, P. D., Larter, N. C., Hervieux, D., Ford, A. T., & Boutin, S. (2021). Trophic consequences of terrestrial eutrophication for a threatened ungulate. *Proceedings of the Royal Society B: Biological Sciences*, 288(1943), 20202811. https://doi.org/10.1098/rspb.2020.2811

Serrouya, R., Mclellan, B. N., Van Oort, H., Mowat, G., & Boutin, S. (2017). Experimental Moose Reduction Lowers Wolf Density and Stops Decline of Endangered Caribou. *Peerj*, 5(8), e3736–e3736. https://doi.org/10.7717/peerj.3736

Shannon, S., Smith, R., Wiltshire, A., Payne, T., Huss, M., Betts, R., Caesar, J., Koutroulis, A., Jones, D., & Harrison, S. (2019). Global Glacier Volume Projections Under High-End Climate Change Scenarios. *Cryosphere*, 13(1), 325–350. https://doi.org/10.5194/tc-13-325-2019

Sharma, A. R., & Dery, S. J. (2016). Elevational Dependence of Air Temperature Variability and Trends in British Columbia's Cariboo Mountains, 1950–2010. *Atmosphere-Ocean*, 54(2), 153–170. https://doi.org/10.1080/07055900.2016.1146571

Sharp, M., Burgess, D. O., Cogley, J. G., Ecclestone, M., Labine, C., & Wolken, G. J. (2011). Extreme melt on Canada's Arctic ice caps in the 21st century. *Geophysical Research Letters*, 38(11). https://doi.org/10.1029/2011GL047381

Shea, J. M., Menounos, B., Moore, R. D., & Tennant, C. (2013). An Approach to Derive Regional Snow Lines and Glacier Mass Change from Modis Imagery, Western North America. *Cryosphere*, 7(2), 667–680. https://doi.org/10.5194/tc-7-667-2013

Shea, J. M., Whitfield, P. H., Fang, X., & Pomeroy, J. W. (2021). The Role of Basin Geometry in Mountain Snowpack Responses to Climate Change. *Frontiers in Water*, 3, nan. https://doi.org/10.3389/frwa.2021.604275

Shugar, D. H., Burr, A., Haritashya, U. K., Kargel, J. S., Watson, C. S., Kennedy, M. C., Bevington, A. R., Betts, R. A., Harrison, S., & Strattman, K. (2020). Rapid worldwide growth of glacial lakes since 1990. *Nature Climate Change*, 10(10), 939–945. https://doi.org/10.1038/s41558-020-0855-4

Shugar, D. H., Clague, J. J., Best, J. L., Schoof, C., Willis, M. J., Copland, L., & Roe, G. H. (2017). River Piracy and Drainage Basin Reorganization Led by Climate-Driven Glacier Retreat. *Nature Geoscience, 10*(5), 370–375. https://doi.org/10.1038/NGEO2932

Siegwart Collier, L. (2020). *Climate change impacts on berry shrub performance in treeline and tundra ecosystems* [Doctoral, Memorial University of Newfoundland]. https://research.library.mun.ca/14436/

Simms, E. L., & Ward, H. (2013). Multisensor Ndvi-Based Monitoring of the Tundra-Taiga Interface (Mealy Mountains, Labrador, Canada). *Remote Sensing, 5*(3), 1066–1090. https://doi.org/10.3390/rs5031066

Simpson, NP., Mach, KJ., Constable, A., Hess, J., Hogarth, R., Howden, M., Lawrence, J., Lempert, RJ., Muccione, V., Mackey, B. (2021) A framework for complex climate change risk assessment. *One Earth, 4*(4), 489–501. https://doi.org/10.1016/j.oneear.2021.03.005

Sinickas, A., Jamieson, B., & Maes, M. A. (2016). Snow Avalanches in Western Canada: Investigating Change in Occurrence Rates and Implications for Risk Assessment and Mitigation. *Structure and Infrastructure Engineering, 12*(4), 490–498. https://doi.org/10.1080/15732479.2015.1020495

Sinnatamby, R. N., Cantin, A., & Post, J. R. (2020). Threats to At-Risk Salmonids of the Canadian Rocky Mountain Region. *Ecology of Freshwater Fish, 29*(3), 477–494. https://doi.org/10.1111/eff.12531

Smit, B., Burton, I., Klein, R.J., Street, R. (1999) The science of adaptation: a framework for assessment. *Mitigation and Adaptation Strategies for Global Change, 4*(3–4), 199–213.

Sobie, S. R. (2020). Future Changes in Precipitation-Caused Landslide Frequency in British Columbia. *Climatic Change, 162*(2), 465–484. https://doi.org/10.1007/s10584-020-02788-1

Sobie, S. R., & Murdock, T. Q. (2022). Projections of Snow Water Equivalent Using a Process-Based Energy Balance Snow Model in Southwestern British Columbia. *Journal of Applied Meteorology and Climatology, 61*(1), 77–95. https://doi.org/10.1175/JAMC-D-20-0260.1

Sobie, S. R., Zwiers, F. W., & Curry, C. L. (2021). Climate Model Projections for Canada: A Comparison of CMIP5 and CMIP6. *Atmosphere-Ocean, 59*(4–5), 269–284. https://doi.org/10.1080/07055900.2021.2011103

Somers, L. D., & McKenzie, J. M. (2020). A review of groundwater in high mountain environments. *WIREs Water, 7*(6), e1475. https://doi.org/10.1002/wat2.1475

St. Pierre, K. A., St. Louis, V. L., Lehnherr, I., Gardner, A. S., Serbu, J. A., Mortimer, C. A., Muir, D. C. G., Wiklund, J. A., Lemire, D., Szostek, L., & Talbot, C. (2019). Drivers of Mercury Cycling in the Rapidly Changing Glacierized Watershed of the High Arctic's Largest Lake by Volume (Lake Hazen, Nunavut, Canada). *Environmental Science & Technology, 53*(3), 1175–1185. https://doi.org/10.1021/acs.est.8b05926

St. Pierre, K. A., Zolkos, S., Shakil, S., Tank, S. E., St. Louis, V. L., & Kokelj, S. V. (2018). Unprecedented Increases in Total and Methyl Mercury Concentrations Downstream of Retrogressive Thaw Slumps in the Western Canadian Arctic. *Environmental Science & Technology, 52*(24), 14099–14109. https://doi.org/10.1021/acs.est.8b05348

Stahl, K., & Moore, R. D. (2006). Influence of watershed glacier coverage on summer streamflow in British Columbia, Canada. *Water Resources Research, 42*(6). https://doi.org/10.1029/2006WR005022

Stahl, K., Moore, R. D., Shea, J. M., Hutchinson, D., & Cannon, A. J. (2008). Coupled modelling of glacier and streamflow response to future climate scenarios. *Water Resources Research, 44*(2). https://doi.org/10.1029/2007WR005956

Staples, K., & Natcher, D. C. (2017). Gender, Decision Making, and Natural Resource Co-management in Yukon. *Arctic, 68*(3), 356. https://doi.org/10.14430/arctic4506

Steffen, W., Broadgate, W., Deutsch, L., Gaffney, O., & Ludwig, C. (2015). The trajectory of the Anthropocene: The Great Acceleration. *The Anthropocene Review, 2*(1), 81–98. https://doi.org/10.1177/2053019614564785

Steiger, R., Knowles, N., Pöll, K., & Rutty, M. (2022). Impacts of climate change on mountain tourism: A review. *Journal of Sustainable Tourism, 1–34.* https://doi.org/10.1080/09669582.2022.2112204

Stevens, S. (2003). Tourism and deforestation in the Mt Everest region of Nepal. *The Geographical Journal, 169*(3), 255–277. https://doi.org/10.1111/1475-4959.00089

Stewart, I. T., Cayan, D. R., & Dettinger, M. D. (2004). Changes in snowmelt runoff timing in western North America under a "business as usual" climate change scenario. *Climatic Change, 62*(1–3), 217–232. https://doi.org/10.1023/B:CLIM.0000013702.22656.E8

St-Louis, A., Hamel, S., Mainguy, J., & Cote, S. D. (2013). Factors Influencing the Reaction of Mountain Goats Towards All-Terrain Vehicles. *Journal of Wildlife Management, 77*(3), 599–605. https://doi.org/10.1002/jwmg.488

Stockdale, C. A., Macdonald, S. E., & Higgs, E. (2019). Forest Closure and Encroachment at the Grassland Interface: A Century-Scale Analysis Using Oblique Repeat Photography. *Ecosphere, 10*(6). https://doi.org/10.1002/ecs2.2774

Stocker-Waldhuber, M., Fischer, A., Keller, L., Morche, D., & Kuhn, M. (2017). Funnel-shaped surface depressions—Indicator or accelerant of rapid glacier disintegration? A case study in the Tyrolean Alps. *Geomorphology, 287,* 58–72. https://doi.org/10.1016/j.geomorph.2016.11.006

Stockner, J., Langston, A., Sebastian, D., & Wilson, G. (2005). The Limnology of Williston Reservoir: British Columbia's Largest Lacustrine Ecosystem. *Water Quality Research Journal, 40*(1), 28–50. https://doi.org/10.2166/wqrj.2005.003

Stocks, B. J., Mason, J. A., Todd, J. B., Bosch, E. M., Wotton, B. M., Amiro, B. D., Flannigan, M. D., Hirsch, K. G., Logan, K. A., Martell, D. L., & Skinner, W. R. (2003). Large forest fires in Canada, 1959–1997. *Journal of Geophysical Research D: Atmospheres, 108*(1). https://doi.org/10.1029/2001jd000484

Stralberg, D., Arseneault, D., Baltzer, J. L., Barber, Q. E., Bayne, E. M., Boulanger, Y., Brown, C. D., Cooke, H. A., Devito, K., Edwards, J., Estevo, C. A., Flynn, N., Frelich, L. E., Hogg, E. H., Johnston, M., Logan, T., Matsuoka, S. M., Moore, P., Morelli, T. L., … Whitman, E. (2020). Climate-change refugia in boreal North America: What, where, and for how long? *Frontiers in Ecology and the Environment, 18*(5), 261–270. https://doi.org/10.1002/fee.2188

Strapazzon, G., Schweizer, J., Chiambretti, I., Brodmann Maeder, M., Brugger, H., & Zafren, K. (2021). Effects of Climate Change on Avalanche Accidents and Survival. *Frontiers in Physiology, 12*. https://www.frontiersin.org/articles/10.3389/fphys.2021.639433

Sun, Y., De Silva, A. O., St Pierre, K. A., Muir, D. C. G., Spencer, C., Lehnherr, I., & MacInnis, J. J. (2020). Glacial Melt Inputs of Organophosphate Ester Flame Retardants to the Largest High Arctic Lake. *Environmental Science & Technology, 54*(5), 2734–2743. https://doi.org/10.1021/acs.est.9b06333

Svoboda, F., & Paul, F. (2009). A New Glacier Inventory on Southern Baffin Island, Canada, from Aster Data: I. Applied Methods, Challenges and Solutions. *Annals of Glaciology, 50*(53), 44521. https://doi.org/10.3189/172756410790595912

Swart, N. C., Cole, J. N. S., Kharin, V. V., Lazare, M., Scinocca, J. F., Gillett, N. P., Anstey, J., Arora, V., Christian, J. R., Hanna, S., Jiao, Y., Lee, W. G., Majaess, F., Saenko, O. A., Seiler, C., Seinen, C., Shao, A., Sigmond, M., Solheim, L., … Winter, B. (2019). The Canadian Earth System Model version 5 (CanESM5.0.3). *Geoscientific Model Development, 12*(11), 4823–4873. https://doi.org/10.5194/gmd-12-4823-2019

Tennant, C., & Menounos, B. (2013). Glacier Change of the Columbia Icefield, Canadian Rocky Mountains, 1919–2009. *Journal of Glaciology, 59*(216), 671–686. https://doi.org/10.3189/2013JoG12J135

Tennant, C., Menounos, B., Wheate, R., & Clague, J. J. (2012). Area Change of Glaciers in the Canadian Rocky Mountains, 1919 to 2006. *Cryosphere, 6*(6), 1541–1552. https://doi.org/10.5194/tc-6-1541-2012

Thomson, L. I., Osinski, G. R., & Ommanney, C. S. L. (2011). Glacier Change on Axel Heiberg Island, Nunavut, Canada. *Journal of Glaciology, 57*(206), 1079–1086. https://doi.org/10.3189/002214311798843287

Toledo, O., Palazzi, E., Cely Toro, I.M. & Mortarini, L. (2022). Comparison of elevation-dependent warming and its drivers in the tropical and subtropical Andes. *Climate Dynamics, 58*, 3057–3074, https://doi.org/10.1007/s00382-021-06081-4

Tolvanen, A., & Kangas, K. (2016). Tourism, biodiversity and protected areas—Review from northern Fennoscandia. *Journal of Environmental Management, 169*, 58–66. https://doi.org/10.1016/j.jenvman.2015.12.011

Trant, A., Higgs, E., & Starzomski, B. M. (2020). A Century of High Elevation Ecosystem Change in the Canadian Rocky Mountains. *Scientific Reports, 10*(9698), 1–10. https://doi.org/10.1038/s41598-020-66277-2

Trant, A. J., & Hermanutz, L. (2014). Advancing Towards Novel Tree Lines? A Multispecies Approach to Recent Tree Line Dynamics in Subarctic Alpine Labrador, Northern Canada. *Journal of Biogeography, 41*(6), 1115–1125. https://doi.org/10.1111/jbi.12287

Trombulak, S. C., & Frissell, C. A. (2000). Review of ecological effects of roads on terrestrial and aquatic communities. *Conservation Biology, 14*(1), 18–30.

Turetsky, M. R., Donahue, W. F., & Benscoter, B. W. (2011). Experimental drying intensifies burning and carbon losses in a northern peatland. *Nature Communications, 2*(1), 514. https://doi.org/10.1038/ncomms1523

Turgeon, G., Kutz, S. J., Lejeune, M., St-Laurent, M. H., & Pelletier, F. (2018). Parasite prevalence, infection intensity and richness in an endangered population, the Atlantic-Gaspésie caribou. *International Journal for Parasitology: Parasites and Wildlife, 7*(1), 90–94. https://doi.org/10.1016/j.ijppaw.2018.02.001

Turner, B., Kasperson, R., Matson, P., McCarthy, J., Corell, R., Christensen, L., Eckley, N., Kasperson, J., Luers, A., Martello, M. (2003) A framework for vulnerability analysis in sustainability science. *Proceedings of the National Academy of Sciences, 100*(14), 8074-8079. https://doi.org/10.1073/pnas.1231335100

UNEP (2022). *Global Peatlands Assessment—The State of the World's Peatlands: Evidence for action toward the conservation, restoration, and sustainable management of peatlands.* https://www.unep.org/resources/global-peatlands-assessment-2022

United Nations Declaration on the Rights of Indigenous Peoples: Resolution/adopted by the General Assembly, A/RES/61/295 § General Assembly (2007). https://www.un.org/esa/socdev/unpfii/documents/DRIPS_en.pdf

van Asselen, S., & Verburg, P. H. (2012). A Land System representation for global assessments and land-use modeling. *Global Change Biology, 18*(10), 3125–3148. https://doi.org/10.1111/j.1365-2486.2012.02759.x

VanShaar, J. R., Haddeland, I., & Lettenmaier, D. P. (2002). Effects of land-cover changes on the hydrological response of interior Columbia River basin forested catchments. *Hydrological Processes, 16*(13), 2499–2520. https://doi.org/10.1002/hyp.1017

Veillard, M., & James, C. (2020). *Status of Whirling Disease in the Crowsnest River 2019: Technical Report.* Government of Alberta, Ministry of Environment and Parks. https://open.alberta.ca/dataset/564d1c08-bf40-4f5e-bef4-b80d2c8d205e/resource/70d3f48e-3a7e-4224-86b7-7ac3bad5e6b1/download/aep-whirling-disease-2019-technical-report-crowsnest-river-2020-09.pdf

Venter, O., Sanderson, E. W., Magrach, A., Allan, J. R., Beher, J., Jones, K. R., Possingham, H. P., Laurance, W. F., Wood, P., Fekete, B. M., Levy, M. A., & Watson, J. E. M. (2016). Sixteen years of change in the global terrestrial human footprint and implications for biodiversity conservation. *Nature Communications, 7*(1), Article 1. https://doi.org/10.1038/ncomms12558

Vionnet, V., Mortimer, C., Brady, M., Arnal, L., & Brown, R. (2021). Canadian historical Snow Water Equivalent dataset (CanSWE, 1928–2020). *Earth System Science Data, 13*(9), 4603–4619. https://doi.org/10.5194/essd-13-4603-2021

Vodden, K., & Cunsolo, A. (2021). Rural and Remote Communities. In *Canada in a Changing Climate: National Issues Report*. Government of Canada.

Vogel, B., Henstra, D., & McBean, G. (2020). Sub-national government efforts to activate and motivate local climate change adaptation: Nova Scotia, Canada. *Environment, Development and Sustainability, 22*(2), 1633–1653. https://doi.org/10.1007/s10668-018-0242-8

Voyer, A., Smith, K., & Festa-Bianchet, M. (2003). Dynamics of Hunted and Unhunted Mountain Goat Oreamnos Americanus Populations. *Wildlife Biology, 9*(3), 213–218.

Wang, X., Helgason, B., Westbrook, C., & Bedard-Haughn, A. (2016). Effect of Mineral Sediments on Carbon Mineralization, Organic Matter Composition and Microbial Community Dynamics in a Mountain Peatland. *Soil Biology & Biochemistry, 103*, 16–27. https://doi.org/10.1016/j.soilbio.2016.07.025

Watson, C. S., & King, O. (2018). Everest's thinning glaciers: Implications for tourism and mountaineering. *Geology Today, 34*(1), 18–25. https://doi.org/10.1111/gto.12215

Watson, J. E. M., Evans, T., Venter, O., Williams, B., Tulloch, A., Stewart, C., Thompson, I., Ray, J. C., Murray, K., Salazar, A., McAlpine, C., Potapov, P., Walston, J., Robinson, J. G., Painter, M., Wilkie, D., Filardi, C., Laurance, W. F., Houghton, R. A., … Lindenmayer, D. (2018). The exceptional value of intact forest ecosystems. *Nature Ecology & Evolution, 2*(4), Article 4. https://doi.org/10.1038/s41559-018-0490-x

Way, R. G., Bell, T., & Barrand, N. E. (2014). An Inventory and Topographic Analysis of Glaciers in the Torngat Mountains, Northern Labrador, Canada. *Journal of Glaciology, 60*(223), 945–956. https://doi.org/10.3189/2014JoG13J195

Way, R. G., Bell, T., & Barrand, N. E. (2015). Glacier Change from the Early Little Ice Age to 2005 in the Torngat Mountains, Northern Labrador, Canada. *Geomorphology, 246*, 558–569. https://doi.org/10.1016/j.geomorph.2015.07.006

Way, R. G., Lewkowicz, A. G., & Zhang, Y. (2018). Characteristics and fate of isolated permafrost patches in coastal Labrador, Canada. *The Cryosphere, 12*(8), 2667–2688. https://doi.org/10.5194/tc-12-2667-2018

Weber, M., Groulx, M., Lemieux, C. J., Scott, D., & Dawson, J. (2019). Balancing the Dual Mandate of Conservation and Visitor Use at a Canadian World Heritage Site in an Era of Rapid Climate Change. *Journal of Sustainable Tourism, 27*(9), 1318–1337. https://doi.org/10.1080/09669582.2019.1620754

Webster, K. L., Beall, F. D., Creed, I. F., & Kreutzweiser, D. P. (2015). Impacts and prognosis of natural resource development on water and wetlands in Canada's boreal zone. *Environmental Reviews, 23*(1), 78–131.

Wehrly, K. E., Wang, L., & Mitro, M. (2007). Field-Based Estimates of Thermal Tolerance Limits for Trout: Incorporating Exposure Time and Temperature Fluctuation. *Transactions of the American Fisheries Society, 136*(2), 365–374. https://doi.org/10.1577/T06-163.1

Wenzel, G. (2013). Inuit and modern hunter-gatherer subsistence. *Études/Inuit/Studies, 37*(2), 181–200. https://doi.org/10.7202/1025716ar

Westerling, A. L., Hidalgo, H. G., Cayan, D. R., & Swetnam, T. W. (2006). Warming and earlier spring increase Western U.S. forest wildfire activity. *Science, 313*(5789), 940–943. https://doi.org/10.1126/science.1128834

Whitaker, D. (2017). Expanded Range Limits of Boreal Birds in the Torngat Mountains of Northern Labrador. *Canadian Field-Naturalist, 131*(1), 55–62. https://doi.org/10.22621/cfn.v131i1.1957

Whitfield, P. H. (2012). Floods in future climates: A review. *Journal of Flood Risk Management, 5*(4), 336–365. https://doi.org/10.1111/j.1753-318X.2012.01150.x

Whitfield, P. H. (2014). Climate Station Analysis and Fitness for Purpose Assessment of 3053600 Kananaskis, Alberta. *Atmosphere-Ocean, 52*(5), 363–383. https://doi.org/10.1080/07055900.2014.946388

Whitfield, P. H., & Pomeroy, J. W. (2016). Changes to Flood Peaks of a Mountain River: Implications for Analysis of the 2013 Flood in the Upper Bow River, Canada. *Hydrological Processes, 30*(25), 4657–4673. https://doi.org/10.1002/hyp.10957

Whyte, K. (2016). *Our Ancestors' Dystopia Now: Indigenous Conservation and the Anthropocene* (SSRN Scholarly Paper No. 2770047). https://papers.ssrn.com/abstract=2770047

Wild, F. J. (2008). Epidemiology of Mountain Search and Rescue Operations in Banff, Yoho, and Kootenay National Parks, 2003–06. *Wilderness & Environmental Medicine, 19*(4), 245–251. https://doi.org/10.1580/07-WEME-OR-141.1

Wildlife Conservation Society Canada. (2021). *Northern Peatlands in Canada An Enormous Carbon Storehouse* [Story Map ArcGIS]. https://storymaps.arcgis.com/stories/19d24f59487b46f6a011dba140eddbe7

Wilkie, K., & Clague, J. J. (2009). Fluvial Response to Holocene Glacier Fluctuations in the Nostetuko River Valley, Southern Coast Mountains, British Columbia. *Geological Society Special Publication, 320*, 199.

Williamson, S. N., Anslow, F. S., Clarke, G. K. C., Gamon, J. A., Jarosch, A. H., & Hik, D. S. (2018). Spring Warming in Yukon Mountains Is Not Amplified by the Snow Albedo Feedback. *Scientific Reports, 8*. https://doi.org/10.1038/s41598-018-27348-7

Williamson, S. N., & Menounos, B. (2021). The influence of forest fires aerosol and air temperature on glacier albedo, western North America. *Remote Sensing of Envi-*

ronment, 267(nan), 112732. https://doi.org/10.1016/j.rse.2021.112732

Williamson, S. N., Zdanowicz, C., Anslow, F. S., Clarke, G. K. C., Copland, L., Danby, R. K., Flowers, G. E., Holdsworth, G., Jarosch, A. H., & Hik, D. S. (2020). Evidence for Elevation-Dependent Warming in the St. Elias Mountains, Yukon, Canada. *Journal of Climate*, 33(8), 3252–3268. https://doi.org/10.1175/JCLI-D-19-0405.1

Wittmer, H. U., Mclellan, B. N., Serrouya, R., & Apps, C. D. (2007). Changes in Landscape Composition Influence the Decline of a Threatened Woodland Caribou Population. *Journal of Animal Ecology*, 76(3), 568–579. https://doi.org/10.1111/j.1365-2656.2007.01220.x

Wittmer, H. U., Serrouya, R., Elbroch, L. M., & Marshall, A. J. (2013). Conservation Strategies for Species Affected by Apparent Competition: Conservation Biology. *Conservation Biology*, 27(2), 254–260. https://doi.org/10.1111/cobi.12005

Wolfe, B. B., Edwards, T. W. D., Hall, R. I., & Johnston, J. W. (2011). A 5200-Year Record of Freshwater Availability for Regions in Western North America Fed by High-Elevation Runoff. *Geophysical Research Letters*, 38(11), 1–5. https://doi.org/10.1029/2011GL047599

Wong, C., Ballegooyen, K., Ignace, L., Johnson, M. J. (Gùdia), & Swanson, H. (2020). Towards reconciliation: 10 Calls to Action to natural scientists working in Canada. *FACETS*, 5(1), 769–783. https://doi.org/10.1139/facets-2020-0005

Wouters, B., Gardner, A. S., & Moholdt, G. (2019). Global Glacier Mass Loss during the GRACE Satellite Mission (2002–2016). *Frontiers in Earth Science*, 7. https://www.frontiersin.org/articles/10.3389/feart.2019.00096

Wu, H., Yan, L., Li, Y., Zhang, K., Hao, Y., Wang, J., Zhang, X., Yan, Z., Zhang, Y., & Kang, X. (2020). Drought-induced reduction in methane fluxes and its hydrothermal sensitivity in alpine peatland. *PeerJ*, 8, e8874. https://doi.org/10.7717/peerj.8874

Wu, J., & Roulet, N. T. (2014). Climate change reduces the capacity of northern peatlands to absorb the atmospheric carbon dioxide: The different responses of bogs and fens: Peatlands switch to C sources by 2100. *Global Biogeochemical Cycles*, 28(10), 1005–1024. https://doi.org/10.1002/2014GB004845

Wyllie De Echeverria, V. R., & Thornton, T. F. (2019). Using Traditional Ecological Knowledge to Understand and Adapt to Climate and Biodiversity Change on the Pacific Coast of North America. *Ambio*, 48(12), 1447–1469. https://doi.org/10.1007/s13280-019-01218-6

Yao, J., Stieb, D. M., Taylor, E., & Henderson, S. B. (2020). Assessment of the Air Quality Health Index (AQHI) and four alternate AQHI-Plus amendments for wildfire seasons in British Columbia. *Canadian Journal of Public Health*, 111(1), 96–106. https://doi.org/10.17269/s41997-019-00237-w

Zdanowicz, C., Karlsson, P., Beckholmen, I., Roach, P., Poulain, A., Yumvihoze, E., Martma, T., Ryjkov, A., & Dastoor, A. (2018). Snowmelt, Glacial and Atmospheric Sources of Mercury to a Subarctic Mountain Lake Catchment, Yukon, Canada. *Geochimica Et Cosmochimica Acta*, 238, 374–393. https://doi.org/10.1016/j.gca.2018.06.003

Zhang, X., Harvey, K. D., Hogg, W. D., & Yuzyk, T. R. (2001). Trends in Canadian streamflow. *Water Resources Research*, 37(4), 987–998. https://doi.org/10.1029/2000WR900357

Zurba, M., Beazley, K. F., English, E., & Buchmann-Duck, J. (2019). Indigenous Protected and Conserved Areas (IPCAs), Aichi Target 11 and Canada's Pathway to Target 1: Focusing Conservation on Reconciliation. *Land*, 8(1), 10. https://doi.org/10.3390/land8010010

Alpine lakes among peaks of the Cayoosh Range in the Coast Mountains. Photo courtesy of Mary Sanseverino, 2022.

CHAPTER 6

Desirable Mountain Futures

CO-LEAD AUTHORS: Keara Lightning, Eric Higgs

CONTRIBUTING AUTHORS: Leon Andrew, Stephen Chignell, Megan Dicker, Erika Gavenus, Murray Humphries, Lawrence Ignace, Aerin Jacob, Gùdia Mary Jane Johnson, Stephen Johnston, Michele Koppes, Shawn Marshall, Graham McDowell, PearlAnn Reichwein, Joseph Shea, Daniel Sims, Niiyokamigaabaw Deondre Smiles, Madison Stevens, Hayden Melting Tallow, Andrew Trant, Gabrielle Weasel Head

"The fox brought the daylight. All of the other animals came after the sun and moon had gone into the sky. All of the animals had come together to make the day, because the earth was covered, like a really foggy day. All of the animals started to jump up to try to tear away that covering on the earth. If you've ever watched in the autumn and winter, the ńthe (fox) jumps high and lands deep in the snow to get what they're hunting. They're very light and they can jump very high. So it was the ńthe (fox) that tore the membrane on this earth. We call that, kamba k'anchäl. When the earth is torn from the membrane and you have the light on the edge of the mountains, or over the prairies, or the ocean. The Raven gave a piece of that sun to the ńthe (red fox). That's why when you look at the tail, it's got white with red all around it, like the sun. That was his gift for giving us the daylight here on earth. The kind of work that everybody has been part of for this mountain assessment, and has thought carefully and critically about, and has celebrated over these last three years, it's sort of like that time, where that daylight is just opening over the side of the earth and the sky. That's the kind of work that this assessment has done, it's given us a little bit of that daylight."—Elder Gùdia (Mary Jane Johnson), Lhu'ààn Mân Ku Dań, 12 January 2023

We have learned a great deal in these three years of the Canadian Mountain Assessment (CMA). Much was already known but not widely shared across the divides of Indigenous and Western knowledge systems. Some was new learning; not new research, but new insights from working together in a project that spanned time, cultures, and landscapes.

We learned that mountains are Homelands. Mountains are unimaginably diverse. Mountains are changing. Mountains are humbling in their vast extents and the scale of cultural knowledge about them. Mountains are boundary zones between peoples, languages, species, and movement, but yet they connect us as well as divide us. Mountains are water towers that nourish lower and drier lands. Mountains are sources of livelihood. Mountains are places of envy and awe, which is why so many people flock to them. Mountains are places where we come to challenge ourselves and seek insight. Mountains are sources of inspiration for art, music, stories and writing. Mountains are spiritual both through long tradition and contemporary wonder. Mountains bear testament to colonial injustices, and cast long shadows.

The CMA had its early glimmers in 2020 as the COVID-19 pandemic was settling in. Mountain researchers and communities in Canada had not taken collective stock of mountains and the importance they place in people's lives, despite efforts to do so in other mountain areas globally; notably, in the Hindu Kush Himalaya. A comprehensive assessment of mountain regions in Canada was overdue. Motivated by the vision of the Project Leader, and with a remarkable team of national and international Advisors, the CMA began to take shape.

It was a daunting task. An early commitment was made to an inclusive approach that brought together people from diverse backgrounds and ways of knowing. This was not to be an assessment of Western academic knowledge alone; it was also about elevating Indigenous knowledges and making space for what might be learned by bringing the two into respectful conversation. Guided by five principles (see Chapter 1, Fig. 1.10)—Service, Inclusivity, Humility, Responsibility, and Action—the work began. Much of it was done in the confines of virtual spaces dotted across mountain areas in Canada, but a face-to-face gathering in Banff in May 2022 brought people and ideas together (Fig. 6.1).

Each core chapter of the CMA was co-led by Indigenous and non-Indigenous individuals to support equitable knowledge co-creation, with many additional Contributing Authors support-

ing the preparation of CMA chapters. Mountain Environments (Chapter 2) described the physical characteristics and environmental significance of mountains in Canada, including their geological evolution and the importance and impact of mountain systems on local and regional climate, and ecosystems and biodiversity. Mountains as Homelands (Chapter 3) provided a vibrant account of those who live among or near mountains, and the complicated legacy of colonial governance, protected areas, private property, access to culturally important lands and waters, and "how science, labour, recreation, and art have shaped perceptions and experiences of mountains as places." Gifts of the Mountains (Chapter 4) accounted for that which mountains provide, as gifts of sustenance, spiritual and cultural expression, and enjoyment. The chapter also acknowledged the importance and obligation

Figure 6.1: CMA contributors coming together in Banff to discuss their diverse knowledges of mountains in Canada, May 2022. Photo courtesy of David Borish.

THE CANADIAN MOUNTAIN ASSESSMENT

of reciprocity, as well as difficulties in manifesting reciprocity in the context of extractive resource activities. Mountains Under Pressure (Chapter 5) examined drivers and impacts of environmental and social change in mountains, including development, recreation, resource extraction, and the cascading consequences of climate change.

More than twenty CMA participants combed through draft versions of these chapters during a workshop on 12 January 2023 to seek emergent themes that might guide us towards desirable futures for mountain people and places. The intention was not to chart exact futures or to describe one path against another, but to articulate how to *think* about desirable mountain futures. We dug deeper into the lessons that the Assessment taught us and emerged with four themes: connectivity; elevating Indigenous knowledges; access and barriers to relationships; and humility. These are ways of approaching the future, ways of guiding the work of people who think and care deeply about mountains.

6.1 Connectivity

Mountains bring connectivity into focus in several ways. The valleys and plains near mountains are places of habitation and use, while at the same time they are forbidding topographic barriers that can restrict those living in these regions from accessing adjacent mountainous regions. Mountains shape the way people and animals move across landscapes. Low points in mountain passes and corridors along ridges and valleys make travel easier. Daunting ranges of mountains, such as those along the Continental Divide, influence cultural, environmental, ecological, hydrological, and climatological transitions. Rivers flow from mountain sources to connect communities and ecosystems hundreds of kilometres apart.

Thinking about connectivity in mountain landscapes also highlights the challenges of fragmentation. Anthropogenic disruption of connectivity, through the building of roads, dams, pipelines and other oil and gas extraction infrastructure, mines, and the harvesting of forests, can produce restricted spaces and isolated communities. This loss of connectivity results in the separation of people and animals from Homelands and homes, isolation from places of learning and from other-than-human teachers and kin, and leads to a divided and an impoverished understanding of mountains and mountain peoples. Political boundaries also disrupt connectivity when people dwell across mountains that are divided by imposed borders. Likewise, fragmentation of space through private ownership and jurisdiction can separate people from access to important mountain places. As well, researchers working on specific problems in the mountains can find it difficult to connect their work because knowledge is often organised by discipline and not by place. Such disciplinary fragmentation challenges efforts to understand mountain systems in more holistic ways. It can also be difficult to connect research insights across space, as most mountain research is focused on specific study areas, limiting understanding that comes from landscape (or larger) scale analyses.

There is a temporal dimension to connectivity, too. People cherish stories and accounts of the past as a way of maintaining deep connections to mountain places. Physical fragmentation disrupts long-standing place-based systems of knowledge transmission and separates people from each other, which can make it harder to share and maintain stories. The persistence of such knowledge requires connection between generations, yet legacies of colonialism, rapid changes in mountain livelihoods, and compromised access to the Land disrupt this continuity. Fragmentation invites us to consider how to reconnect spatially and temporally, ecologically and socially, to allow future generations to find refuge, enjoyment, and meaning in special mountain places.

6.2 Elevating Indigenous Knowledges

This assessment set out to work towards braiding Western academic and Indigenous knowledges of mountains. The relationships that have been built from this process have impacted us all. As authors we believe it important to bring our voices together to enhance our collective understanding of mountains. Throughout this assessment, we observed how many of the pressures and barriers in mountain areas have been caused by the imposition of colonial rule, whether manifest through knowledge systems, economic systems, or land management. In order to create a better future, we must come to terms with and address these issues.

We observed many strengths, but also limitations in the Western academic paradigm. Disciplinary approaches are inherently limited compared to more encompassing approaches that approach mountains as complex systems, including human elements. Many mountain researchers (Indigenous and non-Indigenous) are driven by a felt sense that is not acknowledged in the traditional scientific/academic systems of recording knowledge. Several authors spoke about their own deep spiritual connection to mountain places. There is also a sense that something is deeply wrong in the way mountain spaces are currently treated, an awareness that drives many of us in this work. Non-Indigenous researchers spoke of academic knowledge alone failing to account for the diversity of ways people experience mountains. The process of working across and between knowledge systems is also an internal process of deconstructing key assumptions to evaluate what is worth keeping and what is best to let go.

While the original language used in our process was "knowledge co-creation" and "knowledge braiding," our discussions during the workshop highlighted the importance of *elevating* Indigenous knowledge systems. This does not mean elevating Indigenous knowledges to the exclusion of Western academic knowledge, but rather seeking to unpack such discursive boundaries while prioritising Indigenous-led efforts. For example, the language such as co-creation and braiding can reinforce a binary that obscures the ways that Indigenous knowledge and science have long been entangled and co-produced, such as the presence of processes similar to those used in Western academic inquiry that are already within Indigenous knowledge systems, as well as the widespread scientific methods used by Indigenous communities to benefit their governance and livelihoods. In discussing the importance of building community capacity through scientific training, Gabrielle Weasel Head acknowledged, "Some of the knowledge that [science] is now generating is knowledge that has been held in our communities for thousands of years... there's a lot of stories in our Nations [and] they are the blueprint for our scientific worldview" (LC 6.1).

By casting certain forms of technical and academic knowledge as exclusively non-Indigenous,

Gabrielle Weasel Head, Kainaiwa Nation, Blackfoot Confederacy, 2022, LC 6.1

Brandy Mayes, Kwanlin Dün First Nation, 2022, LC 6.2

a binary view can reinforce a static notion of Indigenous knowledges and constrain the creative capacity of Indigenous knowledge systems in ever-shifting global systems of governance. A few of the Knowledge Holders participating in the Learning Circle referred to the importance of scientific and technical training to support their communities' governance systems. Brandy Mayes (Kwanlin Dün First Nation) described how Kwanlin Dün First Nation members were trained in the skills necessary to run their own resource management projects in their territory: "taking that science-based information and teachings to mentor our own people so we could do this on our own... we are using that science, but we're also being led by some of our own traditional knowledge" as well as "a lands vision from our Elders and our citizens" (LC 6.2). The binary also fails to recognize the individuals who are informed by both Western academic training and Indigenous ways of knowing, which includes many of this CMA's authors, as well as the distinctions between different Indigenous knowledges *and* distinct Western academic traditions. Many Indigenous scholars have made significant contributions and theoretical interventions into Western academic disciplines, which can inform the methods and frameworks used in such disciplines and offer productive avenues of inquiry. Western knowledge systems are similarly diverse, with markedly different cultures and approaches in natural, social, and health sciences.

Elevating Indigenous knowledge systems takes many forms (see e.g., McGregor, 2021). Some ideas of what this looks like are: directing resources towards research and training opportunities within Indigenous communities, supporting Indigenous-led documentation of Indigenous knowledges, enabling the resurgence of Indigenous stewardship practices, and conducting collaborative projects in a way that cultivates Indigenous communities' capacity. For Indigenous students and scholars, employing the tools and techniques of Western scientific methods, in a manner aligned with their philosophies and protocols while addressing questions their communities define, may also serve this purpose. These efforts are necessary to allow research that, rather than using decontextualized Indigenous knowledges to satisfy non-Indigenous curiosities, can instead pursue the questions and issues that are important to Indigenous communities.

Importantly, a focus on elevating Indigenous knowledges does not preclude advancement and continued learning within the context of Western academic institutions and paradigms. Indeed, this assessment has illustrated that among Western academic fields of inquiry there is much we still do not know about the mountains in Canada. For example, this assessment has demonstrated that humanities and social science inquiries into the pressures affecting mountain systems remain limited compared to work in the physical sciences. Limitations in long-term monitoring networks in mountains mean that there is also considerable uncertainty in what the future could hold for mountain hydrological systems, biodiversity, and snow and ice amid rapid environmental change. Enhancing Western academic understandings of mountain systems—particularly by urging academics to work across siloed disciplines and to approach their scholarship with awareness of its underlying assumptions and limitations—will also be crucial to realising desirable mountain futures. Ultimately, we aspire to ensure that "all boats float" when it comes to supporting diverse ways of knowing mountain systems in Canada.

We argue that achieving equitable sharing of knowledges across ways of knowing requires particular attention to elevating First Nations, Métis, and Inuit knowledge systems which have long been delegitimized in the dominant paradigm of producing knowledge. Given the asymmetries in how knowledge is currently defined, a desirable future requires all of us to dig deeper than the goal of acknowledgement or inclusion—to think beyond Western academic constructs to see how different ways of knowing hold a different understanding of where we place ourselves in this world. This is also relevant to thinking about what sustainability might look like as "sustainability requires recognition and restoration of reciprocal relationships between peoples and places (Wildcat, 2013)."

6.3 Access and Barriers to Relationships

Many authors and Learning Circle participants stressed the importance of fostering relationships between people and the mountains. Indigenous contributors expressed the importance of mountains as spaces for ceremony, medicines, food, and as storied places with deep generational connections that are vital for their survival. And most of us depend on mountains for clean water, spiritual connection, mental health and wellbeing, foods and medicines, and more.

Recreational activities such as mountaineering, climbing, skiing, running, canoeing, and kayaking have led many people to develop an appreciation for the gifts of the mountains. Developing this sense of connection to mountain landscapes through recreation can engender a respect and emotional connection to mountains. However, there is also a history of mountains being governed as exclusive spaces. Recreation, tourism, resource development, and sport hunting were encouraged to the exclusion of Indigenous Peoples' access and livelihoods. This exclusivity of space has also extended to exclusion on the basis of racialization, gender, age, class, and ability.

Intergenerational relationships are especially important to uplift going forward, to carry forward the knowledge of the older generations and mentor new generations in mountain knowledge and relationships. Lhu'ààn Mân Ku Dań Elder Gùdia Mary Jane Johnson spoke of how young people generally have more energy and physical strength than older people, while elders carry mental and spiritual strength developed through their years. Just as we bring different forms of

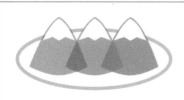

Gùdia Mary Jane Johnson, Lhu'ààn Mân Ku Dań, 2022, LC 6.3

Leon Andrew, Nę K'ə Dene Ts'įlı, 2022, LC 6.4

Gabrielle Weasel Head, Kainaiwa Nation, Blackfoot Confederacy, 2022, LC 6.5

Daniel Sims, Tsay Keh Dene First Nation, 2022, LC 6.6

knowledge together to enhance understanding, bringing these different experiences and abilities together makes our collective efforts stronger and supports the action needed to move forward (LC 6.3).

There is a balance still to be found in considering the negative impacts of human access to mountain places. The language of access can imply an entitlement to the gifts of the mountains. We emphasise that the issue of access is one of identifying barriers to relationships, and importantly, finding ways to enact these relationships that respect the presence and needs of diverse human values in the landscape as well as the needs of other-than-human beings that dwell in mountain places. Nę K'ə Dene Ts'įlı Elder Leon Andrew describes this need to co-exist in partnership between different peoples and wildlife: "One thing we know for sure is Mountain Dene people coexist with wildlife for how long—we're like partners. So now you guys learn to coexist with us too" (LC 6.4).

Animals and plants also depend on mountain spaces. As people take up more and more space, the relative remoteness of mountains has provided vital habitat even to species not originally associated with mountain environments. For the future of ecologically and culturally important species, such as bison and grizzly bears, mountain-dwelling remnant populations and the relative connectivity found across mountain habitats make these places vitally important for the success of ecological restoration efforts. Building relationships to the mountains should thus also embody an ethic of care, reciprocity, and gratitude.

Barriers to relationships include not only those which limit physical access to land in a recreational sense, but also the lack of access to political power needed to carry out the responsibilities of land stewardship that maintain intergenerational relationships to place. Both parks and private land ownership have imposed distant governance systems on Indigenous homelands in mountain spaces. Gabrielle Weasel Head highlighted the ways in which such impositions have infringed on the rights set out in treaties: "Our treaty rights with regards to land access have been infringed on… We need to get a really good understanding of how the legalities of access are structured, and really tie that back to treaty… People's responsibilities to treaty [are] not common knowledge" (LC 6.5). However, as Dr. Daniel Sims (Tsay Keh Dene First Nation) reminds us, not all Indigenous nations in Canada have treaties with the Crown, and many still maintain inherent Indigenous rights. While for treaty Nations, treaties set out a Nation-to-Nation relationship with the Crown, without a treaty, Canada has no legal standing to enforce its presence: "There's no pretence of treaty. It's just we are here, we have always been here, and you guys are the new arrivals" (LC 6.6). This also reminds us that lands that have been constructed by Western culture as wilderness have in reality been occupied by Indigenous Peoples for a very long time. The restoration of such ecosystems is intertwined with the restoration of Indigenous knowledge systems, stewardship, and governance. Some promising areas where this is advancing are Indigenous Protected and Conserved Areas (Artelle et al., 2019; Zurba et al., 2019) as well as Indigenous governance established through land claims such as in Tongait KakKasuangita SilakKijapvinga (Torngat Mountains National Park).

6.4 Humility

Mountains are sacred, old places of ceremony and story, creation and rebirth; they humble us in their size and stature. Looking up at the mountains, they remind us of how small we are as individuals, of how short a time we have to make our contribution in this life.

This assessment set out to evaluate what we know, what we do not know, and what we need to know about mountains in Canada. This has been a humbling task. Over and over again we have come back to recognizing just how much we do not know. We've come across many people and places that are under-represented in the academic literature that is currently available. With humility, the CMA aimed to identify those gaps in order to point directions for future projects and necessary partnerships to move forward together.

This humility extends to the relationships that have been built during the assessment, as we have worked to create a shared body of knowledge from a team of 75 authors from different disciplines, backgrounds, and geographies. Nurturing these relationships with a shared desire to learn and build trust has been crucial to working together to bring together a systematic review of the literature with the knowledge shared in the Learning Circle. The content of this report is the result of collaboration and compromise, and the humility required to allow multiple perspectives and understandings to coexist.

Humility is important in acknowledging the changing dynamics of mountain ecosystems. In writing about desirable mountain futures, we operate from humility and respect for how little we can know about the future. While collecting the best information to plan for the future, we embrace uncertainty. As mountain systems change, we must also change. Lhu'ààn Mân Ku Dań Elder Gùdia Mary Jane Johnson described how to shift our approach to planning: "You need to start from [observing] the roots of the trees and the plants, the soil, the water that comes and feeds them. What kinds of animals come, and need life and sustain themselves on that land and water. And then, you put people beside that, and you say I'm going to manage the people's activity, not the animals. You are not managers of any animals,

Gùdia Mary Jane Johnson, Lhu'ààn Mân Ku Dań, 2022, LC 6.7

any other ones except for yourself" (LC 6.7). As much as we try to plan for, predict, and shape the future, we are going to be living with mountain ecosystems that are full of novelty: novel ecosystems and assemblages of species, as well as new ways of relating to and being in the mountains. Humility calls for each of us to take on our individual and collective responsibilities to the mountains from our respective positions, understanding that while no one person alone can see the whole picture, together with many perspectives, the view becomes clearer.

6.5 Endings as Beginnings

This chapter concludes the Canadian Mountain Assessment, but endings are also beginnings. The CMA brought together people from diverse backgrounds and viewpoints to assess, for the first time, mountain systems in Canada. In the writing of this assessment, boundaries separating disciplines and cultures were traversed, and the result is something new: an account of landscapes where history and experience are shaped by mountains. In many ways this constitutes a baseline, a moment in time, against which future efforts will be compared. In the future we hope people will look back upon this compilation as a reservoir of helpful knowledge, and as a starting point (Fig. 6.2).

Thinking about the assessment as a baseline focuses attention on the *product* of the knowledge and less on the *process* by which it came about. While always intending to present multiple ways of knowing mountains, few participants were prepared for how profound this exchange of knowledges would be, and what it would spark. Working in this space was new terrain for many

Figure 6.2: The CMA provides an opportunity to learn, reflect, and be inspired to work for desirable mountain futures. Photo courtesy of Paul Zizka, 2014.

who contributed to the Assessment, and it has been a learning journey for all involved. As with many significant journeys, the final outcome was often uncertain. As Gùdia remarked, "[S]ometimes when we undertake hard work, we want to see the end result, we want to get it done, but sometimes it doesn't happen quickly. We have to pass it along to the next generation, like a good story."

A mark of accomplishment for the CMA will be the extent to which it finds its way back into the hands of scholars, communities, and policy makers, and from there stimulates efforts that address the needs and opportunities identified in the assessment. As a starting point:

- We ask that mountain researchers, communities, and policy makers in Canada reflect on the findings of the CMA, and resolve to attend to key issues in ways that manifest the spirit and intent of the CMA.

- We emphasise that appropriate and effective inclusion of Indigenous knowledges in these efforts requires recognition of the governance systems and worldviews that underpin such knowledges, which in turn requires support for Indigenous self-determination. This should be foregrounded in conversations about ethical engagements with Indigenous Peoples and their diverse knowledges.

- We challenge the national research community to embrace transdisciplinary approaches to advancing understanding of mountain systems in Canada. Here, meaningful collaboration with local and Indigenous communities; decision-makers; and humanities, social, natural, and health sciences scholars provides an opportunity to improve understanding of many dimensions of mountain systems in the country.

- We call on the Government of Canada to outline commitments to action for mountains in their next Sustainable Development Strategy (and other relevant policy frameworks), and, furthermore, to join the UN's Mountain Partnership. These are important steps in formalising Canada's commitment to the health, well-being, and resilience of mountain systems in the country, and are cogent actions given the findings of the CMA, including the fact that Canada is the 4th most mountainous country globally.
- We request that all levels of government, intergovernmental and non-governmental organisations, and philanthropic groups increase their support for mountain communities and mountain researchers in their efforts to better understand and steward mountain systems in Canada.
- We propose that the CMA should be an ongoing initiative, and that subsequent assessments be conducted every ten years. Like other large-scale assessment platforms (e.g., IPCC, IPBES), this approach will support efforts to track progress in addressing gaps and opportunities identified in earlier reports. Importantly, subsequent iterations of the CMA should build upon and improve (rather than duplicate) the methodology followed herein according to feedback based on this report and in accordance with future norms and aspirations.

- We suggest the establishment of a national institute for mountain studies, which would serve to support, mobilise, and grow the network of mountain researchers, Indigenous Knowledge Holders, and prominent thinkers that the CMA has convened. Such an institute would be a champion for mountain systems in Canada, interface with international efforts such as the Mountain Research Initiative and the UN Mountain Partnership, and could coordinate future iterations of the Canadian Mountain Assessment.
- Finally, we invite those involved with major assessment activities in Canada and abroad to consider how the CMA's approach might inform their own activities going forward. The CMA is not a blueprint to be mapped onto other contexts, but its normative commitments, attendant methodologies, and subsequent findings are instructive and can inform future knowledge assessment initiatives.

We are grateful for the opportunities and learning that the CMA has provided for each of us. Our hope is that what we have prepared will inspire new research, relationships, and actions that help to secure desirable futures for mountain systems in Canada, and beyond. The story is yours to carry forward.

References

Artelle, K. A., Zurba, M., Bhattacharyya, J., Chan, D. E., Brown, K., Housty, J., & Moola, F. (2019). Supporting resurgent Indigenous-led governance: A nascent mechanism for just and effective conservation. *Biological Conservation*, 240, 108284. https://doi.org/10.1016/j.biocon.2019.108284

McGregor, D. (2021). Indigenous knowledge systems in environmental governance in Canada. *KULA*, 5(1), 1–10.

Wildcat, D. R. (2013). Introduction: Climate change and indigenous peoples of the USA. *Climatic Change*, 120(3), 509–515. https://doi.org/10.1007/s10584-013-0849-6

Zurba, M., Beazley, K. F., English, E., & Buchmann-Duck, J. (2019). Indigenous Protected and Conserved Areas (IPCAs), Aichi Target 11 and Canada's Pathway to Target 1: Focusing Conservation on Reconciliation. *Land*, 8(1), 10. https://doi.org/10.3390/land8010010

APPENDIX I: CONTRIBUTOR BIOS

Carolina Adler

I am a dual national from Chile and Australia, living in Switzerland, and enjoy a close relationship with mountains, having lived, played, and worked among them for most of my life. I am an Environmental Scientist and Geographer by training, and obtained my PhD at Monash University (Australia) in 2010, focusing on climate change adaptation and policy processes in mountain regions, receiving the Lasswell Prize for best thesis. In 2017, I became Executive Director at the Mountain Research Initiative (MRI), a global research coordination network based in Switzerland, through which I not only support regional and thematic networks on global change research, but also foster partnerships with various entities including with Future Earth, the Belmont Forum, UN Environment Programme, UNESCO and the Man and the Biosphere Programme, Mountain Partnership, the World Meteorological Organization (WMO), and the Group on Earth Observations. I am also a member of the WMO Executive Council Panel on Polar and High Mountain Observations, Research and Services, and serve as Independent Board Member at the International Centre for Integrated Mountain Development. In 2017 I was appointed as Lead Author for the Intergovernmental Panel on Climate Change, writing and coordinating assessment content on mountains and climate change in its sixth assessment. It is in this capacity that I was also involved in supporting the CMA by sharing these experiences and insights.

Leon Andrew

I am a Shúhtaot'ı̨nę elder with the Tulít'a Dene Band. I am Research Director and Chair of the Nę K'ə Dene Ts'ı̨lı̨ (Living on the Land) Forum. I served as a Special Advisor to the Ɂehdzo Got'ı̨nę Gots'ę́ Nákedı (Sahtú Renewable Resources Board) for many years. I have been an advisor to Aboriginal Affairs and Northern Development Canada and the Government of the Northwest Territories (GNWT) on Transboundary Water negotiations with Alberta. I was an Access and Benefits negotiator and served on the Canol Heritage Trail Committee for the Tulít'a District during 2004–2006. I have also served on the Board of the Tulít'a Land and Financial Corporation. I have provided my research expertise on numerous traditional knowledge studies, assisted and advised GNWT Archeologists from the Prince of Wales Museum, and am also an experienced interpreter in Dene and English languages. I was an active trapper in the Tulít'a area and have first-hand experience of both the positive and negative effects of exploration activities on the environment and traditional economy of the Northwest Territories. Recognized as one of the Sahtú Region's most experienced researchers, I now serve in a leading capacity in various regional, national and international research programs involving research and monitoring: the NWT Water Stewardship Strategy, Mackenzie River Basin Board, the Canadian Mountain Network, Northern Water Futures, and Ǎrramǎt: Biodiversity Conservation and the Health and Well-being of Indigenous Peoples (a network proposed to the New Frontiers in Research Fund of Canada's research Tri-Agency). I represent the SRRB on the NWT Conference of Management Authorities and the NWT Species At Risk Committee

Caroline Aubry-Wake

I am passionate about studying the movement of water in mountain landscapes, encompassing glaciers, snowpack, lakes, and rivers. The captivating beauty of mountain glaciers initially drew me in, but as I delved deeper into their significance for water resources, I became immersed in the field of mountain hydrology. My research journey has taken me across diverse mountain ranges, including the Canadian Rockies, where I currently reside, as well as the Alps, the Andes, and the Himalayas, where I am conducting my postdoctoral research in collaboration with Utrecht University. Among these ranges, the Chic-Chocs of the Gaspé Peninsula hold a special place in my heart as my first encounter with mountains. Exploring these mountain ranges, both scientifically and recreationally, continually deepens my fascination with their unique characteristics. I have come to appreciate that water represents just one facet of the intricate and diverse systems found in these mountains. Moreover, I am grateful for the opportunity to contribute my expertise in mountain water through my involvement in the CMA, enabling me to further explore mountain history, culture, and gain insights from Indigenous perspectives.

David Borish

I am a social science researcher and filmmaker with the Torngat Wildlife, Plants, and Fisheries Secretariat in Labrador, Canada. My work focuses on using audio-visual methodologies to document and communicate Indigenous Knowledge, as well as to explore the human dimensions of ecological change. During my doctoral work, I directed *HERD: Inuit Voices on Caribou*, a research-based documentary film about the impact of caribou population declines on community well-being in Labrador. I am now a core lead on the Nanuk Narratives project, which aims to leverage documentary film as a tool to preserve and communicate Inuit knowledge of polar bears across the Eastern Arctic. As part of these initiatives, I developed a method that blends video editing, qualitative analysis, and community co-creation—all with the goal of making Indigenous Knowledge more accessible and influential in ecological management. Building on this experience, my work with the CMA focused on visually documenting the knowledge shared during the Learning Circle. I have helped to manage and make this audio-visual knowledge accessible for authors to explore in more detail, and ultimately inform various sections of the final assessment.

Stephen Chignell

I am a PhD Candidate in the Institute for Resources, Environment and Sustainability at the University of British Columbia. My interest in mountains stems from my experience growing up in the diverse physical landscape and colonial (knowledge) politics of Hawai'i Island. I have a background in geospatial analysis, social-ecological systems, and critical physical geography, as well as research experience in the Colorado Rocky Mountains, the Bale Mountains in Ethiopia, and the Dry Valleys of Antarctica. I am a White settler, and relatively new to the mountains in Canada, but bring to the CMA an interdisciplinary perspective, curiosity, and excitement to contribute to an effort that reflexively considers knowledge production practices and attempts to weave together multiple ways of knowing.

Ashley-Anne Churchill

Weytkp, xwexweytep, Ashley-Anne Churchill ren skwest. Secwépemc-ken ri7. Te Simpcw re sť7é7kwen. My professional background is in Indigenous Title, Rights, and Interests, working as a technical and research consultant for Indigenous communities and nations for over a decade. I design and facilitate custom technical training for referrals and Consultation staff directly in community and have previously taught the CSTC Referrals Officer Training Program. Recently, I've been collaborating on open-source software for referrals and community data management with the University of British Columbia. I hold an Associate's degree in Environmental Studies and a BA in Geography with a minor in Indigenous Studies. I have academic interests in forest and mountain biogeography, and I have traditional training and interest in genealogy, storied toponymy, and Indigenous plants from the river valleys to the subalpine areas within Secwepemcúl'ecw (Secwépemc territory). I am currently in an interdisciplinary MA program (Geography, Anthropology, Indigenous Law), and a member of the Geographic Indigenous Futures (GIF) lab at the University of Victoria (UVic). My thesis is focused on Secwépemc land-centered relational (kinship) axiology and praxis, in the context of Indigenous Title, Rights, and Interests. Mountains hold embodied stories and relational knowledge, shaping our existence and guiding our movement and dwelling throughout our territory and with our extended kin relations. Secwépemc relational axiology and praxis are inextricably tied to our connection with mountains.

Dawn Saunders Dahl

I am of Red River Ojibway and European (UK, Scandinavian, French) ancestries and am a member of Métis Nation of Alberta. I attended the final TRC in Edmonton and continue to be guided by the responsibilities to care for the land and ensure Indigenous perspectives are present in my projects. I live in Canmore, Alberta, and am an artist creating artwork that reflects my surroundings, my deep interest in place, genealogy, and reconciliation/action. I develop public art opportunities, art exhibitions, and projects with Indigenous arts communities. I attended University of the Arts majoring in painting and ceramics (BFA 1998–99). I started my administration work in art school, volunteering for Untitled Art Society (the Bows) until 2006. I developed The Works Art & Design Festivals' Indigenous Art Program in 2008 and worked in the public art department at the Edmonton Arts Council (2012–15). I currently work at the Whyte Museum of the Canadian Rockies (Banff), and am curator at Galerie Cite (Edmonton) and Indigenous Public Art for Adisoke (Ottawa—opening 2026). I am a board member for the Alberta Craft Council and a BUMP juror (mural festival—Calgary). I am developing Listen Studios and Retreats and am a contributing member of Canmore Land—a not for profit community land trust in Canmore, Alberta.

Goota Desmarais

I grew up on the south shore of Baffin Island in Cape Dorset, Nunavut. My early childhood was spent in a modern Inuit settlement during the winters and in a traditional camp during the summers. I am now an urban Inuk, living in Sherwood Park, Alberta for the past 30 years. I stay connected to my Inuit culture through frequent visits to Nunavut and my involvement on the board of the Edmonton Inuit Cultural Society and Edmontonmiut Inuit. Through my business, Inuit Connections, I have been educating people about Nunavut and Inuit culture for over 20 years. I share personal stories of growing up in the North that illustrate the unique Inuit way of life. I am currently working with Alberta Teachers' Association in their Walking Together: Education for Reconciliation Project.

Megan Dicker

I am an Inuk from Nain, Nunatsiavut on the north coast of Labrador. My family comes from Nain and Makkovik, with roots in Hebron and Nutaak south of the Torngat Mountains. I have been fortunate to spend a lot of time on the land growing up and I still try to get out on the land as much as possible. I am a social-change enthusiast and a climate advocate. For the past two years I worked as the youth leadership program coordinator at the Torngat Mountains base camp and research station, bringing Inuit youth to our ancestral homelands for cultural and leadership activities. It is this program that gave me the opportunity to travel to the Torngait in 2014 and my life has forever changed since then. My love and admiration for the Torngat Mountains led me to where I am today—the connections I have made personally and professionally eventually led to working with the CMA to document the importance of mountains in our homelands.

Karine Gagné

I am an Associate Professor in the Department of Sociology and Anthropology at the University of Guelph. I obtained a PhD in Anthropology from University of Montreal (2015) before holding a Banting Postdoctoral Fellowship at Yale University (2015–2017). My research work is based in the Indian Himalayas where I study a range of issues, including climate change, ethics of care, human-animal relations, state production, citizenship, and climate knowledge. My research has thus far focused on two areas of study. First, I am interested in how climate change is experienced by Indigenous Himalayan communities and how these experiences contend with state rationality. Second, I am interested in the relationships between humans and animals in the Himalayas, and I also aim to understand the political and economic structures that threaten habitats and generate human-animal conflicts. My research work is carried in collaboration with local scholars, artists, farmers, herders, guides, and porters. I am also passionate about visual methodologies and graphic ethnography. My book, *Caring for Glaciers: Land, Animals, and Humanity in the Himalayas* (University of Washington Press) was awarded the 2019 James Fisher Prize for First Books on the Himalayan Region.

Erika Gavenus

I learned to love mountains and all they share with us growing up in Southcentral Alaska surrounded by the Kenai Mountains on lands long stewarded by Nichiłt'ana, Dena'ina, and Sugpiaq peoples. I am currently a PhD candidate at the University of British Columbia within the Institute for Resources, Environment and Sustainability. Through my research I use a lens of food justice to examine how fisheries regulations can challenge food access for coastal First Nations. I bring academic training in public health, nutrition, and food security to this research and deep appreciation for the role of collective well-being and relationships with place. I spend most of my time and research on the ocean and in coastal communities looking up at mountains, and I am thankful the opportunity to travel more intentionally into the mountains through the CMA and Learning Circle. I am a settler-researcher and am grateful to live and learn on the traditional, ancestral, and unceded territory of the Musqueam.

Stephan Gruber

In my work I aim to support wise decisions about adapting to permafrost thaw and to train new experts. I investigate permafrost in polar and mountain areas, and have a deep personal connection to cold environments through wilderness travel and mountaineering. My research bridges field observations and computer simulation aiming to turn the insight derived from both together into products to inform adaptation decisions. I have lived in ten countries, and after 12 years in Switzerland, I came to Canada in 2013 as the Canada Research Chair in Climate Change Impacts/Adaptation in Northern Canada. I work as a Professor of Geography at Carleton University in Ottawa and enjoy the many new relationships, conversations, and insights coming with getting to know and help connect the very diverse Canadian permafrost community better. My experience includes research aimed at discovery and at application, contributions to major assessment reports such as the mountain chapter of the IPCC Special Report on the Ocean and Cryosphere in a Changing Climate or the Hindu Kush Himalaya Assessment, editorial roles, and leadership in large research initiatives such as NSERC PermafrostNet and NSERC CREATE LEAP. Learning makes me happy.

Jiaao Guo

I am a research assistant at Canadian Mountain Assessment (CMA) since 2020. Currently, I'm a full-time geospatial research coordinator working for both University of Calgary and Alberta Biodiversity Monitoring Institute (ABMI). Most of the works that I have done for CMA were during the time when I was a remote sensing analyst at Northwest Territories Centre for Geomatics (2020–2022), in Inuvik, Northwest Territories—a traditional land of Gwich'in First Nations and Inuvialuit Settlement Region. I hope to search and use spatial data/knowledge to better understand the physical, biological, and cultural environments and their interactions within and outside the Canadian mountain systems. I had a background in environmental science and geographic information systems (GIS). Apart from mountain-related researches, my interests and expertise also expand to urban GIS, wildfire and flood mapping, remote sensing analysis using earth-observation satellites, and Light Detection and Ranging (LiDAR) data analysis.

Katherine Hanly

I am a PhD Candidate at the University of Calgary, studying and living in the Bow Valley. My research focuses on the impacts of, and adaptations to, climate-related cryospheric change on mountain recreation in the Canadian Rocky Mountains. Having spent most of my life in the Bow Valley, mountains have always been at the centre of my life, and it is on their trails that I have connected to and learned from friends, family, and the landscape. I approach my research and the CMA with great gratitude for the opportunity to continue to connect, learn, and hopefully contribute to the protection of these magnificent landscapes.

Nina Hewitt

I am an Associate Professor of Teaching in the Department of Geography at the University of British Columbia. I study biogeographical influences on plant species dynamics in temperate forest and alpine ecosystems, and digital tools for experiential field learning within these ecosystems. I have used data from rare historical records and my own contemporary field research to study changes in upper elevation limits of alpine species in the Karakoram-Himalaya. I am co-investigator on a BC Parks Living Lab for

Climate Change and Conservation funded study of alpine plant responses to global change drivers in Garibaldi Park. A passionate educator, I seek to increase accessibility of experiential learning to reach across a diverse student body. I have created numerous immersive virtual and augmented reality experiences in BC forest and alpine environments for teaching, and to provide a modern baseline with which to track vegetation change.

Eric Higgs

I came to mountains as an adult, having grown up in the gently undulating territories near the Haudenosaunee Six Nations of the Grand River and the Saugeen First Nation. My family and I are settlers of northern English, Scottish, Irish and German ancestry. Taking up my first regular faculty position at the University of Alberta in 1990 I teamed up with colleagues to develop the Culture, Ecology and Restoration project that intertwined historical cultural and ecological knowledge in what is now Jasper National Park. It was uncommon at that time to focus on restoration in a national park, especially one iconic for wildness. From this grew the Mountain Legacy Project, which uses historic mountain survey photographs, the largest collection in the world, to study change in mountain landscapes through repeat photography (mountainlegacy.ca). Since 2002 I have been a professor in the School of Environmental Studies at the University of Victoria in the territories of Lekwungen & WSÁNEĆ peoples. My work centres on long-term studies of mountains in service of ecosystem restoration, engaging diverse understanding.

Murray Humphries

I am a Professor of Wildlife Biology at McGill University, located in Montreal, Quebec in the territories of Haudenosaunee and Anishinaabe Peoples. I was born and raised in Brandon, Manitoba in Treaty 2 territory. My family and I are settlers, of Scottish, Irish, and Welsh heritage; the Mitchell side of my family homesteaded and farmed south of Arrow River, Manitoba. I am a flatlander who loves wildlife and wide-open prairie spaces. I came to the mountains looking for wildlife and, along the way, have had the opportunity to meet other people that love land and wildlife in their own way. I am director of

McGill's Centre for Indigenous Peoples' Nutrition and Environment and my research emphasizes community-based partnerships focused on wildlife, environmental change, and local Indigenous food systems. It has been my honour to serve as co-research director of the Canadian Mountain Network of Centres of Excellence from 2020–2023 in support of our mission to support the resilience and health of Canada's mountain peoples and places through research partnerships based on Indigenous and Western ways of knowing that inform decision-making and action.

Rod Hunter

I am an elected councillor of the Bearspaw First Nation for the last 21 years and an accomplished powwow singer. I am the leader of the Eyahey Nakoda powwow world class singers. Eyahey Nakoda has won several singing championships in the last twenty-five years. I have been singing since I was nine years old. I have been a master of ceremony for numerous powwows, round dances, and special events. I am deeply involved in the traditional ways of the Stoney Nakoda. I am a Sundance Maker and have completed four Sundance lodges. I started as a helper for elders and eventually became a pipe holder, medicine holder, and a Sundance maker. Performing a Sundance is extremely difficult and requires total mind and body commitment. The teachings of the elders greatly helped me to achieve Sundance maker status at an early age. I will continue to sing and keep the traditions of my people alive. Eyahey Nakoda was formed in September 1994. The very first powwow they attended, they took home first place in the singing contest. I was educated at Mount Royal College.

Lawrence Ignace

I am an Anishinaabe from Lac Des Milles Lac First Nation in Treaty 3 and grew up in Ignace, Ontario. My family has a deep connection to this area including our last name. I moved to Whitehorse, Yukon about 13 years ago and I have not looked back from living in the mountains. My family taught me how to approach the world in a good way and I have brought this to my work as a PhD student at the School of Environmental Studies with University of Victoria.

Dani Inkpen

I am the product of mixed heritages and I grew up in Treaty Six territory in Edmonton, Alberta. From a young age I loved exploring the trails of the Rocky Mountains and spent much of my early adulthood in the Rockies and Coast Mountains. Since obtaining my PhD in the history of science from Harvard University, I've used my training in environmental history and the history of science to examine the ways that knowledge gets made in and of mountain places. I now live and work in the unceded lands of the Mi'kmaq people in Sackville, New Brunswick where I am assistant professor of history at Mount Allison University. I came to the CMA with a desire to learn more about how people from all walks of life come to know, interact with, and love mountains. It has been an honour to work the people who have realized this project.

Aerin Jacob

Much of my life has been in mountainous regions, particularly the Rocky, Columbia, Mackenzie, and Coast mountains of Canada and the United States, and the Albertine Rift, Eastern Arc Mountains, and Kenya Highlands of Uganda, Tanzania, and Kenya. The juxtaposition of isolation and connectivity in mountain ecology, livelihoods, and conservation have shaped how I think about and approach my work as a conservation scientist. I am the director of science and research and the Weston Family Senior Scientist at the Nature Conservancy of Canada, and an adjunct professor at the University of Northern British Columbia. My work includes research on biodiversity, ecological connectivity, the benefits people get from nature, and the human dimensions of conservation, as well as science communication and the science-policy interface. I was a 2015 Wilburforce Fellow in Conservation Science and a 2016–2018 Liber Ero Fellow, received a PhD from McGill University, conducted post-doctoral research at the University of Victoria, and frequently serve on panels and committees providing scientific advice and guidance to governments, communities, and organizations.

Pnnal Bernard Jerome

I am mostly known as Pn'nal, and am an elder in the community of Gesgapegiag. I am a former chief and have been in leadership positions for my community since 1975. I currently work as the Cultural and Language coordinator in my community and have dedicated my life to the healing and teaching of my community through my work. I am a co-author of a book named *Nta'tugwaqan-minen: our story*. I continue to educate myself and others around me about Gesgapegiag's history and culture.

Patricia Joe

I am from the Tagish Kwan First Nation, the original people where the City of Whitehorse, Yukon is situated. I am from the Dak'laweide Clan (Killer Whale and Wolf Crest) and a proud citizen of the Kwanlin Dun First Nation. I am a teacher, elder and knowledge keeper and an outspoken person for First Nation culture, history, beliefs, and values. I specialize in First Nation oral stories, and I am passionate about delivering authentic stories to students from kindergarten to Grade 12 and to all levels of government to advance First Nation education in Yukon and throughout Canada. I believe that the traditional oral stories will not only develop pride and identity to First Nation students but will help non-Indigenous students to have respect for the people whose Traditional Territory they reside on. In addition to my professional experience as a First Nation Integration Teacher I have worked with all levels of government and have been instrumental in many projects involving Yukon First Nation history and culture. I have been the former Deputy Chief, Chief Land Claims and Self- Government negotiator and I have many years of experience in the areas of politics and business.

Gùdia Mary Jane Johnson

I am a Lhu'ààn Mân Ku Dań Ashaw (Elder) who worked for Parks Canada and Kluane First Nation for over 40 years on protected areas, environment, cultural, and Indigenous language issues. I champion Indigenous language revitalization while partaking in a community that actively lives their culture. I have contributed an objective perspective to the Truth and Reconciliation Commission Report Response Task Force addressing the TRC's Call to Action #70 reporting to the Standing Committee on Canada's Archives; to several boards and committees, I sit as an active committee member on: the Asi Keyi Natural Environment Park Management Plan Steering Committee; the

Pickhandle Lakes Habitat Protection Area Steering Committee; the Canadian Mountain Network—Research Management Committee; the CMA—Canadian Advisory Committee; the Kluane Research Committee; and, the Tutchone Heritage Society. I am retired and am a happy and busy Grandmother of eleven Grandchildren and one Great Grandson.

Linda Johnson

I have lived and worked as an archivist, historian and writer in the Yukon for the past five decades, building a unique blend of cultural knowledge, relationships and contacts with people across the territory, Alaska, northern BC and the Northwest Territories. I have collaborated with Yukon First Nations Elders to record and preserve memories of landscapes, travel, languages, culture, and historical events. I combine oral history and archival research in the development of public history interpretation projects. I have published four books on Yukon history and contributed to several publications documenting diverse aspects of life in Canada's northern mountainous regions.

Stephen Johnston

I have a B.Sc. in Geology from McGill University and an MSc and PhD from the University of Alberta (UAb) in Structural Geology. I have worked in exploration for Shell Canada Ltd.; as a geologist for the BC and Yukon geological surveys; and as a professor at the University of Durban-Westville, South Africa. In 1999 I joined the School of Earth & Ocean Sciences at the University of Victoria, BC, serving as the school's Director from 2011 to 2015. In 2015 I returned to Alberta to serve as the Chair of the Department of Earth & Atmospheric Sciences at UAb. My research focus is on the role of mountain belts in the development of Earth's continental crust; the relationship between the character of our continental crust (for example, its endowment of metals and hydrocarbons) and mountain building processes; and the links between Earth's climate and biosphere and the distribution of continents and mountain systems through deep time (paleogeography). My favourite mountain system, and the one I always return to, is the Cordilleran system of Alberta, BC, and Yukon. I am the son of immigrants, my father a Scot and my mother Irish. I am the first on either side of the family to have attended university. I

am extremely privileged to have had the opportunity to research and teach about mountains given their central role in the development and evolution of all the peoples and cultures of Earth.

Knut Kitching

I am a Senior Researcher in the Indigenous Knowledge Research team at The Firelight Group, an Indigenous-owned consultancy. I am also an Elected Fellow of the Royal Geographical Society, with an MA in Geography from McGill University. I was born in inner-city Toronto and made my way to the mountains of the west coast as quickly as I was able. In my role as a consultant and advisor to Indigenous communities across Canada, I provide strategic advice and research to support communities navigating a wide range of social, ecological, and legal changes. For over a decade, my work has focused on the relationships between people, particularly Indigenous communities, and their environment. Much of this work takes place during environmental impact assessment processes, during which my colleagues and I are focused on the assessment of impacts to culture and rights on the land. Many of my clients, colleagues, friends, and family inhabit the various mountain regions of Canada, and I have seen first-hand the changes they are experiencing. It's been a privilege to be a small part of this exercise.

Michele Koppes

An immigrant of mixed heritage, I am a Professor of Geography and director of the Climate and Cryosphere lab at the University of British Columbia, on traditional and unceded Musqueam territory. My passion is forensic geomorphology: the art of reading landscapes to decipher their stories and the forces that shaped them. My research seeks to combine field and remotely-sensed observations with local perspectives, oral histories, soundscape mapping and storytelling to explore the cascading effects of climate change on glaciated mountain landscapes, waterscapes and people. I have been privileged to have lived in, worked, and been inspired by mountains and mountain peoples all over the world, from the Coast Mountains of BC to the Swiss Alps, Patagonian Andes, Sierra Nevada, Indian and Nepali Himalaya, Tien Shan, and the polar ice sheets of Greenland and Antarctica. I believe deeply that if we are to address the ongoing climate and nature emergency, we need to elevate place-based, indigenous, and embodied understandings of how the lives of the ice, the mountains, the rivers, the people and the more-than-humans who dwell among them are intertwined. I am deeply grateful to the CMA for the opportunity to engage with and learn from these knowledges and knowledge keepers.

Daniel Kraus

I am currently the national director of conservation at Wildlife Conservation Society (WCS) Canada where I get to work with a great team on initiatives that range from Key Biodiversity Areas to the SHAPE (Species, Habitats, Action & Policy Evaluations) of Nature. I led the development of Canada's first list of nationally endemic wildlife (many of which are in mountains!) and have published papers on Canada's "crisis" ecoregions and approaches to endangered species recovery. I'm currently a member of the federal Nature Advisory Committee and I also research and teach about wildlife extinction and recovery at the University of Waterloo. About a decade ago I came to the realization that facts aren't enough halt the biodiversity crisis and have been trying to become a better science communicator ever since. I live and work at the headwaters of Bronte Creek in the Lake Ontario watershed where I enjoy chopping wood and raising happy chickens.

Sydney Lancaster

I am a Prairie-born visual artist and writer, and I have been based in Amiskwacîwâskahikan (Edmonton) most of my life. I am from settler-immigrant-homesteader stock; as such, I perceive myself as an uninvited guest on Turtle Island. My lineage is bound to migration, Dominion Land Survey maps, and the displacement of Indigenous people from their territories. I have spent considerable time in the Rocky Mountains and the foothills over the years, and more recently, in close proximity to the Long Range Mountains, in western Newfoundland. My ongoing research-creation is focused on the potential in liminal states and places to expose gaps in understanding: how the relationships between place, objects, and different types of memory impact notions of history and identity. What is left out of any given story is as important as what is chosen. My MFA research concerned the influence of Dominion Land Survey (DLS) mapping practices on settler thinking in relation to ideas of belonging and affective connection to place. I was interested in the links between measurement, bordering, and Settler-Colonial land ownership as geospatial and political structures that have ongoing implications for relationships between humans, and between humans and more-than-human beings.

Rosemary Langford

I live on Tsleil-Waututh lands in the beautiful space between the ocean and mountains. I have had the extraordinary privilege of spending time in and coming to know mountainous landscapes through my recreational, professional, and academic pursuits. I hold a Masters in Resource Management from Simon Fraser University, where I completed my master's research centred on supporting recreationists in enjoying the winter mountains safely. My passion exists at the intersection of natural sciences, communications, and decision-making, and I care deeply about directing these passions toward efforts that support the well-being of both human and non-human communities.

Keara Lightning

I'm a member of Samson Cree Nation in Maskwacis, Alberta. I'm currently an MA candidate at the University of Alberta, completing a thesis analyzing how scientific constructions of the landscape have worked to obscure Indigenous presence. I am a member of the Indigenous Science, Technology and Society lab at the University of Alberta, a historian laureate with the Beaver Hills Biosphere, and a Lillian Agnes Jones Fellowship recipient. I write about the historic and ongoing role of science in colonization, as well as the potential of Indigenous-led science and environmental management. I'm moving into PhD research focused on wildfire management, with a particular interest in the revitalization of cultural burning practices. I've previously worked in environmental and science education programs, as well as in landscaping, gardening, and agriculture. Outside of the university, I also write interactive stories and animation on the themes of kinship, environmental restoration, and surviving apocalypse.

Lachlan MacKinnon

I am an Associate Professor and Canada Research Chair in Post-Industrial Communities at Cape

Breton University. My research focuses on areas connecting working-class experiences and place identity, including workers' environmentalism, ecological awareness, and occupational memory. In Cape Breton, the deindustrialization of the island's coal and steel industries in the 20th century coincided with the rise of the tourist gaze and the re-making of the province into a premiere travel destination. Part of this process included the re-conceptualization of the mountains in the northernmost parts of the island into "the Highlands" a Scottish-tinged representation that occluded other histories—both Indigenous and settler. My participation in this project has given me the opportunity to reflect upon how convergent notions of mountain landscapes found expression across cultural forms in 20th century Cape Breton, and the collaborative nature ensured that connections could be drawn to similar landscapes across Canada.

Christopher Marsh

Originally from the Canadian Prairies, I have always been drawn to the mountains both recreationally and scientifically. I grew up skiing throughout the Canadian Rockies and Coast mountains, and later in life started hiking and back country camping. I have had the privilege to travel and work throughout the Canadian Cordillera region and Mackenzie mountains, the Pyrenees, and the Alps. My research has focused on how to improve simulations in these complex regions to provide better estimates of snow and water resources. This has been via new numerical modelling methods that allow for incorporating critical process at a high spatial and temporal resolution. Backed by observations and field work, these methods allow for deeper insight into the complex process interactions that drive mountain snowcovers. Improving the predictive capacity for entire mountain ranges is important for water predictions under current climates as well as future climates.

Shawn Marshall

Mountains were not part of my life, growing up in southern Ontario and studying physics at the University of Toronto, but I had the good fortune to "go west" to graduate school, and the even better fortune to study glaciology with Garry Clarke at the University of British Columbia. This

research exposed me to the wonder of glaciers in the St. Elias Mountains, the Canadian Rockies, and Iceland, and I been privileged to spend much of my life in the mountains since that time. I moved from the University of British Columbia to the University of Calgary, where I am a Professor in the Department of Geography and held the Canada Research Chair in Climate Change from 2007–2017. My research group studies glacier-climate processes and glacier response to climate change, including field and modelling studies in western and Arctic Canada. I served as the Departmental Science Advisor at Environment and Climate Change Canada from 2019–2023, and also had the pleasure of contributing to the international Mountain Research Institute over this period, as a member of their Science Leadership Council.

Brandy Mayes

I am a proud descendant of the Tagish Kwan people, the original people of Whitehorse, Yukon, and a beneficiary of Kwanlin Dün First Nation (KDFN). My great-grandparents are Julia Joe from Marsh Lake, Yukon, and Johnny Joe from Hutchi, Yukon. My great-great grandmother is Seke, the eldest daughter of the great Chief Jackie of Marsh Lake. I belong to the Dakhl'aweidí Clan, the Killer Whale and Wolf Clan Crest. The Clan Crest assures me that I am part of the land and part of the water. As a beneficiary of KDFN, my culture is who I am and where I come from. I enjoy everything outdoors including hunting, fishing, snowmobiling, skiing, curling, golfing, and hiking. I also, have a passion for gardening, enjoy cooking and I have been told I am queen of the BBQ and I smoke a mean brisket. My relationship with the mountains goes back to my ancestors. I recall the stories from my Great Grandfather on how all things are related, how the mountain glaciers and snow feed the rivers, creeks, and lakes, which keep all living things alive. I am an avid hiker, including in 2015, I set a goal to reach 21 peaks in Kananaskis Country of Alberta. One of these peaks took me 5 attempts, but I finally made it. I live in the most beautiful place (in my mind), surrounded by what we call in the Yukon, "The Southern Lakes," and the mountains that feed them. I am grateful everyday to my ancestors who took care of this land so we can all enjoy it. I am the Manager of Operations and Fish and Wildlife for KDFN's Heritage, Lands and

Resources, it is not only my job, but my responsibility as a Yukon First Nations person to respect all earth's creations. Our Elders fought hard to get back our land and it's our responsibility to show our respect by practicing good stewardship and to protect and conserve the lands resources for future generations. Implementing our Final Agreements and our citizens' Lands Vision is key in my decisions and how I conduct my work.

Graham McDowell

I live in Canmore, Alberta, on Treaty 7 territory, lands of the Îyârhe (Stoney) Nakoda, Blackfoot Confederacy, and Tsuut'ina First Nation, as well as Métis Nation of Alberta, Region 3. I am a geographer and environmental social scientist with interests in the human dimensions of climate change in high mountain areas, as well as formal knowledge assessment and co-creation methodologies. I have led community-level projects in the Nepal Himalaya, Peruvian Andes, Rocky Mountains, Greenland, and the Canadian Arctic, as well as numerous large-scale assessment initiatives, including the CMA. I have also twice served as a Contributing Author with the Intergovernmental Panel on Climate Change (IPCC), where I led assessments of human adaptation to climate change for mountain focused chapters. In addition, I am an Editorial Board member for the journal *Mountain Research and Development*, a Fellow of the Royal Canadian Geographical Society, and an advisor for numerous initiatives related to mountains and climate change, including as a National Steering Committee member for the UN International Year of Glacier Preservation. I completed a Banting Postdoctoral Fellowship at the University of Zurich and hold degrees from the University of British Columbia (PhD), the University of Oxford (MSc), and McGill University (BA Hons). I am currently affiliated with the Department of Geography at the University of Calgary.

Thomas McIlwraith

I am a settler anthropologist at the University of Guelph, in Guelph, Ontario, Canada. I am interested in the stories people tell about their places, including particularly, the relationships between Indigenous peoples and their communities in British Columbia with mountains, animals, waterways, and landscapes. I am concerned about local

perspectives and appreciate the contributions of knowledge keepers and community experts on sustainable approaches to lands and resources. I try to hear and understand the lessons contained in stories and oral historical accounts, while appreciating the nuances of community responses to development.

Hayden Melting Tallow

I was born and raised on the Siksika Nation part of the Blackfoot Confederacy of southern Alberta. As Blackfoot people do not live within the Miistakis, we are from the prairies but rely on the tributaries that come from the Miistakis that supply us with fish and medicines that grow along its banks. We also go into the Miistakis to collect our medicines, teepee poles, paints for ceremonies, vision quests, to name a few. Although we don't live amongst them, we rely on the abundances they offer. Although we don't live within the Miistakis we support the people that do live there.

Charlotte Mitchell

I am a second year PhD student from the University of Alberta in the Faculty of Kinesiology, Sport and Recreation with a focus of feminist sport history. I have a Masters degree in Gender and Social Justice from the University of Alberta with undergraduate degrees from the University of Calgary in Social and Cultural Anthropology and Women's Studies.

Brenda Parlee

I am a settler scholar and research ally for Indigenous Peoples. I am honoured to have worked with many Indigenous Peoples over 30 years in Canada and internationally. I was born and grew up in northern Ontario in Mushkegowuk Cree territory. The landscape and political economy of this provincial north—impacted by mining, hydro development, forestry, and climate change—has significantly shaped my beliefs and passions for research and teaching on issues of social, economic and environmental justice. I currently share my time between Treaty 6 and Treaty 7 territories of Alberta and make my home in the foothills of the Rocky Mountains. Although I would like to spend more time hiking and meditating in the mountains, I am a busy Mom of two teenage boys and a Professor in the Department of Resource Economics and Environmental Sociology in the Faculty of Agricultural, Life and Environmental Sciences at the University of Alberta. I also co-hold a UNESCO Chair focused on themes of research collaboration, biodiversity, and health which I share with Indigenous scholars from Carleton University and the Sahel/Sahara region of Africa (Tuareg territory). I have led and supported many interdisciplinary and collaborative, and community-based research projects since 2000 on different aspects of social and ecological change. Many of these projects have been in northern Canada and in the Mackenzie River Watershed. In the last ten years, I have been invited to work internationally on major initiatives such as the Intergovernmental Platform on Biodiversity and Ecosystem Services Assessment on the Sustainable Use of Wild Species. I am also co-leading a major research project (2021–2027) funded by the Canadian Tri-Council (NFRF) called Ărramăt. (Ărramăt is an Indigenous [Tuareg] concept meaning the health of people and the environment are interconnected). In the next 6 years the Ărramăt Project will support more than 140 Indigenous-led projects in 70 ecozones/regions around the world to find solutions for improving biodiversity and Indigenous health and well-being. I have a BA from the University of Guelph (1995), an MES in Environmental Studies from the University of Waterloo (1998) and a PhD from the University of Manitoba in Natural Resources and Environmental Management (NREM)

Wanda Pascal

I am from Teetlit Zheh—Fort McPherson, NWT. I was born and raised in Fort McPherson mostly by my grandparents, the late John and Annie Vaneltsi. I am married to Douglas Pascal and has 4 children and 11 grandchildren. I worked for Legal Services for 16 years off and on. I worked at various jobs until I was elected on to Band Council in 1991, and after doing three full terms I made history in my Community. I was elected Chief on June 24, 2016 and re-elected for another term on July 4th, 2016. Being brought up on the land since an early age I have gained a lot of traditional knowledge of my culture as a Teetlit Gwichin woman. I love to sew, hiking, picking berries, and teaching my grandchildren how to live on the land.

Tim Patterson

I was born Morris Coutlee a member of the Lower Nicola Indian Band that belongs to the Scwéxmx ("People of the Creeks") a branch of the Nlaka'pamux (Thompson) Nation of the Interior Salish peoples of British Columbia Canada. I grew up in Revelstoke within the Sn-səlxcin (Sinixt-Lakes) territory and I continue to hike and guide throughout the West Kootenays. I have been an outdoor professional for over 15 years and have hiked and explored both the western parts of Canada and the United States for over 25 years. I am the Indigenous Studies instructor with Timberline Canadian Alpine Academy. I hold a MA in Environmental Education and a BA in Cultural Anthropology, and all have focused on the advancement of First Nations oral narratives and Indigenous Knowledge. My company Zucmin (Zúc'nm) Guiding was developed through the combining of my Academic, Indigenous, and Guiding backgrounds where I focus on Indigenous Knowledge in the mountainous areas of Southern Alberta and British Columbia.

Karen Pheasant

I am Karen Pheasant-Neganigwane (Anishinaabe) of Manitoulin Island of the Wikwemikong First Nations. Eldest daughter of my parents, both who thrived after their Indian Residential School experience. Also, a Nokomis of eight beautiful grandchildren. I attribute my audaciousness to both my parents, first generation to live successfully off-reserve, and remain connected to their land base of Wikwemikong First Nations. I draw on my lived experience, as a young woman who worked in community centres during the height of the Civil Rights movement (AIM), in education (K–12, Post-Secondary) and my continued involvement in the Arts, as an award-winning author, bead'er, dancer, and performer. I spent the past fifty years attaining, studying, and receiving knowledge from the Great Lakes of Anishinaabek of Treaty Three, Treaty Six and currently in Treaty Seven. In 2023, I was selected as an inductee to the Dance Collection Danse: Hall of Fame (Toronto). My education includes a BA in Political Science and English Literature. My graduate studies are in Educational Policy Studies (MEd). I am currently a PhD (c) on the topic of Anishinaabe/Indigenous pedagogy at the University of Alberta. I am currently an Assistant Professor at Mount Royal University, with Humanities and Liberal Arts Education, Calgary, Alberta.

Sophie Pheasant

My name is Sophie Pheasant (Niigani-Bine). I am Bode'wadmi Anishinaabe Kwe, Bineshii dodem from Wiikwemkoong Unceded Territory, the granddaughter of Isedore-bah Pheasant Neganigwane Sr. and Gertrude-bah Nadjiwon and maternal Moses-bah Lavallee and Rosemary (nee Mishibinijima). I am the mother of three children, a graduate of McMaster University and Laurentian University, presently enrolled with Laurier University's certificate program in Decolonizing Education. I received instruction to dance the healing dance of the Jingle Dress at a young age. Spending time learning about the dress and teachings in the Lake of the Woods area and throughout Turtle Island. Retracing my ancestral lands and maintaining connection to the Land Air and Water is of importance to me and my family.

Martin Price

My mountain career started in the Sunshine area of Canadian Rockies in the late 1970s, as an MSc student at the University of Calgary. A few years later, my doctorate at the University of Colorado at Boulder considered the forests of the Colorado Rockies and the Swiss Alps. Through these degrees, my focus shifted from natural to social sciences and I began to consider myself an interdisciplinary scientist. During the 1990s, I reviewed the activities of UNESCO's Man and the Biosphere (MAB) Programme in Europe's mountains and was the focal point for mountains in IUCN's European Programme. In 2000, I established the Centre for Mountain Studies within what is now the University of the Highlands and Islands (UHI), Scotland. In the 2000s and 2010s, I coordinated four assessments of Europe's mountains for different European organisations. Globally, I have been closely involved in the formulation and implementation of Chapter 13—"Protecting Fragile Ecosystems: Sustainable Mountain Development"—of Agenda 21, endorsed by the 1992 Rio Earth Summit; the International Year of Mountains, 2002; the Mountain Forum; and the Mountain Partnership. Ensuring that scientific knowledge is widely understood and used has long been a major concern for me. I have written

and edited 14 books and over 200 reports, papers, book chapters, and articles; and was Book Review Editor of the preeminent mountain science journal *Mountain Research and Development* from 1994 to 2020. I became Chairholder of the UNESCO Chair in Sustainable Mountain Development in 2009, and retired from this, and my role at UHI, in 2021.

PearlAnn Reichwein

I am a historian and Professor at the University of Alberta. My scholarship in Canadian Mountain Studies highlights the history of western Canada. The cultural production of mountains is the compass for my explorations of landscapes as temporally and cross-culturally discursive places of social memory. Studies of the Alpine Club of Canada, National Parks, and Olympic Winter Games, and various individuals, are among my projects. My book *Climber's Paradise: Making Canada's Mountain Parks, 1906–1974* (2014) was awarded the Canadian Historical Association's Clio Prize and was a finalist in the Banff Mountain Film and Book Festival; *Uplift: Visual Culture at the Banff School of Fine Arts* (2020), co-authored with Karen Wall, is my most recent book. Invited guest lectures at University of Innsbruck's Alpine Research Centre Obergurgl and Université Gustave Eiffel steeped my thinking about transnational alpine worlds. I give public talks at libraries and museums. Guiding hikes at Plain of Six Glaciers and planning for cultural resources in Banff National Park and Yoho National Park shaped my early practitioner experience in a UNESCO World Heritage Site. Advocacy for the heritage and health of the North Saskatchewan River—running from its Rocky Mountain headwaters across western farmlands—is a community-engaged interest.

Rachel Reimer

I am a PhD candidate at the School of Human Geography and Sustainable Communities, University of Wollongong. My work is focused on an intersectional feminist approach to inclusion, risk, and psychological safety in the mountain guiding and avalanche professions worldwide. I hold a Master's degree in Leadership Studies from Royal Roads University, and completed a study focused on gender and leadership in wildland fire amongst firefighters in the British Columbia Wildfire Service. Prior to that, my work included community-based Action Research in high-risk conflict zones across the Middle East and Africa for the United Nations and small non-profits. I bring a unique perspective to the mountain-human relationship as a queer neurodiverse academic living in a majority white, cis, hetero mountain town; and, also a practitioner, having worked operationally as a leader in both wildland fire and in the avalanche and guiding industry.

Lauren Rethoret

I am a Faculty Researcher at Selkirk College with a portfolio focused on the policy and planning dimensions of climate change and the environment. My projects are all conducted in partnership with community-based organizations in the mountainous and largely rural Columbia Basin, tackling issues like climate resilience, land use, and the interactions between human communities and 'working' landscapes. I hold a Masters in Resource and Environmental Management (Planning) from Simon Fraser University and a Bachelor of Arts in Geography from Carleton University. I live and work in the Columbia Mountains on the territories of the Sinixt, Ktunaxa, and Syilx peoples.

Gabriella Richardson

I am a Public Issues Anthropology Masters student at the University of Guelph. My Masters dissertation examines how conservation strategies affect relationships between jaguars and people in Ecuador. My research interests include multispecies ethnography, conservation, and the Anthropocene. I am passionate about community development and engagement. I have completed research projects on gender-based violence with non-governmental organizations in Papua New Guinea. I have also developed environmental/conservation education programs for youth in Ecuador's Amazonia and on Christian Island in Ontario, Canada.

Brooklyn Rushton

I am a PhD Candidate at Wilfrid Laurier University living and working in Jasper National Park studying regenerative tourism practices in Canada's mountain regions. My passion for the protection of and care for mountain landscapes is shaped from my experience recreating in and learning from the vast ecosystems that mountain regions offer. I find mountains inspiring and believe

tourism in mountain regions can be an immense opportunity to connect people to nature, if done in a sustainable and regenerative way that gives back to the environment and local communities.

María Elisa Sánchez

I am a wetland scientist born and raised in the Ecuadorian Andes, where finding my love for the mountains came as naturally to me as breathing. I am interested in understanding how mountain wetlands (specifically peatlands) function, and how they are being impacted by humans—including through the current climate emergency. Since 2014 I've been a student and steward of mountain peatlands. I developed my Masters project on carbon flux dynamics in high altitude peatlands in the Ecuadorian Andes. I am currently a PhD candidate studying how climate change is affecting peatlands in the Canadian Rocky Mountains. I have also volunteered as Americas Representative and most recently as Coordinator of Youth Engaged in Wetlands, a volunteer-based network committed to the conservation, protection, and wise-use of wetlands. My objective is to bring visibility to mountain wetlands which are understudied and might not be as extensive as in other ecoregions of the world, but that carry great importance in bringing landscape heterogeneity, biodiversity, and control of hydrological and carbon cycling processes, with far reaching consequences in the ecological health at the basin scale.

Richard Schuster

I am from Austria and grew up with mountains. My whole life mountains have been a fixture for me and if I don't see a mountain something very important is missing. I've have spent my childhood either climbing mountains or riding down on my skis. The passion for mountains has never left me and most of my vacations are spent on or around mountains. I am the Director of Spatial Planning and Innovation at the Nature Conservancy of Canada (NCC). I am responsible for the development and implementation of NCC's conservation planning framework, strategic conservation planning research efforts and new conservation technology initiatives. I also provide leadership to improve best practices and skills for spatial planning practitioners, and to creatively respond to new and emerging conservation questions. I have over 15 years of experience working on systematic conservation planning and spatial modelling for conservation purposes. I have developed innovative techniques to prioritize conservation areas and strategies and have a strong background in technology initiatives such as quantitative ecology and statistics; scientific software development and computing; big spatial data analysis; prioritization and optimization for conservation. I hold a PhD from the University of British Columbia in systematic conservation planning.

Joseph Shea

I am an Associate Professor at the University of Northern British Columbia in Prince George, on the traditional and unceded territory of the Lheidli T'enneh. Mountains are a central theme in my research, and I have been fortunate to travel, work, and play in the mountains for most of my career, with field sites in the Canadian Rockies and Interior Ranges, the north and south Coast Mountains, and the Himalayas. My academic work is focused on the glaciers, snowpacks, meteorology, and hydrology of mountain regions, and the impacts of climate change on each of these components. I bring to the CMA a broad background in mountain science and physical geography, a curious and interdisciplinary viewpoint, and the sense of wonder and humility that the mountains have provided me. And the CMA has brought me a deeper understanding of the importance of Indigenous knowledge and viewpoints, and the motivation to work closely and co-generate knowledge with Indigenous partners, on whose lands I live and work.

Pasang Dolma Sherpa

I am the Executive Director of Center for Indigenous Peoples' Research & Development (CIPRED) and have been working with Indigenous Peoples, Women and Local Communities for the recognition of Indigenous Peoples' knowledge, cultural values and customary institutions that contributed for sustainable management of forest, ecosystem, biodiversity, and climate resilience for more than a decade. I obtained my PhD from Kathmandu University in 2018 on Climate Change Education and its Interfaces with Indigenous Knowledge. I have served as Co-Chair of International Indigenous Peoples' Forum on Climate Change (IIPFCC), Co-Chair of Facilitative Working Group (FWG) of Local Communities and Indigenous Peoples' Platform (LCIP) of the United Nations Framework Convention on Climate Change (UNFCCC), and the board of UN-REDD, Participant Committee of FCPF, World Bank. Presently, I am the Chair of IUCN CEESP Specialist Group on Indigenous Peoples' Customary and Environmental Laws and Human Rights (SPICEH), visiting faculty member at Kathmandu University, and am involved in representing different forums, networks, and institutions at both national and international levels.

Daniel Sims

I am Tsek'ehne, a member of the Tomah-Izony family of the Tsay Keh Dene nation, and academic co-lead of the National Collaborating Centre for Indigenous Health. As an associate professor in First Nations Studies at the University of Northern British Columbia my research focuses on northern British Columbia and I have worked extensively with my own community as well as the related communities of Kwadacha and McLeod Lake. Both Tsek'ehne and Tsay Keh Dene mean people of the "Rocky" mountains. As such, mountains have been central to my work regardless of whether I'm examining the impacts of the W.A.C. Bennett Dam or considering numerous failed economic developments within the Traditional Territory.

Niiyokamigaabaw Deondre Smiles

I am Anishinaabe (Leech Lake Band of Ojibwe) and a member of the Bullhead clan. I am an Assistant Professor in the Department of Geography at the University of Victoria. I have a deep interest in Indigenous geographies and land/place-based knowledge systems. As a visitor to these lands, relationships to mountains and their roles in Indigenous knowledge systems is of keen interest to me, as it is important for me to behave in good relations with the nations that call these lands home. My work in the CMA allows me to act in such good relation.

Tonya Smith

I am currently a postdoctoral research fellow at the University of British Columbia's Faculty of Forestry, where I recently completed my PhD in Forestry. I am a non-binary third generation

Canadian settler of Irish-Scottish-German ancestry residing on the unceded territories of the Lekwungen and Lil'wat Nations. My research is about the relationships between human health and forests. My dissertation work analysed how forestry governance influences these relationships, following lessons from Lílwat First Nation-led research about Indigenous food security and sovereignty. I seek to untangle and inspect the many ways that settler-colonial land management continues to constrain Lílwatúl (citizens of Lil'wat) livelihoods and relationships with the land. This work is done with the intention of supporting the restoration of land-based health practices led by Indigenous peoples. The first of my family to attend university, I am passionate about accountability, reciprocity and relationships in qualitative, community-led research. I am also interested in inclusive and accessible approaches to instruction in university courses. My previous research includes performing sustainability impact assessments on forestry value chains, assessing provincial government practices regarding scientific integrity, documenting Indigenous knowledge about food and medicinal plants and analyzing Payments for Ecosystem Services programs.

Lauren Somers

I am an assistant professor and hydrology researcher at Dalhousie University in the Civil and Resource Engineering Department. My first exposure to mountain research was during my PhD at McGill University, where I focused on groundwater hydrology of the Peruvian Andes. Mountain groundwater continues to be one of my core research themes, which I approach through historical data compilation, field studies in the low mountains of Eastern Canada, and international collaborations focused on the Andes and Himalayas. My other research areas include wetland carbon exchanges and climate change adaptation, all with the goal of supporting sustainable management of our water resources and precious natural landscapes.

Chris Springer

I am an independent researcher and a contracting archaeologist in British Columbia's cultural resource management sector. Broadly speaking, my research interests focus on the social organization and interaction of ancestral First Peoples on the Pacific Northwest Coast of North America. Specifically, my graduate work at Simon Fraser University examined the relationships between past built environments and social networks within the Salish Sea region using a landscape approach that emphasized the concepts of territory, tenure, and territoriality. This experience gave me a greater understanding and appreciation for how past Indigenous communities engaged with their physical world including the high places. Mountains were not simply resource locales and the frames of travel corridors; they were, and continue to be, named places that carry history and make manifest the stories of transformation and creation.

Kyra St. Pierre

Growing up in eastern Ontario, I never fully appreciated the role that mountains played in the landscapes of my youth until I began my undergraduate studies in environmental science. Since then, the mountains have been omnipresent in my life, as I relocated first to Alberta and then British Columbia for my graduate and postdoctoral studies, spending lots of time in the mountains of northern Nunavut, southern Greenland, and coastal British Columbia. Now an assistant professor at the University of Ottawa, my research focuses on the cycles of carbon, nutrients, and contaminants from mountain headwaters to the coastal oceans and back again. Fundamentally, I study connections—between places, land, water, and air—and I feel strongly that bringing together multiple knowledge systems, disciplines and perspectives is what is needed to ensure the health and wellbeing of mountain systems now and in the future.

Madison Stevens

As a European descendant raised in a rural community near Bozeman, on the ancestral homelands of the Apsáalooke (Crow), Tséstho'e (Cheyenne), Siksikaitsitapi (Blackfoot), and Séliš (Salish) Peoples, I grew up profoundly curious about the connection between human communities and the wild mountain places around me. This curiosity has led me to pursue research as a social scientist, focused on community-led biodiversity conservation, ecological restoration, and human-wildlife coexistence, particularly in mountain systems. I earned my PhD in 2023 at the Institute for Resources, Environment, and Sustainability, University of British Columbia, where my research explored environmental decision-making in the contexts of community forest governance in the Indian Himalayas and non-profit conservation planning in Canada. I have helped to coordinate the CMA as the Project Assistant, supporting efforts to respectfully bring together multiple knowledge systems and facilitate communication across our large, diverse project team. I am currently a Postdoctoral Research Scholar at Boise State University working on a project on Indigenous-Led Ecological Restoration (ILER), researching Blackfoot-led restoration of iinnii, buffalo to their transboundary homelands. Away from the desk, I take any chance I get to play outside in the mountains and connect with the wild world.

Karson Sudlow

I am a graduate student at the University of Alberta where I study how melting glaciers affect alpine stream ecosystems. As an alpine biologist, I explore the Rocky Mountains of Alberta and BC to better understand the relationships between glaciers, the streams, and lakes they feed, and the organisms living within them. Mountains have taught me to watch my step crossing alpine streams. You never know what, or who, you might be stepping on.

Yan Tapp

Member and elected councillor of the Micmac Nation of Gespeg, I am the bearer of various political files in terms of community hunting and fishing, land occupancy and commercial fisheries. I graduated last May from a certification in Indigenous governance concerning transformational leadership, my interest in schooling allows me to evolve. Passionate about cultural activities in my community, I am involved in negotiations with the provincial ministry to obtain a camp and a community activity area in the Chic-Chocs reserve. We also currently have new hunting and fishing agreements in the SEPAQ sectors. Involved in commercial fisheries since the Marshall judgment, my experience led me to the organization of MWIFMA. Since 2018, I plan and finance training in commercial or experimental fishing according to the needs of the indigenous communities

of Gespeg, Gesgapegiag and Walostoqiyik Wahsipekuk. My role as an Indigenous Liaison Officer is to collaborate with the Canadian Coast Guard and the respective MWIFMA communities.

Julie M. Thériault

I am a full professor in atmospheric sciences and a Canada Research Chair in Extreme Winter Weather Events at the Department of Earth and Atmospheric Sciences at the Université du Québec à Montréal (UQAM). I received a bachelor's degree in physics from the Université de Moncton (New Brunswick, Canada) and MSc and PhD in atmospheric sciences from McGill University (Québec, Canada). My primary research objective is to better understand winter precipitation formation, distribution, and evolution with climate change. I conducted many research projects to better understand precipitation phase transitions in complex terrain over western Canada and freezing rain over eastern Canada using atmospheric simulations, field experiments, and theoretical approaches. I have trained more than 50 students, including undergraduate, MSc and PhD students, postdocs, and research assistants, many of whom were awarded national and provincial fellowships for their excellent academic records. I published more than 49 publications, along with a book chapter on mountain meteorology. I am also a member of the International Commission on Clouds and Precipitation and the president of the Canadian Meteorological and Oceanographic Society (CMOS) scientific committee.

Andrew Trant

I am an associate Professor in the School of Environment, Resources and Sustainability at the University of Waterloo, in Ontario, on the Traditional Territory of the Neutral, Anishinaabeg, and Haudenosaunee peoples. My research explores the ecological and cultural impacts of long-term environmental change in mountainous regions from the Coast Mountains of British Columbia to the Torngat Mountains of Nunatsiavut, northern Labrador. What I am most interested in is how these ecological changes affect livelihoods and cultural important species, such as caribou. To do this, I use a variety of methods including ethnoecology, repeat photography, dendrochronology, experimental ecology, and remote sensed data analyses. Working closely with Indigenous

Nations, and Territorial/Provincial/Federal governments, my co-developed research makes contributions to ecological theory at regional and global scales, and to the discourse around ecosystem management and conservation policy.

Steven M. Vamosi

I am a second-generation Canadian, born to Hungarian refugees who fled Soviet occupation of their ancestral homelands seeking a better life across the pond. I am Professor of Population Biology in the Department of Biological Sciences and Scientific Director of the Biogeoscience Institute at the University of Calgary. In both roles, I strive to work collaboratively with local Indigenous communities, primarily in Alberta and the Yukon. Between graduate school at the University of British Columbia (1994–2001) and my faculty position at the University of Calgary (2003 to present), I have lived just over half my life near mountain ranges (specifically, Coast and Rocky Mountains). Mountains and the elevational gradients associated with them have long fascinated me. Members of my group and I have published research on montane and foothills species, including insects, plants, trout, and salamanders, often with a focus on evolutionary and conservation ecology. I am particularly concerned by the spread of exotic species, habitat loss, and the implications of climate change for heat-sensitive montane species that are prone to the "escalator to extinction".

Vincent Vionnet

I am a Research Scientist at the Meteorological Research Division of Environment and Climate Change Canada (ECCC) based in Montréal, Québec. I study cold regions hydrology and meteorology with a deep passion for snow and how it interacts with our environment. I grew up in the Jura mountains in Eastern France where I discovered the joys of winter and the beauty of snowy landscapes. I had the chance to actually study mountain snow during my Masters and PhD at the French Meteorological Institute where I spent 4 years observing and modelling blowing snow in the French Alps. I came to Canada for the first time in 2013 to study mountain meteorology in the Canadian Rockies and to test the next generation of meteorological models in this region. Since 2014, I have worked in several research institutions (Snow Research Center, France; University of Saskatchewan, Canada; ECCC, Canada) where snow and mountains have always been at the core of my research.

John Waldron

I grew up in the UK, where I became interested in Earth science through a teenage enthusiasm for collecting fossils. I attended Cambridge and Edinburgh Universities and carried out graduate research in the Taurus Mountains of western Turkey. In 1981, I came to Canada as a postdoctoral fellow at Memorial University of Newfoundland. From 1981 until 2000 I worked at Saint Mary's University, Halifax, Nova Scotia, before moving as a professor to the University of Alberta in Edmonton. I teach introductory Earth science, tectonics, structural and field geology, and I developed an outdoor classroom, the Geoscience Garden, at the University of Alberta. My research deals with the deformed sedimentary rocks of mountain belts from both sedimentary and structural geological perspectives, with a particular focus on the Appalachian orogen of Atlantic Canada and its continuation as the Caledonides of the British Isles. I received the Gesner medal of the Atlantic Geoscience Society in 2009. I have extended this research to studies of sedimentation and tectonics in the Archean of the Slave Craton in the Canadian Shield, in the Cordillera of northern British Columbia, and in the foothills and foreland basin of the Nepal Himalaya.

Gabrielle Weasel Head

Oki my name is Tsa'piinaki, Dr. Gabrielle Weasel Head and I am a member of the Kainai Nation, Blackfoot Confederacy. An Assistant Professor in Indigenous Studies with Mount Royal University, my teaching background includes instructing on topics around First Nation, Métis, and Inuit history and current issues, Indigenous Studies (Canadian and International perspectives), Indigenous cross-cultural approaches, and Indigenous research methods and ethics. Research interests include meaningful assessment in higher education, Indigenous homelessness, intercultural parallels in teaching and learning research, Indigenous lived experience of resilience, Indigenous community-based research, parenting assessment tools reform in child welfare, anti-colonial theory, and anti-racist pedagogy. I am passionate and deeply committed to contributing to Indigenous cultural continuity and sustainability. My work with the CMA is but one area wherein my embodied perspectives on balance and maintaining good relations are mobilized in generative and mutually beneficial ways.

Sonia Wesche

I am an Associate Professor in Environmental Studies, Geography and Indigenous Studies at the University of Ottawa, located on the traditional unceded territory of the Algonquin Anishnaabeg people. As a scholar of settler origins, I work collaboratively with Indigenous communities, organizations, and other partners in Arctic and sub-Arctic environments to better understand local- and regional-scale impacts of environmental change and pathways for fostering adaptive capacity. My interdisciplinary research is primarily community-based, and focuses on linkages among environmental change, food and water security, and health and well-being. I am humbled and awed by mountain environments and am deepening my understanding of human and more-than-human relationships in the mountains of Lhù'àan Mân Ku Dán keyi, Kluane First Nation Traditional Territory, through an ongoing research partnership in the south-west Yukon.

Philippus Wester

I was born in the Netherlands, a low-lying country largely consisting of rivers, canals, polders, and embankments, but grew up in the mountains of the Eastern Highlands Province of Papua New Guinea. This intercultural upbringing instilled a deep respect in me for Indigenous Peoples and cultures and a love for mountains and waters. I studied international land and water management at Wageningen University in the Netherlands and have lived and worked in five continents, sometimes in deltas (Bangladesh, the Netherlands) but more frequently in mountains (Papua New Guinea, Mexico, Ethiopia, Nepal). I joined the International Centre for Integrated Mountain Development (ICIMOD) in 2013, living and working in Kathmandu, Nepal. During this time I coordinated the Hindu Kush Himalayan Monitoring and Assessment Programme (HIMAP), producing the first Comprehensive Assessment of the Hindu Kush Himalaya published in 2019. I also had the honour to serve as Lead Author of Chapter 1 of the Working Group II contribution to the IPCC's Sixth Assessment Report as well as the co-Lead of Cross-Chapter Paper on Mountains in that report. Based on my experience with assessments, I was honoured to be an international advisor to the CMA.

Nicole J. Wilson

I am a white scholar of settler origin. Since 2020, I have been an Assistant Professor and Canada Research Chair Tier II in Arctic Environmental Change and Governance in the Department of Environment and Geography and the Centre for Earth Observation Science at the University of Manitoba. I hold a PhD in Resource Management and Environmental Studies from the University of British Columbia and a MS in Natural Resources from Cornell University. I am an environmental social scientist. My research examines the many ways that Arctic and sub-Arctic Indigenous peoples are asserting their self-determination and revitalizing their governance systems to respond to stressors including climate change. Long-term partnerships with Indigenous governments and organizations are central to my community-based research approach. I am passionate about water governance and politics. Indigenous water rights, responsibilities and authorities are central to my research program. I have worked in partnership with Yukon First Nations to examine the implications of the water rights acknowledged in their modern land claim agreements for water governance and decision-making in the territory. I am also the co-chair of the UM United Nations Academic Impact Hub for Sustainable Development Goal 6 on Clean Water and Sanitation at the University of Manitoba.

Matthew Wiseman

I am a Lecturer in North American Studies in the Department of History at the University of Waterloo. I attained my PhD in History from Wilfrid Laurier University and the Tri-University Graduate Program in History in 2017 before holding a SSHRC Postdoctoral Fellowship at the University of Toronto (2017–19), an AMS Postdoctoral Fellowship at Western University (2019–20), and a Banting Postdoctoral Fellowship at St. Jerome's University (2020–22). As a historian of modern Canada and the United States, my research concentrates on the history of science, technology, and medical research ethics in northern and Arctic contexts. I am the author of a forthcoming monograph entitled *Frontier Science: Northern Canada, Military Research, and the Cold War, 1945–1970* (UTP, 2024), which explores the social and environmental consequences of acclimatization research and other military-sponsored science projects carried out in Indigenous communities near Hudson Bay. My research on the history of science in the Cold War has also appeared in such leading journals as the *Canadian Historical Review, International Journal,* and *Scientia Canadensis.* In addition to my professional work, I volunteer as the Communications Director for the Canadian Science and Technology Historical Association.

Kristine Wray

I am the Canadian Mountain Network Fellow in Indigenous Knowledge and the Decolonization of Science, as well as a PhD Candidate in Environmental Sociology. I am working with Dr. Brenda Parlee in the Faculty of Agriculture, Life and Environmental Sciences (ALES) at the University of Alberta. A proud member of the Métis Nation of Alberta, my graduate work has focused on Indigenous approaches to resource management, specifically commercial and traditional fisheries (Great Slave Lake) and caribou co-management (Porcupine herd). I have a particular interest in the interface of Indigenous Knowledge and science. Finally, I am developing and teaching a new course in ALES called RSOC 260: Indigenous Foundations for the Environmental and Conservation Sciences.

Note: Bios for Melissa Quesnelle and Douglas Kootenay were not available at the time of publication

APPENDIX II: LEARNING CIRCLE CONTRIBUTIONS

Video recordings of oral knowledge contributions from the CMA Learning Circle are alphabetized by last name and formatted according to protocols for citing oral knowledge developed by Lorisia MacLeod, 2021. In-text reference numbers are included in blue in brackets after the citation, prior to the URL.

Andrew, L. Nę K'ə Dene Ts'įłį. Oral teaching, Canadian Mountain Assessment Learning Circle: Mountains as Homelands, 1. Banff, AB. May 24–26, 2022. [LC 3.3, LC 3.12]
https://digitalcollections.ucalgary.ca/AssetLink/68ka5x5bj4vpkq430l5678018qsx0280.mp4

Andrew, L. Nę K'ə Dene Ts'įłį. Oral teaching, Canadian Mountain Assessment Learning Circle: Gifts of the Mountains, 1. Banff, AB. May 24–26, 2022. [LC 4.7, LC 5.33]
https://digitalcollections.ucalgary.ca/AssetLink/a7te0i88l34o3ah24e4n637257k27b0m.mp4

Andrew, L. Nę K'ə Dene Ts'įłį. Oral teaching, Canadian Mountain Assessment Learning Circle: Desirable Mountain Futures, 1. Banff, AB. May 24–26, 2022. [LC 6.4]
https://digitalcollections.ucalgary.ca/AssetLink/4fx685ae11k05keoycfa8087a8381x3f.mp4

Desmarais, G. Inuit, Kinngat, Nunavut. Oral teaching, Canadian Mountain Assessment Learning Circle: Mountains as Homelands, 1. Banff, AB. May 24–26, 2022. [LC 3.13]
https://digitalcollections.ucalgary.ca/AssetLink/8r43by8t82m2o245r0hknpj4v7g6764w.mp4

Desmarais, G. Inuit, Kinngat, Nunavut. Oral teaching, Canadian Mountain Assessment Learning Circle: Gifts of the Mountains, 1. Banff, AB. May 24–26, 2022. [LC 4.10, LC 4.17, LC 4.24]
https://digitalcollections.ucalgary.ca/AssetLink/11b3046y1n15c4uj3bk1urc8x2a760iw.mp4

Desmarais, G. Inuit, Kinngat, Nunavut. Oral teaching, Canadian Mountain Assessment Learning Circle: Gifts of the Mountains, 2. Banff, AB. May 24–26, 2022. [LC 4.11]
https://digitalcollections.ucalgary.ca/AssetLink/ib07464n06064738n6433y0n6jq270so.mp4

Dicker, M. Inuit, Nunatsiavut. Oral teaching, Canadian Mountain Assessment Learning Circle: Mountains as Homelands, 1. Banff, AB. May 24–26, 2022. [LC 3.21, LC 4.19]
https://digitalcollections.ucalgary.ca/AssetLink/05k3e7u7ciqxn58860clwj0d3i2tn22i.mp4

Dicker, M. Inuit, Nunatsiavut. Oral teaching, Canadian Mountain Assessment Learning Circle: Gifts of the Mountains, 1. Banff, AB. May 24–26, 2022. [LC 4.31]
https://digitalcollections.ucalgary.ca/AssetLink/8a3ww703532d11hhgh5qej7ji338u6xo.mp4

Dicker, M. Inuit, Nunatsiavut. Oral teaching, Canadian Mountain Assessment Learning Circle: Gifts of the Mountains, 2. Banff, AB. May 24–26, 2022. [LC 2.16, LC 4.28, LC 4.30]
https://digitalcollections.ucalgary.ca/AssetLink/y3n2wlu3135mgv03n4u3vy0bk486c608.mp4

Jerome, P.N. Micmacs of Gesgapegiag. Oral teaching, Canadian Mountain Assessment Learning Circle: Mountain Environments, 1. Banff, AB. May 24–26, 2022. [LC 2.10, LC 2.17, LC 5.35]
https://digitalcollections.ucalgary.ca/AssetLink/8twnorojmbpo6454g7r7066x21x4p0fd.mp4

Jerome, P.N. Micmacs of Gesgapegiag. Oral teaching, Canadian Mountain Assessment Learning Circle: Mountains as Homelands, 1. Banff, AB. May 24–26, 2022. [LC 3.4]
https://digitalcollections.ucalgary.ca/AssetLink/814y8tck8fx63076ii336436x5vx6h02.mp4

Jerome, P.N. Micmacs of Gesgapegiag. Oral teaching, Canadian Mountain Assessment Learning Circle: Mountains as Homelands, 2. Banff, AB. May 24–26, 2022. [LC 3.18]
https://digitalcollections.ucalgary.ca/AssetLink/8i4mle667umac0t2fxl24r8pm2t2bi5q.mp4

Jerome, P.N. Micmacs of Gesgapegiag. Oral teaching, Canadian Mountain Assessment Learning Circle: Gifts of the Mountains, 1. Banff, AB. May 24–26, 2022. [LC 2.4, LC 2.19, LC 3.8, LC 4.8, LC 4.12, LC 4.22, LC 4.27, LC 5.39]
https://digitalcollections.ucalgary.ca/AssetLink/4oiw2okbwy468vpfo54q25f5myqo154y.mp4

Jerome, P.N. Micmacs of Gesgapegiag. Oral teaching, Canadian Mountain Assessment Learning Circle: Gifts of the Mountains, 2. Banff, AB. May 24–26, 2022. [LC 4.26]
https://digitalcollections.ucalgary.ca/AssetLink/4nwirbtew5771ph4r02103erpnv1d453.mp4

Jerome, P.N. Micmacs of Gesgapegiag. Oral teaching, Canadian Mountain Assessment Learning Circle: Gifts of the Mountains, 3. Banff, AB. May 24–26, 2022. [LC 5.41]

https://digitalcollections.ucalgary.ca/AssetLink/aj27a43x8giu883m72ifa214h5y286jy.mp4

Joe, P. Kwanlin Dün First Nation. Oral teaching, Canadian Mountain Assessment Learning Circle: Mountains as Homelands, 1. Banff, AB. May 24–26, 2022. [LC 2.5, LC 5.36]

https://digitalcollections.ucalgary.ca/AssetLink/i66npq2x6n42q1gjpveupinkq1q62pa5.mp4

Joe, P. Kwanlin Dün First Nation. Oral teaching, Canadian Mountain Assessment Learning Circle: Gifts of the Mountains, 1. Banff, AB. May 24–26, 2022. [LC 2.9, LC 2.20, LC 4.23]

https://digitalcollections.ucalgary.ca/AssetLink/p584805128jje6f7jfiw2qw3cws3o44h.mp4

Johnson, G.M.J. Lhu'ààn Mân Ku Dań. Oral teaching, Canadian Mountain Assessment Learning Circle: Mountain Environments, 1. Banff, AB. May 24–26, 2022. [LC 2.23, LC 5.4, LC 5.5, LC 5.8, LC 5.9, LC 5.13, LC 5.28, LC 5.32, LC 5.43]

https://digitalcollections.ucalgary.ca/AssetLink/j5hp0872u0374p276mvoyq83681u3rih.mp4

Johnson, G.M.J. Lhu'ààn Mân Ku Dań. Oral teaching, Canadian Mountain Assessment Learning Circle: Mountain Environments, 2. Banff, AB. May 24–26, 2022. [LC 2.2, LC 5.1, LC 5.22, LC 5.24, LC 5.30]

https://digitalcollections.ucalgary.ca/AssetLink/v0k5dnpxd88yx8708odd2mawbt0404de.mp4

Johnson, G.M.J. Lhu'ààn Mân Ku Dań. Oral teaching, Canadian Mountain Assessment Learning Circle: Mountain Environments, 3. Banff, AB. May 24–26, 2022. [LC 2.13, LC 3.20, LC 5.10]

https://digitalcollections.ucalgary.ca/AssetLink/7p3q6w315y1capetqv1f2e00jw1hk3rk.mp4

Johnson, G.M.J. Lhu'ààn Mân Ku Dań. Oral teaching, Canadian Mountain Assessment Learning Circle: Mountains as Homelands, 1. Banff, AB. May 24–26, 2022. [LC 2.3, LC 3.1]

https://digitalcollections.ucalgary.ca/AssetLink/4yw840s5i2048jeg61r708b7jyvfh058.mp4

Johnson, G.M.J. Lhu'ààn Mân Ku Dań. Oral teaching, Canadian Mountain Assessment Learning Circle: Gifts of the Mountains, 1. Banff, AB. May 24–26, 2022. [LC 1.1, LC 3.10, LC 3.22, LC 4.1, LC 4.5, LC 4.18]

https://digitalcollections.ucalgary.ca/AssetLink/4f7d426l56002b0b4j4pej085uhc47nd.mp4

Johnson, G.M.J. Lhu'ààn Mân Ku Dań. Oral teaching, Canadian Mountain Assessment Learning Circle: Gifts of the Mountains, 2. Banff, AB. May 24–26, 2022. [LC 2.18, LC 4.15]

https://digitalcollections.ucalgary.ca/AssetLink/u2b2yayq648tloml73208dnl7o7b0732.mp4

Johnson, G.M.J. Lhu'ààn Mân Ku Dań. Oral teaching, Canadian Mountain Assessment Learning Circle: Desirable Mountain Futures, 1. Banff, AB. May 24–26, 2022. [LC 3.24, LC 6.3, LC 6.7]

https://digitalcollections.ucalgary.ca/AssetLink/a4u75hxd2q525k10hq5qqt1hkko31o6f.mp4

Lightning, K.L. Nehiyaw, Samson Cree First Nation. Oral teaching, Canadian Mountain Assessment Learning Circle: Mountains as Homelands, 1. Banff, AB. May 24–26, 2022. [LC 5.14]

https://digitalcollections.ucalgary.ca/AssetLink/imb4opk3dd2hr0b2728r3gpw7br2wg3s.mp4

Lightning, K.L. Nehiyaw, Samson Cree First Nation. Oral teaching, Canadian Mountain Assessment Learning Circle: Gifts of the Mountains, 1. Banff, AB. May 24–26, 2022. [LC 4.9, LC 4.13]

https://digitalcollections.ucalgary.ca/AssetLink/jfu4bxk8m52b57r7w8y228wpj76o0044.mp4

Lightning, K.L. Nehiyaw, Samson Cree First Nation. Oral teaching, Canadian Mountain Assessment Learning Circle: Desirable Mountain Futures, 1. Banff, AB. May 24–26, 2022. [LC 2.14]

https://digitalcollections.ucalgary.ca/AssetLink/eurxmd108c658068l6v4kn31kh2bsjp5.mp4

Mayes, B. Kwanlin Dün First Nation. Oral teaching, Canadian Mountain Assessment Learning Circle: Mountain Environments, 1. Banff, AB. May 24–26, 2022. [LC 2.7, LC 2.21, LC 4.20, LC 5.2, LC 5.3, LC 5.27]

https://digitalcollections.ucalgary.ca/AssetLink/fsp7ljmp5804soo05a5g41xefo62840i.mp4

Mayes, B. Kwanlin Dün First Nation. Oral teaching, Canadian Mountain Assessment Learning Circle: Mountain Environments, 2. Banff, AB. May 24–26, 2022. [LC 5.23]

https://digitalcollections.ucalgary.ca/AssetLink/3qsxarj56e161o1n2mdt75d8nile842l.mp4

Mayes, B. Kwanlin Dün First Nation. Oral teaching, Canadian Mountain Assessment Learning Circle: Mountain Environments, 3. Banff, AB. May 24–26, 2022. [LC 5.25, LC 5.31]

https://digitalcollections.ucalgary.ca/AssetLink/4i2078s863f1c6e2o3e0du030s2621gm.mp4

Mayes, B. Kwanlin Dün First Nation. Oral teaching, Canadian Mountain Assessment Learning Circle: Mountains as Homelands, 1. Banff, AB. May 24–26, 2022. [LC 3.5]

https://digitalcollections.ucalgary.ca/AssetLink/s2kc0y8k3rfo6654hr0u4o047885557x.mp4

Mayes, B. Kwanlin Dün First Nation. Oral teaching, Canadian Mountain Assessment Learning Circle: Gifts of the Mountains, 1. Banff, AB. May 24–26, 2022. [LC 4.4]

https://digitalcollections.ucalgary.ca/AssetLink/o7y47m6v6d83306401h6225xd3832qav.mp4

Mayes, B. Kwanlin Dün First Nation. Oral teaching, Canadian Mountain Assessment Learning Circle: Desirable Mountain Futures, 1. Banff, AB. May 24–26, 2022. [LC 6.2]

https://digitalcollections.ucalgary.ca/AssetLink/dpij5by4b3111ho351hq3088hb751485.mp4

Melting Tallow, H. Siksika Nation, Blackfoot Confederacy. Oral teaching, Canadian Mountain Assessment Learning Circle: Mountain Environments, 1. Banff, AB. May 24–26, 2022. [LC 5.7]

https://digitalcollections.ucalgary.ca/AssetLink/20656bqi6sao36x742w368681010211g.mp4

Melting Tallow, H. Siksika Nation, Blackfoot Confederacy. Oral teaching, Canadian Mountain Assessment Learning Circle: Mountain Environments, 2. Banff, AB. May 24–26, 2022. [LC 2.12, LC 5.29]

https://digitalcollections.ucalgary.ca/AssetLink/mv04l767g7p28311l3tm331st21ert3w.mp4

Melting Tallow, H. Siksika Nation, Blackfoot Confederacy. Oral teaching, Canadian Mountain Assessment Learning Circle: Mountain Environments, 3. Banff, AB. May 24–26, 2022. [LC 5.19]

https://digitalcollections.ucalgary.ca/AssetLink/1e60t1780o1661e2p44eh537r00663no.mp4

Melting Tallow, H. Siksika Nation, Blackfoot Confederacy. Oral teaching, Canadian Mountain Assessment Learning Circle: Mountains as Homelands, 1. Banff, AB. May 24–26, 2022. [LC 2.1, LC 3.9, LC 3.11, LC 3.16]

https://digitalcollections.ucalgary.ca/AssetLink/t4tqsf4r2uw77bt4sh4fqn802x21hd6n.mp4

Melting Tallow, H. Siksika Nation, Blackfoot Confederacy. Oral teaching, Canadian Mountain Assessment Learning Circle: Mountains as Homelands, 2. Banff, AB. May 24–26, 2022. [LC 2.8]

https://digitalcollections.ucalgary.ca/AssetLink/01ts4184kaw0xk73s718p803m65w128e.mp4

Melting Tallow, H. Siksika Nation, Blackfoot Confederacy. Oral teaching, Canadian Mountain Assessment Learning Circle: Mountains as Homelands, 3. Banff, AB. May 24–26, 2022. [LC 3.2]

https://digitalcollections.ucalgary.ca/AssetLink/4yw840s5i2048jeg61r708b7jyvfh058.mp4

Melting Tallow, H. Siksika Nation, Blackfoot Confederacy. Oral teaching, Canadian Mountain Assessment Learning Circle: Mountains as Homelands, 4. Banff, AB. May 24–26, 2022. [LC 2.6]

https://digitalcollections.ucalgary.ca/AssetLink/ach1vpap5482k35ke463b237678x7xn6.mp4

Melting Tallow, H. Siksika Nation, Blackfoot Confederacy. Oral teaching, Canadian Mountain Assessment Learning Circle: Gifts of the Mountains, 1. Banff, AB. May 24–26, 2022. [LC 4.6]

https://digitalcollections.ucalgary.ca/AssetLink/803h5h836m0kih3fef15s5533ro2mud1.mp4

Melting Tallow, H. Siksika Nation, Blackfoot Confederacy. Oral teaching, Canadian Mountain Assessment Learning Circle: Desirable Mountain Futures, 1. Banff, AB. May 24–26, 2022. [LC 1.2]

https://digitalcollections.ucalgary.ca/AssetLink/q64ktn74ur8x2h7q62f45lah875407nc.mp4

Pascal, W. Teetl'it Gwich'in. Oral teaching, Canadian Mountain Assessment Learning Circle: Gifts of the Mountains, 1. Banff, AB. May 24–26, 2022. [LC 2.11, LC 2.22, LC 5.6, LC 5.26, LC 5.37]

https://digitalcollections.ucalgary.ca/AssetLink/w54h4pc1qo884a8xscasn4e5d31nb10q.mp4

Pascal, W. Teetl'it Gwich'in. Oral teaching, Canadian Mountain Assessment Learning Circle: Gifts of the Mountains, 2. Banff, AB. May 24–26, 2022. [LC 4.14]

https://digitalcollections.ucalgary.ca/AssetLink/2keq327fo223e20yw2l08006qgtyj6f6.mp4

Patterson, T. Lower Nicola Indian Band, Scw̓éxmx, Nlaka'pamux (Thompson) Nation. Oral teaching, Canadian Mountain Assessment Learning Circle: Mountain Environments, 1. Banff, AB. May 24–26, 2022. [LC 5.21]

https://digitalcollections.ucalgary.ca/AssetLink/v662nueh2711e0n0r33q31jpbax0fl5k.mp4

Patterson, T. Lower Nicola Indian Band, Scw̓éxmx, Nlaka'pamux (Thompson) Nation. Oral teaching, Canadian Mountain Assessment Learning Circle: Mountains as Homelands, 1. Banff, AB. May 24–26, 2022. [LC 4.21]

https://digitalcollections.ucalgary.ca/AssetLink/ck83sfqy3y552jgb3722cr03tyrsrc88.mp4

Pheasant, S. Anishinaabe. Oral teaching, Canadian Mountain Assessment Learning Circle: Gifts of the Mountains, 1. Banff, AB. May 24–26, 2022. [LC 4.25]

https://digitalcollections.ucalgary.ca/AssetLink/cl6a2k5204qc3i180kcd7l1adxkf0044.mp4

Saunders Dahl, D. Métis (Red River Ojibway). Oral teaching, Canadian Mountain Assessment Learning Circle: Mountain Environments, 1. Banff, AB. May 24–26, 2022. [LC 5.11, LC 5.12, LC 5.15, LC 5.44]

https://digitalcollections.ucalgary.ca/AssetLink/1f041dq7e03k26314812hplw2m8wr5m2.mp4

Sims, D. Tsay Keh Dene First Nation. Oral teaching, Canadian Mountain Assessment Learning Circle: Mountains as Homelands, 1. Banff, AB. May 24–26, 2022. [LC 5.20]

https://digitalcollections.ucalgary.ca/AssetLink/1r3qd1tnukos6gnlb050sh5m57r508hj.mp4

Sims, D. Tsay Keh Dene First Nation. Oral teaching, Canadian Mountain Assessment Learning Circle: Gifts of the Mountains, 1. Banff, AB. May 24–26, 2022. [LC 2.15, LC 4.2, LC 5.34]

https://digitalcollections.ucalgary.ca/AssetLink/d251mb4u20tl3x2o77uw5pfvf3y4d450.mp4

Sims, D. Tsay Keh Dene First Nation. Oral teaching, Canadian Mountain Assessment Learning Circle: Gifts of the Mountains, 2. Banff, AB. May 24–26, 2022. [LC 4.29]

https://digitalcollections.ucalgary.ca/AssetLink/8c75y325u4ypuaadnaq862u2y6d4sq62.mp4

Sims, D. Tsay Keh Dene First Nation. Oral teaching, Canadian Mountain Assessment Learning Circle: Desirable Mountain Futures, 1. Banff, AB. May 24–26, 2022. [LC 3.17, LC 3.23]

https://digitalcollections.ucalgary.ca/AssetLink/2fngxlr4p05y6648ut3qioey7vvnu45e.mp4

Sims, D. Tsay Keh Dene First Nation. Oral teaching, Canadian Mountain Assessment Learning Circle: Desirable Mountain Futures, 2. Banff, AB. May 24–26, 2022. [LC 6.6]

https://digitalcollections.ucalgary.ca/AssetLink/jp1u4if07pr7556dw026fnf6w0s52jrc.mp4

Tapp, Y. Gespeg First Nation. Oral teaching, Canadian Mountain Assessment Learning Circle: Mountain Environments, 1. Banff, AB. May 24–26, 2022. [LC 5.16, LC 5.42]

https://digitalcollections.ucalgary.ca/AssetLink/o1bs4r2xurnm7pksp7hn5rttlg7ed012.mp4

Tapp, Y. Gespeg First Nation. Oral teaching, Canadian Mountain Assessment Learning Circle: Mountains as Homelands, 1. Banff, AB. May 24–26, 2022. [LC 3.6, LC 3.14, LC 3.19]

https://digitalcollections.ucalgary.ca/AssetLink/253852pt6w17ai7kprpr2x13v853qc6i.mp4

Tapp, Y. Gespeg First Nation. Oral teaching, Canadian Mountain Assessment Learning Circle: Gifts of the Mountains, 1. Banff, AB. May 24–26, 2022. [LC 5.17, LC 5.40]

https://digitalcollections.ucalgary.ca/AssetLink/1k1wggn03l8xqetlti68w7m87g836302.mp4

Weasel Head, G. Kainaiwa Nation, Blackfoot Confederacy. Oral teaching, Canadian Mountain Assessment Learning Circle: Mountain Environments, 1. Banff, AB. May 24–26, 2022. [LC 5.18]

https://digitalcollections.ucalgary.ca/AssetLink/7s41ale1f4q04vn50dy2otghnp08lnh6.mp4

Weasel Head, G. Kainaiwa Nation, Blackfoot Confederacy. Oral teaching, Canadian Mountain Assessment Learning Circle: Gifts of the Mountains, 1. Banff, AB. May 24–26, 2022. [LC 1.3, LC 5.38]

https://digitalcollections.ucalgary.ca/AssetLink/8s2085shi43k76qtp16sy8xfjv3gr1qb.mp4

Weasel Head, G. Kainaiwa Nation, Blackfoot Confederacy. Oral teaching, Canadian Mountain Assessment Learning Circle: Gifts of the Mountains, 2. Banff, AB. May 24–26, 2022. [LC 4.3, LC 4.16]

https://digitalcollections.ucalgary.ca/AssetLink/60x0cwd0kg5oyj5a14uc0q4e7s2k8356.mp4

Weasel Head, G. Kainaiwa Nation, Blackfoot Confederacy. Oral teaching, Canadian Mountain Assessment Learning Circle: Gifts of the Mountains, 3. Banff, AB. May 24–26, 2022. [LC 3.15, LC 4.16]

https://digitalcollections.ucalgary.ca/AssetLink/253852pt6w17ai7kprpr2x13v853qc6i.mp4

Weasel Head, G. Kainaiwa Nation, Blackfoot Confederacy. Oral teaching, Canadian Mountain Assessment Learning Circle: Desirable Mountain Futures, 1. Banff, AB. May 24–26, 2022. [LC 6.1, LC 6.5]

https://digitalcollections.ucalgary.ca/AssetLink/46gm0a858vdx04jw374boja7n818778k.mp4

Weasel Head, G. Kainaiwa Nation, Blackfoot Confederacy. Oral teaching, Canadian Mountain Assessment Learning Circle: Desirable Mountain Futures, 2. Banff, AB. May 24–26, 2022. [LC 3.7]

https://digitalcollections.ucalgary.ca/AssetLink/gd2v04jkw5reqdsdsijqmf6y8o11245q.mp4

APPENDIX III: MAP DATA

Canadian Mountain Assessment (CMA) maps were designed by Chris Brackley and Angi Goodkey (As the Crow Flies cARTography), as well as Jiaao Guo for Figures 1.1, 1.2, 1.3, 1.4, and 1.11.

Data below are for maps produced by the CMA. Data for a limited number of other maps that were not produced by the CMA are not included here, as data sources are cited in map captions.

Base data for maps

Natural Earth. (2021). Prisma Shaded Relief (Version 4.2). Retrieved from https://www.naturalearthdata.com/50m-prisma-shaded-relief/prisma-shaded-relief/

Natural Resources Canada. (2016). Boundary Polygons; Boundary Lines, Atlas of Canada National Scale Data 1:5,000,000. Retrieved from: https://open.canada.ca/data/en/dataset/b8477997-51db-5ee8-91c8-52af2a2d7a96

Chapter 1

Figure 1.1

McDowell, G., & Guo, J. (2021). A Nationally Coherent Characterization and Quantification of Mountain Systems in Canada. *Mountain Research and Development*, *41.0*(2), R21–R31. https://doi.org/10.1659/MRD-JOURNAL-D-20-00071.1

Sayre, R., Karagulle, D., Krauer, J., Payne, D., Adler, C., & Cress, J. (2020). Global Mountain Explorer. Retrieved from https://rmgsc.cr.usgs.gov/gme/

Figure 1.2

McDowell, G., & Guo, J. (2021). A Nationally Coherent Characterization and Quantification of Mountain Systems in Canada. *Mountain Research and Development*, *41.0*(2), R21–R31. https://doi.org/10.1659/MRD-JOURNAL-D-20-00071.1

Native-Land.ca (2020). Native-Land API. Retrieved from https://native-land.ca/api-docs/

Figure 1.3

McDowell, G., & Guo, J. (2021). A Nationally Coherent Characterization and Quantification of Mountain Systems in Canada. *Mountain Research and Development*, *41.0*(2), R21–R31. https://doi.org/10.1659/MRD-JOURNAL-D-20-00071.1

Native-Land.ca (2020). Native-Land API. Retrieved from https://native-land.ca/api-docs/

Figure 1.4

McDowell, G., & Guo, J. (2021). A Nationally Coherent Characterization and Quantification of Mountain Systems in Canada. *Mountain Research and Development*, *41.0*(2), R21–R31. https://doi.org/10.1659/MRD-JOURNAL-D-20-00071.1

CIESIN. (2020). Gridded Population of the World, Version 4 (GPWv4): Population Density, Revision 11. Palisades, NY: NASA Socioeconomic Data and Applications Center (SEDAC). Retrieved from https://doi.org/10.7927/H49C6VHW

Figure 1.8

Canadian Mountain Assessment primary data (2023).

Figure 1.11

McDowell, G., & Guo, J. (2021). A Nationally Coherent Characterization and Quantification of Mountain Systems in Canada. *Mountain Research and Development*, *41.0*(2), R21–R31. https://doi.org/10.1659/MRD-JOURNAL-D-20-00071.1

Sayre, R., Karagulle, D., Krauer, J., Payne, D., Adler, C., & Cress, J. (2020). Global Mountain Explorer. Retrieved from https://rmgsc.cr.usgs.gov/gme/

Agriculture and Agri-Food Canada (2016). Terrestrial Ecozones of Canada. Ottawa, Canada: Retrieved from https://open.canada.ca/data/en/dataset/7ad7ea01-eb23-4824-bccc-66adb7c5bdf82020.

Chapter 2

Figure 2.3

Hasterok, D., Halpin, J. A., Collins, A. S., Hand, M., Kreemer, C., Gard, M. G., & Glorie, S. (2022). New Maps of Global Geological Provinces and Tectonic Plates. Earth-Science Reviews, 231, 104069. https://doi.org/10.1016/j.earscirev.2022.104069

Figure 2.7

Global Volcanism Program. (2023). Volcanoes of the World (Version v. 5.1.0). Smithsonian Institution. https://doi.org///doi.org/10.5479/si.GVP.VOTW5-2023.5.1

Natural Resources Canada. (2022). *Major Volcanoes* [PDF, JPG]. Retrieved from https://open.canada.ca/data/en/dataset/de376fde-8893-11e0-bee7-6cf049291510

Figure 2.9
Hersbach, H., Bell, B., Berrisford, P., Hirahara, S., Horányi, A., Muñoz-Sabater, J., ... Thépaut, J. (2020). The ERA5 global reanalysis. *Quarterly Journal of the Royal Meteorological Society, 146*(730), 1999–2049. https://doi.org/10.1002/qj.3803

Figure 2.11
Carrera, M. L., Bélair, S., & Bilodeau, B. (2015). The Canadian Land Data Assimilation System (CaLDAS): Description and Synthetic Evaluation Study. *Journal of Hydrometeorology, 16*(3), 1293–1314. https://doi.org/10.1175/JHM-D-14-0089.1

Fortin, V., Roy, G., Stadnyk, T., Koenig, K., Gasset, N., & Mahidjiba, A. (2018). Ten Years of Science Based on the Canadian Precipitation Analysis: A CaPA System Overview and Literature Review. *Atmosphere-Ocean, 56*(3), 178–196. https://doi.org/10.1080/07055900.2018.1474728

Figure 2.12
Mekis, É., & Vincent, L. A. (2011). An Overview of the Second Generation Adjusted Daily Precipitation Dataset for Trend Analysis in Canada. *Atmosphere-Ocean, 49*(2), 163–177. https://doi.org/10.1080/07055900.2011.583910

Vincent, L. A., Wang, X. L., Milewska, E. J., Wan, H., Yang, F., & Swail, V. (2012). A second generation of homogenized Canadian monthly surface air temperature for climate trend analysis: Homogenized Canadian Temperature. *Journal of Geophysical Research: Atmospheres, 117*(D18), n/a-n/a. https://doi.org/10.1029/2012JD017859

Figure 2.13
Vionnet, V., Marsh, C. B., Menounos, B., Gascoin, S., Wayand, N. E., Shea, J., ... Pomeroy, J. W. (2021). Multiscale snowdrift-permitting modelling of mountain snowpack. *The Cryosphere, 15*(2), 743–769. https://doi.org/10.5194/tc-15-743-2021

Figure 2.14
Vionnet, V., Mortimer, C., Brady, M., Arnal, L., & Brown, R. (2021). Canadian historical Snow Water Equivalent dataset (CanSWE, 1928–2020). *Earth System Science Data, 13*(9), 4603–4619. https://doi.org/10.5194/essd-13-4603-2021

Figure 2.15
Mudryk, L. R., Derksen, C., Kushner, P. J., & Brown, R. (2015). Characterization of Northern Hemisphere Snow Water Equivalent Datasets, 1981–2010. *Journal of Climate, 28*(20), 8037–8051. https://doi.org/10.1175/JCLI-D-15-0229.1

Figure 2.16
Pfeffer, W. T., Arendt, A. A., Bliss, A., Bolch, T., Cogley, J. G., Gardner, A. S., ... The Randolph Consortium. (2014). The Randolph Glacier Inventory: A globally complete inventory of glaciers. *Journal of Glaciology, 60*(221), 537–552. https://doi.org/10.3189/2014JoG13J176

Figure 2.17
Gruber, S. (2012). Derivation and analysis of a high-resolution estimate of global permafrost zonation. *The Cryosphere, 6*(1), 221–233. https://doi.org/10.5194/tc-6-221-2012

Figure 2.21
Beck, H. E., De Roo, A., & Van Dijk, A. I. J. M. (2015). Global Maps of Streamflow Characteristics Based on Observations from Several Thousand Catchments. *Journal of Hydrometeorology, 16*(4), 1478–1501. https://doi.org/10.1175/JHM-D-14-0155.1

GloH2O. (n.d.). Global Streamflow Characteristics Dataset. Retrieved from https://www.gloh2o.org/gscd

Figure 2.25
Hermosilla, T., Wulder, M. A., White, J. C., & Coops, N. C. (2022). Land cover classification in an era of big and open data: Optimizing localized implementation and training data selection to improve mapping outcomes. *Remote Sensing of Environment, 268*, 112780. https://doi.org/10.1016/j.rse.2021.112780

Chapter 3

Figure 3.1
Native-Land.ca (2020). Native-Land API. Retrieved from https://native-land.ca/api-docs/

Natural Resources Canada. (2017). Aboriginal Lands of Canada Legislative Boundaries [Vector]. Retrieved from https://open.canada.ca/data/en/dataset/522b07b9-78e2-4819-b736-ad9208eb1067

U.S. Geological Survey's Center for Earth Resources Observation and Science. (1996). Digital Elevation—Global 30 Arc-Second Elevation (GTOPO30). https://doi.org///doi.org/10.5066/F7DF6PQ

Figure 3.4
Native-Land.ca (2020). Native-Land API. Retrieved from https://native-land.ca/api-docs/

Natural Resources Canada. (2017). Aboriginal Lands of Canada Legislative Boundaries. Retrieved from https://open.canada.ca/data/en/dataset/522b07b9-78e2-4819-b736-ad9208eb1067

U.S. Geological Survey's Center for Earth Resources Observation and Science. (1996). Digital Elevation—Global 30 Arc-Second Elevation (GTOPO30). https://doi.org///doi.org/10.5066/F7DF6PQ

Figure 3.5

Native-Land.ca (2020). Native-Land API. Retrieved from https://native-land.ca/api-docs/

Natural Resources Canada. (2017). Aboriginal Lands of Canada Legislative Boundaries. Retrieved from https://open.canada.ca/data/en/dataset/522b07b9-78e2-4819-b736-ad9208eb1067

U.S. Geological Survey's Center for Earth Resources Observation and Science. (1996). Digital Elevation—Global 30 Arc-Second Elevation (GTOPO30). https://doi.org ///doi.org/10.5066/F7DF6PQ

Chapter 5

Figure 5.1

Hersbach, H., Bell, B., Berrisford, P., Blavati, G., Horányi, A., Muñoz Sabater, J., ... Thépaut, J. N. (2023). ERA5 monthly averaged data on single levels from 1940 to present. Copernicus Climate Change Service (C3S) Climate Data Store (CDS). https://doi.org/10.24381/cds.f17050d7

Figure 5.4

Swart, N. C., Cole, J. N. S., Kharin, V. V., Lazare, M., Scinocca, J. F., Gillett, N. P., ... Winter, B. (2019). The Canadian Earth System Model version 5 (CanESM5.0.3). *Geosci. Model Dev., 12*(11), 4823–4873. https://doi.org/10.5194/gmd-12-4823-2019

Swart, Neil Cameron, Cole, J. N. S., Kharin, V. V., Lazare, M., Scinocca, J. F., Gillett, N. P., ... Sigmond, M. (2019a). *CCCma CanESM5 model output prepared for CMIP6 Scenario-MIP ssp126.* Earth System Grid Federation. https://doi.org/10.22033/ESGF/CMIP6.3683

Swart, Neil Cameron, Cole, J. N. S., Kharin, V. V., Lazare, M., Scinocca, J. F., Gillett, N. P., ... Sigmond, M. (2019b). *CCCma CanESM5 model output prepared for CMIP6 Scenario-MIP ssp585.* Earth System Grid Federation. https://doi.org/10.22033/ESGF/CMIP6.3696

Figure 5.5

Swart, N. C., Cole, J. N. S., Kharin, V. V., Lazare, M., Scinocca, J. F., Gillett, N. P., ... Winter, B. (2019). The Canadian Earth System Model version 5 (CanESM5.0.3). *Geosci. Model Dev., 12*(11), 4823–4873. https://doi.org/10.5194/gmd-12-4823-2019

Swart, Neil Cameron, Cole, J. N. S., Kharin, V. V., Lazare, M., Scinocca, J. F., Gillett, N. P., ... Sigmond, M. (2019a). *CCCma CanESM5 model output prepared for CMIP6 Scenario-MIP ssp126.* Earth System Grid Federation. https://doi.org/10.22033/ESGF/CMIP6.3683

Swart, Neil Cameron, Cole, J. N. S., Kharin, V. V., Lazare, M., Scinocca, J. F., Gillett, N. P., ... Sigmond, M. (2019b). *CCCma CanESM5 model output prepared for CMIP6 Scenario-MIP ssp585.* Earth System Grid Federation. https://doi.org/10.22033/ESGF/CMIP6.3696

Figure 5.8

Locke, H., Ellis, E. C., Venter, O., Schuster, R., Ma, K., Shen, X., ... Watson, J. E. M. (2019). Three global conditions for biodiversity conservation and sustainable use: An implementation framework. *National Science Review, 6*(6), 1080–1082. https://doi.org/10.1093/nsr/nwz136

Figure 5.11

Hugonnet, R., McNabb, R., Berthier, E., Menounos, B., Nuth, C., Girod, L., ... Kääb, A. (2021). Accelerated global glacier mass loss in the early twenty-first century. *Nature, 592*(7856), 726–731. https://doi.org/10.1038/s41586-021-03436-z

Figure 5.12

Aubry-Wake, C., and Pomeroy, J. W. (2023) Predicting Hydrological Change in an Alpine Glacierized Basin and its Sensitivity to Landscape Evolution and Meteorological Forcings, *Water Resources Research.* https://doi.org/10.1029/2022WR033363

Milton Keynes UK
Ingram Content Group UK Ltd.
UKHW021019091123
432249UK00010B/62